T0188914

Communications
in Computer and Information Science   1737

More information about this series at https://link.springer.com/bookseries/7899

Mrutyunjaya Panda · Satchidananda Dehuri ·
Manas Ranjan Patra · Prafulla Kumar Behera ·
George A. Tsihrintzis · Sung-Bae Cho ·
Carlos A. Coello Coello (Eds.)

Innovations in Intelligent Computing and Communication

First International Conference, ICIICC 2022
Bhubaneswar, Odisha, India, December 16–17, 2022
Proceedings

 Springer

Editors
Mrutyunjaya Panda 🔟
Utkal University
Bhubaneswar, Odisha, India

Manas Ranjan Patra
Berhampur University
Berhampur, Odisha, India

George A. Tsihrintzis
University of Piraeus
Piraeus, Greece

Carlos A. Coello Coello
CINVESTAV-IPN
Mexico City, Mexico

Satchidananda Dehuri
Fakir Mohan University
Balasore, Odisha, India

Prafulla Kumar Behera 🔟
Utkal University
Bhubaneswar, Odisha, India

Sung-Bae Cho 🔟
Yonsei University
Seoul, Korea (Republic of)

ISSN 1865-0929   ISSN 1865-0937 (electronic)
Communications in Computer and Information Science
ISBN 978-3-031-23232-9   ISBN 978-3-031-23233-6 (eBook)
https://doi.org/10.1007/978-3-031-23233-6

This Springer imprint is published by the registered company Springer Nature Switzerland AG
The registered company address is: Gewerbestrasse 11, 6330 Cham, Switzerland

Preface

A hearty welcome to the proceedings of the International Conference on Innovations in Intelligent Computing and Communications (ICIICC 2022) which was held at Utkal University, Vani Vihar, Odisha, India, during December 16–17, 2022.

The aim of ICIICC 2022 was to provide a platform for researchers from industry and academia, practitioners, and scientists across the globe to discuss the latest solutions, innovative and scientific methods, and applications in intelligent computing, communications, machine learning, and data analytics to solve the real issues of the today's world.

ICIICC 2022 received a total 78 submissions from authors in several counties, and each submission was reviewed by at least three reviewers in a single-blind process. Based on the reviewers' recommendations, finally 31 papers were selected for presentation at the conference with an acceptance rate of 40%. The conference proceedings are published in Springer's CCIS series, which is indexed in Scopus, DBLP, etc. The papers in this proceedings are divided into three tracks:

- Track 1 - Intelligent Computing, consisting of 12 papers,
- Track 2 - Communications, consisting of 6 papers, and
- Track 3 - Machine Learning and Data Analytics, consisting of 13 papers.

ICIICC 2022 was organized successfully due to support and hard work of many people. First and foremost, we thank all the authors for their research contributions to the conference, and for their presentations and discussion during the conference. Our thanks go to the Technical Program Committee members and reviewers for their sincere efforts in carefully reviewing the submitted articles. We would also like to thank SERB, Government of India, and WB-OHEPEE, Utkal University, for providing seminar grants to conduct the conference successfully. Our special thanks go to the following keynote speakers for exciting and motivational keynote addresses:

- Ajith Abraham, Machine Intelligence Research Laboratories, USA
- Sung Bae-Cho, Yonsei University, South Korea
- Carlos A. Coello Coello, CINVESTAV-IPN, Mexico
- Aniket Mohanty, University of Auckland, New Zealand
- Umamaheswar A Kakinada, Charter Communications, USA
- Ganapati Panda, CVR Global University, India
- Siba K. Udgata, University of Hyderabad, India
- Saroj Ku. Meher, Indian Statistical Institute, Bangalore, India

We express our sincere thanks to the session chairs and local organizing committee members for helping us to formulate a rich technical program. We are immensely grateful to our Honorable Vice-Chancellor, Registrar, Comptroller of Finance, Directors, and other administrative officers of Utkal University for allowing us to organize the conference.

Finally, our sincere gratitude goes to Lakhmi C. Jain, Founder of KES International, UK, for his continuous support and kind guidance in the process of technical collaborations, and to the Springer CCIS series team, for their guidance in bringing the conference proceedings in a timely manner and with good quality.

We hope that the readers of this proceedings will find it enjoyable.

December 2022

Mrutyunjaya Panda
Manas Ranjan Patra
Satchidananda Dehuri
Prafulla Kumar Behera
George A. Tsihrintzis
Sung-Bae Cho
Carlos A. Coello Coello

Organization

Chief Patron

Sabita Acharya Utkal University, India

Patrons

Durga Sankar Pattnaik Utkal University, India
Avaya Kumar Nayak Utkal University, India
Shri Gautama Pradhan Utkal University, India

Convenor

Mrutyunjaya Panda Utkal University, India

Finance Committee

Biswojit Nayak Utkal University, India
Sanjaya Kumar Sarangi Utkal University, India

Publishing Committee

Prafulla Kumar Behera Utkal University, India
Manas Ranjan Patra Berhampur University, India
Satchidananda Dehuri Fakir Mohan University, India
Haraprasad Naik Utkal University, India
Sanjaya Kumar Sarangi Utkal University, India
N. Adhikari Utkal University, India

Organizing Committee

Prafulla Kumar Behera Utkal University, India
Mrutyunjaya Panda Utkal University, India
N. Adhikari Utkal University, India
Lalatendu Muduli India
Biswojit Nayak Utkal University, India
Haraprasad Naik Utkal University, India
Purna Chandra Sethi Rama Devi Women's University, India

Omm Prakash Jena	Ravenshaw University, India
Sanjaya Kumar Sarangi	Utkal University, India

Advisory Committee

Ajith Abraham	Machine Intelligence Research Labs, USA
Ganapati Panda	IIT Bhubaneswar, India
P. K. Meher	NTU, Singapore
S. K. Patra	IIIT Vadodara, India
Milli Pant	IIT Roorkee, India
S. K. Udgata	University of Hyderabad, India
A. K. Bisoi	Utkal University, India
J. Dandpat	Utkal University, India
P. K. Hota	Utkal University, India
N. Das	Utkal University, India
S. K. Pradhan	Utkal University, India
B. S. Panda	IIT New Delhi, India
B. Majhi	VSSUT, India
P. K. Mohapatra	Utkal University, India
Prasanta K. Jana	IIT(ISM) Dhanbad, India
Srikanta Patnaik	SOA, India
B. K. Tripathy	VIT, India

Program Chairs

Mrutyunjaya Panda	Utkal University, India
Satchidananda Dehuri	Fakir Mohan University, India
Prafulla Kumar Behera	Utkal University, India
Manas Ranjan Patra	Berhampur University, India
George A. Tsihrintzis	University of Piraeus, Greece
Sung-Bae Cho	Yonsei University, South Korea
Carlos A. Coello Coello	Cinvestav-IPN, Mexico

Technical Program Committee

Aniket Mahanti	University of Auckland, New Zealand
Nashwa El-Bendary	Arab Academy of Science, Technology and Maritime Transport, Egypt
Milli Pant	IIT Roorkee, India
D. P. Mohapatra	National Institute of Technology, Rourkela, India
Lalatendu Muduli	Utkal University, India
B. Acharya	National Institute of Technology, Raipur, India

S. K. Panda	National Institute of Technology, Warangal, India
S. K. Meher	Indian Statistical Institute, Bangalore, India
Abhinav Tomar	Netaji Subhas University of Technology, New Delhi, India
Pratyay Kuila	National Institute of Technology, Sikkim, India
Nabajyoti Mazumdar	International Institute of Information Technology, Allahabad, India
P. K. Biswal	International Institute of Information Technology, Bhubaneswar, India
Rahul Pramanik	Birla Institute of Technology, Dubai, UAE
S. K. Mishra	Birla Institute of Technology, Mesra, India
Md Azaruddin	Aliah University, India
Partha Sarkar	JIS College of Engineering, India
P. M. Khilar	National Institute of Technology, Rourkela, India
S. K. Udgata	University of Hyderabad, India
Nibedita Adhikari	Utkal University, India
Bijayananda Patnaik	National Institute of Technology, Raipur, India
Pulak Sahoo	Silicon Institute of Technology, India
Sourav Bhoi	Parala Maharaja Engineering College, India
Harish Kumar Sahoo	VSSUT, India

Keynote Speakers

Ajith Abraham	Machine Intelligence Research Labs, USA
Sung-Bae Cho	Yonsei University, South Korea
Carlos A. Coello Coell	Cinvestav-IPN, Mexico
Aniket Mohanty	University of Auckland, New Zealand
Ganapati Panda	IIT Bhubaneswar, India
Umamaheswar A. Kakinada	Charter Communications, USA
Saroj Kumar Meher	Indian Statistical Institute, Bangalore, India
Siba Ku. Udgata	University of Hyderabad, India
Bhawani Sankar Panda	IIT Delhi, India
Sadhna Rana	Tata Consultancy Services, India

Sponsors

Science and Engineering Research Board (SERB), Government of India

Odisha Higher Education Programme for Excellence and Equity (WB-OHEPEE), Utkal University, India

Keynote Address

Industry 4.0 Meets Data Science: The Pathway for Society 5.0

Ajith Abraham

Machine Intelligence Research Labs (MIR Labs), Scientific Network
for Innovation and Research Excellence, USA

Abstract. We are blessed with the sophisticated technological artifacts that are enriching our daily lives and the society. Industry 4.0 is the current trend of automation and data exchange in manufacturing technologies, which also includes a close integration of cyber-physical systems, the Internet of things and cloud computing. In this talk, the concept of Industry 4.0 and Society 5.0 will be presented and then various research challenges from several application perspectives will be illustrated. Some real world applications involving the analysis of complex data/applications would be the key focus.

Continual Learning for Intelligent Systems in Changing Environments

Sung-Bae Cho

Yonsei University, South Korea

Abstract. Intelligent systems are expected to learn new knowledge incrementally without forgetting in an ever-changing environment. Due to the critical limitation accompanied by amazing success of deep learning, a lot of continual learning methods have been proposed with different approaches. In this talk, I will give the general definition and three key approaches of continual learning, and present an idea of exploiting extra memory for working out the catastrophic forgetting of the knowledge learned with the previous tasks. Experimental results with several benchmark datasets such as MNIST, CIFAR-10 and CIFAR-100 will show the possibilities and challenges of the continual learning in changing environments.

Where is the Research on Evolutionary Multi-objective Optimization Heading to?

Carlos A. Coello Coello

Investigador Cinvestav 3F, CINVESTAV-IPN, Mexico

Abstract. The first multi-objective evolutionary algorithm was published in 1985. However, it was not until the late 1990s that so-called evolutionary multi-objective optimization began to gain popularity as a research area.

Throughout these 37 years, there have been several important advances in the area, including the development of different families of algorithms, test problems, performance indicators, hybrid methods and real-world applications, among many others. In the first part of this talk we will take a quick look at some of these developments, focusing mainly on some of the most important recent achievements.

In the second part of the talk, a critical analysis will be made of the by analogy research that has proliferated in recent years in specialized journals and conferences (perhaps as a side effect of the abundance of publications in this area).

Much of this research has a very low level of innovation and almost no scientific input, but is backed by a large number of statistical tables and analyses.

In the third and final part of the talk, some of the future research challenges for this area, which, after 37 years of existence, is just beginning to mature, will be briefly mentioned.

Designing a Software Framework Based on an Object Detection Model and a Fuzzy Logic System for Weed Detection and Pasture Assessment

Aniket Mohanty

University of Auckland, New Zealand

Abstract. Artificial Intelligence (AI) has provided advanced and precise tools for processing agricultural data called agreprecision. Pasture processing is one of the main applications of agriprecision to provide automation and saving labour tasks for dairy farmers. By weeds as the main issue of pastures, dairy farmers need to invest a tremendous amount of time for pasture monitoring for weed destroying. This paper proposes designing a software framework based on an object detection model and a fuzzy logic system for weed detection and pasture assessment. Weed density and empty spots are two main factors of reducing pasture productivity. By considering these two factors as pastoral input variables, we ingest them to our system to process the pastures and score the state of pasture's productivity. With the aid of our software system, we can produce 2D weed density maps, 2D bareness maps, and scoring maps, which provides a much better insight into the pastures. The types of 2D maps and the yield score can help and support dairy farmers to schedule, organize, and manage pastoral weeds.

An Overview of Machine Learning Based Intelligent Computing and Applications

Ganapati Panda[1,2]

[1] IIT, Bhubaneswar
[2] C.V. Raman Global University, Bhubaneswar, India

Abstract. In recent years, Machine Learning Techniques have played a significant role for decision making, reasoning and finding appropriate solution by analyzing the available data from experiments, communication receivers, finance, agriculture, health care and manufacturing. Pre-processing of the data comprising of de-noising and normalization plays a vital role. Subsequently, features are extracted from the raw data and then selection/reduction of features is carried out. The selected features are then used as inputs to the intelligent decision making process for classification, prediction, pattern recognition, inverse modeling, detection and optimization, operation. The proposed talk will cover all these aspects in details. In addition, various important soft computing, evolutionary computing and machine learning techniques (supervised and unsupervised) will be dealt in brief. The different application areas pertaining to each intelligent operation will also be illustrated.

Semisupervised Learning with Spatial Information and Granular Neural Networks

S. K. Meher

Indian Statistical Institute, Bangalore, India

Abstract. The effectiveness of a classification model depends primarily on two things. One is the accurately labeled samples, and the other is the number that should be significant. Without these, the model's estimation of posterior probability and class conditional probability density functions becomes erroneous. However, getting a large number of accurately labeled samples for real-time applications, e.g., remote sensing, healthcare, and telecommunication, is cumbersome. To address these issues, semisupervised learning strategies are adopted that can exploit unlabeled and labeled samples in the learning process and lead to the performance improvement of a classification model. Here, we discuss a semisupervised classification model with spatial information-based self-learning methodology for pattern classification. The model uses a granular neural network (GNN) as the base classifier because of its customizable network architecture that is functionally interpretable and costs less computational complexity. The architecture of GNN is governed by fuzzy if-then rules generated from fuzzy granulation of input feature space. The model has used an improved spatial neighborhood learning method to understand data distribution in a semisupervised framework better. The technique collects the information with collaborative opinions of two independent information extraction approaches, i.e., based on mutual neighborhood criteria and class maps of unlabeled samples. A case study on remote sensing images is provided at the end.

IoT Based General Purpose Sensing Application for Smart Home Environment

Siba K. Udgata

WiSECom Lab, School of Computer and Information Sciences,
University of Hyderabad (Institute of Eminence), Hyderabad, India

Abstract. General Purpose Sensing is an approach towards developing a universal sensor used to detect different facets of an environment. In this approach a single enhanced sensor is used which can monitor a vast context without requiring direct object instrumentation. The most natural and traditional form of sensing relies on direct and distributed sensing wherein one single sensor is utilized to monitor a single aspect of an environment. General purpose sensing helps in developing and creating smart sensing environments. This also overcomes many of the issues faced by earlier methods and helps a normal environment to become smart environments. In this, we discuss our experience on developing a general purpose sensing application to detect combination of different day-to-day events and combination of events in a room environment. We also discuss how general purpose sensing can be used to estimate the energy consumption in a room. For this, we use different sensor modules like MPU6050, HMC5833L, BH1750, INMP441, HC-SR501, DHT11 together with ESP8266 controller to generate a dataset for linear acceleration, angular acceleration, magnetic values along the 3 axis coordinates (X, Y, Z), light intensity, audio frequencies, movement detection, temperature and humidity values while performing combination of different general activities like Hand shake and Face touch, Raise hand and Face touch, Raise hand and hand shake, Face touch and hand shake, Face touch and Raise hand, Shake hand and Raise hand among a few others. The developed module is also used to generate a data set for combination of events in a room environment like fan on, lights on, AC on, person walking, computer on and combination of these activities. We also estimated the energy consumption in a room environment using the general purpose sensor module which records sensor values while performing certain activities which are then converted and analyzed by a model to classify the activities. This is accomplished by using adaptive threshold based data segmentation and different classification methods.

Emerging Topics in Wireless and Network Communications – A Standards Perspective

Umamaheswar A. Kakinada

Emerging Technologies - Research and Development,
Charter Communications, Colorado, USA

Abstract. We probably are in the initial stages of many promising evolving technologies such as AR/VR/XR, Metaverse, AI/ML based various network functions such as network automation, quality of experience, end user privacy and security and federated learning is just to name a few. Many of these technologies are in the early stage of development and many of the essential enablers for these technologies such as low latency, high throughput, ultra-reliable fail-safe communications, and various sensory devices are still in the various stages of development and realization. The standards, protocols, and reference architectures developed by various Standards Development Organizations (SDOs) play an important role in development of these technologies, also enabling harmonious coexistence of different components of this somewhat disparate ecosystem; to realize these ambitious goals. In this presentation we will explore a few of these being developed by 3GPP and other SDOs.

Emerging Topics in Wireless and Network Communications – A Standards Perspective

B. S. Panda

Indian Institute of Technology Delhi, Hauz Khas, New Delhi, India

Abstract. With the boom in technologies and mobile networks in recent years, online social networks have become an integral part of our daily lives. Nowadays, various Online Social Networks (OSNs) like Twitter, Facebook, Instagram, etc., have enabled the world into a hyper-connected global world and provide virtual platforms on which various social interactions occur between the users. These OSNs offer users an ideal platform to share and promote new ideas, products, or information. An online social network can be modeled as a graph, where V denotes a set of people or entities present in the network, and E represents edges. The edge between two entities on a social network corresponds to a virtual acquaintance like friendship and follow-followee relationships. Due to the presence of many users from different parts of the world on these social networks, they help facilitate the dissemination of information at a faster rate. Virtual networks connect people worldwide and provide them excellent platforms for promoting their products and ideas. It is often the case that certain users are more influential than others present on social networks. The process of efficiently recognizing influential users to maximize a particular piece of information across a network is known as Influence Maximization (IM). Influential nodes are the nodes with high spreading capability, and a piece of information originating from them can reach a maximum extent in the network by triggering an information diffusion cascade. Identifying influential nodes for the task of influence maximization is one of the popular research topics in the field of network science. Viral marketing is one of the popular applications of influence maximization where companies intend to reach a large number of users from initially chosen influential seed nodes through diffusion cascade. In this talk, we will discuss some recent solutions to influence maximization in complex networks.

Contents

Communications

Machine Learning and Data Analytics

Intelligent Computing

Ensemble Learning Model for EEG Based Emotion Classification

Sanjit Kumar Dash[1(✉)], Sambit Subhasish Sahu[1], J. Chandrakant Badajena[1], Sweta Dash[1], and Chinmayee Rout[2]

[1] Odisha University of Technology and Research, Bhubaneswar, Odisha, India
`sanjitkumar303@gmail.com`
[2] Ajay Binay Institute of Technology, Cuttack, Odisha, India

Abstract. Emotion and feelings are recently becoming popular concepts in the everyday life. It not only affects human health but also plays an essential role in the decision-making processes. For this reason, emotion classification is one of the important aspects to deal with the problems like mental disorders, suicidal activities and judgmental process. Electroencephalogram (EEG) signal is one of the physiological signals which can be collected from the human brain activity while a person performing various mental and physical task. In this paper, the DEAP dataset has been implemented with the deep learning model for the classification process. In the process of developing models, for the extraction of the important features from the unprocessed EEG signals, Fast Fourier Transformation is used. Three ensemble deep learning models are tested and compared to get the best accuracy result for emotion classification. Furthermore, by the best model we can classify four emotional regions in the valance-arousal plane: HVHA, HVLA, LVHA and LVLA can be classified. The experimental results show that among all the three deep learning models, 1D-CNN-GRU achieved the highest training accuracy of 96.54% as compared to LSTM and 1D-CNN, which is the best model to classify emotions in this context.

Keywords: EEG · Emotion classification · Feature extraction · LSTM · GRU · Fast fourier transformation

1 Introduction

Now a days several industries have adopted the implementation of emotion recognition and classification on their employees. When the human resources fields start gain the emotional state of the employee, they could take the advantages from it to improve the quality of taking decision regarding their organization and it will also help to make judgment regarding employees' work. Emotion is physiological process triggered due to the environmental and personal conditions, which affects the mood, behavior, character and motivations. It also plays an important role in the daily conversation and behavior which affects the decision-making process, personal and professional workflow. Nowadays, the emotional state of a person takes a very crucial position in life, which is associated with their mental and physical health, daily lifestyle, decisions about the future and

M. Panda et al. (Eds.): ICIICC 2022, CCIS 1737, pp. 3–16, 2022.
https://doi.org/10.1007/978-3-031-23233-6_1

many more. The Valence, Arousal, and Dominance (VAD) dimensions are another way to divide up emotion. A measure of pleasantness known as valence can originate from very good (pleasure) or very negative emotions (displeasure). Arousal, on the other hand, is the level of feeling that a situation elicits and can range from positive excitement to calmness (negative). Last but not least, dominance is the degree of control demonstrated in response to a stimulus [1]. The popular Circumplex Model of Affect is depicted in Fig. 1 and categories emotions into two groups: Low valence or negative valence emotions (such as fear, tension, rage, sadness, boredom, etc.) and High valence or pleasant valence emotions (happy, calm, delighted, excited, etc.).

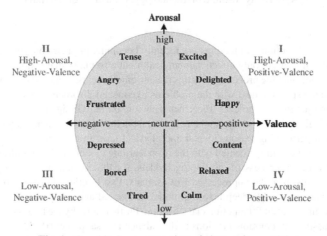

Fig. 1. Graphical representation of circumplex model

In the present scenario, it has become increasingly significant to analyze a person's emotional state which can be apprehended from social networking websites, blogging platforms like twitter, online review sites and so on. However, in order to facilitate emotion classification, the use of EEG data is an emerging field of study. The EEG is (Electroencephalogram) which is used on the scalp surface to record electric current using metallic electrodes and conductive media [2]. By using the electrodes, the different electric waves forming according to different mental states inside the brain could be collected as EEG signals. This can help to have a better understanding of a person's mental state.

Recently, various researchers are using different data sets like AMIGOS, DREAMER, Seed according to their field of experiment, but for emotion recognition DEAP dataset is highly recommended. The EEG dataset is not used for emotion classification but also different fields of BCI like wheel chair, Telemedicine, stock market prediction etc. In different studies different researchers are using different processing and feature extraction methods and different machine learning models. In our paper we are using Fast Fourier Transformation as the feature extraction model before feed into the Deep learning model. CNN and RNN are used for the classification purpose. We also propose 3 models, likely 1D-CNN, LSTM and a combination of two neural networks CNN and RNN as 1D-CNN-GRU.1D-CNN is chosen from CNN and LSTM and GRU are chosen from RNN. All the models are tested in the training and testing process to check the accuracy and loss value and will be compared.

The remainder of the paper is structured as follows. Section 2 discusses the related works which helped us to get the fundamental knowledge about the research work. Section 3 describes System Model and Methodology. Section 4 describes the Dataset description used in the paper. In Sect. 5, the complete environmental setup and results were elaborated, including the model accuracy and data loss. Section 6 concludes the paper with detailed future work and limitations.

2 Related Works

The C-RNN deep learning hybrid model, which combines CNN & RNN, was introduced by Xiang Li et al. (2016) for the aim of recognizing emotions [3]. The data is pre-processed using continuous wavelet transformation & body production before being taught inside the model. For the arousal and valence dimensions, this test's overall performance is 74.12% and 72.06%, respectively. In their deep learning architecture, they used DEAP dataset [4] for emotion recognition, Alhagry et al. (2017) recommended LSTM. According to this method, the average accuracy for the arousal, valence, and liking classes is 85.65%, 85.45%, and 87.99%, respectively.

Lin et al. performed emotional state classification in CNN using end -to-end learning method and DEAP Dataset [5]. The datasets were turned into six grayscale images that included frequency and time information, and the previously identified characteristics were then taught using the AlexNet version. For arousal and valence, this study gives accuracy of 87.30% and 85.50%, respectively. Li et al. (2017) used the DEAP dataset to perform their emotion recognition task using a hybrid CNN and LSTM RNN (CLRNN) [6]. Already converted into a series of Multidimensional Feature Images is the dataset. With the hybrid neural networks suggested inside the study, every event may be accurately classified as having a common emotion 75.21% of the time. In order to accomplish emotion classification tasks, Acharya et al. (2020) examined the general performance of CNN and LSTM models and performed feature extraction using FFT [7]. The test outcome was excellent for LSTM and CNN model with an accuracy of 88.6% and 87.2% respectively for the liking emotion.

Zhang et al. (2020) discussed different deep learning models like CNN, DNN, LSTM, and combination of CNN and LSTM model along with their applications to the research field of EEG-based emotion classification [8]. This study made substantial use of the DEAP dataset, and many capabilities, including mean, maximum value, standard deviation, minimum value, skewness, and kurtosis, were retrieved from it. The CNN model with 90.12% accuracy and CNN-LSTM model with 94.17% accuracy shows excellent ability to complete this task. Anubhav et al. (2020) investigated the EEG signals with the goal of creating a headgear version for tracking real-time emotions [9]. From the DEAP dataset band energy and frequency domain were recovered, and the accuracies for valence and arousal dimensions were calculated with accuracy of 94.69% 93.13% respectively using LSTM.

A 2D-CNN structure was suggested by Dar et al. (2020) to systematic EEG indications for emotion recognition [10]. The DREAMER & AMIGOS datasets are utilized for this test and before being input into CNN, each statistic is converted into 2D function matrix (PNG format). The multi-modal emotion reputation system also uses different peripheral physiological markers, such as ECG and GSR, in addition to EEG. Only 76.65% accuracy can be attained using the EEG modality, and multi-modal fusion is required to achieve the overall maximum accuracy of 90.8% and 99.0% for DREAMER and AMIGOS dataset respectively.

3 System Model and Methodology

Figure 2 shows the system model for emotion classification. There are 4 phases in the process, initially collected DEAP dataset with proper approval which is publicly available. Then it will be passed through the Feature Extraction process in the second phase, which extract the main features from the unprocessed EEG data. Thirdly the data will split into Train and Test data, training data will be passed through the three different models; 1D-CNN, LSTM, 1D-CNN-GRU to check testing accuracy and all other parameters. In the end phase the best model will be implemented as the classification model for the classification of four emotional regions from valance arousal plane.

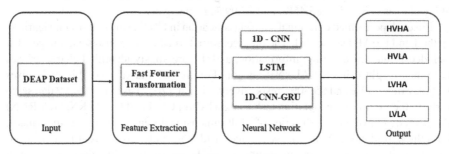

Fig. 2. System model

3.1 Feature Extraction

For feature extraction, Fast Fourier Transformation (FFT) was used which is best in all tradition feature extraction models to extract the important features for the classification purpose, which reduces the number of computation data needed for an experiment from actual data of size N and the final result was achieved (58560,70) dimension from (40,40,8064) which allows for faster training and higher accuracy.

The extracted features contain five frequency bands: Delta, Theta, Alpha, Beta and Gamma with frequency 1–4, 4–8, 8–14, 14–31, and 31–50 Hz respectively. The PyEEG python package was used to extract these five out of 70 characteristics in total. The signal domain is transformed from time to frequency on the x-axis using FFT. This is based on the idea of discrete fourier transform (DFT) on time series data. Calculating the DFT coefficients in an iterative approach will reduce both computational time and complexity. It also helps to reduce round-off errors in computations.

3.2 Deep Learning Model Implementation

In this section, three deep learning models have been implemented: 1D-CNN (One Dimensional Convolutional Neural Network), LSTM (Long Short-Term Memory), and a hybrid model of 1D-CNN and GRU (Gated Recurrent Unit). Preprocessed version of the DEAP dataset used in the models. The models were trained to categorise each emotion individually using different train-test splits, such as arousal, valence, dominance, and liking. The following is a description of model implementations using Keras (Chollet (2015) [11]):

A. 1D-CNN Model

1D-CNN is used to extract the significant features from the DEAP dataset. CNN works good on the time series data which are the 1D signals. In Conv1D the kernel slides along one dimension only. This is one of the key justifications for using 1D-CNN in our research. As shown in Fig. 3, out of the 10 classes, we employed three conv1D, three dense layers that were completely coupled, and one dense layer with SoftMax activation. The first convolution layer employs the Rectified linear unit (ReLU) as its activation function and has 164 filters and a kernel of size 3. After hyperparameter tuning, optimization with Grid Search and manual adjustments, the number and size of filters are determined. A shape of (70,1) with the same padding and stride of one is feed into Conv1D's first layer. To reduce network overfitting, dropout on the dense layer outputs is implemented with 0.2 dropout probability. Following this dense layer of 21 ReLU-activated neurons with a 0.2 dropout probability is a layer of 42 Tanh-activated neurons with a 0.2 dropout probability. At the end Dense layer of 10 neurons with a SoftMax activation function produces the network's final output.

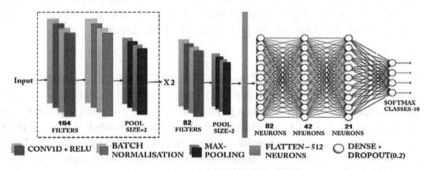

Fig. 3. 1D - CNN architecture

B. LSTM Model

Long Short-Term Memory Networks (LSTMs) is one type of recurrent neural network (RNN), first introduced in 1997 by Hochreiter and Schmidhuber [12]. It solves the problem of short-term memory. It has a built-in gate that can recognize which information in a sequence has to be kept and which information can be discarded.

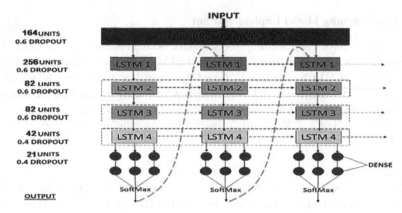

Fig. 4. LSTM architecture

Figure 4 shows the model architecture of LSTM, which consists of two dense layers, four LSTM layers, and one bi-directional layer. The initial bi-directional LSTM layer contains 164 units. It involves adding a second LSTM layer on top of the first one in the network. The first receives the input sequence, and the second receives a reverse copy to the next layer. The dropout layer, which has a probability of 0.6, comes next. Inputs are randomly set to 0 which helps to prevent overfitting. The following layer is a 256-neuron LSTM layer, followed by a 0.6 dropout layer. Two LSTM layers with 82 neurons each make up the next four layers, which are then followed by a dropout layer. There were 0.6 and 0.4 percent dropout rates, respectively. 42 neurons make up the final LSTM layer with a dropout layer of 0.4 following that 21 units of dense layers is applied. ReLU is the activation method employed in this case. The SoftMax activation function is then applied to dense layer of 10 classes, which gives a multiclass probability distribution. Using argmax find out the class output is done after knowing the probability of all the classes.

C. 1D-CNN-GRU Model

This variant is a hybrid model of the 1D-CNN and GRU of deep learning architectures. The network's first input size is 256 units, followed by two seconds of the time-stamped signal with 256 data points, 128 units of convolutional filters, and a kernel size of 3. Rectified linear unit (ReLU) activation function is used in the first convolution layer. The precise number and size of filters are identified after extensive hyperparameter optimization using Grid Search and manual adjustments. Conv1D's first layer receives as its input a shape of the form (70,1) with the same padding. The outputs of the first layer are normalized using a batch normalized layer, which has a mean value zero and a standard deviation value of one. The input is down sampled in the following layer, dropout of 0.2 after a Max pooling 1D layer with a pool size of 2 and the second convolutional layer, which is same as the first one. The implementation of GRU comes after the convolutional layers with an input length of 256 units and 32 units. At the end of every GRU layers a dropout layer of 0.2 has been set. A flattening operation is implemented to send the features into the

1D feature vector prior to dense layer. The dense layer is set to 32 units and ReLU is used as the activation function. To represent the 4 labels of classification 4 units of dense layer has been set. The activation function for the dense layer is SoftMax. In this model 379,594 units of trainable parameter used. The details model architecture of 1D-CNN-GRU is given in Fig. 5.

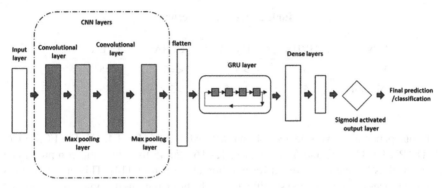

Fig. 5. 1D - CNN?+?GRU architecture

4 Dataset Description

The DEAP dataset [13] used in the experiment is publicly available for researchers for their experiments. This data set contains both EEG and EMG signals. To collect the data 32 participants as engaged. In the dataset the physiological recordings and participant evaluations of 32 individuals (s01-s32) are covered. These physiological clips are already in BioSemi.bdf format and have not been processed. For each of them, 40 films were presented which makes 40 channels in total. Depending on the rating, the emotion is either stronger or weaker; the stronger the emotion, the higher the rating. Table 1 contains each subject's information, which contains two arrays: data and label, which contains the array shape and the content of each file.

Table 1. Pre-processed dataset description

Array name	Array shape	Array contents
Data	40 :40 :8064	video/trial * Channel * Data
Labels	40 :4	video/trial * label (valence, arousal, dominance, liking)

The data was filtered by a band-pass filter with a bandwidth of 4–45 Hz and down sampled by 128 Hz. In addition to these, the collection includes listings and links to YouTube music videos. Questions to ask before testing are contained in the participant questionnaire file, each trial or video was given a rating on a scale of 1 to 9. The dataset is divided into four classes, which is subsequently labelled as: High-Valence Low-Arousal (HVLA), Low-Valence High-Arousal (LVHA), and Low-Valence Low-Arousal (LVLA) are four different types of arousal The Table 2 contains all the four classes and two labels, the threshold value for this classification is 5. If the value is greater than 5, then it will be classified as high and low if it is less than 5.

Table 2. Label classification

Label	HVHA	HVLA	LVHA	LVLA
Valence	>5	>5	<=5	<=5
Arousal	>5	?<=5	>5	<=5

In our paper we have selected 14 channels AF3, AF4, F3, F4, F7, F8, FC5, FC6, T7, T8, P7, P8, O1, O2 and 5 bands 4, 8, 12, 16, 25, 45 to reduce the computational cost as well as for the better result for emotion classification [14]. This entire channel selection process is based on the significance of the brain regions that make up emotional states. When we divided the label into the four categories of HVHA, HVLA, LVHA, and LVLA, the paper was considered to be complete. But for now, as a result, models will be compared on the basis of an increase in training accuracy while decreasing validation loss for the selection of a better classification model.

5   Experimental Setup and Results

Google Collaboratory was used to compute 1D – CNN, LSTM, GRU classifiers because, it uses Jupyter notebook service that needs no installation and gives unrestricted access to computing tools, such as GPUs. Python is the python version (3.7.13). The current version of TensorFlow is 2.8.0. Pandas: 1.3.5, numpy: 1.21.6, sklearn: 1.0.2, plotly: 5.5.0. A laptop is used to run the code. Nvidia K80s, T4s, P4s, and P100s are common GPUs seen in CoLab. To get an amazing result, hyperparameter should be tuned adequately. Conv1D layers are utilized in the CNN architecture because they are best suited for data in time series. Both maximum and average pooling were used, however maximum pooling produced better results, as predicted by the literature. For the CNN, LSTM, and 1D-CNN-GRU architectures, the finalized epoch size is 200 and batch size of 256. The models are trained on 80–20 train–test splits and 10-fold cross validation is also employed to determine the best metrics-accuracy. To update the weights during back-propagation, used Adam as the optimizer and category cross entropy as the loss function. In both cases, SoftMax performs the activation of the last layer. Separate decisions were made for each of the three models, including the number of layers, hidden layers, filter size, number of filters, pool size for the CNN model, and hidden neurons, dropout rates, and layers for the LSTM and GRU models separately. Both grid search and manual testing are used to finalize everything.

Overall performance of the three models can be elaborated and analyzed on the basic of accuracy and loss value. Table 3 contains test accuracy and test loss of each model. It can be inferred that, the 1D-CNN-GRU model architecture provide the best test accuracy of 96.54%, 41.3% of test loss with an 80–20 train test split as compared to the LSTM model architecture's accuracy of 89.6%, test loss of 39.6% with an 80–20 train test split and the 1D-CNN model architecture's accuracy of 90.65%, test loss of 42.2% with an 80–20 train test split. All these three experiments were designed to test the overall performance of each model for classification of emotion.

Table 3. Test accuracy and test loss comparison

Classifier	Test accuracy	Test loss
1D - CNN	90.65%	42.2%
LSTM	89.6%	39.6%
1D CNN?+?GRU	96.54%	11.4%

Above discussed models performed exceptionally well at generalizing findings since they classified each emotion with an accuracy rate of more than 80%. The loss function is categorical cross entropy. Overfitting on training data was avoided by the use of dropout layers, which also enhanced model results. Batch normalization layers also significantly affect model accuracy. By altering the number of epochs, data units and input layers the accuracy affects. When we implemented the GRU architecture we got a very less accuracy, but after implementing the hybrid model of 1D-CNN and GRU, it crossed all the levels.

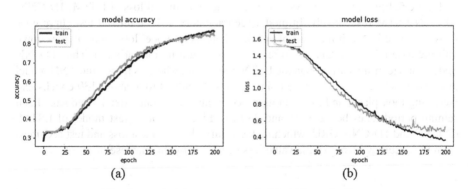

Fig. 6. (a) Model accuracy and (b) Model loss of LSTM

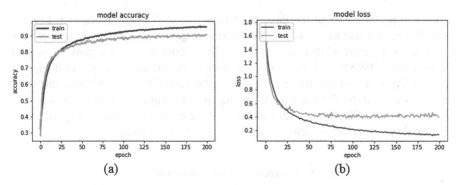

Fig. 7. (a) Model accuracy and (b) Model loss of 1D-CNN

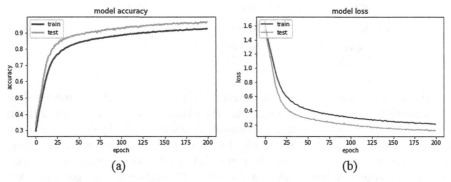

Fig. 8. (a) Model accuracy and (b) Model loss of 1D-CNN-GRU

Figure 6, Fig. 7, Fig. 8 shows model accuracy and model loss of LSTM, 1D-CNN, 1D-CNN-LSTM respectively. In model accuracy curves the train and test curve goes up award direction with increase of epoch, where as in model loss figure it goes down with increase of epoch. Curves were found to have a minor variation, The 1D-CNN model starts learning earlier than the LSTM model and where as it took the CNN model about 50 epochs to reach a stable point, the LSTM model took about 130 epochs. No overfitting took place, and the training process came to an end after 165 epochs. Each training period takes between 16 and 330 ms. Figure 9 shows test model of LSTM, 1D-CNN and 1D-CNN-GRU, which makes a curve between test loss and test accuracy, when the accuracy increases the value loss decreases by the increase of epoch.

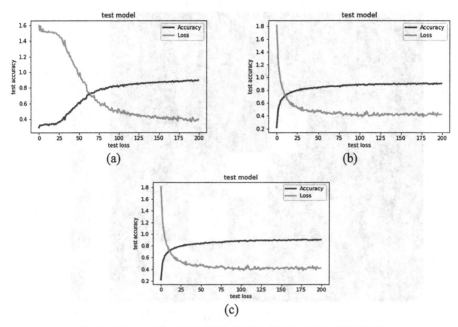

Fig. 9. Test model of (a) LSTM, (b) 1D-CNN, (c) 1D-CNN-GRU

Dropout and batch normalisation layers have a big impact on the model's accuracy. Additionally, we constructed a confusion matrix in Fig. 10 to explore the discrepancy between the predicted and actual value. Each model's F1-Score and recall value are close to one, which shows that this model has good quality.

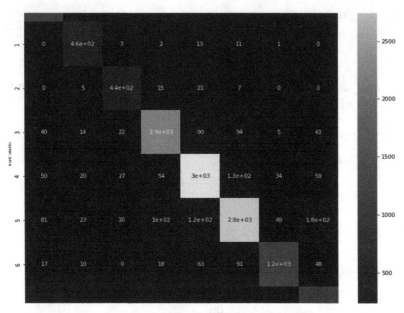

a.   LSTM

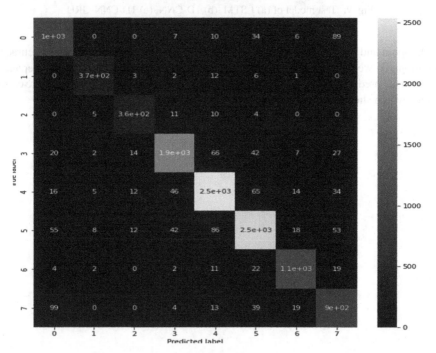

b. 1D-CNN

Fig. 10. Confusion matrix of LSTM, 1D-CNN, 1D-CNN-GRU

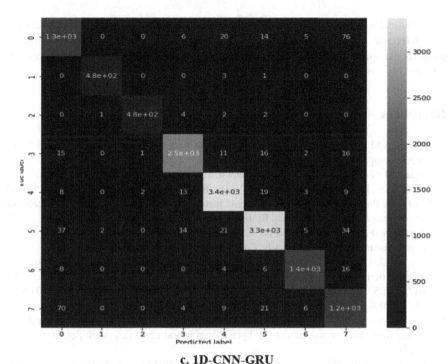

c. 1D-CNN-GRU

Fig. 10. (*continued*)

6   Conclusion

In this paper we have discussed the simplest feature extraction method with the best classification model for emotion classification using DEAP dataset. In this paper, we have described three deep learning models: 1D-CNN, LSTM, and 1D-CNN-GRU. As compared to normal feature extraction strategies, FFT increased accuracy and extracted crucial characteristics. The 1D-CNN design has proven to be best model to extract EEG signal features. The 1D-CNN architecture has a classification accuracy of 90.8% which is somewhat better than the 89.2% classification accuracy of the LSTM model. From all the three models the 1D – CNN – GRU gives the best accuracy of 96.54%.

Bi-LSTMs were able to preserve data from the past as well as the future, which contributed to increase the accuracy in the LSTM model. Even though the emotion classification test showed that our model worked remarkably well, we still wish to assess it further in additional datasets like DREAMER and AMIGOS and enhance our model. More particular, while this version no longer undergoes testing on various people, it was best trained using the DEAP dataset only.

In future we would try to work on quick output of the EEG data processing in real-time online analysis systems, which limits calculation time. We will concentrate on a multi-task cascaded-hybrid LSTM and CNN model in the future, which will combine their features and improve the efficacy of the emotion classification model. The system to detection of emotion can improve human experiences by minimizing the gap between computational technology and human emotions and allowing computers, BCI system and robots to receive emotional feedback in real-time. Even with the help of this technology, therapists can more thoroughly evaluate their patients and learn how to spot depression early and prevent it before any outward situation occurs.

References

1. Alarcao, S.M., Fonseca, M.J.: Emotions recognition using EEG signals: a survey. IEEE Trans. Affect. Comput. **10**(3), 374–393 (2017)
2. Teplan, M.: Fundamentals of EEG measurement. Measur. Sci. Rev. **2**(2), 1–11 (2002)
3. Li, X., Song, D., Zhang, P., Yu, G., Hou, Y., Hu, B.: Emotion recognition from multi-channel EEG data through convolutional recurrent neural network. In: 2016 IEEE International Conference on Bioinformatics and Biomedicine (BIBM), pp. 352–359. IEEE (2016)
4. Alhagry, S., Fahmy, A.A., El-Khoribi, R.A.: Emotion recognition based on EEG using LSTM recurrent neural network. Int. J. Adv. Comput. Sci. Appl. **8**(10), 355–358 (2017)
5. Lin, W., Li, C., Sun, S.: Deep convolutional neural network for emotion recognition using EEG and peripheral physiological signal. In: Zhao, Y., Kong, X., Taubman, D. (eds.) ICIG 2017. LNCS, vol. 10667, pp. 385–394. Springer, Cham (2017). https://doi.org/10.1007/978-3-319-71589-6_33
6. Li, Y., Huang, J., Zhou, H., Zhong, N.: Human emotion recognition with electroencephalographic multidimensional features by hybrid deep neural networks. Appl. Sci. **7**(10), 1060 (2017)
7. Acharya, D., et al.: Multi-class emotion classification using EEG signals. In: Garg, D., Wong, K., Sarangapani, J., Gupta, S.K. (eds.) IACC 2020. CCIS, vol. 1367, pp. 474–491. Springer, Singapore (2021). https://doi.org/10.1007/978-981-16-0401-0_38
8. Zhang, Y., et al.: An investigation of deep learning models for EEG-based emotion recognition. Front. Neurosci. **14**, 622759 (2020)
9. Nath, D., Singh, M., Sethia, D., Kalra, D., Indu, S.: An efficient approach to EEG-based emotion recognition using lstm network. In: 2020 16th IEEE International Colloquium on Signal Processing and its Applications (CSPA), pp. 88–92. IEEE (2020)
10. Dar, M.N., Akram, M.U., Khawaja, S.G., Pujari, A.N.: CNN and LSTM-based emotion charting using physiological signals. Sensors **20**(16), 4551 (2020)
11. Chollet, F. (2017). Keras (2015)
12. Hochreiter, S., Schmidhuber, J.: Long short-term memory. Neural Comput. **9**(8), 1735–1780 (1997)
13. https://www.eecs.qmul.ac.uk/mmv/datasets/deap/readme.html
14. Al-Qazzaz, N.K., Sabir, M.K., Ali, S., Ahmad, S.A., Grammer, K.: Effective EEG channels for emotion identification over the brain regions using differential evolution algorithm. In: 2019 41st Annual International Conference of the IEEE Engineering in Medicine and Biology Society (EMBC), pp. 4703–4706. IEEE (2019)

Foundation for the Future of Higher Education or 'Misplaced Optimism'? Being Human in the Age of Artificial Intelligence

Ashraf Alam$^{(\boxtimes)}$ ⓘ and Atasi Mohanty ⓘ

Rekhi Centre of Excellence for the Science of Happiness, Indian Institute of Technology Kharagpur, Kharagpur, West Bengal, India
`ashraf_alam@kgpian.iitkgp.ac.in`

Abstract. Several publications from across the globe have noted the rapid growth of the field of Artificial Intelligence in Education (AIEd). Even though it has been around for over 30 years, many professors are still confused about its implementation in their classrooms. This research surveys the existing literature on this issue by means of a systematic review. Only 112 of the 2984 articles identified between 2006 and 2021 met the exclusion and inclusion criteria necessary for incorporation in the final synthesis. Descriptive results show that STEM and subjects related to computer science predominate in AIEd articles and that 'quantitative methods' predominate in empirical research. The findings are arranged into 4 categorical groupings: (1) intelligent tutoring systems; (2) personalization and adaptive systems; (3) evaluation and assessment; and (4) prediction and profiling, all of which can be applied to institutional and administrative services, academic support services, and assessment and evaluation. The findings call for firm attention towards the lack of critical thinking on the challenges and risks of AIEd and towards the necessity for more comprehensive research on ethical and pedagogical techniques in the deployment of AIEd in higher education.

Keywords: Smart tutoring systems · Machine learning · Pedagogy · Artificial intelligence · Curriculum · Smart campuses · Teaching · Learning · Educational technology

1 Introduction

In recent years, there has been a lot of buzz about how artificial intelligence (AI) may be used in classrooms. The 2018 Horizon report cites artificial intelligence and adaptive learning technologies as major advances in EdTech [1, 27]. Experts forecast a 43% increase in the use of AI in education between 2018 and 2022. Netherlands' Technical University of Eindhoven has announced plans to hire 50 new faculty members to work for a new 'Institute for Artificial Intelligence Systems' dedicated to AI education and research [2, 3, 28]. Studies on the implementation of AI in classrooms date back around 30 years [4, 29].

M. Panda et al. (Eds.): ICIICC 2022, CCIS 1737, pp. 17–29, 2022.
https://doi.org/10.1007/978-3-031-23233-6_2

This year will be the 20th time the AIEd conference has been conducted by the International AIEd Society [5, 6, 30]. The development of AI applications in higher education raises new ethical challenges and risks [7, 31]. Managers, for instance, may be tempted to replace training with more profitable automated AI solutions in times of financial strain [8, 32]. Chatbots, expert systems, and intelligent tutors could cause concern among educators, teaching assistants, counsellors, and administrators who work in the education sector [9, 33]. While AI has the potential to enhance learning analytics, the fact that these systems demand huge volumes of data, particularly sensitive information about professors and students, creates major privacy and data protection problems. Several groups, including the Analysis & Policy Observatory in Australia, have recently published a framework for the ethical regulation of AI in educational settings [10, 34].

Every AI researcher has to be concerned about how their findings will be interpreted morally. We are interested in learning about the novel ethical risks and repercussions that have been envisioned by researchers and authors working in the field [11, 12, 35]. The goal of this research article is to offer a synopsis of studies that examine AI's potential contributions to higher education.

Using a systematic review, this paper focuses on the following three areas of inquiry:

1. When looking back, how scholarly articles on AI have evolved?
2. Which ethical concerns, challenges, and potential hazards are taken into consideration when imagining the role of AI in teaching?
3. In what ways might AI be used, and how broadly, in the context of higher education?

Though the origins of AI lie in computer science and engineering, other disciplines, including philosophy, cognitive science, neurology, and economics, have had substantial impacts on the area. Even though many academics are unaware of the breadth and, more crucially, what is included, AI-based educational and pedagogical tools are being introduced into higher education.

2 Education Using Artificial Intelligence (AIEd)

The first workshop on artificial intelligence (AI) was hosted in the 1950s by John McCarthy at Dartmouth College in the United States. McCarthy first used the term artificial intelligence in the 1956 workshop proposal [13, 36]. Artificial intelligence studies will continue on the premise that every aspect of learning or any other attribute of intelligence may, in principle, be so perfectly characterized that a computer can be built to reproduce it [14, 37]. The term artificial intelligence (AI) is often used to describe robots that can do cognitive tasks, such as learning and problem-solving, that is traditionally done by people. Machine learning, NLP, data mining, neural networks, and algorithms all fall under the general category of artificial intelligence. There is no one technology that is synonymous with AI [15, 38]. Machine learning (ML) is used to determine whether students will pass a course or whether they will be accepted into a program [16, 39]. ML makes use of pattern recognition and prediction software to apply learned patterns to problems [17, 40].

The concept of intelligent machines acting rationally is fundamental to AI. Everything that can detect its environment and respond to it using some kind of actuator is considered an agent [18, 41]. Specialists in the subject make a distinction between weak and strong artificial intelligence as well as particular and wide artificial intelligence. Whether computers can think for themselves, as opposed to just acting logically and mimicking the human mind, is still a philosophical question open to debates and discussions [19, 42]. An AI as advanced and comprehensive as this one appears unlikely to appear very soon. In academia, intelligent agents and information systems are referred to as GOFAI, which stands for "good old-fashioned AI". John Haugeland, a philosopher, came up with this term [20, 43].

There are now three types of AI software solutions utilized in education: intelligent virtual reality, intelligent aid for group learning, and intelligent personal tutors. Intelligent tutoring systems (ITS) have the potential to mimic in-person, one-on-one tutoring [21, 44]. Based on learner models, algorithms, and neural networks, they could choose the student's learning path and the content to be taught. Cognitive scaffolding and teacher-student communication are two further benefits [22, 45]. The vast majority of research indicates that education is best accomplished in a group setting. Collaboration and discussion are crucial to the educational process. It is essential, however, to facilitate and govern digital teamwork [23, 46]. Assisting adaptive group construction based on learner models, AIEd may also promote online group engagement or summarise talks that a human teacher may use to guide students toward the course's aims and objectives [24, 47]. Collaborative learning may be aided by all these methods. Intelligent virtual reality (IVR), which also makes use of ITS, is used to immerse students in realistic VR and game-based learning environments [25, 48]. In remote or online labs, simulated humans may play the roles of teachers, facilitators, or even other students [26, 49].

Artificial intelligence can provide immediate assessments and suggestions [21, 50]. Instead of relying only on periodic assessments, teachers may integrate AIEd into their lesson plans for continuous monitoring of student progress [8, 51]. Algorithms have been employed with a high degree of accuracy to predict whether a student would fail an assignment or withdraw from a course [19, 52]. Learner-facing, teacher-facing, and system-facing are the three primary perspectives from which to examine AI technologies in education [13, 53].

Learner-facing artificial intelligence technologies include software used by students to study a subject, such as adaptive or personalized learning management systems [18, 54]. Teacher-facing technology help reduce the workload of the educator by automating tasks like course management, student assessment, instructor feedback, and plagiarism checking [23, 55]. Teachers may monitor their students' progress in their lessons with the help of AIEd technologies and then respond accordingly with guidance and support. System-facing helps managers and administrators gather data at the institutional level [8, 56].

In this paper, we apply the concept of the student life cycle to the setting of higher education as a theoretical model for describing the many services anchored in AI, available both for administrative and institutional purposes and to support the academic teaching and learning process.

3 Methods

A systematic review seeks to address specific issues by using a clear, consistent, and repeatable search strategy to identify relevant studies for inclusion or exclusion. Next, we summarise the findings, discuss how they may be used in practice, and call attention to any gaps or inconsistencies by retrieving and codifying data from the included study. This article provides a map of 112 papers dealing with AI in academic settings.

3.1 Search Strategy

Although problems exist in the peer-review process, our assessment restricted itself to articles published in peer-reviewed journals due to their credibility and rigorous review standards. The first search was performed in January of 2021 and 2984 records were located. After weeding out the duplicates, it was agreed that only articles published in 2006 or later would be included. It was also decided that the corpus would only include articles that dealt with the application of AI to academic settings.

3.2 Reliability of Agreement Amongst Raters

At this stage of screening, sensitivity rather than specificity was necessary, therefore articles were included rather than rejected after being examined by a team of four coders. Sessions were held often to discuss the first 80 entries and determine their inclusion or exclusion. The coding decisions made by the four coders (A, B, C, and D) were evaluated using Cohen's kappa (κ), a coefficient for consistency across raters, to determine inter-rater reliability. Random selection led to the examination of twenty papers. Overall, the Kappa values for the four coders were quite high (between 0.81 and 0.89). Therefore, it is reasonable to conclude that there is high inter-rater reliability.

After the first screening, 268 articles met the criteria to go on to the full-text phase. Unfortunately, 81 publications could not be retrieved due to issues with the library's order system or with contacting the authors. A total of 189 articles were retrieved, screened, and coded, however only 112 were included in the final synthesis.

3.3 Collection, Codification, and Analysis of Data

EPPI Reviewer, a tool used for systematic reviews, was loaded with all of the articles. Articles were evaluated according to their research methodology (empirical vs. descriptive, academic setting) and primary author's area of study. AI applications were also considered. The concept of AI and any references to its benefits and downsides in the papers were also coded. Descriptive analysis was conducted in R, using the tidyr tool for handling data.

3.4 Limitations

Although every effort was made to ensure the accuracy of the included studies, the methods used in each research always result in some degree of error, and this systematic review is no exception. Although the three databases of educational research that were chosen are large and worldwide in reach, this analysis did not include research on AI that had been published in other languages. This was accomplished by focusing on English-language, peer-reviewed papers. Papers published in journals that were not indexed in any of the three databases were not included in this review. Additional databases, publication types, and language versions of publications might be used in future research to increase the study's breadth. This would need a thorough evaluation of the project's available resources and the feasibility of conducting the review.

4   Results

The term artificial intelligence (AI) is used to describe computer systems or intelligent agents that exhibit human-like intelligence by mimicking human cognitive abilities such as learning, memory, perception, and interaction with the environment, as well as language [15, 57]. Artificial intelligence, or AI, refers to machines that can simulate human intelligence. The purpose of this wide-ranging academic discipline is to learn about the inner workings of the human brain so that we might apply those discoveries to the development of better technological tools [8, 58]. Artificial intelligence (AI) may play the role of either a teacher or a student in a language class.

The incorporation of agent-based, individualized instruction raises serious concerns about personal data privacy [19, 59]. Agents may pick up on a wide variety of learner attributes, like preferences and aptitude, without any human input. Data pertaining to an individual's identity is, in fact, confidential [4, 60].

Many learners are uncomfortable with the idea that their individual characteristics may be made public. If they are struggling academically, students with special education needs may feel their teachers will treat them differently. For this reason, the issue of privacy must be resolved before employing agent-based systems [24, 60]. Many public schools cannot afford the time and money needed to develop and execute AI-based techniques, which is another barrier to its usage [13, 61].

We have utilized the concept of a student's life-cycle as a framework to define the many AI-based services provided at the institutional and administrative level, such as admission, counselling, and library services, and at the academic support level, such as evaluation, feedback, and tutoring [26, 62]. The following four domains of artificial intelligence use were identified using a comprehensive literature study and iterative coding procedure: affirmative action and personalization, evaluation and assessment, profiling and prediction, and intelligent tutoring systems [5, 63].

4.1   Forecasting and Characterising

Many AI tools rely on learner models or profiles to make predictions, such as which students are more likely to enroll in a program or to drop out, and to provide students with timely assistance, feedback, and guidance on content-related concerns as they go through their studies [12]. Dropout/retention, student models/performance, and admission/scheduling are the three main subsets of profiling/prediction [24, 32].

Research in this area has made use of machine learning strategies for classifying patterns, modelling student profiles, and making forecasts. Several machine learning techniques, such as artificial neural networks (ANN), support vector machines (SVM), random forests, and neural networks, are used to assess the overall prediction accuracy of conventional logistic regression. In terms of percentage classification accuracy, machine learning approaches exceed logistic regression [12, 33]. Classifier performance may also be evaluated using the F1-score, which takes into consideration the proportion of correctly classified positive cases, erroneously classified negative instances, and incorrectly classified positive instances [3, 34].

It is crucial to have a reliable evaluation of students' academic performance for use in admissions decisions and to boost educational services [5, 35]. The applications might be sorted using the support vector machine (SVM) method, which has a 95% accuracy rate. SVM may be used to find geographical patterns that provide prospective students from specific places an edge in the college admissions process [19, 36].

Using a model trained with data from one state or province, an ANN may make predictions about registration rates in other parts of the country [14, 37]. A student's course selection might be affected by several factors, including the quality of the course and the instructor, the amount of work involved, the mode of delivery, and the scheduling of the examination. Since admissions decisions can often be predicted with high accuracy, an AI solution might free up administrative staff from routine tasks so that they can focus on more complex cases [21, 38].

As a consequence of studies on student attrition and re-enrollment, early warning systems have been developed to spot potentially disengaged freshmen. Predicting attrition may be done using classification methods like logistic regression, decision trees (DT), and artificial neural networks (ANN) [26, 39]. Students' demographic, academic, and economic characteristics should all be included in the data (e.g., age, sex, ethnicity, GPA, etc.). The ANN model has the highest performance with an accuracy rating of over 80% which is checked after 10 rounds of cross-validation [15, 40].

Technology based on AI is helping with student profiling and modelling learning behaviours for the purpose of predicting academic achievement [20, 41]. Several machine learning algorithms are used to analyze student behavioural data from the virtual learning environment to predict student involvement [6, 42]. Smart prescriptive algorithms enable automated detection of disinterested learners and prompt intervention. Students' progress on projects is evaluated in workshops using face tracking and hand tracking [20, 43]. The outcomes supplied by multimodal data may help educators get insight into critical features of project-based learning activities. How undergraduates learn to code may be analyzed by looking at the code transcripts they write for software development projects [11, 44]. Algorithms based on artificial intelligence may predict students' academic motivation based on their actions in a virtual classroom [21, 45]. Studying AI-based models helps tremendously in creating intelligent tutoring systems and flexible learning environments [5, 46].

4.2 Curriculum Technology that Uses Artificial Intelligence

Teaching-learning is the main priority for intelligent tutoring systems (ITS). In contrast, there are some that have been institutionalized and given an administrative setting. The first known ITS was the SCHOLAR system, which was established in 1970 and allowed for question-and-answer sessions between professors and students but did not provide continuous interaction [9, 47]. ITS is more efficient than other methods of instruction, including lectures, textbooks, online reading, and homework [14, 48]. ITS provides students with course materials and supports them via adaptive feedback, question-specific strategies, and the capacity to identify when a student is struggling [7, 49]. The ITS enables this by keeping tabs on where each student is at any given time.

Errors may be identified and corrected with the help of a discussion between the learner and the machine using an instructional conversation toolkit-based tutoring system or a pervasive interactive teaching robot with question recognition-based speech [9, 50]. The ITS acts as a peer mentor, collaborating with a student to find solutions to their issues. They can talk, sign, and organize their messages. They do not get tutoring but rather engage in cooperative problem-solving [24, 51]. A possible label for this scenario is 'cooperation amongst peers'. With the data gathered from each student's participation in the course, ITS can tailor their assistance to each individual's needs while they are enrolled in an online course [17, 52]. With this information, the system can recommend the best books to read, exercises to do, and other individualized plans of action. A smart assistant is stationed in a simulated statistical mechanics laboratory, where it presents activities, assesses students' understanding of the topic, and tailors its presentation of the information to each individual learner [19, 53].

The basic purpose of ITS is to promote academically fruitful conversation movements in online collaborative learning debates [23, 54]. It helps to encourage collaborative writing by automatically generating questions, providing automated feedback, and analyzing the process. Teachers are able to act when necessary, thanks to intelligent assistants who compile summaries of each student's progress and engagement in group work, alert notifications based on the identification of conflict situations, and data regarding each student's preferred method of learning [17, 55]. The ITS breaks up the tutoring obligations of the instructors by automating chores and offering timely feedback, leaving the instructors responsible for supplying new clues and the correct responses. As a result, it makes the lives of teachers easier [13, 56].

4.3 Constant Re-Evaluation

Artificial intelligence is used to determine how well students have retained the information and applied what they have learned [5, 57]. Learners may benefit from using tools like Latent Semantic Analysis and ePortfolios to map out unique courses of study. Semantic web technology may be used to translate student credentials from different universities to facilitate credit transfers [8, 58]. Course descriptions and syllabi may be made available using these technologies as well. Algorithms may be used to pair up prospective students with the skills and knowledge employers are looking for, allowing instructors to tailor their lessons to the specific demands of the workforce. When it comes to making judgments and evaluations, AI programs are highly precise and efficient. However, due to the calibration and training requirements of supervised machine learning systems, they are best suited for large-enrollment classes or programs. Automated grading and feedback systems, assessing students' knowledge, engagement, and academic integrity, and evaluating teachers' efficacy are the four main types of AI assessment and evaluation used in the classroom [21, 59, 64].

Student essays may be graded automatically with the use of open-source Java software used in automated grading, commonly known as Automated Essay Scoring (AES) systems [18, 60]. Using AES would be challenging in small schools because of the large number of pre-scored exams required for calibration, and AES may not be appropriate for all forms of writing. One of the benefits of using algorithms to analyze text responses is that it shifts the focus of evaluation away from students' knowledge and abilities and toward their ability to rewrite and improve their work [18, 61].

Intelligent agents provide reminders or help to pupils when they become lost or stuck in their tasks. Aspiring pilots may now use software that will alert them if they start to lose situational awareness in the air [23, 62]. The cognitive load on students is reduced since lexical properties in machine learning systems give automatic feedback and help students create better essays [8, 18]. For example, an adaptive testing-based automated feedback system selects the most appropriate answers for each student based on Bloom's taxonomy of cognitive domains and then recommends related reading and exercises [9, 22]. Tools have been developed to help students evaluate their conceptual understanding and get individualized instruction. These formulas factor in students' performance on tests and other assessments, as well as their activity in the virtual learning environment [11, 16]. Academic integrity is assessed by using machine learning algorithms to identify instances of possible plagiarism in student work [8, 17]. Data mining techniques are used to analyze course evaluations and determine an instructor's effectiveness based on several different classification strategies [7, 18]. Comparatively speaking, using an algorithm to evaluate instructional approaches yields more accurate results [19, 26].

4.4   A System that May Change to Fit the USER'S Needs

Biology, computer science, environmental education, and even animation design are just some of the many areas that benefit from the usage of adaptive systems in the classroom [8, 20]. Adaptive systems profile students' behaviours and then provide them with individualized assignments, resources, and content. E-learning recommendation systems help students make informed course selections [21, 24]. Adaptive recommendation systems are useful in massive open online courses (MOOCs) because they provide students with suggestions for further assignments, resources, and other users based on their individual interests [22, 26]. Having access to students' academic information helps teachers with diagnostic tasks and personalize learning plans for each student [5, 23]. It also helps with performance assessment and offers individualized help and criticism [11, 24].

5   Conclusion and Way Forward

This article looks at the field of AIEd. In this research, we provide a summary of the many ways AI might be used to improve the educational experience for college students, teachers, and administrators. Profiling and prediction, intelligent tutoring systems, assessment and evaluation, and adaptive systems and customization were the four main themes under which they were studied. In order to better conceptualize and comprehend

AIEd practice and research, a framework was developed via a systematic review. On the other hand, there is still a substantial window of opportunity for educators to pursue innovative and significant research and practice with AIEd that may have an effect on teaching and learning in higher education due to the scarcity of longitudinal studies, the predominance of descriptive and pilot studies from a technological standpoint, and the predominance of quantitative methods, particularly quasi-experimental methods. There is a dearth of research on the effects of policies and their actual implementation.

Throughout the various stages of a student's academic career, AI-based tools and services can be extremely helpful for all parties involved. This is important for universities with a large student body, like open and remote learning colleges. It could be helpful to provide options for adaptable, interactive, and personalized education. This may, for example, relieve teachers of the burden of manually grading hundreds, if not thousands, of assignments, enabling them to focus on their core duty, i.e., providing sympathetic human instruction. It is crucial to underline the need of considering not just the technological elements of AIEd, but also the pedagogical, ethical, social, cultural, and economic ones. The danger, of course, is in taking data and code at face value. Due to education's inherent complexity, it cannot be reduced to a set of purely quantitative variables and methods. Digital data, like all digital technologies, may seem like a simple technological solution to educational problems, but despite the promising results, they do not offer such a solution.

Pedagogically sound goals, rather than technically feasible ones, should be pursued. In China, teachers are already able to see data about their students' participation and emotions in class thanks to face recognition technology displayed on a dashboard. Sometimes, even the most sophisticated AI systems may make a mistake. An AI system cannot acquire intelligence without the training data used to develop it. Every one of the many issues discussed in the new UNESCO study on the prospects and obstacles of AIEd for sustainable development is laden with important educational, societal, and ethical implications. For example, it discusses how to assure inclusion and equality in AIEd, how to educate teachers for AI-powered education, how to construct high-quality and inclusive data systems, and how to be ethical and transparent while collecting, utilizing, and distributing data.

The most surprising aspect of this assessment is the astounding lack of critical consideration of the potential dangers and educational implications of using AI technologies in higher education. Recently conducted empirical research seldom addressed privacy problems in terms of ethical consequences. Educators and learning designers need to perform more research on how to include AI applications throughout the student lifecycle in order to take advantage of the immense potential that these technologies have for constructing intelligent learning and teaching systems. Our systematic review's absence of authors with links to education departments demonstrates the need for a pedagogical lens to be applied to these innovations in technology. Possible consequences of this theoretical vacuum for the whole area of educational technology are discussed. More than forty percent of the studies in three premier journals for educational technology lacked any practical application. Explicit educational views were missing from the papers that were reviewed. Unfortunately, there is currently no evidence to back the development of psychological and pedagogical theories of learning in connection with technologies anchored in artificial intelligence.

References

1. Chatterjee, S., Bhattacharjee, K.K.: Adoption of artificial intelligence in higher education: a quantitative analysis using structural equation modelling. Educ. Inf. Technol. **25**(5), 3443–3463 (2020)
2. Alam, A.: Challenges and possibilities in teaching and learning of calculus: a case study of India. J. Educ. Gifted Young Sci. **8**(1), 407–433 (2020)
3. Bates, T., Cobo, C., Mariño, O., Wheeler, S.: Can artificial intelligence transform higher education? Int. J. Educ. Technol. High. Educ. **17**(1), 1–12 (2020). https://doi.org/10.1186/s41239-020-00218-x
4. Dilmurod, R., Fazliddin, A.: Prospects for the introduction of artificial intelligence technologies in higher education. Academicia: Int. Multi. Res. J. **11**(2), 929–934 (2021)
5. Knox, J.: Artificial intelligence and education in China. Learn. Media Technol. **45**(3), 298–311 (2020)
6. Alam, A.: Designing XR into higher education using immersive learning environments (ILEs) and hybrid education for innovation in HEIs to attract UN's education for sustainable development (ESD) Initiative. In: 2021 International Conference on Advances in Computing, Communication, and Control (ICAC3), pp. 1–9. IEEE (2021)
7. Guan, C., Mou, J., Jiang, Z.: Artificial intelligence innovation in education: a twenty-year data-driven historical analysis. Int. J. Innovation Stud. **4**(4), 134–147 (2020)
8. Chen, X., Xie, H., Zou, D., Hwang, G.J.: Application and theory gaps during the rise of artificial intelligence in education. Comput. Educ.: Artif. Intell. **1**, 100002 (2020)
9. Alam, A.: Educational robotics and computer programming in early childhood education: a conceptual framework for assessing elementary school students' computational thinking for designing powerful educational scenarios. In: 2022 International Conference on Smart Technologies and Systems for Next Generation Computing (ICSTSN), pp. 1–7. IEEE (2022)
10. Alyahyan, E., Düştegör, D.: Predicting academic success in higher education: literature review and best practices. Int. J. Educ. Technol. High. Educ. **17**(1), 1–21 (2020). https://doi.org/10.1186/s41239-020-0177-7
11. Rampersad, G.: Robot will take your job: innovation for an era of artificial intelligence. J. Bus. Res. **116**, 68–74 (2020)
12. Chen, L., Chen, P., Lin, Z.: Artificial intelligence in education: a review. Ieee Access **8**, 75264–75278 (2020)
13. Cope, B., Kalantzis, M., Searsmith, D.: Artificial intelligence for education: knowledge and its assessment in AI-enabled learning ecologies. Educ. Philos. Theory **53**(12), 1229–1245 (2021)
14. Alam, A.: Mapping a sustainable future through conceptualization of transformative learning framework, education for sustainable development, critical reflection, and responsible citizenship: an exploration of pedagogies for twenty-first century learning. ECS Trans. **107**(1), 9827 (2022)
15. Yilmaz Ince, E., Kabul, A., Diler, İ: Distance education in higher education in the COVID-19 pandemic process: A case of Isparta Applied Sciences University. Int. J. Technol. Educ. Sci. **4**(4), 345–351 (2020)
16. Alam, A. (2022). Employing Adaptive Learning and Intelligent Tutoring Robots for Virtual Classrooms and Smart Campuses: Reforming Education in the Age of Artificial Intelligence. In: Shaw, R.N., Das, S., Piuri, V., Bianchini, M. (eds) Advanced Computing and Intelligent Technologies. Lecture Notes in Electrical Engineering, vol 914. Springer, Singapore

17. Holmes, W., Bialik, M., Fadel, C.: Artificial Intelligence in Education (2020)
18. Wang, T., Cheng, E.C.K.: Towards a tripartite research agenda: a scoping review of artificial intelligence in education research. In: Cheng, E.C.K., Koul, R.B., Wang, T., Xinguo, Y. (eds.) Artificial Intelligence in Education: Emerging Technologies, Models and Applications. LNDECT, vol. 104, pp. 3–24. Springer, Singapore (2022). https://doi.org/10.1007/978-981-16-7527-0_1
19. Nemorin, S., Vlachidis, A., Ayerakwa, H.M., Andriotis, P.: AI hyped? A horizon scan of discourse on artificial intelligence in education (AIED) and development. Learn., Media Technol. 1–14 (2022). https://doi.org/10.1080/17439884.2022.2095568
20. Alam, A.: Cloud-based e-learning: scaffolding the environment for adaptive e-learning ecosystem based on cloud computing infrastructure. In: Computer Communication, Networking and IoT: Proceedings of 5th ICICC 2021, vol. 2, pp. 1–9. Springer Nature Singapore, Singapore (2022)
21. Holmes, W., Porayska-Pomsta, K. (eds.): The Ethics of Artificial Intelligence in Education: Practices, Challenges, and Debates. Taylor & Francis (2022)
22. Chen, X., Zou, D., Xie, H., Cheng, G., Liu, C.: Two decades of artificial intelligence in education. Educ. Technol. Soc. 25(1), 28–47 (2022)
23. Paek, S., Kim, N.: Analysis of worldwide research trends on the impact of artificial intelligence in education. Sustainability 13(14), 7941 (2021)
24. Akgun, S., Greenhow, C.: Artificial intelligence in education: addressing ethical challenges in K-12 settings. AI and Ethics 2, 431–440 (2021). https://doi.org/10.1007/s43681-021-00096-7
25. Bhimdiwala, A., Neri, R.C., Gomez, L.M.: Advancing the design and implementation of artificial intelligence in education through continuous improvement. Int. J. Artif. Intell. Educ. 32(3), 756–782 (2022)
26. Alam, A.: Test of knowledge of elementary vectors concepts (TKEVC) among first-semester bachelor of engineering and technology students. Periódico Tchê Química 17(35), 477–494 (2020)
27. Ouyang, F., Jiao, P.: Artificial intelligence in education: the three paradigms. Comput. Educ.: Artif. Intell. 2, 100020 (2021)
28. Holmes, W., et al.: Ethics of AI in education: towards a community-wide framework. Int. J. Artif. Intell. Educ. 32(3), 504–526 (2022)
29. Megahed, N.A., Abdel-Kader, R.F., Soliman, H.Y.: Post-pandemic education strategy: framework for artificial intelligence-empowered education in engineering (AIEd-Eng) for lifelong learning. In: International Conference on Advanced Machine Learning Technologies and Applications, pp. 544–556. Springer, Cham (2022)
30. Dickler, R., Dudy, S., Mawasi, A., Whitehill, J., Benson, A., Corbitt, A.: Interdisciplinary approaches to getting ai experts and education stakeholders talking. In: Rodrigo, M.M., Matsuda, N., Cristea, A.I., Dimitrova, V. (eds.) Artificial Intelligence in Education. Posters and Late Breaking Results, Workshops and Tutorials, Industry and Innovation Tracks, Practitioners' and Doctoral Consortium. AIED 2022. Lecture Notes in Computer Science, vol. 13356. Springer, Cham (2022). https://doi.org/10.1007/978-3-031-11647-6_20
31. Alam, A.: Positive psychology goes to school: conceptualizing students' happiness in 21st century schools while 'minding the mind!' are we there yet? evidence-backed, school-based positive psychology interventions. ECS Trans. 107(1), 11199 (2022)
32. Wang, T., Cheng, E.C.K.: An investigation of barriers to Hong Kong K-12 schools incorporating artificial intelligence in education. Comput. Educ.: Artif. Intell. 2, 100031 (2021)
33. Chan, L., Hogaboam, L., Cao, R.: Artificial intelligence in education. In: Applied Artificial Intelligence in Business, pp. 265–278. Springer, Cham (2022)

34. Khosravi, H., et al.: Explainable artificial intelligence in education. Comput. Educ.: Artif. Intell. **3**, 100074 (2022)
35. Alam, A.: A digital game based learning approach for effective curriculum transaction for teaching-learning of artificial intelligence and machine learning. In: 2022 International Conference on Sustainable Computing and Data Communication Systems (ICSCDS), pp. 69–74. IEEE (2022)
36. Schiff, D.: Out of the laboratory and into the classroom: the future of artificial intelligence in education. AI & Soc. **36**(1), 331–348 (2020). https://doi.org/10.1007/s00146-020-01033-8
37. Sadiku, M.N., Musa, S.M., Chukwu, U.C.: Artificial Intelligence in Education. iUniverse (2022)
38. Lameras, P., Arnab, S.: Power to the teachers: an exploratory review on artificial intelligence in education. Information **13**(1), 14 (2021)
39. Ezzaim, A., Kharroubi, F., Dahbi, A., Aqqal, A., Haidine, A.: Artificial intelligence in education-State of the art. Int. J. Comput. Eng. Data Sci. **2**(2), 1–11 (2022)
40. Alam, A.: Possibilities and apprehensions in the landscape of artificial intelligence in education. In: 2021 International Conference on Computational Intelligence and Computing Applications (ICCICA), pp. 1–8. IEEE (2021)
41. Bozkurt, A., Karadeniz, A., Baneres, D., Guerrero-Roldán, A.E., Rodríguez, M.E.: Artificial intelligence and reflections from educational landscape: a review of AI studies in half a century. Sustainability **13**(2), 800 (2021)
42. Sharples, M.: Automated essay writing: an AIED opinion. Int. J. Artif. Intell. Educ. **32**(4), 1119–1126 (2022). https://doi.org/10.1007/s40593-022-00300-7
43. Biswas, G., Bull, S., Kay, J., Mitrovic, A. (eds.): AIED 2011. LNCS (LNAI), vol. 6738. Springer, Heidelberg (2011). https://doi.org/10.1007/978-3-642-21869-9
44. Ye, R., Sun, F., Li, J.: Artificial intelligence in education: origin, development and rise. In: Liu, X.-J., Nie, Z., Jingjun, Y., Xie, F., Song, R. (eds.) ICIRA 2021. LNCS (LNAI), vol. 13016, pp. 545–553. Springer, Cham (2021). https://doi.org/10.1007/978-3-030-89092-6_49
45. Alam, A.: Should robots replace teachers? Mobilisation of AI and learning analytics in education. In: 2021 International Conference on Advances in Computing, Communication, and Control (ICAC3), pp. 1–12. IEEE (2021)
46. Zhang, K., Aslan, A.B.: AI technologies for education: Recent research & future directions. Comput. Educ.: Artif. Intell. **2**, 100025 (2021)
47. Khazanchi, R., Khazanchi, P.: Artificial intelligence in education: a closer look into intelligent tutoring systems. In: Handbook of research on critical issues in special education for school rehabilitation practices, pp. 256–277. IGI Global (2021)
48. Nalbant, K.G.: The importance of artificial intelligence in education: a short review. J. Rev. Sci. Eng. **2021**, 1–15 (2021)
49. Zheng, Y., Zhou, Z., Blikstein, P.: Towards an inclusive and socially committed community in artificial intelligence in education: a social network analysis of the evolution of authorship and research topics over 8 years and 2509 papers. In: Rodrigo, M.M., Matsuda, N., Cristea, A.I., Dimitrova, V. (eds.) Artificial Intelligence in Education. AIED 2022. Lecture Notes in Computer Science, vol. 13355. Springer, Cham (2022). https://doi.org/10.1007/978-3-031-11644-5_34
50. Lameras, P., Paraskakis, I., Konstantinidis, S.: A rudimentary progression model for artificial intelligence in education competencies and skills. In: Auer, M.E., Tsiatsos, T. (eds.) IMCL 2021. LNNS, vol. 411, pp. 927–936. Springer, Cham (2022). https://doi.org/10.1007/978-3-030-96296-8_84
51. Alam, A.: Social robots in education for long-term human-robot interaction: socially supportive behaviour of robotic tutor for creating robo-tangible learning environment in a guided discovery learning interaction. ECS Trans. **107**(1), 12389 (2022)

52. Hamal, O., El Faddouli, N.E., Harouni, M.H.A., Lu, J.: Artificial intelligent in education. Sustainability **14**(5), 2862 (2022)
53. Campbell, C.: Artificial intelligence in education: contributors, collaborations, research topics, and challenges. Educ. Technol. Soc. **25**(1), 28–47 (2022)
54. Ungerer, L., Slade, S.: Ethical considerations of artificial intelligence in learning analytics in distance education contexts. In: Prinsloo, P., Slade, S., Khalil, M. (eds.) Learning Analytics in Open and Distributed Learning: Potential and Challenges, pp. 105–120. Springer Nature Singapore, Singapore (2022). https://doi.org/10.1007/978-981-19-0786-9_8
55. Corbeil, M.E., Corbeil, J.R.: Establishing trust in artificial intelligence in education. In: Paliszkiewicz, Joanna, Chen, Kuanchin (eds.) Trust, Organizations and the Digital Economy: Theory and Practice, pp. 49–60. Routledge, New York (2021). https://doi.org/10.4324/978 1003165965-5
56. Xia, Q., Chiu, T.K., Lee, M., Sanusi, I.T., Dai, Y., Chai, C.S.: A self-determination theory (SDT) design approach for inclusive and diverse artificial intelligence (AI) education. Comput. Educ. **189**, 104582 (2022)
57. Alam, A.: Possibilities and challenges of compounding artificial intelligence in India's educational landscape. Int. J. Adv. Sci. Technol. **29**(5), 5077–5094 (2020)
58. Dai, C.P., Ke, F.: Educational applications of artificial intelligence in simulation-based learning: a systematic mapping review. Comput. Educ.: Artif. Intell. **3**, 100087 (2022)
59. Yang, S.J., Ogata, H., Matsui, T., Chen, N.S.: Human-centered artificial intelligence in education: seeing the invisible through the visible. Comput. Educ.: Artif. Intell. **2**, 100008 (2021)
60. Alam, A.: Investigating sustainable education and positive psychology interventions in schools towards achievement of sustainable happiness and wellbeing for 21st century pedagogy and curriculum. ECS Trans. **107**(1), 19481 (2022)
61. Channa, F.R., Sarhandi, P.S.A., Bugti, F., Pathan, H.: Harnessing artificial intelligence in education for preparing learners for the 21st century. Elementary Educ. Online **20**(5), 3186 (2021)
62. Xu, W., Ouyang, F.: The application of AI technologies in STEM education: a systematic review from 2011 to 2021. Int. J. STEM Educ. **9**(1), 1–20 (2022)
63. Alam, A.: Pedagogy of calculus in India: an empirical investigation. Periódico Tchê Química **17**(34), 164–180 (2020)
64. Chaudhry, M.A., Kazim, E.: Artificial intelligence in education (AIEd): a high-level academic and industry note 2021. AI and Ethics **2**(1), 157–165 (2022)

AI Enabled Internet of Medical Things Framework for Smart Healthcare

Jyoti Srivastava[1,2] and Sidheswar Routray[1(✉)]

[1] Department of Computer Science and Engineering, School of Engineering, Indrashil University, Rajpur, Mehsana, Gujarat, India
[2] Department of Computer Engineering, Unitedworld School of Computational Intelligence, Karnavati University, Gandhinagar, India

Abstract. Internet of Medical Things (IoMT) is basically the use of the Internet of Things (IoT) in Smart Healthcare where automation in health monitoring is provided using Artificial Intelligence (AI) so that without visiting the hospital for every small problem an individual can get consultancy from doctors remotely. As per the pandemic situation visiting the hospital an individual can result in contact with harmful viruses, so using this Smart HealthCare System (SHS) without visiting the hospital an individual can monitor their day-to-day health record and can take preliminary precautions accordingly. Three major health domains are defined in this work where AI-based SHS can help the individual depending on the patient's health situation they can belong to one of these domains. Now, SHS deals with highly sensitive patient health data so few parameters must be satisfied by this system i.e., data security, data accuracy, system efficiency, Quality of Service (QoS), System Reliability, etc. In this work, we will elaborate discussion about these parameters and provide a comparison table to analyze the work done by different researchers in this era to improve the performance of an Artificial Intelligence (AI) based SHS using the IoMT framework.

Keywords: Internet of medical things (IoMT) · Smart healthcare system (SHS) · Artificial intelligence (AI) · Data accuracy · Energy efficiency · Quality of service (QoS)

1 Introduction

The demand for advanced medical treatment is increasing everyday to ensure better health and protectiveness from both tangible and non-tangible viruses thereby accelerating the need for automation in Healthcare System. On top of the new healthcare era, the AI-based Internet of Medical Things (IoMT) framework is developing with various new creative and smart solutions to various real-world problems [1]. Various organizations and researchers are showing their interest in the Internet of Things (IoT) to enhance their scope of work and throughput. IoT seems to be the new generation technology with a universal applicability in almost every market field with increasing integration degree of end products, systems, and services. IoT is basically a collection of nodes (computers, laptops, Smartphones, or other smart devices) having their unique IDs connected via

© The Author(s), under exclusive license to Springer Nature Switzerland AG 2022
M. Panda et al. (Eds.): ICIICC 2022, CCIS 1737, pp. 30–46, 2022.
https://doi.org/10.1007/978-3-031-23233-6_3

wired or wireless medium and able to communicate without any human intervention. IoT can be used in various fields for providing automation in the implementation of smart techniques for the betterment of society [2]. Figure 1 shows the use of IoT in different eras including agriculture services [3], healthcare services [1], educational institutes [4], traffic management [5], etc.

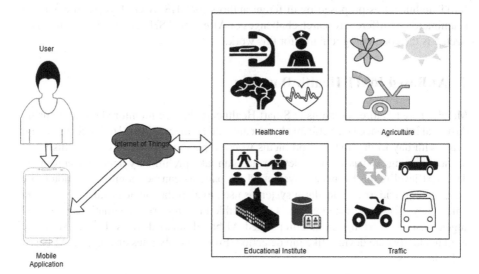

Fig. 1. Role of IoT in various market fields.

Artificial Intelligence gives the automation for providing essential features in IoMT framework-based Smart Healthcare systems, System Security where AI can be used to identify the intrusion within the system [6], detect immediate security attacks [7], Web-based security assessment [8], etc. AI can also be used to provide an automatic alert to all the respective medical staff for immediate actions in emergencies [9]. Along with the patients, this technique will be beneficial for the doctors also as using AI doctors will be able to easily maintain and monitor patient's health records and can provide remote medical advice.

Therefore, considering the susceptibility of patients' health data we are motivated to provide this comparative analysis of AI-based SHS using IoMT architecture using the following parameters: data security, data accuracy, system efficiency, Quality of Service (QoS), and System Reliability. The major contributions of the work are as follows.

- To discover the role of AI in different health domains of the IoMT framework along with their application in SHS.
- To examine different IoMT architectures of AI-based SHS.
- To present a comparative analysis of various accurate data collection techniques thereby creating a reliable AI-based SHS.
- To scrutinize different Data Security techniques to ensure protectiveness in AI-based SHS.

- To present an extensive examination of different system efficiency algorithms for an AI-based SHS.
- To present a comparative analysis of different QoS parameters for an AI-based SHS

This work consists of total 5 sections where Sect. 2 represents different AI-based health domains with their application in SHS, Sect. 3 elaborates on different AI-enabled IoMT architectures proposed by different authors for SHS, Sect. 4 gives an extensive examination of different research challenges of AI-enabled SHS and the last section i.e., Sect. 5 is the concluding remarks for this work.

2   AI Based IoMT Health Domains

Mainly there are three domains in Smart Healthcare that are monitored remotely using Artificial Intelligence i.e., Selfcare, Acute care, and Homecare [10]. The Selfcare system deals with day-to-day medical problems where a person can easily monitor his regular health using AI-based smart devices and can take preliminary actions accordingly. The next level is the Homecare system where patients can be monitored remotely by healthcare providers and an alarm system is used to alert the medical staff in case of an emergency. The acute care system is responsible only for critical situations that need urgent responses from wearable/implanted AI-based smart devices that are specially used in elderly care devices like fall detection. Figure 2 elaborates on all three AI-based SHS domains.

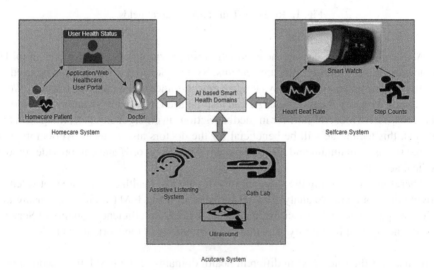

Fig. 2. AI enabled smart healthcare domains

All three domains use different types of sensors or collections of different sensors to fetch accurate medical data about the individual. For example, LM35 senses body temperature usually used in self-care systems, DHT11 is also a humidity and temperature sensor used in Homecare Systems and AD8232 is an Electrocardiogram Sensor usually used in Acute care Systems [11].

3   AI Enabled IoMT Architectures for Smart Healthcare Systems

In most AI-enabled Smart Healthcare Systems as shown in Fig. 3, the whole architecture consists of three basic layers, where the bottommost one is primarily used for collecting patients' health records from wearable/implanted sensors on the human body, the middle layer primarily analyses and does the processing on the collected data using some AI algorithms and the topmost layer mostly deals with the AI results display to the end user using some interface. But depending on different system requirements, names, protocols, and features can be added or removed by different authors.

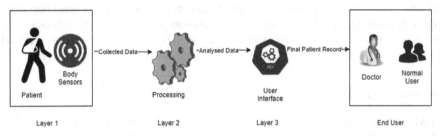

Fig. 3. AI enabled IoMT architectures for smart healthcare systems

Sun et al. [1] introduces a security protocol using AI where a three-tier architecture is used namely the Sensor level, and Personal server level, Medical Server level where medical server layer consists of various core algorithms and programs, and the sensor level deals with sensors and medical devices and personal server level is a collection of few personal servers for internal process and data storage [33]. Kumar et al. [12] proposed a three-layered end-to-end architecture for connecting IoT sensors to smart healthcare i.e., the Data storage layer, Data collection layer, and Data processing Layer. The data collection layer consists of IoT devices for sensing medical data, then the data storage layer is used to store this record on a wider range, and the last one i.e., the data processing layer does an analysis of received data [34]. Sun et al. [13] proposed an AI-based IoMT architecture mainly consisting of three layers namely, the Network Layer, Perceptual Layer, and the Application Layer. The perceptual layer collects medical data from the on-body sensors and transforms it into important information. The next layer i.e., the network layer is responsible for platform and interface-related services required for implementing particular data transmission techniques. The topmost layer i.e., the application layer deals with different healthcare equipment and utilizes all collected medical information for managing patient healthcare data remotely.

4   Research Challenges of AI Enabled Smart Healthcare Systems

AI-enabled IoMT framework for smart healthcare systems ensures automation and flexibility for the end user but to create a such real-time framework, the developing team needs to tackle various research challenges. There can be various research challenges that are to be monitored during the development of AI-enabled SHS like amount of energy consumed, packet delivery ratio, battery lifetime, quality of service, body movements, temperature change, range of transmission, heterogeneous environment, power drain, network throughput, delay, transmission rate, etc. In this research paper, we are focusing on a few of these challenges and the rest can be explored in future work. The challenges that occurred during IoMT system development differ from the wireless network as it deals with very sensitive real-time medical data of the patients and a small delay, data loss, or inconsistency in this healthcare system can result in severe health issues and can be very risky for someone's health. All these challenges need to be handled with care during the development of AI-enabled SHS using the IoMT framework for a better user experience. This system works upon very sensitive medical data of various patients using small and ultra-low power wearable/implanted smart IoMT devices therefore most of the real-time development challenges are handled in network and protocol designing techniques considering effective topology, energy consumption, and effective channel. So, this section provides a scrutinized analysis of different research challenges that occurred during the development of the AI-based SHS system using the IoMT framework.

4.1 Data Accuracy

An AI-enabled SHS works with highly sensitive medical records and the AI algorithm will predict efficient results only when it gets accurate medical data. If there is any inconsistency in fetching the medical record from the patient's body it can result in severe physical and financial loss and can thereby end up with total system failure. Hence in this section, we are elaborating Data accuracy parameter of an SHS. The data accuracy comparison has been illustrated in Fig. 4. Table 1 shows a comparative analysis of various work done regarding data accuracy in AI-enabled Smart Healthcare systems. Tekieh MH et al. [14], 2015 proposed an electronic health record approach for the collection of data using various techniques based on system requirements to accomplish the accuracy of collected data. Shahin A et al. [15], 2014 also use an electronic health record approach for data collection considering two parameters error rate and accuracy of the collected data. Yang L et al. [16], 2016 use a Rule-Based approach to improve data gathering speed maintaining the accuracy of collected data. Mdaghri Z A., et al. [17], 2016 proposed a support system for clinical decisions improving accuracy within the collected data. Roy S et al. [18], 2016 proposed a new technique i.e., correlation-based ratio analysis gathers medical information using parameters correlation and accuracy. Rao AR et. al. [19], 2016 use an open dataset for prediction and accuracy having better visualization because of GUI.

Table 1. Data accuracy in AI enabled smart healthcare system

Sr. No.	Authors and publication years	Parameters	Data collection technique	Advantages	Disadvantages
1	Tekieh MH et al. [14], 2015	Accuracy	Electronic health record (EHR)	Few EHR based techniques were discussed so that based on the problem statement optimal solution can be choosed	Future work not suggested
2	Shahin A et. al. [15], 2014	Accuracy and error rate	EHR	Case study	Can be applied only to special environmental conditions
3	Yang L et al. [16], 2016	Accuracy	Rule – based approach	Improvement in speed of data collection	Still improvement in accuracy needed
4	MdaghriZA et al. [17], 2016	Accuracy	Clinical decision support system	Collected data is more accurate	Missing Values not handled properties
5	Roy S et al. [18], 2016	Accuracy and correlation	Correlation based ratio analysis	Correlation helps in collecting specific medical record	Missing Values not considered in this work
6	Rao AR et. al. [19], 2016	Accuracy and prediction	Used open dataset	Improved GUI helps in improved visualization	Missing Values not considered in this work

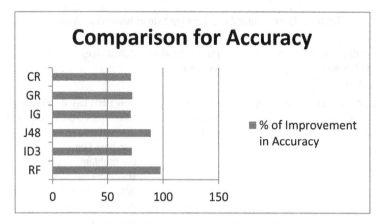

Fig. 4. Accuracy comparison

4.2 Data Security

AI-based SHS mostly uses the cloud for storage of data so that we can get fast access to medical data whenever required but it can lead to security threats of highly sensitive medical data. Any security breach within an SHS can result in the tempering of sensitive patient's medical data and thereby causing treatment failure as well as users' faith in using smart IoMT devices. Table 2 shows a scrutinized analysis of different work done regarding security in AI-enabled Smart Healthcare systems. Moosavi, S. R., et al. [20], 2015 proposed techniques to Encrypt system information and used biometric identification and two-factor authentication for system security against unauthorized access. Sun, Y., et al. [1], 2019 implement secure routing algorithms to avoid routing attacks where the Attacker modifies the route of traffic to a new destination. This paper also uses encryption and an intrusion detection system, builds redundancy in infrastructure, and uses region mapping, authentication, and egress filtering to avoid Denial of Service (DoS) attacks where the attacker generates so much network traffic that the SHS halts; generally caused by a compromised node. Verma, G., et al. [21], 2021 uses advanced techniques to Encrypt links and the network layer preventing message disclosure where attacker targets sensitive information disclosure to access a patient's log file. This paper also uses hashing and digital signatures to avoid message modification by unauthorized users where an attacker can modify messages between a patient and a healthcare provider. Also, the author discusses encryption, segmentation, and implementation of network access control (NAC) techniques to avoid eavesdropping, and reply attacks where the attacker listens to information through an open SHS communication channel and can forward modified information. Verma, G., et al. [21], 2021 also uses symmetric key security algorithms for compromised node attack where the attacker hacks into openly deployed sensor nodes and injects false information into them. Sun, Y., et. al. [1], 2019 use multi-path, multi-base data forwarding, identity verification protocols, and cryptography to avoid Hello Flooding where the attacker uses a compromised node with high transmission power to compromise all of its neighbors.

Table 2. Data Security in AI enabled smart healthcare system

Sr.No	Authors & publication years	Attack or threat	Description	Counter measures
1	Moosavi, S. R., et al. [20], 2015	Unauthorized access	Attacker gains access to a system by using another authorized user's credentials	Encrypt system information, use biometric identification or two-factor authentication
2	Sun, Y., et. al. [1], 2019	Routing attacks	Attacker modifies the route of traffic to a new destination	Implement secure routing algorithms
3	Verma, G., et al. [21], 2021	Message disclosure	Attacker targets sensitive information disclosure to access a patient's log file	Encrypt links and the network layer
4	Verma, G., et al. [21], 2021	Message modification	Attacker modifies messages between a patient and healthcare provider	Use hashing and digital signatures
5	Verma, G., et al. [21], 2021	Eavesdropping	Attacker listens to information through an open SHS communication channel	Use encryption, segmentation, and implement network access control (NAC)
6	Verma, G., et al. [21], 2021	Replying attack	Attacker forwards modified information after eavesdropping	Use encryption, segmentation, and implement NAC
7	Verma, G., et al. [21], 2021	Compromised node attack	Attacker hacks into openly deployed sensor nodes and injects false information	Use symmetric key security algorithms
8	Sun, Y., et. al. [1], 2019	Denial of service (DoS) attack	Attacker generates so much network traffic that the SHS halts; generally caused by a compromised node	Use encryption and an intrusion detection system, build redundancy in infrastructure, and use region mapping, authentication, and egress filtering

(continued)

Table 2. (*continued*)

Sr.No	Authors & publication years	Attack or threat	Description	Counter measures
9	Sun, Y., et. al. [1], 2019	Hello flooding	Attacker uses a compromised node with high transmission power to compromise all of its neighbors	Use multi-path, multi-base data forwarding, identity verification protocols, and cryptography
10	Algarni, A. [10], 2019	Black and gray hole attack	Attacker inserts a malicious node into a network that changes routing tables so that neighboring nodes send the compromised node all their data. Black hole attacks don't reply to the neighboring nodes; gray hole attacks reply with non-critical data	Use a time-based threshold mechanism, track pending packet tables and node rating tables, and make sure all nodes have different IDs
11	Algarni, A. [10], 2019	Sybil attack	Attacker uses a malicious sensor that masquerades as multiple sensors to modify the routing table	Validate sensors at a central authority or by using sensor graph connectivity characteristics
12	Algarni, A. [10], 2019	Social engineering	Attacker influences users to reveal information or perform an action that benefits the attacker	Raise awareness of security concerns through training, auditing, and adequate security policies

Algarni, A. [10], 2019 uses a time-based threshold mechanism, to track pending packet tables and node rating tables, and make sure all nodes have different IDs to avoid Black and Gray hole attacks where the attacker inserts a malicious node into a network that changes routing tables so that neighboring nodes send the compromised node all their data. Black hole attacks don't reply to the neighboring nodes; Gray hole attacks reply with non-critical data. This paper uses various techniques to validate sensors at a central authority or by using sensor graph connectivity characteristics to avoid a Sybil attack where the attacker can use a malicious sensor that masquerades as multiple sensors to modify the routing table. It also Raises awareness of security concerns through training, auditing, and adequate security policies for social engineering where the attacker influences users to reveal information or perform an action that benefits the attacker.

4.3 System Efficiency

The efficiency of an SHS will determine the size of the IoMT device, battery lifetime, and usability of the smart devices which is usually very small hence the energy optimization is handled by the routing protocol only. The energy consumption comparison has been illustrated in Fig. 5. Therefore, a comparative analysis of various work done regarding system efficiency is shown in Table 3 for an AI-enabled SHS. AI-enabled Smart Healthcare System collects data either from an implant or wearable smart healthcare devices. Now the implant devices must maintain a long battery life of approx. 10–15 years to prevent multiple surgery repetition [16]. Even if we consider wearable devices battery lifetime is again very important because repeatedly changing the battery will reduce the usability of smart devices. Rehman, A., et al. [22], 2021 proposed a new Energy efficient IoT e-health model using AI with a homomorphic secret sharing technique for better Packet delivery ratio, Delivery time, energy consumption, and Data leakage of an IoMT device. Sodhro et. al. [23], 2021 proposed another energy-efficient technique for better system efficiency to improve battery life while consuming minimal energy. Lazarevska et al. [24], 2018 show a New Objective Function (NEWOF) for improved energy consumption and total control of traffic overhead. Saba, T., et al. [25], 2020 projected another energy-efficient and secure e-healthcare technique to present a highly secure healthcare system with increased medical data delivery with minimum energy consumption. AbdulmohsinHammood D., et. al. [26], 2019 proposed an inter-WBAN cooperation algorithm for an IoMT environment giving increased energy efficiency and outage probability.

Table 3. System efficiency in AI enabled smart healthcare system

Sr.no	Author and publication year	Parameters	Efficiency measurement technique	Advantages	Disadvantages
1	Rehman A., et. al. [22], 2021	Packet Delivery Ratio (PDR), Delivery time, energy consumption and data leakage	Energy efficient IoT e-health model using AI with homomorphic secret sharing	1. Disease diagnosis system maintainability increased 2. Secure communication with medical cloud	1. Increased PDR under very high load scenario 2. Different IoT nodes energy consumptions are different 3. Low intelligence to avoid packet collision

(*continued*)

Table 3. (*continued*)

Sr.no	Author and publication year	Parameters	Efficiency measurement technique	Advantages	Disadvantages
2	Sodhro et. al. [23], 2021	Charge dissipation, energy dissipation, battery lifetime and energy discharge	Energy efficient algorithm for better system efficiency	Increased battery lifetime consuming minimal energy	Computational load is high
3	Lazarevska et. al. [24], 2018	PDR, network lifetime, energy consumption, total control traffic overload (TCTO)	New objective function for system energy	1.Better energy efficiency 2. Improved TCTO 3. Better PDR	20% loss during mobility plugin
4	Saba, T., et. al. [25], 2020	E2E delay, throughput, packet loss, link breakages and energy consumption	Energy-efficient and secure e-healthcare technique	1. Reduced energy consumption 2. Increased data delivery 3. Minimum network delay with high security	1. Mobility parameter not considered 2. Inter-WBAN data transformation requires improvement in security and energy consumption parameters
5	AbdulmohsinHamood D., et. al. [26], 2019	Outage probability, power consumption, energy efficiency, transmission rate	Inter-WBAN cooperation algorithm for efficient IoMT framework	Highly efficient with high outage probability for symmetric transmission	Low outage probability during asymmetric transmission

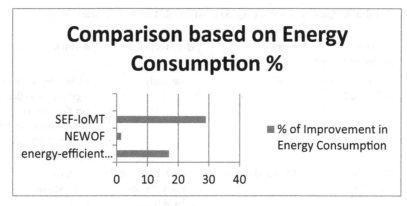

Fig. 5. Energy consumption comparison

4.4 Quality of Service

AI enables SHS applications that deal with highly sensitive real-time medical data like ECG which is susceptible to execution timing and data loss. To fulfill such real-time medical demand Quality of service (QoS) requirements must be justified in an AI-enabled IoMT framework for SHS. To maintain system usability the sensing devices of SHS have fixed memory and computational capabilities, so the QoS measures must be adapted by the routing protocols. Table 4 shows a comparative analysis of various work done regarding QoS in AI-enabled Smart Healthcare systems. Kumar, A., et al. [27], 2022 proposed a case study of various algorithms to improve the QoS of the IoMT framework. Patan, R., et al. [28], 2020 proposed an AI-driven IoMT eHealth architecture implying a grey filter Bayesian convolution neural network that will improve accuracy during medical data analysis. Agnihotri, S., et al. [29], 2019 proposed the CARA-IoT algorithm using ACO (AntColony Optimization) approach to choose the best consistent and smart routing path depending firstly on the channel noise and secondly on communicating content. Singh, P. D. et al. [30], 2021 proposed an ensemble-based classifier algorithm that combines AI with Fog computing for smart health of early covid-19 detection and also takes shared storage peer-to-peer, time stamping advantages of blockchain. Khodkari, H., et al. [31] use multi-attribute decision-making techniques specifically the simple weighting technique for better QoS, and due to the integration of cloud and IoT, this SHS system gains the support of the new developers in this era. Sodhro, A. H., et. al. [32]. 2021 proposed a new adaptive QoS computation algorithm (AQCA) to monitor the performance indicators fairly and efficiently.

Table 4. Quality of service (QoS) in AI enabled smart healthcare system

Sr.No	Authors & publication years	Parameters	QoS Technique	Advantages
1	Kumar, A., et al. [27], 2022	QoS	Case study	Elaborated various algorithms so that as per the project requirement, the best suitable technique can be opted
2	Patan, R., et al. [28], 2020	Time and overhead	An AI driven IoMT framework for e-Health architecture using Grey filter Bayesian convolution neural network	1. Design suggestions elaborated considering accuracy, overhead and execution time in comparison with state-of-the-art methods 2. Accurate medical data analysis
3	Agnihotri, S., et al. [29], 2019	Packet loss and delay	CARA-IoT algorithm using ACO (AntColony Optimization) approach	This algorithm will choose the best consistent and smart routing path depending firstly on channel noise and then on the communicating content
4	Singh, P. D. et al. [30], 2021	1. Network delay, RAM and network usages 2. Aaccuracy, precision, recall, kappa static and root mean square error	Ensemble-based classifier	1. Combination of AI and fog computing for smart health enabling early covid-19 detection 2. Advantage of blockchain is utilized like shared storage, peer-to-peer connection and time stamping 3. Better classification technique as per the results

(*continued*)

Table 4. (*continued*)

Sr.No	Authors & publication years	Parameters	QoS Technique	Advantages
5	Khodkari, H., et al. [31], 2018	QoS measures, sensor data, big data, IoT protocols and Cloud interface parameters	Multi attribute decision making algorithm	1. Due to the integration of cloud and IoT, most of the recent developers of this era shows their interest in this system 2. The IoT paradigms improves QoS of the system
6	Sodhro, A. H., et. al. [32]. 2021	1. Transmission power, route selection and duty cycle 2. AQCA and Quality of experience (QoE) used for QoS measurement	Adaptive QoS Computation algorithm (AQCA)	High visualization, battery lifetime and power optimization

5   Conclusion

Artificial Intelligence (AI) gives automation to the system to increase ease and simplicity within a system. AI can be used in the Internet of Medical Things (IoMT) framework to incorporate automation in the healthcare sector which is also known as Smart Healthcare. As per the current scenario, every day new harmful viruses are coming leading to severe health degradation. A person visiting hospitals or other healthcare for every small health problem may get infected by these harmful viruses and therefore Smart Healthcare System (SHS) is introduced. In SHS without visiting the hospital a person can measure his regular health records using wearable/implanted smart devices and can take preliminary precautions on their own. A doctor can also monitor his patient's health from remote areas using SHS applications. Based on the patient's health scenario SHS can be divided into three domains as discussed in this work. AI-based SHS using the IoMT framework usually have three layers in their architecture namely the bottommost sensor level for collection of medical data by means of wearable/ implanted smart devices, the middle layer used for processing of these data with a set of algorithms, and the topmost layer used for the end-user interface. This work gives an explanative analysis of different AI-based SHS architectures proposed by various authors based on their system requirements. SHS deals with highly sensitive medical records of various patients and also requires quick responses from the system therefore few research challenges need to be defined and tackled effectively. A comparative analysis of these research challenges namely

Data security, Data accuracy, System efficiency, Quality of Service (QoS), and System reliability has been discussed in this paper.

References

1. Sun, Y., Lo, F.P.W., Lo, B.: Security and privacy for the internet of medical things enabled healthcare systems: a survey. IEEE Access **7**, 183339–183355 (2019)
2. Chen, S., Xu, H., Liu, D., Hu, B., Wang, H.: A vision of IoT: applications, challenges, and opportunities with china perspective. IEEE Internet Things J. **1**(4), 349–359 (2014)
3. Sinha, B.B., Dhanalakshmi, R.: Recent advancements and challenges of Internet of Things in smart agriculture: a survey. Future Gener. Comput. Syst. **126**, 169–184 (2022)
4. Al-Emran, M., Malik, S.I., Al-Kabi, M.N.: A survey of Internet of Things (IoT) in education: opportunities and challenges. In: Hassanien, A.E., Bhatnagar, R., Nour Eldeen, M., Khalifa, M.H., Taha, N. (eds.) Toward Social Internet of Things (SIoT): Enabling Technologies, Architectures and Applications. SCI, vol. 846, pp. 197–209. Springer, Cham (2020). https://doi.org/10.1007/978-3-030-24513-9_12
5. Elkin, D., Vyatkin, V.: IoT in traffic management: review of existing methods of road traffic regulation. In: Silhavy, R. (ed.) Applied Informatics and Cybernetics in Intelligent Systems: Proceedings of the 9th Computer Science On-line Conference 2020, vol. 3, pp. 536–551. Springer International Publishing, Cham (2020). https://doi.org/10.1007/978-3-030-51974-2_50
6. Routray, S., Mao, Q.: A context aware-based deep neural network approach for simultaneous speech denoising and dereverberation. Neural Comput. Appl. **34**(12), 9831–9845 (2022)
7. Mohamed Shakeel, P., Baskar, S., Sarma Dhulipala, V.R., Mishra, S., Jaber, M.M.: Maintaining security and privacy in health care system using learning based deep-Q-networks. J. Med. Syst. **42**(10), 1–10 (2018)
8. Alsubaei, F., Abuhussein, A., Shandilya, V., Shiva, S.: IoMT-SAF: internet of medical things security assessment framework. Internet of Things **8**, 100123 (2019)
9. Routray, S., Mao, Q.: Phase sensitive masking-based single channel speech enhancement using conditional generative adversarial network. Comput. Speech Lang. **71**, 101270 (2022)
10. Algarni, A.: A survey and classification of security and privacy research in smart healthcare systems. IEEE Access **7**, 101879–101894 (2019)
11. Padhy, S., Dash, S., Routray, S., Ahmad, S., Nazeer, J., Alam, A.: IoT-based hybrid ensemble machine learning model for efficient diabetes mellitus prediction. Compu. Intell. Neurosci. **2022**, 1–11 (2022). https://doi.org/10.1155/2022/2389636
12. Kumar, N.: IoT architecture and system design for healthcare systems. In: 2017 International Conference on Smart Technologies for Smart Nation (SmartTechCon), pp. 1118–1123. IEEE (2017)
13. Sun, L., Jiang, X., Ren, H., Guo, Y.: Edge-cloud computing and artificial intelligence in internet of medical things: architecture, technology and application. IEEE Access **8**, 101079–101092 (2020)
14. Tekieh, M.H., Rashemi, B.: Importance of data mining in healthcare. In: Proceedings of 2015 IEEE/ACM international conference advances in social networks analysis and mining 2015—ASONAM'15, pp 1057–1062 (2015)
15. Shahin, A., Moudani, W., Chakik, F., Khalil, M.: Data mining in healthcare information systems case studies in Northern Lebanon. In: 2014 Third International Conference e-Technologies Networks Devices, pp 151–155 (2014)
16. Yang, L., Li, Z., Luo, G.: MH-Arm: a multimode and high-value association rule mining technique for healthcare data analysis. In: 2016 International Conference on Computational Science and Computational Intelligence, no. 71432002, pp. 122–127 (2016)

17. Mdaghri, Z.A., El Yadari, M., Benyoussef, A., El Kenz, A.: Study and analysis of data mining for healthcare. In: 2016 4th IEEE International Colloquium on Information Science and Technology (CiSt), pp. 77–82 (2016)
18. Roy, S., Mondal, S., Ekbal, A., Desarkar, M.S.: CRDT: correlation ratio based decision tree model for healthcare data mining. In: 2016 IEEE 16th International Conference on Bioinformatics, Bioengineering, pp. 36–43 (2016)
19. Rao, A.R., Clarke, D.: A fully Integrated open-source toolkit for mining healthcare bigdata: architecture and applications. In: Proceedings on 2016 IEEE international conference on healthcare informatics, ICHI 2016, pp. 255–261 (2016)
20. Moosavi, S.R., et al.: SEA: A secure and efficient authentication and authorization architecture for IoT-based healthcare using smart gateways. Procedia Comput. Sci. **52**(1), 452–459 (2015)
21. Verma, G., Prakash, S.: Internet of Things for healthcare: research challenges and future prospects. In: Hura, G.S., Singh, A.K., Hoe, L.S. (eds.) Advances in Communication and Computational Technology. LNEE, vol. 668, pp. 1055–1067. Springer, Singapore (2021). https://doi.org/10.1007/978-981-15-5341-7_80
22. Rehman, A., Saba, T., Haseeb, K., Larabi Marie-Sainte, S., Lloret, J.: Energy-efficient IoT e-health using artificial intelligence model with homomorphic secret sharing. Energies **14**(19), 6414 (2021)
23. Sodhro, A.H., et al.: Decentralized energy efficient model for data transmission in IoT-based healthcare system. In: 2021 IEEE 93rd Vehicular Technology Conference (VTC2021-Spring), pp. 1–5. IEEE (2021)
24. Lazarevska, M., Farahbakhsh, R., Shakya, N.M., Crespi, N.: Mobility supported energy efficient routing protocol for IoT based healthcare applications. In: 2018 IEEE Conference on Standards for Communications and Networking (CSCN), pp. 1–5. IEEE (2018)
25. Saba, T., Haseeb, K., Ahmed, I., Rehman, A.: Secure and energy-efficient framework using Internet of Medical Things for e-healthcare. J. Infect. Public Health **13**(10), 1567–1575 (2020)
26. AbdulmohsinHammood, D., Rahim, H.A., Alkhayyat, A., Ahmad, R.B.: Body-to-body cooperation in internet of medical things: toward energy efficiency improvement. Future Internet **11**(11), 239 (2019)
27. Kumar, A., Joshi, S.: Applications of AI in healthcare sector for enhancement of medical decision making and quality of service. In: 2022 International Conference on Decision Aid Sciences and Applications (DASA), pp. 37–41. IEEE (2022)
28. Patan, R., Ghantasala, G.P., Sekaran, R., Gupta, D., Ramachandran, M.: Smart healthcare and quality of service in IoT using grey filter convolutional based cyber physical system. Sustain. Cities Soc. **59**, 102141 (2020)
29. Agnihotri, S., Ramkumar, K.R.: Content based routing algorithm to improve QoS in IoMT networks. In: Saha, A., Kar, N., Deb, S. (eds.) Advances in Computational Intelligence, Security and Internet of Things: Second International Conference, ICCISIoT 2019, Agartala, India, December 13–14, 2019, Proceedings, pp. 195–206. Springer Singapore, Singapore (2020). https://doi.org/10.1007/978-981-15-3666-3_17
30. Singh, P.D., Kaur, R., Dhiman, G., Bojja, G.R.: BOSS: A new QoS aware blockchain assisted framework for secure and smart healthcare as a service. Expert Syst. e12838 (2021)
31. Khodkari, H., Maghrebi, S.G., Asosheh, A., Hosseinzadeh, M.: Smart healthcare and quality of service challenges. In: 2018 9th International Symposium on Telecommunications (IST), pp. 253–257. IEEE (2018)
32. Sodhro, A.H., Malokani, A.S., Sodhro, G.H., Muzammal, M., Zongwei, L.: An adaptive QoS computation for medical data processing in intelligent healthcare applications. Neural Comput. Appl. **32**(3), 723–734 (2019). https://doi.org/10.1007/s00521-018-3931-1

33. Srivastava, J., Routray, S., Ahmad, S., Waris, M.M.: Internet of Medical Things (IoMT)-based smart healthcare system: Trends and progress. Comput. Intell. Neurosci. **2022**, 1–17 (2022). https://doi.org/10.1155/2022/7218113

34. Malla, P.P., Sahu, S., Routray, S.: Investigation of breast tumor detection using microwave imaging technique. In 2020 International Conference on Computer Communication and Informatics (ICCCI), pp. 1–4. IEEE (2020)

Metaverse and Posthuman Animated Avatars for Teaching-Learning Process: Interperception in Virtual Universe for Educational Transformation

Ashraf Alam$^{(\boxtimes)}$ (iD) and Atasi Mohanty (iD)

Rekhi Centre of Excellence for the Science of Happiness, Indian Institute of Technology Kharagpur, Kharagpur, West Bengal, India
ashraf_alam@kgpian.iitkgp.ac.in

Abstract. It has been quite some time that the attention of teachers has been focused on the incorporation of Metaverse in education. Since Facebook's announcement that it will be rebranding and promoting itself as Meta, there has been much interest in this subject. To the best of our knowledge, no research as of date has systematically synthesised the results associated with the implementation of Metaverse in education, even though several studies have conducted literature reviews on Metaverse in general. This research does a detailed literature assessment on how the Metaverse might be used in the classroom in order to fill this knowledge gap. Research trends, focal points, and limitations of this 'study subject' are revealed using both bibliometric analysis and text analysis. It is evident from the collected data that lifelogging for educational metaverse merits additional research. The results indicate that research into mobile-, hybrid-, and micro-learning environments are still in its infancy. There is no study on the effectiveness of utilising metaverse to educate children with special needs. In order to widen the attraction of metaverse to educators throughout the globe and to improve their capacity to assist successful learning and teaching in the virtual environment, more in-depth research shall be carried out along the proposed roadmap as suggested by the results of the current investigation.

Keywords: Metaverse · Virtual avatars · Review article · Education · Curriculum · Pedagogy · Teaching-learning · E-learning · Educational technology · Schools · Universities

1 Introduction

The inkling of Metaverse is not very new; it has been explored in works of science fiction such as Snow Crash and has recently received increased attention with the release of the film which is an adaptation of the book, Ready Player One [1, 31]. Second Life and World of Warcraft were already out there as well-known and well-liked examples [2, 7]. Mark Zuckerberg's public unveiling of Metaverse in October 2021, however, sparked a surge in the platform's popularity [3, 46]. Many instructors and researchers have begun

© The Author(s), under exclusive license to Springer Nature Switzerland AG 2022
M. Panda et al. (Eds.): ICIICC 2022, CCIS 1737, pp. 47–61, 2022.
https://doi.org/10.1007/978-3-031-23233-6_4

outlining potential future agendas and implementation scenarios in their teaching and research methods [4, 19]. The virtual environment, which depicts people as realistically as possible, may enhance the interpersonal aspects of education, contributing to the rising popularity of online courses [5]. Since 'Metaverse' is still a relatively new term, the current investigation addresses the need to evaluate the current state of research on the topic [6].

Avatars, which are digital representations of real-world humans, administer the economy and conduct daily activities in the 3D virtual environment known as the Metaverse [7]. Instead of being a platform built by a single corporation, which would inevitably lead to monopolisation, the word 'Metaverse' describes a whole ecosystem. It denotes a whole new dimension of life that is not just beyond the purview of any nation's or company's governing bodies, but of all governments altogether [8]. Metaverse offers opportunities for immersion, collaboration, and involvement, all of which contribute to the expansion of social experiences and the birth of 'parallel worlds' [9]. The growth of the metaverse requires the following three stages: (1) digital twins, which permit simulating and modelling the physical environment digitally [10]. Numerous academics and thinkers have already explored the educational potential of the Metaverse [11]. The integration of Metaverse with Second Life as a learning management system was previously explored in the context of enhancing educational outcomes [12]. The Metaverse, which emphasises the virtuality component, might be the next place where people congregate and form social connections; as such, institutions of higher learning should take the initiative to use it for educational purposes [13].

Mirror worlds, lifelogging, AR, and virtual worlds are the four branches of the metaverse technology tree [14]. Through the use of digital data superimposed on top of the user's perception of the actual world, augmentation technology enhances the environment with a new visual element [15]. In contrast, simulation technology creates and alters models of the actual world in order to give virtual interactions and experiences [16]. The other group focuses on the interplay between the internal and exterior spheres [17]. Information regarding the user's external environment and methods for influencing it are presented to emphasise the importance of this aspect of the technology [18]. When these two dimensions are combined, four distinct variations of the Metaverse emerge [19]. Thanks to the technologies present in the Augmented Reality Metaverse, we now design smart environments dependent on location networks, like Pokémon Go [20]. Lifelogging Metaverse collects daily details about people and things using augmented reality applications like Facebook and Instagram [21]. The technique generates virtual maps and models in the Metaverse of Mirror Worlds using GPS data from programmes like Google Earth and Google Maps [22]. Digitally interactive avatars representing a wide variety of identities form the basis of the technology powering the Metaverse of Virtual Worlds [23].

González Crespo and colleagues utilised OpenSim to research the potential of virtual worlds as a platform for knowledge exchange and education [4, 9, 13, 24]. After seeing the potential of augmented reality and mobile education for the classroom, Reyes and colleagues developed the Metaverse for the purpose of teaching mathematics [24]. The findings suggested that incorporating Metaverse into mathematics education has the potential to boost students' achievement [25]. Park and Kim also categorised the many sorts of instructional Metaverse worlds with different genres such as survival, labyrinth, multi-choice, racing/jump, and escape room [8, 12, 17, 22].

2   Objectives of the Research and Knowledge Gap

What we know about the Metaverse now is based on the widespread perception among members of Generation Z that their digital persona is identical to their ideal one. In other words, people believe that their online digital identities are reflected and represented in their offline physical selves. The researchers argue that the development and influence of Generation Z need a new definition of the term 'Metaverse', as it has evolved from its previous iteration. Furthermore, the speedy growth of deep learning and mobile technology has made the Metaverse more accessible from any place at any time, improved the precision of visual and linguistic recognition, and created more immersive environments than ever before. Thus, it is crucial to examine the evolution of the Metaverse in teaching, the structure of the Metaverse, and the current trends in historical research.

Many questions, such as what sort of Metaverse is utilised in education, what kinds of learning circumstances are used, and what kinds of assessment methodologies are used, remain unanswered. This study employs bibliometric and content analysis to provide a thorough assessment of the literature about the Metaverse's use in the classroom, filling a need that has so far gone unfilled. Content analysis was used to conduct a comprehensive review of the papers that were analysed in order to determine the research subjects that researchers choose to emphasise while discussing the educational applications of the Metaverse. The following research questions are addressed in this investigation:

1. What is the educational trend in the Metaverse?
2. What sorts of metaverses are employed in classrooms?
3. Where and at what grade level can these learning scenarios be used?
4. What technologies have been used, and how does the Metaverse represent the pupils' digital identities?
5. In what ways Metaverse is used to effectively educate students?
6. What concerns arise from the Metaverse's potential influence on schooling?

3   Methods and Methodology

The current investigation uses qualitative and quantitative synthesis techniques to investigate the literature on teaching using the Metaverse. A human evaluation is more likely to introduce outcome reporting bias, and results that are obtained from interpretation are likely to be subjective, than an automated review. Therefore, a mixed-method review including content analysis and bibliometric analysis is necessary to systematically recognize and classify the evolution and knowledge base of a subject matter. PRISMA guidelines were followed in this systematic literature review.

The databases Web of Science (WOS) and Scopus were combed using the search phrase "education and metaverse" to locate scholarly articles. All scholarly articles published as of September 25, 2022, are included in this analysis. The research articles were not considered if they did not meet all three of the following criteria: (1) be written in English, (2) deal with Metaverse in general, and (3) be available online. Consequently, 21 articles were in the Scopus database, and 36 publications were located in the WOS database.

The research used both bibliometric analysis and content analysis. The evaluation and interpretation of the data employed data triangulation techniques to provide a more holistic perspective and strengthen the reliability of the study's findings. The VOSviewer software was used to do the bibliometric analysis and synthesis by categorising and mapping the phrases taken from the keywords, titles, and abstracts into a similarity matrix based on their level of relatedness.

4   Results and Discussion

The results are discussed in light of each of the aforementioned research questions.

4.1   Educational Metaverse: A Categorical Analysis

The first academic investigations towards Metaverse implementation in teaching started in 2007. Research in the WOS database increased after 2008, with the number of research reaching a peak of five per year in 2009, 2010, and 2013. There is a precipitous fall beginning in 2013, with no new studies being uncovered in 2014. In 2015, the highest number of studies ever recorded occurred, with six in total. From 2015 to 2019, there was a precipitous drop in the number of published study findings, and in 2019, no new studies were conducted at all. In 2020 and 2021, researchers conducted an average of four investigations each year. Using regression analysis, we found that the Metaverse's popularity in the WOS database fluctuated from 2007 to 2021, but has generally been on the increase in recent years. The highest number of studies that were published in the Scopus database occurred in the year 2009, with a total of four articles published in 2001 and 2013. After 2013, the number of research published annually decreased. There was a notable increase in the number of scientific publications published from four in 2019 to six in 2020. The year 2021 saw a decline in the number of studies, with just three being uncovered. Recent years, especially after Covid-19 pandemic, have seen increased metaverse research activity in both databases, perhaps as a consequence of the widespread use of simulated worlds. The first wave of Metaverse study, which lasted from 2007 to 2013, has been compared to both Web 2.0 and to earlier examples like Second Life. The investments made in Metaverse technology explain the sudden surge in 2021, which marks the beginning of the third wave (2021 onwards). Web 3.0 and emerging technologies like augmented and virtual reality (AR/VR), as well as the rise in processing data and the ability to display virtual worlds, are responsible for the second wave (2014–2020) (e.g., Facebook).

When it comes to publication type, conference proceedings constitute the bulk of publications discussing the spread of Metaverse in educational research. There are twice as many studies of the article type in the WOS database than there are in the Sco-pus database. The search rates for books and scholarly journals are equivalent in both databases. Both databases show a preponderance of conference papers as the primary source for Metaverse research. Shorter publication schedules of conference proceedings explain the popularity of conference papers.

There was an assumption that the author's nationality revealed where the concept of the Metaverse first emerged inside the realm of educational research. The United States, Brazil, Japan, Spain, and South Korea led the world in research activity. It is worth noting that there has not been a research done on the efficacy of the Metaverse as a teaching tool in either the Arab world or Africa. This may be because these countries' inadequate infrastructure hinders them from introducing such technologically advanced educational environments. This raises the question of whether or not this kind of classroom really deepens the digital divide rather than helping to bridge it via offering an accessible education for all students. The potential of openness and open educational resources must be continuously used to keep the Metaverse of education welcoming and accessible to everyone.

Since the study of the metaverse is still in its infancy, almost half (41.7%) of the studies just summarised previous works and expounded on theories without actually conducting any tests. Twenty-eight percent of the studies used a hybrid design, followed by eighteen percent each that used quantitative and qualitative methodologies. The research found that the two most often cited types of data collecting were interviews and surveys. This is largely attributable to the speed with which information may be gathered via participant interviews and surveys. Log data may also document how students engaged with the Metaverse settings and progressed, offering better insights throughout the whole learning process compared to surveys or interviews alone.

4.2 A Wide Variety of Virtual Worlds for Use in Education

Most studies included sophisticated modelling and close interaction tools, suggesting a preference for the Virtual Worlds (VW) Metaverse [26]. VW employs a system that makes use of 3D technology to virtually portray elaborate computer graphics works [27]. VW articles used language and translation grids as the basis for a virtual reality debate and communication platform, among other educational elements from the VW Metaverse category [28]. Because they include virtual simulations of environments that are either expensive to create (like aircraft simulators for student training) or challenging (like learning about nuclear energy and safety) for students (because of high risk), VW Metaverse types have proven to have useful educational implications [29].

Augmented reality (AR) is the process of superimposing computer-generated imagery (CGI) onto a user's view of the real world to create a more lifelike, three-dimensional effect [30]. One such use is the transformation of a real-world book page into something like a 3D movie 31]. Examined studies included those that used Microsoft HoloLens to instruct students in aircraft maintenance or those that used augmented reality projects including the scanning of QR codes to get students interested in the material [31]. The articles as a whole did not make effective use of AR Metaverse's educational potential [32]. As an example, none of the publications we read advocated for the use of simulated, digitally presented three dimensions to educate students about intangible concepts [33].

According to the literature we reviewed, Lifelogging and Mirror Worlds are the two Metaverse categories that are used least often in the classroom [34]. Lifelogging

Metaverse is the practise of using social media for learning purposes in order to record, collate, and analyse one's day-to-day activities, thoughts, and relationships with others [35]. Lifelogging metaverse research is a kind of study that combines augmented reality with personal communication via voice interaction and recognition [36]. Because of its potential instructional value in enhancing one's ability to represent and use knowledge appropriately in response to criticism from other users in the network, this fits the criteria for a Lifelogging Metaverse [37]. Lifelogging students can use their critical thinking and creative imagination to explore the site's diverse data and reconstruct knowledge through the power of the group [36].

The final type of Metaverse is called Mirror Worlds (MW), and it is used to overcome geographical and physical barriers to education by extending real-world settings through networking technologies and GPS [38]. Only one study was classified as a MW Metaverse, and that was because it used a game-based approach to immersive learning by gathering students in a traditional classroom and mirroring the physical space onto an online platform [39]. The research did not make full use of the MW Metaverse, while reflecting what Kye termed as 'efficient expansion' approach for modelling the physical world [3, 7, 16, 21]. For example, MW users may work together on significant projects and even play games with others who are thousands of miles away from them [40].

The bulk of studies in the field of education have focused on Virtual Worlds Metaverse, while just a small number have made use of Augmented Reality Metaverse, and an even smaller number have made use of Lifelogging and Mirror Worlds Metaverses [41]. The outcomes are discussed in this article [42]. Nonetheless, 3D technologies were employed in the papers to either use or explain virtual worlds [43]. However, as the Metaverse road map indicates, the technology was not completely used or explained in the reviewed publications [44]. Lifelogging may give novel forms of data that may be analysed to probe hitherto unexplored areas of blending psychology and educational technology [45]. Those who have developed advanced digital skills may also benefit from using MW technology, making them worthy of special attention to the ways in which they learn in the MW Metaverse [46].

4.3 Situations for Learning, Tiers of Education, and VR Learning Environments

Fifty-three percent of Metaverse researches were in the fields of natural science, mathematics, and engineering, while fifteen percent were in the realms of general education and eleven percent were in the arts and humanities [47]. The Metaverse may provide technical assistance to the STEM disciplines by way of 3D modelling software for use in the classroom, by helping students draw parallels between real-world experiments and virtual things, and by offering data-mining-driven, autonomous tutoring systems [48]. For these and other reasons, several disciplines might benefit from integrating Metaverse into their work [49]. For this reason, the arts and humanities have made substantial use of Metaverse for language learning, since it may allow users to communicate with speakers of various languages [17]. Metaverse has the potential to merge the virtual world with traditional classrooms, therefore fostering novel avenues for interdisciplinary and problem-based learning [23]. Only 6% of social scientists use Metaverse, which is notable [29]. In reality, the Metaverse may also be quite useful in these areas [36]. For instance, students may form virtual networks in the subject of archaeology via the use of the Metaverse, which can be accessed during online e-learning sessions [38].

It was found that 62.9% of Metaverse research was conducted involving students who were at the university level [41]. The findings prove that Metaverse can be used in higher education to give students and faculty access to interactive and immersive experiences that open the door to exploring novel pedagogical practises, ICTs, and emerging technologies [46]. From this vantage point, it appears that the Metaverse may help alleviate the limitations and inefficiencies of traditional 2D online education [49]. However, there has only been a modest amount of research into the Metaverse in primary, secondary, and tertiary institutions [7]. No studies were found that specifically addressed disabled students, so more studies are needed to determine how to create inclusive and accessible Metaverse in educational environments [12]. The emergence of virtual freedom in space and time may allow students with impairments and special needs to engage more fully [18].

Metaverse provides several opportunities for the development of educational situations [25]. The findings showcase nine different pedagogical settings where the Metaverse is used for learning [28]. Online education received the most study (31.3%), followed by problem-based education, gaming-based education, collaborative education, and project-based learning (PBL) [31]. Metaverse provide pupils with a more engaging and interactive setting, as well as the opportunity for more collaborative study [35]. By analysing the Metaverse's applications in a variety of contexts, it may help both educators and students improve their use of the platform for instruction [38]. This means that proposals for innovative methods of instruction and evaluation will be made, and that plans for their use in virtual reality settings will be explored [41]. How can innovative tools like eye-tracking and voice-recognition software be incorporated into the instructional design process?

When it comes to online education, the Metaverse is where it is at. This is largely due to the fact that students can engage with various digital resources through virtual worlds, made possible by the Metaverse and high-performance servers [45]. Meanwhile, collaborative learning is frequently combined with virtual learning scenarios [48]. Through the Metaverse's built-in social networks, students can communicate with one another and exchange course-related knowledge to promote cooperative learning [3]. Metaverse's simulated environment is ubiquitous in modern blended-learning setups [7]. The results demonstrate the usefulness of integrating real-world experiments involving the Metaverse and virtual systems with online lectures and tutorials [8]. According to Kanematsu's study, using Metaverse (Second Life) for virtual course lectures is a viable option for students enrolled in science, technology, engineering, and mathematics (STEM) programmes [5, 7, 11, 19]. In this way, the teacher can guide the students through the STEM curriculum experiment in the physical classroom while also providing them with support in the Metaverse [13].

Using the same principles as game-based education, the Metaverse offers a virtual, engaging environment for learning [11]. Getchell and colleagues showed how Metaverse pioneers new-fangled possibilities for game-based teaching-learning by letting teachers develop flexible game-based learning environments and providing students more control over their education at a cheaper price [2, 6, 18, 25]. Estudante and Dietrich, in their study, propose utilising the free software Metaverse to create a VR game for mobile devices [3, 8, 15, 19]. The students are taught to think like physicists while solving issues [19]. This game may help students get a deeper understanding of chemistry concepts like the periodic table, chemical equilibrium, and molar mass while having fun at the same time [22]. As a result, the Metaverse's platform might be utilised to improve students' drive to study and their capacity for collaboration via the use of game-based instruction [28].

Students are given brief lectures and faced with topics connected to nuclear power, and they actively engage in problem-solving via Metaverse chat sessions led by their lecturers [33]. According to the findings, including Metaverse in PBL courses has the potential to raise interest, stimulate debate, and improve students' level of understanding [36]. As a matter of fact, by using the Metaverse, these learning scenarios may pique the interest of both students and instructors while providing the optimal environment for their teaching and learning activities [41]. The Metaverse's built virtual world is able to change the static conventional teaching paradigm into a dynamic one in these different learning settings since it provides learning materials and timely evaluations [46]. Collaboration among students is made possible by this [49].

4.4 Students' Avatars (Digital Personas) in the Metaverse

It is believed that as students build their digital identities in metaverse settings, they will have a greater social presence, or be seen as more authentic by their peers [1]. 'Digital Identity' is characterised by student's choice or building of avatars and interaction patterns as the self-image or inner goals [6]. In the Metaverse, avatars may be either immersive, present, or representative [8]. Avatars were a way for students to share their digital selves in the Metaverse and were allowed in the evaluated papers [12]. Particularly, a few studies allowed participants to choose an avatar from a pool of pre-made ones [16]. Students may create and customise their own avatars in several other classes [19]. From this, we might infer that pupils tailor their avatars to reflect their own qualities [21]. According to the findings from González Crespo's research, students may express their individuality and taste via the creation of customised digital avatars [6, 14, 19, 23]. In order to engage with the virtual environment, students may draw upon a wide range of skills, such as walking, flying, purchasing products, and personalising their appearance [25]. In addition, the Metaverse's social chatting feature allows students to successfully convey their ideas to one another via the use of both overt and covert references to real-world objects, locations, and emotions [29]. Thanks to the digital avatar's integration of real-world objects, characters, and settings, the user is immersed in a highly realistic, three-dimensional simulation [34].

Metaverse characters often have the ability to blink, which encourages rigorous coursework and more student participation [36]. Video games are another popular medium where digital avatars appear [41]. Most research shows that students use their digital avatars to participate in class discussions and form relationships with their peers in Second Life [45]. Students who spend significant time in the virtual world of Second Life will be able to create digital avatars that take on a variety of jobs, including socializers, and so expand their social circles [49]. In addition, future research might investigate how students of different cultures use avatars [3]. Improving the educational Metaverse's gaming options is a top priority [8].

The Metaverse provides a wealth of pedagogical and technical resources for educators, allowing students to participate in immersive learning that has been shown to boost engagement and motivation [11]. The seven types of technological resources are as follows: wearable, immersive, educational, modelling and simulation, gaming applications, artificial intelligence, mobiles, and sensors [15]. The Metaverse is used to provide students with hands-on experience, which not only encourages collaboration and skill development but also keeps them interested and involved in what they are learning [12]. Virtual reality, augmented reality, mixed reality, and other similar virtual technologies must be combined to provide a truly immersive experience [27]. The benefit of multimodal immersion is further shown by the emergence of technologies that open portals to and transport us inside Metaverse realms [36]. The aforementioned four technologies are the most widely used immersive interfaces in the Metaverse, and they have the potential to enhance classroom instruction by immersing pupils psychologically and so promoting transferable skills [46]. In their study, Siyaev and Jo discuss how MR may be used in the Metaverse to enhance learning via the use of deep learning voice interaction modules, bringing together the real and virtual worlds [5, 9, 11, 18]. To help students form more meaningful relationships with the digital world, MR may focus largely on the voice interaction that happens during the learning process [11]. To further facilitate students' access to immersive learning, VR allows for the administration of virtual worlds and the development of shareable avatars [21]. Students in the Metaverse may control their own avatars in line with the shown environment, make social connections with other students, and create custom avatars utilising virtual reality to provide an immersive experience [34].

Games are another popular kind of application utilised in the Metaverse to provide meaningful learning opportunities [38]. In terms of gaming apps, Pokémon Go has been the most popular recently [27]. As a result of advancements in real-time virtual reality and augmented reality, fictitious interactive 3D avatars can now be created and used to lure Pokémon inside games [19]. When the Metaverse is employed in the classroom, the immersive surroundings may play a crucial role in teaching various subjects and make it easier to draw connections between different areas of knowledge [24]. If blended with learning management systems [30]. Rapanotti and Hall have integrated the Metaverse with the Second Life platform to provide a more immersive virtual world platform for higher education [2, 9, 17, 24]. Using the resources supplied by Second Life, students may construct a 3D virtual avatar, resulting in an immersive learning experience [41]. Students fashion their own digital avatars in Second Life and engage in virtual interactions with other students and can spend virtual cash to buy or manufacture the resources [44]. Together, the institution's LMS, HotPotatoes, Massive Open Online Course (MOOC), Moodle, Teleduc, Eduquito, and Sloodle form a hybrid learning platform in the Metaverse for teaching and learning [48]. The Metaverse and MOOCs have made it possible for numerous students to have free and simultaneous access to a wealth of topical material to expand their understanding [43]. The use of virtual labs is common in the teaching of natural sciences, mathematics, and engineering [4]. By providing a dynamic, collaborative, and interactive learning environment, VLL increases students' motivation to learn and value their education [8]. Moodle, a modern learning management system, may improve upon traditional methods of distributing course materials and encourage student interaction [45].

Estudante and Dietrich developed software for Apple and Google smartphones that may be used to construct an augmented reality version of the Metaverse [21]. The OpenSim platform may be used with geographic mobility to provide content tailored to each organization's needs and methods of operation [24]. Connectivity to the internet and data sharing in public virtual worlds are also made feasible by geospatial mobility [5]. Metaverse on mobile devices might help students study if they use their avatars [47]. Another popular resource in the Metaverse is the Blinking system, which keeps track of students' blink rates using specialised software [13]. When a student's emotions are up in the air, the blinking mechanism causes them to blink more often, which helps teachers decipher their responses [19].

AI provides a foundation for the Metaverse's central concept—the analysis of its complex data for interpretation, supervision, control, and planning [13]. Neuro-symbolic AI might fill the role of subject-matter experts in aviation maintenance courses, providing guidance on technical matters and providing access to all the materials needed for effective training and teaching [19]. To improve learning efficiency, convolutional neural networks are increasingly being used to process not just visual and textual data, but also audio data, such as commands and language recognition [31]. To help users navigate virtual spaces, Web 3.0 often uses a combination of machine learning and semantic database modelling [41]. The AI possibilities of the Metaverse allow for the creation of new roles for intelligent NPCs to play as mentors, peers, and mentees [37].

Many different types of technology have been used in the creation of a thriving ecosystem in Metaverse, as has previously been mentioned [11]. There are, however, a number of state-of-the-art technologies that are not being used [13]. As one possible solution to the problems of cheating and insecure user data, a blockchain-based educational system is being created [25]. It is also feasible to wonder whether the ICT-based competencies mentioned in the literature are sufficient to prepare students and teachers for this new educational environment ('Metaverse in Education'), or if additional abilities are necessary for enhanced teaching and learning [42]. Along with the new learning possibilities presented by technological advancements, users may be vulnerable to threats [10]. Privacy may be compromised by sensors designed to read pupils' emotions and activities [26]. The potential for privacy breaches also increases in a digital classroom where physical items may be used to track user activity [34]. These risks should be taken into account by educators and researchers when they design Metaverse applications for use in the classroom [39].

4.5   Alterations in Educational Multiverse

One of the primary challenges with using Metaverse in the classroom is the technology and tactics used for immersion [12]. There are likely many classroom settings in which the Metaverse may be helpful [8]. For instance, the Metaverse's escape game built on the VR platform might be a useful tool for facilitating mobile learning in the context of a game-based classroom [9]. The findings show that students are more invested in their education when using games in the Metaverse as a means of instruction, and that they are eager to use smart gadgets for scientific practise [23]. Teaching in a metaverse environment, such as Second Life, is also effective [37]. It has the potential to enhance student learning by encouraging cross-lingual interaction and discussion [28].

The Metaverse is helpful for students in a wide variety of disciplines. The studies show that the Metaverse may help students connect, become more motivated and engaged, and broaden the possibilities of learning [14]. When combined, these features expand the educational potential of the Metaverse considerably [8]. Students majoring in aviation maintenance now have an affordable online alternative to flying, thanks to metaverse, which not only allows them to engage with one another but also to undertake fake aircraft repair [3]. The translation system will also allow for more direct interactions between students, adding to the advantages of the metaverse for language instruction, and the language grid system can be integrated with Second Life [15]. Finally, students in a Metaverse-powered classroom may have trouble distinguishing fiction from fact [13]. Therefore, it is reasonable to assume that the students in the class will form a new set of social networks for learning, resulting in novel scholastic opportunities [29].

Various pedagogical, technological, and other types of challenges have been associated with using the Metaverse in the classroom [22]. Technically speaking, the biggest factor was network congestion (21.1%), followed by smartphone interface design problems (8.2%) and blink capture problems (5.9%). Getchell emphasised the significance of punctuality in network communications and the increased demands they place on the host server and the overall network infrastructure [8, 11, 17, 26]. Because of the current state of the network connection size, the results of student evaluations may be skewed. There is further evidence from studies conducted on smartphones that the Metaverse has an interface problem that is independent of the Metaverse app [5, 9, 16, 23]. It has been suggested that if too few children use smartphones at once, this might have a negative impact on their ability to work together and communicate [32]. This is due to the small size of smartphone screens [40].

Dáz argues that the structure of the Metaverse could give students access to interesting digital resources, encourage them to interact with educational material, and inspire them to invent exciting new activities [1, 7, 19, 25]. Educators are responsible for developing, refining, and supplying the Metaverse server administrators with digital resources for students to utilise [33]. It is worth noting that both students' time management and the Metaverse's implementation in the classroom present challenges [38]. Students have trouble accessing the Metaverse due to the increased difficulty in managing their time and the many technical barriers that exist [4]. Students often lack the technical proficiency and expertise necessary to effectively apply what they have learned [27]. Finally, the amount of work, planning, and experimentation necessitated to successfully deploy Metaverse in the classroom are limitations on its growth [38].

5   Conclusion and Way Forward

This study demonstrates the fundamental limitations of the Metaverse, despite the solid groundwork it provides for its implementation in the classroom. For instance, this systematic review has certain restrictions due to the databases and keywords used. Non-English studies on the use of the Metaverse in education were excluded from this analysis. In addition, there were not many publications covering this issue in the leading journals for educational technology, which may be an indication of how new this field is. Because of this, the current study contributes to the body of knowledge among academics and practitioners on potential avenues for future research on this topic, specifically the use of the Metaverse in teaching and learning.

This study provides an in-depth analysis of how the Metaverse may be used in the classroom. The findings suggest that the Metaverse might be used to solve real-world problems in a virtual setting, opening up new educational opportunities that were previously unattainable due to constraints of time, place, and resources. Furthermore, they reveal the gap in knowledge about the use of lifelogging in metaverse education. More research is needed to determine how using Metaverse affects students with disabilities. It must be delineated that providing teachers with technical support, encouraging teacher training in both asynchronous and synchronous ways, and providing pupils with a collaborative, engrossing, and dynamic computer-simulated platform is extremely essential for the successful integration of Metaverse in education.

However, although Metaverse technology is not new, it has evolved considerably during the last two decades. With the advancement of technology comes the return of both its advantages and its drawbacks. Many of the papers we looked at, for example, focused more on the benefits of the Metaverse than the threats it brought. With the backing of large technology companies, it is becoming more popular, but caution is warranted since it poses potential threats to schools. In spite of its short existence, this technology is extremely vulnerable due to its developmental stage. For instance, how can we ensure the safety and privacy of our users? How does one make money in a virtual setting that generates copious amounts of data? In a world dominated by algorithms and AI, how do we define right and wrong? What kind of social and physiological implications may we foresee from the Metaverse, a realm where physical and digital realities merge? We need to scientifically explore the benefits of the Moreover, the analysed research makes it clear that Metaverse in education is based on cutting-edge technology, which may be a gift for schools or universities with cutting-edge infrastructure but a curse for people who are affected by it, especially in poor nations. Metaverse may be made more accessible and inclusive for every learner in order to contribute to the Sustainable Development Goals (SDGs), especially SDG-4 addressing quality education.

These findings underscore the fact that application of Metaverse in classroom teaching is still in its early stages, with all the associated benefits and drawbacks that it entails. Further, vital concerns remain unanswered. For instance, in light of the impact of EdTech firms, how will we ensure that students are given the tools they need to succeed? How do we ensure their safety in a world where computers make all the important decisions? Is this a brave new world where everything goes, or are we all bound by digital restraints? Before we rush into the Metaverse, perhaps we should take a moment to reflect on the costs we have already incurred. Is Metaverse a user that mines and profits from user-produced data, or we, as its products, are the users? Will there be a swarm of metabots out to fool people, or will only humans have access? When we are cut off from the real world like this, do we have the resources to deal with cyber pathologies in these games? If we wish to use the artificial Metaverse for educational reasons, do we have a plan to humanise these processes? Although the novelty of the Metaverse may tempt us to go in headfirst, there are still many serious issues to think about before making a permanent transition there.

References

1. Alam, A.: Challenges and possibilities in teaching and learning of calculus: A case study of India. Journal for the Education of Gifted Young Scientists **8**(1), 407–433 (2020)
2. Mughal, M.Y., Andleeb, N., Khurram, A.F.A., Ali, M.Y., Aslam, M.S., Saleem, M.N.: Perceptions of teaching-learning force about metaverse for education: a qualitative study. Journal of Positive School Psychology **6**(9), 1738–1745 (2022)
3. Mystakidis, S.: Metaverse. Encyclopedia **2**(1), 486–497 (2022)
4. Mustafa, B.: Analyzing education based on metaverse technology. Technium Social Sciences Journal **32**, 278–295 (2022)
5. Alam, A.: Pedagogy of Calculus in India: An Empirical Investigation. Periódico Tchê Química **17**(34), 164–180 (2020)
6. Zhong, J., Zheng, Y.: Empowering future education: learning in the Edu-METAVERSE. In: 2022 International Symposium on Educational Technology (ISET), pp. 292–295. IEEE (2022 July)
7. Fitria, T.N., Simbolon, N.E.: Possibility of metaverse in education: opportunity and threat. SOSMANIORA: Jurnal Ilmu Sosial dan Humaniora **1**(3), 366–376 (2022)
8. Barráez-Herrera, D.P.: Metaverse in the context of virtual education. Metaverse **3**(1), 9 (2022)
9. Alam, A.: Possibilities and challenges of compounding artificial intelligence in India's educational landscape. Int. J. Adv. Sci. Technol. **29**(5), 5077–5094 (2020)
10. Wang, H., Chen, D., Deng, Q.: The formation, development and research prospect of educational metaverse. Educ. J. **11**(5), 260–266 (2022)
11. Phakamach, P., Senarith, P., Wachirawongpaisarn, S.: The metaverse in education: the future of immersive teaching & learning. RICE J. Creative Entrepreneu. Manage. **3**(2), 75–88 (2022)
12. Yu, J.E.: Exploration of educational possibilities by four metaverse types in physical education. Technologies **10**(5), 104 (2022)
13. Alam, A.: Test of knowledge of elementary vectors concepts (TKEVC) among first-semester bachelor of engineering and technology students. Periódico Tchê Química **17**(35), 477–494 (2020)
14. Lee, H., Hwang, Y.: Technology-enhanced education through VR-making and metaverse-linking to foster teacher readiness and sustainable learning. Sustainability **14**(8), 4786 (2022)
15. Areepong, T., Nilsook, P., Wannapiroon, P.: A study of a metaverse interdisciplinary learning community. In: 2022 Research, Invention, and Innovation Congress: Innovative Electricals and Electronics (RI2C), pp. 290–296. IEEE (2022 August)
16. Alam, A.: Designing XR into Higher Education using Immersive Learning Environments (ILEs) and Hybrid Education for Innovation in HEIs to attract UN's Education for Sustainable Development (ESD) Initiative. In: 2021 International Conference on Advances in Computing, Communication, and Control (ICAC3), pp. 1–9. IEEE (2021)
17. Zhai, X., Chu, X., Wang, M.: Education metaverse: innovations and challenges of the new generation of internet education formats. Metaverse **3**(1), 13 (2022)
18. Singh, J., Malhotra, M., Sharma, N.: Metaverse in Education: An Overview. Applying Metalytics to Measure Customer Experience in the Metaverse, 135–142 (2022)
19. Alam, A.: Possibilities and Apprehensions in the Landscape of Artificial Intelligence in Education. In: 2021 International Conference on Computational Intelligence and Computing Applications (ICCICA), pp. 1–8. IEEE (2021)

20. Burnett, G.E., Harvey, C., Kay, R.: Bringing the Metaverse to Higher Education: Engaging University Students in Virtual Worlds. In: Methodologies and Use Cases on Extended Reality for Training and Education, pp. 48–72. IGI Global (2022)

21. Fernandes, F.I.L.I.P.E., Werner, C.L.Á.U.D.I.A.: A Systematic Literature Review of the Metaverse for Software Engineering Education: Overview, Challenges and Opportunities. Preprint, Sep. (2022)

22. Alam, A.: Should Robots Replace Teachers? Mobilisation of AI and Learning Analytics in Education. In: 2021 International Conference on Advances in Computing, Communication, and Control (ICAC3), pp. 1–12. IEEE (2021)

23. Contreras, G.S., González, A.H., Fernández, M.I.S., Martínez, C.B.: The importance of the application of the metaverse in education. Mod. Appl. Sci. **16**(3), 1–34 (2022)

24. Rospigliosi, P.A.: Metaverse or simulacra? roblox, minecraft, meta and the turn to virtual reality for education, socialisation and work. Interact. Learn. Environ. **30**(1), 1–3 (2022)

25. Alam, A.: A digital game based learning approach for effective curriculum transaction for teaching-learning of artificial intelligence and machine learning. In: 2022 International Conference on Sustainable Computing and Data Communication Systems (ICSCDS), pp. 69–74. IEEE (2022)

26. Mistretta, S.: The Metaverse—An Alternative Education Space. AI, Computer Science and (2022)

27. Dahan, N.A., Al-Razgan, M., Al-Laith, A., Alsoufi, M.A., Al-Asaly, M.S., Alfakih, T.: Metaverse framework: a case study on E-learning environment (ELEM). Electronics **11**(10), 1616 (2022)

28. Alam, A.: Educational robotics and computer programming in early childhood education: a conceptual framework for assessing elementary school students' computational thinking for designing powerful educational scenarios. In: 2022 International Conference on Smart Technologies and Systems for Next Generation Computing (ICSTSN), pp. 1–7. IEEE (2022)

29. Wang, M., Yu, H., Bell, Z., Chu, X.: Constructing an Edu-metaverse ecosystem: a new and innovative framework. IEEE Transactions on Learning Technologies (2022)

30. Batnasan, G., Gochoo, M., Otgonbold, M.E., Alnajjar, F., Shih, T.K.: ArSL21L: arabic sign language letter dataset benchmarking and an educational avatar for metaverse applications. In: 2022 IEEE Global Engineering Education Conference (EDUCON), pp. 1814–1821. IEEE (2022 March)

31. Alam, A.: Employing adaptive learning and intelligent tutoring robots for virtual classrooms and smart campuses: reforming education in the age of artificial intelligence. In: Shaw, R.N., Das, S., Piuri, V., Bianchini, M. (eds) Advanced Computing and Intelligent Technologies. Lecture Notes in Electrical Engineering, vol 914. Springer, Singapore (2022)

32. Jovanović, A., Milosavljević, A.: VoRtex metaverse platform for gamified collaborative learning. Electronics **11**(3), 317 (2022)

33. Hwang, G.J., Chien, S.Y.: Definition, roles, and potential research issues of the metaverse in education: An artificial intelligence perspective. Computers and Education: Artificial Intelligence, 100082 (2022)

34. Alam, A.: Investigating Sustainable Education and Positive Psychology Interventions in Schools Towards Achievement of Sustainable Happiness and Wellbeing for 21st Century Pedagogy and Curriculum. ECS Trans. **107**(1), 19481 (2022)

35. Arpaci, I., Karatas, K., Kusci, I., Al-Emran, M.: Understanding the social sustainability of the Metaverse by integrating UTAUT2 and big five personality traits: A hybrid SEM-ANN approach. Technology in Society, 102120 (2022)

36. Lee, H., Woo, D., Yu, S.: Virtual reality metaverse system supplementing remote education methods: based on aircraft maintenance simulation. Appl. Sci. **12**(5), 2667 (2022)

37. Alam, A.: Mapping a sustainable future through conceptualization of transformative learning framework, education for sustainable development, critical reflection, and responsible citizenship: an exploration of pedagogies for twenty-first century learning. ECS Trans. **107**(1), 9827 (2022)

38. Wang, Y., Lee, L.H., Braud, T., Hui, P.: Re-shaping Post-COVID-19 Teaching and Learning: A Blueprint of Virtual-Physical Blended Classrooms in the Metaverse Era. arXiv preprint arXiv:2203.09228 (2022)

39. Alam, A.: Positive Psychology Goes to School: Conceptualizing Students' Happiness in 21st Century Schools While 'Minding the Mind!' Are We There Yet? Evidence-Backed. School-Based Positive Psychology Interventions. ECS Transactions **107**(1), 11199 (2022)

40. Yang, J., Zhou, Y., Huang, H., Zou, H., Xie, L.: Metafi: device-free pose estimation via commodity wifi for metaverse avatar simulation. arXiv preprint arXiv:2208.10414 (2022)

41. Sutopo, A.H.: Developing Teaching Materials Based on Metaverse. Topazart (2022)

42. Alam, A.: Social robots in education for long-term human-robot interaction: socially supportive behaviour of robotic tutor for creating robo-tangible learning environment in a guided discovery learning interaction. ECS Trans. **107**(1), 12389 (2022)

43. Teng, Z., Cai, Y., Gao, Y., Zhang, X., Li, X.: Factors Affecting Learners' Adoption of an Educational Metaverse Platform: An Empirical Study Based on an Extended UTAUT Model. Mobile Information Systems (2022)

44. Gupta, Y.P., Chawla, A., Pal, T., Reddy, M.P., Yadav, D.S.: 3D networking and collaborative environment for online education. In: 2022 10th International Conference on Emerging Trends in Engineering and Technology-Signal and Information Processing (ICETET-SIP-22), pp. 1–5. IEEE (2022 April)

45. Alam, A.: Cloud-Based E-learning: Scaffolding the Environment for Adaptive E-learning Ecosystem Based on Cloud Computing Infrastructure. In: Satapathy, S.C., Lin, J.CW., Wee, L.K., Bhateja, V., Rajesh, T.M. (eds) Computer Communication, Networking and IoT. Lecture Notes in Networks and Systems, vol 459. Springer, Singapore (2023). https://doi.org/10.1007/978-981-19-1976-3_1

46. Kim, K., Jeong, Y., Ryu, J.: Does the real face provision improve the attention and social presence in metaverse as learning environments?. In: Society for Information Technology & Teacher Education International Conference, pp. 1760–1765. Association for the Advancement of Computing in Education (AACE) (2022 April)

47. Lim, S., Byun, H.: Development of Learning Analysis Framework on Metaverse

48. Hines, P., Netland, T.H.: Teaching a Lean masterclass in the metaverse. International Journal of Lean Six Sigma, (ahead-of-print) (2022)

49. Jagatheesaperumal, S.K., Ahmad, K., Al-Fuqaha, A., Qadir, J.: Advancing Education Through Extended Reality and Internet of Everything Enabled Metaverses: Applications, Challenges, and Open Issues. arXiv preprint arXiv:2207.01512 (2022)

Tuning Functional Link Artificial Neural Network for Software Development Effort Estimation

Tirimula Rao Benala[1]([⊠]) [iD] and Satchidananda Dehuri[2] [iD]

[1] Department of Information Technology, JNTU-GV College of Engineering, Vizianagaram, Jawaharlal Nehru Technological University, Gurajada-Vizianagaram 535003, Andhra Pradesh, India
b.tirimula@gmail.com

[2] Department of Computer Science, Fakir Mohan University, Vyasa Vihar, Janugnai, Balasore 756019, Odisha, India

Abstract. Software development effort estimation (SDEE) is a critical task in project management for accurate planning, staffing, resource allocation, scheduling, and cost estimation. Detailing nonlinear correlations between cost drivers and project costs using conventional parametric methodologies is difficult. In this context, we evaluated methods based on foundation-centered swarm intelligence and functional link neural networks for SDEE. The primary objective of this study was to investigate the use of functional link artificial neural networks for improving the predictability of SDEE. The findings are presented as computational intelligence methods for SDEE.

Keywords: Functional link artificial neural network · Software development effort estimation (SDEE) · Chebyshev polynomial · Particle swarm optimization · Genetic algorithm · Back-propagation

1 Introduction

The use of modern software procedures has helped software development companies provide high-quality software on time and minimize cost. Therefore, precise cost/effort estimation is crucial in the early stage of the software development life cycle. Accurate effort estimation influences several fundamental project management tasks, including budgeting, personnel, and resource allocation. Various cost estimation methods have been proposed. Conventionally, these methods are separated into algorithmic and nonalgorithmic software cost estimation methodologies. SLIM [9] and COCOMO are two well-known algorithmic approaches [8, 10]. The most prevalent nonalgorithmic strategies include expert judgment, estimation by analogy [5, 11, 12], and machine learning techniques [13–15]. Machine-learning-based techniques, such as artificial neural networks, analogy-based estimates, support vector regression, and classification and regression trees have been used as an alternative to software effort prediction models.

© The Author(s), under exclusive license to Springer Nature Switzerland AG 2022
M. Panda et al. (Eds.): ICIICC 2022, CCIS 1737, pp. 62–81, 2022.
https://doi.org/10.1007/978-3-031-23233-6_5

Artificial neural networks (ANNs) are used to solve complex, mathematically ill-defined problems. The higher-order neural network (HON) is a unique neural network that has attracted considerable research attention because it helps overcome the limitations of many non-HONs. The functional link neural networks (FLANN) is an extension of the HON. Therefore, examining HON characteristics is critical, even though this study focuses mainly on the CFLANN. A feed-forward neural network is inadequate for use in several applications. Therefore, a two-layer neural network with threshold activation is used. Minsky and Papert [16] revealed that the network always converges to linearly separable functions such as AND, OR, and NOT but cannot represent or learn XOR. Thus, feed-forward neural networks exhibit limited expressiveness. A hidden layer with an arbitrary activation function was introduced to address this bottleneck. This architecture was characterized by a feed-forward neural network with many layers. Multilayer perceptron with BP learning is the most widely used method. Under finite norms, the error in approximating any bounded continuous function can be arbitrarily small if sufficient hidden units are accessible in an MLP [17, 18]. MLP can express numerous nonlinear functions, and except for gradient descent, it does have any other limitations. When calculating partial derivatives, the function is assumed to be continuous in BP learning.

Consequently, the approach is seldom helpful. Second, BP learning increases the computation cost of MLP, which slows convergence. Several local minimums exist along the cost-function surface in the weight space for complex computer workloads. According to a mathematical study, the gradient descent technique of BP converges to a local minimum [19–22]. Lyapunov's stability theory states that the output tracking error cannot converge to zero [23]. The determination of many design factors of neural network architecture, such as the number of hidden units and neurons in a hidden unit, is challenging. Designing the architecture of a neural network is complex [24].

Numerous alternative neural network topologies have been proposed for nonlinear systems based on the Lyapunov stability theory to solve the aforementioned instability and convergence problems [25]. The explicit, hidden layer of the normal feed-forward neural network is eliminated, and an implicitly hidden layer is established by equipping the input layer with higher-order units known as functional expansions [26, 27]. Thus, an entirely novel neural network paradigm known as HONs, which includes FLANNs [28–31] and ridge polynomial neural networks (RPNNs) [32], has been proposed.

We investigated software development effort estimation (SDEE) methods based on ANNs with functional links. FLANN's learning algorithms incorporate genetic algorithm (GA), particle swarm optimization (PSO), adaptive PSO (APSO), and improved PSO (ISO), in addition to BP, to reduce computation load and speed convergence rate relative to MLP. The orthogonal basis function is the polynomial functional expansion of the Chebyshev polynomial. The FLANN is a neural network with a single layer and no hidden layers. Chebyshev's polynomial orthogonal basis function (functional link unit) introduces nonlinearity and increases the dimension of the input vector. Therefore, the FLANN requires lower processing power compared with MLP. A set of linearly independent functional expansion units (nonlinear units) are used to generate hyperplanes to improve discrimination in the input pattern space. A notable aspect of the FLANN architecture for predicting software development effort is the generation of the output (effort) by expanding the inputs (cost drivers) using orthogonal basis functions. Based on the information in the network, the FLANN hidden layer can be used to predict the effort required to construct software.

The rest of the paper is organized as follows: Sect. 2 covers the FLANN. Section 3 presents swarm-intelligence-based learning algorithms for the FLANN. Section 4 contains the performance metrics that were used to evaluate SDEE accuracy. Section 5 details the COCOMO'81 test suite from the promise repository. The results of the proposed SDEE models performance studies using the COCOMO'81 test suite are discussed in Sect. 6. Finally, Sect. 7 presents the conclusion of the study.

2 Functional Link ANN-based SDEE

The FLANN is a HON introduced by Klassen and Pao in 1988 [33]. It is a single-layer feed-forward neural network for creating arbitrary complex decision regions with an input layer and an output layer. By analyzing the final output layer to forecast output and increasing the input vector (cost drivers), the FLANN model incorporates non-linear input–output interactions (effort in Person-Months). Furthermore, an implicitly concealed unit is produced after the input vector (cost driver) has been expanded using the Chebyshev polynomial. Therefore, the weighted summation closely represents the software development effort. Swarm-intelligence-based learning techniques train the network and improve the output.

The block diagram of an n-dimensional input FLANN architecture is displayed in Fig. 1. A nonlinear network with only one visible layer is used. In this method, the input space is expanded into a high-dimensional feature space using a functional expansion block or functional link (Chebyshev orthogonal polynomial). To evaluate the input pattern, as opposed to the linear weighting of the linear links in an MLP, the functional links produce a set of linearly independent orthogonal basis functions (nonlinear functions). To accommodate the nonlinear characteristics of the problem, this phenomenon increases the dimension of the input pattern. Therefore, prediction accuracy may increase in the expanded feature space [24, 34]. FLANN learning can be considered an approximation function that is approximating or interpolating a continuous, multivariate function. The FLANN is a collection of orthogonal basis functions with a fixed number of weight parameters. The functional expansion unit improves the discrimination capability of the FLANN by increasing the dimension of an n-dimensional input pattern in the m-dimensional feature space. The problem is obtaining the weight parameters that extend the best possible approximation of the set of input–output examples after completing the measure design issue of selecting the basis function [35]. Using the Stone–Weierstrass theorem, Chen et al. [1] in 2008 revealed that the FLANN could be used as a universal approximator.

Let k be the number of input–output pattern pairs that the FLANN should learn. The input–output relationship of the FLANN can be described as follows. Let us consider a set of basic functions $\Upsilon = \{\Phi(A)\}_{i \in N}, N = \{1, 2, \dots\}$ be the set of basis functions, where A is a subset of n-dimensional Euclidean space $\Re^n$, ,, with the following properties: (1) $\phi_1 = 1$ and the subset $\Upsilon_j = \{\phi_i \in \Upsilon\}_{i=1}^j$ is a linearly independent set, that is, if $\sum_{i=1}^N (\theta_i \phi_i) = 0$, then $\theta_i = 0$ for all $i = 1, 2, \dots, j$, and $sup_j \left[\sum_{i=1}^j \|\phi_i\|_A^2\right]^{1/2} < \infty$.

Thus, the FLANN consists of N basis functions $\{\phi_1, \phi_2, \ldots, \phi_N\} \in \Upsilon_N$, with the following input–output relationship for the jth output:

$$\hat{y}_j = \rho(s_j); \tag{1}$$

where $s_j = \sum_{i=1}^{N}(\theta_{ji}\phi_i(I))$, $I \in AC\Re^n$, i.e., $I = [i_1, i_2, \ldots, i_n]^T$ is the input pattern vector, $\hat{y} \in \Re^m$, that is, $\hat{y} = [\hat{y}_1, \hat{y}_2, \ldots, \hat{y}_n]^T$ is the output vector, and $\theta_j = [\theta_{j1}, \theta_{j2}, \ldots, \theta_{jN}]$ is the weight vector associated with the jth output of the FLANN. Here, $\rho(.) = \tanh(.)$ is a nonlinear function (.).

Consider the m-dimensional output vector (1), which can be expressed as

$$O = \theta\Phi, \tag{2}$$

where θ is a $(m \times N)$ weight matrix of the FLANN depicted by $\theta = [\theta_1, \theta_2, \ldots, \theta_m]^T$, $\Phi = [\phi_1, \phi_2, \ldots, \phi_N]^T$ is the basis function vector, and $O = [O_1, O_2, \ldots, O_N]^T$ is a matrix of the linear outputs of the FLANN. The m-dimensional output vector $\hat{y}$ can be expressed as follows:

$$\hat{y} = \rho(O) = h_\theta(x), \tag{3}$$

Assume the input pattern vector I_k be of dimension n and the output o_k be a scalar. The training patterns are denoted by (I_k, o_k) and the network weight is $\theta(k)$, where k is the iteration number. According to (4), the jth output of the FLANN at iteration k is expressed as follows:

$$\hat{y}_j(k) = \rho\left(\sum_{i=1}^{N}(\theta_{ji}(k)\phi_i(X_k))\right) = \rho\left(\theta_j(k)\phi^T(X_k)\right), \tag{4}$$

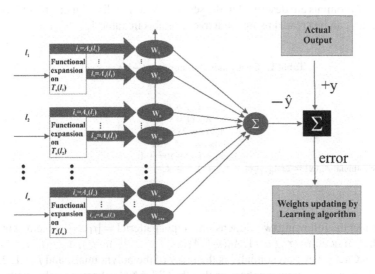

Fig. 1. Functional link neural networks (FLANN) architecture

For all $I \in A$ and $j = 1, 2, \ldots, m$, where $\phi(X_k) = [\phi_1(X_k), \phi_2(X_k), \ldots, \phi_N(X_k)]$.
Let $e_j(k) = y_j(k) - \hat{y}_j(k)$ denote the corresponding error

When using the BP algorithm for a single layer, the update rule for all FLANN weights is represented as follows:

$$\theta(k+1) = \theta(k) + \mu\delta(k)\varnothing(X_k), \tag{5}$$

where $(\theta(k))_{m \times N}$ is the FLANN weight matrix, and δ and μ are the error and learning rates, respectively.

2.1 Justification of the Use of Chebyshev Polynomial as the Orthogonal Basis Function

The nonlinear approximation capacity of the Chebyshev orthogonal polynomial is potent according to the approximation theory [6]. Chebyshev polynomial was combined with the FLANN to obtain the CFLANN [7]. The Weierstrass theorem states that a polynomial is always arbitrarily close to any continuous function. Notably, polynomial power series interpolation can be used to obtain an excellent estimate of a function with only a few data points. A good fit with little error requires a polynomial of extremely high degree, which is computationally not feasible and restricts the application of power series. Unlike power series with slow convergence problems, the Chebyshev polynomials exhibit a high computational economy with fast convergence. Thus, the Chebyshev series is considerably more competent than other power series of the same degree. The efficacy of Chebyshev polynomial orthogonal basis functions concerning convergence criteria is superior to that of other orthogonal polynomials [6]. Moreover, Chebyshev polynomials involve simple computation compared with trigonometric polynomials. These characteristics motivated us to use the CFLANN for approximating the target function for SDEE [24, 36, 37].

The polynomials are described in the section. Additionally, higher-order Chebyshev polynomials can be created using recursive formulas in Table 1.

Table 1. Chebyshev polynomials $(-1 \leq x \leq 1)$.

$$A_0(x) = 1$$
$$A_1(x) = x$$
$$A_2(x) = 2x^2 - 1$$
$$A_3(x) = 4x^3 - 3x$$
$$A_4(x) = 8x^4 - 8x^2 + 1$$

Recursive formula: $A_n(x) = 2xA_{n-1}(x) - A_{n-2}(x), n \geq 2$.

Consider the following two-dimensional input pattern $\mathrm{I} = [i_1, i_2]^T$ obtained by using Chebyshev functions: $\tau = [1, A_0(x_1), A_1(x_1), \ldots; 1, A_0(x_2), A_1(x_2), \ldots]$ where $A_i(x_j)$ is a Chebyshev polynomial, i is the order of the polynomials, and $j = 1, 2$.

The following theorem emphasizes that the CFLANN is homomorphic with a feed-forward MLP.

Theorem. Assume a feed-forward MLP neural network with only one hidden layer and a linear activation function for the output layer. If all activation functions of the hidden layer satisfy the Riemann integrable condition, the feed-forward neural network can be represented as a Chebyshev neural network. Lee et al. (1998) provided a detailed proof of the theorem.

3 Swarm Intelligence-Based Learning Algorithms for the CFLANN

This section provides an overview of four learning algorithms, namely classical PSO, adaptive PSO, improved PSO, and GA.

3.1 Classical PSO

PSO is a stochastic population-based swarm intelligence algorithm that was developed for function optimization by James Kennedy and Russell Eberhart in 1995 [47]. Each solution in PSO can be modeled as a particle flying through the hyper-space problem. In the uniform random search space, a population of particles is initialized with random positions $\vec{x}_k$ and velocity $\vec{v}_k$. The PSO algorithm traverses the search space by using the fitness function. The root mean square error is used as a fitness function. In every iteration, the fitness function for each particle is evaluated with its current position, and this information is used to adjust the trajectory of the particle by determining the best particle in the sub-swarms and the entire swarm population [38]. The position and velocity of a particle are updated using the following equations in the classical PSO algorithm at iteration t.

$$\vec{v_k}(t+1) = w \otimes \vec{v_k}(t) + \vec{c_1} \otimes \vec{r_1}(t) \otimes \left(\vec{p_k}(t) - \vec{x_k}(t)\right)$$
$$+ \vec{c_2} \otimes \vec{r_2}(t) \otimes \left(\vec{p_g}(t) - \vec{x_k}(t)\right), \tag{6}$$

$$\vec{x_k}(t+1) = \vec{x_k}(t) + \vec{v_k}(t+1), \tag{7}$$

In Eq. (6), symbol $\otimes$ represents point-by-point vector multiplication. A value less than one "w" is referred to as inertia. Here, c_1 and c_2 are real constants that are non-negative. Venter and Sobieski (Shi Y and Eberhart RC 1999) labeled c_1 as "self-confidence" and c_2 as "swarm confidence." Furthermore, $\vec{r_1}$ and $\vec{r_2}$ are two uniformly distributed random numbers in the range $[-1,1]$. In the original PSO algorithm, $w = 1, c_1 = 2$, and $c_2 = 2$ were used. Here, $\vec{p_k}(t)$ represents the best position found by the given particle, $\vec{p_g}(t)$ refers to the best position found by any particle, and the corresponding fitness values are referred to as the best of the particle and global best, respectively. The process of evaluating fitness function, velocity update, and updating position is repeated until a stopping criterion is reached. The objective of the algorithm is to change the particle position (weight vectors) in each iteration until the maximum change in the best fitness value is less than the specified threshold value for a given number of iterations as follows:

$$\left|f\left(\vec{p_g}(t)\right) - f\left(\vec{p_g}(t-1)\right)\right| \leq \epsilon, \quad t = 2, 3, \ldots, I \tag{8}$$

Pseudo Code of the proposed PSO-CFLANN:
The proposed PSO for training the CFLANN developed for SDEE is as follows:
The particle encoding of the proposed CFLANN's weights is as follows:

$$[w_{13}w_{14}w_{23}w_{24}]$$

Step 1: Initialize
 Set Particle size = 20.
    Set constants $w = 0.9, c_1 = 2, c_2 = 2$ (Kennedy et al., 2001)
    Set $t = 0$ (iteration number)

Step 2: Particle encoding of the CFLANN weights.

Step 3: Create the initial population of particles at random between [-1,1]. Each element of a particle's location vector corresponds to its biases and weights in the CFLANN.

Step 4: Randomly generate the particle velocities in the range [-1,1].

Step 5: Each individual particle is evaluated by the fitness function $f(.)$. We have selected RMSE as the fitness function and PSO is designed to minimize the fitness function.

$$RMSE = \sqrt{\frac{1}{n}\sum_{i=1}^{n}(y_i - \hat{y}_i)}, \tag{9}$$

where y_i is the actual ouput, $\hat{y}_i$ is the predcited output, and n is the number of training examples over which RMSE is compared.

Step 6:
$$if\ f(\vec{x}_k(t+1)) \leq f(\vec{p}_k(t))\ then\ \vec{p}_k(t+1) = \vec{x}_k(t+1), \vec{p}_k(t), \tag{10}$$

$$if\ f(\vec{x}_k(t+1) \leq f(\vec{p}_g(t))\ then\ \vec{p}_g(t+1) = \vec{x}_k(t+1), \vec{p}_g(t), \tag{11}$$

Step 7: Update weights (position) of the particle and change weights (velocity) of the particle based on eqns. 6 and 7.

Step 8: If the stopping condition mentioned in Eqn. (8) is satisfied, then go to Step 11.

Step 9: Increment "t".

Step 10: Go to Step 5.

Step 11: EXIT.

3.2 Improved PSO Technique

Based on classical PSO, an ISO improves search efficiency and increases the likelihood of obtaining the global optimum without considerably reducing the speed of convergence or the simplicity of the PSO structure. The mathematical model of ISO is as follows:

$$\vec{v_k}(t+1) = \lambda \otimes \vec{v_k}(t) + \vec{c_1} \otimes \vec{r_1}(t) \otimes (\vec{p_k}(t) - \vec{x_k}(t))$$
$$+ \vec{c_2} \otimes \vec{r_2}(t) \otimes (\vec{p_g}(t) - \vec{x_k}(t)), \tag{12}$$

$$\vec{x_k}(t+1) = \vec{x_k}(t) + \vec{v_k}(t+1), \tag{13}$$

where λ is the newly defined adaptive inertia weight whose value decreases with each iteration. The inertia weight decreases linearly until Gen1 and nonlinearly from Gen1 + 1 to Gen2, as presented in eqns. (14) and (15). The inertia weight adaptation mechanism enables the IPSO algorithm to achieve the best results by balancing the trade-off between exploration and exploitation [24].

Adaptive Inertia Weight (λ):
The following equations describe the adaptive inertia weight proposed by Dehuri et al. [28]:

$$\lambda_1 = \lambda_0 - \left(\left(\frac{\lambda_1}{Gen1} \right) \times i \right) \quad \forall i = 1..Gen1, \tag{14}$$

$$\lambda_1 = (\lambda_0 - \lambda_1) \times \exp \left(\frac{(Gen1 + 1) - i}{i} \right) \quad \forall i = Gen1 + 1..Gen2, \tag{15}$$

where λ_0 represents the initial weight, λ_1 represents the end point of linear selection, Gen1 represents the number of generations during which inertia weight is decreased linearly, and Gen2 represents the maximum generation. The values of λ_0 and λ_1 are based on empirical observations.

The more the particle improves, the smaller the area it should explore. The exploration capability of PSOs is greater than the exploitation capability. Therefore, the model outperforms local search in terms of global search. With a high probability, the self-adaptive evolutionary strategy generates small Gaussian and Cauchy perturbations suitable for local search optimization. The model improves the particle by calibrating PSO solutions.

Self-adaptive Cauchy Mutation: A random variable has Cauchy distribution ($C(t)$), if its density function is as follows:

$$C(t) = \frac{t}{\pi(t^2 + x^2)}, \quad -\infty < x < +\infty \tag{16}$$

The self-adaptive Cauchy mutation is represented as follows:

$$v_{ki}(t + 1) = v_{ki} \times \exp \left(\tau' \times C_{gi}(0, 1) + \tau \times C_{ki}(0, 1) \right), \tag{17}$$

$$x_{ki}(t + 1) = x_{ki}(t) + v_{ki}(t + 1), \tag{18}$$

Pseudo Code of the ISO-CFLANN:

The ISO algorithm used to train the CFLANN developed for SDEE is described in the following steps:

The particle encoding of the proposed CFLANN's weights is as follows:

$$[w_{13}w_{14}w_{23}w_{24}]$$

Step 1: Initialize
    Set particle size = 20.
    Set constants $c_1 = 2, c_2 = 2$ (Kennedy et al., 2001)
    Set adaptive inertia weight λ as described in eqns. (14) and (15).
    Set $t = 0$ (iteration number)

Step 2: Particle encoding of the CFLANN weights.

Step 3: Create the initial population of particles at random between $[-1,1]$. Each element of a particle's location vector corresponds to its biases and weights in the CFLANN.

Step 4: Randomly generate the particle velocities in the range $[[-1,1]$.

Step 5: Each individual particle is assessed by fitness function $f(.)$. We selected RMSE as the fitness function and PSO is designed to minimize the fitness function.

$$RMSE = \sqrt{\frac{1}{n}\Sigma_{i=1}^{n}(y_i - \hat{y}_i)}, \tag{19}$$

where y_i is the actual ouput, $\hat{y}_i$ is the predcited output, and n is the number of training examples over which RMSE is compared.

Step 7: Calculate the adaptive inertia weight as per eqns. (14) and (15).

Step 8:

$$if\ f(\vec{x}_k(t+1)) \leq f(\vec{p}_k(t))\ then\ \vec{p}_k(t+1) = \vec{x}_k(t+1), \vec{p}_k(t), \tag{20}$$

$$if\ f(\vec{x}_k(t+1) \leq f(\vec{p}_g(t))\ then\ \vec{p}_g(t+1) = \vec{x}_k(t+1), \vec{p}_g(t) \tag{21}$$

Step 9: Update weights (position) of the particle and change weights (velocity) of the particle based on eqns. 12 and 13.

Step 10: Apply Cauchy mutation alternatively to update the position and velocity of the particle as per eqns. (17) and (18), respectively, if the position of the global best solution is not improved for a successive number of pre-specified generations.

Step 11: If the stopping condition as specified in eqn. (10) is satisfied, then go to step 13.

Step 11: Increment "t".

Step 12: Go to Step 5.

Step 13: EXIT.

3.3 Adaptive PSO

APSO is an advancement over PSO that improves search efficiency and increases the likelihood of reaching the global optimum by dynamically varying the inertia weight based on population fitness variance. The inertia weight determines how the previous velocity of the particle influences its velocity at the current time step [39, 40]. The inertia weight w_i is updated by calculating the population fitness variance as follows:

$$\tau = \sqrt{\sum_{i=1}^{M} \left(\frac{f_i - f_{avg}}{f} \right)^2}, \tag{22}$$

where f_{avg} = average fitness of the population, f_i = fitness of the ith particle in the population, and M = total number of particles.

$$f = -\max\{\|f_i - f_{avg}\|\} \; i = 1, 2, \ldots, M, \, if \; \max\{\|f_i - f_{avg}\|\} > 1 \tag{23}$$

$$= -1 \; if \; \max\{\|f_i - f_{avg}\|\} < 1 \tag{24}$$

If τ is significant, then the population is in exploration aptitude (global search), whereas small τ enhances the exploitation capability (local search) of the swarm. To circumvent this problem, the inertia weight is adjusted as follows:

$$w(k) = \lambda w(k-1) + (1 - \lambda)\tau \tag{25}$$

A forgetting factor λ is selected as 0.95 for faster convergence.

Pseudo Code of the APSO-CFLANN:
The APSO algorithm used to train the SDEE CFLANN is as follows:
The particle encoding of the proposed CFLANN's weights is as follows:

$$[w_{13}w_{14}w_{23}w_{24}]$$

Step 1: Initialize
      Set particle size = 20.
      Set constants $c_1 = 2, c_2 = 2$ (Kennedy et al., 2001)
      Set $t = 0$ (iteration Number)
Step 2: Particle encoding of the CFLANN weights.
Step 3: Create the initial population of particles at random between [-1,1]. Each element of a particle's location vector corresponds to its biases and weights in the CFLANN.
Step 4: Randomly generate the particle velocities in the range $[-1,1]$.
Step 5: Each individual particle is assessed by the fitness function $f(.)$. We selected RMSE as the fitness function and PSO is designed to minimize the fitness function.

$$RMSE = \sqrt{\frac{1}{n}\Sigma_{i=1}^{n}(y_i - \hat{y}_i)}, \tag{26}$$

where y_i is the actual ouput, $\hat{y}_i$ is the predcited output, and n is the number of training examples over which RMSE is compared.
Step 7: Calculate the adaptive inertia weight as per eqn. (25).

Step 8:

$$if\ f\big(\vec{x}_k(t+1)\big) \leq f\big(\vec{p}_k(t)\big)\ then\ \vec{p}_k(t+1) = \vec{x}_k(t+1), \vec{p}_k(t), \tag{27}$$

$$if\ f(\vec{x}_k(t+1) \leq f\big(\vec{p}_g(t)\big)\ then\ \vec{p}_g(t+1) = \vec{x}_k(t+1), \vec{p}_g(t), \tag{28}$$

Step 9: Update weights (position) of the particle and change weights (velocity) of the particle based on the eqns. 2 and 3.
Step 10: If stopping condition is satisfied as specified in eqn. (10), go to step 13.
Step 11: Increment "t".
Step 12: Go to Step 5.
Step 13: Stop.

3.4 GA

Inspired by biological evolution, Holland created the GA in 1975 [2]. The GA is a probabilistic search algorithm based on Darwin's principle of biological evolution through reproduction and "survival of the fittest" [3]. The algorithm begins with a randomly generated population of individuals (chromosomes). The search for a global optimum is managed by shifting from an initial population of individuals to a new population using genetics-like operators such as selection, crossover, and mutation. The explanation of the proposed genetic-CFLANN algorithm pseudo-code is as follows:

Pseudo Code of the Genetic-CFLANN:
The following steps describe the GA used to train the CFLANN developed for SDEE:
The particle encoding of the proposed CFLANN's weights is as follows:

$$[w_{13} w_{14} w_{23} w_{24}]$$

Step 1: Initialize:

Set population size = 10 V, where V is the number of features in the input pattern (Huang and Chiu, 2006; Chiu and Huang, 2007).

Set crossover rate = 0.8

Set Mutation rate = 0.1

Set t = 0 (Iteration number)

Step 2: Encoding of the CFLANN weights on chromosomes.

Step 3: Generate the starting population of chromosomes at random within the interval $[-1,1]$.

Step 4: Each individual chromosome is assessed by the fitness function $f(.)$ in the GA. RMSE is selected as the fitness function and GA is designed to minimize the fitness function.

$$RMSE = \sqrt{\frac{1}{n}\sum_{i=1}^{n}(y_i - \hat{y}_i)}, \tag{29}$$

where y_i is the actual ouput, $\hat{y}_i$ is the predcited output, and n is the number of training examples over which RMSE is compared.

Step 5: The standard roulette wheel technique is adapted to select 10-V chromosomes from the current population.

Step 6: Arithmetic crossover and uniform mutation operations are performed on the chosen parent chromosomes with crossover and mutation rates, respectively, to yield offspring with higher fitness value.

Step 7: The fitness value of each offspring is evaluated in the population.

Step 8: Elitist strategy: The chromosome with the highest fitness value is copied to the next generation. The other chromosomes of the next generation (new populations) are reproduced from older population

Step 9: Stopping criteria: The population is evolved by the GA algorithm until the number of generations is equal to or exceeds 1000 or the best fitness value did not change in the last 200 generations. If the stopping criteria are satisfied, then go to step 12.

Step 10: Increment "t".

Step 11: Go to Step 4

Step 12: Stop.

3.5 BP

BP is a fundamental neural network platform that was first used in the 1960s and popularized in 1989 by Rumelhart, Hinton, and Williams. BP is used to train feed-forward neural networks and is applicable to other ANNs and functions. When fitting a neural network, BP is used to efficiently compute the gradient of the loss function for the network weights for a single input–output sample. To train multilayer networks, gradient methods can be used to update weights to minimize loss. Gradient descent and stochastic gradient descent are popular methods. In BP, the chain rule is used to calculate the gradient of the loss function for each weight one layer at a time, iterating backward from the last layer to avoid unnecessary calculations of intermediate terms [41]. The proposed BP-CFLANN algorithm pseudo-code is as follows:

Pseudo Code of the BP-CFLANN:

The BP algorithm used to train the CFLANN developed for SDEE is described in the following steps:

x: Input Vector

y: Output

C: loss function or cost function

Squared error loss is typically used in the regression.

L: the number of layers

a_j^l is the activation value of layer l, unit (neuron j)

$$a_j^l = g\left(\left(\overline{w}_j^l\right) * \overline{a}_j^{l-1} + b_j^l\right)$$

g is the sigmoid activation function at layer l, parameters w and b of layer l and unit j.

The training set pairs (x_i, y_i). The loss of the model on each input–output pair in the training set is the difference between the predicted and target outputs.

BP computes the gradient for a fixed input–output pair (x_i, y_i) with variable weights. The chain rule can compute each gradient component but applying this rule for each weight is wasteful. BP avoids repeated calculations and unneeded intermediate values by computing the gradient of each layer from back to front.

---

4 Performance Evaluation Metrics

This section presents a few metrics for the performance evaluation of the proposed models widely used in existing SDEE literature. To evaluate the efficacy of proposed swarm intelligence-based SDEE models, the following performance metrics are considered to provide a powerful performance evaluation: standardized accuracy (SA) [43], mean magnitude of relative error (MMRE), median magnitude of relative error (MdMRE), and PRED (0.25) [42]. When the MMRE and MdMRE values are at most 0.25, and the PRED value is at least 0.75, the SDEE model performs well. MREs are defined as MMRE. The MRE of the ith project is defined as follows:

$$MRE_i = \left|\frac{y_i - \hat{y}_i}{y_i}\right|, \tag{30}$$

Therefore, $MMRE = \sum_{i=1}^{n} MRE_i/n$

MdMRE, a global error measure, is defined as the median of all MREs and is less sensitive to outliers.

$$MdMRE = median(BRE_i), \tag{31}$$

PRED(x) is described as the percentage of predictions falling within the actual known value x, specified as follows:

$$PRED(x) = \frac{100}{N} \times \sum_{i=1}^{N} D_i, \tag{32}$$

$$D_i = \begin{cases} 1 & if \quad MBRE < \frac{x}{100} \\ 0 & otherwise \end{cases}, \tag{33}$$

when $x = 25$, the PRED metric is defined as PRED (0.25).

MAE, a non-symmetric evaluation criterion, is used as an error indicator. The MAE is determined using Eqs. (34) and (35). Because the residuals are not standardized, the model with MAE as a performance measure is difficult to understand. To avoid this difficulty, Sheppred and McDonell created a new metric called SA, as expressed in Eq. (36). To estimate the effect size, Eq. (37) is used. SA measures whether a prediction model is relevant and outperforms random guessing. It is a percentage (0–100 scale) or number (0–1 scale). Higher SA values indicate the superiority of a model to random guessing, which explains how well the strategy works. The effect size DELTA (Δ) checks if the prediction models are by accident or by choice by comparing them to a random guess model. A value larger than 0.5 is better than that less than 0.2 (Shepperd and MacDonell 2012; Azzeh, M. et al. 2015).

$$AE_i = |y_i - \hat{y}_i|, \tag{34}$$

$$MAE = \frac{\sum_{i=1}^{N} AE_i}{N}, \tag{35}$$

$$SA = 1 - \frac{MAE}{\overline{MAE_{P_0}}}, \tag{36}$$

$$\Delta = \frac{MAE - \overline{MAE_{P_0}}}{s_{P_0}}, \tag{37}$$

- Actual and projected project efforts are y_i and $\hat{y}_i$. The mean absolute error of the prediction model is MAE. $\overline{MAE_{P_0}}$ is the mean of many random guesses. a $\hat{y}_i$ for the target case t is predicted by random sampling (with equal probability) over all the remaining $n - 1$ case and considering $y_t = y_r$, where r is taken from $1, \ldots\ldots, n \bigwedge r \neq t$.

5 Description of the Dataset

In this part, the COCOMO'81 Dataset from the prospective repository test suite was used to benchmark the prospective model. Boehm conceived the idea for COCOMO'81 (1981) [8]. COCOMO is an open-source, well-documented algorithmic cost model. COCOMO'81 is the most practical, well-known, and often-cited conventional model. Boehm illustrated the "fundamental," "intermediate," and "detailed" levels of project estimation. Initially, a preliminary estimate is made. The first estimate is refined in two steps [44]. The most frequently used model is the intermediate COCOMO. The intermediate COCOMO model considers the following parameters, in addition to the product size: (a) software product size, (b) project development mode B (scaling factor), and (c) 15 cost drivers (effort multipliers). Organic, semi-detached, and embedded development are three problematic modes, with the values 1.05, 1.12, and 1.20, respectively. Next,

15 effort multipliers are used to modify the software development effort based on its qualities. The cost drivers are the multiplying factor, that is, very low, low, nominal, high, very high, and extra high. Based on the factor's effect on productivity, an actual number (effort multiplier) is assigned to each rating.

6 Experiments and Results

We tested four CFLANN models. First, PSO-CFLANN trains CFLANN with PSO. Second, ISO-CFLANN tweaks CFLANN's weights using ISO. Third, the APSO-CFLANN model fine-tunes weights. Fourth, genetic-CFLANN optimizes CFLANN weights using a GA. The proposed techniques are compared with well-known techniques such as functional link artificial neural networks with BP learning and ANNs with back-propagation learning. Method validity depends on selecting and creating experimental circumstances. This section describes the circumstances of the experiment. The proposed solutions are implemented on a PC with an Intel Core i5- 2410M, 2.30 GHz CPU, 4 MB RAM, and MATLAB 8.3 programming environment. Using min-max normalization in the interval [0, 1] eliminates the unequal feature effect [45]. The dataset is randomly partitioned into training and testing subsets. Leave-one-out cross-validation is used to assess model accuracy. The algorithm is trained on $N-1$ random occurrences and validated on one. Cross-validation is repeated N times [46]. The training set constructs the model, the validation set tweaks to control parameters, and the test set predicts model performance.

The outcomes of the strategies outlined in Sect. 3 are reported. The outcomes of simulations using the COCOMO dataset for PSO-CFLANN, APSO-CFLANN, ISO-CFLANN, Genetic-CFLANN, BP-CFLANN, and BP-ANN are presented in Tables 2 and 3. According to Table 2, the MMRE and MdMRE results revealed that PSO-CFLANN is superior to all other approaches, with values of 0.000259 and 8.49E−05, respectively. PRED (0.25) delivers identical results across all approaches. Because the research on SDEE indicates that MMRE and PRED are biased performance indicators, SA and DELTA are used to determine the optimal technique, and results are depicted in Table 3. At PSO-CFLANN, the SA and DELTA values are greater, with SA = 99.94 (in percentage) and DELTA = 3.4895, thereby confirming the superiority of the PSO-CFLANN to other approaches.

The comparison of the prediction models used for the COCOMO'81 Dataset is displayed in Figs. 2, 3, and 4. The efficacy of each model is determined using three distinct types of graphs. The first graph is a 2Dplot of MAE values for a line graph, whereas the second is a histogram. On the x-axis of each MAE graph, the number of COCOMO dataset simulation projects is indicated. The MAE graphs reveal that for PSO-CFLANN and ISO-CFLANN, the generalization error assessed over the validation examples increases until project number 20, and subsequently steadily decreases as the number of projects increases, overcoming the overfitting issue (low training error and high testing error). By contrast, numerous strategies exhibit overfitting concerns (low training error and high testing error). The MAE graphs reveals that as the number of training examples increases, PSO-CFLANN and ISO-CFLANN become better suited to handle overfitting concerns. Figure 4 depicts the boxplot of all approaches, indicating that ISO, GA, and BP CFLANNs have more error dispersion than other approaches.

Compared with those of APSO and BP CFLANNs, PSO-CFLANNs's boxplots have the shortest interquartile distance and are normally distributed. Therefore, alternative methods are preferred.

Table 2. Outcomes and comparisons of all techniques on the COCOMO81 dataset

	MMRE			MdMRE			PRED (0.25)		
	Training	Validation	Testing	Training	Validation	Testing	Training	Validation	Testing
PSO-CFLANN	6.96E−05	0.000355	0.000259	0.000903	0.000141	8.49E−05	1	1	1
APSO-CFLANN	0.003111	0.00467	0.006586	0.00236	0.001302	0.001905	1	1	1
ISO-CFLANN	0.004959	0.000786	0.010225	0.004335	0.004416	0.010225	1	1	1
Genetic-CFLANN	0.008699	0.01085	0.008252	0.007867	0.001392	0.001929	1	1	1
BP-CFLANN	0.00463	0.004696	0.011901	0.000469	0.000286	0.000655	1	1	1
BP-ANN	0.009619	0.004001	0.024008	0.009502	0.001354	0.002902	1	1	1

Table 3. Outcomes and comparisons of all techniques on the COCOMO81 dataset

	SA			DELTA		
	Training	Validation	Testing	Training	Validation	Testing
PSO-CFLANN	0.99986	0.99928	0.99947	0	2.7627	3.4895
APSO-CFLANN	0.99986	0.99982	0.9999	0	3.4424	2.7082
ISO-CFLANN	0.99981	0.99997	0.99985	0	0.933	1.0638
Genetic-CFLANN	0.99962	0.99959	0.99988	0	0.26906	0.5378
BP-CFLANN	0.99982	0.99982	0.99982	0	0.17986	0.202
BP-ANN	0.99965	0.99985	0.99964	0	0.59613	0.1208

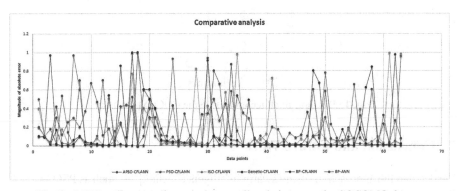

Fig. 2. MAE outcomes and comparison to all techniques on the COCOMO dataset

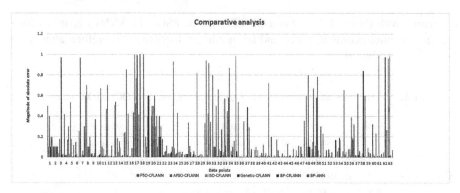

Fig. 3. MAE outcomes and comparison to all techniques on the COCOMO dataset

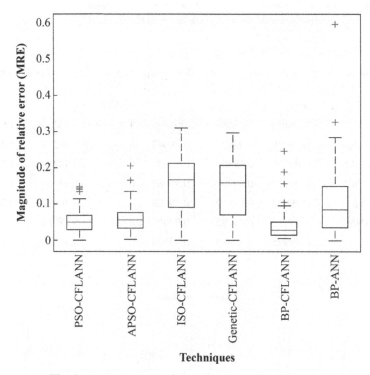

Fig. 4. Boxplots of all techniques on the COCOMO dataset

7   Conclusion and Future Work

We detailed the approach for using swarm intelligence techniques, such as PSO, APSO, ISO, and GA, to optimize the weight parameters of the CFLANN. The approaches antic-ipate the software development effort by using the optimum weight value acquired by swarm intelligence techniques and the set of Chebyshev polynomials orthogonal basis functions selected for the functional expansion of feature vectors. The results of the empirical study revealed that the strategies of swarm intelligence enhance the performance of CFLANN. In most instances, the PSO-CFLANN model provided outcomes that were comparable or superior to the best results obtained by the APSO-CFLANN, ISO-CFLANN, genetic-CFLANN, BP-CFLANN, and BP-ANN. The PSO-CFLANN model's architectural complexity is considerably less than that of MLP and is the same as or less than that of the CFLANN with BP. This feature of PSO-CFLANN may encourage SDEE researchers to perform additional studies in this domain. Future studies should concentrate on the symbiotic interaction between swarm intelligence and other soft computing techniques, as well as the concurrent growth of architecture and weights with a Pareto set of solutions for the next generation of SDEE. Calibration of input patterns from low to high dimension utilizing clones of HONs such as ridge polynomial neural networks and pi-sigma neural networks is another research direction.

Acknowledgment. Dr. Satchidananda Dehuri, Professor of Computer Science (Erstwhile P. G. Department of Information and Communication Technology), Fakir Mohan University would like to thank SERB, Govt. of India for financial support under Teachers' Associateship for Research Excellence (TARE) fellowship vide file no. TAR/2021/000065 for the period 2021–2024.

References

1. Chen, C.H., Lin, C.J., Lin, C.T.: A functional-link-based neurofuzzy network for nonlinear system control. Fuzzy Systems, IEEE Transactions on **16**(5), 1362–1378 (2008)
2. Holland, J.H.: Adaption in Natural and Artificial Systems. The University of Michigan Press, Ann Arbor (1975)
3. Michalewicz, Z.: Genetic Algorithms + Data Structures = Evolution Programs. Springer, Heidelberg (2013). https://doi.org/10.1007/978-3-662-03315-9
4. Chiu, N.H., Huang, S.J.: The adjusted analogy-based software effort estimation based on similarity distances. J. Syst. Softw. **80**(4), 628–640 (2007)
5. Huang, S.J., Chiu, N.H.: Optimization of analogy weights by genetic algorithm for software effort estimation. Inf. Softw. Technol. **48**(11), 1034–1045 (2006)
6. Lee, T.T., Jeng, J.T.: The Chebyshev-polynomials-based unified model neural networks for function approximation. IEEE Trans. Syst. Man Cybern. Part B Cybern. **28**(6), 925–935 (1998)
7. Pao, Y.H., Takefuji, Y.: Functional link net computing: theory, system, architecture and functionalities. IEEE Comput. 76–79 (1992)
8. Boehm, B.W.: Software Engineering Economics, vol. 197. Prentice-Hall, Englewood Cliffs (1981)
9. Putnam, L.H., Myers, W.: Measures for Excellence: Reliable Software on Time, Within Budget. Prentice Hall Professional Technical Reference (1991)
10. Huang, X., Ho, D., Ren, J., Capretz, L.F.: Improving the COCOMO model using a neuro-fuzzy approach. Appl. Soft Comput. **7**(1), 29–40 (2007)
11. Shepperd, M., Schofield, C.: Estimating software project effort using analogies. IEEE Trans. Softw. Eng. **23**(11), 736–743 (1997)
12. Auer, M., Trendowicz, A., Graser, B., Haunschmid, E., Biffl, S.: Optimal project feature weights in analogy-based cost estimation: improvement and limitations. IEEE Trans. Softw. Eng. **32**(2), 83–92 (2006)
13. Heiat, A.: Comparison of artificial neural network and regression models for estimating software development effort. Inf. Softw. Technol. **44**(15), 911–922 (2002)

14. Shin, M., Goel, A.L.: Empirical data modeling in software engineering using radial basis functions. IEEE Trans. Softw. Eng. **26**(6), 567–576 (2000)
15. Oliveira, A.L.: Estimation of software project effort with support vector regression. Neurocomputing **69**(13), 1749–1753 (2006)
16. Minsky, M., Papert, S.: Perceptrons. MIT Press, Cambridge (1969)
17. Hornik, K., Stinchcombe, M., White, H.: Multilayer feed-forward networks are universal approximators. Neural Netw. **2**(5), 359–366 (1989)
18. Cybenko, G.: Approximations by superpositions of a sigmoid function. Math. Controls Sig. Syst. **2**, 303–314 (1989)
19. Guillermo, V.: A distributed approach to neural network simulation program. Master thesis, The University of Texas at El Paso, TX (1998)
20. Zurada, J.M.: Introduction to Artificial Neural System. West Publishing Company, St. Paul (1992)
21. Beale, R., Jackson, T.: Neural Computing: An Introduction. Hilger, Philadelphia (1991)
22. AlBataineh, A., Kaur, D., Jalali, S.M.J.: Multi-layer perceptron training optimization using nature inspired computing. IEEE Access **10**, 36963–36977 (2022)
23. Man, Z., Wu, H.R., Liu, S., Yu, X.: A new adaptive back-propagation algorithm based on Lyapunov stability theory for neural networks. IEEE Trans. Neural Netw. **17**(6), 1580–1591 (2006)
24. Dehuri, S., Cho, S.B.: A comprehensive survey on functional link neural networks and an adaptive PSO–BP learning for CFLNN. Neural Comput. Appl. **19**(2), 187–205 (2010)
25. Kosmatopoulos, E.B., Polycarpou, M.M., Christodoulou, M., Ioannou, P.: High-order neural network structures for identification of dynamical systems. IEEE Trans. Neural Netw. **6**(2), 422–431 (1995)
26. Giles, C.L., Maxwell, T.: Learning, invariance and generalization in higher-order neural networks. Appl. Opt. **26**(23), 4972–4978 (1987)
27. Pao, Y.H.: Adaptive Pattern Recognition and Neural Network. Addison-Wesley, Reading (1989)
28. Dehuri, S., Roy, R., Cho, S.B., Ghosh, A.: An improved swarm optimized functional link artificial neural network (ISO-FLANN) for classification. J. Syst. Softw. **85**(6), 1333–1345 (2012)
29. Mirea, L., Marcu, T.: System identification using functional link neural networks with dynamic structure. In: 15th Triennial World Congress, Barcelona, Spain (2002)
30. Cass, R., Radl, B.: Adaptive process optimization using functional link networks and evolutionary algorithms. Control EngPract. **4**(11), 1579–1584 (1996)
31. Pao, Y.-H., Philips, S.M.: The functional link net learning optimal control. Neurocomputing **9**, 149–164 (1995)
32. Shin, Y., Ghosh, J.: Ridge polynomial networks. IEEE Trans. Neural Netw. **6**(2), 610–622 (1995)
33. Klasser, M.S., Pao, Y.H.: Characteristics of the functional linknet: a higher order delta rule net. In: IEEE proceedings of 2nd Annual International Conference on Neural Networks, San Diago, CA (1988)
34. Elyounsi, A., Tlijani, H., Bouhlel, M.S.: ISAR-image recognition using optimized HONN by a Metaheuristic algorithm. In: 2022 IEEE 9th International Conference on Sciences of Electronics, Technologies of Information and Telecommunications (SETIT), pp. 97–103. IEEE, May 2022
35. Patra, J.C., Van den Bos, A.: Modeling of an intelligent pressure sensor using functional link artificial neural networks. ISA Trans. **39**(1), 15–27 (2000)
36. Qi, Y., Pan, L., Liu, S.: A Lyapunov optimization-based online scheduling algorithm for service provisioning in cloud computing. Futur. Gener. Comput. Syst. **134**, 40–52 (2022)

37. Vilsen, S.B., Stroe, D.I.: Transfer learning for adapting battery state-of-health estimation from laboratory to field operation. IEEE Access **10**, 26514–26528 (2022)
38. Barrera, J., Coello, C.A.C.: A review of particle swarm optimization methods used for multimodal optimization. In: Lim, C.P., Jain, L.C., Dehuri, S. (eds.) Innovations in Swarm Intelligence, vol. 248, pp. 9–37. Springer, Heidelberg (2009). https://doi.org/10.1007/978-3-642-04225-6_2
39. Gad, A.G.: Particle swarm optimization algorithm and its applications: a systematic review. Arch. Comput. Methods Eng. 1–31 (2022)
40. Nickabadi, A., Ebadzadeh, M.M., Safabakhsh, R.: A novel particle swarm optimization algorithm with adaptive inertia weight. Appl. Soft Comput. **11**(4), 3658–3670 (2011)
41. Backpropagation – Wikipedia, 1 August 2022. https://en.wikipedia.org/wiki/Backpropagation
42. Cohen, J.: A power primer. Psychol. Bull. **112**, 155–159 (1992)
43. Shepperd, M., MacDonell, S.: Evaluating prediction systems in software project estimation. Inf. Softw. Technol. **54**(8), 820–827 (2012)
44. Mall, R.: Fundamentals of Software Engineering. PHI Learning Pvt. Ltd., New Delhi (2018)
45. Kocaguneli, E., Menzies, T.: Software effort models should be assessed via leave-one-out validation. J. Syst. Softw. **86**(7), 1879–1890 (2013)
46. Kohavi, R., John, G.H.: Wrappers for feature subset selection. Artif. Intell. **97**(1–2), 273–324 (1997)
47. Kennedy, J., Eberhart, R.C.: Particle swarm optimization. In: Proceedings of the IEEE International Conference on Neural Networks, Perth, Australia, pp. 1942–1948 (1995)

METBAG – A Web Based Business Application

Nannapaneni Akshaj and B. K. Tripathy(✉) ⓘ

School of Information Technology Engineering, VIT, Vellore, India
tripathybk@vit.ac.in

Abstract. Digitization has made the online business in the domain of core sector of metals, minerals and ores more competitive. A lot of web and mobile applications are available to make the process smooth. However, a user has to follow the price trend and analyse it in order to make the right choice. This and possible repetition of the process leads to its slowing down. Also, from the company perspective the operations and transactions involved makes the process complex. So, automation in generating the Irrevocable cooperate purchase order (ICPO) and Sales and Purchase Agreement (SPA), invoices and Non Circumvention and Non-Disclosure Agreement (NCNDA) forms is highly recommended. For increment in business accurate data analytics plays an important role. It is our aim in this paper to focus on developing an automated web application to frame a transaction integrated with all necessary features which is user-friendly from the letter of intent till the generation of invoice for the user and an auto generated dashboard for the company. The process includes the price prediction for the products and also takes care of the security of user credentials in view using hashing and multi-lingual jumbled salting.

Keywords: Predictive analysis · LSTM · Regression · F1-Score · SHA-512 · Salting · Descriptive analysis

1 Introduction

The competition in the online business in the domain of core sector of metals, minerals and ores has increased extensively due to the businesses moving digital [1]. Many industrial companies do not have e-commerce websites, they have struggled to fully embrace this strategy because of the complexities involved, particularly those related to distributor management, and thus they remain stuck at the pilot stage. Direct e-commerce sales can help industrial companies, as it gives them more of a connection to end customers and their needs. The analysis framework has proved to be useful for assessing the power of every considered methodology to affect the planning of business processes in web applications. Requirements for methodology to design business processes are representing component activities, describing possible workflows, defining and managing state of web transaction, specifying which activities can be suspended or resumed, describe how two or more users are related in a transaction, specify how content navigation and operation affect each other, which contents will be provided to user to support execution of an activity, defining which information objects are affected by executing the activity

© The Author(s), under exclusive license to Springer Nature Switzerland AG 2022
M. Panda et al. (Eds.): ICIICC 2022, CCIS 1737, pp. 82–94, 2022.
https://doi.org/10.1007/978-3-031-23233-6_6

and describing how the activity will be customized. Three dimensions of analysis framework are the business requirements, user requirements and system requirements. The user requirements include a simple user interface, all necessary features and tools for completing the transaction, security of credentials, etc. Business requirements mainly include the track of user activity on the platform, business performance using numbers and statistics and reduced work load for repetitive work. But the web applications in this sector lack a lot of user requirements like lack of proper UI, integrated analytics system [9] for the admin because of which they go to third-party tools, credential security and other user utilities. For the security of the credentials, SHA-512 hash algorithm has become popular because of complex hash generated by it [10]. But hashes can be cracked using guess and check technique [7]. Therefore, salting along with it is used to enhance security. Also, the price prediction systems are of great use for the business transactions and can be largely seen in a number of applications. But for this accurate price based on recent market dynamics are needed to be predicted. Also, there are number of other utilities which are to be included in order to provide a good experience to the user [2]. Also, providing a data analytical system [6] and dashboard to the business admin helps in taking data-driven decisions and prevents them from going to third-party for the services. So, this application focuses on an automated web application to frame a transaction integrated with all necessary features which is user-friendly from the letter of intent till the generation of invoice for the user and an auto generated integrated dashboard for the company [8]. The process includes the price prediction for the products based on recent market dynamics and also takes care of the security of user credentials in view using hashing and multi-lingual jumbled salting.

2 Literature Review

Many industrial companies do not have an e-commerce web application, they find it difficult to fully implement this strategy due to the complexity involved, particularly related to the management of distributors, and are therefore stuck in the pilot phase. Many of them do not meet all user requirements, such as getting real-time prices of products, user-friendly interface, lack of complete information, ease of activities to be performed like submission of LOI & ICPO, reordering etc. Often these things become the reason for loss of business. Direct selling by e-commerce can help industrial companies because it allows them to be closer to the end customer and his needs.

2.1 Gaps and Solutions

Gaps in the current system are:

- Lack of user utilities
- Lack of integrated analytics systems because of which businesses go for third-party tool, thus increasing their expenditure.
- Price prediction for the products being sold.
- Simple user interface.
- Security of the user credentials.

So, this system takes care of the above-mentioned gaps and develops a system with the objective of:

- Develop metal price prediction model using the market price values to get relevant predicted price values.
- Using techniques like SHA-512 hashing [3] and multi-lingual jumbled salting for security of the user credentials [4]
- Use of technologies like bootstrap, chart.js, HTML, CSS and jQuery for designing and developing a good user interface.
- Applying the SQL techniques and plotting techniques to extract the valuable information from the collected user data and putting it in the form of dashboards and tables.

If provided with right computational power, the system can be implemented to a number of different sectors and the number of domains can also be increased. Also, the prediction model can be scaled to any number of domains, even then producing highly accurate results.

2.2 Deep Neural Networks (DNN) and LSTM

Neural networks are uncertainty based models, which have been developed to mimic the functionalities of the human brain. Of late Deep Neural Network which are neural networks with deep learning concept embedded into them (In fact the number of hidden layers have been increased to a good number) ([12, 21]. There are several types of DNNs like Convolutional Neural Networks (CNN) [13], recurrent Neural Networks (RNN) [12], generative Adversarial Neural Networks (GAN) [12] and so on. There are a number of applications of these nets, mainly for image classification ([14–19]). LSTM is a special kind of recurrent neural network capable of handling long-term dependencies ([20, 21]). In this work we use LSTM in the price prediction component.

3 Architecture of the System

The architecture of the proposed system comprises of two main components; from user side and from admin side.

3.1 Architecture of the User Side of the System

The user side system architecture is provided in Fig. 1. The below figure explains the flow user follows in order to complete a transaction. This also dives the flow of data in and out of the database. Thus giving a brief about the user side of the application.

Description of Modules

- About: This module describes about the company, their operations and about the CEO of the company.

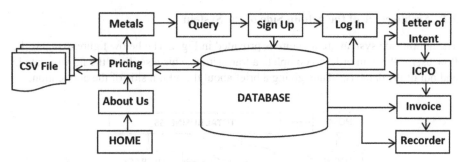

Fig. 1. Architecture of the user side of the system

- Pricing: This module displays the price trends. The module also gives the option of price conversions to desired currencies along with the option of price prediction of the product chosen by the user and the price prediction using the different domains of provided based on the user input. The domains are the different products and each domain has a separate data of prices which is a time-series data, which would be the input for the model after processing.
- Metals: This module displays all the products with the analysis of each product and the query tab.
- Query: This module is for the user to clear his queries regarding a particular product that he wishes to know about.
- Registration: This module is for the user signup. The entered password is hashed and also a random multi-lingual salt generated is also hashed and then both the hashes are concatenated in alternative jumbled manner to generate a 256 characters long password string. Other details like the username and email are also collected.
- Login: The username and password are required for authentication. Password entered is hashed and then the password stored in database is extracted and sliced to match with the entered password hash.
- LOI: After selecting product the user fills the LOI form with the LOI PDF. After submitting, the user will receive Sales and Purchase Agreement and the ICPO and Sales and purchase Agreement link after reviewing LOI.
- ICPO: This module is for the order submission. The user enters all the details of the order and submits the order. After placing the Order, the user will receive NCNDA form and the invoice.
- Reorder: The user can click on the reorder tab against each order displayed in the user login. After clicking, the user gets the auto filled ICPO form and the user can place the order.

3.2   Architecture of the Admin Side of the System

The admin side system architecture is provided in Fig. 2 The below figure explains the flow user follows in order to complete a transaction. This also dives the flow of data in and out of the database. Thus giving a brief about the admin side of the application.

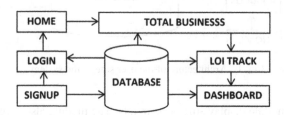

Fig. 2. Architecture of the system- Admin side

Description of the Modules

- Registration: This module is for the admin signup. The entered password is hashed and also a random multi-lingual salt generated is also hashed and then both the hashes are concatenated in alternative jumbled manner to generate a 256 characters long password string. Other details like the username and email are also collected.
- Login: The username and password are required for authentication. Password entered is hashed and then the password stored in database is extracted and sliced to match with the entered password hash.
- Total Business: This module shows the amount of each product sold and amount of revenue total generated by each product
- LOI Track: This module shows the list of all the LOI pending to be converted with the download option of each LOI file.
- Dashboard: This is the visualization module displaying the business analytical dashboard

4   Workflow Diagrams

We provide the workflow diagrams of the system in two components in this section (Fig. 3 and Fig. 4).

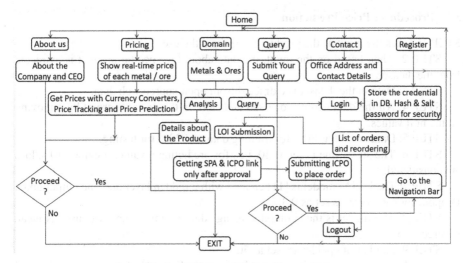

Fig. 3. Workflow diagram- Users' side

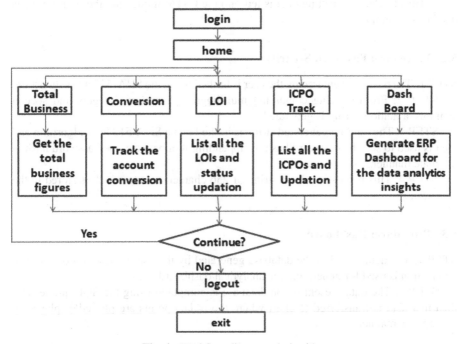

Fig. 4. Workflow diagram admin side

5 Procedures

The entire procedure is divided into 3 parts; price prediction, password security and dashboard. We provide the three procedures below.

5.1 Procedure: Price Prediction

STEP 1: Takes the input as the product name from the user.

STEP 2: Then based on the input, the data about the specific product is extracted from the dataset.

STEP 3: Data in the dataset is extracted from open-source web data.

STEP 4: All the data is pre-processed and store in the desired format by removing all the null values.

STEP 5: Data is split as 80% for training data and 20% for testing.

STEP 6: The step value is set as 40, i.e., for predicting a value, previous 40 values are considered.

STEP 7: The LSTM model is [11] created with 2 hidden layer and one output node. Dropout for each layer is set as 0.3.

STEP 8: The model is then compiled using adam optimizer and loss used is mean squared error.

STEP 9: number of epochs are set as 50.

STEP 10: The testing data is prepared by using the last 20% of the data concatenated with the last 40 values of the training dataset.

STEP 11: Then the testing data is fed into the LSTM model and the future price is displayed as output.

5.2 Procedure: Password Security

STEP 1: The password entered by the user is hashed using the SHA-512 hash algorithm.

STEP 2: From a string containing multilingual characters, integers and special symbols, a random string is generated.

STEP 3: The random generated string is hashed using SHA-512 hash algorithm and then is used to salt the password hash by appending it in between the password hash in alternate manner.

STEP 4: This results in a hash string of 256 characters long which is stored in the database.

5.3 Procedure: Dashboard

STEP 1: The data stored in the database generated by the user transaction on the web application is used for generating the analytical dashboard.

STEP 2: The data present in the database is computed using the SQL queries and then that data is transferred to chart where those data points are plotted/displayed in appropriate manner.

6 Result Analysis

6.1 Price Prediction

The performance metrics used are Confusion matrix and the F1-Score. Confusion matrix consists of:

- True Positive: a true positive is an outcome where the model correctly predicts the positive class.
- True Negative: a true negative is an outcome where the model correctly predicts the negative class.
- False Positive: A false positive is an outcome where the model incorrectly predicts the positive class.
- False Negative: False Negatives (FN) are negative outcomes that the model predicted incorrectly.

The Technique used was regression, but for testing on the basis of the confusion matrix, the output has to be of the classification type. So, to convert the output and original array of prices to binary form, the elements of the arrays were normalized. Then the normalized values were rounded to the nearest integers, therefore all the values were either 0 or 1 using the formula

$$round \left(\frac{\text{Element of the Prediction Price Array - min(Prediction Price Array)}}{\text{max(Prediction Price Array) - min(Prediction Price Array)}} \right) \quad (1)$$

The F-score, also called the F1-score, may be a measure of a model's accuracy on a dataset. It is used to evaluate binary classification systems, which classify examples into 'positive' or 'negative'.

$$F1 - score = \frac{TP}{TP + \frac{1}{2}(FP + FN)} \quad (2)$$

Value of the F1-Score is between 0 and 1. Higher the value better is the model. We use python language for the implementation of the system [5]. The dataset used is presented in Fig. 5.

	A	B	C	D	E	F	G	H	I
1	Unnamed: 0	id	silver_5000oz	palladium	platinum	comex_gold	iron_ore	time_stamp	date
2	0	161	25.99	2951.5	1083.1	1995	156.95	11-03-2022 15.27	11-03-2022 0.00
3	1	162	25.99	2955	1082.9	1995	156.95	11-03-2022 15.37	11-03-2022 0.00
4	2	183	25.81	2687	1071	1976.7	155.36	14-03-2022 12.20	14-03-2022 0.00
5	3	184	25.81	2687	1071	1976.7	155.36	14-03-2022 12.23	14-03-2022 0.00
6	4	185	25.81	2687	1072	1976.7	155.36	14-03-2022 12.27	14-03-2022 0.00
7	5	186	25.81	2687	1071.5	1976.7	155.36	14-03-2022 12.30	14-03-2022 0.00
8	6	187	25.81	2691.5	1073.1	1976.7	155.36	14-03-2022 12.33	14-03-2022 0.00
9	7	188	25.81	2691.5	1071	1976.7	155.36	14-03-2022 12.37	14-03-2022 0.00
10	8	189	25.81	2691.5	1071	1976.7	155.36	14-03-2022 12.40	14-03-2022 0.00
11	9	190	25.81	2691	1069.1	1976.7	155.36	14-03-2022 12.43	14-03-2022 0.00
12	10	191	25.81	2691	1069.1	1976.7	155.36	14-03-2022 12.47	14-03-2022 0.00
13	11	192	25.81	2691	1071.2	1976.7	155.36	14-03-2022 12.50	14-03-2022 0.00
14	12	193	25.81	2691	1071	1976.7	155.36	14-03-2022 12.53	14-03-2022 0.00
15	13	194	25.81	2681	1072	1976.7	155.36	14-03-2022 12.56	14-03-2022 0.00
16	14	195	25.81	2681	1070	1976.7	155.36	14-03-2022 13.00	14-03-2022 0.00
17	15	196	25.81	2681	1070.8	1976.7	155.36	14-03-2022 13.04	14-03-2022 0.00
18	16	197	25.81	2681	1069.8	1974.7	155.36	14-03-2022 13.07	14-03-2022 0.00
19	17	198	25.81	2691	1070.5	1974.7	155.36	14-03-2022 13.10	14-03-2022 0.00
20	18	199	25.81	2691	1069.7	1974.7	155.36	14-03-2022 13.14	14-03-2022 0.00
21	19	200	25.81	2691	1070.3	1974.7	155.36	14-03-2022 13.17	14-03-2022 0.00
22	20	201	25.81	2676	1070.3	1974.7	155.36	14-03-2022 13.20	14-03-2022 0.00
23	21	202	25.81	2675.5	1071.5	1974.7	155.36	14-03-2022 13.23	14-03-2022 0.00
24	22	203	25.94	2673.5	1071.5	1974.7	155.36	14-03-2022 13.26	14-03-2022 0.00
25	23	204	25.94	2673.5	1073	1974.7	155.36	14-03-2022 13.30	14-03-2022 0.00
26	24	205	25.94	2673.5	1071	1974.7	155.36	14-03-2022 13.33	14-03-2022 0.00

Fig. 5. Dataset

The screen shots of user input is as presented in Fig. 6.
The building of the model is as in Fig. 7.
Figure 8 shows the screen output and Fig. 9 shows the performance matrix.

Fig. 6. User Input

```
Model: "sequential"

Layer (type)                Output Shape              Param #
=================================================================
lstm (LSTM)                 (None, 40, 50)            10400

dropout (Dropout)           (None, 40, 50)            0

lstm_1 (LSTM)               (None, 40, 50)            20200

dropout_1 (Dropout)         (None, 40, 50)            0

lstm_2 (LSTM)               (None, 50)                20200

dropout_2 (Dropout)         (None, 50)                0

dense (Dense)               (None, 1)                 51

=================================================================
Total params: 50,851
Trainable params: 50,851
Non-trainable params: 0
```

Fig. 7. Model Building

MetBag
About Us
Domains
Pricing
Contact & Address
Query
USD
INR
EUR
AUD
Predict
in USD
METAL
PRICE (USD)
Silver 5000oz
21.57
22.65
Palladium
1844.0
Platinum
935.0
COMEX Gold
1835.6
Iron Ore
135.69

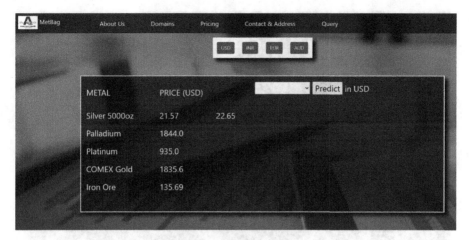

Fig. 8. Output on the Screen

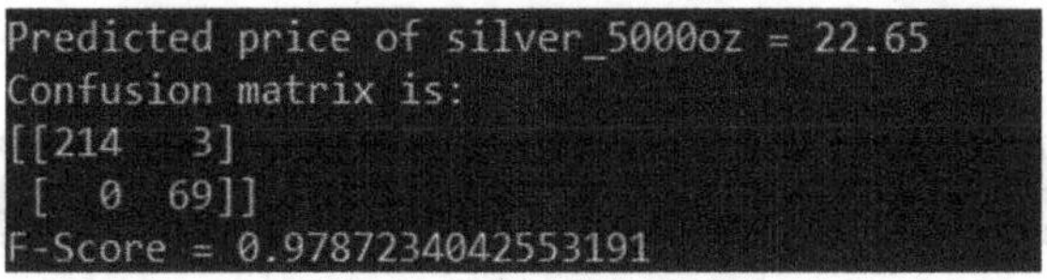

Predicted price of silver_5000oz = 22.65
Confusion matrix is:
[[214 3]
[0 69]]
F-Score = 0.9787234042553191

Fig.9. Performance Metrics

6.2 Password Security

The resultant password after salting and hashing is 256 characters long and padded with the noisy salt characters. Although Hash is irreversible, the attackers try "guess and Check" method to crack the password. They hash a random generated string and match with the hashed password. So as this password will now have the noisy characters, this will become more difficult to guess the password string.

The user registration is shown in Fig. 10, The password generated salt and password using hashing is shown in Fig. 11. A resultant password is shown in Fig. 12.

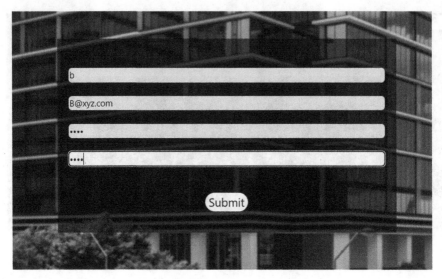

Fig. 10. Registration

Salt is: k1&% beWV2
Salt Hash is: fd499fb77091b6cf58069973d2af12d556b477bac8308796c29dcba197f9ff44b88e15099b78ae9624bc82f4b1f96d81e9334f66fa3e51b235ecba041ce1ea9d
Origional Password is: 1234
Hash Password is: d404559f602eab6fd602ac7680dacbfaadd13630335e951f097af3900e9de176b6db28512f2e000b9d04fha5133e8b1c6e8df59db3a8ab9d60be4b97cc9e81db

Fig. 11. The generated salt and password hashes

Final Password is: fdd4409495f56427760d921eba46c0ff5d060b420a8c733d828a4fa1c2bdf5a5a6db6d173f6b1a6c30335de4075916fc82997dacfb3e418907c499dfef142f6b9d68de6125605919bf728e0fe0086b204db0c4bf2bfa49b233436e05d4b81
ceone18344f35b0afpa33ad0a1bb92d369a0ccb4ab0947fcc ce4acc6a394db

Fig. 12. The resultant password

7   Conclusions and Future Work

We developed a system for a complete business transaction with all the necessary modules available to the user at a single place. It reduces the tedious task for the user to go for different websites in search of market price research and analysis, which many a times leads to losing the client. Also, using regression model and LSTM, which is the best when it comes to dealing time series data, the prices prediction of the metals helps the user to get the insight of the next price, whether it would increase or decrease. It is seen that the model performance evaluated using F1-score is coming to be 0.963855421686747 for iron ore, 0.997289972899729 for COMEX gold, 0.9642857142857143 for platinum, 0.90032153408306 for palladium and 0.9939393939393939 for Silver 5000oz. The security of the credentials is also a major concern. providing security using SHA-512 hashing which itself is a highly preferred security practice and in addition to that multi-lingual jumbled salting provides a higher security to the credentials. An integrated analytical dashboard provides ease to the administration to take data-driven decisions by sharing the analysis with the stakeholders. The visualization dashboard giving a holistic view of the business makes it easier for them to under-stand. In future, the data collected from the user transactions to be used for the prediction of future business growth using the machine learning models. Larger dataset can be created for further enhancing the accuracy and performance of the models. Text extraction script for content of document submitted by the user to a get the summary of the document.

References

1. Distante, D., Rossi, G., Canfora, G.: Modelling business processes in web applications: an analysis framework. In: Proceedings of the 2007 ACM symposium on applied computing, pp. 1677–1682 (2007)
2. Verma, J., Shahrukh, M., Krishna, M., Goel, R.: A critical review on cryptography and hashing algorithm SHA-512. Int. Res. J. Modernization Eng. Technol. Sci. **03**(12), 1760–1764 (2021)
3. Sumagita, M., Riadi, I., Sh, J.P.D.S., Warungboto, U.: Analysis of secure hash algorithm (SHA) 512 for encryption process on web-based application. Int. J. Cyber-Security and Digital Forensics (IJCSDF) **7**(4), 373–381 (2018)
4. Kharod, S., Sharma, N., Sharma, A.: An improved hashing-based password security scheme using salting and differential masking. In: 2015 4th International Conference on Reliability, Infocom Technologies and Optimization (ICRITO), (Trends and Future Directions), pp. 1–5. IEEE (2015)
5. Nagpal, A., Gabrani, G.: Python for data analytics, scientific and technical applications. In: 2019 Amity international conference on artificial intelligence (AICAI), pp. 140–145. IEEE (2019)
6. Thomas, D.M., Mathur, S.: Data analysis by web scraping using python. In: 2019 3rd International conference on Electronics, Communication and Aerospace Technology (ICECA), pp. 450–454. IEEE (2019)
7. De Guzman, F.E., Gerardo, B.D., Medina, R.P.: Implementation of enhanced secure hash algorithm towards a secured web portal. In: 2019 IEEE 4th International Conference on Computer and Communication Systems (ICCCS), pp. 189–192. IEEE (2019)
8. Manjushree, B.S., Sharvani, G.S.: Survey on Web scraping technology. Wutan Huatan Jisuan Jishu **16**(6), 1–8 (2020)
9. Appelbaum, D., Kogan, A., Vasarhelyi, M., Yan, Z.: Impact of business analytics and enterprise systems on managerial accounting. Int. J. Account. Inf. Syst. **25**, 29–44 (2017)
10. Gupta, P., Kumar, S.: A comparative analysis of SHA and MD5 algorithm. Int. J. Comp. Sci. Info. Technol. **5**(3), 4492–4495 (2014)
11. Liu, S., Liao, G., Ding, Y.: Stock transaction prediction modelling and analysis based on LSTM. In: 2018 13th IEEE Conference on Industrial Electronics and Applications (ICIEA), pp. 2787–2790. IEEE (2018)
12. Bhattacharyya, S., Snasel, V., Hassanian, A.E., Saha, S., Tripathy, B.K.: Deep learning research with engineering applications. De Gruyter Publications (2020). https://doi.org/10.1515/9783110670905
13. Maheswari, K., Shaha, A., Arya, D., Tripathy, B.K., Rajkumar, R.: Convolutional neural networks: a bottom-up approach. In: Bhattacharyya, S., Hassanian, A.E., Saha, S., Tripathy, B.K. (eds.) Deep Learning: Research and Applications, pp. 21–50. De Gruyter Publications (2020). https://doi.org/10.1515/9783110670905-002

14. Bose, A., Tripathy, B.K.: Deep learning for audio signal classification. In: Bhattacharyya, S., Hassanian, A. E., Saha, S., Tripathy, B. K. (eds.) Deep Learning: Research and Applications, pp. 105–136. De Gruyter Publications (2020). https://doi.org/10.1515/9783110670905-00660

15. Adate, A., Tripathy, B.K.: A Survey on Deep Learning Methodologies of Recent Applications. In: Acharjya, D.P., Mitra, A., Zaman, N. (eds.) Deep Learning in Data Analytics. SBD, vol. 91, pp. 145–170. Springer, Cham (2022). https://doi.org/10.1007/978-3-030-75855-4_9

16. Kaul, D., Raju, H., Tripathy, B.K.: Deep Learning in Healthcare. In: Acharjya, D.P., Mitra, A., Zaman, N. (eds.) Deep Learning in Data Analytics. SBD, vol. 91, pp. 97–115. Springer, Cham (2022). https://doi.org/10.1007/978-3-030-75855-4_6

17. Tripathy, B.K., Parikh, S., Ajay, P., Magapu, C.: Brain MRI segmentation techniques based on CNN and its variants. In: Chaki, J. (ed.) Brain Tumor MRI Image Segmentation Using Deep Learning Techniques, Chapter-10, pp. 161–182. Elsevier publications (2022). https://doi.org/10.1016/B978-0-323-91171-9.00001-6

18. Bhardwaj, P., Guhan, T., Tripathy, B.K.: Computational biology in the lens of CNN, studies in big data. In: Roy, S.S., Taguchi, Y.-H. (eds.) Handbook of Machine Learning Applications for Genomics, (Chapter 5), vol. 103 (2021). ISBN: 978-981-16-9157-7 496166_1_En

19. Prabhavathy, P., Tripathy, B.K., Venkatesan, M.: Analysis of diabetic retinopathy detection techniques using CNN models. In: Mishra, S., Tripathy, H.K., Mallick, P., Shaalan, K. (eds.) Augmented Intelligence in Healthcare: A Pragmatic and Integrated Analysis. Studies in Computational Intelligence, vol. 1024, pp. 87–102. Springer, Singapore (2022). https://doi.org/10.1007/978-981-19-1076-0_6

20. Sandhu, S.S., Tripathy, B.K., Jagga, S.: KMST+: A K-Means++-Based Minimum Spanning Tree Algorithm. In: Panigrahi, B.K., Trivedi, M.C., Mishra, K.K., Tiwari, S., Singh, P.K. (eds.) Smart Innovations in Communication and Computational Sciences. AISC, vol. 669, pp. 113–127. Springer, Singapore (2019). https://doi.org/10.1007/978-981-10-8968-8_10

21. Adate, A., Tripathy, B.K.: S-LSTM-GAN: Shared Recurrent Neural Networks with Adversarial Training. In: Kulkarni, A.J., Satapathy, S.C., Kang, T., Kashan, A.H. (eds.) Proceedings of the 2nd International Conference on Data Engineering and Communication Technology. AISC, vol. 828, pp. 107–115. Springer, Singapore (2019). https://doi.org/10.1007/978-981-13-1610-4_11

Designing Smart Voice Command Interface for Geographic Information System

Shivam Pant[1] and Narayan Panigrahi[2(✉)]

[1] Intern, Centre for Artificial Intelligence and Robotics, Post Graduate Student,
Gautam Buddha University, Noida, India
17iec044@gbu.ac.in
[2] Scientist-G, Centre for Artificial Intelligence and Robotics, Bangalore, India
pani.cair@gov.in

Abstract. Voice based command activation has gained momentum as a feature of user interface replacing the mouse or pointing device-based menu selection. Among various software driven systems such as internet of things, search engines and robotic systems use the voice command interface as the primary interaction between the user and the system keeping the conventional user interface as secondary. Voice command interface has much pay offs and advantages over conventional menu driven user interface or mouse-driven user interface. This paper presents the research landscape on voice command interface and proposes a design of voice-based interface for a GIS (Geographic Information System). Further we compare the proposed voice command interface with open source and COTS (Commercial Off-The-Shelf) voice command interface models. The proposed voice interface model has significant reduction in the word error rate by 3.49% compared to existing models.

Keywords: Virtual assistant · VOS viewer · ASR · Computer science · IOT · GIS

1 Introduction

The voice-based command is integrated in most of the IOT based device these days for the ease of the user. The purpose to work in design and implementation of such a device for defence is because the normal graphic user interface (GUI) and mouse that is used, usually needs the attention of the user. There are many times when the user might be stuck in a situation where the user may not be capable enough to focus on all the tasks at the same. Some of the scenarios to name are: - while navigating and driving, while handling different kind of machineries at the same time. In this moment it'll be better if the user can get the assistance side by side so that the cognitive abilities of user can be divided fairly towards the more important things that needs to be focused upon at that moment of emergency.

Some of the key applications of voice assistant are as follows: -

Unmanned aerial vehicle operations: - The voice command can play a very effective role in Unmanned aerial vehicle operations by simply making the Unmanned aerial

M. Panda et al. (Eds.): ICIICC 2022, CCIS 1737, pp. 95–112, 2022.
https://doi.org/10.1007/978-3-031-23233-6_7

vehicle operate several functions just by uttering the respective query attached to that function instead of manually maneuvering over the physical console.

Pilot Communication & autopilot with the voice-enabled console: - There are times when the Pilot might be switching to autopilot mode and would require accessing some emergency buttons even in the autopilot mode. So, in such a tough situation, the voice command interface can come handy so that the pilot need not have to think much on dealing with the physical panel rather he would just utter the command to initiate the whole process smoothly.

Specially abled person: - This voice command interface can work as a boon for almost every specially abled individual so that they can make use of the system to perform several functions where in no physical assistance would be required from the user's end.

Health check-in and communication: - This voice command interface can also be integrated with a health-based application which can easily maneuver the cardinal state of a person in a situation where they might be collapsing or on the verge of getting collapsed more over the interface can detect and directly communicate the same with their emergency contact.

The voice assistant comes with the ability to render through the queries of user within seconds even when there is a lot of disturbance and noise. The organization for which even one second can cost a life and pride of the country, this becomes a crucial role to leave the minor tasks in an automated mode and focus on the tasks that really needs a cognitive attention to work with. The assistant can really work it out at times when the human needs to open a particular application say "maps" or needs to see how much time it will take to hop on from not 1 but 5 different locations at the same time by rendering over the maps and providing the user an output that is backed by facts. There is no limit to what a voice assistant can be capable of doing for the user.

1.1 Review of Literature on Voice Command Interface

A search of research literature on "dimensions.com" was carried out. It has resulted in 1500 + numbers of papers developed in Java programming language; VOS viewer is simply a tool which is used to create maps that are based on network data. It can create three types of map-based visualizations, which are as follows:

- Network Visualization
- Overlay Visualization
- Density Visualization

The 3 visualizations that was created by using CSV file of related topic of the research will be shown and then a theoretical inference would be generated out of it.

In Fig. 1, it is shown that out of all the keywords present in form of text in our publications, only these are the relevant keywords that have occurred more than ten times in every paper. The relevance score has been generated with the help of a machine learning algorithm that is working in the backend of the model [1]. The Network map diagram of the review literature on voice command interface gives the collaborative picture of area

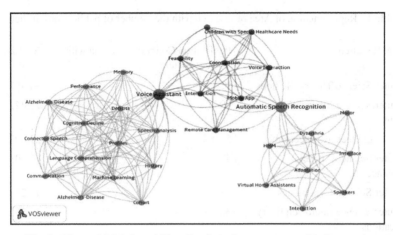

Fig. 1. Network Map-based Visualization of most co-occurring keywords

of research on voice command interface versus other technologies. Prominent amongst the other area of study are tabulated below (Table 1).

The outcome which came after data exploration of the top cited paper in the field of research proves that the all the five keywords present in the Fig. 2 are very much related and relevant to the voice assistant and is in constant integration with the smart voice based assistant. [2].

2   Design and Implementation

After describing the architecture, the model's implementation will be thoroughly discussed under this heading, along with the scenarios that have been created to check the efficiency of the same.

2.1   Review of Literature on Voice Command Interface

The dataset for the voice-based command model NAKSHA includes every query-based command utilized by the model. The model has been evaluated to see how it performs using examples of instructions that relate to real-world situations and can be used to generate real-world scenarios.

Following are the commands for the smart voice-based system:

- Wake-up command will help the system and will listen and greet with a given set of commands, in this case, which is "Hello Naksha".
- For online search for a particular website the query named "Website" is used wherein the user can speak "open the website" along with the respective website that user wants the assistant to open. e.g., "Naksha Open Website Facebook" as a result assistant will open.

Table 1. Representation of Area of research with the number of publications affiliated

Area Of Research	Publication Count in Common with Voice Assistant	% of 267
Computer Science Theory Methods	92	34.457
Computer Science Information Systems	60	22.472
Engineering Electrical Electronic	59	22.097
Computer Science Artificial Intelligence	47	17.603
Computer Science Cybernetics	38	14.232
Computer Science Interdisciplinary Applications	33	12.36
Telecommunications	32	11.985
Computer Science Software Engineering	27	10.112
Acoustics	14	5.243
Business	14	5.243
Imaging Science Photographic Technology	12	4.494
Medical Informatics	12	4.494
Health Care Sciences Services	11	4.12
Psychology Multidisciplinary	9	3.371
Computer Science Hardware Architecture	8	2.996
Engineering Multidisciplinary	8	2.996
Geriatrics Gerontology	6	2.247
Gerontology	6	2.247
Psychology Applied	6	2.247
Public Environmental Occupational Health	6	2.247
Education Educational Research	5	1.873
Engineering Biomedical	5	1.873
Engineering Industrial	5	1.873
Linguistics	5	1.873

- Similarly, there's an "Open maps" query which once spoken will redirect the user to the map location of the Centre for Artificial Intelligence and Robotics, DRDO, Bangalore that is where this model was developed.

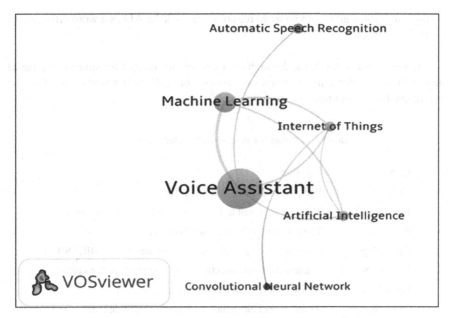

Fig. 2. Relationship among keywords

- If the user wants to shut down the system, then the user can simply speak "Bye" and the voice assistant will greet the user goodbye and the system will stop.
- For additional activities a query named "music" is also included, wherein a user can request to play a track of their choice and the assistant will play the track for the user which for now is targeted in a location inside a directory of the local machine.
- There's another feature where if a user is interested in closing or opening a new tab while the user is working online, can do so by just speaking "open new tab" and "close this tab".
- "Introduction" is another query wherein the assistant will brief the user about its origin and the purpose for which it is built (Xie et al., 2019) [5].

This was the brief theoretical knowledge about the dataset i.e., the query-based voice commands that is being used in this proposed model.

Designing a voice-based command interface for a system has many dependencies and factor. The prime factor being: -

(a) **Response time**: - The response time is an efficient parameter in the designing of the voice command interface, which decides that how quick the interface is responding to the given query. The Naksha AI has a response time of 5 s in which it listens to the query and responds with an answer within 5 s time.

(b) **Error rate**: - The error rate is simply defined as the number of errors divided by the total number of words. This parameter defines the efficiency of the voice assistant. Lower the word error rate more structured would be the input, hence, the output of the voice assistant would be more reliable. The Naksha AI has a word error rate of 16.5% respectively.

Below is provided the Table 2 which comprises of the dataset for smart voice-based command interface for a menu-driven system describing all the functions in brief for the given query-based common system pointwise.

Table 2. Dataset for voice-based command system

S No	Query	Function
1	Hello	Wake word & Assistant will greet
2	Introduce	The Assistant will tell the user about it's origin & purpose
3	Bye	The assistant will shutdown the process
4	Open Maps	Assistant will open the base map location for CAIR, DRDO
5	Youtube Search	The assistant will directly youtube search the given phase
6	Open New Tab	Assistant will open a new tab in google.com
7	Close this tab	Assistant will close the existing tab on google.com
8	The time	The assistant will tell us the time according to IST
9	Website	The assistant will open a website
10	Music	The assistant will play the music from a local directory inside the system
11	Google Search	It will google search the phrase that user said

2.2 Modules Used

Datetime Module

- In python programming language the python datetime module can be used to provide a specific date and time in the python code.
- The classes that are supplied by the datetime module provide functions that are used to deal with dates and times.
- The Date Time module is an inbuilt module of python.

Web Browser Module

- This module allows user to access content from web easily.
- This module with the help of open() function allows user to open a certain application which is accessible online.

- With the help of this module we can easily open and close a particular application through open() and close() function.

Pyttsx3 Module

- It is a python-based module.
- It is used to convert text into speech.
- Pyttsx3 works offline unlike other libraries which require intern connectivity.
- This module is compatible with both versions, python2 and python3.
- This particular module is supported by two voices i.e., male and female for windows.

2.3 Methodology

The explanation of the proposed voice command-based model for a menu driven system that has been constructed end to end on visual studio code has been explained through a flow chart.

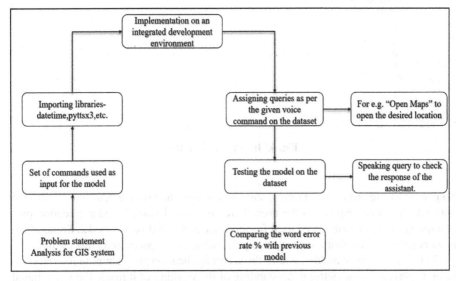

Fig. 3. Block diagram of the proposed model

Therefore, a reader can comprehend how to construct a comparable type of model by analysing Fig. 3. The flowchart demonstrates each step of the model development process, from the input of the given set of commands as depicted from the Table 2, to importing the libraries that have been explained in detail in Subsect. 2.2, implementation of the model explained in Subsect. 2.4 and further analyzing and testing the model in different scenarios explained in detail in the Subsect. 3.1. For a comparative study please refer the Subsect. 3.3. Therefore, from comprehending the issue statement to creating a dataset, to implementing and coding the model to improve an existing automatic speech recognition system [6].

The above methods will now be illustrated step by step, along with snippets from the programs.

2.4   Implementation

Step 1: First, understand the problem statement, which was to create a voice-based command system that could function without the need to define each command line by line accurately, instead providing a query for a function to be executed.

Step 2: Flowchart of the proposed model has been created to better understand the logic behind creating it and the complexities that needs to get resolved with it.

Step 3: Installed the respective libraries on Visual Studio Code where the model has been coded (Fig. 4).

```
from datetime import datetime
import webbrowser
import datetime
from winreg import QueryInfoKey
import pyttsx3
import speech_recognition as sr
import os
import wikipedia
import smtplib
import keyboard
import pywhatkit
```

Fig. 4. Importing Libraries

Step 4: After importing the libraries, now the voice module for the assistant is imported with which it will respond to the user, there are several voice-based application programming interface that can be used for the voice command-based model. Some of the most popular models that are used are sapi5, kaladi, deep speech and Alexa skills.

In Fig. 5, the voice architecture of the server application programming interface has been displayed for the better understanding of the working of it inside the voice-based command system. Here the managed app and native app both are interacting with the application programming interface and system.speech* which further interacts with a speech engine that recognizes and synthesizes the voice signal programming interface and system.speech which further interacts with a speech engine which recognizes and synthesize the voice signal (Fig. 6).

Step 5: The function has been defined which will help the assistant understand how to speak after understanding the voice command it can speak and execute the task according to the given rules.

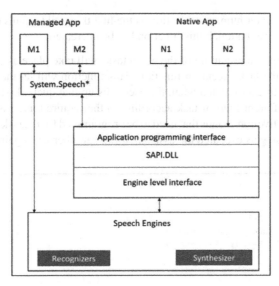

Fig. 5. Diagram of voice architecture

```
Assistant = pyttsx3.init('sapi5')
voices = Assistant.getProperty('voices')
print(voices)
Assistant.setProperty('voices',voices[0].id)
Assistant.setProperty('rate',170)#Speech rate
```

Fig. 6. Importing voice

Step 6: Wishme() function has been created to greet the user on the basis of IST i.e. Indian standard time.

Wherein time-wise greeting is assigned to the user:

- If the time is greater than 0:00 h and less than 12:00 then greet with "Good Morning".
- If the time is greater than or equal to 12:00 h and less than 18:00 then greet with "Good Afternoon".
- Else greet with "Good Evening"

These are the following program that has been coded inside the wish me function.

Therefore, whenever the code will run this would be the initial voice commands that the assistant will use to greet the user after which it'll take the further queries of the user and execute them. This is one of the essential functions that need to get included inside the assistant for a better human interaction as the first thing all humans do is greet each other. In order to give it a touch this function has been created.

Step 7: In this step, the execution of the given tasks will take place as shown in Fig. 7. With the help of the task execution function. This function will let the assistant know which task needs to get executed when the user calls up that query. Inside this function user can add a different kind of task according to the required use case and then can provide the respective commands that need to be programmed for the task to get executed. As soon as the task gets executed the assistant awaits another task again.

```
def TaskExe():

    def Music():
        Speak("Tell Me the name of the Song!")
        musicName = takecommand()
        if 'India' in musicName:
            os.system('E:\\Music_Naksha\\India.mp3')
        Speak("Enjoy your song, sir")


    def OpenApps():
        Speak("yes sir,Please wait a second")

        if 'maps' in query:

webbrowser.open('https://www.google.com/maps/d/edit?mid=1_EL7WKPhWL7
Z_2BLtQKhymX6x3mjGnA&ll=12.988053272785052%2C77.66889376994948&z=18'
)

        elif 'GIS' in query:
            webbrowser.open('https://qgis.org/en/site/')
        Speak("Here is your result sir!")
```

Fig. 7. Task execution function

Step 9: In this step we will simply define different kind of smart voice-based command/query- based command that we will be using as an input to train and test the model. The model will be provided with several queries and will be tested in a noisy environment to check how quick it understands and interprets the voice signal to generate the given query in the output.

Some of the given voice-based command on this model are (Fig. 9):

• "Hello","Music","Open Maps","YouTube search","Google search","Wikipedia search","Open GIS"

```
query = takecommand()

    if 'hello' in query:
        Speak("Jai Heend! sir , I am Naksha .")
        Speak("Your Personal Assistant!,ready for the mission sir")
        Speak("How may I help you today,Sir!")

    if 'introduce' in query:
        Speak("Hello Sir, My name is Naksha.")
        Speak("I am a virtual assistant, that is being build for the     sole purpose of providing service to
my country, India")
        Speak("I'm still under process,but I believe I'll soon be working for the benifit of my country sir
and that makes me feel proud!!")

    elif 'say it' in query:
        Speak("My motto is that Strength's Origin is in Science")

    elif 'take a break' in query:
        Speak("ok Sir,I'll be ready and up whenever you'll need me")
        break
```

Fig. 8. Query based command

```
elif 'open GIS' in query:
        OpenApps()

        elif 'open maps' in query:
            OpenApps()

        elif 'close GIS' in query:
            CloseAPPS()

        elif 'close this tab' in query:
            keyboard.press_and_release('ctrl + w')

        elif 'open new tab' in query:
            keyboard.press_and_release('ctrl +t')
```

Fig. 9. Chrome automation query

The Fig. 8 demonstrates the takecommand() function, different kind of queries are taken for the assistant and then respective responses for every query is given so that the assistant respond when that particular query is called upon by the user at the time of testing the model. Figure 10 gives a demonstration of all the chrome automation query that has been coded in the model so that whenever the user is working with the chrome engine then the user can use this command.

As a result, this is the entire scenario, starting with how the problem statement was understood and how the dataset for the problem statement was selected to build the functions that allow the assistant to speak and understand any command the user gives.

The query here is the voice-based commands which get executed when the user says them in the system.

Therefore, this paper gives an overview of the design and implementation that took place in this voice-based command interface for a menu-driven system.

3   Results and Discussion

The term "voice recognition devices" is not new; in fact, these devices have been around since the late 1980s (Terzopoulos et al.,2020) [7]. The training that has been done on the model with increasingly modern datasets at each and every iteration has been what has ultimately contributed to it achieving better results over time. While the model is being trained on a substantial amount of data, it is able to comprehend the distinctions that exist between each and every phrase, word, and phenome.

3.1   Testing Model by Creating a War Zone like Environment

In order to check the reliability, and responsiveness of the model and if it is feasible to get deployed for the use in defense sector, we create a warzone like environment to test out model.

Inside a room an environment has been created which is somewhat similar to a war zone where there is a lot of disturbance.

- An audio[27] is adapted from YouTube[28] of a war sound which is played in full volume on the mobile phone that is, iPhone 13, which generates 104.7dBA ~ 105dBA when it is at it's full volume.
- The audio was played for approximately five minutes.
- Meanwhile, two commands were given to the assistant first "Open Maps" and other "Open new tab"
- The model was able to interpret both the commands in that scenario and was able to execute the tasks.
- The snippet of the same is shown below in Fig. 8 where the model successfully opened the base location in the map along with the other 2 new tabs.

Therefore, we have achieved the end result, by testing our model in this environment.

Fig. 10. Result of warzone like experiment

3.2 Spectrogram and Waveform Samples for Spoken Voice

The spectrogram in Fig. 11, and Fig. 13 and waveform in Fig. 12, and Fig. 14 depicts the waveform of the audio signal and audio quality of the voice signal being generated from the assistant respectively. The color shade in Fig. 11 and Fig. 13 shows the heat in the voice signal generated by the assistant. This gives an idea of how impactful the generated voice signal is.

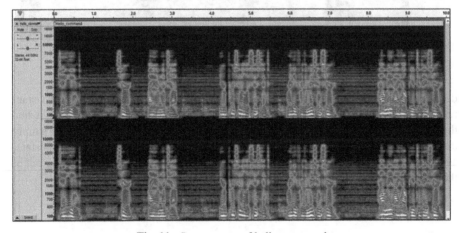

Fig. 11. Spectrogram of hello command

This measure has been evaluated and visualized to understand the audio quality and the audibility of the assistant's speech. The frequency on the y axis of the Fig. 14

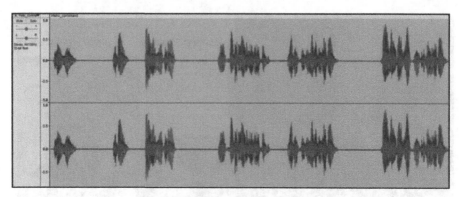

Fig. 12. Waveform of hello command

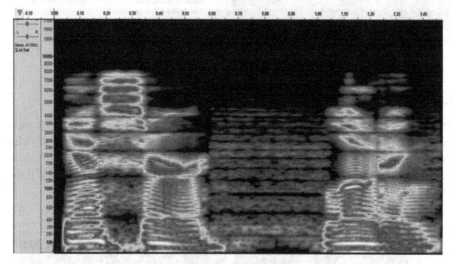

Fig. 13. Spectrogram of google website query

describes the frequency rate for the voice signal that is being generated when the assistant responds to the user on a google website query. The Fig. 13 shows the voice signal when the google website query response is being uttered by the assistant. The Fig. 14 simply defines when and with how much pressure the voice is being generated from the assistant. This will help to gather the information about the quality of audio that is coming out of the assistant so that when it will work in a real-time scenario it works correctly.

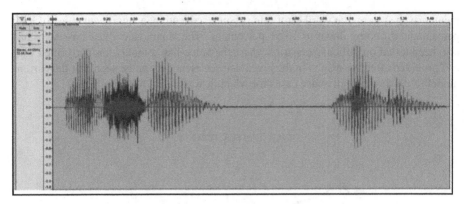

Fig. 14. Waveform of google website query

3.3 Comparative Analysis Based on Word Error Rate

The word error rate is a parameter which is used to check the efficiency of a speech recognition model that is being used in several voice assistant such as Kaladi, Siri, Alexa, Cortana, and Naksha. The Mathematical formula to calculate the basic word error rate is as follows:

$$Word - Error - Rate = \frac{Selection + Inserton + Deletion}{TotalNumberofWordsSpoken} \tag{1}$$

Here, the word error rate of the model has been compared with an existing model in the organisation to show how much the proposed model has progressed in contrast to the earlier automatic speech recognition model.

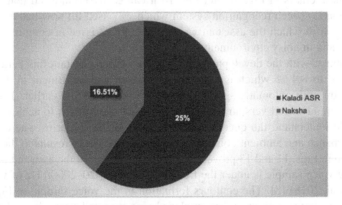

Fig. 15. Graph containing word error rate %

Figure 15 shows that the word error rate of the kaladi based automatic speech recognition model when trained and tested on the dataset is getting a word error rate of 25 percentage and the same when did with the Naksha- smart voice-based assistant for the menu driven system, the word error rate is being reduced by a significant value of 8.49 percentage, dropping down to 16.51 percentage. The smart voice-based assistant has also been tested on difficult scenarios where the voice-based model has performed well and provided effective results in the given dataset. Hence it can be seen that the current model fulfils the respective use cases for which it was meant to be built.

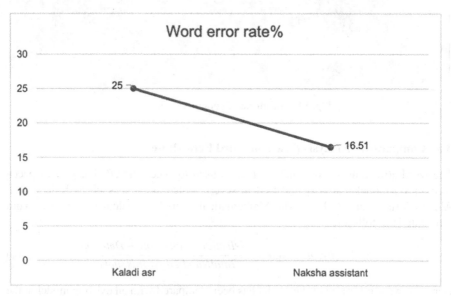

Fig. 16. Line chart displaying the difference in word error rate

From these charts in Fig. 15 and Fig. 16 it can easily be inferred that the kaladi based automatic speech recognition system which was used till now had a word error rate of 25%, with which the assistant was facing a lot of issue in comprehending the voice command in noisy environment.

On contrary, with the development of Naksha - voice assistant this parameter has been reduced to 8.49% which is a significant change and upliftment in the features of the already built automatic speech recognition model (ASR) earlier. The purpose of building an advanced version of this kaladi based system was to achieve a system which could understand the query-based command in the scenarios where there is a lot of disturbance and ambient noise and can provide the better results to the user. The spectrogram in Figs. 11 and 13 proved that the voice quality of the assistant is up to the mark as the voice sample is under the frequency range of 20–20000 Hz of voice band (Bentley et al.,2018) [8]. The contours formation in the voice sample of Fig. 11 and Fig. 13 proves that as and when the sample is being executed every single detail of the voice is clearly visible which tends towards the conclusion that user can comprehend the voice of the assistant clearly.

4 Conclusion

The main goal of this research was to build a model that can easily work on a machine that is safe and secure and for working in geographic information system data. This voice-based model has many pros if compared with the already existing model in the organization. The speech model when tested in different scenarios could easily comprehend what the user said and was able to execute the respective command given by the user. The word error rate of the proposed model was approximately 8% less than the previous model which made it easier to interpret the words quickly (Belanche et al.,2019) [9].

The best part of this model is that many of the things that the user was not able to change earlier now have full ability to change according to user's will. The model can be re-created according to the given use case.

The automatic speech recognition[30] model is not a new concept rather it has been in existence since the 1950s but as and when the time passed now every industry or organization simply uses it according to their problem statement and needs. Similarly, this research has been created to fill the void of having a smart voice-based assistant that could fulfil the needs of defence organizations (Yan et al.,2022) [10].

Further on I'd like to start by quoting one of the famous quotes said by famous scientist Albert Szent-Györgyi "Research is to see what everybody else has seen, and to think what nobody else has thought". Moving on the same line it can be figured that some of the work that could be done to improve the voice assistant is by integrating a layer of authenticity so that nobody instead the authoritative user can only have the access to whole system just by the tone of voice which will be a far more advanced step in this field where passcode, fingerprint or retina-based authentication are in use that can easily be breached or manipulated by allies for an illegal purpose (Hansen *et al.*,2015) [3]. With the help of a powerful voice-based authentication system soon one can not only automate and multitask but can also safely work even in the tough environment where there's a risk of leaking of the data (Kepuska *et al.*,2018) [4].

Acknowledgement. Authors are thankful to Director, CAIR-DRDO for his support to carry out this research. This research did not receive any specific grant from funding agencies in the public, commercial, or not-for-profit sectors.

References

1. Panigrahi, N., Mohanty, S.P.: Brain Computer Interface. CRC Press (2022)
2. App.dimensions.ai (n.d.)
3. Hansen, J.H.L., Hasan, T.: IEEE Signal Process. Mag. **32**, 74 (2015)
4. Kepuska, V., Bohouta, G.: 2018 IEEE 8th Annual Computing and Communication Workshop and Conference (CCWC) (2018). https://doi.org/10.1109/ccwc.2018.8301638
5. Xie, B., Charness, N., Fingerman, K., Kaye, J., Kim, M.T., Khurshid, A.: J. Aging Soc. Policy **32**, 460 (2020)
6. Amershi, S., et al., Proceedings of the 2019 CHI Conference on Human Factors in Computing Systems - CHI '19 (2019). https://doi.org/10.1145/3290605.3300233

7. Terzopoulos, G., Satratzemi, M.: Informatics in Education **19**, 473 (2020)
8. Bentley, F., Luvogt, C., Silverman, M., Wirasinghe, R., White, B., Lottrjdge, D.: Proceedings of the ACM on Interactive. Mobile, Wearable and Ubiquitous Technologies **2**, 1 (2018)
9. Belanche, D., Casaló, L.V., Flavián, C., Schepers, J.: Serv. Ind. J. **40**, 203 (2019)
10. Yan, C., Ji, X., Wang, K., Jiang, Q., Jin, Z., Xu, W.: ACM Comput. Surv. (2022). https://doi.org/10.1145/3527153
11. Panigrahi, N.: Geographical Information Science. Boca Raton Crc Press (2018)
12. Panigrahi, N., Computing in Geographic Information Systems. CRC Press (2014)

Smart Garbage Classification

Aviral Jain⬤, Vidipt Khetriwal⬤, Hitesh Daga⬤, and B. K. Tripathy$^{(\boxtimes)}$⬤

School of Information Technology and Engineering, VIT, Vellore, TN, India
tripathybk@vit.ac.in

Abstract. Garbage recycling is a key aspect of maintaining our environment in good condition. Poor waste management has the potential to have a significant negative effect on the environment, on public health, and on the economy of the nation. The garbage must be separated into groups with similar recycling processes to make the recycling process much more effective and faster. Recycling, needless to say, is a very important task for all the countries. Garbage categorization is the most basic stage in enabling cost-effective recycling among the tasks required for recycling. Some of the well-known deep learning models for trash categorization include Densenet121, DenseNet169, InceptionResnetV2, MobileNet and Xception architecture. In this article, we propose a procedure to recognize single trash objects in images and categorize them into one of the recycling categories. A Convolutional Neural Network (CNN) with transfer learning is used. An analysis of the results obtained from the study shows that the EfficientNet-b0 CNN performs well under this scenario. The trash categorization problem for the target database can be efficiently handled using deep learning approaches as they offer a reliable foundation for image recognition with high consistency. Once a waste is put into the bin, the top compartment scans and predicts which type of waste it is, and then the respective lid of the bottom compartment opens, pushing the waste down. This prototype model of the system is proposed, which can be used in real-time implementation.

Keywords: Recycling · Convolutional neural network · Transfer learning · EfficientNet · Deep learning

1 Introduction

Recycling is quickly gaining traction as a necessary component of a sustainable society. However, there is a significant hidden cost associated with the entire recycling process. This is due to the selection, classification, and processing of recycled materials. Even though many customers nowadays can sort their own garbage, they might not be sure of which waste category to select when getting rid of a variety of items. In today's industrial and information-based society, finding an automated solution to recycling is incredibly beneficial since it provides both environmental and economic advantages. Using computer vision and artificial intelligence (AI), recognition, removal, and sorting of things on a moving conveyor is possible. The vast majority of today's best object identification networks use CNN features ([20, 21]). The convolutional neural network

(CNN), a widely used image classifier, is based on biological neural networks ([17, 18]), which include many layers with neurons connected directly to neurons in the next layer [26]. The use of CNN has the advantage of being independent of prior knowledge and requiring less work in extracting features and design ([19, 22]). In image detection and classification, the CNN has been a significant success ([23, 24]). A pre-trained model is used as the basis for a new model in the machine learning technique known as transfer learning [3]. A CNN named EfficientNet-B0 was trained by using more than a million images from the ImageNet database. The network can categorize images into a thousand different object categories. Hence, using this in our model as a base layer would lead to faster optimization and hence better results. No human workforce is required in the adopted and implemented methodology. Trash items can be directly thrown into the main container, which acts as a common space for attached separate dustbins and where segregation takes place ([4, 5]).

2 Literature Review

In the paper by Lam, K.N. et al. [9], by using SSD-MobileNetv2, the server can identify and classify 3 types of garbage: bottles, nylon, and scrap paper. The SSD architecture is a single convolution network that learns to anticipate and classify bounding box locations in a single run. As a result, SSD can be trained from beginning to end. All garbage has been labeled and the position is returned to the Four Degrees Of Freedom (4 DoF). 4 DoF can pick up and return the garbage to the correct trash bin. With SSD-MobileNetv2, the recognition and classification of garbage have achieved an elevated level of accuracy. A system has been developed that effectively visually classifies and separates several types of waste, a task that would typically require manual labor. It does this by utilizing the most recent innovations in computer vision, robot control, and other sectors and taking advantage of their maturity as proposed by Salmandor et al. [2] and Adedeji et al. [10]. A system that can analyze pictures from a camera and command a robot arm and conveyer belt to automatically classify several types of waste has been developed using current technology according to A. P. Puspaningrum et al. [1] and White et al. [14]. To detect and classify domestic garbage, a novel deep CNN based on the multimodal cascading method was developed in the papers by Simonyan et al. [7], Meng et al. [12] and Thanawala et al. [13]. They created a smart trash bin system as the platform's front-end carrier of household garbage disposal, communicating directly with residents and providing data support. They also gathered 30 000 rubbish pictures from homeowners as a dataset for model training and identified 52 distinct types of waste. A multi-target detection model for garbage pictures was also established at the same time to improve detection precision. The trials revealed that the suggested method can improve detection precision by more than 10% on average, and it also performs well in terms of model size and detection time. In the paper by Kang et al. [15], ResNet-34 was found to perform the best and was tweaked to perfection. Resnet34 is a 34-layer convolutional neural network that can be used to create a cutting-edge image classification model. This model has been pre-trained on the ImageNet dataset, which contains 100,000+ images from 200 different classes. However, it differs from traditional neural networks in that it uses residuals from each layer in the subsequent connected layers. Three modifications were made to the ResNet-34 model, including multi-feature fusion, residual unit feature reuse, and optimization of the activation function, to address the problem of trash classification. The changes are put to the test on a trash dataset containing 14 different sorts of garbage items. The original model has a precision of 0.9859. ResNet34-A's accuracy has been improved to 0.9941 using multi-feature fusion. ResNet-34-B's residual unit accuracy has been enhanced to 0.9995. With the changed activation function, the accuracy of ResNet-34-C has increased to 0.9928. The highest accuracy is 0.9996 for ResNet-34-ALL, which integrates all three modifications. The automatic trash classification system is completed with the suggested algorithm and associated hardware. This system's average cycle time for classifying is 0.95 s, and its accuracy for classifying is 0.9996.

2.1 Gaps in Literature

In [9], the performance of the model can be improved by the following methods: A. The performance of classification can be improved by training more models. B. The labeling of images should be done carefully. C. This model can recognize only 3 types of garbage, which is not enough according to the real-world scenario. So, more types should be added to compare and evaluate the training model. In the paper by Li et al. 2022 [6], the accuracy of the model can be further improved. Waste detection and automatic sorting need more attention. The method proposed by Kang et al. [15] has several limitations: The classification in the case of small targets has a scope for improvement. The classification criteria can further be extended, including more categories such as kitchen waste, etc. Overall, a general gap that is observed is the lack of classification categories, lower accuracy scores, and complex structures. These are some points researchers are aiming to improve upon. We have tried to provide solutions to some of the limitations in our work.

3 System Details

The overall architecture of the system is shown through a prototype and can be described in the following steps. The name of the prototype which we have made is 'smart dustbin'.

3.1 Waste Scanning Through Camera

The waste is scanned by using a web camera as in Fig. 1. When a person puts a waste in the bin, the camera is ready to scan the waste so that it can be classified by the dustbin. We have also provided a light source, so that there is no problem in scanning even when it is dark.

3.2 Waste is Segregated and the Lid Opens

The waste is segregated from the image produced in Fig. 1. This is shown in (Fig. 2). Here, after scanning, the waste is classified as one of the items, and then the respective lid to that compartment opens.

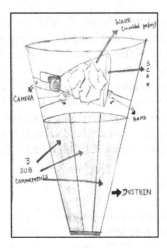

Fig. 1. Waste scanning through camera

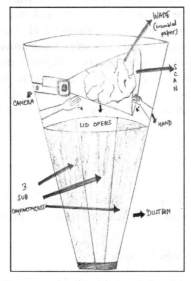

Fig. 2. Waste is segregated and the lid opens

3.3 Moving of Hands and Trash Being Put into Respective Compartment

Once the lid is opened, two hands move in both the direction to push the waste down the opened compartment. This is shown in Fig. 3.

The workflow of the system is depicted in Fig. 4.

As stated in the diagrams, and the workflow, when a garbage is thrown, there is a camera present to capture an image of the garbage. The image is then processed to the CNN model. After the image is identified, it is classified into one of the categories. After

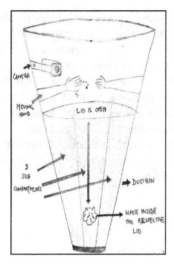

Fig. 3. Successful classification

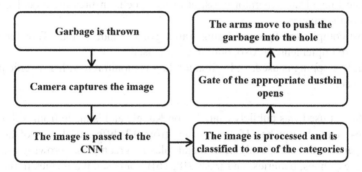

Fig. 4. Workflow diagram

this, the lid of the appropriate dustbin opens and the arms move to push the garbage into the opened compartment.

4 Component Modules and Description

The overall system works on three modules. The first one is the hardware component, that is, the main container which is being used. The trash is to be thrown in this custom-made container. The top level has a camera attached, and the second level of the container is internally sub-divided into various sections that will be used to segregate the waste into distinct categories. Images of the trash are taken with the high-resolution camera and transferred to the integrated Raspberry Pi controller for further analysis. The container has some other components, like an LED light and robotic arms. The battery-powered LED focuses on the trash to make sure that the trash is visible even in the dark. The robotic arms can be said to be another sub-module which is responsible for pushing the waste into its respective container upon successful classification. Firstly, the arm moves from left to right, sweeping the product to the extreme right, allowing it to fall into its respective container, and then it moves from right to left for a similar sweep. Eventually, the item will reach its respective container after both arm movements are completed. The second main module is the software component, that is, the model that is being used to classify the waste item. A deep neural network is used for this purpose, and the best fitting model is saved as a ".h5" file. Now, this file is loaded into the Raspberry Pi module, which is the third module connecting hardware and software components by providing a control structure for the process of classification. It runs the machine learning models for the classification process [11]. According to the classification results, the respective lid opens, and hand movements begin.

5 Algorithmic Steps

Step 1: Data collection is done for waste classification.
Step 2: The practical imbalanced data is then processed and re-sampled.
Step 3: Augmentation, standardization, and preprocessing are done on the dataset.
Step 4: The ImageDataGenerator class, at every epoch, ensures the model gets fresh iterations of the images.
Step 5: Post-completion of preprocessing, training of the model is done. Transfer learning principles are implemented. Also, optimizers are used.
Step 6: Early stopping is used, and validation loss is monitored with a specific patience level or value.

The dataset used was publicly available on Kaggle and is made from web scraping the images. This dataset has 15,150 images from 12 different classes of household garbage: paper, cardboard, biological, metal, plastic, green-glass, brown-glass, white-glass, clothes, shoes, batteries, and trash. ([8, 26]) Some sample images in the dataset are shown in Fig 5.

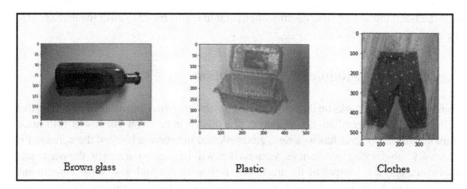

Fig. 5. Sample images in dataset

The algorithm used for image classification is straightforward. The process starts with the creation of a dataset and preprocessing. The dataset was found to be highly imbalanced and hence the distribution was improved by re-sampling the dataset [16].

The images are captured inside the main container in an isolated environment, so there is no need for segmentation (to separate the object from the background). Image augmentation is a method of altering original images by applying various transformations to them, resulting in many altered copies of the same image. These picture augmentation approaches not only increase the amount of the dataset but also add variance to it, allowing the model to generalize better on unknown data. The images are preprocessed using ImageDataGenerator. It offers a variety of augmentation options, including standardization, rotation, shifts, flips, brightness changes, and more. It is designed to provide real-time enhancement of the data. In other words, it generates augmented images while the model is still learning. The ImageDataGenerator class ensures that the model gets fresh iterations of the images at every epoch [25]. The input image must be resized in accordance with the classifier input layer before being fed to the classifier.

After preprocessing is done, the image is passed to the network and hence the model is trained. The concept of transfer learning is used here. Basically, as an optimization, a model trained on one job is reconfigured on a second, similar job, allowing for rapid progress while creating a model for the second job. The pre-trained model used here is EfficientNet-B0, which is relevant to our system as it has learned rich feature representations for a wide range of images. A flatten layer and a dense layer are further added to the network and the model is compiled using the Adam optimizer. Optimizers are modules that adjust model attributes like weights and learning rates to minimize losses. Optimizers are generally preferred during training as they aid in obtaining faster outcomes.

During the training of the model, the concept of early stopping is used, where validation loss is monitored with a patience of 10. Basically, it stops the model fitting before the total number of epochs if the model isn't improving. The best trained model is saved to a ".h5" file and is used to perform classification in real time.

6   Result and Analysis

An accuracy of 99% was achieved on the training dataset, 92% on the validation dataset, and 93% on the training dataset. To understand the exact distribution of the predictions made by the model, we can generate a classification report using sklearn.metrics. This provides different metrics like precision, recall, f1-score etc. to evaluate the performance of the model.

Accuracy is a metric for classification models that measures the number of predictions that are correct as a percentage of the total number of predictions that are made.

Precision counts the percentage that is correct among everything that has been predicted as a positive; Recall counts the number which the model succeeds to find from among everything that actually is positive. Mathematically,

$$\mathrm{Pr}\,ecision = \frac{\#of\ True\ Positives}{\#of\ True\ Positives + \#of\ False\ Positives} \tag{1}$$

$$Recall = \frac{\#of\ True\ Positives}{\#of\ True\ Positives + \#of\ False\ Negatives} \qquad (2)$$

$$F1\ score = 2 * \frac{Pr\ ecision * Recall}{Pr\ ecision + Recall} \qquad (3)$$

Precision is used to indicate the model's performance. It determines the quality of a 'positive prediction' that is obtained from the model. The recall is the measure of our model's correctly identifying true positives. The F1 Score gives the weighted average of precision and recall. As a result, the F1 score accounts for both false positives and false negatives. The classification report generated is shown in Fig. 6. It is observed that items in some categories like clothes, shoes, trash, etc. are getting classified with high accuracy. However, classification for items like metal and plastic is not performing very well. This is due to the imbalanced nature of the dataset.

```
Classification Report
                precision    recall  f1-score   support

     battery       0.96      0.98      0.97        96
  biological       0.94      0.99      0.96       104
 brown-glass       0.91      0.92      0.92        53
   cardboard       0.94      0.94      0.94        84
     clothes       0.96      0.96      0.96        74
 green-glass       0.95      0.95      0.95        61
       metal       0.85      0.86      0.85        78
       paper       0.91      0.96      0.94       105
     plastic       0.90      0.88      0.89        88
       shoes       0.99      0.94      0.97       103
       trash       0.99      0.96      0.97        72
 white-glass       0.92      0.84      0.88        81

    accuracy                          0.93       999
   macro avg       0.93      0.93      0.93       999
weighted avg       0.93      0.93      0.93       999
```

Fig. 6. Classification report

The table in Fig. 6 provides the classification of trash into different classes in the first 12 rows. While the columns under precision, recall and F1-measure are as explained in the formulae provided, the last three are on the whole data set of 999 elements. The last column provides the distribution of 999 elements into different classes (mentioned in the first column) in the 12 rows.

The simulated working of the model is depicted in Fig. 7 and Fig. 8. We can see that in this case, the model correctly classified the items as 'plastic' and 'clothes'.

So, as we can see, the camera detection analysis helps us recognize the type of waste successfully. This shows that the model was trained effectively and, hence, the object identification and detection were made possible in a matter of seconds. The accuracy

Fig. 7. Plastic bottle being classified as 'plastic'

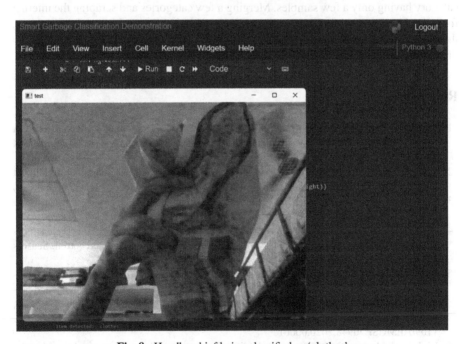

Fig. 8. Handkerchief being classified as 'clothes'

in some of the classes is better than in others. This smart, quick, and efficient method of classification makes segregation a lot easier and faster. We are the future generation, and it is our responsibility to look after the plant and dump waste in the allotted bins (biodegradable or non-biodegradable). Only if we take care of the planet will our future generations be able to thrive in a stable way.

As the outcomes of this study show, the problem of trash picture categorization may be solved with high accuracy using deep learning algorithms. The achieved accuracy was 93% on the testing dataset. The use of EfficientNet-B0 and the Adam optimizer helped to attain this accuracy score. This accuracy can be improved by further preprocessing the dataset.

7 Conclusions

This paper focuses highly on how we can segregate waste and differentiate it into particular kinds so that each kind can be identified and recycled. Every kind is re-used in some way or other and we save our planet. The proposed model is much simpler than the other proposals and the number of categories is increased to 12, which allows a more realistic real-world implementation. The twelve categories include: battery, biological, brown-glass, cardboard, clothes, green-glass, metal, paper, plastic, shoes, trash and white-glass. Currently, the size of the dataset is relatively small and there are 12 categories, with each category having only a few samples. Merging a few categories and scraping the internet for more data can result in better accuracy. Even though the neural network is complex, the process of real-time classification is amazingly fast, which increases the efficiency of the proposed system.

References

1. Puspaningrum, A.P., et al.: Waste classification using support vector machine with SIFT-PCA feature extraction. In: 2020 4th International Conference on Informatics and Computational Sciences (ICICoS), pp. 1–6 (2020). https://doi.org/10.1109/ICICoS51170.2020.9298982
2. Salmador, A., Pérez Cid, J., Rodríguez Novelle, I.: Intelligent garbage classifier. Intelligent Garbage Classifier. Int. J. Interact. Multimedia and Artificial Intelligence 1(1), 31–36 (2008)
3. Gao, M., Qi, D., Mu, H., Chen, J.A.: Transfer residual neural network based on resnet-34 for detection of wood knot defects. Forests 12, 212 (2021)
4. Gondal, A.U., et al.: Real time multipurpose smartwaste classification model for efficient recycling in smart cities using multilayer convolutional neural network and perceptron. Sensors 21, 4916 (2021). https://doi.org/10.3390/s21144916
5. Wang, H.: Garbage recognition and classification system based on convolutional neural network vgg16garbage recognition and classification system based on convolutional neural network VGG16. In: 2020 3rd International Conference on Advanced Electronic Materials, Computers and Software Engineering (AEMCSE), pp. 252–255 (2020). https://doi.org/10.1109/AEMCSE50948.2020.00061
6. Li, J., et al.: Automatic detection and classification system of domestic waste via multimodel cascaded convolutional neural network. IEEE Trans. Industr. Inf. 18(1), 163–173 (2021)
7. Simonyan, K., Zisserman, A.: Very Deep Convolutional Networks for Large-Scale Image Recognition, in arXiv:1409.1556 [cs], San Diego, CA, USA, pp. 1–14 (2015)
8. Mostafa, M.: Garbage Classification (12 classes). Dataset on Kaggle (2020). https://www.kaggle.com/mostafaabla/garbage-classification

9. Lam, K.N., et al.: Using artificial intelligence and IoT for constructing a smart trash bin. In: Dang, T.K., Küng, J., Chung, T.M., Takizawa, M. (eds.) FDSE 2021. CCIS, vol. 1500, pp. 427–435. Springer, Singapore (2021). https://doi.org/10.1007/978-981-16-8062-5_29

10. Adedeji, O., Wang, Z.: Intelligent waste classification system using deep learning convolutional neural network. Procedia Manuf. **35**, 607–612 (2019). https://doi.org/10.1016/j.promfg.2019.05.086

11. Khan, R., et al.: Machine learning and IoT-based waste management model. Comput. Intell. Neurosci. **2021**, 1–11 (2021)

12. Meng, S., Chu, W.T.: A study of garbage classification with convolutional neural networks. In: 2020 Indo–Taiwan 2nd International Conference on Computing, Analytics and Networks (Indo-Taiwan ICAN), pp. 152–157. IEEE (2020)

13. Thanawala, D., Sarin, A., Verma, P.: An approach to waste segregation and management using convolutional neural networks. In: Singh, M., Gupta, P.K., Tyagi, V., Flusser, J., Ören, T., Valentino, G. (eds.) ICACDS 2020. CCIS, vol. 1244, pp. 139–150. Springer, Singapore (2020). https://doi.org/10.1007/978-981-15-6634-9_14

14. White, G., Cabrera, C., Palade, A., Li, F., Clarke, S.: WasteNet: Waste classification at the edge for smart bins. arXiv preprint arXiv:2006.05873 (2020)

15. Kang, Z., Yang, J., Li, G., Zhang, Z.: An automatic garbage classification system based on deep learning. IEEE Access **8**, 140019–140029 (2020). https://doi.org/10.1109/ACCESS.2020.3010496

16. Ziouzios, D., Tsiktsiris, D., Baras, N., Dasygenis, M.: A distributed architecture for smart recycling using machine learning. Future Internet **12**(9), 141 (2020)

17. Bhattacharyya, S., Snasel, V., Hassanian, A.E., Saha, S., Tripathy, B.K.: Deep Learning Research with Engineering Applications. De Gruyter Publications (2020). https://doi.org/10.1515/9783110670905

18. Maheshwari, K., Shaha, A., Arya, D., Rajasekaran, R., Tripathy, B.K.: 2 Convolutional neural networks: a bottom-up approach. In: Bhattacharyya, S., Snasel, V., Hassanien, A.E., Saha, S., Tripathy, B.K. (eds.) Deep Learning: Research and Applications, pp. 21–50. De Gruyter (2020). https://doi.org/10.1515/9783110670905-002

19. Bose, A., Tripathy, B.K.: Deep learning for audio signal classification. In: Bhattacharyya, S., Hassanian, A.E., Saha, S., Tripathy, B.K. (eds.) Deep Learning Research and Applications, pp. 105–136. De Gruyter Publications (2020). https://doi.org/10.1515/9783110670905-00660

20. Adate, A., Tripathy, B.K.: A survey on deep learning methodologies of recent applications. In: Acharjya, D.P., Mitra, A., Zaman, N. (eds.) Deep Learning in Data Analytics. SBD, vol. 91, pp. 145–170. Springer, Cham (2022). https://doi.org/10.1007/978-3-030-75855-4_9

21. Kaul, D., Raju, H., Tripathy, B.K.: Deep learning in healthcare. In: Acharjya, D.P., Mitra, A., Zaman, N. (eds.) Deep Learning in Data Analytics. SBD, vol. 91, pp. 97–115. Springer, Cham (2022). https://doi.org/10.1007/978-3-030-75855-4_6

22. Tripathy, B.K., Parikh, S., Ajay, P., Magapu, C.: Brain MRI segmentation techniques based on CNN and its variants. In: Brain Tumor MRI Image Segmentation Using Deep Learning Techniques, pp. 161–183. Elsevier (2022). https://doi.org/10.1016/B978-0-323-91171-9.00001-6

23. Prabhavathy, P., Tripathy, B.K., Venkatesan, M.: Analysis of diabetic retinopathy detection techniques using CNN models. In: Mishra, S., Tripathy, H.K., Mallick, P., Shaalan, K. (eds.) Augmented Intelligence in Healthcare: A Pragmatic and Integrated Analysis, pp. 87–102. Springer Nature Singapore, Singapore (2022). https://doi.org/10.1007/978-981-19-1076-0_6

24. Adate, A., Tripathy, B.K.: S-LSTM-GAN: shared recurrent neural networks with adversarial training. In: Kulkarni, A.J., Satapathy, S.C., Kang, T., Kashan, A.H. (eds.) Proceedings of the 2nd International Conference on Data Engineering and Communication Technology. AISC, vol. 828, pp. 107–115. Springer, Singapore (2019). https://doi.org/10.1007/978-981-13-1610-4_11

25. Subramanian, M., Narasimha Prasad, L.V., Sathishkumar, V.E.: Hyperparameter optimization for transfer learning of VGG16 for disease identification in corn leaves using bayesian optimization. Big Data **10**(3), 215–229 (2021)
26. Lu, W., Chen, J.: Computer vision for solid waste sorting: a critical review of academic research. Waste Manage. **142**, 29–43 (2022)

Optical Sensor Based on MicroSphere Coated with Agarose for Heavy Metal Ion Detection

Asesh Kumar Tripathy[1]([envelope]) [iD] and Sukanta Kumar Tripathy[2] [iD]

[1] Department of Computer Science and Engineering (H), Koneru Lakshmaiah Education Foundation, Vaddeswaram, Vijayawada 522502, AP, India
asesh.tripathy@gmail.com
[2] Department of Physics, Berhampur University, Bhanja Bihar, Berhampur 760007, Odisha, India
skt.phy@buodisha.edu.in

Abstract. Micronutrients are essential for plants to flourish sustainably. For optimum plant growth, the heavy meatal ions like Zn^{2+}, Cu^{2+}, Ni^{2+}, etc. must be present in the right amounts. For example, $0.69 mgKg^{-1}$ is the critical limit of Zn^{2+} ions in plants. It is the most restricting micronutrient for wetland rice, and its absence poses a serious nutritional challenge. Zinc deficiency in edible plant parts causes micronutrient deficiencies by impeding growth. In this paper, we show the best way to build up a microsphere coated in agarose gel for the detection of heavy metal (Zn^{2+}) ions. Using the Finite-Difference Time-Domain approach, the optimal configuration of the sensor is then created in order to calculate the concentration of Zn^{2+} ion. The proposed sensor is shown to have a sensitivity and LOD for Zn^{2+} ion detection of $3.1021 au/ppm$ and $0.01924 ppm$, respectively.

Keyword: Heavy metal Zn^{2+} ion sensor, Agarose coated, Microsphere, Resonance

1 Introduction

A decent crop in plants can be ensured by the soil's optimal zinc concentration. All living things require zinc, a micronutrient important for growth, development, and defence. According to Indira Sarangthem et al. (2018), the critical limits in soil nutrients, such as Zn^{2+} characteristics, to distinguish between adequacy and deficiency are $0.69 mgKg^{-1}$. Rastegarzadeh and Rezaei (2008) designed an optical sensor to detect Zn^{2+} ion by spectrophotometry. He used Zincon as a sensing agent. The procedure metnoined requires laboratory set up and the method has a limit of detection of $0.16M$. Aksuner et al. (2011) developed a sensor membrane, in laboratory, that is capable of determining Zn^{2+} ions with a LOD of $1.6 \mu gL^{-1}$. Hassana et al. (2021) used cystalline optical fibers as a sensor for the Zn^{2+} ion concentration using the image processing method.

M. Panda et al. (Eds.): ICIICC 2022, CCIS 1737, pp. 125–136, 2022.
https://doi.org/10.1007/978-3-031-23233-6_9

The sensor showed a sensitivity of about 73.47%. Gupta et al. (2016) synthesized 2-((5-methylpyridin-2-ylimino)methyl)phenol (L1) chemosensor, in laboratory, for detection of Zn^{2+} ions with a LOD of $1.13 \times 10^{-7} M$. Abbasitabar et al. (2011) showed how to determine Zn^{2+} using a very accurate and reversible optical chemical sensor that uses dithizone as the chromoionophore immobilised within a plasticized carboxylated PVC sheet.

The development of optical sensors has received significant analytical attention due to its advantages in terms of size, cost, ease of sample preparation, speed of measurement, and lack of dependence on a reference solution as mentioned by Fen et al. (2013). Ramdzan et al. (2020) mentions that future development of innovative sensing composites with outstanding sensitivity and selectivity for heavy metal ion detection and other practical sensing applications may greatly benefit from the development of biopolymers and conducting polymers with SPR sensors. Lim and Yoon (2015) emphasized on vigorous pursuance of research into the creation of a water-quality measurement device that will allow us to determine the potability of water swiftly and precisely at a reasonable cost for the general population. An experimentally proven fiber-optic interferometric sensor for Ni^{2+} detection was proposed by Raghunandhan et al. (2016). The lower detection limit was found to be $0.1671 M$, while the detection sensitivity was found to be $0.05537 nm/M$. In the concentration range up to $500 M$, the suggested sensor displays a linear response. Heavy metal ion detection using an optrode, an optic-chemical sensor, has been developed by Czolk et al. (1992). Ions like Cd(II), Pb(II), or Hg(II) can be complexed to produce distinct absorbance spectra, which alters the sensor's reflection behaviour. In the instance of Cd, the impact of immobilisation on the dye's complexation properties has been investigated (H). For Cd, the sensor's detection limit is $3 \times 10^{-6} mol/l$, and it is reversible (U). Zhang et al. (2020) summarized progress of optical fiber heavy metal ion sensors through various measurement methods based on optical absorbance, fiber grating, modal interference, plasmonic and fluorescence. The sensing characteristics of fiber-optic heavy metal ion sensor were also analyzed. With the sensor reported by Klimant and Otto (1992) , heavy metal ions in the concentration range of 3×10^{-6} to $3 \times 10^{-5} M$ can be determined quickly and simply. To be fully reversible, the sensor must be regenerated using diluted HNO_3. The sensor may be used for the online measurement of the total concentration of heavy metal ions in industrial waste water. In their investigation of heavy metal pollution in various Indian soils, Kumar et al. (2019) revised prior knowledge on both the average heavy metal contamination in soil. The review by Lu et al. (2018) provides an overview of current developments in the use of electrodes modified with inorganic materials for the electrochemical detection of heavy metal ions (HMIs) in contaminated soils and other mediums. In this study, Jeong and Kim (2015) investigated whether aminosilane (APTES) might be used as a colorimetric detecting agent for heavy metal ions in the aqueous phase. The amine group in APTES has a strong affinity for bivalent metal ions and is easily synthesised into the metal-amine complex, which might be transformed into metal nanoparticles, through self-seed generation with silanization of APTES.

The discussion shows that there is a need for highly accurate, reasonably priced, and user-friendly HM ion concentration sensors. The organisation of this document is as follows. The Sect. 2 describes the intended device's sensing idea. Section 3 discusses the device design process. The results are examined and our proposed sensor is compared with other sensors that are already being used in the literature in the Sect. 4. Section 5 concludes the discussion.

2   Sensing Principle

The FDTD approach, which is based on the Yee (1966) algorithm, is used to investigate electromagnetic wave propagation since it reduces the amount of compute and memory needed, according to Qiu and He (2000) and Qiu and He (2001). An area of space is selected for field sampling in both space and time. At $t = 0$, all fields in the sample region are zero. Examining mode radiation makes use of the central difference approximation. The following update equations from Sundaray et al. (2018) are used in our simulation.

$$
\begin{aligned}
\tilde{D}\Big|_{i,j}^{\frac{n+1}{2}} = \tilde{D}\Big|_{i,j}^{\frac{n-1}{2}} + \frac{\Delta t}{\Delta y.\sqrt{\mu_0\omega_0}} \left(H_y\Big|_{\frac{i+1}{2},j}^{n} - H_y\Big|_{\frac{i-1}{2},j}^{n} \right) \\
- \frac{\Delta t}{\Delta x.\sqrt{\mu_0\omega_0}} \left(H_x\Big|_{i,\frac{i+1}{2}}^{n} + H_x\Big|_{i,\frac{i-1}{2}}^{n} \right)
\end{aligned}
\tag{1}
$$

$$
\begin{aligned}
H_x\Big|_{i,\frac{i+1}{2}}^{(n+1)} = H_x\Big|_{i,\frac{i+1}{2}}^{n-1} \\
- \frac{\Delta t}{\Delta z.\sqrt{\mu_0\omega_0}} \left(E_z\Big|_{i,(j+1)}^{\frac{n+1}{2}} + E_z\Big|_{i,j}^{\frac{n+1}{2}} \right)
\end{aligned}
\tag{2}
$$

$$
\begin{aligned}
H_x\Big|_{\frac{i+1}{2},j}^{(n+1)} = H_x\Big|_{\frac{i+1}{2},j}^{(n-1)} \\
- \frac{\Delta t}{\Delta z.\sqrt{\mu_0\omega_0}} \left(E_z\Big|_{(i+1),j}^{\frac{n+1}{2}} + E_z\Big|_{i,j}^{\frac{n+1}{2}} \right)
\end{aligned}
\tag{3}
$$

The x and y coordinate axes of the lattice space increments are referred to as Δx and Δy. The coordinates of the sample sites are represented by the numbers i and j, which stand for x and y, respectively. The time increment is represented by Δt and coupled to the number n to localise a predetermined observation interval. A perfectly matched layer (PML) was employed to ensure the uniqueness and validity of the numerical solution of Maxwell's equations inside the computation domain. In this study, the spatial step $(\Delta x, \Delta y)$ is $\frac{\lambda}{40}$ and the temporal step (Δt) is $2 \times 10^{-12} s$. λ is the signal wavelength. Additionally, stability is attained when the following conditions are met:

$$
\Delta t < \frac{1}{c} \left(\frac{1}{\Delta x^2} + \frac{1}{\Delta y^2} \right)^{-\frac{1}{2}}
\tag{4}
$$

where c is the speed of light. Here, the loss in the proposed sensor caused by transmission-related absorption or scattering is not taken into account. A correction factor is included in the simulation to account for these losses.

According to Baaske and Vollmer (2012) optical microcavities have developed into one of the most sensitive micro/nanosystems biodetection technology. Light enters our proposed structure through the glass rod and the microsphere. According to Tripathy et al. (2022), light is trapped inside the micro-sphere and circulates for many tens of thousands of times because of the material's predominate absorption loss. If scattering losses at the microsphere's boundary are controlled and light absorption in the transparent material is kept to a minimum, photons can go around their orbit thousands of times before exiting the microsphere via the loss mechanism. According to Soria et al. (2011), the long duration of imprisoned light is correlated with a long optical path length due to the resonant character of the event. Additionally, a whispering gallery mode (WGM) often has many more total internal reflections per orbit than is shown in the Fig. 1 , making the polygonal optical route more similar to a circular optical path that circles the microsphere's surface. This straightforward illustration guides us to the general WGM resonance condition:

$$N \times \frac{\lambda_r}{n} = 2\pi R \tag{5}$$

It asserts that a circular optical route with a length $2\pi R$, a microsphere radius R, and a microsphere refractive index n must fit an integer N number of wavelengths λr. The WGM's resonant frequency is then determined as follows:

$$\overline{w} = 2\pi f = 2\pi \frac{c}{\lambda_r} = \frac{cN}{nR} \tag{6}$$

Even while all solutions have the same concentration, they all have different refractive indices. As stated in Sun et al. (2019), carrier absorption is the likely cause. The small optical resonator is utilised to detect changes in the WGM resonance frequency that occur when Zn^{2+} ions attach to the Dithizone($C_{13}H_{12}N_4S$) coating. Figure 2 demonstrates how a Zn^{2+} ion's binding slightly affects the resonance frequency. The shift takes place as a result

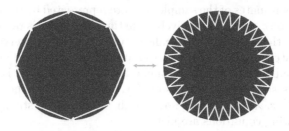

Fig. 1. Micro-Sphere with Total Internal Reflection

of the connected Zn^{2+} ion "pulling" a piece of the optical field outside of the microsphere, lengthening the route by $2\pi\Delta l$. According to:

$$\frac{\Delta\overline{\omega}}{\overline{\omega}} = -\frac{2\pi\Delta l}{2\pi R} = -\frac{\Delta l}{R} \tag{7}$$

this increase in path length results in a shift in the resonance frequency $\Delta\overline{\omega}$.

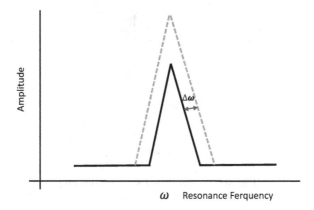

Fig. 2. The WGM path length is lengthened when a Zn^{2+} ion binds to the Dithizone coating on the surface of the microsphere, and this is seen as a $\Delta\omega$ resonance frequency shift.

3   Sensor Design

Figure 3 depicts the proposed sensor's configuration. By first coating the sphere with agarose gel and subsequently with Zinc ion binding Dithizone, a novel optical microscopic sphere sensor that can detect the concentration of Zinc ions indirectly was proposed. We investigated micro-sphere sensing with various sphere and cylinder radii as well as its various lengths in order to determine the best sensor parameters; the spectra are given in Figs. 4, 5, and 6.

According to Fig. 4, the sphere's radius is $0.65mum$ and the wavelength with the least reflected intensity is $640nm$. Therefore, the speher's diameter is kept at $130\mu m$. As stated in Han et al. (2019) , the microsphere is coupled with a solid cylinder made of silicon dioxide (SiO_2). The cylindrical glass rod's radius and length were adjusted, and it was found from Figs. 5 and 6 that a radius of $30\mu m$ and a length of $150\mu m$, respectively, at $565nm$ and $640nm$, offered the least amount of reflection. The diameter and length of the cylindrical rod were calculated to be $60\mu m$ and $150\mu m$, respectively. It is first coated with precast Agarose gel with RI 1.3661 and then with Zinc ion binding Dithizone with RI 1.684.

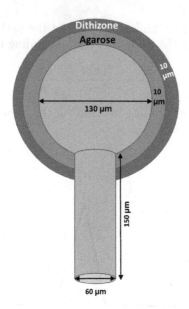

Fig. 3. The proposed sensor's design

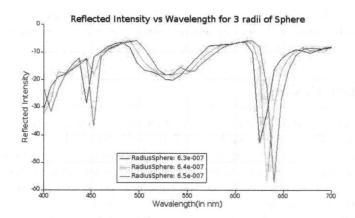

Fig. 4. Interference spectra at various radii of Sphere

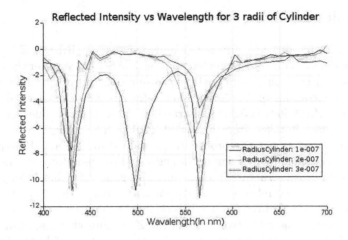

Fig. 5. Interference spectra at various radii of Cylinder

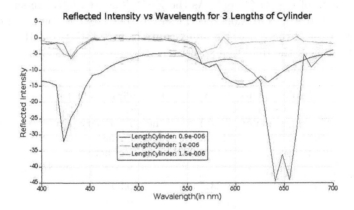

Fig. 6. Interference spectra at various lengths of Cylinder

The cylinder allows a plane wave with a wavelength between $400nm$ and $700nm$ to pass through. The microsphere absorbs some of the light at resonance, reflecting back some of the remaining light. The modification of Zn^{2+} ions in soil can alter the resonance environment, which moves the reflection spectrum's fringe. As a result, by keeping an eye on the reflection spectrum of the suggested structure at the cylinder's end, the Zn^{2+} ion concentration can be demodulated.

4   Results and Discussions

The concentration of Zn^{2+} affects the Refractive index (R.I.) of Zn^{2+}. Therefore, in the device arrangement depicted in Fig. 3 of Sect. 3, we alter the refractive
index of a thin layer surrounding the Agarose coating in order to replicate the
various concentrations of Zn^{2+} ions. The refractive index changes as the concentration of Zn^{2+} ions rises, as illustrated in Table 1. The values less than or
equal to 70 ppm is taken from Fen et al. (2011). The values greater than 70
ppm is calculated as per the procedure mentioned in Tan and Huang (2015).
Due to the very small diemension of the suggested configuration, it is possible to
place the cylindrical structure into one end of a glass tube that is long enough.
The sensor's observed reflection spectra for Zn^{2+} ions with different refractive
indices are shown in Figures 7 and 8. It is clear that the characteristic wavelength
changes whenever the refractive index of the Zn^{2+} ions changes, primarily as a
result of changes in the resonant state. Agarose is a type of hydrophilic poly-
mer, and as a result, it will take up water molecules from the soil, raising the
refractive index of the Zn^{2+} ions. As the Zn^{2+} ions' refractive index rises and
the wavelength of the reflection spectra shifts, the resonant condition changes.
According to Fig. 8 the refractive index shifts from 1.3317 to 1.3318, causing a
0.00057 nm shift in the reflection spectrum.

Table 1. Variation of Zn^{2+} ions' refractive indices

Concentration of Zn^{2+} ion (in ppm)	Real Part of the Refractive index, n (± 0.0005)	Imaginary part of the Refractive index, k (± 0.0002)
0.5	1.3317	0.0002
1	1.3317	0.0002
10	1.3318	0.0005
30	1.3318	0.0009
50	1.3318	0.0009
70	1.3318	0.0020
90	1.3319	0.0028
110	1.3320	0.0046
130	1.3321	0.0056
150	1.3322	0.0061
170	1.3323	0.0065

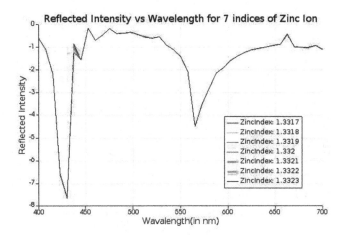

Fig. 7. Interference spectra with different RI of $Zn^{2+}ions$

Table 2. Recent Literature On Sensor Performance For Zn^{2+} Ion Detection

Range	LOD	Sensitivity	Ref
$0.76 - 30.60\mu M$	$0.16\mu M$	Not Mentioned	Rastegarzadeh et al.
2.5×10^{-8} to $5.8 \times 10^{-8} molL^{-1}$	$8.0 \times 10^{-9} molL^{-1}$	Not Mentioned	Abbasitabar et al.
$0 - 10ppm$	$0.01ppm$	Not Mentioned	Daniyal et al.
$0 - 170ppm$	0.01924 ppm	$3.1021au/ppm$	Our proposed Sensor

The Fig. 8 shows that the reflection spectra shift monotonically as the Zn^{2+} ion concentration increases. As stated in Han et al. (2019), the sensitivity for the Zn^{2+} ion concentration measurement using spectral shift may be described as the ratio of the variation in reflection wavelength to the variation in Zn^{2+} ion concentration, i.e. $S = \frac{d\lambda_{res}}{dZn^{2+}Concentration}$. According to calculations, the sensor's sensitivity is $3.1021au/ppm$, and its Limit of Detection (LOD) is $0.01924ppm$. Table 2 demonstrates that our suggested sensor is the most sensitive to the concentration of the Zn^{2+} ion. As a result, it may be used to find the soil's critical limit of the Zn^{2+} ion. Because the Zn^{2+} ion will only stick to the Dithizone, the coating ensures the sensor's specificity. The Zn^{2+} ions are the only ones that change the Refractive Index (RI), as other metal ions do not bind to the Dithizone coating.

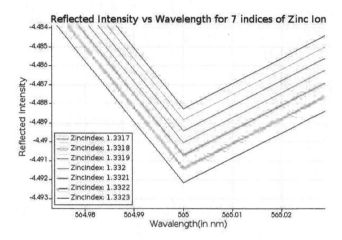

Fig. 8. When the plot in Fig. 7 is magnified for the tip at wavelength 565 nm, the shift is clearly visible.

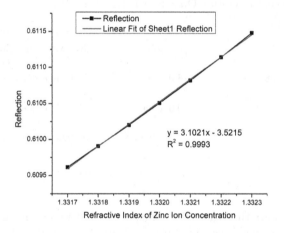

Fig. 9. Linear fitting of the Reflection and Zinc ions concentration of the sensor

5   Conclusion

Finally, a novel design of a Zn^{2+} ion detection sensor based on an Agarose Coated Micro-Sphere Resonator has been put forth. It was demonstrated that the sensor could detect Zn^{2+} ion concentrations between $0ppm$ and $170ppm$. The sensor's sensitivity to ion concentration is $3.1021au/ppm$. The predicted lowest detectable Zn^{2+} ion concentration is $0.01924ppm$.

References

Abbasitabar, F., Zare-Shahabadi, V., Shamsipur, M., Akhond, M.: Development of an optical sensor for determination of zinc by application of PC-ANN. Sens. Actuators, B Chem. **156**(1), 181–186 (2011). https://doi.org/10.1016/j.snb.2011.04.011

Aksuner, N., Henden, E., Yenigul, B., Yilmaz, I., Cukurovali, A.: Highly sensitive sensing of zinc (II) by development and characterization of a PVC-based fluorescent chemical sensor. Spectrochim. Acta Part A Mol. Biomol. Spectrosc. **78**(3), 1133–1138 (2011). https://doi.org/10.1016/j.saa.2010.12.065

Baaske, M., Vollmer, F.: Optical resonator biosensors: molecular diagnostic and nanoparticle detection on an integrated platform. ChemPhysChem **13**(2), 427–436 (2012). https://doi.org/10.1002/cphc.201100757

Czolk, R., Reichert, J., Ache, H.: An optical sensor for the detection of heavy metal ions. Sens. Actuators B Chem. **7**(1–3), 540–543 (1992). https://doi.org/10.1016/0925-4005(92)80360-A

Fen, Y.W., Yunus, W.M.M., et al.: Characterization of the optical properties of heavy metal ions using surface plasmon resonance technique. Opt. Photonics J. **1**(03), 116–123 (2011). https://doi.org/10.4236/opj.2011.13020

Fen, Y.W., Yunus, W.M.M., Talib, Z.A., Yusof, N.A.: Fabrication and evaluation of surface plasmon resonance optical sensor for heavy metal ions detection. In: 2013 IEEE 4th International Conference on Photonics (ICP), pp. 114–116 IEEE (2013). https://doi.org/10.1109/ICP.2013.6687085

Gupta, V.K., Singh, A.K., Kumawat, L.K., Mergu, N.: An easily accessible switch-on optical chemosensor for the detection of noxious metal ions Ni (II), Zn (II), Fe (III) and UO$_2$ (II). Sens. Actuators, B Chem. **222**, 468–482 (2016). https://doi.org/10.1016/j.snb.2015.08.063

Han, C., Ding, H., Zhao, C., Chen, C.: Ultrafast miniature humidity sensor based on single-sided microsphere resonator. J. Lightwave Technol. **37**(21), 5493–5499 (2019). https://doi.org/10.1364/JLT.37.005493

Hassana, O.S., Al-azawi, R.J., Mahdi, B.R.: Image processing technique for zinc ion sensing using a crystalline fiber sensor. Eng. Technol. J. **39**(10), 1539–1543 (2021). https://doi.org/10.30684/etj.v39i10.2136

Indira Sarangthem, L., Sharma, D., Oinam, N., Punilkumar, L.: Evaluation of critical limit of zinc in soil and plant. Int. J. Curr. Res. Life Sci. **7**(08), 2584–2586 (2018)

Jeong, U., Kim, Y.: Colorimetric detection of heavy metal ions using aminosilane. J. Ind. Eng. Chem. **31**, 393–396 (2015). https://doi.org/10.1016/j.jiec.2015.07.014

Klimant, I., Otto, M.: A fiber optical sensor for heavy metal ions based on immobilized xylenol orange. Microchim. Acta **108**(1), 11–17 (1992). https://doi.org/10.1007/BF01240367

Kumar, V., et al.: Pollution assessment of heavy metals in soils of india and ecological risk assessment: a state-of-the-art. Chemosphere **216**, 449–462 (2019). https://doi.org/10.1016/j.chemosphere.2018.10.066

Lim, S.-H., Yoon, S.: Sensors and devices for heavy metal ion detection. In: Kyung, C.-M. (ed.) Smart Sensors for Health and Environment Monitoring. KRS, pp. 213–232. Springer, Dordrecht (2015). https://doi.org/10.1007/978-94-017-9981-2_9

Lu, Y., Liang, X., Niyungeko, C., Zhou, J., Xu, J., Tian, G.: A review of the identification and detection of heavy metal ions in the environment by voltammetry. Talanta **178**, 324–338 (2018). https://doi.org/10.1016/j.talanta.2017.08.033

Qiu, M., He, S.: Numerical method for computing defect modes in two-dimensional photonic crystals with dielectric or metallic inclusions. Phys. Rev. B **61**(19), 12871 (2000). https://doi.org/10.1103/PhysRevB.61.12871

Qiu, M., He, S.: FDTD algorithm for computing the off-plane band structure in a two-dimensional photonic crystal with dielectric or metallic inclusions. Phys. Lett. A **278**(6), 348–354 (2001). https://doi.org/10.1016/S0375-9601(00)00795-7

Raghunandhan, R., et al.: Chitosan/PAA based fiber-optic interferometric sensor for heavy metal ions detection. Sens. Actuators, B Chem. **233**, 31–38 (2016). https://doi.org/10.1016/j.snb.2016.04.020

Ramdzan, N.S.M., Fen, Y.W., Anas, N.A.A., Omar, N.A.S., Saleviter, S.: Development of biopolymer and conducting polymer-based optical sensors for heavy metal ion detection. Molecules **25**(11), 2548 (2020). https://doi.org/10.3390/molecules25112548

Rastegarzadeh, S., Rezaei, V.: An optical sensor for zinc determination based on zincon as sensing reagent. Sens. Actuators, B Chem. **129**(1), 327–331 (2008). https://doi.org/10.1016/j.snb.2007.08.016

Soria, S., et al.: Optical microspherical resonators for biomedical sensing. Sensors **11**(1), 785–805 (2011). https://doi.org/10.3390/s110100785

Sun, P., Chen, Y., Gao, C., Liu, X., Yang, X., Xu, M.: Heavy metal ion detection on a surface plasmatic resonance based on the change of refractive index. In: 9th International Symposium on Advanced Optical Manufacturing and Testing Technologies: Optoelectronic Materials and Devices for Sensing and Imaging, vol. 10843, pp. 365–373 SPIE (2019). https://doi.org/10.1117/12.2506976

Sundaray, M., Tripathy, S., Das, C.: FDTD analysis of diffraction efficiency in a hologram for application in optical fiber communication. Optik **154**, 325–330 (2018). https://doi.org/10.1016/j.ijleo.2017.10.003

Tan, C.-Y., Huang, Y.-X.: Dependence of refractive index on concentration and temperature in electrolyte solution, polar solution, nonpolar solution, and protein solution. J. Chem. Eng. Data **60**(10), 2827–2833 (2015). https://doi.org/10.1021/acs.jced.5b00018

Tripathy, A.K., Tripathy, S.K., Sundaray, M.: An ultra-sensitive optical sensor based on agarose coated microscopic sphere to detect cu^{2+} ion in soil. Comput. Electron. Agric. **202**, 107424 (2022). https://doi.org/10.1016/j.compag.2022.107424

Yee, K.: Numerical solution of initial boundary value problems involving Maxwell's equations in isotropic media. IEEE Trans. Antennas Propag. **14**(3), 302–307 (1966). https://doi.org/10.1109/TAP.1966.1138693

Zhang, Y.-N., Sun, Y., Cai, L., Gao, Y., Cai, Y.: Optical fiber sensors for measurement of heavy metal ion concentration: a review. Measurement **158**, 107742 (2020). https://doi.org/10.1016/j.measurement.2020.107742

Influential Factor Finding for Engineering Student Motivation

Sourajit Ghosh[1], Aritra Sinha[2]([✉]) [iD], Arpita Roy[2] [iD], and Biswarup Neogi[2] [iD]

[1] Department of Computer Science and Engineering, JIS University, Kolkata, WB, India
[2] Department of Electronics and Communication Engineering, JIS College of Engineering, Kalyani, WB, India
get.aritra94@gmail.com, biswarup.neogi@jiscollege.ac.in

Abstract. The case study encompasses the evaluation of the motivational factors of a student to pursue and complete his/her engineering degree program. In order to analyze the factors, a large amount of data have been collected from the students of various engineering institutes. Two categories of factors have been found and the most influential attribute has also been realized by a statistical analysis of the data set. The two categorized factors are: Intrinsic and Extrinsic. And, either of them has been seen to influence the motivation of the students. The study shows that students are mostly bothered by the anxiety of being outperformed by their fellow classmates.

Keywords: Motivation · Data · Factor analysis · Attributes · Linear regression · Student motivation · Intrinsic · Extrinsic

1 Introduction

Motivation is a word, that is derived from the word 'motive', which means the need of a person. It also means the desire, wants, or drive of a human being [1]. It is the process of motivating people to achieve their personal or collective goals [2]. This study has tried to find the most influential factor in the motivation of engineering students [3].

The engineering degree program is a robust, rigorous process that runs for four years in India. The motivation level of a student can't be the same for the whole four years. Sometimes students are highly motivated, sometimes they are not. Different levels of motivation have been observed during various phases of the course. This motivation level [4] does fluctuate because of some external reasons or attributes. In this study, we have analyzed those attributes and categorized them into factors and in the end, will find the most influential factor in engineering students' motivation. In order to do this analysis,

i. a questionary was prepared in accordance with educators and psychologists. It was distributed amongst different students of various engineering institutes excluding 1st-year students. There was no bar on gender or stream of engineering. After getting enough responses from the students, accepting more entries was stopped.

ii. After that, the data were analyzed with a statistical tool [5]. From the analysis, the data were categorized into two major factors.
iii. Then, the study tried to find out the most influential attribute that impacts engineering student motivation the most.

While browsing through hitherto relevant studies on the means and the strategies [6] to motivate students, it has found a lack of analysis regarding the assessment of the influential factors in student motivation and the assessing the dominating attribute.

Here, the related studies are reported in section II, followed by the experiment in section III. Sections IV and V are the discussion and conclusion respectively.

2 Related Studies

Adam N. Kirn a Ph.D. scholar at Clemson University has disserted a study on the motivation of students in his work [7]. His work tells, about a sequential explanatory study of various methods that can motivate engineering students. How the current behavior of engineering students is influenced by long-term motivation. The most common indicator of students' performance is academic performance and it does not consider the needed fundamental motivation. Students can use their logical resources efficiently as it is somewhat triggered by academic performance. The relevant features (e.g. Expectations, values, future scopes) of student motivation in relation to students' long-term goals and short-term work assignments were examined in the first stage of the study. In the second stage, three more factors of student motivation, are expectations of success in engineering courses, current recognition as a student of an engineering program, and ideas about their future as an engineer come under the study. Along with these their problem-solving ability also comes under the scrutiny of this study. The third stage of the study inspects the motivational profiles of senior engineering students in important and key subjects.

In order to do the study, a specific group was formed. The first phase result showed that the expectation of students and their insights about the future differentiate students with different long-term goals. In the second stage, it was seen that students' technical problem-solving ability correlates with the recognition of students' future. The senior engineering students were divided into groups according to their expectations, problem-solving ability, and their future perceptions. Long-term goals and measures of students were asked in the fourth stage of the study. This phase is a continuation study on previous works by inspiring the engineering student experience with their Future Temporal Outlook (FTP). The result of the fourth stage showed that some of the students had a clear perception on the FTP and some others didn't have a specific goal beyond completion of the course program.

Development of plans beyond just completing the course with a large variety is also seen in the study. Also, a well-defined future for students creates greater aspects of their current works and tasks. It helps them to improve their own performance.

Understanding the relationship between student motivation and current behavior helps engineering educators raise their interest in engineering and prepare students to become effective engineers. In the final phase of this work, they explore how students looked upon a technical problem to solve the problem efficiently. The result shows that motivation across the different time scales actually determines the students' perception of problem-solving. In addition, assessment by the students of engineering issues may be based on the student's integrated cultural observation of engineering issues.

In her research on student motivation [8], Linda S. Lumsden of ERIC Clearinghouse on Educational Management, Eugene, and Oreg have summarized regaining student motivation. She has some offer-specific strategies that can be used in the classroom, etc. Address issues outside the classroom and admit this throughout the school Policies and practices can also stimulate or satisfy a student's hunger for learning. James P. Rafini [9] encourages educators to investigate the idea of "win or lose" in many schools. He makes a suggestion for structural changes and classroom strategies aimed at empowering students' motivation. Recalling that "classrooms are not islands," Martin L.[10] Mar and Carol Migily have school-wide policies, practices, and procedures that affect student motivation. They suggest the process by which the principal can start moving the school Apart from emphasizing relative abilities "Learning, Achievement, Effort." How does Carol A. Ames focus? Motivational concepts and processes are suitable for everyday use Teacher issues and decisions. Jere Brophy shows this example Four categories of motivational strategies available to teachers stimulate your interest in learning. (1) Taking care of students' Expectations for success; (2) Provide external motivation. (3) Take advantage of existing essential motivations. (4) Stimulate Student motivation to learn. Hermione H. Marshall [11] clearly different motivational directions for the three-fifth graders' teachers.

After going through several previous pieces of research on this very ground, it was found that all of them comprise the ways to motivate students and the relevant strategies as well [12]. No hitherto study has been found that analyzes what are the influential factors that impact the students' motivation and which attribute is predominant. Therefore, we made our research in this very arena to assess the aforementioned.

3   Experiment

In order to do this analysis, some questions were set that can extract the students' perspectives [13] on their program. The questions were set in such a way, that students will answer the questions without knowing the purpose. Keeping this in mind, with the help of consultation of psychiatrists and educators, a questionary was set, in which there were some demographical questions and some of them were motivation-oriented. Amongst the twenty-two questions, eighteen questions were taken for the analysis (Table 1).

Table 1. Questions and corresponding variables.

Sl. no.	Question	Variable Name
1	I am enjoying learning engineering	V1
2	My personal goals and objectives are linked to my learning	V2

(continued)

Table 1. (*continued*)

Sl. no.	Question	Variable Name
3	It has always bothered me that, other students will outperform me in the evaluation process	V3
4	It makes me concerned about how I will fare on the engineering exam	V4
5	I try to figure out why I'm having trouble learning engineering subjects	V5
6	I'll be nervous when it's time to take the test(s)	V6
7	It is critical and valuable for me to achieve high grades in the exam(s)	V7
8	I am very interested in my study and put in a lot of effort to learn it	V8
9	I use a variety of approaches to ensure that I fully understand the course	V9
10	The subject I'm learning can help me find a great job	V10
11	I expect to outperform other students in a technical subject(s)	V11
12	It worries me to think about poor performance in the exam(s)	V12
13	I am concerned about how my Engineering performance will affect my overall grade	V13
14	I despise even thinking about the evaluation	V14
15	It is important to me how I will apply the engineering that I study in my daily life and in the future	V15
16	All of my technical knowledge is related to or relevant to my existence	V16
17	I am confident in my course abilities and competencies	V17
18	I am satisfied with my progress in understanding the subject(s)	V18

The other four questions were kind of demographical, from where students' demographical presence can be looked upon. Those questions were (Table 2):

Table 2. Demographical questions

1	Year	First/second/third/fourth
2	Gender	Male/Female
3	Last semester marks	
4	I study to	Learn/Stay Away from social humiliation/Peer or family pressure/Earn or rewarded

From the above-mentioned questions, a google form was created and distributed amongst the students of different engineering institutes to collect data. The window was kept open for around 15 days so that the responses from the students could be received and registered. Students' response was collected on a Likert scale of 5 scales, where 1 denotes very low, 2 stands for low, 3 is moderate, 4 implies high and 5 means very high.

In this period, 638 student responses were collected and put in Raosoft to check the data sufficiency. The recommended sample size is directly proportionate with the sample size, remarks Raosoft. It suggests that at least a sample size of 377 is necessary to carry out a study on a large amount of population. A larger sample size ensures a lower margin regarding the error and a higher confidence level as well. From now on, the questions will be called attributes, that influence a student's motivation. In the first phase of analysis, a reliability test was run on the data set to check the reliability. During the reliability tests, Chronbach's Alpha value of 0.9 was maintained which indicates the data's reliability (Table 3).

Table 3. Chronbach's alpha values

Rotation	Chronbach's alpha
1st	0.913
2nd	0.905
3rd	0.900

Cronbach's alpha is a measure of internal consistency, or how closely related a group of items is. It is regarded as a scale reliability metric. Then, the attributes were analyzed to be categorized by factor analysis. For reliability testing and factor analysis, a statistical tool named Statistical Package for Social Science [SPSS] was used. SPSS is a tool [14], that provides descriptive and inferential statistics on the data researchers have collected from surveys or observations. It can analyze a huge pool of data with ease and this is very much user-friendly also [15].

The received data set was opened in SPSS and run the factor analysis method on the said dataset so that relevant attributes can be extracted and the irrelevant attributes can be eliminated by finding out the attributes with low communalities, cross-loading, or low item-total correlation.

In the first phase of the factor analysis, the dataset was to be checked if it was significant to run the factor analysis. For this, a KMO & Bartlett's test was done. The critical measurement of KMO sampling adequacy is 0.6, i.e., the value needs to be above 0.6 to be significant. From the given data set it was seen the KMO sampling adequacy is well above 0.9, this tells the dataset is substantial (Table 4).

From the first rotation of the factor analysis method, it can be stated that there are two dominating factors in which all our attributes can be categorized. And from the pattern matrix of the first rotation, it was seen that only one attribute (V13) has cross-loading. Therefore, the attribute was removed from the list and the second rotation of factor analysis was run. From the second rotation, no low communality attribute or low

Table 4. KMO sampling adequacy

Rotation	KMO sampling adequacy
1st	0.931
2nd	0.927
3rd	0.922

item-total correlation was found amongst the attributes. V7 attribute once again showed cross-loading. Therefore, it had to be removed as well. After removing the V7 and V13, the factor analysis was run for the third time, and no attributes with low commonality, cross-loading, and low item-total correlation were found. Thus, after the third rotation, the attributes can be clearly categorized into two broad categories (Table 5).

Table 5. Two factors

Factor 1	Factor 2
I am enjoying learning engineering	It has always bothered me that, other students outperform me in the evolution process
My personal goals and objectives are linked to my learning	It makes me concerned about how I will fare on the engineering exam
I am very interested in my study and put a lot of effort to learn it	I try to figure out why I'm having trouble learning engineering subjects
I use a variety of approaches to ensure that I fully understand the course	I'll be nervous when it's time to take the test(s)
The subject I am learning can help me find a great job	It worries me to think about poor performance in the exam(s)
I expect to outperform other students in a technical subject(s)	I despise even thinking about the evolution
It is important to me how I will apply the engineering that I study in my daily life and in the future	
All my technical knowledge is related to or relevant to my existence	
I am confident in my course abilities and competencies	
I am satisfied with my progress in understanding the subjects	

After analyzing the two factors, it can be seen that the attributes under Factor 1 are occurring from a student's own self, which we named Intrinsic and the attributes under Factor 2 are caused due to external effects like family or peer pressure. Those are named extrinsic. The scree plot also graphically acknowledges the two-factor theory. The scree plot graphs the eigenvalue against the factor number. From the third factor on, it can be seen that the line is almost flat, meaning each successive factor is accounting for smaller and smaller amounts of the total variance (Fig. 1):

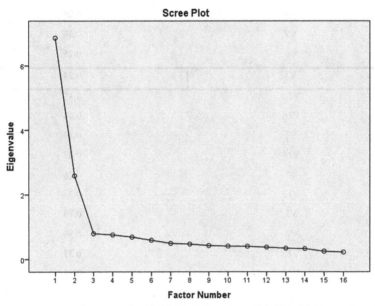

Fig. 1. Scree plot

At this stage, the method proposed two clear factors that are influencing engineering student motivation: 1. Intrinsic Factors. 2. Extrinsic factors.

Now in the next phase, the most influential attribute of all is to be found. To find this the linear regression [16] method was applied in SPSS. From the output of linear regression, the standard error values of the attributes were compared.

3.1 Logistic Regression

In statistics, the method used for modeling a relationship between a scalar response and one or more dependent or independent variables (also known as explanatory variables), is known as linear regression. In linear regression, when there is one explanatory variable present, the model is known as simple linear regression; on the other hand, if there are more than one explanatory variable present, it is called multiple linear regression [17].

The first regression analysis method that undergoes in-depth research and sees a lot of use in actual application is linear regression [18]. This is because models with linear dependency on their unknown parameters are simpler to fit than models with non-linear dependency on their parameters and because it is simpler to determine the statistical characteristics of the resulting estimators.

Table 6. Standard error

Variable	Std. Error
V13	0.36
V17	0.44
V4	0.29
V9	0.38
V6	0.25
V3	0.24
V10	0.33
V16	0.38
V2	0.33
V14	0.27
V7	0.26
V12	0.26
V5	0.26
V8	0.36
V18	0.37
V15	0.36
V11	0.33

Linear regression is one of the most vital algorithms in supervised machine learning [19]. It is applied in model predicting, forecasting, etc [20].

By applying the linear regression algorithm in the dataset, a list of standard errors of each of the attributes was made. Table 6 depicts that the standard error value of the V3 attribute is the least. This indicates that V3 is the nearest attribute to the predicted model or regression line. That means this is the very attribute that influenced engineering student motivation the most. This is empirical by the study as it can be noted that the present-day rat race, the cut-throat competition in every sector, the fear of being undervalued or being left out during the process of achieving career goals in the future, or even securing a job as per his capability and crave-all of these and more serve to be the reason behind the fluctuating and sometimes, depleting motivation levels during different phases of engineering students' career.

The V3 attribute falls under the Extrinsic Factor category.

4   Discussion

The focus of our study was to find the most influential factor in engineering students' motivation, i.e., the attribute which drives the engineering students' motivation [19–24] the most in their four-year marathon course. From the analysis, we have found the attributes fall under two categories of Factors: 1. Intrinsic and 2. Extrinsic and the most influential attribute (V3) that motivates the students, the most is also determined.

From the received answers the attributes were analyzed for factor analysis and factor finding. Since the questionary was distributed amongst very few localized institutes, the results received may contain location bias. To get even more precise results the study may be carried out on a broader scale all over the state or the country.

The collected data used in the study comprises every stream of engineering course, therefore, there was no scope for specification in the analysis. But there is an aspect to doing this analysis on every particular stream of engineering or any general course. From the received dataset we can categorize the data into two genders: Male and Female. A huge difference was found between male and female students' input. This implies that engineering is still a male-dominated sector of education at least in our locality. If this study can be done over a larger number of students, over a broader region like a state or a country, the numbers can differ and upon that analysis can be done [4, 22, 25–29].

Therefore, there is still a lot of scope for research in the future on this topic. Our data can be very much gender-biased or region biased. We can further do trade-based analysis, gender-based analysis, or region-based analysis on the same topic. In that case, the dataset can be used to assess the reason for the engineering trade being male-dominated. That can give far more precise results regarding our research topic.

5 Conclusion

While analyzing the database, only two attributes were eliminated through factor analysis. After factor analysis was done, the attributes were classified into two following categories, the first one being the intrinsic factor and the other one being extrinsic factor.

After analyzing the standard error of each attribute, to find out which one influenced a student to keep motivated toward the course program, the attribute with the least standard error should have the highest impact on the students. The study found that the V3 attribute "It has always bothered me that, other students outperform me in the evaluation process" is the most impactful on students' motivation. Now, from the previous factor analysis, the V3 attribute can be classified under the extrinsic factor.

References

1. Atkinson, J.W.: An introduction to motivation. Van Nostrand, Princeton, N.J. (1964)
2. Geen, R.G.: Social motivation. In: Colman, A.M. (ed.) Companion Encyclopedia of Psychology, pp. 522–541. Routledge (2019). https://doi.org/10.4324/9781315002897-30
3. Savage, N., Birch, R., Noussi, E.: Motivation of engineering students in higher education. Eng. Educ. **6**(2), 39–46 (2011)
4. Mubeen, S., Norman, R.E.İD.: The measurement of motivation with science student. Eur. J. Educ. Res. **3**(3), 129–144 (2014)
5. Pivk, M., Le Diberder, F.R.: Plots: a statistical tool to unfold data distributions. Nucl. Instrum. Methods Phys. Res., Sect. A **555**(1–2), 356–369 (2005)
6. Yusuf, M.: The impact of self-efficacy, achievement motivation, and self-regulated learning strategies on students' academic achievement. Procedia Soc. Behav. Sci. **15**, 2623–2626 (2011)

7. Kirn, A.N.: The influences of engineering student motivation on short-term tasks and long-term goals. Doctoral dissertation, Clemson University (2014)
8. Lumsden, L.S.: Student Motivation. Research Roundup, vol. 10, issue (3), n3 (1994)
9. Raffini, J.P.: Winners Without Losers: Structures and Strategies for Increasing Student Motivation to Learn. Allyn & Bacon, 160 Gould Street, Needham Heights, MA 02194 (1993)
10. Maehr, M.L., Midgley, C.: Enhancing student motivation: a schoolwide approach. Educ. Psychol. 26(3–4), 399–427 (1991)
11. Marshall, H.H.: Motivational strategies of three fifth-grade teachers. Elem. Sch. J. 88(2), 135–150 (1987)
12. Cho, M.H., Heron, M.L.: Self-regulated learning: the role of motivation, emotion, and use of learning strategies in students' learning experiences in a self-paced online mathematics course. Distance Educ. 36(1), 80–99 (2015)
13. Babo, R., Dey, N., Ashour, A.S. (eds.): Workgroups eAssessment: Planning, Implementing and Analysing Frameworks. Springer (2021)
14. Bala, J.: Contribution of SPSS in social sciences research. Int. J. Adv. Res. Comput. Sci. 7(6), 250–254 (2016)
15. Acharjya, D., Anitha, A.: A comparative study of statistical and rough computing models in predictive data analysis. Int. J. Ambient Comput. Intel. 8(2), 32–51 (2017)
16. Dey, N., Wagh, S., Mahalle, P.N., Pathan, M.S. (eds.): Applied Machine Learning for Smart Data Analysis. CRC Press (2019)
17. Freedman, D.A.: Statistical Models: Theory and Practice. Cambridge University Press, Cambridge (2009). https://doi.org/10.1017/CBO9780511815867
18. Krupinski, E.A.: Medical imaging. In: Chen, J., Cranton, W., Fihn, M. (eds.) Handbook of Visual Display Technology, pp. 545–558. Springer, Cham (2016). https://doi.org/10.1007/978-3-319-14346-0_186
19. Bindu, K.H., Raghava, M., Dey, N., Rao, C.R.: Coefficient of Variation and Machine Learning Applications. CRC Press (2019)
20. Das, S.K., Das, S.P., Dey, N., Hassanien, A.E. (eds.): Machine Learning Algorithms for Industrial Applications. Springer, Cham (2021)
21. Labib, W., Abdelsattar, A., Ibrahim, Y., Abdelhadi, A.: What motivates students to study engineering? a comparative study between males and females in Saudi Arabia. Educ. Sci. 11(4), 147 (2021)
22. Saadon, N.F.S.M., Ahmad, I., Pee, A.N.C., Hanapi, C.: The implementation of augmented reality in increasing student motivation: a systematic literature review. In: IOP Conference Series: Materials Science and Engineering, vol. 854, no. 1, p. 012043. IOP Publishing (2020)
23. Benson, L., Morkos, B.: Student motivation and learning in engineering. In ASEE 120th Annual Conference, p. 13 (2011)
24. Brown, P.R., Matusovich, H.M.: Unlocking student motivation: development of an engineering motivation survey. In: 2013 ASEE Annual Conference & Exposition, pp. 23–1284 (2013)
25. Ng, B.L., Liu, W.C., Wang, J.C.: Student motivation and learning in mathematics and science: a cluster analysis. Int. J. Sci. Math. Educ. 14(7), 1359–1376 (2016)
26. Rahman, A., Muktadir, M.G.: SPSS: an imperative quantitative data analysis tool for social science research. Int. J. Res. Innov. Soc. Sci. V, 300–302 (2021)
27. Sweet, S.A., Grace-Martin, K.: Data Analysis with SPSS, vol. 1. Allyn & Bacon, Boston, MA, USA (1999)
28. Basto, M., Pereira, J.M.: An SPSS R-menu for ordinal factor analysis. J. Stat. Softw. 46, 1–29 (2012)
29. Liu, R.X., Kuang, J., Gong, Q., Hou, X.L.: Principal component regression analysis with SPSS. Comput. Methods Programs Biomed. 71(2), 141–147 (2003)

30. Bennett, C., Ha, M.R., Bennett, J., Czekanski, A.: Awareness of self and the engineering field: student motivation, assessment of 'fit' and preparedness for engineering education. In: Proceedings of the Canadian Engineering Education Association (CEEA) (2016)
31. Panisoara, G., Duta, N., Panisoara, I.O.: The influence of reasons approving on student motivation for learning. Procedia Soc. Behav. Sci. **197**, 1215–1222 (2015)
32. Yacob, A., Saman, M.Y.M.: Assessing the level of motivation in learning programming among engineering students. In: The International Conference on Informatics and Applications (ICIA2012), pp. 425–432. Malaysia:[sn] (2012)

Prediction of Software Reliability Using Particle Swarm Optimization

Getachew Mekuria Habtemariam[1], Sudhir Kumar Mohapatra[2(✉)],
and Hussien Worku Seid[1]

[1] Addis Ababa Science and Technology University Addis Ababa, Addis Ababa, Ethiopia
getachewmekuria19@gmail.com, hussien.seid@aastu.edu.et
[2] Sri Sri University, Cuttack, Odisha, India
sudhir.mohapatra@srisriuniversity.edu.in

Abstract. The quality of Software comprises many features constituting of software reliability. Estimating of software reliability in the initial stage of platform establishment will allow a software professional in originating tables well as defect long-suffering software. Testing and maintaining Software is terribly exorbitant and strenuous, and it has been predicted that about half of software establishment expenses are designated to validating of the software. In view of this we propose nature inspires methods of Particle Swarm Optimization (PSO) based model to predict software failure. The proposed model is compared with some existing benchmark techniques like Neural Networks (NN), Support Vector Machine (SVM), Logistic Regression, K-Nearest Neighbour (KNN), Random Forest, and genetic algorithm (GA). The dataset considered for experiments are taken from NASA Promise Software Engineering Repository projects. The prediction generated by PSO is more accurate as compared with other benchmark techniques.

Keywords: Software reliability · Particle swarm optimization · Parameter estimation

1 Introduction

A reliability of software is one of the indispensable attribute of system perfection. In consideration of that, more and more scholars are giving attention to it. Various researchers are investigating the reliability prediction of software utilizing various search algorithms, as a consequence of our dependability on software systems is rising, we are coming to have more exposure to the impairment caused because of software collapses. Software dependability is a quality element and establishing a sound software creation is a challenging duty. Consequently, reliability is a quality cornerstone and is recognized as the capability of a software to achieve its expected functions adequality in a period of given time and a given circumstance. Performance of software declines may happen in accordance with environmental factors, but gracefully [1].

The measurement of software reliability is intended to help in the subsequent ways:

i. Determining if a proper amount of evaluation is done or not; if done then we should move to next stage, if not continue evaluating. For instance, we can determine to stop the checking when the reliability reaches its margins.
ii. Organizing our maintenance task according to the acquired data or in some cases we can predict the possible scenarios for the subsequent type of the product; i.e., should the subsequent type be functioned as expected or not.
iii. As a complication of optimization character of the problems meticulously investigate and evaluate all possible fact and figure in order to reach accurate and sound prediction.

Increasing gains or decreasing disasters has always been a prime importance in software reliability issues. For various area of discipline, acomplication of enhancement issues which maximizes science and technology advancement. Frequently, instances of computing issues which might be need an optimization method in software engineering particularly in software reliability and other like in power energy renovation and delivery, in electronic design, in interconnected structure deign, and in reload of atomic activator. To increase or decrease a performance in order to identify the best, solution for a given problem, there are various methods that could be accomplish optimization methods. Even though a broad scope of optimization procedures that could be applied, which is not the vital one that is recognized to a promising of the best for any situation. In an optimization approach which is appropriate for one problem might not be so fit for another problem; it relies on various elements, for instance, in case the operation is dissimilar and its concavity which is convex or concave. So as to settle an issue, we have to recognize variety optimization approaches therefore, the system developer good enough for choosing the procedure which is the most tailored through the characteristic of the optimized problem [2, 3].

Concentration in using developmental data processing to settle software reliability prediction as well as software reliability problems prolonged in the current years. The evaluation of the model parameters employing Genetic Algorithms and Particle Swarm Optimization for Software developments is straightforward as well as simple to learn [4].

Particle swarm optimization encompasses a very simple idea, and models which are executed with a small number of lines of computer code. It requires simply elementary computational operators and is analytically economical in connection with both storage and speed requirements. The initial testing has found the application to be efficient with various types of problems [5, 6].

In the next section, we discuss some of the related work for our research. In Sect. 3 we address the proposed PSO model followed by the experiment and result discussion in Sect. 4. Section 5 also discuss concludes and future insight of the research.

2   Related Work

Reliability of software has regularly been among the major issues to the scholars for elongated a period of time. Fenton discusses about the software measurement and metrics

[7]. Reliability has been eminently determining humankind ever meanwhile we adapted to form groups or communities among ourselves. Communitie sreveal the interrelationship; as well reliability is at the centre of interrelationship. Nowadays, software has tend to the indispensable parts of our lives. Evaluating or estimating reliability has ever been an intuitive operation. In the event of software, investigates have been perform to create this operation more scientific instead of intuitive. The current paper enhances a bit in this series of investigates [10].

Software reliability is an optimization problem which is no single model can answer the problem of software reliability which mean one model fit for one problem it may not be fit for another problem. Therefore, following optimization techniques for solving such type problem is crucial. Optimization approaches motivated by Swarm intelligence have tend to more common during the previous decade. Swarm intelligence perhaps used to various aspects of software engineering [10].

Developmental intelligence-based approaches, for instance Genetic Algorithm and Particle Swarm Optimization perhaps an answer to such type issues. PSO is a search space method utilized in computing discipline and in engineering field to obtain the appropriate answers to optimization the problems and that was innovative through the community characteristics of bird swarming and fish schooling. PSO has its origins in imitation of life and community way of thinking, as well in engineering field and computing technology.It exploits a community of individual that glide over the problem hyperspace within given paces [8].

In current assessments, Particle Swarm Optimization (PSO) is another search method, and regularly outshined from Genetic Algorithm as when used to several problems. This takes up the request of how PSO challenges with Genetic Algorithms in the context of developmental structural testing [9].

PSO plan of action is exploited to pay attention of software establishment undeviating quality development exhibiting issues to a great degree applied as a part of the documenting in the Logarithmic, Exponential, Power, S-Formed and Converse polynomial model [2].

Particle swarm enhancement, as a novel global optimization technique, has been used in parameters estimation and quadratic programming. So, it is available for Particle swarm enhancement to optimize different type software reliability models parameters [11].

3   Reliability Prediction Algorithm Using PSO

Software reliability prediction proposed algorithm.

Algorithm 1.   Initializing the particle
2.   Repeat
2.   Calculate the fitness value (ft)of each particle
3.   if ft > pBest

   Update pBest with ft

4.   Assigned best pBest value of the particle to gBest

5. Calculate velocity and update the position
6. Until no updation is possible in gBest

The above PSO algorithmstops when there is no update in the gBest value. The initial value are the software error of individual projects.The fitness function is the normalised mean squre error(NRMSE).

$$NRMSE = \sqrt{\left.\sum_{i=1}^{n}\left(y_i' - y_i\right)^2 \middle/ \sum_{i=1}^{y} y_i^2\right.} \tag{1}$$

The software error data is a pair having time and cumulative software failure information is present. In Eq. 1, n is represent the number of failure data of a software, and y_i represent is the actual error data of particle I where as y_i' is the predicted error.

4 Experimental Result and Comparison

The algorithm is implemented on python language. The experiment is carried out in a 11th Gen Intel(R) Core(TM) i7-1165G7 @ 2.80 GHz 2.80 GHz machine. For our research purpose, we use the following Metric Data Program (MDP) [12] dataset from NASA Promise Software Engineering Repository projects which support software developers in inspection test status and estimating schedules and used to verifying software reliability models (Table 1).

Table 1. Metric data program (MDP) dataset

	Project	Language	KLoc	No. module	Defect module
0	CM1	C	20	505	10.0
1	KC3	Java	18	458	9.0
2	KC4	Perl	25	125	49.0
3	MC1	C&C++	63	9466	0.7
4	MC2	C	6	161	32.0
5	MW1	C	8	403	8.0
6	PC1	NaN	40	1107	7.0
7	PC2	NaN	26	5589	0.4
8	PC3	c	40	1563	10.0
9	PC4	NaN	36	1458	12.0
10	PC5	c	164	17168	3.0

Figure 1 shows the lines of code, number of module size and defect module which is important for our research in order to exhibit the efficiency of detecting of error capacity by different software reliability methods.

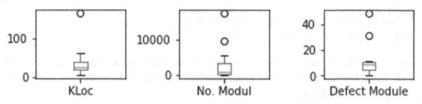

Fig. 1. Metric data program (MDP) dataset

Based on the above dataset we were chosen seven classic Software Reliability pre-diction technique to calculate detection of error accuracy. The testing results we obtained on each data extracted from its formulas and algorithms which is the maximum capacity of detecting software error.

Table 2. Detecting error capacity of the techniques

Detecting error capacity							
Deft. module	NN	SVM	Logitic.reg	KNN	Ran.forst	GA	PSO
CM1 (10)	78.89	92.01	85.23	87.5	91.7	92.67	93.89
KC3 (9)	88.01	77.56	78.98	90.23	77.89	90.67	91.78
KC4 (49)	83.12	91.03	81.45	83.56	88.61	73.35	89.56
MC1 (.7)	91.03	88.23	90.32	78.76	90.12	77.36	93.02
MC2 (32)	87.89	90.68	90.56	77.89	86.45	91.61	92.01
MW1 (8)	83.45	79.67	88.36	82.29	73.36	91.45	93.65
PC1 (7)	86.28	86.37	91.07	82.57	85.21	89.51	90.57
PC2 (.4)	74.84	78.31	81.27	82.24	87.31	91.25	94.01
PC3 (10)	82.23	85.23	87.23	90.01	77.25	88.25	93.12
PC4 (12)	78.23	76.12	83.35	81.59	84.21	90.78	92.35
PC5 (3)	90.12	89.45	90.37	78.29	89.27	91.38	93.45

From Table 2, we use ten-fold cross-validation technique and average the results over the folds. We made a comparison to our algorithm with seven different machine learning techniques such as Neural Networks (NN), Support Vector Machine (SVM), Logistic Regression, K-Nearest Neighbour (KNN), Random Forest, Genetic Algorithm (GA) and Particles Swarm Optimization (PSO). The outcome indicates that Particles Swarm Optimization achieve the maximum result. As we know software reliability is an optimization problem and results shows that PSO outshines in each project we examined Thus, PSO have shown their ability to provide an adequate and best error detecting capacity for predicting reliability of a software (Fig. 2).

Table 3 displays the Statistical Summary of mean, standard deviation, minimum and maximum result of the experiment which shows Particles Swarm Optimization achieve the maximum result (Fig. 3).

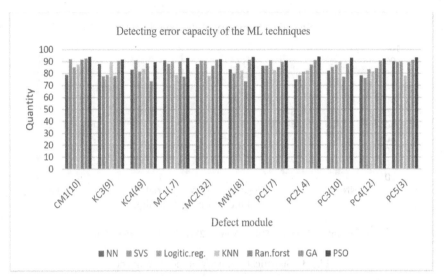

Fig. 2. Detecting error capacity of the ML techniques

Table 3. Statistical summary of the experiment

	NN	SVS	log. r	KNN	rad. f	GA	PSO
Count	11	11	11	11	11	11	11
Mean	84.01	84.2	86.2	83.18	84.67	88.03	92.49
Std	5.2	5.98	4.37	4.37	5.96	6.43	1.42
Min	74.84	76.12	78.98	77.89	73.36	73.35	89.56
25%	80.56	78.99	82.4	80.18	81.05	88.88	91.9
50%	83.45	86.37	87.23	82.29	86.45	90.78	93.02
75%	87.95	90.06	90.34	85.53	88.94	91.41	93.55
Max	91.63	92.01	91.07	90.23	91.7	92.67	94.01

Finally, we conclude from the above experiment Particle Swarm Optimization is broadlyemployed in multiple researchdomains and real-world utilizationas a tremendous optimization practicewhich is imitating the natural behaviour, of swarm as well Particle Swarm Optimization technique has a collection of swarm particles that fly around n dimensional problem space in search of an optimal solution.

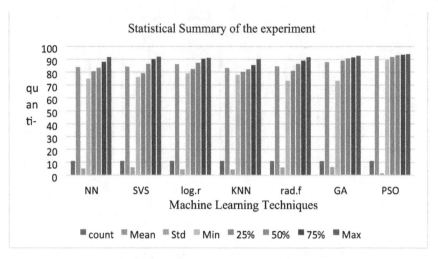

Fig. 3. Statistical summary of the experiment

It is regularly noble for us to assess the relationships of the attributes in our dataset using Particle Swarm Optimization into machine learning project as some machine learning techniques like linear regression and logistic regression will perform inadequately if we have hugely associated with attributes. Figure 4 shows the relationships between each machine learning techniques (Table 4).

Table 4. Relationships between each machine learning techniques

	NN	SVS	log. r	KNN	rad. F	GA	PSO
NN	1	0.38	0.53	−0.31	0.02	−0.25	−0.26
SVS	0.38	1	0.49	−0.23	0.61	−0.36	−0.2
log. r	0.53	0.49	1	−0.56	0.12	0.08	0.14
KNN	−0.31	−0.23	−0.56	1	−0.44	0.12	−0.02
rad. f	0.02	0.61	0.12	−0.44	1	−0.29	−0.06
GA	−0.25	−0.36	0.08	0.12	−0.44	1	0.54
PSO	−0.26	−0.36	0.14	−0.02	−0.06	0.54	1

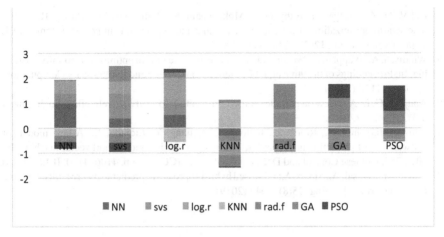

Fig. 4. Correlations between each machine learning techniques

5 Conclusions

Because of the increasing desire of software with highly reliable and safety software, therefore, software reliability prediction emerges as more and more important. Software reliability is a vital component of software quality. Here we design a novel concept of particle swarm optimization (PSO) algorithm which is used for software reliability prediction. The proposed model is tested with 11 number of dataset taken from NASA Promise Software Engineering Repository. The prediction given by PSO is comparatively more accurate as compared to other techniques. The error-detecting capability is varying from 89.56% to 94.01%. Whereas in other models it is much comparatively less.

References

1. Malhotra, R., Negi, A.: Reliability modeling using particle swarm optimization. Int. J. Syst. Assur. Eng. Manage. **4**(3), 275–283 (2013)
2. Shin, S.M., Uroosa, S.: Predicting software reliability using particle SWARM optimization technique. Asia-Pac. J. Convergent Res. Interchange **1**(3), 17–30 (2015)
3. de Almeida, B.S.G., Leite, V.C.: Particle swarm optimization: a powerful technique for solving engineering problems. In: Ser, J.D., Villar, E., Osaba, E. (eds.) Swarm Intelligence – Recent Advances, New Perspectives and Applications. IntechOpen (2019)
4. Sheta, A.: Reliability growth modeling for software fault detection using particle swarm optimization. In: 2006 IEEE International Conference on Evolutionary Computation, pp. 3071–3078. IEEE (2006)
5. Eberhart, R., Kennedy, J.: A new optimizer using particle swarm theory. In: MHS'95. Proceedings of the Sixth International Symposium on Micro Machine and Human Science, pp. 39–43. IEEE (1995)
6. Kennedy, J., Eberhart, R.: Particle swarm optimization. In: Proceedings of ICNN'95-international conference on neural networks, vol. 4, pp. 1942–1948. IEEE (1995)
7. Fenton, N.: Software measurement: a necessary scientific basis. IEEE Trans. Software Eng. **20**(3), 199–206 (1994)

8. Del Valle, Y., Venayagamoorthy, G.K., Mohagheghi, S., Hernandez, J.C., Harley, R.G.: Particle swarm optimization: basic concepts, variants and applications in power systems. IEEE Trans. Evol. Comput. **12**(2), 171–195 (2008)
9. Windisch, A., Wappler, S., Wegener, J.: Applying particle swarm optimization to software testing. In: Proceedings of the 9th Annual Conference on Genetic and Evolutionary Computation, pp. 1121–1128 (2007)
10. Ahuja, N.G.T.: A review on particle swarm optimization for software reliability. Environment **3**(3), 213–214 (2014)
11. Can, H., Jianchun, X., Ruide, Z., Juelong, L., Qiliang, Y., Liqiang, X.. A new model for software defect prediction using particle swarm optimization and support vector machine. In: 2013 25th Chinese Control and Decision Conference (CCDC), pp. 4106–4110. IEEE (2013)
12. Banga, M., Bansal, A., Singh, A.: Proposed hybrid approach to predict software fault detection. Int. J. Performability Eng. **15**(8), 2049 (2019)

An Effective Optimization of EMG Based Artificial Prosthetic Limbs

Dwarika Nath Choudhury$^{(\boxtimes)}$ and Narayan Nayak

Silicon Institute of Technology, Bhubaneswar, India
narayan@silicon.ac.in

Abstract. Humans value with their physical parts are the greatest of all the possessions. The human hand is capable of a broad range of dexterous maneuvers that allow us to interact with our surroundings and communicate with one another. In this paper our main aim is to attempt for restoration of amputated limbs with artificial limbs for millennia. The difficulty of replacing a lost human limb, particularly a hand, lets one properly understand the complexities in a human. In this paper, early designs are drawn in order to finalize the model for 3d modelling. 3d models are then designed using CATIA v5 modelling software. The size of modelled limbs are same as that of a human being. Using a 3d printer, each component of the limb is printed. 3d printed components are cured with light in order to remove moisture from it. Actuators are then set up with the limbs. The controller is then programmed with the EMG sensors. The analog signals from the EMG sensors are amplified resulting in motion of the limbs. The angular rotation angles are then recorded by keeping different subjects on it. Grasping capacity is calculated and compared with that of human limbs. The optimized result is recorded.

1 Introduction

A number of ancient prosthetic devices from many cultures throughout the world have been found, illustrating the development of prosthetic technology. The development of prosthetic limb design has been somewhat gradual up until recently. Simple prosthetic devices can be looked of as early breakthroughs like the wooden leg. History demonstrates that prostheses have traditionally been passive tools that provide nothing in the way of control or movement. Modern prosthetic hands have been created to closely resemble natural limbs in terms of both shape and function. Although the bionic hand has lately been lauded as a victory of engineering prowess, it still falls short of the genuine thing and as a result, there are a number of obstacles preventing the upper limb amputee community from adopting it. The prosthetic hand is unable to achieve the complete acceptance of its users, which is the ultimate objective of any prosthesis. The topic of myoelectric prosthetic arms will be covered in this thesis. The goal is to create a machine that performs human arm functions.

M. Panda et al. (Eds.): ICIICC 2022, CCIS 1737, pp. 157–171, 2022.
https://doi.org/10.1007/978-3-031-23233-6_12

A large amount of prosthesis are present in current world. Some of them are as follows:

1. Passive Prostheses

   Simple, immobile limbs known as passive prostheses are designed to help amputees regain their fundamental functioning and aesthetic appeal. A straight-forward passive prosthesis is an item like a wooden "pirate" peg leg.

2. Mechanical Control Prostheses

   Control of mechanical powered prosthesis is accomplished through a harness fastened to the user. They typically consist of a straight forward tool like a hook that is connected to shoulder and elbow. Although these gadgets are very straight forward, they continue to be the most common kind of prosthesis in use today.

3. Myo-signal Controlled Prostheses

   Myo-signal controlled prostheses track the electromyography signals that are produced when muscles contract. Through electrodes attached to the muscle, these impulses are monitored.

   These signals are then modulated and sent to the controller. These signals are then amplified and processed by micro-controllers for proper control of the limbs.

4. Brain Interface

   The best type of control is through brain signals. Generally, EEG sensors are used to fetch the neural signals. These are signals are then amplified and passed through certain instructions so as to work ideally.

2 Literature Review

Kato et al. [1] proposed a model of communication between brain and prosthetic limbs using myo-sensors. The signals were then modulated and amplified using a controller board. The relation between muscle readings and movement of the limbs were then established. Hussein et al. [2] introduced manufacturing of tiny parts related to prosthesis using 3d printer. In North America small manufacturers constructed mechanical limbs using 3d printed parts. Moreno et al. [3] implemented cheap and affordable mechanism of prosthesis. He also introduced leg prosthesis. They proposed a IOT embedded real time operating system for the prosthesis. The paper throws more light on circuits to process and achieve ideal prosthesis. Melchiorri et al. [4] focuses on development of prosthetic hands. The paper is well suited to a single domain. The use of these type of hand can also be implemented in humanoid robots. Full replication of human hand is targeted to achieve through this publication.Clement et al. [5] emphasizes on design of light weight prosthetic hands and weight distribution of the prosthetic limbs. The control of lateral balancing while movement of hand is Kaplanoglu et al. [6] The shape memory alloy (SMA) wires that make up the finger tendon act as muscle pairs to flex and extend the finger joints as needed. Three finger's four degrees of freedom are actively used. Abhishek et al. [7] introduced introduced the use of mathematical-algorithms to recognize human gestures. They how gestures of hand can turn pages, scroll up and down, etc. Atique et al. [8] introduces a cost effective prosthetic hand using myoelectric signals. Analog signals are simulated and result is improvised using x and y coordinates. The motions of limbs are processed accordingly.

3   Design and Manufacturing

A prosthetic tendon's design was finalized after examining several actuation strategies. The wires (green lines) attach to the fingers and are tightened by the motors. The fingers open and close by a result of pulling on the tendons. To make it more portable and attachable, the electric motors are entirely enclosed within. The ideal location for these motors is as close to the fingers (Figs. 1 and 2).

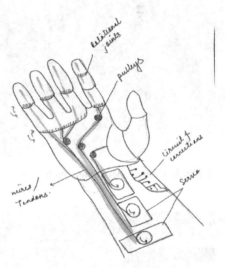

Fig. 1. Early design mechanism (1)

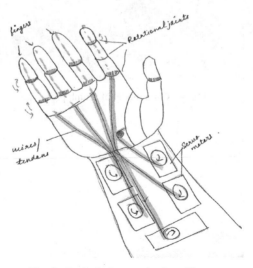

Fig. 2. Early design mechanism (2)

3.1 Cad Model

Catia is the application software used in modelling of prosthetic limbs (Figs. 3, 4, and 5).

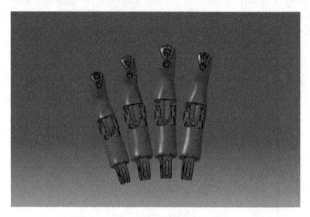

Fig. 3. Catia model offinger prototype

Fig. 4. Catia model of thumb prototype

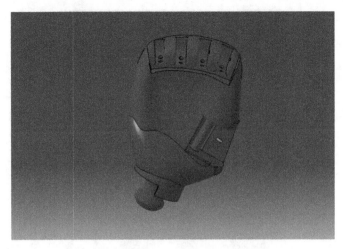

Fig. 5. Catia model of palm prototype

The below-displayed closed loop is made by the tendons wrapping around specially made, 3D-printed servo horn. The tendon is pulled while the servo motor turns in one direction, closing the finger (Table 1). The motor is turned counterclockwise to release the finger (Figs. 6 and 7).

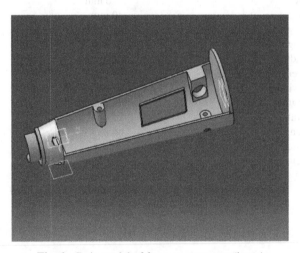

Fig. 6. Catia model of forearm prototype (inner)

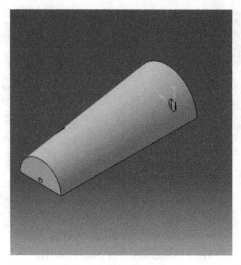

Fig. 7. Catia model of forearm prototype (outer)

Table 1. Parameters of CAD modelling

Parameter	Dimensions
Length of profile	370 mm
Thumb (height)	40 mm
Thumb (width)	18.5 mm
Index-finger (length)	75 mm
Index-finger (width)	24 mm
Middle-finger (length)	78 mm
Middle-finger (width)	27 mm
Ring-finger (length)	73 mm
Ring-finger (width)	24 mm
Pinkie-finger (length)	64 mm
Pinkie-finger (width)	20 mm
Forearm (height)	163 mm
Forearm (width)	60 mm
Wrist size	42 mm
Palm (height)	58 mm
Palm (width)	53 mm

3.2 Manufacturing and Assembly

All components have been printed using Flashforge Creator pro 2. This type of 3-D printer produces small parts with high precisions. The printer automatically prints an outer cover for each part as a layer of protection. Each of the screws used within the model like finger joints, are 3mm in diameter. Polypropylene is used for 3-D printing.

Pin-holes were done using a drill after printing. The printer is perfect for printing of tiny subjects. It gives very high precision while printing (Figs. 8, 9 and 10).

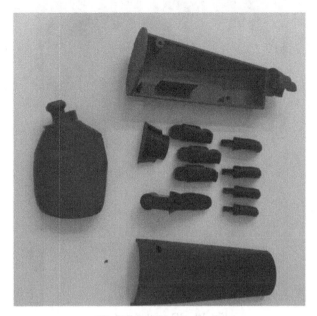

Fig. 8. 3D printed part (i)

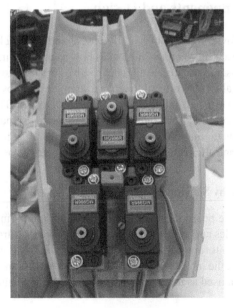

Fig. 9. 3D printed parts (ii)

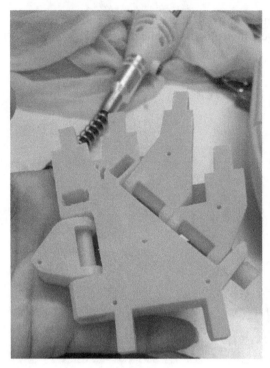

Fig. 10. 3D printed part (iii)

4 Electrical Components and Design

These motors can movie around 360° in clockwise and anticlockwise direction. The angular accuracy of each servo motor influences how each finger moves when the limbs move to open and close finger. Relatively cheap servos are used to decrease production cost. Using higher quality servos would increase strength of limbs and accuracy.

The Arduino Uno is used initially for as micro-controller. The EMG sensors are connected with the controller. The controller receives analog signals in real time which after processing results in rotation of servos, ultimately resulting in movement of limbs. Initially this micro-controller is used in order to make the mib cost-effective.

4.1 Electromyography Sensing

Electromyogram device board is used for detecting and monitoring live activity of the muscle. Three electrodes and a tiny PCB are included. Three electrodes are used as: two electrodes help in monitoring voltage potential, while the third one is used as ground point. As a user flexes, the interior systems converts electrical signals into a corresponding ironed signal, then used as input to a microcontroller's analogue to digital convertor (Fig. 11).

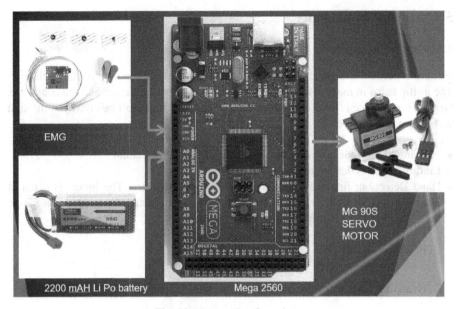

Fig. 11. Connection flow chart.

When a user flexes, it creates an analog signal that is amplified by the EMG sensor. The Arduino board uses this analog signal to create a movement. This moves servos by whose tension, the limbs cause the limbs to move (Fig. 12).

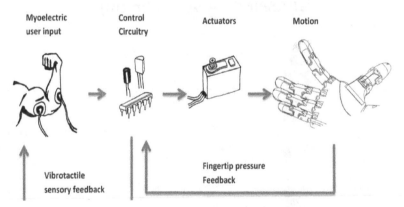

Fig. 12. Servo processor interfacing

The following code says that the signal pin is connected to pin 10 (pwm) in aurduino will turn a servo motor from 0° to 360, wait for 15ms delay, then turn it back from 360 to 0° back.

5 Artificial Intelligence

5.1 Gesture Recognition

Gesture focus is the method used to apprehend and analyze human physique behavior. The in-flip helps in making a channel between the computing device and the consumer. Gesture cognizance is helpful in processing the records that can't be conveyed through verbal or written content.

- Training library contains different hand gestures used in training.
- Library includes determination of the centroid.
- Hand Detection: first the photo is taken from web camera. The image is taken at 30 frames per second. The distance between the camera and the hand should range between 30 cm to 120 cm.

    TEST AND RESULTS

5.2 Grasping Capacity (According to Size)

Testing with small essential objects and comparing it with grasping capacity of human hand and plotting a graph.

Aim of the experiment:- To test the maximum grasping capacity of our designed prosthetic limb.

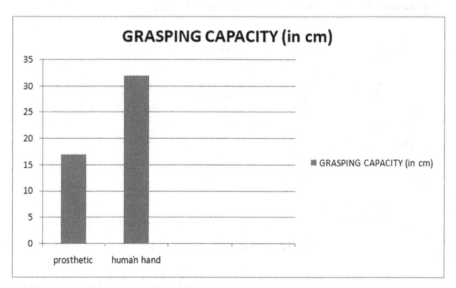

Fig. 13. Flow chart of grasping capacity

Procedure:- small objects which are really essential for an amputee or prosthetic limb user were taken into account such as glass of water, pen, pendrive, wallet, etc.

These objects were taken for the experiment and then their circumference were noted down by the traditional thread and ruler method and noted down. Then for each object it was marked upto what circumference our hand can grasp objects. After all readings were taken a graph was plotted to compare it with the functionality of the human hand (Fig. 13) (Table 2).

Table 2. Weight of different parts of prosthetic hand

Parts	Weight (in g)
3D printed parts	156
Servomotors (5)	5 * 13 = 65
Lithium Polymer battery	180
Rest parts: Wires, Tendons, Arduino Nano	50
Total	451

5.3 Analysis of EMG Signals

Analysis of EMG signals that are detected from the user muscles have been analyzed by taking the EMG signals of 10 different persons (Subject) to check the rotation of servomotor, as the EMG signals vary from person to person.

As physiological, anatomical and biochemical characteristics of persons are different from each other, so that the range of EMG signals changes from person to person. Some factors like height, weight of a person, strength of muscles, placement of electrodes also influence the values of EMG signals. So, to analyses the changing value the readings of EMG signals for 15 s of different 10 persons have been taken and presented in graph (Tables 3, 4 and 5).

Table 3. Basic data list taken from different persons

Subject	Height	Weight (kg)	Arm length (cm)
01(M)	5'3"	92	25
02	5'5"	88	24
03	5'8"	61	27
04	6'	66	27.3
05	6'	110	27
06	5'10"	100	26.4

(continued)

Table 3. (*continued*)

Subject	Height	Weight (kg)	Arm length (cm)
07	5'11"	73	24.5
08	4'9"	39	23.6
09	4'8"	52	23
10	5'3"	61	23.6

Table 4. EMG Signals of different subjects in each second and rotation angle (a)

Time (s)	Subject-1	Subject-2	Subject-3	Subject-4	Subject-5	Servo rotation angle (°)
1	408	405	276	234	208	170
2	377	370	279	210	201	170
3	380	382	284	199	202	170
4	395	392	290	208	195	170
5	380	325	286	244	199	170
6	343	340	290	239	207	170
7	331	328	297	236	212	170
8	342	340	283	222	224	170
9	311	250	292	238	242	170
10	309	108	279	241	225	170
11	309	208	273	232	229	170
12	322	120	285	241	235	170
13	320	150	298	238	237	170
14	323	310	283	245	228	170
15	319	122	274	241	231	170

From the above characteristics, it is observed that the servo mechanism performs almost the same for all subjects (i.e., subject-1, subject-2, subject-3, subject-4, subject-5, subject-6, subject-7, subject-8, subject-9, sub-10) irrespective of their body weight, height and arm length. Though the servo mechanism holds good for all different subjects, it gives a good response for the operation. So, it can be concluded that this setup can easily be used for any amputees (Fig. 14).

Table 5. Signals of different subjects in each second and rotation angle of servo motor (b)

Time (s)	Subject-6	Subject-7	Subject-8	Subject-9	Subject-10	Servo rotation angle (°)
1	158	250	208	246	209	170
2	178	256	216	236	211	170
3	159	236	213	235	225	170
4	15	260	212	224	229	170
5	154	265	200	258	227	170
6	152	261	194	256	210	170
7	181	287	184	254	237	170
8	161	290	188	243	239	170
9	160	268	189	256	222	170
10	131	261	193	258	235	170
11	153	252	195	256	248	170
12	135	250	200	242	244	170
13	131	244	252	242	234	170
14	144	246	255	242	235	170
15	146	246	253	230	236	170

6 Conclusion

This project aims in design of the ideal prosthetic limbs controlled by EMG signal. Each of the finger has three axis of rotation. Each finger is powered by using servo motors controlled by micro-controller. The prosthetic limb is processed by the EMG signals. The described EMG setup can operate only one finger so if we want to operate all five fingers of the designed prototype then we need 5 EMG sensors as well as 15 electrodes. This implies that a total of 11 electrodes are required while complete functioning of the limbs.

When EMG signals of 10 different persons were taken it is observed that the servo mechanism performs almost the same for all persons irrespective of their body weight, height and arm length. The servo motor is rotating about 170° which helps to move the finger of the prosthetic hand.

Though the servo mechanism holds good for all different subjects, it gives a good response for the operation. So, it can be concluded that this setup can easily be used for any amputees without any maloperation.

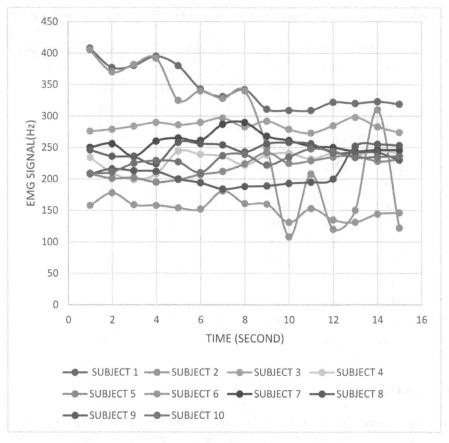

Fig. 14. Characteristics cure of EMG signals

References

1. Kato, R., Yokoi, H., Arai, T.: Real-time learning method for adaptable motion-discrimination using surface EMG signal. In: 2006 IEEE International Workshop on Intelligent Robots and Systems (IROS), pp. 2127–2132 (2006)
2. Ahmed, S.F., Kamran Joyo, M., Mahdi, H.F., Kiwarkis, I.J.: Muscle fatigue detection and analysis using EMG sensor. In: 2020 IEEE 7th International Conference on Engineering Technologies and Applied Sciences (ICETAS), pp.1–4 (2020)
3. Cifuentes, C.A., Braidot, A., Frisoli, M., Santiago, A., Frizera, A., Moreno, J.: Evaluation of IMU ZigBee sensors for upper limb rehabilitation. In: Converging Clinical and Engineering Research on Neurorehabilitation, pp. 461–465 (2013)
4. Palli, G., Scarcia, U., Melchiorri, C., Vassura, G.: Development of robotic hands: the UB hand evolution. In: 2012 IEEE/RSJ international conference on intelligent robots and systems, pp. 5456–5457
5. Clement, R.G.E., Bugler, K.E., Oliver, C.W.: Bionic prosthetic hands: a review of present technology and future aspirations. Surgeon 336–340 (2011)

6. Akgun, G., Cetin, A.E., Kaplanoglu, E.: Exoskeleton design and adaptive compliance control for hand rehabilitation. In: Transactions of the Institute of Measurement and Control, pp. 493–502 (2020)
7. Rai, V., Sharma, A., Rombokas, E.: Mode-free control of prosthetic lower limbs. In:2019 International Symposium on Medical Robotics (ISMR), pp. 1–7 (2019)
8. Atique, M.D., Moin, M.S., Siddique, R.: A cost-effective myoelectric prosthetic hand, journal of prosthetics and orthotics, pp. 231–235 (2018)

Communications

Performance Analysis of Fading Channels in a Wireless Communication

Pradyumna Kumar Mohapatra[1](✉) [ID], Saroja Kumar Rout[2] [ID], Ravi Narayan Panda[3], Anudeep Meda[4], and Banoj Kumar Panda[5]

[1] Department of ECE, Vedang Institute of Technology, Bhubaneswar, Odisha, India
er_pradyumna@yahoo.co.in
[2] Department of IT, Vardhaman College of Engineering (Autonomous), Hyderabad, Telangana, India
[3] Department of ECE, GIFT, Bhubaneswar, Odisha, India
[4] Department of IT, Vardhaman College of Engineering (Autonomous), Hyderabad, India
[5] Department of ECE, GIET, Gunupur, Odisha, India

Abstract. Wireless communication relies heavily on system performance. It is very important to consider channel behavior when designing wireless communication systems. Fading, scattering, interference, and other channel aspects affect the received signal quality. In MATLAB 2015 simulations, Rayleigh, Rician, and Nakagami fading channel models were compared for fading envelope, signal power, and channel capacity. Multipath fading environments require the use of parameters such as source velocity and pdf to analyze and design digital communication systems. The present study analyzes and simulates wireless channel behavior under different distributions of fading.

Keywords: Fading channel · Channel capacity · Nakagami channel

1 Introduction

Although wireless technology has exploded in popularity, some unavoidable conditions, signal attenuation, and barriers have made it difficult for the system to achieve its best results. An antenna that transmits and receives wireless signals from a simple line of sight to complex barriers like buildings, mountains, etc. In contrast to fixed channels, mobile channels are unpredictable and very different, due to their randomness. Faded communication is characterized by several multipath mechanisms' different times of arrival at the receiver, which is particularly bothersome in wireless communications [1–3]. The mobility of the transmitter and receiver as well as the signal bandwidth are a few of the parameters that can have an impact on a channel's fading and multipath delay nature [4]. In wireless communication, some of the undesired signals may interfere with the useful signal which may affect the performance of the channel. An effective channel equalizer is needed which is positioned at the receiver side to eliminate these multipath effects. Thus the role of the equalizer is one of the vital parts of wireless communication. Channel equalization itself is an optimization problem [5]. In training neural networks

© The Author(s), under exclusive license to Springer Nature Switzerland AG 2022
M. Panda et al. (Eds.): ICIICC 2022, CCIS 1737, pp. 175–183, 2022.
https://doi.org/10.1007/978-3-031-23233-6_13

for channel equalization, evolutionary algorithms were used extensively [6–11]. The node location algorithm adopts distance measurement as a TDOA technique and the static sensor node can localize when it comes into the reception range of the channel [12].

Using a vehicular environment, this paper develops Rayleigh, Rician, and Nakagami-m fading algorithms. Frequency selective fading is categorized under multipath time delay spread in addition to flat fading. Fast fading is observed on the channel when its coherence time is small compared to its delay constraint. In the Nakagami fading model, multipath scattering with large delays is considered, with multiple reflected waves clustered together. Each reflected wave within a cluster has a random phase, but all waves have approximately equal delay times. Hence, each cumulated cluster signal has a rayleigh envelope. Multipath reception is considered the cause of Rayleigh fading. Using a Rayleigh distribution, the Rayleigh fading model predicts that a signal's magnitude will vary randomly through the transmission medium. A Rayleigh fading effect is most commonly observed when line-of-sight propagation is not dominant between transmitters and receivers. As a result of the Rician model, the dominant wave is composed of several dominant signals, for instance, the line of sight and the ground reflection. A deterministic process is then used to treat the combined signal, with shadow attenuation also applying to the dominant wave.

The rest of this work is structured as follows:

The technique for Signal propagation is affected by fading channels described in Sect. 2. In Sect. 3, the study's findings are given and thoroughly discussed. Section 4 marks the conclusion of the research work.

2   Fading Channels

Signal propagation is affected by fading channels due to elements including shadowing, multipath propagation, and geographic conditions. Rayleigh, Rician, and Nakagami, channels [13] are some of the fading channels that are commonly used.

The following expressions can be used to determine the capacity of the Rayleigh, Rician, and Nakagami fading channels:

$$C = log_2 \left\{ det\left(I_n + \frac{1}{\sigma^2}HR_xH\right) \right\} \frac{bits}{Hz} \qquad (1)$$

Here, C refers capacity of the channel, mutual information denoted as I_n whereas the channel matrix identified as H and the signal envelope mentioned as R_x.

2.1   Performance Analysis of Rayleigh Fading

The transmission and reception of wireless signals are subject to LOS conditions. However, in specific towns LOS conditions are difficult to achieve; consequently, the receiver detects multipath signals. The amplitudes and phases of these multipath signals are distributed. In the absence of LOS, these signals are subject to Rayleigh fading at the receiver side [14] Summation of two Gaussian noise signals in quadrature is governed by Rayleigh distributions [15–17]:

$$f_h(h) = p(h) = \frac{h}{\sigma^2} e^{-\left(\frac{h^2}{2\sigma^2}\right)} h \geq 0 \qquad (2)$$

Ithis case, σ is the root mean square of the voltage signal received before envelope detection. In-phase and quadrature components of the received signal are demodulated. Using the following formula, we can calculate the envelope of a received signal:

$$x(t) = \sqrt{P^2(t) + Q^2(t)} \qquad (3)$$

Here, $P(t)$ and $Q(t)$. Ardefined as the in-phase and quadrature Signal. Based on the central limit theorem, signals can be entirely described by their means and autocorrelation functions,

2.2 Description of the Performance of Rician Fading Channel

An envelope distribution that exhibits fading at small scales is rician when the majority of the signal component is stationary (non-fading), such as a line-of-sight transmission channel. In this case, a dominating signal that is steady has random multipath components that are coming at various angles superimposed on it. This has the result of increasing the random multipath's dc component at the output of an envelope detector. Several weaker multipath signals interact to produce the Rician distribution. An enveloped Rayleigh signal is formed when the dominant signal becomes weaker. Rician distributions degenerate into Rayleigh distributions when the dominant component disappears. The transmitted signal can be written as the following equation when such a path exists.

$$c(t) = \sum_{j=1}^{N-1} l_j \cos(w_c t + w_{sj} t + \varphi_j) + k_s \cos(w_c t + w_s t) \qquad (4)$$

Here, k_s is denoted as the strength of the direct component, w_s represents the Doppler shift along the LOS path [18, 19].

The pdf's derivation in this situation is comparable to that in the Rayleigh scenario. It is possible to identify the mean and autocorrelation function of Q(t) and P(t) if N is large enough. They are independent Gaussian processes. The presence of the direct component in the Rician situation prevents the mean values of P(t) and Q(t) from being zero. By demodulating the signal s(t), the envelope r(t) of P(t) and Q(t) is derived [2]. In this instance, the Rician density function of the envelope is given by:

$$f_h(h) = p(h) = \frac{h}{\sigma^2} \exp\left\{-\frac{h^2 + k_s^2}{2\sigma^2}\right\} I_0\left(\frac{hk_s}{\sigma^2}\right) h \geq 0 \qquad (5)$$

2.3 Performance Analysis of NAKAGAMI-M Fading Channel.

Channel estimation is lacking in the Rayleigh and Rician distributions over long distances and at higher frequencies. Nakagami distributions, on the other hand, include a density function coupled to a parametric gamma distribution. As a condition for evaluating channel behaviour, A LOS component must exist between the transmitter and receiver. [16, 20].

Here, m is the scaling parameter that describes the amount of fading. As soon as m goes to ∞, the Nakagami fading channel is no longer available. Equation (6) showed the probability density function for the said channel:

$$f_h(h) = p(h) = \frac{2}{\Gamma(m)}\left(\frac{m}{\Omega}\right)mh^{2m-1}e^{-\left(\frac{mh^2}{\Omega}\right)}h \geq 0 \tag{6}$$

Here,

$$m = \frac{\Omega^2}{E\left[\left(h^2 - \Omega\right)\right]^2} \tag{7}$$

In Eq. (7), the spread parameter is represented as Ω where $\Omega = E\left[h^2\right]$ (Fig. 1).

3 Experimentation and Result Analysis

3.1 Simulation and Discussion of Rayleigh Fading Channel

In Fig. 2, we can see the envelope of fading and power of the Rayleigh channel. The signal envelope shows a gradual increase in fading when the user's speed increases. Thus, fading is a key problem in wireless communication. In the 2nd part of this figure, signal power is maximum then substantially decreases. Figure 3 also shows the channel capacity of the Rayleigh channel with or without channel state information of both transmitter and receiver.

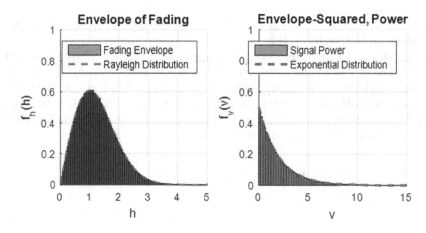

Fig. 1. Fading envelope and power for a Rayleigh channel

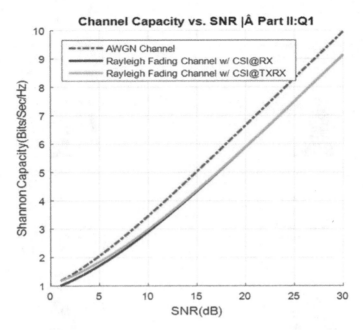

Fig. 2. Channel capacity

3.2 Simulation Results of Rician Fading Channel

Since the same signal is created for both this fading and the preceding Rayleigh example, the components, envelope, and RF signal values will all be the same. For the Rician distribution, the probability density function plot will resemble that in Fig. 3.

3.3 Simulation Results of Nakagami-M Fading Channel

Fading parameter for Nakagami channel denoted as m (m $\geq$ 0.5). It is also called a shape parameter and the standard Gamma function is identified as $\Gamma(.)$. A variety of fading circumstances are covered by the Nakagami-m distribution, it is a one-sided Gaussian distribution when m = 0.5. The condition for Rayleigh distribution when m = 1, when m < 1, a more severe fading scenario than Rayleigh fading is used by the Nakagami model (Fig. 4 and Fig. 5). The capacity variation to SNR is depicted in Fig. 6. In general, channel state information describes how power decays with distance,

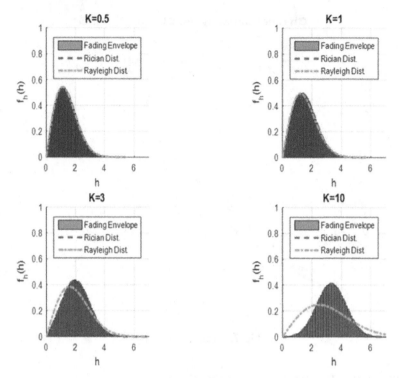

Fig. 3. Comparison of fading envelope of Rician and Rayleigh distribution for different value K

interference, fading, scattering, etc. Knowing CSI improves the reliability of the signal transmitted compared to not knowing CSI. As a result, it plays a significant role in defining the communication relationship. From transmitter to receiver and from receiver to transmitter, the CSI varies. A comparison graph between the Nakagami and AWGN channel with CSI of both transmitter and receiver is also shown in Fig. 6.

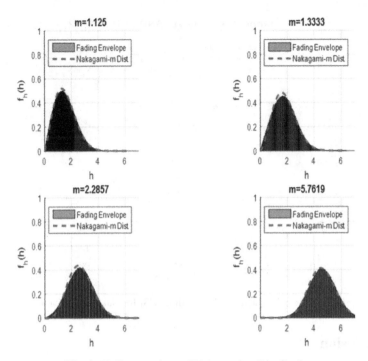

Fig. 4. Fading envelope of Nakagami-m Distribution

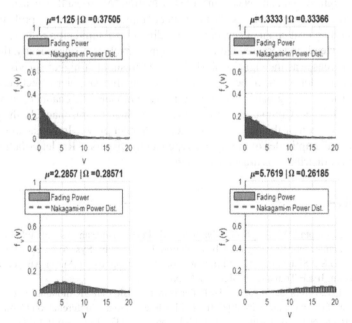

Fig. 5. Fading Power of Nakagami-m Distribution

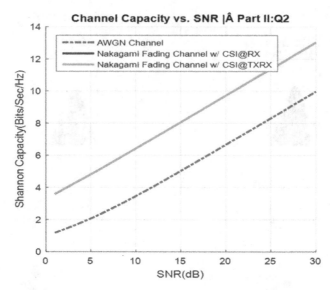

Fig. 6. Channel capacity with or without CSI for Nakagami- channel

4 Conclusion

Using Rayleigh, Rician, and Nakagami-m Distributions of probability density functions for respective fading channel models, this paper compares the respective probability density functions against channel capacity. According to the simulation results, increasing vehicle speed leads to increased fading in the signal envelope. Consequently, the amount of fading increases as the signal sinks below the threshold at higher speeds. However, some fading models perform better than others even after Doppler Effect degrades the channel capacity. Using better distribution in these models, the channel's capacity can be further enhanced. Compared to Rayleigh and Ricchian fading channels, the probability density function of the Nakagami-m fading channel grows. In Nakagami-m fading channel, signal amplitudes of multiple independently dispersed Rayleigh-fading signals with identical distributions are added together.

References

1. Kumar, S., Gupta, P.K., Singh, G., Chauhan, D.S.: Performance analysis of rayleigh and rician fading channel models using matlab simulation. Int. J. Intelli. Sys. Appl. **5**(9), 94 (2013)
2. Prabhu, G.S., Shankar, P.M.: Simulation of flat fading using MATLAB for classroom instruction. IEEE Trans. Educ. **45**(1), 19–25 (2002)
3. Khan, M. J., Singh, I., Tayal, S.: BER Performance using BPSK modulation over rayleigh and rician fading channel. In: 2022 IEEE 11th International Conference on Communication Systems and Network Technologies (CSNT), pp. 434–437. IEEE (April 2022)
4. Bellorado, J., Ghassemzadeh, S., Kavcic, A.: Approaching the capacity of the MIMO Rayleigh flat-fading channel with QAM constellations, independent across antennas and dimensions. IEEE Trans. Wireless Commun. **5**(6), 1322–1332 (2006)

5. Mohapatra, P.K., Jena, P.K., Bisoi, S.K., Rout, S.K., Panigrahi, S.P.: Channel equalization as an optimization problem. In: 2016 International Conference on Signal Processing,
   Communication, Power and Embedded System (SCOPES), pp. 1158–1163. IEEE (October
   2016)
6. Mohapatra, P.K., Rout, S.K., Bisoy, S.K., Sain, M.: Training Strategy of Fuzzy-Firefly based
   ANN in Non-linear Channel Equalization. IEEE Access (2022)
7. Panda, S., Mohapatra, P.K., Panigrahi, S.P.: A new training scheme for neural networks and
   application in non-linear channel equalization. Appl. Soft Comput. **27**, 47–52 (2015). https://
   doi.org/10.1016/j.asoc.2014.10.040
8. Mohapatra, P., Samantara, T., Panigrahi, S.P., Nayak, S.K.: Equalization of Communication
   Channels Using GA-Trained RBF Networks. In: Saeed, K., Chaki, N., Pati, B., Bakshi, S.,
   Mohapatra, D.P. (eds.) Progress in Advanced Computing and Intelligent Engineering. AISC,
   vol. 564, pp. 491–499. Springer, Singapore (2018). https://doi.org/10.1007/978-981-10-6875-
   1_48
9. Mohapatra, P., Sunita, P., Panigrahi, S.P.: Equalizer Modeling Using FFA Trained Neural
   Networks. In: Soft Computing: Theories and Applications, pp. 569-577. Springer, Singapore
   (2018)
10. Pradyumna, M., et al.: Shuffled Frog-Leaping Algorithm trained RBFNN Equalizer. Int. J.
    Comp. Info. Sys. Indu. Manage. Appl. **9**, pp. 249–256 (2017)
11. Kumar Mohapatra, P., et al.: Application of Bat Algorithm and Its Modified Form Trained
    with ANN in Channel Equalization. Symmetry **14**(10), 2078 (2022)
12. Rout, S.K., Rath, A.K., Bhagabati, C.: Energy efficient dynamic node localization technique
    in wireless sensor networks. Indian J. Sci. Technol. **10**(15), 1–8 (2017)
13. Panchal, A., Dutta, A.K.: Performance analysis and design of MIMO power NOMA with
    estimated parameters error statistics along with SIC and hardware imperfections. IEEE Trans.
    Veh. Technol. **70**(2), 1488–1500 (2021)
14. Narayana, M., Bhavana, G.: Performance analysis of MIMO system under Fading Channels
    (Rayleigh and Rician) Using SVD PCA and FSVD. journal of engineering technology **5**(2),
    116–126 (2016)
15. Zhang, D., Zhou, P., Jiang, C., Yang, M., Han, X., Li, Q.: A stochastic process discretization
    method combing active learning Kriging model for efficient time-variant reliability analysis.
    Comput. Methods Appl. Mech. Eng. **384**, 113990 (2021)
16. Tang, L., Hongbo, Z.: Analysis and simulation of Nakagami fading channel with MAT-
    LAB. In: Asia-Pacific Conference on Environmental Electromagnetics, 2003. CEEM 2003.
    Proceedings, pp. 490–494. IEEE (November 2003)
17. Gvozdarev, A.S.: The novel approach to the closed-form average bit error rate calculation for
    the Nakagami-m fading channel. Digital Signal Processing **127**, 103563 (2022)
18. Sijbers, J., den Dekker, A. J., Scheunders, P., Van Dyck, D.: Maximum-likelihood estimation
    of Rician distribution parameters (2004)
19. Mounika, I.S.D., Sharma, D., Sharma, P.K.: Analysis of different detection techniques of
    MIMO in future generation of wireless communication. In: international journal of pure and
    applied mathematics **114**(12), 419–426 (2017)

Power Conscious Clustering Algorithm Using Fuzzy Logic in Wireless Sensor Networks

Sanjaya Kumar Sarangi[1]($\boxtimes$), Arabinda Nanda[2], Manas Ranjan Chowdhury[3], and Subhadra Mishra[4]

[1] Department of Computer Science and Applications, Utkal University, Bhubaneswar, Odisha, India
sanjaya.res.cs@utkaluniversity.ac.in
[2] Department of Computer Science and Engineering, Krupajal Engineering College, Bhubaneswar, Odisha, India
[3] Department of Computer Science and Engineering, Trident Academy of Technology, Bhubaneswar, Odisha, India
[4] Department of Computer Science and Applications, Odisha University of Agriculture and Technology, Bhubaneswar, Odisha, India

Abstract. The most challenging difficulties in Wireless Sensor Networks (WSNs) is energy conservation. Data fusion is the process of combining data from several sources to produce a single scenario. It has the ability to save a large amount of sensor energy while simultaneously enhancing sensing data accuracy. Reduced energy usage is mainly essential and difficult examination issue in WSNs. Computational intelligence (CI) principles like localization, grouping, power-sensitive routing, job arrangement, and protection are now widely employed WSNs & other applications. WSNs are organized into clusters to optimize data-collecting efficiency while minimizing energy dissipation. Clustering allows you to organize a deployed network into a connected hierarchy while simultaneously balancing network load and increasing the system's lifespan. Each sensor node in a cluster-based WSN sends the data it has acquired to the cluster coordinator for the cluster in which it is located. The expanse among cluster heads & events, with the energy of clusters, is fuzzified in order to choose clusters for data uploading and fusing using fuzzy logic. The cluster heads apply the fugitive logic technique in confined resolution building as well, and the outcomes of the local decision-making are then relayed to the base station. As a result of this research, a fuzzy logic-based power-conscious active clustering method is developed, that amplifies system duration assessed by means of Last Node Dies (LND). Results of this simulations carried out illustrate the usefulness of this approach.

Keywords: Wireless sensor networks · Fuzzy logic · Cluster head

© The Author(s), under exclusive license to Springer Nature Switzerland AG 2022
M. Panda et al. (Eds.): ICIICC 2022, CCIS 1737, pp. 184–193, 2022.
https://doi.org/10.1007/978-3-031-23233-6_14

1 Introduction

Many new applications, such as armed surveillance, environmental supervising, & intellectual shipping system, have been made possible as a result of recent advancements in low-WSN, which are becoming increasingly common. As a typical WSN application, event detection has received a great deal of attention in the past few years. Diverse wireless sensor networks (DWSN) are systems that are made up of different types of sensors that differ in terms of energy consumption, computing power, and storage space, among other characteristics. Cluster leader is dominant than cluster associate in terms of all assets, including control, storage, communiqué, & data dispensation; this reduces the transparency of cluster associate by allowing cluster heads to perform all of the expensive computations, thereby reducing the overhead of cluster members. In particular, when using a Hierarchical Wireless Sensor Networks(HWSN), for example a cluster dependent system, cluster leader [1] is more influential than cluster component in terms of every source, including control, storage, communiqué, & information processing. Thus, load-balancing capability and network lifetime can both be significantly enhanced as a result. It is widely used in a variety of fields, including sensor network, robotics, video & image processing [2], and it is particularly effective in combining information from multiple sources into a single unified picture. Data fusion has several advantages at WSN because it is an efficient way to collaborate between several sensors. As a physical data fusion design, clustering has become increasingly popular, as it set sensors into numerous groups so as to accomplish the system scalability goal [3]. Clustering is a frequently used physical architecture of data fusion. Each group has a cluster head (CH), which performs and acts as a relay for data fusion. The cluster head therefore use more power than the usual sensors; a stronger sensor is therefore more possible to chosen as the cluster head. With the introduction of the membership concept [4], it is possible to handle faulty data in a proper manner. Data fusion theoretical thinking framework that adds a new notion of membership and allows for the right handling of flawed data is known as fuzzy reasoning. Because the sensing information from a solitary sensor is frequently indistinct & incomplete, it is complicated to derive the last fusion result from these imperfect data by performing an exact quantitative calculation on the imperfect data, as is the case with many other types of sensing data in general. To produce fuzzy output, fuzzy logic makes use of the membership degree to fuzzily transform partial data. This data is then combined with fuzzy system to create even more fuzzy production. Using it is a simple and effective method of dealing with data that contains some degree of uncertainty. It establish the novel concept of association degree, that allows for the appropriate handling of imperfect data.[5] fuzzy reasoning is a supposed analysis system for information integration that set up the narrative concept of association quantity, which allows for the appropriate handling of imperfect data. Because the sensing information from a particular antenna is frequently indistinct & incomplete, it is hard to derive the last fusion result from these imperfect data by performing an exact quantitative calculation on the imperfect data. To produce fuzzy output, fuzzy logic makes use of the membership degree to fuzzily transform partial data. This data is then combined with fluffy system to create even more fuzzy production. Using it is a simple and effective method of dealing with data that contains some degree of uncertainty.

The organized papers are as follows: Sect. 2. Related Works, Sect. 3. Proposed Model, Sect. 4. Simulation Setup and evaluation, Sect. 5. Conclusions.

2 Related Works

Low-energy adaptive clustering hierarchy (LEACH) [6, 7] is a steering practice that uses a grouping system wherein cluster arrangement is random, adaptive, & self configuring in the field of routing protocols. Application-specific data transmission is controlled at the local level. All of the sensor nodes in LEACH are grouped into clusters, with a cluster head at the centre of each cluster (CH). The CH transfers collected information to the base station (BS) using code division multiple access (CDMA), wherever the data is desirable, using TDMA (time division multiple access) scheduling. When the access point is by far the clusters and the amount of data would be sent is big, it suffers from a disadvantage. in this case, the data transmission process consumes a lot of energy. Another disadvantage is that, due to the adaptive nature of the clusters, the initialization stage for group a specified round will have little impact on LEACH's overall performance.

Centralized LEACH (LEACH-C) [8] is a centralized approach that provides an improved cluster by using a consistent grouping stage of the CH collection. It have stable stage, just like LEACH. For larger networks, however, they lack scalability and robustness. Using Multi Criteria Decision-production, a strategy called Reliability based Enhance Techniques for Ordering Preference by Ideal Similarity Solutions (RE-TOPSIS) [9] in blend with Fuzzy supports viable and dependable CH choice (MCDM). It likewise utilizes the notable LEACH convention to take into consideration one time CH choice or planning dependent on RE-TOPSIS rank file esteem in each group. During each round of the LEACH arrangement state period, this methodology dispenses with the requirement for CH choice. The Gupta convention [10], which depends on 3 parameters: centrality, focus, and energy for concentrated bunch head political race, has been proposed to conquer LEACH's limits. As indicated by reenactment results, the organization lifetime was altogether expanded, beating LEACH. It proposes a fluffy rationale based bunch head political decision system (CHEF). Neighborhood distance and energy levels were utilized by CHEF. As indicated by reenactment results, bunch heads are appropriated more equally than LEACH. Subsequently, the organization's future has been broadened. The fundamental disadvantage of CHEF is that it can't be utilized to assemble multi-jump courses in CHs.[11] suggested a power, regression routing algorithm to enhance lifetime of the network, assuming the cluster members has no resource constraints and more power than some other sensors. It proposes a technique for modeling the multiple step information broadcast problem in WSNs, which is caused by more data failure & low power competence, with the goal of providing reliable end-to-end information broadcast at a lower price. The authors proposed a Distributed Learning Automaton (DLA) based algorithm to conserve the difficulty as best route trouble with numerous limitations. DLA's ability to find the smallest number of nodes while maintaining the required QoS specifications is exploited in the proposed solution [12] to find the smallest number of nodes while still maintaining the required QoS specifications. Develop and demonstrate a data gathering scheme for wireless sensor networks (WSNs) that ensures service quality while also optimizing system concert metrics such as power expenditure, operation competence, and overall reliability. EPDC adjusts the prospect of group head appointment & evenly allocate the cluster leader diagonally the system in order to provide connectivity between cluster members, but it is not practical for practical WSNs due to its computational complexity. When using the Energy competent group arrangement procedure (ECGA), cluster leader was chosen based on the amount of data transmitted among every node and neighboring elements. [13] Has proposed an algorithm for forming energy-efficient clusters of atoms and molecules. The projected technique necessitates compound matrix procedures, which was never capable of being performed by sensor nodes. When using the FLGAP procedure, the stable condition stage is the similar as when using the LEACH. The lone time there is a conflict is during the early stages of cluster organization. With the FLGAP (Fuzzy Logic group arrangement procedure), a cluster head (CH) was selected for non-CH members using Fuzzy Logic. The CH chance value was calculated using three parameters in order to select a cluster head (CH). A solution to the problem of sensors with uniform distinctiveness, which is inconvenient for a wide range of applications, has been proposed in [14]. It is necessary for both regions to gather responsive &non-responsive data in a manner that is separate from one another. Suitable for sensible purposes such as sensors with mixed characteristics (i.e., where each sensor node has a different characteristic from the others). The authors [15] have anticipated two methods, one is based on the central (Fuzzy–C) approach which was central grouping algorithm dividing the entire network into a predetermined quantity of spectral partitioning strategy clusters. The sink node is supposed to have total information regarding system arrangement. The descend node is divided the sensors into k-numbers groups and connects to all the CHs. The others use a disseminated grouping method by using the neighboring information of a node. A central algorithm is used as benchmarks for the evaluation of the performance of the distributed algorithm. The centralized algorithm can improve performance with full knowledge of network topology. A Fuzzy Logic (MCFL) [16] Multi-clustering Strategy was developed to reduce energy dissipation and boost network life. The MCFL approach combines sensor nodes with multiple clustering algorithms at different times, reducing the number of messages that are sent from each node and base station to other nodes and maintaining network energy. The authors [17] used fuzzy approach with the input to the fuzzy system are angle, distance and energy and output is the chance of Cluster head selection. After the cluster head selection, IDA* search algorithm is used to find the shortest path to send the data packets from source node to sink node via cluster head node. In [18] the authors used mamdani fuzzy inference method to select the cluster head (CH) node. Once after the cluster head is selected, the Best first search algorithm is used to find the shortest route path to send data to reach at the sink node.

3 Proposed Model

A. Preliminaries
The derived system model is implicated for the proposed sensor network.

1. The sensors don't have GPS projections; therefore they were not aware of their location (node localization algorithm used to find location of node).

3 Proposed Model

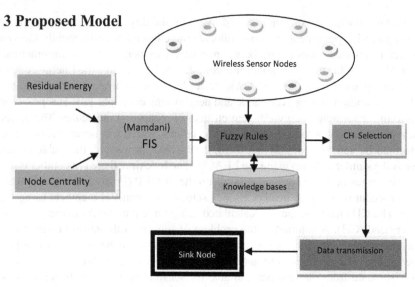

Fig. 1. Proposed model

2. The nodes have the ability to adjust the broadcast control based on the expanse.
3. Radio relations are symmetric, which means that in any situation, two sensors X & Y will converse by means of the equivalent broadcast authority.
4. The strength of the wireless radio signal can be used to calculate distance.
5. The most common cause of node failure is power exhaustion (Fig. 1).

B. Fuzzy Inference System

This method uses widely accepted and simplest Mamdani FIS. The inputs to the system are residual energy and node centrality. The output of the system is fuzzy cost.

Residual Energy

The residual energy of node calculated using Eq. 1.

$$E_{re} = E_{in} - E_{co} \tag{1}$$

where,

E_{re} : Residual Energy
E_{in} : Initial Energy of a node
E_{co} : Consumed Energy of a node

Node Centrality

Node centrality is calculated as the sum of distance of the shortest paths between the node and all other neighboring nodes in the networks shown in Eq. 2.

$$N_c(x) = \frac{1}{\sum_z d(z, x)} \tag{2}$$

where, $d(z, x)$ is the distance between the node and neighboring node.

The Mamdani FIS has the following steps:

1. *Fuzzification:*

   This is the first step of Mamdani FIS. In this step convert the crisp inputs residual energy, node centrality and output fuzzy cost into fuzzy membership grade using triangular and trapezoidal fuzification method (Table 1) and (Fig. 2).

Table 1. Parameters and membership grade

Parameters		Membership Grade
Inputs	Residual Energy	poor, good, excellent
	Node Centrality	poor, good, excellent
Output	Fuzzy Cost	VeryPoor(VP), MediumPoor (MP), poor, NoMedium (NM), Medium(M), Mediumgood (MG), Good, Very Good(VG), excellent

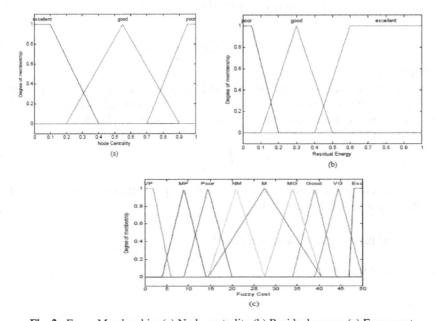

Fig. 2. Fuzzy Membership: (a) Node centrality (b) Residual energy (c) Fuzzy cost

2. *Rule generation and Rule Evaluation*

   Fuzzy if...then rules are generates are shown in Table 2. For an example, Rule1 can be read as: *If* (residual energy) is poor *and* (node centrality) is poor *then* fuzzy cost is very poor.

Table 2. Fuzzy If...Then Rules

Rules	Residual Energy	Node Centrality	Fuzzy Cost
Rule1	Poor	Poor	VP
Rule2	Poor	good	poor
Rule3	poor	excellent	MP
Rule4	good	poor	M
Rule5	good	good	NM
Rule6	good	excellent	good
Rule7	excellent	poor	MG
Rule8	excellent	good	verygood
Rule9	excellent	excellent	excellent

The fuzzy if...then rules are evaluated using the Eqs. (3) and (4).

$$\mu_{XUY(z)} = Max\big[\mu_{X(z)}, \mu_{Y(z)}\big] \tag{3}$$

$$\mu_{X \cap Y(z)} = Min\big[\mu_{X(z)}, \mu_{Y(z)}\big] \tag{4}$$

3. Defuzzification

This is the final stage of FIS. The evaluated fuzzy rules are changes to crisps value. The output of the defuzzification is the node cost. The centroid method is used for defuzzification. The defuzzified value Z* using COA is shown in Eq. 5.

$$Z^* = \int \frac{\mu_A(x).x.dx}{\mu_A(x).dx} \tag{5}$$

The output of defuzzification value is less than or equal to the pre-assigned threshold, then the node is selected as cluster head.

Proposed fuzzy based clustering approach:

Step-1: [Initial Round]

1. Start
2. BS choose CHs arbitrarily & transmit the CH_Msg
3. Cluster arrangement & information transmission will be done in this step
4. Every sensor calculate the remaining power & node centrality and propel this information to BS from CH
5. End

Step-2: [General Rounds]

1. Start
2. fuzzy cost ← measured by BS by means of sensor centrality & residual power

3. BS select CHs depending on the cost of fuzzy & transmit the message
4. Cluster arrangement & information transmission will be done in this step
5. Every sensor calculate the remaining power & node centrality and propel this information to BS from CH
6. End

4   Simulation Setup and Evaluation

The proposed model is evaluatexd using Network Simulator NS-2. An area of (1000 * 1000) square meter has been set aside for the installation of network test beds for 400 nodes. The proposed system is assessed with respect to energy efficiency and total data received. The simulation parameters are shown in Table 3 below:

Table 3. Simulation parameters

Sl. No	Parameters	Description
1	Network Area	(1000x 1000) sq.m
2	Number of Nodes	400
3	Data Packet size	2500 bytes
4	Channel bandwidth	2 Mbps
5	Energy	100 J / node
6	No of Cycle Simulations	10

Figure 3 shows that, when compared to LEACH, this Fuzzy Power Conscious Clustering Algorithm (FPCCA) can process about 26.8% more data if FND (First Node Dies) is taken into account, although the BS receives roughly 15.3% and 17.9% more data through Half of Nodes Alive (HNA) and Last Node Dies (LND).

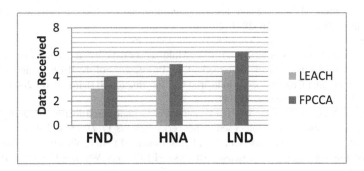

Fig. 3. Data received through Base Station (BS) during FND, HNA and LND

Figure 4 shows energy consumption of nodes. It is clear from the below figure, the energy consumption of FPCCA is less as compared to LEACH as the node increases.

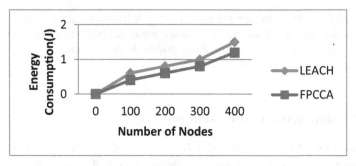

Fig. 4. Energy consumption

5 Conclusions

WSNs routing has gotten a lot of attention recently, and it presents a distinct problem when evaluated to typical information routing in wired networks. We significantly analyzed research findings on grouping in WSN using fuzzy logic. We discussed an energy-efficient dynamic clustering methodology in this research. The softness of the fuzzy approach allows it to be easily modified for various network and node conditions by simply shaping the fuzzy sets. Sensor nodes are grouped together in a cluster-based routing system to ensure that sensed data is efficiently sent to the sink. The selection of cluster heads is centralized here, although data collecting is spread. When compared to LEACH, our method will extend the sensor system's lifetime while also ensuring the optimal quantity of groups in each round. This algorithm is straightforward and requires little computing power. As a result, this technique can be employed effectively in larger WSNs. More research will be done to extend this method to suit the QoS (Quality of Service) requirements for WSNs.

References

1. Abbasi, Younis, M.: A survey on clustering algorithms for wireless sensor networks. Comput. Commun. **30**(14–15), 2826–2841 (2017)
2. Zadeh, A.: Fuzzy sets. Inf. Control **8**(3), 338–353 (1965)
3. Manjunatha, P, Verma, A.K., Srividya, A.: Multi-sensor data fusion in cluster based wireless sensor networks using fuzzy logic method. In: Proceedings of the IEEE Region 10 and the 3rd International Conference on Industrial and Information Systems (ICIIS 2008), pp. 1–6. IEEE, Kharagpur, December (2018)
4. Zhang, Y., Wang, J., Han, D.: Wu Hand Zhou R: Fuzzy-logic based distributed energy-efficient clustering algorithm for wireless sensor networks. Sensors **17**(7), 1554 (2017)
5. Heinzelman, W.B., Chandrakasan, A.P., Balakrishnan, H : An application-specific protocol architecture for wireless microsensor networks. IEEE Trans. Wireless Commun. **1**(4), 660–670 (2012)
6. Wang, Q., Guo, S., Hu, J., Yang, Y.: Spectral partitioning and fuzzy C- means based clustering algorithm for big data wireless sensor networks, EURASIP J. Wireless Commun. Netw. 1, 54 (2018)

7. Murugaanandam, S., Ganapathy, V.: Reliability-based cluster head selection methodology using fuzzy logic for performance improvement in WSNs. IEEE Access, **7**, 87357–87368 (2019)

8. Gupta, I., Riordan, D., Sampalli, S.: Cluster-head election using fuzzy lsogic for wireless sensor networks. In: Proceedings of 3rd **Annual Communication Networks** Services **Research Conference**, vol. 255, no. 260, 255–260, May 2005

9. Mostafaei, H.: Energy-efficient algorithm for reliable routing of wireless sensor networks. IEEE Trans. Ind. Electron. **66**(7), 5567–5575 (2019)

10. Younis, O., Fahmy, S.: HEED: a hybrid, energy-efficient, distributed clustering approach for ad hoc sensor networks. IEEE Trans. Mobile Comput. **3**(4), 366–379 (2014)

11. Aslam, N., Phillips, W., Robertson, W., Sivakumar, S.: A multi-criterion optimization technique for energy efficient cluster formation in wireless sensor networks. Inf. Fusion **12**(3), 202–212 (2018)

12. El Alami, H., Najid, A: Fuzzy logic based clustering algorithm for wireless sensor networks. Int. J. Fuzzy Syst. Appl. **6**(4), 63–82 (2017)

13. Wang, Q., Guo, S., Hu, J., Yang, Y.: Spectral partitioning and fuzzy C-means based clustering algorithm for big data wireless sensor networks. EURASIP J. Wireless Commun. Netw. 54–64 (2018)

14. Mirzaie, M., Mazinani, S.: M: MCFL: an energy efficient multi- clustering algorithm using fuzzy logic in wireless sensor network. Wireless Netw. **24**(6), 2251–2266 (2018)

15. Lenka, S., Nanda, A., Pradhan, S.K.: QoS provisioning based cost-effective routing in WSN based IoT Network using fuzzy IDA* technique. In: IEEE 2021 8th International Conference on Computing for Sustainable Global Development (INDIACom), pp. 591–595 (2021)

16. Lenka, S., Pradhan, S.K., Nanda, A.: Quality of service (QoS) enhancement of IoT based wireless sensor network using fuzzy best first search approach. In: IEEE 2022 International Conference on Intelligent Controller and Computing for Smart Power (ICICCSP), pp. 1–6 (2022)

Cryptanalysis on "An Improved RFID-based Authentication Protocol for Rail Transit"

Suresh Devanapalli[1]([✉])[iD] and Kolloju Phaneendra[2]

[1] Department of Mathematics, Rajiv Gandhi University of Knowledge Technologies, Basar 504107, Telangana, India
dsuresh7799@gmail.com
[2] Department of Mathematics, University College of Science, Osmania University, Hyderabad 500004, India

Abstract. In recent years, Radio-Frequency Identification (RFID) systems are widely used in many applications. RFID-based authentication protocol plays a major role in data protection network communication. So, authentication protocol should ensure security against all well-known attacks such as password guessing attacks, insider attacks, and impersonation attacks. In the literature, several protocols are proposed to address the problem of authentication using RFID-tags. In this paper, we analyze the recently proposed Zhu et al.'s protocol and show that it is vulnerable to a known session-specific temporary information attack and impersonation attack. In addition, it shows that their scheme is lack scalability.

Keywords: Security · RFID · Authentication · Key agreement

1 Introduction

In the recent days, Radio Frequency Identification (RFID) technology becomes more popular due to a contactless automatic identification of object and also its low cost. The advantage of RFID system is that it will simultaneously recognize massive amounts of information. Therefore, RFID-based solutions are widely applying to many applications, includes healthcare to monitor patient's health. However, the most important problem with the RFID system is that an adversary can access the tag information, which gives rise to privacy and forgery problems. After decades of development, RFID technology has gradually become the mainstream technology for various identification applications. At present, researchers have put forward a variety of solutions for the potential security problems in RFID systems.

In 2005, Rhee et al. [1] proposed challenge-response based authentication protocol based-on static identity that changes a tag response using a hash function and the random number. In the same year, Lee et al. [2] proposed low-cost authentication protocol that improves database operation quantity for resynchronization while solving an asynchronous problem between a tag and a database. However, later Lim et al. [3] pointed out the forward security issue, in Lee et al. [2] proposed protocol, which rise because of usage of XOR operation to update the identity. In addition, if an attacker intentionally blocks the previous communicated message, the same value is given as a response to a query of a reader so as not to satisfy indistinguishability and allow location tracing. Dimitriou et al. [4] proposed a Lightweight RFID protocol to protect against traceability and cloning attacks that can ensure forward security by updating a tag identity using a one-way hash function. Later, Lim et al. [3] pointed out that if we keep a current tag ID (identity) only, a database needs additional hash operations as many as the number of saved tags every time to identify a tag. Moreover, despite its design based on a dynamic ID, a database cannot distinguish a tag when the last message is blocked by an attacker, because it does not consider control of asynchronous status and resynchronization. Further, Lim et al. [3] proposed a dynamic ID-based mutual authentication protocol designed to meet requirements of both indistinguishability and forward security by ensuring the unlinkability of tag responses among sessions. Henrici et al. [5] proposed a simple and efficient authentication protocol for low-cost RFID system. Their protocol is based on a hash function embedding in a tag and a random number generator on a back-end server to protect the user information privacy, the user location privacy, and the replay attack. Their scheme also provides a simple method for the data loss. However, later Yang et al. [6] pointed out that Henrici et al. [5] proposed protocol can not resist against the man-in-the-middle attack. The attacker can be located between a legitimate tag and a legitimate reader and obtain the information from the tag. Thus, the attacker easily can be authenticated by the legitimate reader before the next session. Weis et al. [7] proposed two hash-based authentication schemes: hash-lock scheme and extended hash-lock scheme. However, Yang et al. [6] pointed out the major security drawbacks in Weis et al. [7] proposed scheme that they are insecure against eavesdropping attack since the attacker can track ID and impersonate the tag to a legitimate reader. Further, Yang et al. [6] proposed an enhanced authentication protocol for low-cost RFID, which describe privacy and security risks and how they apply to the unique setting of low-cost RFID devices. Cho et al. [8] proposed protocol to secure against brute-force attack: a hash-based RFID mutual authentication protocol using a secret value which emerged with the de-synchronization problem. Tsudik [9] proposed a YA-TRAP: Yet Another Trivial RFID Authentication Protocol, with objective to provide tracing resistance tag authentication through monotonically increasing timestamps on the tag.

Recently, the medical field is becoming an emerging area of research, particularly RFID technology in healthcare applications. In the recent years, several authentication protocols are presented in the literature for medical applications. In 2007, Chien et al. [10] proposed mutual authentication protocol for RFID conforming to Electronic Product Code(EPC) Class 1 Generation 2 standards. But, in 2010, Yeh et al. [11] showed that Chien et al. [10] proposed protocol is vulnerable to DoS attacks. Due to the bad properties, the claimed security objectives are also not met. Moreover, in each time of tag access, all records kept in the database needs to be computed and verified one by one to pinpoint the matching record which overloads the database and pulls down the overall performance. Then, Yeh et al. [11] proposed a securing RFID systems conforming to EPC Class 1 Generation 2 standard. Unfortunately, In 2011, Habbi et al. [12] proved that Yeh et al. [11] proposed scheme is vulnerable to tracing attacks, obtains the most important secret value, does not provide backward untraceability and untraceability of a tag. Further, Habbi et al. [12] proposed an improvement on Yeh et al. [11] proposed scheme. Later, Alavi et al. [13] found that some vulnerabilities still there in Yeh et al. [11] proposed scheme, such as traceability and forward traceability attacks. In 2013, Khedr's [14] proposed SRFID: A hash-based security scheme for low cost RFID systems. Dehkordi et al. [15] proposed an improved version of Cho et al.'s protocol [16] that eliminates weaknesses of Cho et al.'s [16]. Later, Alavi et al. [13] showed that the protocols proposed in [14–16] are still has some privacy concerns and are not resistance against backward traceability and forward traceability attacks. Hoque et al. [17] proposed enhancing privacy and security of RFID system with serverless authentication and search protocols in pervasive environments. However, Deng et al. [18] pointed out that protocol cannot offer any protection against data desynchronization attack. Chen et al.'s [19] proposed a novel mutual authentication scheme based on quadratic residues for RFID systems. However, Doss et al. [20] showed that Chen et al.'s [19] proposed protocol is insecure against the tag impersonation attacks, replay attacks and location privacy compromise.

In 2015, Srivastava et al. [21] proposed a hash-based RFID mutual authentication protocol for TMIS, and claimed that the protocol is effective against a various active and passive attacks such as forged attacks, replay attacks, and so on. However, Li et al. [22] pointed out the weaknesses of Srivastava et a.l [21] RFID tag authentication protocol such as reader stolen/lost attacks, lack of mutual authentication between reader and server, low efficiency. Later, Zhou et al. [23] and Benssalah et al. [24] analyzed the security flaws of Li et al. [22] that it fails to protect against tag and reader anonymity, strong forward traceability attack, replay attack, de-synchronization attack, data integrity vulnerability and impersonation attack. Next, Zhou et al. [23] proposed a quadratic residue-based RFID authentication protocol with enhanced security for TMIS. Benssalah et al. [24] proposed an enhanced authentication protocol. In 2018, Zheng et al. [25] proposed a new mutual authentication protocol in mobile RFID for smart campus and claimed that their protocol will provide forward security, anti-counterfeit, anti-replay, anti-tracking, anti-eavesdropping, anti-man-in-the-middle attack, de-synchronize, anti-DoS. But, in 2019, Safkhani et al. [26] proved that Zheng et al. [25] protocol is vulnerable to impersonation attack, replay attack, traceability attack, anonymity and the attacks that the adversary can control the time.

In 2019, Safkhani et al. [26] proposed a new secure authentication protocol for TIMS and smart campus. They claimed that their protocol is secured against various known attacks and provides distinguished properties. But, in 2020, Feng

[27] and Zhu et al. [28] analyzed the security flaws of Safkhani et al.'s protocol [26] and showed that it fails to provide forward secrecy. Next, Feng [27] proposed a new authentication protocol based on quadratic residues for RFID systems. Recently, Zhu et al. [29] proposed an improved RFID-based authentication protocol in order to withstand these security issues, and claimed that their scheme is secure against all possible known attacks.

1.1 Motivation and Contribution

The contribution of this paper is manyfold:

- We analyze the security limitations of the recently proposed Zhu et al.'s RFID-based authentication and key agreement scheme, and this scheme is, unfortunately, fails to prevent known session temporary information attack.
- In addition, we have demonstrated that their protocol lack of scalability.

1.2 Organization of the Paper

The rest of the paper is organized as follows: Sect. 2 presents the preliminaries, including the Secure Requirements and the threat model. We then review the recently proposed Zhu et al.'s scheme [29] in Sect. 3. In Sect. 4, we show that Zhu et al.'s scheme [29] is vulnerable to various attacks. Finally, we wind up the paper in Sect. 5.

2 Preliminary

2.1 Secure Requirements

To secure a RFID system, the applied authentication protocol should meet the following security demands.

1. **Untraceability:** A tag should not be traced, e.g., by correlating the tag's messages in two different sessions.
2. **Resistance to replay attacks:** An adversary cannot get any benefits by replaying old messages.
3. **Forward secrecy:** Even if the secrets of a tag is exposed to an adversary, the adversary can hardly identify the previous messages of the tag.
4. **Mutual authentication:** The protocol parties should authenticate with each other so as to prevent any impersonation attack.
5. **Synchronization:** If a protocol relies on shared values for authentication, an adversary may cause desynchronization problems. For example, if the server updates the shared values but the tag does not, the server may not be able to authenticate the tag in future. Such desynchronization attacks should be resisted.
6. **Scalability:** If a protocol requires the server to use exhaustive search for authentication, the protocol is of low efficiency. Worse than that, an adversary can launch a time measurement attack [30], e.g., tracing a tag based on its authentication time.

2.2   Threat Model

This article considers the widely accepted Dolev-Yao threat model [31] in which an adversary has control over the communication channels between the protocol parties, i.e., the tag-to-reader channel and the reader-to-server channel, and can eavesdrop, modify, delete or add messages in between the communication.

Table 1. The symbols in Zhu et al.'s scheme [29]

Symbols	Description
$ID_k,$	: the identity of kth tag
$RID_k,$	: the identity of kth Reader
T	: a time stamp
ΔT	: the time delay
$E_{skS}(.)$	: encryption function with private key skS
$D_{pkS}(.)$	: decryption function with public key pkS
R_x	: the random number generated by x
G	: a cyclic group
g	: a generator of G
$H(.)$	: a secure one-way collision avoiding hash function
$\oplus$	: the bitwise XOR operation
$\parallel$	: a concatenation

3   Review of Zhu et al.'s Protocol

In this section, we briefly review Zhu et al.'s scheme [29]. Their scheme has the following phases:set up phase, authentication phase. The symbols used in Shuming et al's. scheme are listed in Table 1.

3.1   Set up Phase

The server chooses the cyclic group G with a generator g, and publishes them.

3.2   Authentication Phase

In this phase, we briefly review the authentication and key agreement of Zhu et al. protocol. The summary of the authentication phase is shown in Fig. 1.

Step1: As the start, the tag generates a fresh random number R_t and computes g^{R_t} , then the tag sends the query and g^{R_t} to the reader.

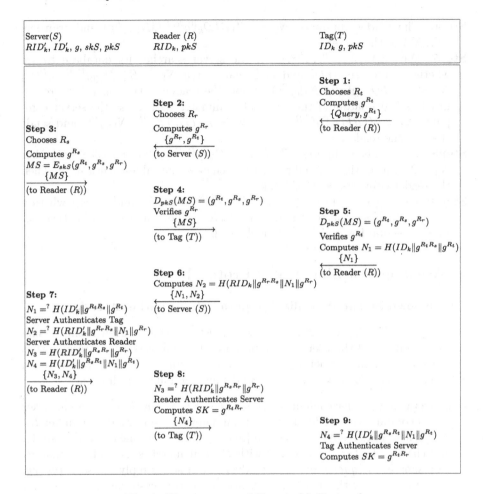

Fig. 1. The summary of Zhu et al.'s Protocol

Step2: When the reader receives the message from the tag, the reader stores g^{R_t} for later use. Then the reader generates a random number R_r, computes g^{R_r} and sends it with g^{R_t} to the server.

Step3: Upon receiving g^{R_r} and g^{R_t}, the server generates a random number Rs and computes g^{R_s}. The server signs $\{g^{R_t}, g^{R_s}, g^{R_r}\}$ with its private key skS and send the signed message MS to the reader.

Step4: With public key pkS, the reader can decrypt the message MS and check whether the message is legal. If so, the reader transfers the message MS to the tag.

Step5: When receiving the message MS from the reader, the tag check whether the message is legal.If so, the tag computes $N_1 = H(ID_k\|g^{R_tR_s}\|g^{R_t})$ and sends it to the reader.

Step6: The reader computes $N_2 = H(RID_k\|g^{R_rR_s}\|N_1\|g^{R_r})$ and transfers (N_1, N_2) to the server.

Step7: With $(N_1, N_2, g^{R_t}, g^{R_s}, g^{R_r})$, the server searches its database to see whether there are RID'_k and ID'_k that match $N_1 = H(ID'_k\|g^{R_tR_s}\|g^{R_t})$, $N_2 = H(RID'_k\|g^{R_rR_s}\|N_1\|g^{R_r})$. If not, the reader or the tag will be recognized as legitimate and the protocol terminates. Otherwise the server computes $N_3 = H(RID'_k\|g^{R_sR_r}\|g^{R_r})$, $N_4 = H(ID'_k\|g^{R_sR_t}\|N_1\|g^{R_t})$ and sends them to the reader.

Step8: The reader computes $N'_3 = H(RID_k\|g^{R_sR_r}\|g^{R_r})$ and checks whether $N'_3 = N_3$, if so, the tag and the server achieves mutual authentication. Then the reader transfers N_4 to the tag.

Step9: The tag computes $N'_4 = H(ID_k\|g^{R_sR_t}\|N_1\|g^{R_t})$ and checks whether $N'_4 = N_4$, if so, the reader and the server achieve mutual authentication. Finally session key $SK = g^{R_tR_r}$ is defined.

4   Weakness of Zhu et al.'s Protocol

4.1   Known Session-Specific Temporary Information Attack

According to [32–36] all the session keys must be secured even if the session random numbers of the user are compromised to an adversary A. Assume that the session random number R_t chosen by tag is unexpectedly revealed to an attacker A. Then, Zhu et al.'s [29] Protocol has the following drawback:

- Since tag and reader computes a session key SK as $SK = g^{R_tR_r}$, an attacker A can compute the session key SK using known session random number R_t.
- Adversary A intercepts the message $\{query, g^{R_t}\}$ sent to the reader (In step1), and checks whether g^{R_t} matches with R_t. If it matches, A confirms that R_t corresponds to $\{query, g^{R_t}\}$. The adversary A sends reply message $\{query, g^{R_t}\}$ to reader without any modifications. In this case, neither server nor reader can identify the message $\{query, g^{R_t}\}$ as a replied one. From the message $MS = \{g^{R_t}, g^{R_s}, g^{R_r}\}_{skS}$, the adversary A can decrypt the message MS with public key pkS. And also, the adversary A knows g^{R_r}, and he/she can compute SK as $SK = g^{R_tR_r}$ using g^{R_t}. As a result, A can successfully impersonate the legal tag.

4.2   Lack of Scalability

Zhu et al.'s protocol uses exhaustive search for authentication. In the step 7, the server searches for a match ID'_k that satisfies $N_1 = H(ID'_k\|g^{R_tR_s}\|g^{R_t})$. To do so, the server has to retrieve each ID'_k from its database, computes $H(ID'_k\|g^{R_tR_s}\|g^{R_t})$ and compares it with N_1. Similarly, the server has to retrieve each RID'_k, computes $N_2 = H(RID'_k\|g^{R_rR_s}\|N_1\|g^{R_r})$ and compares it with N_2. Assume that there are m readers and n tags in the system. The server has to perform $\frac{m+n+2}{2}$ hash operations on average to find the match ID'_k and RID'_k. It is obvious that the computation cost is linear with the number of readers and tags in the system so this protocol is lack of scalability. In addition, as mentioned in Sect. 2.1, because the server needs to perform exhaustive search operation to authenticate the reader and the tag, this protocol also suffers from time measurement attacks.

5 Conclusion

In this paper, we have first reviewed the recently proposed Zhu et al. protocol and then shown that their protocol fails to prevent known session temporary information attack. Also, we have demonstrated that their protocol lack of scalability. In the future, we aim to design a novel and more secure RFID-based authentication protocol using Elliptic curve cryptography for Telecare Medicine Information System to withstand the security flaws found in Zhu et al. Scheme.

References

1. Rhee, K., Kwak, J., Kim, S., Won, D.: Challenge-response based RFID authentication protocol for distributed database environment. In: Hutter, D., Ullmann, M. (eds.) SPC 2005. LNCS, vol. 3450, pp. 70–84. Springer, Heidelberg (2005). https://doi.org/10.1007/978-3-540-32004-3_9
2. Lee, S.M., Hwang, Y.J., Lee, D.H., Lim, J.I.: Efficient authentication for low-cost RFID systems. In: Gervasi, O., et al. (eds.) ICCSA 2005. LNCS, vol. 3480, pp. 619–627. Springer, Heidelberg (2005). https://doi.org/10.1007/11424758_65
3. Lim, J., Oh, H., Kim, S.: A new hash-based RFID mutual authentication protocol providing enhanced user privacy protection. In: Chen, L., Mu, Y., Susilo, W. (eds.) ISPEC 2008. LNCS, vol. 4991, pp. 278–289. Springer, Heidelberg (2008). https://doi.org/10.1007/978-3-540-79104-1_20
4. Dimitriou, T.: A lightweight RFID protocol to protect against traceability and cloning attacks. In: First International Conference on Security and Privacy for Emerging Areas in Communications Networks (SECURECOMM2005), pp. 59–66. IEEE (2005)
5. Henrici, D., Muller, P.: Hash-based enhancement of location privacy for radio-frequency identification devices using varying identifiers. In: IEEE Annual Conference on Pervasive Computing and Communications Workshops, 2004. Proceedings of the Second, pp. 149–153. IEEE (2004)
6. Yang, J., et al.: Mutual authentication protocol for low-cost RFID. In: Workshop on RFID and Lightweight Crypto, pp. 17–24. WRLC (2005)
7. Weis, S.A., Sarma, S.E., Rivest, R.L., Engels, D.W.: Security and privacy aspects of low-cost radio frequency identification systems. In: Hutter, D., Müller, G., Stephan, W., Ullmann, M. (eds.) Security in Pervasive Computing. LNCS, vol. 2802, pp. 201–212. Springer, Heidelberg (2004). https://doi.org/10.1007/978-3-540-39881-3_18
8. Cho, J.S., Yeo, S.S., Kim, S.K.: Securing against brute-force attack: a hash-based RFID mutual authentication protocol using a secret value. Comput. Commun. **34**(3), 391–397 (2011)
9. Tsudik, G.: Ya-trap: yet another trivial RFID authentication protocol. In: Fourth Annual IEEE International Conference on Pervasive Computing and Communications Workshops (PERCOMW2006), p. 4. IEEE (2006)

10. Chien, H.-Y., Chen, C.-H.: Mutual authentication protocol for RFID conforming to EPC class 1 generation 2 standards. Comput. Stand. Interfaces **29**(2), 254–259 (2007)
11. Yeh, T.-C., Wang, Y.-J., Kuo, T.-C., Wang, S.-S.: Securing RFID systems conforming to EPC class 1 generation 2 standard. Expert Syst. Appl. **37**(12), 7678–7683 (2010)
12. Habibi M.H., Gardeshi, M.: Cryptanalysis and improvement on a new RFID mutual authentication protocol compatible with EPC standard. In: 2011 8th International ISC Conference on Information Security and Cryptology, pp. 49–54. IEEE (2011)
13. Alavi, S.M., Baghery, K., Abdolmaleki, B., Aref, M.R.: Traceability analysis of recent RFID authentication protocols. Wireless Pers. Commun. **83**(3), 1663–1682 (2015)
14. Khedr, W.I.: SRFID: a hash-based security scheme for low cost RFID systems. Egyptian Inf. J. **14**(1), 89–98 (2013)
15. Masoud Hadian Dehkordi and Yousof Farzaneh: Improvement of the hash-based RFID mutual authentication protocol. Wireless Pers. Commun. **75**(1), 219–232 (2014)
16. Cho, J.-S., Jeong, Y.-S., Park, S.O.: Consideration on the brute-force attack cost and retrieval cost: a hash-based radio-frequency identification (RFID) tag mutual authentication protocol. Comput. Math. Appl. **69**(1), 58–65 (2015)
17. Hoque, M.E., Rahman, F., Ahamed, S.I., Park, J.H.: Enhancing privacy and security of RFID system with serverless authentication and search protocols in pervasive environments. Wireless Pers. Commun. **55**(1), 65–79 (2010)
18. Deng, M., Yang, W., Zhu, W.: Weakness in a serverless authentication protocol for radio frequency identification. In: Wang, W. (ed.) Mechatronics and Automatic Control Systems. LNEE, vol. 237, pp. 1055–1061. Springer, Cham (2014). https://doi.org/10.1007/978-3-319-01273-5_119
19. Chen, Y., Chou, J.-S., Sun, H.-M.: A novel mutual authentication scheme based on quadratic residues for RFID systems. Comput. Netw. **52**(12), 2373–2380 (2008)
20. Doss, R., Sundaresan, S., Zhou, W.: A practical quadratic residues based scheme for authentication and privacy in mobile RFID systems. Ad Hoc Netw. **11**(1), 383–396 (2013)
21. Srivastava, K., Awasthi, A.K., Kaul, S.D., Mittal, R.C.: A hash based mutual RFID tag authentication protocol in telecare medicine information system. J. Med. Syst. **39**(1), 153 (2015)
22. Li, C.-T., Weng, C.-Y., Lee, C.-C.: A secure RFID tag authentication protocol with privacy preserving in telecare medicine information system. J. Med. Syst. **39**(8), 77 (2015)
23. Zhou, Z., Wang, P., Li, Z.: A quadratic residue-based RFID authentication protocol with enhanced security for TMIS. J. Ambient. Intell. Humaniz. Comput. **10**(9), 3603–3615 (2019)
24. Benssalah, M., Djeddou, M., Drouiche, K.: Security analysis and enhancement of the most recent RFID authentication protocol for telecare medicine information system. Wireless Pers. Commun. **96**(4), 6221–6238 (2017)
25. Zheng, L., et al.: A new mutual authentication protocol in mobile RFID for smart campus. IEEE Access **6**, 60996–61005 (2018)
26. Safkhani, M., Vasilakos, A.: A new secure authentication protocol for telecare medicine information system and smart campus. IEEE Access **7**, 23514–23526 (2019)
27. Zhu, F.: SecMAP: a secure RFID mutual authentication protocol for healthcare systems. IEEE Access **8**, 192192–192205 (2020)

28. Zhu, F., Li, P., He, X., Wang, R.: A novel lightweight authentication scheme for RFID-based healthcare systems. Sensors **20**(17), 4846 (2020)
29. Zhu, R., He, X., Xie, J., Zhang, Z., Wang, P.: An improved RFID-based authentication protocol for rail transit. In: 2020 IEEE 14th International Conference on Big Data Science and Engineering (BigDataSE), pp. 65–72. IEEE (2020)
30. Avoine, G., Coisel, I., Martin, T.: Time measurement threatens privacy-friendly RFID authentication protocols. In: Ors Yalcin, S.B. (ed.) RFIDSec 2010. LNCS, vol. 6370, pp. 138–157. Springer, Heidelberg (2010). https://doi.org/10.1007/978-3-642-16822-2_13
31. Dolev, D., Yao, A.: On the security of public key protocols. IEEE Trans. Inf. Theory **29**(2), 198–208 (1983)
32. SK Hafizul Islam: Design and analysis of an improved smartcard-based remote user password authentication scheme. Int. J. Commun Syst **29**(11), 1708–1719 (2016)
33. He, D., Kumar, N., Khan, M.K., Lee, J.-H.: Anonymous two-factor authentication for consumer roaming service in global mobility networks. IEEE Trans. Consum. Electron. **59**(4), 811–817 (2013)
34. Canetti, R., Krawczyk, H.: Analysis of key-exchange protocols and their use for building secure channels. In: Pfitzmann, B. (ed.) EUROCRYPT 2001. LNCS, vol. 2045, pp. 453–474. Springer, Heidelberg (2001). https://doi.org/10.1007/3-540-44987-6_28
35. Cheng, Z., Nistazakis, M., Comley, R., Vasiu, L.: On the indistinguishability-based security model of key agreement protocols-simple cases. Cryptology ePrint Arch. **2005**, 129 (2005)
36. Mishra, D., Das, A.K., Mukhopadhyay, S.: A secure user anonymity-preserving biometric-based multi-server authenticated key agreement scheme using smart cards. Expert Syst. Appl. **41**(18), 8129–8143 (2014)

A Novel Approach to Detect Rank Attack in IoT Ecosystem

Amardeep Das[1,2]([✉]), Nibedita Adhikari[1], Pradeep Kumar Bhale[3], and S. K. Rath[4]

[1] Department of Computer Science and Applications, Utkal University, Bhubaneswar 751004, India
amardeepcvrp@gmail.com, nibedita.cs@utkaluniversity.ac.in
[2] Department of Computer Science and Engineering, C.V. Raman Global University, Bhubaneswar 752054, India
[3] Department of Computer Science and Engineering, Indian Institute of Technology, Guwahati 781039, India
pradeepkumar@iitg.ac.in
[4] Department Admin/Computer Science, BPUT, Rourkela 769015, India

Abstract. Internet of Things (IoT) is a popular technology in which everyday objects are converted into intelligent gadgets. These gadgets have sensing, computation, and networking capabilities. These gadgets, equipped with a variety of IoT applications, are primarily focused on automating various functions and are attempting to give inanimate physical things the ability to behave independently of any human interaction. Existing and future IoT applications are extremely promising for enhancing consumer convenience, productivity, and automation. To build such an IoT ecosystem in an ever-expanding manner, we require high levels of security, privacy, and authentication. The IoT ecosystem and associated routing protocols are composed of several threads. In an IoT network, a lightweight Rank attack detection system is suggested by this research. With the aid of the Contiki Cooja simulator, we implement our proposed lightweight security solution. Experiments using simulation demonstrate that the proposed method is lightweight and can detect the Rank attack with comparable performance.

Keywords: Internet of Things · Rank attack · Intrusion Detection System (IDS) · Contiki Cooja simulator

1 Introduction

Kevin Ashton, a British technological innovator, is credited with inventing the *Internet of Things (IoT)*. The IoT is a huge network of machines/objects that are all connected to each other. The connected machine/objects may be low-resource devices that share and communicate to one another via wired or wireless connections [1]. A different study says that IoT ecosystem evolution market share and prospects have grown by 31% since 2016 and that 8.4 billion IoT-enabled objects will be in use in 2017 [2, 3]. According to the information gathered from the resources, the ecosystem of the Internet of Things will expand by the year 2020, when there will be 30 billion gadgets. This demonstrates

M. Panda et al. (Eds.): ICIICC 2022, CCIS 1737, pp. 204–221, 2022.
https://doi.org/10.1007/978-3-031-23233-6_16

both how quickly we are integrating them into our daily lives and why it is so important to treat their security seriously.

The vast majority of Internet of Things ecosystem components and applications are dependent on Internet Protocol version 6, which was released to support these technologies (IPv6). Because the sensor nodes have limited resources, the routing protocol that is employed must be as efficient as possible in terms of both the amount of energy it consumes and the amount of computational power it can muster. The routing protocol for the IoT ecosystem is also known as Low-power and Lossy Networks (RPL) [4]. It was developed to address routing issues in the IoT ecosystem. RPL has been designated by the Internet Engineering Task Force (IETF) as the preferred routing protocol for the IoT ecosystem [5]. Thus, RPL is widely employed in several IoT applications. This protocol was designed from the ground up to work well over slow and error-prone connections, and it succeeds admirably. Among RPL's multiple impressive characteristics are its adaptability to different routing metrics and goal functions; its ability to handle complicated interconnections and multi-topology routing operations; and the adaptability of its trickling method and control message style and frequency.

RPL contains a number of configurable security measures to safeguard its control messages. These approaches ensure authenticity, integrity, and confidentiality. Assailants are nevertheless able to get control of the genuine nodes despite the fact that they are not immune to being tampered with and are not physically protected [6]. Threats that lower the quality of IoT applications service can be launched using these compromised nodes.

RPL is utilized in numerous IoT applications and can be attacked in different ways [7, 8]. Cyber-attacks like Rank, black-hole, Sybil, and Sinkhole attacks are able to target the RPL mostly because of design defects in the topology generation of the RPL [9–12] All of the above assaults are the most significant obstacles to the actual use of RPL in the IoT ecosystem. Despite the protection provided by the MAC layer, RPL continues to struggle significantly with the issue of internal assaults. Destructive attacks like the rank attack occur when an attacker node successfully creates a fake topology and coerces its neighbors into rerouting traffic to itself. Despite the fact that the rank attack has been the subject of a noteworthy amount of analysis in the routing path, no study has investigated the consequences of assaults of this kind on the different topologies of the IoT network. Additionally, no study covers how this assault on the RPL networks is made viable. This gave us the motivation to carry out this study and close the noted research gap. The highlights and new contributions of our study are outlined here.

We examine both the non-attack and the attack scenario in relation to rank estimation using the objective functions (OFs) and the DODAG Information Object (DIO) communication methods.

We analyze rank attack change with threshold modifications introduced by the Rank change scenario with minimum computational and communication overhead.

The suggested method offers novel lightweight security solutions to improve Rank attack detection in IoT ecosystems. It gives High True Negative Rate (TNR) and True Positive Rate (TPR) with minimum energy consumption.

The suggested solution is implemented on both small- and large-scale IoT networks to examine the effectiveness and efficiency of the desired solution.

The comprehensive analysis of the suggested security solution that was carried out using the Contiki cooja simulation.

The remainder of the paper is structured as follows. Section 2 introduces the generic IoT network architecture, RPL as IoT routing protocol, Rank attack in IoT ecosystem, and Intrusion Detection System (IDS) for IoT ecosystem. The relevant research is presented and discussed in Sect. 3. In Sect. 4, an explicit overview of the proposed security model is presented. The experiments and results are described in Sect. 5. The research paper is finally ended in Sect. 6, which also discusses conceivable future directions.

2 Background

In this section, we offer a concise introduction to the architecture of the IoT net- work, RPL as routing protocol, rank attack, and IDS for the IoT ecosystem.

2.1 Generic IoT Network Architecture

There are five parts to the IoT network architecture: Business, Application, Processing, IoT-Internet Connection, IoT Access Network, and Perception. The network stack remains the same, as illustrated in Fig. 1, with the exception of the upsurge of the adaption layer, modification of the routing strategy at the IoT access network layer, use of IEEE 802.15.4 as the MAC layer, and other similar changes.

The layers and functions associated with each layer are depicted in Fig. 1. With the exception of the extra adaption layer, the IoT access network layer is functionally equivalent to the network layer in conventional networks. The Application layer of the Internet of Things commonly implements a protocol known as CoAP (Confined Application Protocol). This protocol was designed particularly for limited devices such as LLN devices and is used by the majority of IoT applications. In the part on the RPL algorithm that came before this one, [13, 14] you may find a description of the routing protocol that is used.

2.2 RPL Protocol

IoT ecosystems that are built on Low Power and Lossy Networks (LLN) will use this routing protocol. As a practical protocol, RPL supports a variety of communication modes, including [15]. Reactive and proactive RPL are the two classes of RPL that could be found in the IoT ecosystem. RPL provides path as needed. The disadvantage is that the time needed to find a path to an IoT node increases as more and more connections are made. The routes are provided by proactive RPL before another IoT node needs them. In addition to this, it engages in the trading of various control messages in order to get access to local knowledge about the area and find new routes [16]. RPL procedure as displayed in Fig. 2.

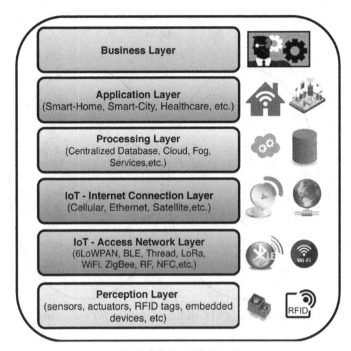

Fig. 1. Generic IoT network architecture

2.3 Rank Attack in IoT

This section's main goal is to talk about the two most important routing-based attacks. As shown in Fig. 3, attacks can be put into three groups based on the IoT ecosystem resources, IoT ecosystem topology, and IoT ecosystem traffic. This research paper used an IoT ecosystem scenario to test and look at the rank attack.

2.4 IDS for IoT Ecosystem

It consists of cooperating elements that detect attacks and harmful behavior in the IoT ecosystem. IDSs are as follows:

– Payload-based IDS (PIDS): It analyses inbound/outbound payload information. Packets are statistically tested.
– Header-based IDS (HEIDS): It analyses only the packet header portion of network packets. Comparing the other IDS, its tests and uses the perceived network packet payload.
– Statistical anomaly-based IDS (SAIDS): It collects the IoT ecosystem information and learns what normal user behavior is. Statistical tests are used to figure out if a behaviour is right or wrong based on how it is seen. SAIDS can be categorized into two main groups like profile-based anomaly detection and threshold-based anomaly detection.

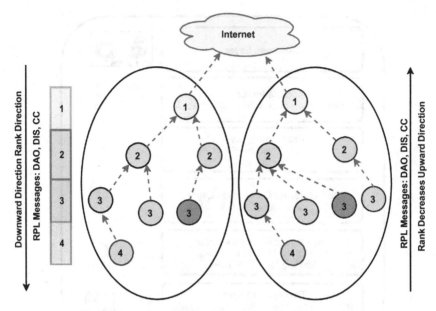

Fig. 2. Execution of RPL routing protocol in IoT ecosystem.

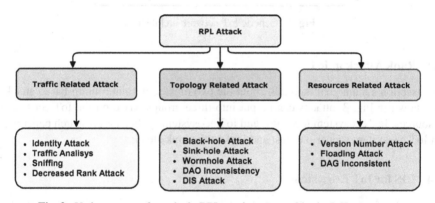

Fig. 3. Various types of attacks in RPL routing protocol in the IoT ecosystem

- Signature-based IDS (SIDS): This type of IDS uses a database of intrusion detection signatures that have already been seen. Every intrusion leaves a trail, such as the files and folders that were accessed, the type of data packets that were sent, and failed logins, etc. This IDS compares the behavior of known attack imprints in the IoT ecosystem. If attack imprints or signature match is found, a notification is given so that the right steps can be taken.
- Network-based IDS (NIDS): Analyses network traffic and monitors many hosts to identify malicious activities.

– Host-based IDS (HIDS): In order to identify potentially malicious behaviour, a HIDS will monitor file-system changes, system calls, and application logs (such as binaries, password files, and so on), as well as host-based actions and states.

3 Related Work

Kamble et al. [17] enclose recently provided a survey on various protection methods against vulnerabilities and safe routing algorithms in RPL-based Internet of Things technology. They divided the attacks into two basic categories (i.e., direct and indirect assault). In the case of an explicit invasion, the assailants are actively involved in the attack. Examples of direct assaults in the IoT Ecosystem include routing table overflow assaults and flooding attacks. When an invasion occurs, it is not the intruder who is attacking directly. Therefore, the malicious node relies on other nodes to overwhelm IoT networks with assaults such as increasing rank attacks, version number attacks, and inconsistency in DAG formation attacks.

Raoof et al. [16] include different forms of routing-related attacks in the IoT ecosystem: Sybil attacks, Selective forward attacks, Black-hole attacks, etc. It is important to note that several metrics are used for evaluating various assaults (e.g., data packet delivery rate, data packet delay, power consumption, etc.). This research study lessens the severity of the effects of a routing assault without adding any additional defence measures to the routing protocol. But the low TPR and TNR are a weakness of this paper.

Le et al. [18] recognized attacks including rank, sinkhole, DIS and local repair using IDS. The Extended Finite State Machine (EFSM) in this IDS was produced using a semi-automatic characterization approach. The DIO suppression attack, a brand-new method of attacking the RPL protocol, was first described by Perazzo et al. [19]. This attack targets the ability of IoT nodes to send and receive updated DIO control messages, which are necessary for the discovery of optimal routing pathways and the elimination of inefficient or erroneous paths.

Wallgren et al. [20] utilized the Cooja simulation in order to carry out a variety of attacks on RPL. These attacks included a selective forwarding attack as well as a sinkhole attack. They have also exhibited many capabilities of the IPv6 protocol and its application in the IoT enable IDS. This method's primary drawback is that it consumes more power than local processing.

Glissa et al. [21] presented SRPL, a safe routing mechanism utilized by RPL routing protocol. This approach prevents deviant nodes from generating a false topology by altering node rankings. They have implemented a rank threshold and hash chain authentication approach to thwart internal attacks likes selective forwarding attacks, blackhole attacks, and sinkhole attacks. This research paper concludes that internal attacks depending on malicious RPL metrics must be avoided. The SRPL strategy, meanwhile, has several shortcomings. First and foremost, regulated messages produced by SRPL incur more overhead in contrast to RPL. Additionally, it requires greater processing power and storage space.

Osman et el. [22], an ML-based model was introduced that uses the Light Gradient Boosting Machine (LGBM) to find VN attacks. Methodology components focused on creating a dataset of VN attacks, extracting features from that dataset, using a logistic regression-based classification technique, and optimizing the algorithm's specifications were presented. The suggested model performed well but required at least 347,530 bytes of memory, which is beyond the capability of most IoT devices. This suggests that in order to execute the model in a centralized fashion, this system requires additional devices with significant memory resource capacities.

In order to protect the RPL routing mechanism against rank and VN at- tacks, the authors of [23] developed a blockchain-based structure. ML A-based detection systems modules in RPL network are connected securely through the blockchain network. To identify potential rank and VN attacks, it deploys an XGBoost classifier on a private blockchain network. After that, smart contracts are utilized to evaluate these efforts and provide real-time warnings to harmful nodes in the IoT networks. The outcomes of the performance tests demonstrated that the blockchain-based solution that was offered boosted the accuracy reached by the ML algorithms when it came to forecasting the assault.

Loo et al. [24] demonstrated a new type of routing attack known as a Topology Attack, which alters node operation by separating the optimum topology of the nodes. Local Repair Attack and Rank Attack are two subtypes of Rank at- tack. They have furthermore implemented an IDS architecture that makes use of RPL finite state machines in order to keep an eye on the nodes. Nevertheless, this strategy has the drawback of using more memory and consuming more power than necessary. IoT network and RPL attacks have been studied by et al. [25]. They have demonstrated that several assaults are practicable on low-resource devices due to the simplicity and small size of IoT protocols.

In [26], the authors provide a lightweight solution which they call INTI (Intrusion detection of SiNkhole attacks on 6LoWPAN for Internet of Things). This strategy, which combines trust, reputation, and sinkhole attack detection using Rooming IDS in the IoT ecosystem with a watchdog, is a sandwich of many approaches. When developing the solution for the Internet of Things, they took the nodes' ability to move around in the network into account. FNR, FPR, and resource utilisation are all regarded as performance criteria by the INTI. The biggest drawback of this technique is that it requires more resources and computational power. As a result, this method shortens the IoT ecosystem's lifespan.

In [27] describes how the researchers developed four assault models and evaluated how they affected important network metrics relating to the attacker's topological loca- tion. However, this study solely addressed static networks and did not offer any feasible defenses against the rank assault. The effects of a ranked assault utilizing a fictitious IP address were examined by the authors of [28]. However, the specific consequences of the rank attack on the RPL procedure are not specifically examined in this study. The enhanced rank assault was initially presented by Shukla et al. [29], who also proposed an ego-based mitigation strategy. However, this study focuses on a topology with just 12 nodes rather than taking into account a realistic topology. Additionally, mobile nodes were not included in this study.

4 Proposed Security Approach

This section describes the proposed rank attack security solution for detecting rank attacks in the IoT network. It consists of many IoT devices with various processing and storage capacities. Our intended security approach employs the lightweight IDS. Additionally, it utilizes minimum energy during the execution of the proposed technique to detect rank and rank-related attacks.

4.1 Proposed Approach Assumption

We would want to consider the following assumptions before we discuss the lightweight security mechanism and the methodologies.

We presume that every device with a resource limitation has a finite quantity of available power.

- In the IoT ecosystem, every single device is different in terms of its resource limitations (i.e. communication capacity, computation, memory, and battery power).
- Despite this, it is possible that billions or even trillions of IoT devices are connected to the IoT ecosystem via wireless network. Nevertheless, we will provide our strategy for a IoT ecosystem that is capable of holding a fixed quantity of the IoT devices like 8 to 128 IoT devices.

4.2 Security Model

The IoT network is made up of both genuine and malicious nodes (MN). The border router (6BR) serves as the point of entry for the IoT. In addition, 6BR acts as a connection point among the private and the public Internet network. The 6BR is a powerful hub that may take the form of a portable computer. There is currently no computer or laptop hardware that can be considered an equivalent to IEEE 802.15.4 devices. For this reason, we run the Linux platform based communicate with the Cooja simulator [30]. The IoT setup configuration for our investigation is shown in Fig. 4.

4.3 Proposed Rank Attack Detection Solution

The suggested lightweight security solution based on rank change threshold. We endorse both static rank attack detection IDS module and lightweight nature is deploy them through 6BR routers. Based on the features of IoT network characteristics like battery power, resource-constrained, and lossy. Fig. 5 utilized to identify rank assault. Based on residual energy, we calculate the lifetime of the network.

5 Experiments and Results Analysis

5.1 Setup and Execution of Experiments

Our proposed security solution is implemented in Contiki cooja [30] emulation settings and presumes that the IoT ecosystem comprises various type of sensor like Tmotes Sky,

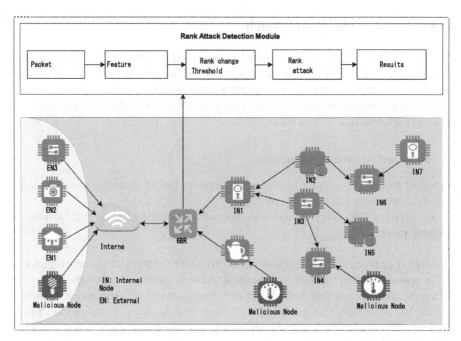

Fig. 4. IoT experiment setup and rank attack detection IDS module architecture

and sky mote which is CC2420 IEEE 802.15.4-compatible radio chips [31]. 6BR device features an additional piece of hardware and increased processing power. To support the intended solution to identifying Rank attacks. The IoT network is depicted in Fig. 4. We conduct three different types of experiments in the experiment section. A thorough justification of each experiment is provided below. Table 1 lists the simulation settings with values for Contiki cooja.

Experiments 1: Non-rank Attack in IoT Ecosystem: IN this experiment, we take into account various node counts (i.e., 4 to 128 node). The settings utilised to simulate the environment are listed in Table 1 and the simulation's network architecture is illustrated in Fig. 4. Fig. 6(a), 6(b), and 6(c), respectively, depict the topology, DODAG, and power consumption profile. When there are no malicious nodes that are lowering the rank and causing the network to function normally, we noticed that the nodes' power usage is lower.

At several nodes, the IoT network traffic is examined utilizing collect view techniques. Fig. 7 displays the throughput achieved in this experiment. The figure depicts that as the nodes number rises, the average throughput gradually declines. Additionally, we can see the avg. energy utilization per node and the network's overall energy utilization in Figs. 8 and 9. RPL alone and RPL collect modules are used in the IoT paradigm for power and energy analysis.

Experiments 2: Rank Attack in IoT Ecosystem: IN a situation involving a rank attack, the same amount of nodes are used to perform an attack. At different nodes,

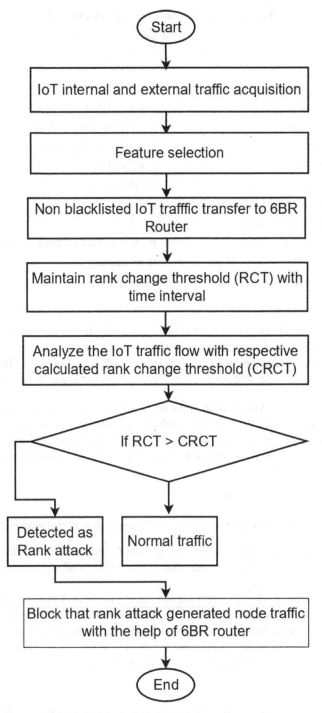

Fig. 5. Flowchart of rank attack detection process

Table 1. Cooja simulator settings with values [3]

Name of setting	Value
OS	Contiki NG, Contiki 3.0 OS
Simulator	Cooja
Target area	100 m × 100 m
Radio environment	UDGM with distance loss
Sensor node type	Tmot Sky and sky mote
IoT routing protocol	Contiki RPL
Adaptation layer	6LoWPAN
Transmitter power output (TPO)	(dBm) 0–25
Receiver sensitivity threshold	(dBm) - 94
Radio frequency (RF)	IEEE 802.15.4 CC2420 2.4 GHz
Type of attack	Rank attack
Simulation duration	60 min

collect view methods are used to gather and analyse IoT traffic in real time. We noticed a significant decrease in throughput together with an increase in the typical amount of power consumed by each node of 41–54%. Specifically, as seen in Fig. 10 and Fig. 11, respectively. Figure 12 emphasizes a 37.8% increase in energy use for the whole network.

Experiment 3: Rank Attack with Security Solution: To identify a rank assault, we execute a security solution based on the rank change threshold. Experiment 1 and Experiment 2 are repeated numerous times along a varying number of connected IoT devices in IoT networks and power usage overview with the help of Contiki Cooja Simulator's Collect-View application.

5.2   After Proposed Security Solution Implementation Performance Analysis

We provide a security solution to the widely-used *Contiki* OS [9] in order to safeguard the Io network. The following are the measures that will be used to evaluate performance:

- Average energy usage: All IoT enabling device in the IoT ecosystem are battery-powered device. As a result, there is a finite amount of energy. Here we compute power depletion at node-level as well as system-level. For this purpose, we employ *powertrace* on sky motes to estimate the power depletion. The *powertrace* output shows system execution time with respective total time.

- Memory usage (RAM/ROM): It shows the percentage of memory utilization of the IoT devices to run the proposed security solution throughout the experimentation.

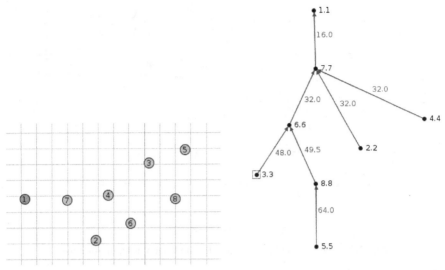

(a) Topology for normal network

(b) The DODAG protocol for the normal IoT ecosystem

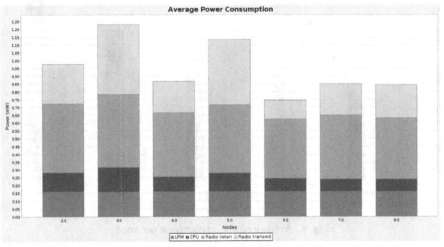

(c) Power usage profiles during Seven good nodes and zero bad ones

Fig. 6. Topology, DODAG, and power profiling are utilized to study non-rank assaults.

– TNR and TPR: The True Negative Rate (TNR) and True Positive Rate (TPR) are estimated utilising sensitivity and specificity correspondingly. Sensitivity predicts the number of legitimate nodes (LN) that are quickly and precisely recognised, whereas specificity counts the quantity of rank attack generated nodes like (CN) that are consistently discovered. Both sensitivity and specificity fit within the following

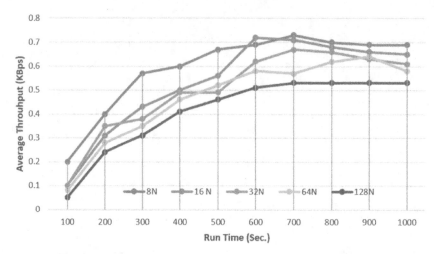

Fig. 7. Average throughput different IoT node with different run time

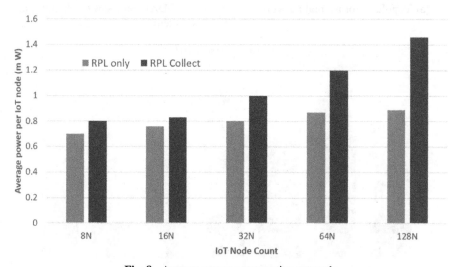

Fig. 8. Average power consumption per node

descriptions:

$$Senstivity = \frac{m}{m+n} \qquad (1)$$

and

$$Specificity = \frac{x}{x+y} \qquad (1)$$

where $m = CN$ correctly recognise, $n = Falsely$ labelled as authentic by CN, $x = LN$ correctly recognise. $y = LN$ labelled wrongly as malicious.

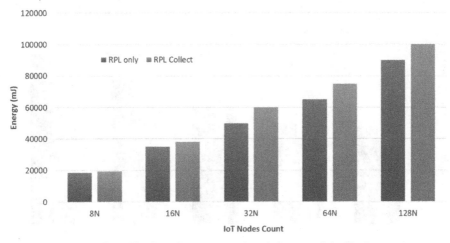

Fig. 9. Utilization of energy over the whole network in 60 min.

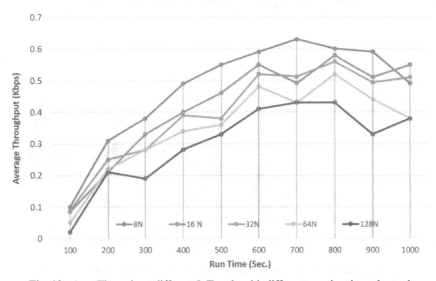

Fig. 10. Avg. Throughput different IoT node with different run time in rank attack

5.3 Comparison of the Suggested Security Solution to Similar Works

In this section, a comparison is made based on memory usage, TNR, TPR, Avg. power usage, and IoT traffic. As depicted in Table 2, the comparative analysis of the suggested technique and the most recent current solutions. The suggested technique uses additional ROM and RAM for the memory utilization analysis. Every configuration has a different baseline since it is based on a different Contiki system component. A 6BR router, for instance, requires more memory usage than other IoT nodes. Nevertheless, 1760 and 365 bytes of total ROM and RAM are anticipated to be used to implement the suggested

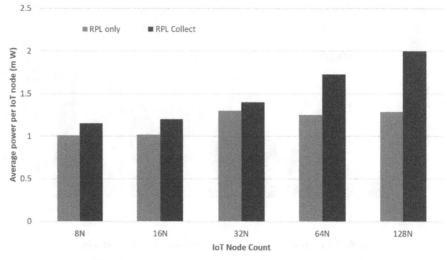

Fig. 11. Avg. Power consumption per node in rank attack

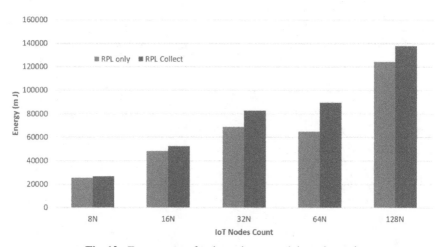

Fig. 12. Energy usage for the entire network in rank attack

strategy on IoT nodes. In experiment 3, 64 IoT nodes were run for 60 min while 9834 and 54256 bytes of RAM/ROM consumption were observed, respectively.

The avg TNR and TPR attained using the proposed approach are 94.12% and 95.34% correspondingly. Most comparable solutions demonstrated in the literature have lower detection rates than the rank attack detection rate [23, 28, 29]. However, when the IoT network grows (in terms of size and device count), the TPR declines as a result of the massive network topologies. Additionally, it takes some time for the network to stabilize and grow enough to get a more increased TNR and TPR. In experimentation work, the rank attack case, it takes 128 nodes 60 min to obtain the same TPR and TNR as 64 nodes do in 30 min.

The average energy consumption of the whole IoT ecosystem for 60 min, during which our experiment was conducted with a certain number of devices with limited resources. Energy usage increases as the number of IoT nodes in- creases from 8 to 128 nodes. Our proposed approach reduces energy consumption by up to 70000 mJ.

Table 2. Comparing proposed method to current works

Research paper	Simulation	Memory usage (in byte)		Avg. energy utilization (mJ)	Rank attack detection (%)	
		ROM	RAM		TPR	TNR
[17]	Contiki Cooja	47137	15883	75522	78.98%	93.11%
[26]	Contiki Cooja	51045	12894	76320	92.45%	93.93%
[28]	Contiki Cooja	74914	14587	74567	93.34%	93.05%
[23]	Contiki Cooja	70534	12544	71801	95.86%	94.31%
[22]	Contiki Cooja	60476	11837	70480	96.11%	95.81%
[29]	Contiki Cooja	56137	10383	62133	93.68%	92.22%
Proposed method	**Contiki Cooja**	**54256**	**9834**	**48391**	**95.34%**	**94.12%**

6 Conclusion

The goal of the research is to provide rank change threshold-based security solutions that monitor IoT network traffic and offer security against rank attacks. The execution of the suggested security solution is assessed in contiki cooja with three types of network scenarios, like non-rank attack, rank attack, and security solution with rank attacks. We also included a comparison with recently developed solutions and closely related work. Results from experiments demonstrate that the suggested system is capable of detecting rank attacks. As a result, rank attacks are depreciated since the proposed security solution uses the rank change threshold-based security solution to identify the rank attack. The performance of accuracy and reaction time was superior to other security solutions. In comparison to the closely linked work, the findings reveal that the average energy usage, memory usage (RAM/ROM), TPR, and TNR are comparable 47540 mJ, 9834/54256 in Byte, 95.34% and 94.12% respectively. In the future, the effort will incorporate the IoT network's lightweight security solution and evaluate the enhanced defence mechanism by fending off multiple mixed attacks.

Acknowledgments. The network security and systems lab, IIT Guwahati, India; Utkal University, Bhubaneswar, India; and BPUT, Bhubaneswar, India have all been the sites of the study activity. IIT Guwahati, Utkal University, Bhubaneswar, and BPUT, Bhubaneswar are all thanked by the authors for their assistance.

References

1. Ashton, K., et al.: That 'internet of things' thing. RFID J. **22**(7), 97–114 (2009)
2. Sharma, N., Shamkuwar, M., Singh, I.: The history, present and future with IoT. In: Balas, V.E., Solanki, V.K., Kumar, R., Khari, M. (eds.) Internet of Things and Big Data Analytics for Smart Generation. ISRL, vol. 154, pp. 27–51. Springer, Cham (2019). https://doi.org/10.1007/978-3-030-04203-5_3
3. Bhale, P., Dey, S., Biswas, S., Nandi, S.: Energy efficient approach to detect sinkhole attack using roving ids in 6lowpan network. In: Rautaray, S.S., Eichler, G., Erfurth, C., Fahrnberger, G. (eds.) I4CS 2020. CCIS, vol. 1139, pp. 187–207. Springer, Cham (2020). https://doi.org/10.1007/978-3-030-37484-6_11
4. Kharrufa, H., AlKashoash, H.A., Kemp, A.H.: RPL-based routing protocols in IoT applications: a review. IEEE Sens. J. **19**(15), 5952–5967 (2019)
5. Sheng, Z., Yang, S., Yu, Y., Vasilakos, A.V., McCann, J.A., Leung, K.K.: A survey on the IETF protocol suite for the internet of things: standards, challenges, and opportunities. IEEE Wirel. Commun. **20**(6), 91–98 (2013)
6. Zhang, Z.K., Cho, M.C.Y., Wang, C.W., Hsu, C.W., Chen, C.K., Shieh, S.: IoT security: ongoing challenges and research opportunities. In: 2014 IEEE 7th International Conference on Service-Oriented Computing and Applications, pp. 230–234. IEEE (2014)
7. Bhale, P., Biswas, S., Nandi, S.: Liene: lifetime enhancement for 6lowpan network using clustering approach use case: smart agriculture. In: Krieger, U.R., Eichler, G., Erfurth, C., Fahrnberger, G. (eds.) I4CS 2021. CCIS, vol. 1404, pp. 59–75. Springer, Cham (2021). https://doi.org/10.1007/978-3-030-75004-6_5
8. Kuna, B., Fu, A., Susilo, W., Yu, S., Gao, Y.: A survey of remote attestation in internet of things: attacks, countermeasures, and prospects. Comput. Secur. **112**, 102498 (2022)
9. Bang, A.O., Rao, U.P., Kaliyar, P., Conti, M.: Assessment of routing attacks and mitigation techniques with RPL control messages: A survey. ACM Comput. Surv. (CSUR) **55**(2), 1–36 (2022)
10. Alsukayti, I.S., Singh, A.: A lightweight scheme for mitigating RPL version number attacks in IoT networks. IEEE Access (2022)
11. Ray, D., Bhale, P., Biswas, S., Nandi, S., Mitra, P.: DAISS: design of an attacker identification scheme in COAP request/response spoofing. In: TENCON 2021–2021 IEEE Region 10 Conference (TENCON), pp. 941–946. IEEE (2021)
12. Goyal, M., Dutta, M.: Intrusion detection of wormhole attack in IoT: a review. In: 2018 International Conference on Circuits and Systems in Digital Enterprise Technology (ICCSDET), pp. 1–5. IEEE (2018)
13. Krčo, S., Pokrić, B., Carrez, F.: Designing IoT architecture (s): a European perspective. In: 2014 IEEE World Forum on Internet of Things (WF-IoT), pp. 79–84. IEEE (2014)
14. Radanliev, P., De Roure, D., Nicolescu, R., Huth, M.: A reference architecture for integrating the Industrial Internet of Things in the Industry 4.0. arXiv preprint arXiv:1903.04369 (2019)
15. Nandhini, P., Kuppuswami, S., Malliga, S.: Energy efficient thwarting rank attack from RPL based IoT networks: a review. Materials Today: Proceedings (2021)
16. Raoof, A., Matrawy, A., Lung, C.H.: Routing attacks and mitigation methods for RPL-based internet of things. IEEE Commun. Surv. Tutor. **21**(2), 1582–1606 (2018)
17. Kamble, A., Malemath, V.S., Patil, D.: Security attacks and secure routing protocols in RPL-based Internet of Things: survey. In: 2017 International Conference on Emerging Trends and Innovation in ICT (ICEI), pp. 33–39. IEEE (2017)
18. Le, A., Loo, J., Chai, K.K., Aiash, M.: A specification-based IDS for detecting attacks on RPL-based network topology. Information **7**(2), 25 (2016)

19. Perazzo, P., Vallati, C., Anastasi, G., Dini, G.: DIO suppression attack against routing in the internet of things. IEEE Commun. Lett. **21**(11), 2524–2527 (2017)
20. Wallgren, L., Raza, S., Voigt, T.: Routing attacks and countermeasures in the RPL- based internet of things. Int. J. Distrib. Sens. Netw. **9**(8), 794326 (2013)
21. Glissa, G., Rachedi, A., Meddeb, A.: A secure routing protocol based on RPL for Internet of Things. In: 2016 IEEE Global Communications Conference (GLOBE-COM), pp. 1–7. IEEE (2016)
22. Osman, M., He, J., Mokbal, F.M.M., Zhu, N., Qureshi, S.: Ml-LGBM: a machine learning model based on light gradient boosting machine for the detection of version number attacks in RPL-based networks. IEEE Access **9**, 83654–83665 (2021)
23. Sahay, R., Geethakumari, G., Mitra, B.: A novel block chain based framework to secure IoT-LLNS against routing attacks. Computing **102**(11), 2445–2470 (2020)
24. Le, A., Loo, J., Luo, Y., Lasebae, A.: Specification-based IDS for securing RPL from topology attacks. In: 2011 IFIP Wireless Days (WD), pp. 1–3. IEEE (2011)
25. Pongle, P., Chavan, G.: A survey: attacks on RPL and 6LoWPAN in IoT. In: 2015 International Conference on Pervasive Computing (ICPC), pp. 1–6. IEEE (2015)
26. Cervantes, C., Poplade, D., Nogueira, M., Santos, A.: Detection of sinkhole attacks for supporting secure routing on 6lowpan for internet of things. In: 2015 IFIP/IEEE International Symposium on Integrated Network Management (IM), pp. 606–611. IEEE (2015)
27. Le, A., Loo, J., Lasebae, A., Vinel, A., Chen, Y., Chai, M.: The impact of rank attack on network topology of routing protocol for low-power and lossy networks. IEEE Sens. J. **13**(10), 3685–3692 (2013)
28. Rai, K.K., Asawa, K.: Impact analysis of rank attack with spoofed IP on routing in 6lowpan network. In: 2017 Tenth International Conference on Contemporary Computing (IC3), pp. 1–5. IEEE (2017)
29. Shukla, S., Singh, S., Kumar, A., Matam, R.: Defending against increased rank attack on RPL in low-power wireless networks. In: 2018 Fifth International Conference on Parallel, Distributed and Grid Computing (PDGC), pp. 246–251. IEEE (2018)
30. IoT-Simulator: Cooja. https://anrg.usc.edu/contiki/index.php/Cooja~Simulator. Accessed 29 July 2019
31. Bhale, P., Biswas, S., Nandi, S.: Ml for IEEE 802.15. 4e/TSCH: Energy efficient approach to detect DDoS attack using machine learning. In: 2021 International Wireless Communications and Mobile Computing (IWCMC), pp. 1477–1482. IEEE (2021)

Energy Efficient Adaptive Mobile Wireless Sensor Network in Smart Monitoring Applications

Seli Mohapatra[1,2](✉) and Prafulla Kumar Behera[1]

[1] Utkal University, Vani Bihar, Bhubaneswar, Odisha, India
selimohapatra@gmail.com
[2] C. V. Raman Global University, Mahura, Bhubaneswar, Odisha, India

Abstract. The Mobile Wireless Sensor Networks (MWSNs) owe its name due to mobile sinks or mobile sensor nodes as one category of heterogeneous networks with induced mobility of nodes making it autonomous and more suitable for smart monitoring applications. The possible application in their implementation context in home and disaster management involves the integration of mobile WSN in ubiquitous computing. With the enormous growth of smart devices, the data sharing among entities lead to hotspot problem nearby sink, that requires a powerful computing, communicating and storage capable mobile devices, can benefit network in terms of scalability, efficiency and data delivery speed. In this paper, we proposed an adaptive heterogeneous multi-tiered architecture based mobile sensor network and analyzed its performance and routing efficiency with respect to the static wireless sensor network. The performance metrics used help in validating our proposed method suitable for smart data collecting and dissemination for monitoring applications. Again, the low power wireless personal area network (6LoWPAN) plays a vital role in interconnecting these IoT devices and implementing mobility of nodes with appropriate data rate for robust communication and achieving desired Quality of Service.

Keywords: Mobile wireless sensor network · Mobile hotspot · Heterogeneous multi-tier model · Clustering · M-LEACH

1 Introduction

Smart Monitoring Applications is a great revolutionary aspect of the decade, made more accountable and intelligent by embedding sensors and providing communication among the network. The integration of IoT(Internet of Things) with wireless sensor networks gives a vast range of application perspectives for monitoring like smart home, field or environment monitoring, smart disaster management, or industrial automation. Moreover, various companies have also supported the integration of IoT with wireless sensor network. The crucial element of the Internet of Things is wireless communication across different platforms and devices without human-to-human or human-to-device interaction. It is important to think of a quick and flexible way to experiment with the

© The Author(s), under exclusive license to Springer Nature Switzerland AG 2022
M. Panda et al. (Eds.): ICIICC 2022, CCIS 1737, pp. 222–235, 2022.
https://doi.org/10.1007/978-3-031-23233-6_17

behaviour of an application, a protocol, and in a repeatable manner due to unforeseen events and the physical features of wireless propagation and the internet of things. Thus, it becomes a multi-objective optimization problem, resolved by constrained numerical methods. To achieve the coverage as a major objective, connectivity and mobility are considered as constraint, including energy optimization and improvement in network lifetime. As a result, the Mobile Wireless Sensor Network coordinates the operation of sensors to enable long-term monitoring of the environment over a vast surface area [1]. The sinks and sensor nodes are presumed to be static in the conventional wireless sensor network with heterogeneous nodes. These devices are energy efficient, reliable, and commercial implementation is straightforward in their homogeneous counterpart. However, in a large-scale network and real-time monitoring session, the static network lacks data gathering and data dissemination. Thus, the self-organizing robots or randomly deployed nodes that can be made mobile under certain circumstances become more effective leads the implementation of mobile wireless sensor network [2]. Finally, the integration of two distinct network entities, such as the data acquisition network and a data dissemination network, seems to be how WSNs are best defined at a higher level. Due to the numerous technologies involved, it might be challenging to choose the components work for such complicated networks [3]. In order to create a consistent, reliable, and strong overall system, these networks are monitored and controlled by the control center. as shown in Fig. 1.

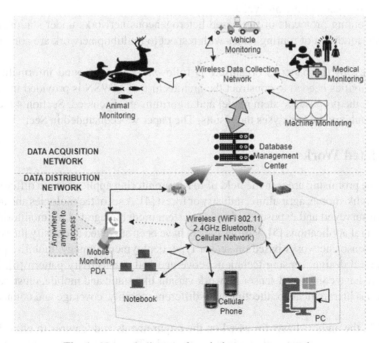

Fig. 1. Network diagram for wireless sensor networks

The major challenges in integrating the MWSN to IoT is the data collection and data sharing with energy management. Hence, various topology control and routing schemes based on clustering has been incorporated. The issue we deal with here begins with a coverage area's random distribution of heterogeneous nodes. The first step is to organize the networked in different cluster groups depending on energy distribution among nodes. Assuming the nodes in a group contain at least one cluster head or routing node and other sensing nodes, the network gets connected as a whole including the sink node. However, some routing nodes undergoes controlled mobility pattern depending on the data dissemination to the sink node, that aims to integrate the Internet of Things with the Mobile Wireless Sensor Network.

The main contribution to our paper is to exploit the IoT based applications on MWSN (mobile wireless sensor network) context which can be possible with the node heterogeneity in mobile sensors. The main objective of our paper proposals are summarized as follows.

- A system model for level based heterogeneous mobile network is proposed that signifies a better QoS.
- To initiate the criteria of energy and mobility model on heterogeneous network on the basis of threshold parameter and received signal strength indicator.
- The performance parameters for energy utilization and lifetime maximization in heterogeneous network of different variants suitable for basic IoT applications with static and mobile sensors are analyzed.
- Other routing protocols of tier based heterogeneous networks under stationary and mobile condition of routing nodes with respect to multihop network are compared.

The rest of the paper is organised as follows. The background information and related activities needed to construct the architecture of MWSN is provided in Sect. 2. In Sect. 3, the proposed system model and algorithm are discussed. Section 4 then sets up the simulation and analyses the results. The paper was concluded in Sect. 5.

2   Related Works

One of the promising areas in the field of IoT is monitoring applications in different real time fields like home, agriculture, industry or forest [4]. A set of technologies and devices has been surveyed and exposed to develop system model integrated for monitoring and architectural applications [5]. Various papers have been surveyed to classify the types of wireless sensor networks based on sensor type, deployment strategy, mobility pattern, architectural design, sensing technique, coverage and connectivity pattern [6]. In our paper, we have considered sensor network variant like static and mobile, clustered heterogeneous hierarchical architecture with different mobility, coverage and connectivity pattern.

In [7], the authors have discussed on the requirements and features to offer diverse and heterogeneous tools and services on testbeds. But there existed some gaps and difficulties to choose a static or mobile sensor network depending on needs. However, the authors from [8] focused on the deployment and working of static wireless sensor in homogeneous and heterogeneous scenario.

The coverage and connectivity among the nodes are important perspective of sensor networking and has been addressed by several authors in different methods adapted. In [9], authors developed a decentralized solution for adjustment and improving the coverage and connectivity for prolonging the lifetime in sensor network. Snagwan et. al [10] addresses the problem of supervision of at least one node at targeted region. The sensing ability and energy consumption features are described to define the network lifetime. However, based on the category of sensor network the mobility based on placement of nodes in robots and its coverage pattern is observed in [11]. The author Tirandazi et. al [12] created a dynamic network by robot path planning algorithm where the nodes are placed on mobile robots in two steps. With local phase and global phases analysis reveals the combined connected coverage performance that effect the overall network operation.

The spatially distributed set of autonomous connected sensor nodes create hotspot problems near the sink node. So, the dynamic heterogeneous network issues some routing strategy to mitigate this problem and enhance the energy efficiency and network longevity. The authors Khalaf et. al in [13] explained the dynamic and unequal clustering technique by providing solution to hotspot problem from various parameters like cluster head selection, number of clusters, zone formation and different routing parameters. Hence, clustering methods become an important and reliable method in static and mobile wireless sensor network which various authors have focused with different routing strategies. The Cluster Head selection methods are addressed by many researchers based on different criterion over LEACH (Low-energy adaptive clustering hierarchy). The distance-based approach [14] optimizes energy, in Cluster Head (CH) Selection, by equal distribution of network load. The residual energy distribution for CH selection is another important criterion explained by Behera et.al in [15]. Similarly, the statistical methods have also significantly improved the network lifetime and energy efficiency as discussed in the paper Mohapatra et al. [16].

The major contributions of this paper are as follows.

- The network development is initiated with a random deployment of nodes which may not be connected. Thus, the first objective is to ensure the full connectivity among the nodes within appropriate coverage level.
- Based on communication range cluster groups are formed with selection of Cluster Head based on statistical based residual energy of nodes.
- The data collected from remote node are disseminated at the sink node via Cluster head. However, if the communication distance between CH and Sink node is large, then in accordance to greedy algorithm, some group of nodes or the Cluster Head node provide adaptive logic in greedy direction towards Sink Node for further processing.

The performance evaluation of our proposed method then evaluated with two basic scenarios, with respect to static and mobile wireless sensor network with or without clustering.

3 Proposed Method

The design of low power and low delay mobile wireless sensor network is a challenging task, as in such network's topology is moderately dynamics and the mobile sensor nodes are equipped with poor sensing and processing capabilities. So, it is required to develop a hierarchical or tiered based heterogeneous model with controlled mobility to achieve the requirement of energy consumption and data delay. In the paper, we proposed a mobile wireless sensor network model with three tier architecture in which some sensor nodes are mobile by adaptive method as discussed below. For this work we have considered following assumptions.

- After the random deployment of nodes, the node positions are determined on initialization. The heterogeneity is maintained based on non-uniform energy distribution.
- Nodes with higher energy levels are preferred for cluster head formation. However, it is assumed that the distribution of nodes is such that in each group at least one CH is possible. Also, these nodes are GPS enabled to track the location.
- Based on the distance of nodes to higher energy node Cluster Head or Sink Node the node gets mobility associated with greedy algorithm to destination.
- The sink node is allocated at the center of the network and is considered as the base station.

3.1 Mobile Sensor Node Architecture

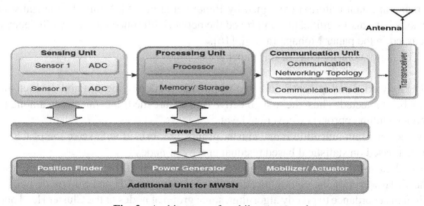

Fig. 2. Architecture of mobile sensor node

The mobile sensor node architecture is almost identical to that of a regular sensor node, with the inclusion of a few extra elements like locators, power sources, and mobilizers. The sensing unit uses one or more sensors to provide basic sensing. Similar to this, the processing unit contains memory and motes processors to execute signal processing on digitized data with considering data aggregation into account. Once more, the communication unit identifies the routing path and chooses the appropriate radio range.

To identify the position, generate more electricity for nodes like solar cells, and control the mobility of sensor nodes, additional units are however employed. The architecture of Mobile sensor node is shown in Fig. 2. The majority of MWSN considers large-scale applications made up of numerous sensor and sink nodes, where the mobility of the nodes depends on the application's specific requirements. The key factor for the design of a MWSN are scalability and topology, data routing, mobility and residual energy utilization [17]. Our proposed model is based on three phases (a)Establishment Phase (b)Routing and Clustering phase.

3.1.1 Establishment Phase

The topology of MWSN is considered dynamic as the connectivity among the CHs to sensor nodes varies with time due to its mobility as and when desired[18]. The position finder helps to place the nodes throughout the area is proper distribution. The sensor nodes can be placed distributed randomly. So, if N nodes are put in an area of $A = LxL$ sq. m, so the sensor node density can be $\rho = \frac{N}{A}$. The sensing range r, determines the forwarding of data between nodes which must be at most the communication range 2r. If the nodes are uniformly distributed then the probability that there are m nodes within the space S is Poisson distributed as

$$P(m) = \frac{(\rho S)^m}{m!} e^{-\rho S} \tag{1}$$

where $S = \pi r^2$ for 2-D Space. Thus, the probability that the monitored space is covered by at least one sensor node is given by

$$Pcov = 1 - P(0) = 1 - e^{-\rho S} \tag{2}$$

. The sensor node computes the distance between its post deployment location and the locations associated with the pre distributed units. The smaller distance having higher priority over larger distance between adjacent nodes.

3.1.2 Routing and Clustering Phase

Another essential area for mobile WSN is routing and clustering. The network is driven into a structure by the routing protocols to achieve stability, scalability, and energy efficiency. The cluster head, nodes with high residual energy, coordinate cluster operations and forward information among sensor nodes and sink nodes. This class of routing protocol causes clustering. These cluster heads can be seen as dynamic, nevertheless, depending on the situation. Mobility to the sensor nodes can be performed using mobilizers to change places, wheels, or robots through the use of an suitable mobility pattern. [19]. Mobile nodes' dynamic topology depicts how routing, MAC, and physical characteristic implementation are used in the network. Again, static WSN is inefficient owing to energy exhaustion or device failure, but MWSN reorganizes the network. The ideal routing protocol is one that never uses up too much network resources while still covering all network states. The MWSN routing strategies can be both traditional and optimized. When designing a routing protocol for MWSNs, consideration is given to the network topology, sensor node mobility, energy consumption, network coverage, data transmission techniques, quality of service (QoS), connectivity, data aggregation, sensor node and communication link heterogeneity, scalability, and security. As a result, it's crucial to select a mobile node that can prolong network lifetime and attain better energy efficiency [20].

Consider a network with N sensor nodes which is deployed over the sensor field with remote/sensing nodes followed by advanced excluding the Sink Node. The levelled based heterogeneous nodes are defined as

$$N_r = 0.7 * N \text{ and } N_a = 0.3 * N \tag{3}$$

where Nr represents normal nodes with 20% being GPS enabled and rest 80% are without GPS and Na are the advanced node.

After deployment the nodes configure their respective locations with coordinate value (x_i, y_i). If r_c is the communication range and r_s is the sensing range of node N. then

$$r_c = 10^{\frac{P_t - P_{th}}{10\eta}} \tag{4}$$

$$r_c \leq 2r_s \tag{5}$$

with P_t being transmitter power and P_{th} being minimum threshold received power required by nodes and η is the path loss factor.

The network nodes begin monitoring events that take place within sensing range and report to CH using single-hop and multi-hop methods. However, nodes may cluster in some areas and may generate coverage holes where nodes are not available when sensors are randomly distributed in hostile target fields, resulting in network partitioning. Therefore, it is necessary to find and fix the network's gaps. In order to locate the holes, it is reported to the base station or sink. In order to obtain a complete connectivity network, the nodes are re-localized by introducing mobility into advanced nodes or sink nodes. Either the sink node instructs the CH to travel a specific distance till the entire network is joined to solve this issue.

When remote nodes and reference nodes are deployed at random, the nodes are localized by calculating their distance from reference nodes using the total of their shortest-path communication ranges. And utilizing the Angle of Arrival approach to assess the sites. Nodes also identify coverage gaps and unconnected networks by examining the distribution of nearby neighbor nodes. To achieve the desired coverage, node density should be properly considered as in Eq. (6).

$$\rho = \frac{N}{A} = \frac{Nr + Na}{\pi r_0^2} \tag{6}$$

where $r_0 = \frac{r_s}{1.066}$ =Minimal sensing Radius of heterogeneous nodes.

Every initial GPS enabled node broadcasts location information (x,y) and r_{c_i} to neighbour nodes. The neighbour nodes store this information and add its own r_{c_j}. If $r_{c_i} + r_{c_j} \leq r_{c_{th}}$, then nodes disseminate them together with reference node positions. By attempting to segregate only the nearest reference nodes, the $r_{c_{th}}$ minimizes the impact of asymmetric bent routes on distance estimations. Following the submission of this data, neighbour nodes check to see if the reference node information has already been saved in their neighbor data. The received reference node location and Critical Range sum are updated in the neighbor information if it corresponds to a new node. The received sum of r_c is compared to the stored value if the obtained node information has already been saved, and the lowest of these two r_c values is saved along with the location data. Each node will have the locations of the reference nodes and the associated minimum value of the sum of the r_c from the reference node to itself at the completion of this stage [21].

4   Simulation and Result Analysis

In this section, we have simulated and analyzed our proposed method for various performance metrics with its static sensor network counterpart. We have considered LEACH and SEP under static scenario and with M-LEACH as mobile scenario and compared them with our proposed implemented Mob M-LEACH.

4.1   Simulation Set Up

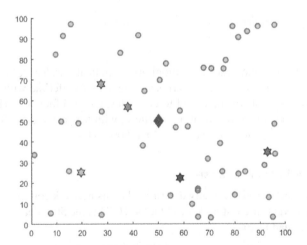

Fig. 3. A three tier heterogeneous network

The simulation work is carried out in MATLAB2020b with Intel core i5 processor, 64-bit operating system with 1.8 GHz frequency [22]. After the random deployment of nodes, the three-tiered heterogeneous network is represented as in Fig. 3 and the required simulation parameters is cited in Table 1.

4.2   Experimental Analysis

The paper focus of two basic simulation environment, static or dynamic sensor node in small coverage area like smart home or office and adaptive mobile sensor network

Table 1. Simulation parameters

Sl No.	Parameters	Font Size and Style
1	Number of nodes (N)	10, 50, 100, 200, 400, 600, 800, 1000
2	Topography	$500 \times 500 \ m^2$, $500 \times 500 \ m^2$
3	Communication range (d_0)	87 m
4	Simulation time	300 s
5	No. of rounds(r)	6000
6	Initial energy of normal node (E_0)	1J
7	Packet Length	500 bits, 127 bytes
8	Mobility model	Controlled with velocity 10 m/s
9	E_{TX} (nJ/bit)	50
10	E_{RX} (nJ/bit)	50
11	E_{elec} (nJ/bit)	50
12	E_{DA} (nJ/bit/f rame)	5
13	ε_{fs} (pJ/bit/m2)	10
14	ε_{mp} (pJ/bit/m4)	0.0013

in large coverage area like smart farm monitoring applications. Thus, the performance metrics [23] considered for these scenarios are the network lifetime with network convergence factor, speed of coverage, end-to-end delay, energy efficiency. The analysis of the mobility is based on above mentioned criteria with $500 \ m^2$ and $5000 \ m^2$ coverage area with network size variations between 50 to 800 nodes.

4.2.1 Network Lifetime Analysis

The lifetime of a network is basically determined by its network convergence expressed in Eq. 1 where LND is the last node dead factor, HND is the 50% dead factor and FND is the first node dead factor.

$$NCI = \frac{LND - HND}{HND - FND} \tag{7}$$

The network lifetime indicates the longevity of sensor nodes of the network which can be illustrated from the availability of nodes to carry out data processing task in the network. As shown in Fig. 4(a) our proposed MSWN can sustain for large rounds of operation for performing its task as the all-dead nodes are obtained considering maximum rounds than other methods. However, the network lifetime is better analyzed from its convergence factor as shown in Fig. 4(b). It is seen that the network sustainability is better in our proposed MWSN in comparison to other protocols for any variation of nodes. However, in a coverage area of 100 sqm, as the number of nodes increases the convergence factor decreases due to inefficient data handling capability with more interference levels. It also ensures that to implement an IoT in coverage area of 100 sqm. we need to choose a proper scalable network suitable for smart applications.

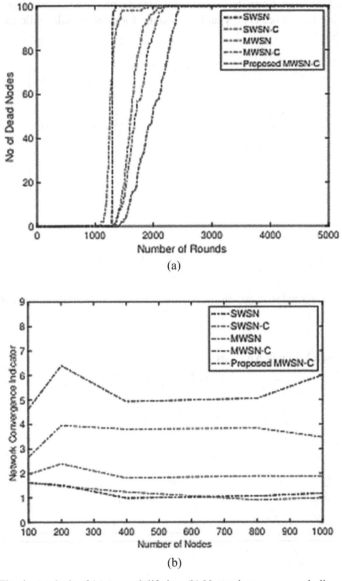

(a)

(b)

Fig. 4. Analysis of (a) network lifetime (b) Network convergence indicator

4.2.2 Residual Energy Analysis

The residual energy analysis indicates the energy remains in the entire network by advanced node for different coverage area. Figure 5 represents the residual energy distribution over 100 sqm. From the graph it indicates the proposed mobile sensor network with clustering have more energy and can sustain for more rounds while choosing the cluster heads.

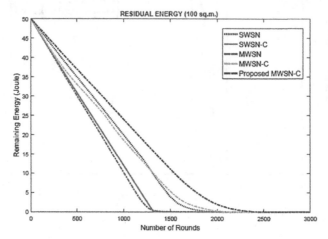

Fig. 5. Analysis of residual energy distribution for 100 nodes in the entire network with 100 m^2

4.2.3 Network Latency Analysis

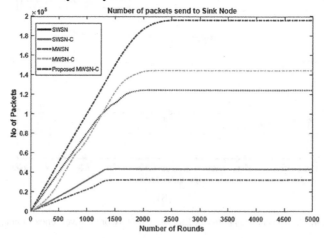

Fig. 6. Analysis of packets sent to sink node from CH with coverage area 100 m^2

The network latency analysis directs the way in which robust data packets reach the server as fast as possible. This factor signifies under the above-mentioned criteria, the basic monitoring applications must utilize the method where data gathering and delivery to sink node should be very fast with minimal loss [23]. In the paper, we compared our proposed model with the its static and mobile sensor network Fig. 6 indicates the packets sent to the sink node for the entire simulation duration. It is observed the adaptive movement of sensor nodes in our proposed method gives the maximum data to the sink node for any coverage area. Thus, it becomes suitable for monitoring based IoT applications in different scenarios. Similarly, the time elapsed for network indicates the computational complexity as shown in Fig. 7.

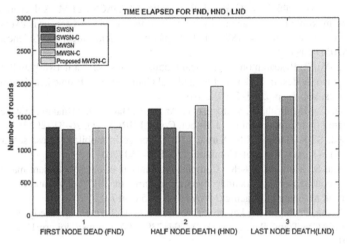

Fig. 7. Analysis of time elapsed for data delivery of network with coverage area 100 m^2

5   Conclusion

With the advent of new technologies in the last few years, the integration of IoT and Mobile Wireless Sensor Network has envisaged the ability of entities and environment to recognize, communicate and share the data. The heterogeneity of nodes in an adaptive mobile platform can be controlled via remote access. In this paper, we have proposed a new adaptive method to develop mobile wireless senor network, specifically designed for monitoring based IoT applications. The architectural implementation of layered based clustered heterogeneous network with adaptive mobility of sensor node, followed by analysis of performance related issues on the aspect of mobility is discussed. It is observed that, our proposed hierarchical clustered mobile wireless sensor network is more efficient than its static and mobile sensor network and it is also scalable to a variety of network size. It reveals the fact that our proposed model is more useful in different IoT based monitoring applications, from smart home to smart farm monitoring scenario. Again, the energy efficiency and data dissemination over the network properly address the effective data flow throughout the network to achieve the desired quality of service (QoS).

References

1. Reddy, V., Gayathri, P.: Integration of internet of things with wireless sensor network. Int. J. Elec. Comput. Eng. (IJECE), **9**, 439 (2019)
2. Tonneau, A.-S., Mitton, N., Vandaele, J.: How to choose an experimentation platform for wireless sensor networks? a survey on static and mobile wireless sensor network experimentation facilities
3. Mhatre, V., Rosenberg, C.: Homogeneous vs heterogeneous clustered sensor networks: a comparative study. In: 2004 IEEE International Conference on Communications (IEEE Cat. No.04CH37577), vol. 6, pp. 3646–3651 (2004)
4. Etancelin, J.-M., Fabbri, A., Guinand, F., Rosalie, M.: DACYCLEM: A decentralized algorithm for maximizing coverage and lifetime in a mobile wireless sensor network. Ad Hoc-Networks, vol. 87, pp. 174–187 (2019). https://www.sciencedirect.com/science/article/pii/S1570870518309430
5. Chen, X., Yu, P.: Research on hierarchical mobile wireless sensor network architecture with mobile sensor nodes. In: 2010 3rd International Conference on Biomedical Engineering and Informatics, vol. 7, pp. 2863–2867 (2010)
6. Hermanu, C., Maghfiroh, H., Santoso, H.P., Arifin, Z., Harsito, C.: Dual mode system of smart home based on internet of things. J. Robot. Control (JRC) **3**(1), 26–31 (2022)
7. Mohamed, S.M., Hamza, H.S., Saroit, I.A.: Coverage in mobile wireless sensor networks (M-WSN): a survey. Comput. Commun. **110**, 133–150 (2017)
8. Mohapatra, S., Mohapatra, R.K.: Comparative analysis of energy efficient mac protocol in heterogeneous sensor network under dynamic scenario. In; 2017 2nd International Conference on Man and Machine Interfacing (MAMI), pp. 1–5 (2017)
9. Liu, D., Ning, P.: Improving key predistribution with deployment knowledge in static sensor networks. ACM Trans. Sen. Netw. **1**(2), 204–239 (2005). https://doi.org/10.1145/1105688.1105691
10. Huang, C.-F., Tseng, Y.-C., Wu, H.-L.: Distributed protocols for ensuring both coverage and connectivity of a wireless sensor network. ACM Trans. Sen. Netw.**3**(1), p. 5–es (2007). https://doi.org/10.1145/1210669.1210674
11. Sangwan, A., Singh, R.P.: Survey on coverage problems in wireless sensor networks. Wireless Pers. Commun. **80**(4), 1475–1500 (2015)
12. Tirandazi, P., Rahiminasab, A., Ebadi, M.: An efficient coverage and connectivity algorithm based on mobile robots for wireless sensor networks. J. Ambient Intell. Humanized Comput., 1–23 (2022)
13. Khalaf, O.I., Romero, C.A.T., Hassan, S., Iqbal, M.T.: Mitigating hotspot issues in heterogeneous wireless sensor networks. J. Sens. (2022)
14. Rajput, M., Sharma, S.K., Khatri, P.: Energy-Efficient multihop cluster routing protocol for WSN. In: Poonia, R.C., Singh, V., Singh Jat, D., Diván, M.J., Khan, M.S. (eds.) Proceedings of Third International Conference on Sustainable Computing. Advances in Intelligent Systems and Computing, vol 1404, pp. 77–84. Springer, Singapore (2022). https://doi.org/10.1007/978-981-16-4538-9_8
15. Behera, T.M., Mohapatra, S.K., Samal, U.C., Khan, M.S., Daneshmand, M., Gandomi, A.H.: Residual energy-based cluster-head selection in WSNs for IoT application. IEEE Int. Things J. **6**(3), 5132–5139 (2019)
16. Mohapatra, S., Behera, P.K.: Statistical approach based cluster head selection in heterogeneous networks for IoT applications. In: Behera, P.K., Sethi, P.C. (eds.) Digital Democracy – IT for Change. CSI 2020. Communications in Computer and Information Science, vol 1372, pp. 77–84. Springer, Singapore (2021). https://doi.org/10.1007/978-981-16-2723-1_4

17. Atay, N., Bayazit, B.: Mobile wireless sensor network connectivity repair with K-Redundancy. In: Chirikjian, G.S., Choset, H., Morales, M., Murphey, T. (eds.) Algorithmic Foundation of Robotics VIII. Springer Tracts in Advanced Robotics, vol 57, pp. 35–49. Springer, Heidelberg (2009). https://doi.org/10.1007/978-3-642-00312-7_3
18. Sahoo, P.K., Hwang, I.-S.: Collaborative localization algorithms for wireless sensor networks with reduced localization error. Sensors **11**(10), 9989–10009 (2011). https://www.mdpi.com/1424-8220/11/10/9989
19. Buehrer, R.M., Wymeersch, H., Vaghefi, R.M.: Collaborative sensor network localization: algorithms and practical issues. Proc. IEEE **106**(6), 1089–1114 (2018)
20. Sara, G.S., Sridharan, D.: Routing in mobile wireless sensor network: a survey. Telecommun. Syst. **57**(1), 51–79 (2014)
21. Tolba, F.D., Ajib, W., Obaid, A.: Distributed clustering algorithm for mobile wireless sensors networks. SENSORS. IEEE **2013**, 1–4 (2013)
22. Amine, D., Nassreddine, B., Bouabdellah, K.: Energy efficient and safe weighted clustering algorithm for mobile wireless sensor networks. Proc. Comput. Sci. **34**, 63–70 (2014). The 9th International Conference on Future Networks and Communications (FNC 2014)/The 11th International Conference on Mobile Systems and Pervasive Computing (MobiSPC 2014)/Affiliated Workshops. https://www.sciencedirect.com/science/article/pii/S1877050914008953
23. Mohapatra, S., Kanungo, P.: Performance analysis of AODV, DSR, OLSR and DSDV routing protocols using NS2 simulator. In: Procedia Engineering, vol. 30, pp. 69–76 (2012). International Conference on Communication Technology and System Design (2011). https://www.sciencedirect.com/science/article/pii/S1877705812008454

Orthogonal Chirp Division Multiplexing: An Emerging Multi Carrier Modulation Scheme

Mohit Kumar Singh$^{(\boxtimes)}$ and Ashish Goel

ECE Department, Jaypee Institute of Information Technology, Noida, India
{19402019,ashish.goel}@mail.jiit.ac.in

Abstract. OCDM, a MCM scheme compatible to widespread OFDM, has been proposed in the literature. It provides maximum spectral efficiency for chirp spread spectrum system and outperforms over OFDM. In this paper, we have discussed the generation of OCDM system and its implementation using OFDM system with some minor correction. The computational complexity analysis of OCDM system is also carried out in this paper and its comparison with OFDM system is also done. It has been found that like OFDM, OCDM system also suffers from the problem of high PAPR. Some of the popular schemes for PAPR reduction applicable to OCDM system have been discussed and its performance analysis in terms of PAPR and BER performance is also carried out in this paper. Further, applications of OCDM for wireless communication, optical fiber communication, UWA communication and MIMO system is also presented in detail.

Keywords: Chirp Signal · DFnT · OCDM · PAPR

1 Introduction

Chirp, a kind of signal whose phase changes with time, being of spread spectrum nature guarantees secure and robust communication. X. Ouyang et al. [1] introduced an Multi Carrier Modulation (MCM) technique for high-speed communication and named it Orthogonal Chirp Division Multiplexing (OCDM). In OCDM, N orthogonal chirps of same bandwidth are multiplexed. Fresnel transform is the fundamental mechanism behind OCDM. Implementation of OCDM system in digital domain is obtained by Discrete Fresnel Transform (DFnT). At the transmitter side, OCDM signal is generated using Inverse Discrete Fresnel Transform (IDFnT) while at the receive side, OCDM signal is recovered using DFnT. Similar to Orthogonal Frequency Division Multiplexing (OFDM) [2], OCDM system sends the modulated signals block-wise. Between two consecutive blocks, Guard Interval (GI) is inserted to avoid Inter Symbol Interference (ISI). To fill the GI, Zero Padding (ZP) and Cyclic Prefix (CP) both can be used. For modulation, amplitude and/or phase of each chirp are modulated therefore QAM and PSK can be used as modulation scheme in OCDM system. Being a MCM scheme, OCDM system also suffers from high Peak-to-Average Power Ratio (PAPR). Various PAPR reduction, equalization and channel estimation schemes presented in the literature for OFDM system are applicable for OCDM system also [1] and various precoding matrices can be used to implement precoded OCDM [3].

© The Author(s), under exclusive license to Springer Nature Switzerland AG 2022
M. Panda et al. (Eds.): ICIICC 2022, CCIS 1737, pp. 236–246, 2022.
https://doi.org/10.1007/978-3-031-23233-6_18

Partial Transmit Sequences (PTS) [4] is an attractive distortion less PAPR reduction technique because there is no limitation on number of subcarriers but the transmitter is required to send the optimum phase rotation factors, which is used to provide the minimum PAPR, to the receiver. These phase factors are known as Side Information (SI). Sending SI to receiver reduces the spectrum efficiency and it is very difficult to receive the correct SI in multipath environment. Different PTS based schemes have been proposed to eliminate the requirement of transmitting SI to the receiver. Multipoint square mapping (MSM) combined with PTS (M-PTS) [5] and Concentric Circle Mapping-based PTS (CCM-PTS) [6] are two of them.

In this paper, authors have presented the overview of OCDM along with its applications in various communication system. The main contribution of this paper is to analyze the performance of OCDM system using PTS based PAPR reduction schemes like M-PTS and CCM-PTS. Computational complexity of these PTS based systems are also analyzed and their PAPR reduction capabilities along with their SER performance over AWGN and Rayleigh fading channels are also given. OFDM is also simulated for comparison. PAPR performance of OCDM and OFDM is same without any PAPR reduction scheme. PTS, M-PTS and CCM-PTS provide almost same reduction in PAPR for OCDM and OFDM both. SER performance of OCDM with PTS, M-PTS and CCM-PTS is identical to the performance of OFDM with PTS, M-PTS and CCM-PTS respectively over AWGN channel. Over multipath Rayleigh fading channel, performance of OCDM slightly degraded in the low SNR region whereas OCDM shows much better performance compared to OFDM in high SNR region.

Rest of the paper is arranged as follows: Sect. 2 explains the compatibility of OCDM with OFDM. Section 3 explains the computational complexity of OCDM. Section 4 provides various applications of OCDM. Section 5 provides results of computer simulation and finally conclusion is drawn in Sect. 6.

2   Compatibility with OFDM

The discrete time OCDM signal [1] is given by

$$x = \phi^H s \tag{1}$$

Here $s = \begin{bmatrix} s_0, s_1, s_2 \ldots \ldots, s_{N-1} \end{bmatrix}^T$ is information carrying symbol vector, $x = \begin{bmatrix} x_0, x_1, x_2 \ldots \ldots, x_{N-1} \end{bmatrix}^T$ is OCDM symbol vector and ϕ is DFnT matrix. The $(n, k)^{th}$ entry of $N \times N$ DFnT matrix ϕ is given by

$$\phi(n, k) = \frac{1}{\sqrt{N}} e^{-j\frac{\pi}{4}} X \begin{cases} e^{j\frac{\pi}{N}(n-k)^2} for\ even\ N \\ e^{j\frac{\pi}{N}\left(n-k+\frac{1}{2}\right)^2} for\ odd\ N \end{cases} \tag{2}$$

The discrete time OFDM signal is given by

$$y = W_N^{-nk} s \tag{3}$$

Here $y = [y_0, y_1, y_2 \ldots\ldots, y_{N-1}]^T$ is OFDM symbol vector and W_N^{nk} is DFT matrix. The $(n, k)^{th}$ entry of $N \times N$ DFT matrix W_N^{nk} is given by

$$W_N^{nk} = \frac{1}{\sqrt{N}} e^{-j\frac{2\pi}{N}nk} \tag{4}$$

Inspecting Eq. (2) and (4), we can say that DFnT in Eq. (2) consists of DFT of Eq. (4) with additional quadratic phases given by.

$$\Phi_1(n) = e^{-j\frac{\pi}{4}} X \begin{cases} e^{j\frac{\pi}{N}n^2} \ even\ N \\ e^{j\frac{\pi}{4N}} e^{j\frac{\pi}{N}(n^2+n)} \ odd\ N \end{cases} \tag{5}$$

and

$$\Phi_2(k) = \begin{cases} e^{j\frac{\pi}{N}k^2} \ even\ N \\ e^{j\frac{\pi}{N}(k^2-k)} \ odd\ N \end{cases} \tag{6}$$

So, one can find the DFnT using DFT in three steps:

Step 1: Multiple with quadratic phase Φ_1.

Step 2: Perform DFT by FFT algorithm.

Step 3: Multiple with 2nd quadratic phase Φ_2.

Here Φ_1 and Φ_2 are the diagonal matrices having m^{th} diagonal entries $\Phi_1(m)$ and $\Phi_2(m)$ respectively.

Using above three steps, one can integrate OCDM into the widespread OFDM system with minor modifications (colored boxes) as shown in Fig. 1. [1].

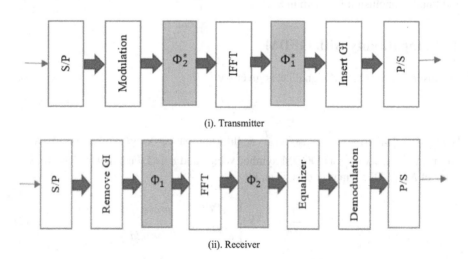

(i). Transmitter

(ii). Receiver

Fig. 1. OCDM Integration into OFDM System

3 Computational Complexity

Transmitter and receiver both are considered to compute the computational complexity of OCDM and OFDM with PTS, M-PTS and CCM-PTS schemes. Computational complexity is calculated by counting the total number of complex multiplications and additions.

3.1 Computational Complexity of OCDM

In OCDM, with N chirps and L oversampling factor, one LN point IDFnT is calculated for each sub-block at transmitter which require $2LN + \frac{1}{2}LN\log_2(LN)$ complex multiplications and $LN\log_2(LN)$ complex additions [1]. Therefore, for M sub-blocks, $2MLN + \frac{1}{2}MLN\log_2(LN)$ complex multiplications and $MLN\log_2(LN)$ complex additions are required. With K phase factors, K^{M-1} searches are performed to find the OCDM signal with minimum possible PAPR and $(M-1)LN$ complex additions are required to combine M sub-blocks per search [7]. Therefore, $K^{M-1}(M-1)LN$ complex additions are required to combine the sub-blocks in K^{M-1} searches. At the receiver, one LN point DFnT is calculated for OCDM symbol detection which requires $2LN + \frac{1}{2}LN\log_2(LN)$ complex multiplications and $LN\log_2(LN)$ complex additions and for demapping of information carrying symbols, DN complex multiplications and $2DN$ complex additions per OCDM symbol are also required [7]. Here D is the total number of decision regions.

Therefore, total number of complex multiplications and additions required in OCDM with PTS, M-PTS and CCM-PTS schemes are as follows:

Total complex multiplications: $2MLN + \frac{1}{2}MLN\log_2(LN) + 2LN + \frac{1}{2}LN\log_2(LN) + DN$.

Total complex additions: $MLN\log_2(LN) + K^{M-1}(M-1)LN + LN\log_2(LN) + 2DN$.

3.2 Computational Complexity of OFDM

In OFDM, with N subcarriers and L oversampling factor, one LN point IDFT is calculated for each sub-block at transmitter which require $\frac{1}{2}LN\log_2(LN)$ complex multiplications and $LN\log_2(LN)$ complex additions [1]. Therefore, for M sub-blocks, $\frac{1}{2}MLN\log_2(LN)$ complex multiplications and $MLN\log_2(LN)$ complex additions are required. With K phase factors, K^{M-1} searches are performed to find the OFDM signal with minimum possible PAPR and $(M-1)LN$ complex additions are required to combine M sub-blocks per search [7]. Therefore, $K^{M-1}(M-1)LN$ complex additions are required to combine the sub-blocks in K^{M-1} searches. At the receiver, one LN point DFT is calculated for OFDM symbol detection which requires $\frac{1}{2}LN\log_2(LN)$ complex multiplications and $LN\log_2(LN)$ complex additions and for demapping of information carrying symbols, DN complex multiplications and $2DN$ complex additions per OFDM symbol are also required [7].

Therefore, total number of complex multiplications and additions required in OFDM with PTS, M-PTS and CCM-PTS schemes are as follows:

Total complex multiplications: $\frac{1}{2}MLN\log_2(LN) + \frac{1}{2}LN\log_2(LN) + DN$.

Total complex additions: $MLN\log_2(LN)+K^{M-1}(M-1)LN+LN\log_2(LN)+2DN$.

Table 1 summarize the computational complexity of OCDM and OFDM with PTS, M-PTS and CCM-PTS.

Table 1. Computational Complexity of OCDM and OFDM with PTS, M-PTS and CCM-PTS

System	Total Complex Multiplications	Total Complex Additions
OCDM	$(1+M)LN\left\{2+\frac{1}{2}\log_2(LN)\right\}+DN$	$LN\{(1+M)\log_2(LN)+K^{M-1}(M-1)\}+2DN$
OFDM	$(1+M)\frac{1}{2}LN\log_2(LN)+DN$	$LN\{(1+M)\log_2(LN)+K^{M-1}(M-1)\}+2DN$

4 Applications of OCDM

This section presents the various applications of OCDM proposed in literature.

4.1 OCDM for Wireless Communication

In [1], OCDM is proposed for wireless multipath channel and simulated for PAPR performance and BER performance with (a). ZF and MMSE equalizers (b). Insufficient GI (c). Iterative block DFE (IB-DFE) and (d). Forward error coding (FEC). For comparison, OFDM, DFT-P-OFDM and SC-FDE are also considered. DFT-P-OFDM provides the best PAPR performance while the OFDM and OCDM systems have the identical PAPR characteristics. As per simulation results, OCDM is superior to the traditional OFDM and it also exhibits a higher anti-interference ability which occurs due to insufficient GI.

4.2 OCDM for Optical Fiber Communication

In [3], OCDM is proposed for coherent optical communication. Digital implementation of coherent optical OCDM (CO-OCDM) system is realized using DFnT. The relation between DFnT and DFT, given in Sect. 2, is utilized to integrate the CO-OCDM into the conventional CO-OFDM with some additional operations. In [2], CO-OCDM is simulated for PAPR performance, average Q factor and OSNR penalties with different GI lengths at different transmission distance and BER performance. CO-OFDM is also considered for comparison. OCDM and OFDM have the same PAPR performance under the same conditions. In CO-OFDM, the Q factors of the subcarriers fluctuate, but in OCDM, all chirps have same Q factors. However, for identical GI and transmission distance, the averaged Q factors of CO-OCDM and CO-OFDM are same. Performance of the CO-OCDM system is better as compared to CO-OFDM systems in terms of transmission distance at the same GI length, OSNR penalty and BER. Performance of CO-OCDM is better as compared to CO-OFDM because OCDM is less sensitive to the channel impairments. As CO-OFDM does, CO-OCDM is also able to compensate the chromatic dispersion. Similar to precoded OFDM, various precoding matrices can be used to implement precoded OCDM.

4.3 OCDM for IM/DD Based Short Reach Systems

In [8, 9], DSB modulated OCDM is introduced for intensity modulation and direct detection (IM/DD) based short reach systems. IM/DD system has one dimension only for modulation therefor the OCDM signal of complex values is not feasible for it. Passband signal is obtained from complex baseband signals using Digital up conversion (DUC) technique. Real part of passband signal which is equivalent to DSB modulated OCDM signal is reserved for IM and imaginary part is rejected. At receiving end, digital down conversion (DDC) converts back the passband signal to baseband signal for demodulation. Due to presence of DUC and DDC techniques, complexity of IM/DD OCDM system is increased.

In [8, 9], open loop IM/DD OCDM and in [9] closed-loop IM/DD OCDM are simulated for BER performance with different data rates at different transmission distance. DMT-OFDM is also considered for performance comparison. For open loop system, the IM/DD OCDM system consistently perform better than the DMT OFDM system in all instances. For high modulation levels and at long transmission distances, the IM/DD-OCDM signal has a clear benefit. Because subcarriers of high frequencies are more sensitive to fading induced by chromatic dispersion, the SNR performance of OFDM subcarriers of high frequencies begins to drop with the increase in transmission distance. In contrast, OCDM chirps are unaffected by these defects, with flat SNRs and relatively slight deterioration. As a result, IM/DD OCDM system performance is superior to DMT OFDM. If channel state information (CSI) is available at the transmitter, most of the imperfections may be addressed therefore the IM/DD OCDM system shows only a slight improvement over DMT OFDM in closed loop scenario. In comparison to open loop system, the closed loop system shows a significant improvement for both systems.

4.4 OCDM for Underwater Acoustic Communication

In [10, 11,12] OCDM is proposed for underwater acoustic communication (UWAC). In [10, 11], fully and underloaded OCDM are simulated for BER performance over static and dynamic UWAC channels. For comparison, conventional OFDM and SC with an iterative FDE (SC-FDE) are also considered. Over static UWAC channel, due to enhanced diversity exploitation, the fully-loaded OCDM system gives an SNR gain compared to fully-loaded OFDM. In underloaded configuration, both OFDM and OCDM systems give an improved BER performance described by the spread spectrum effect. However, underloaded OCDM outperformed the fully/underloaded OFDM significantly, particularly in the low SNR region. Over dynamic UWAC channel, SC-FDE system provides the best performance and fully-loaded OFDM outperform the fully-loaded OCDM. Poor performance of OCDM is because MMSE equalizer enhances the noise in the event of Doppler spread. Underloaded OCDM outperformed the underloaded OFDM by a large margin for low values of SNR, however, the BER performance of SC-FDE is comparable with underloaded OFDM. With reduction in load ratio, OCDM delivers improved BER performance and converged to the AWGN boundary because underloaded OCDM provides spreading gain as well as diversity gain while OFDM performance increased marginally because underloaded OFDM provides enhanced robustness against carrier frequency offset (CFO) only which is caused by increased inter carrier spacing. By exploiting the multipaths diversity of the channel, underloaded OCDM provides good robustness than OFDM but at the cost of reduced data rate.

Orthogonality of the subcarriers is destroyed by the Doppler effect therefore OCDM reacts to Doppler spread and ICI. Hence, Doppler compensation algorithm is required. In [12], Data Pick Rake OCDM, or DP-Rake OCDM, is proposed to remove ICI at short GI and increase the data rate. The basic purpose of rake receiver is to determine the ideal rake finger which minimize the ICI. The computational complexity of the receiver can be considerably increased by using number of rake fingers. In [12], DP-Rake OCDM is simulated over static and dynamic UWA channels. Static UWA channel is based on the measured data of Xiamen Port Shallow Water and dynamic UWA channel is based on the Water Mark Time-varying (WMT) channel. For comparison, SC-FDE, OFDM and OCDM are also considered.

As FEC coding, Doppler estimation, and phase correction techniques remove the Doppler shift introduced by channel variations, the BER performance of OFDM and SC-FDE with these techniques is same over WMT channel. OCDM outperform OFDM over WMT channel because it provides diversity and spreading gain both through its chirp-based signal. The BER performance of DP Rake OCDM is the best, although the performance improvement against OCDM is not considerable because WMT channel's delay spread is tiny in comparison to the CP, causing no severe ICI. Since the ICI caused by delay spread has severe impact on MCM, BER performance of OCDM and OFDM are poor over Xiamen Port SW channel, however, OCDM slightly outperforms OFDM. With the addition of data pick-based rake receiver, which effectively eliminates ICI, BER performance of DP Rake OFDM and DP Rake OCDM systems enhanced considerably, however, the performance of DP Rake OFDM lies between DP Rake OCDM and OCDM.

4.5   OCDM for Baseband Data Communication

In [13], OCDM is proposed for baseband data communication. OCDM signal of complex values is not feasible for baseband data communication. Therefore, four types of modified OCDM schemes which permit baseband data communication, i.e., transmission and reception of real-valued symbols, are proposed. In [13], four modified OCDM schemes are simulated for PAPR performance and BER performance over AWGN, ABGN, PLC with AWGN and PLC with ABGN environments. HS-OFDM along-with SC-CP is considered for performance comparison. SC-CP has the best PAPR characteristics, while the four OCDM schemes and HS-OFDM have the same PAPR performance. Proposed OCDM schemes provide better BER performance as compared to HS-OFDM and SC-CP but has greater computational complexity.

4.6   OCDM for MIMO Communication

In [14], OCDM in MIMO with different space time coding (STC) is proposed and simulated for URLLC. In addition to Alamouti and Cyclic Delay Diversity (CDD), authors have used Alamouti with CDD (ACDD) also for transmit diversity while Maximum Ratio Combining (MRC) is adopted for receive diversity. For comparison, OFDM is also simulated. Since OCDM spreads the symbols uniformly in frequency, FER performance of

OCDM is better than OFDM in all scenarios, for $N_t = 1, 2, 4$ or 8 and $N_r = 1$ or 2, with CDD as well as ACDD. ACDD outperforms CDD for $N_t \geq 2$. With $N_r = 2$, performance improvement is very large, in all situations, compared with $N_r = 1$. With the increase in N_t in CDD, frequency selectivity of SISO channel improves and favors the spreading feature of OCDM. Therefore, the performance difference between OCDM and OFDM increases with increase in N_t. In ACDD, the performance difference between OCDM and OFDM begins to widen when N_t takes value greater than 2 because CDD begins to show its influence for $N_t > 2$ only. Authors expect that, in more realistic situation, the performance difference between CDD and ACDD will widen which will make ACDD more attractive diversity technique compared to CDD.

5   Simulation Results

We have simulated OCDM and OFDM with $N = 256$ chirps/subcarriers, oversampling factor $L = 4$ and 10,000 OCDM/OFDM symbols to investigate their PAPR performance. QPSK modulation is used to modulate the chirps/subcarriers in original OCDM/OFDM. PTS, M-PTS and CCM-PTS are applied for PAPR reduction. SER performance of PTS, M-PTS and CCM-PTS over AWGN and Rayleigh fading channel is also investigated. For PTS operation, we have taken $K = 4$ phase factors $\{1, -1, j, -j\}$ and data symbols are divided into $M = 4$ sub-blocks using adjacent partition methods. QPSK modulation is used to modulate the chirps/subcarriers in OCDM/OFDM with PTS.

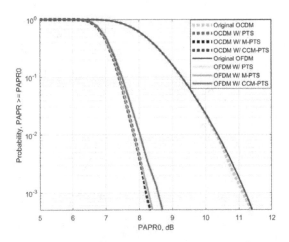

Fig. 2. PAPR Performance of OCDM and OFDM Signals

Figure 2 shows the PAPR performance of OCDM and OFDM with PTS, M-PTS and CCM-PTS. It is clear from Fig. 2 that OCDM and OFDM have same PAPR performance. Reduction in PAPR provided by PTS, M-PTS and CCM-PTS is almost same and is approximately equal to 3 dB at CCDF $= 10^{-3}$.

Figure 3 shows the SER performance of OCDM and OFDM with PTS, M-PTS and CCM-PTS over AWGN channel. In Fig. 3, analytical expression for SER of QPSK, M-PTS [7] and CCM-PTS [7] have been used to validate the simulation results. As shown in

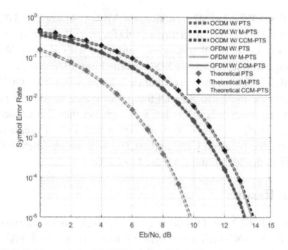

Fig. 3. SER Performance of OCDM and OFDM Signals over AWGN Channel

Fig. 3, SER performance of OCDM with PTS, M-PTS and CCM-PTS is same as that of OFDM with PTS, M-PTS and CCM-PTS respectively over AWGN channel. CCM-PTS and M-PTS require almost 3.5 dB and 4 dB more bit energy (E_b) compared to PTS at SER = 10^{-5}.

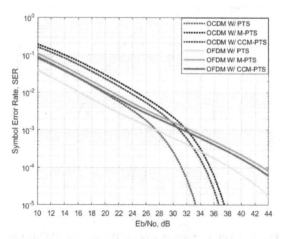

Fig. 4. SER Performance of OCDM and OFDM Signals over Rayleigh Fading Channel

Figure 4 shows the SER performance of OCDM and OFDM with PTS, M-PTS and CCM-PTS over a 3-tap multipath Rayleigh fading channel having path delays [0 μs, 0.5 μs, 1 μs] and average path gains [0dB, -5dB, -10dB]. An OCDM/OFDM system with $N = 256$ chirps/subcarriers, cyclic prefix length $L_{CP} = 4$ and 10000 OCDM/OFDM symbols are considered. FDE is used for equalization. As shown in Fig. 4, SER performance of OCDM slightly degrades in low SNR region whereas OCDM shows much better performance than OFDM in high SNR region for all the three schemes. OCDM with PTS, M-PTS and CCM-PTS outperforms for SNR > 28 dB, 32 dB and 31 dB respectively. M-PTS and CCM-PTS require almost 4 dB and 3.5 dB more bit energy (E_b) compared to PTS at SER = 10^{-5}.

6 Conclusion

OCDM is a MCM technique in which N orthogonal chirps having same bandwidth are multiplexed. OCDM provides maximum spectral efficiency for chirp spread spectrum system but suffers from high PAPR. Various PAPR reduction, equalization and channel estimation schemes presented in the literature for OFDM are applicable to the OCDM also. With minor additional operations, OCDM system can be obtained from OFDM. Computational complexity of OCDM is higher than the OFDM. OCDM outperforms OFDM for wireless communication, coherent OFC, IM/DD-based short reach system, UWA communication, baseband data communication and MIMO communication. Thus, for high-speed communication OCDM is an attractive solution.

PAPR performance of OCDM is same as that of OFDM. Reduction in PAPR offered by PTS, M-PTS and CCM-PTS is almost same for OCDM and OFDM both. Over AWGN channel, SER performance of OCDM with PTS, M-PTS and CCM-PTS is identical to the performance of OFDM with PTS, M-PTS and CCM-PTS respectively but CCM-PTS and M-PTS require more bit energy (E_b) compared to PTS to achieve the same SER. Performance of OCDM slightly degrades in low SNR region over multipath Rayleigh fading channel but it shows much better performance as compared to OFDM in high SNR region. M-PTS and CCM-PTS discard the requirement of sending any SI to the receiver at the cost of increased SER compared to PTS.

References

1. Ouyang, X., Zhao, J.: Orthogonal chirp division multiplexing. IEEE Trans. Commun. **64**(9), 3946–3957 (2016)
2. Wu, Y., Zou, W.Y.: Orthogonal frequency division multiplexing: a multi-carrier modulation scheme. IEEE Trans. Consum. Elec. **41**(3), 392–399 (1995)
3. Ouyang, X., Zhao, J.: Orthogonal chirp division multiplexing for coherent optical fiber communications. J. Lightwave Technol. **34**(18), 4376–4386 (2016)
4. Muller, S.H., Huber, J.B.: OFDM with reduced peak-to-average power ratio by optimum combination of partial transmit sequences. Electron. Lett. **33**(5), 368–369 (1997)
5. Zhou, Y., Jiang, T.: A novel multi-point square mapping combined with PTS to reduce PAPR of OFDM signals without side information. IEEE Trans. Broadcast. **55**(4), 831–835 (2009)
6. Goel, A., Gupta, P., Agrawal, M. : Concentric circle mapping based PTS for PAPR reduction in OFDM without side information. In: Proceedings of 2010 Sixth International Conference on Wireless Communication and Sensor Networks, Allahabad, India, pp. 1–4, December 2010
7. Goel, A., Gupta, P., Agrawal, M.: SER analysis of PTS based techniques for PAPR reduction in OFDM systems. Digit. Signal Proc. **23**(1), 302–313, January 2013
8. Ouyang, X., Tall, G., Power, M., Townsend, P.: Experimental demonstration of 112 Gbit/s orthogonal chirp-division multiplexing based on digital up-conversion for IM/DD systems with improved resilience to system impairments. In: Proceedings of 2018 European Conference on Optical Communication, Rome, Italy, pp. 1–3, September 2018

9. Ouyang, X., Talli, G., Power, M., Townsend, P.: Orthogonal chirp division multiplexing for IM/DD-based short-reach systems. Opt. Expr. **27**(16), 23620–23632 (2019)
10. Bouvet, P.J., Auffret, Y., Aubry, C.: On the analysis of orthogonal chirp division multiplexing for shallow water underwater acoustic communication. In: Proceedings of OCEANS 2017, Aberdeen, UK, pp. 1–5, June 2017
11. Bai, Y., Bouvet, P.J.: Orthogonal chirp division multiplexing for underwater acoustic communication. Sensors **18**(11), 3815 (2018)
12. Zhu, P., Xu, X., Tu, X., Chen, Y., Tao, Y.: Anti-multipath orthogonal chirp division multiplexing for underwater acoustic communication. IEEE Access **8**, 13305–13314 (2020)
13. de M.B.A. Dib, L., Colen, G.R., de L. Filomeno, M., Ribeiro, M.V.: Orthogonal chirp division multiplexing for baseband data communication systems. IEEE Syst. J. **14**(2), 2164–2174, June 2020
14. Bomfin, R., Chafii, M., Fettweis, G.: Performance assessment of orthogonal chirp division multiplexing in MIMO space time coding. In: Proceedings of 2019 IEEE 2nd 5G World Forum, Dresden, Germany, pp. 220–225, October 2019

Machine Learning and Data Analytics

COVID-19 Outbreak Estimation Approach Using Hybrid Time Series Modelling

Soham Chakraborty, Sushruta Mishra$^{(\boxtimes)}$, and Hrudaya Kumar Tripathy

School of Computer Engineering, Kalinga Institute of Industrial Technology, Deemed to be University, Bhubaneswar, India
{sushruta.mishrafcs,hktripathyfcs}@kiit.ac.in

Abstract. In the beginning of March 2020, coronavirus was claimed to be a worldwide pandemic by the World Health Organization (WHO). In Wuhan, a region in China, around December 2019, the Corona virus, also known as the novel COVID-19 was first to arise and spread throughout the world within weeks. Depending upon publicly available data-sets, for the COVID-19 outbreak, we have developed a forecasting model with the use of hybridization of sequential and time series modelling. In our work, we assessed the main elements to forecasting the potential of COVID-19 outbreak throughout the globe. Inside the work, we have analyzed several relevant algorithms like Long short-term memory (LSTM) model (which is a sequential deep learning model), used to predict the tendency of the pandemic, Auto-Regressive Integrated Moving Average (ARIMA) method, used for analyzing and forecasting time series data, Prophet model an algorithm to construct forecasting/predictive models for time series data. Based on our analysis outcome proposed hybrid LSTM and ARIMA model outperformed other models in forecasting the trend of the Corona Virus Outbreak.

Keywords: Epidemic transmission · Time series forecasting · Machine learning · Corona-virus · LSTM networks · ARIMA

1 Introduction

It is believed that every infectious disease shows some design or pattern which must be identified to forecast the outbreak of such diseases. We can define a different category for the spread of disease such as concerning time i.e., seasonal change [1]. Generally, it is found that their forwarding from person to person can be represented with the help of the non-linear system. We have found that in the previous studies using the data-driven method either linear or non-linear components are captured. Since they depend on both linear and non-linear, hence, they are not able to get hold of the situation of the transmittance of these infective health risks completely. Here we aim to build a intelligent statistical model that can capture both the linear and non-linear components in the trend. Purely Statistical techniques like moving average methods primarily depend on use cases and these techniques are tedious to forecast the actual rate of transmissions. There is a large array of a statistical and mathematical model which have been proposed for the

M. Panda et al. (Eds.): ICIICC 2022, CCIS 1737, pp. 249–260, 2022.
https://doi.org/10.1007/978-3-031-23233-6_19

broadcast of the covid-19 [2, 3]. In a general situation, the accuracy and prediction of such a model are low because the model is unable to fit samples in an accurate manner [4]. So, a deep learning approach is presented to address transmission in real-time, which beats the barrier of the statistical approach [5]. Since much research has been done on the same domain so after some intensive research using different methods like ARIMA, SARIMAX we found that the demographic-based trend curve has some non-linear characteristics which can't be determined by the existing 3 models. Our research work is based on the hypothesis that LSTM model and ARIMA can together capture the non-linearity under the forecasting data. The main objective of the work is to build a logical forecast for developing an intuition over the trend of coronavirus outbreaks [6].

We have also compared our algorithm with similar methods like seasonal ARIMA, which can be claimed to learn the non-linear representation of the time-series data. But again due to the unpredictable non-seasonality occuring in the curve it fails to represent or learn the actual underlying distribution, rather it tries to map it to the nearest possible seasonal cycles. Thus, we conclude to move forward with a combination of LSTM ()for capturing non-linearity and non-seasonality) and ARIMA (for capturing the linear trend components).

The rest of the work has arranged as follows. In Sect. 2 we have given a detailed overview of the dataset. In Sect. 3 we have discussed the basics of time-Series Modelling. In Sect. 4 the LSTM model for time series models their detailing, definitions, and related terms have been discussed. In Sect. 5, the ARIMA model detailing, definitions, and related terms have discussed. In Sect. 6 We have proposed a model for forecasting the coronavirus trend using the LSTM model and the ARIMA model and formed a hybrid model from both the model. In Section VII We have discussed the detailed implementation and the results of our research work.

2 Background

It Time-series interpretation is a statistical procedure for processing time-series data or trend study. There are three types of data.

- Time series data - Observation results of variables taking values at varying times [7].
- Cross-sectional data - When info of single or multiple parameters gathered at the similar instance.
- Pooled data - A mixture of time stamped and hybrid information.

2.1 LSTM Network for Modelling Time Series

Most samples in the real world are temporary in nature. The data collected at regular intervals are time series (TS) records where every record is evenly distributed. TS analysis is to predict future patterns for predefined past data set with basic characteristics [8–10]. TS samples may be cracked down to seasonal error. If it does not depend on time components such as trend and seasonal influence, called a stationary series. If TS data has a trend of seasonal influence and changes over time the TS data is considered non-stationary.

2.2 ARIMA Model

ARIMA stands for Autoregressive Integrated Moving Average. Different ARIMA metrics are:

- Auto-regressive constituent [11] - This metric is represented as p. If p = 0, no autocorrelation in the sequence is noted and if p = 1, it signifies presence of auto-correlation in sequence.
- Integration - In the ARIMA, the integration is represented by d. If d = 0, it signifies that the set is stable, and we don't require to make the difference. If d = 1, it signifies the set not to be stationary.
- Moving average constituent - It is denoted by q. In ARIMA, the moving average q = 1, signifies an error and time auto correlation is there.
- Decomposition - It relates to dividing the time series into trends, seasonal impacts, and residual variability.

2.3 Seasonal ARIMA Model

- Seasonal Autoregressive Integrated Moving Average, SARIMA or Seasonal ARIMA, is an extension of ARIMA that explicitly supports univariate time series data with a seasonal component.
- It adds three new hyperparameters to specify the autoregression (AR), differencing (I) and moving average (MA) for the seasonal component of the series, as well as an additional parameter for the period of the seasonality [12].

3 Proposed Model

It Time-series interpretation is a statistical procedure for processing time-series data or trend study. There are three types of data.

- Time series data - Observation results of variables taking values at varying times [13].
- Cross-sectional data - When info of single or multiple parameters gathered at the similar instance.
- Pooled data - A mixture of time.

Because of the automatically extracting significant feature nature of the Deep learning method like recurrent neural network (RNN) it is observed to be a powerful technique for the forecast [14]. In this the previous step's activation is taken and is given is input to the current time step and network self-connection. To eliminate the shortcoming long short-term memory RNN structure was designed that regulates the data pass and memory cell in the current hidden layer [15–17]. The framework of the LSTM constitutes 4 gates i.e., input gate, forget gate, control gate, and output gate. The main job of the input gate is to make a decision depending on which details can be transported to the cell. The forget gate decides which details from the input of the previous memory are to neglected. The work of the control gate is to control the updating of the cell. The output layer is accountable for updating the hidden layer(ht-1) and also updating the output. The LSM model is shown in Fig. 1.

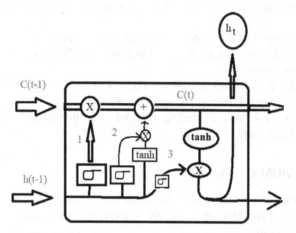

Fig. 1. A basic representation of the LSTM model

In the proposed model we consider the dataset from Kaggle which contains a list of daily Corona affected people, the daily number of deaths, in different provinces. These data points are considered as observational points in multidimensional vector space. These observational points are then fed into the ARIMA model and LSTM model separately. The ARIMA model is fitted to the data to learn the moving average and the trends in the data. Then the multidimensional vectors are fed into the LSTM algorithm, which generates an embedding. The ARIMA output and its corresponding residual embedding vector are concatenated in the final stage and down-projected by passing through a linear function to generate the next data points sequentially. The proposed model flow diagram has been shown in the following Fig. 2.

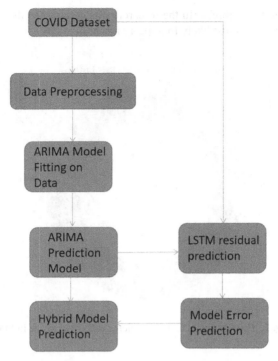

Fig. 2. A simple representation of the proposed model

4   Implementation and Results Discussion

In this section we will give a detailed exploratory data analysis overview of the complete dataset. A sample of the used COVID-19 dataset has given in Table 1. We have provided 3 samples from the available data sets. The methods utilized here are predicated on data-supervised methods which vary from precedent research work [18–21]. This forecasting model can be used to pre-assume the outbreak trend of COVID-19 outbreak which can

Table 1.   A Sample of India COVID-19 Dataset

S no.	Period	Time	State	Confirm cases	Confirm abroad cases	Cure	Life lost	Confirm
1	Jan 30, 2020	Evening	Kerala	1	0	0	0	1
2	Jan 31, 2020	Evening	Kerala	1	0	0	0	1
3	Fev 1st, 2020	Evening	Kerala	2	0	0	0	2

help in controlling the outbreak. In the research, it is determined that norms and rules formed by the regime is most likely to impact present outbreak.

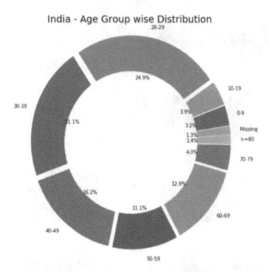

Fig. 3. Distribution of COVID patients according to age in India

From the Fig. 3, age-wise distribution of the India population, we infer that out of 100% the most affected group is between the age of 20 to 29 with having approximately 25% of the total cases while the least cases have been found in the group of old people having age above 80. The people between the ages group 30 to 39 occupy the second position to easily get infected with 21% of the total cases. Next, comes the age group of the 40 to 49 people having 16% of the total cases.

From the Fig. 4(a), we found that the total number of confirmed cases along with the recovery is increasing exponentially, while the death rate is increasing slowly with respect to time. From the graph it can be refer that the total number of cases by the end of August has reached 3500000 which is very threatening. But one good thing can we gather from the graph that the recovery rate is also increasing so we can hope for the best. In Fig. 4(b). we compared the situation of few countries facing global pandemics like China, the US, Italy, Spain, France, And India [22–24]. From the graph, we found that the total number of cases in India and the US are increasing rapidly with time, while countries like China, Italy and France, and Spain have somewhat controlled their condition so the total number of cases is increasing but a bit slow.

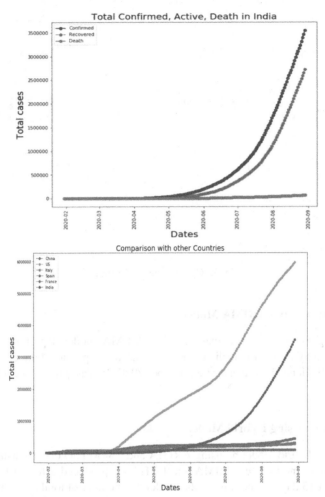

Fig. 4. a. Distribution of COVID patients according to age in India b. Graph for comparison with other countries.

4.1 Prediction Using LSTM Model

LSTM forms a recurrent network for storing previous outcomes into its storage units and in training phase, it discovers to utilize its memory [25, 26]. From the Fig. 6(a) we can observed that the proposed model performed well. It is able to accurately follow the inclination. Also, our model predicted the upcoming next month's trend. Hence, by the end of September 2020, the cases in India could touch up to 5000000. Figure 5 shows the growth rate of 15 states of India.

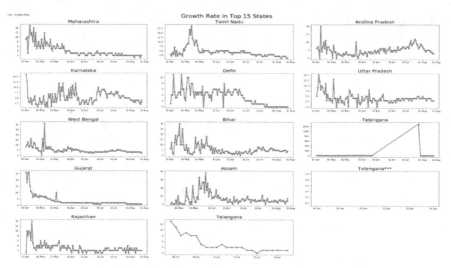

Fig. 5. Growth rate for 15 states

4.2 Prediction Using ARIMA Model

From the Fig. 6(b), it is clear that by using ARIMA model it performs well. It is able to accurately follow the inclination. Also, our model predicted the upcoming next month's trend. Hence by the end of September 2020, the cases in India could touch up to 57,00,000.

4.3 Prediction Using Hybrid Model

Figure 7 is the hybrid model by using ARIMA and LSTM network. By using the combination of both models i.e. ARIMA and LSTM we produced a forecast of the total cases for next 15 days. According to the model, the number of total cases will increase exponentially, until or unless some strict step will not be taken. Of course, it is not the exact prediction but based upon the trend.

(a)

(b)

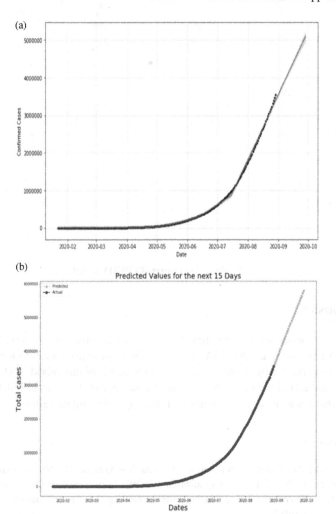

Fig. 6. a. Prediction using LSTML model b. Prediction using ARIMA model

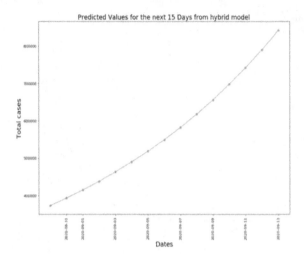

Fig. 7. Prediction using HYBRID model

5   Conclusion

In this research paper we have predicted the trend of coronavirus for next 15 days by using the LSTM model and ARIMA model and their combined model to form a hybrid model which worked better than the two. From the result of the hybrid model, it can be seen that by the end of the month September the number of the cases in India will cross 5000000, which is a close approximation of the original estimate value.

References

1. World Health Organization. Naming the Coronavirus Disease (COVID-19) and the Virus that Causes it. World Health Organization (2020). https://www.who.int/emergencies/dis eases/novelcoronavirus-2019/technical-guidance/naming-the-coronavirus-disease-(covid-209)-and-the-virus-thatcauses-it
2. Coronaviridae Study Group: The species Severe acute respiratory syndrome-related coronavirus: classifying 2019-nCoV and naming it SARS-CoV-2. Nat. Microbiol. **5**, 536 (2020)
3. Lu, H., Stratton, C.W., Tang, Y.W.: Outbreak of pneumonia of unknown etiology in Wuhan China: the mystery and the miracle. J. Med Virol. **92**, 401–402 (2020)
4. Klompas, M.: Coronavirus disease 2019 (COVID-19): protecting hospitals from the invisible. Ann. Intern. Med. **172**, 619–620 (2020)
5. Roser, M., Ritchie, H., Ortiz-Ospina, E.: Coronavirus Disease (COVID-9)–Statistics and Research. Our World Data (2020)
6. Rath, M., Mishra, S.: Security approaches in machine learning for satellite communication. In: Hassanien, A.E., Darwish, A., El-Askary, H. (eds.) Machine Learning and Data Mining in Aerospace Technology. SCI, vol. 836, pp. 189–204. Springer, Cham (2020). https://doi.org/10.1007/978-3-030-20212-5_10
7. Dutta, A., Misra, C., Barik, R.K., Mishra, S.: Enhancing mist assisted cloud computing toward secure and scalable architecture for smart healthcare. In: Advances in Communication and Computational Technology, pp. 1515–1526s. Springer, Singapore (2021)

8. Mishra, S., Tripathy, H.K., Panda, A.R.: An improved and adaptive attribute selection technique to optimize dengue fever prediction. Int. J. Eng. Technol. **7**, 480–486 (2018)
9. Roy, S.N., Mishra, S., Yusof, S.M.: Emergence of drug discovery in machine learning. In: Technical Advancements of Machine Learning in Healthcare, pp. 119–138). Springer, Singapore (2021)
10. Salinas, D., Flunkert, V., Gasthaus, J., Januschowski, T.: DeepAR: Probabilistic forecasting with autoregressive recurrent networks. Int. J. Forecast. (2019). https://doi.org/10.1016/j.ijforecast.2019.07.001
11. Oreshkin, B.N., Carpov, D., Chapados, N., Bengio, Y.: N-BEATS: neural basis expansion analysis for interpretable time series forecasting. arXiv 2019, arXiv:1905.10437
12. Adhikari, R., Agrawal, R.K.: An introductory study on time series modeling and forecasting. arXiv 2013, arXiv:1302.6613
13. Tripathy, H.K., Mishra, S., Thakkar, H.K., Rai, D.: CARE: a collision-aware mobile robot navigation in grid environment using improved breadth first search. Comput. Electr. Eng. **94**, 107327 (2021)
14. Sahoo, S., Mishra, S., Mishra, B.K.K., Mishra, M.: Analysis and implementation of artificial bee colony optimization in constrained optimization problems. In: Handbook of Research on Modeling, Analysis, and Application of Nature-Inspired Metaheuristic Algorithms, pp. 413–432. IGI Global (2018)
15. Anastassopoulou, C., Russo, L., Tsakris, A., Siettos, C.: Data-based analysis, modelling and forecasting of the COVID-19 outbreak. PLoS ONE **15**, e0230405 (2020)
16. Kane, M.J., Price, N., Scotch, M., Rabinowitz, P.: Comparison of ARIMA and Random Forest time series models for prediction of avian inflfluenza H5N1 outbreaks
17. Gelper, S., Fried, R., Croux, C.: Robust forecasting with exponential and Holt-Winters smoothing. J. Forecast. **29**, 285–300 (2010)
18. Mishra, S., Mallick, P.K., Tripathy, H.K., Jena, L., Chae, G.-S.: Stacked KNN with hard voting predictive approach to assist hiring process in IT organizations. Int. J. Electr. Eng. Educ., February 2021. https://doi.org/10.1177/0020720921989015
19. Harvey, A.C., Peters, S.: Estimation procedures for structural time series models. J. Forecast. **9**, 89–108 (1990)
20. Mishra, S., Tadesse, Y., Dash, A., Jena, L., Ranjan, P.: Thyroid disorder analysis using random forest classifier. In: Mishra, D., Buyya, R., Mohapatra, P., Patnaik, S. (eds.) Intelligent and Cloud Computing. SIST, vol. 153, pp. 385–390. Springer, Singapore (2021). https://doi.org/10.1007/978-981-15-6202-0_39
21. Chaudhury, P., Mishra, S., Tripathy, H.K., Kishore, B.: Enhancing the capabilities of student result prediction system. In: Proceedings of the Second International Conference on Information and Communication Technology for Competitive Strategies pp. 1–6, March 2016
22. Jena, L., Mishra, S., Nayak, S., Ranjan, P., Mishra, M.K.: Variable optimization in cervical cancer data using particle swarm optimization. In: Mallick, P.K., Bhoi, A.K., Chae, G.-S., Kalita, K. (eds.) Advances in Electronics, Communication and Computing. LNEE, vol. 709, pp. 147–153. Springer, Singapore (2021). https://doi.org/10.1007/978-981-15-8752-8_15
23. Mishra, S., Dash, A., Jena, L.: Use of deep learning for disease detection and diagnosis. In: Bio-inspired Neurocomputing, pp. 181–201. Springer, Singapore (2021)
24. Madhu, G., et al.: Imperative dynamic routing between capsules network for malaria classification. CMC-Comput. Mater. Continua **68**(1), 903–919 (2021)

25. Chakraborty, S., Sahoo, K.S., Mishra, S., Islam, S.M.: AI Driven cough voice-based COVID detection framework using spectrographic imaging: an improved technology. In: 2022 IEEE 7th International conference for Convergence in Technology (I2CT), pp. 1–7. IEEE, April 2022
26. Mishra, S., Thakkar, H.K., Singh, P., Sharma, G.: A decisive metaheuristic attribute selector enabled combined unsupervised-supervised model for chronic disease risk assessment. Comput. Intell. Neurosci. (2022)

Analysis of Depression, Anxiety, and Stress Chaos Among Children and Adolescents Using Machine Learning Algorithms

Satyananda Swain$^{(\boxtimes)}$ and Manas Ranjan Patra

Department of Computer Science, Berhampur University, Berhampur, Odisha, India
sswaincse1985@gmail.com, mrpatra.cs@buodisha.edu.in

Abstract. In recent times, the pandemic seems to have a serious impact on the mental health of people around the world across all age groups. This has been manifested in the form of unstable mental conditions, depression, anxiety, stress, and many other similar mental illnesses among individuals. In this study, we explore the use of machine learning classification algorithms to detect and classify children and adolescents with unstable mental conditions such as depression, stress, and anxiety through the Covid-19 period based on demographic information and characteristics using the DASS-21 Scale. Using a dataset of 2050 Chinese participants, an attempt has been made to classify their depression, stress, and anxiety behavior into different levels (Normal, Moderate, and Severe). The classification algorithms considered are Support Vector Machines, KNN, Naive Bayes, and Decision Trees. It is observed that the Support Vector Machine is the most effective method for the classification of mental depression, anxiety, and stress conditions. The goal of the study is to build a classification model for accurate categorization of unknown samples into appropriate psychological chaos levels.

Keywords: Anxiety · DASS-21 · Decision tree · Depression · KNN · Naïve bayes · Stress · Support vector machine

1 Introduction

The COVID-19 pandemic and frequent lockdowns led to fear and anxiety around the world. This phenomenon has given rise to short-term and long-term psychological and mental health implications like depression, anxiety, and stress both in children and adolescents. The nature and scale of impact on individuals depending on factors such as age, educational position, pre-existing mental health conditions, etc. This necessitates a scientific study to analyze the impact and develop a strategy to deal with the psychosocial and intellectual health issues of susceptible children and adolescents during the pandemic and post-pandemic period.

The COVID-19 outbreak provided a scenario to study the correlation between stressful life, their resulting psychological responses, and addictive behaviors. Through our study, we demonstrate that an increased level of depression, anxiety, and stress caused due to COVID-19 which can be established using the Depression, Anxiety, and Stress Scale popularly called the DASS-21 Scale.

© The Author(s), under exclusive license to Springer Nature Switzerland AG 2022
M. Panda et al. (Eds.): ICIICC 2022, CCIS 1737, pp. 261–272, 2022.
https://doi.org/10.1007/978-3-031-23233-6_20

1.1 Background

Depression (D)

Depression is a mood-based temperament illness that causes a sense of sadness and loss of attention. In medical terms, depression can be specified as a major depressive disorder that can affect how an individual feels, anticipates, and acts which can lead to a variety of emotional and bodily hitches. Depression is not a common illness, and it should not be taken casually.

Anxiety (A)

Anxiety is a feeling of strong, undue, tenacious apprehension and fear about unremarkable situations. In a worrying situation, anxiety is usually obvious. When feelings become extreme, all-consuming, and hinder daily living then a check on anxiety issues is a must which indicates an underlying disease.

Stress (S)

Stress is a sensation of emotive or bodily strain. It's a reaction of our body to a challenge or claim. In a medical sense, post-traumatic stress chaos is a psychological health disorder that is caused by a petrifying incident either undergoing it or perceiving it.

Depression, anxiety, and stress may require long-term treatment but most people with these mental disorders feel better with medication, psychotherapy, or both. Early detection is usually required for a proper diagnostic evaluation so that treatment can be provided before severe mental distortions occur.

DASS-21 Details

DASS-21 has been an established psychometric screening tool with acceptable validity and reliability. DASS-21 is a set of three self-report scales designed to measure the emotional states of depression, anxiety, and stress. Each of the three DASS-21 scales contains seven items, divided into subscales with similar content. The depression scale assesses dysphoria, hopelessness, devaluation of life, self-deprecation, lack of interest/involvement, anhedonia, and inertia. The anxiety scale assesses autonomic arousal, skeletal muscle effects, situational anxiety, and subjective experience of anxious affect. The stress scale is sensitive to levels of chronic non-specific arousal. It assesses difficulty in relaxing, nervous arousal, and being easily upset/agitated, irritable/over-reactive, and impatient. Scores for depression, anxiety, and stress are calculated by summing the scores for the relevant items [1].

The questions used for the DASS-21 test are described in Table 1 [1]. Table 2 presents the cut-off scores for all three conventional severity labels as normal, moderate, and severe which are considered to evaluate a person with these mental disorders[1].

Table 1. DASS-21 question set with question type specification (D-Depression, A-Anxiety, and S-Stress Chaos). [*Adopted from Reference-1*]

DASS-21 Questions	Type
I found it hard to wind down	S
I was aware of the dryness of my mouth	A
I couldn't seem to experience any positive feelings at all	D
I experienced breathing difficulty (e.g. Excessive rapid breathing, breathlessness in the absence of physical exertion)	A
I found it difficult to work up the initiative to do things	D
I tended to overreact to situations	S
I experienced trembling (e.g., in my hands)	A
I felt that I was using a lot of nervous energy	S
I was worried about situations in which I might panic and make a fool of myself	A
I felt that I had nothing to look forward to	D
I found myself getting agitated	S
I found it difficult to relax	S
I felt downhearted and blue	D
I was intolerant of anything that kept me from getting on with what I was doing	S
I felt I was close to panic	A
I was unable to become enthusiastic about anything	D
I felt I wasn't worth much as a person	D
I felt that I was rather touchy	S
I was aware of the action of my heart in the absence of physical exertion (e.g., sense of heart rate increase, heart missing a beat)	A
I felt scared without any good reason	A
I felt that life was meaningless	D

Table 2. DASS-21 cut-off scores for severity labels [*Adopted from Reference-1*]

	Depression	Anxiety	Stress
Normal	0–9	0–7	0–14
Mild	10–13	8–9	15–18
Moderate	14–20	10–14	19–25
Severe	21–27	15–19	26–33
Extremely Severe	28 +	20 +	34 +

1.2 Motivation and Objective of the Work

The goal of this research is to analyze the level of mental chaos among Chinese children and adolescents with unstable mental conditions during the pandemic situation and develop a classification model to categorize them into normal, moderate, or severe mental illness levels. It is intended to address some of the following research questions:

- How machine learning algorithms can be adopted for the classification of mental chaos or illness based on psychological features?
- How DASS-21 features can be used to ensure the categorization of Chinese children and adolescents with unstable mental conditions as per the Machine Learning algorithm?
- Which Machine Learning algorithm can be employed that guarantees optimal classification results?
- How to develop a classification framework for the accurate categorization of unknown samples into appropriate psychological chaos levels?

2 Literature Review

S. Aleem, N. U. Huda, et al. discussed the idea of using machine learning methodologies in the mental health domain to predict the probabilities of mental disorders and tried to adopt potential treatment outcomes from the prediction. They proposed a general model for depression detection using machine learning procedures [2].

S. A. H. M. Alim, M. G. Rabbani, et al. discussed a cross-sectional and descriptive study to access depression, anxiety, and stress among medical students. As per their studies, almost eighty-one percent of students either had depression, anxiety, or stress alone or in combination. The combination of depression, anxiety, and stress was highest among students [3].

L. Evans, K. Haeberlein, and A. Chang suggests that DASS-A and DASS-D provide a good convergence validity and may be suitable for identifying adolescents with a significant amount of anxiousness and depression [4].

V. Farnia, D. Afshari, et al. presented a study on the effect of substance abuse on anxiety, depression, and stress in epileptic patients. They also showed that psychological symptoms have an important role in the development of addiction among epileptic patients [5].

S. H. Hamaideh, H. Al-Modallal, M.A. Tanash, and A. Hamdan Mansour prescribe the prevalence and predictors of depression, anxiety, and stress among university students during home quarantine due to COVID-19. They found a strong correlation between depression, anxiety, and stress with demographic, health-related lifestyle variables [6].

E. Kakemam, E. Navvabi, and A.H. Albelbeisi proposed a study for examining the psychometric properties of the Persian version of DASS-21 for nurses. They properly evaluated and confirmed that DASS-21 is considered to be a valid and reliable tool for evaluating depression, anxiety, and stress among Iranian nurses [7].

R. B. Khalil, R. Dagher, and M. Zarzour demonstrate the psychological impact of the lockdown in Lebanon. Lockdown and other stressful life events are major factors in developing depression, anxiety, and stress in individuals. The DASS-21 score was found to be correlated with the impact of lockdown to develop such drastic mental disorders [8].

I. Marijanović, M. Kraljević, T. Buhovac, et al. showed that the COVID-19 pandemic affected depression, anxiety, and stress levels in oncological staff in BiH. They monitored and provided support to staff members for their wellbeing and retention at a time of global crisis in the healthcare sector [9].

Oli Ahmed, Rajib Ahmed Faisal, Sheikh M. A. H. Mostafa Alim, Tanima Sharker, and Fatema Akhter Hiramoni demonstrate their research work to access mental health status in various situations among Bangladeshi adults. They used the Bangla version of the DASS-21 to access psychometric properties by utilizing both classical test theory and item response theory. Their main idea is to propose a psychometrically sound tool to access depression, anxiety, and stress in the non-clinical sample of Bangladesh [10].

P. Sharif-Esfahani, R. Hoteit, C. El Morr, and H. Tamim, provide the relationship between fear of COVID-19 and depression, anxiety stress, and PTSD among Syrian refugee parents in Canada. They found severe levels of depression, anxiety, and stress in the participants [11].

R. S. Vaughan, E. J. Edwards, and T. E. MacIntyre provide initial support for use of the DASS-21 as an operationalization of mental health symptomology in athletes. They examine the internal consistency, factor structure, invariance, and convergent validity of the DASS-21 scale in two athlete samples [12].

3   Methodology

3.1   Data Set Description

A self-reported, cross-sectional survey was conducted among Chinese children and adolescents aged between 6 to 18 years. Participants responded to questionnaires containing DASS-21 information and internet usage characteristics like internet use frequency before COVID and after COVID, degree of internet usage, etc. A total of 2050 participants participated in the survey. The demographic measures include gender, age, DOB, frequency of internet use, depression, anxiety, stress, and many other features. The DASS-21 was used to screen mental issues from three different mental perspectives. Accordingly, the DASS-21 scale defines the categorization principle of categorizing persons into normal, moderate, and severely affected individuals with depression, anxiety, or stress (Figs. 1, 2, 3).

3.2   Implementation

Step-1: The problem is described as a classification problem that attempts to classify persons with depression, anxiety, or stress into normal, moderate, or severely affected individuals based on the demographic data gathered through the DASS-21 test (Fig. 4).

Step-2: The original data sample pertains to school-going children and youngsters from three different zones (central, east, and north) of China. In addition to details like age, gender, education, parent details, income, etc., the DASS-21 scale questionnaires were used to observe different symptoms of depression, anxiety, or stress. DASS-21 is

	DASS3	DASS5	DASS10	DASS13	DASS16	DASS17	DASS21
0	3	2	1	1	2	2	2
1	2	2	2	2	2	2	2
2	1	1	1	1	1	1	1
3	2	2	2	2	2	2	1
4	1	1	1	1	1	1	1
...	...	...	...	...	...	...	...
2045	1	2	1	1	1	1	1
2046	1	1	1	1	1	1	1
2047	2	1	1	1	1	1	1
2048	2	3	1	1	1	1	1
2049	1	1	1	1	1	1	1

[2050 rows x 7 columns]

Fig. 1. Sample data set for depression

	DASS2	DASS4	DASS7	DASS9	DASS15	DASS19	DASS20
0	3	2	1	1	1	2	1
1	2	2	2	2	2	2	2
2	1	1	1	1	1	1	1
3	2	2	2	2	1	2	3
4	2	1	1	1	1	1	2
...	...	...	...	...	...	...	...
2045	2	1	1	1	1	1	2
2046	1	1	1	1	1	1	1
2047	1	1	1	1	1	1	1
2048	3	1	1	1	1	1	1
2049	1	1	1	1	1	1	1

[2050 rows x 7 columns]

Fig. 2. Sample data set for anxiety

	DASS1	DASS6	DASS8	DASS11	DASS12	DASS14	DASS18
0	2	2	2	2	1	1	2
1	2	2	2	2	2	2	2
2	1	1	1	1	1	1	1
3	2	3	2	1	2	2	2
4	1	1	1	1	1	1	1
...	...	...	...	...	...	...	...
2045	1	1	2	1	1	1	2
2046	1	1	1	1	2	2	1
2047	2	1	1	2	2	1	1
2048	3	1	1	1	1	1	1
2049	1	1	1	1	1	1	1

[2050 rows x 7 columns]

Fig. 3. Sample data set for stress

a scale with 21 basic questions with three subgroupings. Each response is recorded on a 0–3 point scale. According to DASS-21, participants were classified into Normal (1), Moderate(2), and Severe (3) predictable label groups.

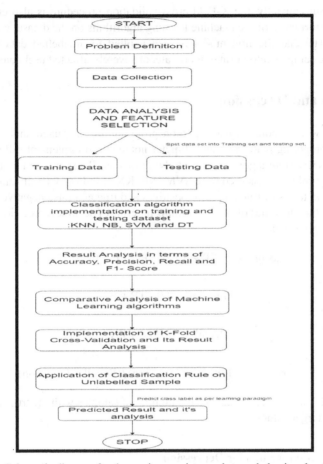

Fig. 4. Schematic diagram for depression, anxiety, and stress behavior classification.

Step-3: Based on the available raw data, a comprehensive analysis has been done to evaluate each feature with its respective values and an attempt has been made to determine parameters that are used as classification criteria. The features that appeared prominent, promising, and selected for learning were the 21 items of the DASS-21 scale. Based on these features, classification labels were defined to categorize individuals into different class labels.

Step-4: After feature selection, the data set is divided into the training set and testing set in the ratio of 70:30.

Step-5: Various machine learning classification algorithms, viz., SVM, NB, KNN, and DT are employed for training and testing.

Step-6: The accuracy, precision, recall, and F1-score are computed as performance measures for the chosen classification algorithms.

Step-7: A comparative study of the classifiers is done to judge their relative performance on the dataset.

Step-8: Subsequently, the K-Fold cross-validation procedure is also employed to assess the performance of the machine learning algorithms on the dataset with K = 10.

Step-9: The classification model is then applied to unlabelled data samples to categorize the samples into normal, moderate, or severely affected user categories.

4 Results and Discussion

Experiments were conducted using python programming language and a web-based interactive computing platform called Jupyter notebook to implement different supervised machine learning algorithms for studying mental illness in children and adolescents. The algorithms considered were SVM, NB, KNN, and DT. Classification matrices were defined in terms of true and false positives and true and false negatives. Obtained results depict the outcomes of ML algorithms in terms of accuracy, precision, recall, F1 scores, and support where:

$$Accuracy = (TP + TN)/(TP + FP + FN + TN) \tag{1}$$

$$Precision = TP/(TP + FP) \tag{2}$$

$$Recall = TP/(TP + FN) \tag{3}$$

$$F1\ Score = 2 * (Recall * Precision)/(Recall + Precision) \tag{4}$$

Further, the support factor defines the number of samples with the true responses in each class of target values.

4.1 Classification Results for Depression

Overall, the SVM algorithm demonstrates the highest accuracy of *0.997* as compared to other classification algorithms. KNN and NB yield an accuracy of 0.964 and 0.938 respectively. The lowest performance was observed in the case of DT with a minimal accuracy score of 0.896. The classification result for depression behavior is depicted in Table 3. Figure 5 indicates the supremacy of SVM over other classifiers with an accuracy score of 0.997.

Table 3. Depression behavior classification results

Algo. Name	Accuracy	Precision	Recall	F1Score	Support
SVM	**0.997**	**0.997**	**0.997**	**0.997**	615
KNN	0.964	0.964	0.964	0.963	615
NB	0.938	0.95	0.938	0.941	615
DT	0.896	0.865	0.896	0.879	615

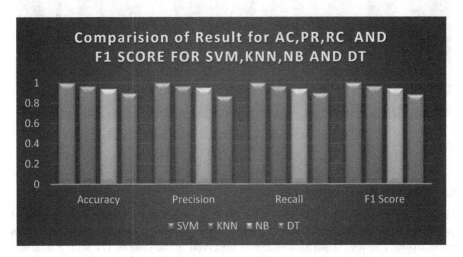

Fig. 5. Comparative analysis of classification results for depression

4.2 Classification Results for Anxiety

For anxiety also, the SVM algorithm demonstrates the highest accuracy of 1.0 as compared to other classification algorithms. KNN and NB yield an accuracy of 0.94 and 0.912 respectively. The lowest performance was observed in the case of DT with a minimal accuracy score of 0.893. The classification result for anxiety behavior is depicted in Table 4. Figure 6 also indicates the efficacy of SVM over other classifiers with an accuracy score of 1.0 for anxiety chaos.

Table 4. Anxiety behavior classification results

Algo. Name	Accuracy	Precision	Recall	F1Score	Support
SVM	1	1	1	1	615
KNN	0.94	0.937	0.94	0.935	615
NB	0.912	0.943	0.912	0.912	615
DT	0.893	0.846	0.893	0.868	615

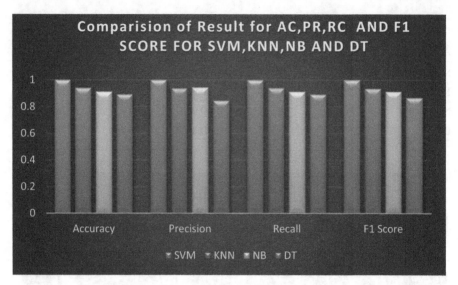

Fig. 6. Comparative analysis of classification results for anxiety

4.3 Classification Results for Stress

The SVM algorithm again demonstrates the highest accuracy of 0.997 as compared to other classification algorithms. KNN and NB yield an accuracy of 0.959 and 0.938 respectively. The lowest performance was observed in the case of DT with a minimal accuracy score of 0.925. The classification result for stress behavior is presented in Table 5. Figure 7 indicates the supremacy of SVM yet again over other classifiers with an accuracy score of 0.997 for stress chaos.

Table 5. Stress behavior classification results

Algo. Name	Accuracy	Precision	Recall	F1Score	Support
SVM	**0.997**	**0.997**	**0.997**	**0.997**	615
KNN	0.959	0.954	0.959	0.953	615
NB	0.938	0.971	0.938	0.947	615
DT	0.925	0.921	0.925	0.923	615

4.4 Cross-Validation Results for Depression, Anxiety, and Stress Behaviour

The performance of the classifiers SVM, KNN, NB, and DT using 10-fold cross-validation is presented in Table 6. Once again SVM emerges as the best performer concerning accuracy in classification for all three aspects of our study, namely, depression, anxiety, and stress stages.

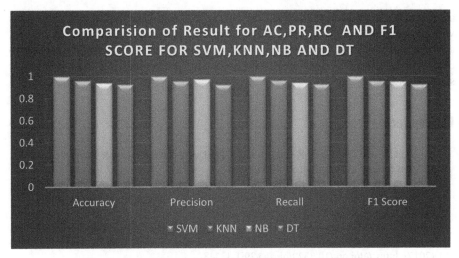

Fig. 7. Comparative analysis of classification results for Stress

Table 6. 10-Fold cross-validation results for depression, anxiety, and stress behaviour.

Algo Name	Depression		Anxiety		Stress	
	Acc. (Mean)	Std. Dev.	Acc. (Mean)	Std. Dev.	Acc. (Mean)	Std. Dev.
SVM	**0.99**	0.004	**0.986**	0.009	**0.987**	0.005
KNN	0.943	0.02	0.901	0.016	0.915	0.025
NB	0.968	0.011	0.953	0.14	0.969	0.007
DT	0.959	0.017	0.967	0.01	0.955	0.014

5 Future Work

In future, we will investigate the impact of deep learning techniques like CNN and RNN on depression, anxiety, and stress issues which are expected to provide better classification results and for DASS-21 scaled features. Also, suitable ensemble models will be looked at, to build effective and robust classification models.

6 Conclusions

The COVID-19 epidemic situation had a visible impact on the behavior of children and adolescents because of the digital shift from offline to online modes of working. Our study investigated Chinese children and adolescents for depression, anxiety, and stress issues during the lockdown period. We have classified the individuals into normal, moderate, and severely affected categories based on the DASS-21 scale which comprises of 21 questions related to the behavioral aspects of children and adolescents. The classification algorithms considered were SVM, KNN, NB, and DT which provide interesting results with classification accuracies of 0.997, 1.0, and 0.997 in the case of SVM for depression, anxiety, and stress chaos respectively. Thus, one can use these classification models to classify new behavioral data samples accurately for predicting depression, anxiety, or stress disorders.

References

1. Lovibond, S.H., Lovibond, P.F.: Manual for the Depression Anxiety & Stress Scales. (2nd Ed.) Psychology Foundation, Sydney (1995)
2. Aleem, S., Huda, N.U., Amin, R., Khalid, S., Alshamrani, S.S., Alshehri, A.: Machine learning algorithms for depression: diagnosis, insights, and research directions. Electronics 11(7), 1111 (2022). https://doi.org/10.3390/electronics11071111
3. Alim, S.A.H.M., et al.: Assessment of depression, anxiety, and stress among first-year MBBS students of a public medical college, Bangladesh. Bangladesh J. Psychiatry 29(1), 23–29 (2017). https://doi.org/10.3329/bjpsy.v29i1.32748
4. Evans, L., Haeberlein, K., Chang, A., Handal, P.: Convergent validity and preliminary cut-off scores for the anxiety and depression subscales of the DASS-21 in US adolescents. Child Psychiatry Hum. Dev. 52(4), 579–585 (2020). https://doi.org/10.1007/s10578-020-01050-0
5. Farnia, V., et al.: The effect of substance abuse on depression, anxiety, and stress (DASS-21) in epileptic patients. Clinical Epidemiology and Global Health 9, 128–131 (2021)
6. Hamaideh, S.H., Al-Modallal, H., Tanash, M. A., Hamdan-Mansour, A.: Depression, anxiety, and stress among undergraduate students during COVID-19 outbreak and "home quarantine". Nursing Open 9(2), 1423-1431 (2022)
7. Kakemam, E., Navvabi, E., Albelbeisi, A.H.: Psychometric properties of the persian version of depression anxiety stress scale-21 Items (DASS-21) in a sample of health professionals: a cross-sectional study. BMC Health Serv Res 22, 111 (2022). https://doi.org/10.1186/s12913-022-07514-4
8. Khalil, R.B., et al.: The impact of lockdown and other stressors during the COVID-19 pandemic on depression and anxiety in a Lebanese opportunistic sample: an online cross-sectional survey. Current Psychology, 1-11 (2022)
9. Marijanović, I., et al.: Use of the depression, anxiety, and stress scale (DASS-21) questionnaire to assess levels of depression, anxiety, and stress in healthcare and administrative staff in 5 oncology institutions in Bosnia and Herzegovina during the 2020 COVID-19 pandemic. Medical Science Monitor: Int. Medical J. Experimental Clinical Res. 27, e930812–e930821 (2021)
10. Ahmed, O., Faisal, R.A., Alim, S.M.A.H.M., Sharker, T., Hiramoni, F.A.: The psychometric properties of the depression anxiety stress scale-21 (DASS-21) Bangla version. Acta Psychologica 223, 103509 (2022). ISSN 0001-6918, https://doi.org/10.1016/j.actpsy.2022.103509
11. Sharif-Esfahani, P., Hoteit, R., El Morr, C., & Tamim, H. (2022). Fear of COVID-19 and Depression, Anxiety, Stress, and PTSD among Syrian Refugee Parents in Canada. Journal of Migration and Health, 100081
12. Vaughan, R.S., Edwards, E.J., MacIntyre, T.E.: Mental health measurement in a post Covid-19 World: psychometric properties and invariance of the DASS-21 in athletes and non-athletes. Front. Psychol. 11, 590559 (2020). https://doi.org/10.3389/fpsyg.2020.590559

Sentiment Analysis from Student Feedbacks Using Supervised Machine Learning Approaches

Preeti Routray[1] , Chinmaya Kumar Swain[1(✉)] ,
and Rakesh Chandra Balabantaray[2]

[1] Department of CSE, SRM University, Amaravati, Andhra Pradesh, India
`chinmayakumar.s@srmap.edu.in`
[2] Department of CSE, IIIT Bhubaneswar, Bhubaneswar, Odisha, India
`rakesh@iiit-bh.ac.in`

Abstract. Human life experiences a radical change due to the availability of all kinds of information on the World Wide Web. This phenomenon makes the life of each individual easier and better than before. This flooding of information also contains huge amount of people's opinions about their used products or services. The massive flow of information in terms of opinions and views need to be analyzed to know the efficacy of the products and/or services. The subjective expressions, which are known as opinions describes the peoples' feelings or sentiments towards the service or product. The opinion can be either positive or negative, depending on the evocation that the product or service has created. Similarly, in the realms of education, initiatives are being taken by Govt. Organizations as well as private organizations to know the effectiveness of the contemporary teaching-learning process. The present undertaking of the investigation is to evaluate the academic transaction by eliciting the students' subjective expressions and analyzing the same as their feedback. The scope of this paper is to analyze the student's feedback, which covers the teaching quality, style of delivery by the faculty, the components of the course, and the overall ambiance in which the academic activities are conducted. The present study investigates the applicability of different supervised machine learning approaches for sentiment analysis from students' subjective feedback. The chosen supervised machine learning approaches are Naive Bayes (NB), N-gram, Support Vector Machine (SVM), and Maximum Entropy (ME). These four approaches are applied only for binary sentiment classifications and to obtain a comparative analysis that would help to build a superior teaching and learning process.

Keywords: Sentiment analysis · Supervised learning · Student feedback

1 Introduction

The sharing of textual information on the Internet has ushered in substantial changes in human life [1]. The change is so pervasive that it is doubtful if any aspect of life is untouched by the web. The paradigm shift in Information and Communication Technology (ICT) has become a regular phenomenon nowadays [5, 7]. The World Wide Web is

M. Panda et al. (Eds.): ICIICC 2022, CCIS 1737, pp. 273–288, 2022.
https://doi.org/10.1007/978-3-031-23233-6_21

flooded with opinions or reviews shared in many forms. The huge collections of reviews or opinions in textual and other forms make person's life simple in many ways. One of the fundamental benefit is to know about the quality of a product or service, which is already being used by others. The opinion of other users play an important role for drawing any conclusion about the quality of the product. Opinions about a product or service is the subjective expression which describes the person's sentiment towards that product or service. The subjective expression can be positive or negative, that depends on the quality of the product or service [17].

In most of the research on natural language processing aim at processing of textual information, that is retrieval or mining of information [2–4]. Incidentally, the quantum of research has overlooked the emotional response towards a product or service, which is more spontaneous than rational thinking. Consequently, scant attention and research have been directed towards sentiment analysis to improve the teaching-learning process. Now the need is being felt that ICT recognizes the usefulness of the sentiment analysis, also known as opinion mining, to make decisions based on the opinions of others [8].

The World Wide Web evolved the way people share their opinions or views. Now, a person can post his perspective on web sites and express anything in the Internet forums, groups, and blogs. These opinions or user-generated content can be used in many practical applications. If a person wants to buy a product, he is going to ask his friends to know about the product, but due to the user- generated content on the web, he can get access to those opinions for buying the products. This is quite helpful not only for the individuals but also for the organizations. To obtain opinions about a product, organizations besides relying on the surveys, they are extracting the feedbacks from the opinion polls and use those feedbacks to improve the quality of the product or service [6].

The monitoring of opinions about a product or service on the web is a challenging task as large amount of textual information available on the web and that are from diverse sources. It is not effortless for a person to collect the opinions from all the sources and extract the relevant opinions, summarize them and organize them into usable forms [9]. So there is a need for automated opinion discovery and summarization system [10], which will help the user to make decisions faster [11]. This would immensely benefit the user and the organizations from the inevitable chaos of information overload.

Sentiments can be described as opinions, judgments, emotions, or ideas prompted [13]. The word sentiment and opinion are used interchangeably in technical writings. But in the context of this paper, sentiments refer to the complexities of very subtle and refined human feelings like tenderness, admiration and subdued resentment, etc. Such subjective conditions of fellow beings hold immense value in the academic arena. The trainer and the trainees, the teacher and the students form a sustained face-to-face relationship and interaction between them based on the course held in a controlled environment. Receiving only opinions from the students may not do optimal justice to the feedback system. That is why the history of feedback is growing by the day and yet remains chequered.

The unitary body of research on opinion mining or sentiment analysis is to extract opinions (positive/negative) from the text documents. Against this backdrop, there is little research on scattered sentiments of students in the teaching- learning process. Possibly this could be due to the variations in the perceptive- cognitive levels of the students in a class. The trainer or the instructor faces this problem of addressing the collective student group with a standardized content delivery without any discrimination. Today's education system is a choice-based credit system that hardly leaves any room for negotiation in the academic calendar. The present study has future promises of benefiting the educational system in India. At this juncture, it is not elementary to ignore the element of student's subjective feedback as the students and teachers are groomed in a varied cultural and linguistic matrix.

In general, an opinion is a message expressing a belief or skepticism or cynicism or bias or exaltation about a wide range of products and services- from a sports car to an android OS. This subjectivity, often deeply rooted and held with confidence but may not be validated or substantiated by knowledge or proof [11]. In many cases, opinions are shrouded in emotional articulations and embedded in long forum posts and blogs. Obviously, it is not very easy for a human reader to retrieve relevant sources, extract the desired information from the voluminous opinions. Consequently, it becomes a tiring and hesitant struggle to process them and bring them in to usable form. Thus it is imperative today that automated opinion discovery and summarization systems are urgently developed [15], which would address the sentiment analysis of students hailing from diverse cultural complexes and varied native languages in a country like India [12, 14].

The rest of the paper organized as follows. Section 2 discusses basic back- ground and related works in this area of research. Section 3 discusses four machine learning approaches used for sentiment analysis. The experimentation and results are discussed in Sect. 4. Finally, Sect. 5 discusses about the conclusion and future direction of this research.

2   Background

In the past few years, extensive studies were being carried out about sentiment analysis. The reported studies classified the approaches in three categories like (a) lexicon-based approach, (b) machine learning approach, and (c) hybrid approach.

The lexicon-based approach uses lexicon containing sentiment polarity of the words to determine the sentiment of a given textual document. The sentiment lexicon can be constructed either automatically or manually with list words and their associated sentiment polarity. In this context Hu and Liu [18] utilized WordNet to predict the semantic orientation of a word. There is several domain-specific and general-purpose lexicons (MPQA subjectivity lexicon, Word Counts database, Linguistic Inquiry, Harvard General Inquirer, etc.) have been constructed for the extraction of the semantic orientation of words. However, this type of lexicon misses the domain-specific and contextual orientation of a word. Rajput and Haider [19] used a lexicon-based approach to determine the semantic polarity of the student's feedback. They have used an academic domain-specific lexicon for this purpose and also suggested that the domain-specific lexicon gives the better result as compared to the general-purpose lexicon. Fernández et al. [21] used the dependency parsing technique for reporting the semantic orientation of the unstructured text. The proposed method used sentiment lexicon, which was constructed using a semi-automatic polarity expansion algorithm.

Sentiment analysis using machine learning approaches relies on building the model using training data set and evaluation of those models using test data set. The machine learning approaches can be classified as unsupervised and supervised methods based on the availability of the labeling of data set. Qiang Ye et al. [29] used supervised machine learning approaches for sentiment classification from the travel destinations reviews. The same way Turney [20] proposed an unsupervised approach for sentiment analysis. Altrabsheh et al. [38] analyzed the sentiment from student's feedback using three supervised learning approaches.

However, the hybrid approach is the combination of a lexicon-based approach and a machine learning-based approach. Zhang et al. [10] used a hybrid approach for sentiment analysis of Twitter data. They have used an opinion lexicon for labeling the data set and used those to train the prediction model. Appel et al. [24] used a hybrid approach for the sentiment analysis at the sentence level. They used SentiWordNet a sentiment lexicon and fuzzy set theory to know the sentiment polarity of a sentence.

This study is intended to apply four supervised machine learning approaches for sentiment analysis from students' feedback collected during an academic session.

3 Machine Learning Approaches

Machine learning approaches proved to be very promising approaches for natural language processing, specifically for sentiment analysis [29]. In this work we focus on the four machine learning approaches (Naive Bayes, Support Vector Machine (SVM), N-gram model, and Maximum Entropy (ME)) to classify the sentiment of the student's feedback. The overall process is represented in Fig. 1.

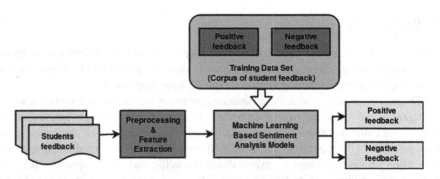

Fig. 1. Overview of supervised machine learning approaches

3.1 Naive Bayes Model

The popular Naive Bayes model is used for text classification and performs well in various domains of study [25]. The Naive Bayes model uses stochastic model of document generation during its operation. In order to predict the class of a new document Bayes rules are used. In this paper, multinomial event model [26] is used to generate the documents. Each document (d_i) is represented as a vector $v_i = (f_{i1}, f_{i2}, ..., f_{ik})$, where f_{ik} represents the frequency of the kth word of the vocabulary set in i^{th} document. The vocabulary set V consists of all the words present in the documents under study, i. e. $V = w_1, W_2,...., w_k$. Given with the model parameter $P(w_k c_j)$ and class prior probabilities $P(c_j)$ with the assumption that the words are independent, the most likely class of the document d_i is computed as

$$c^*(d_i) = \underset{j}{\text{argmax}}\, P(c_j)P(d|c_j) = \underset{j}{\text{argmax}}\, P(c_j) \prod_{k=1}^{|V|} P(w_k|c_j)^{n(w_k, d_i)} \qquad (1)$$

where $n(w_k, d_i)$ represents the frequency of the word w_k in document d_i. The terms P $(w_k c_j)$ and $P(c_j)$ are estimated from the documents used in training, whose class labels are known apriori. The terms are estimated as follows:

$$P(w_k|c_j) = \frac{1 + \sum_{d_i \in c_j} n(w_k, d_i)}{|V| + \sum_{k=1}^{|V|} \sum_{d_i \in c_j} n(w_k, d_i)}$$

$$P(c_j) = \frac{|c_j|}{\sum_{l=1}^{|C|} |c_l|}$$

3.2 Support Vector Machine (SVM)

It has been observed that SVM is one of the highly effective models for text categorization, and it performs better than other traditional approaches [27]. SVM segregates the positive and negative documents which are represented through vectors ($\vec{v}$). The hyperplanes represented by vectors segregated with maximum margin, as shown in Fig. 2. The approach is to find the desired hyperplane, which can be made by solving a constraint optimization problem. Let x_i takes the value $+1(-1)$, if the document d_i belongs to positive or negative class. The representative solution can be written as:

$$\vec{v} = \sum_{i=1}^{n} \lambda_i^* x_i \vec{d}_i \qquad (2)$$

where $\lambda_i \geq 0$ and the values of λ_i^* can be obtained by solving a dual optimization problem. The weight vector of the hyperplane can be constructed with a linear combination of $\vec{d}_i$ using Eq. 2. The document vectors whose corresponding $\lambda_i \geq 0$ are call support vectors as those document vectors contribute to the calculation of $\vec{v}$. The performance of the SVM mostly affected by the kernel it uses. The well-known kernel methods used in SVM are linear, polynomial, and radial basis functions. In our experimentation, we used a radial basis kernel (SVM RB) as it is mostly used and flexible also [36].

3.3 N-gram Based Character Language Model

There is another popular model called the N-gram character language model used in natural language processing [30]. This model is derived from the popular N- gram language models. This model considers character as the basic units instead of considering words as the basic units. The probability distribution of a string $s \in \Sigma^*$ over a fixed

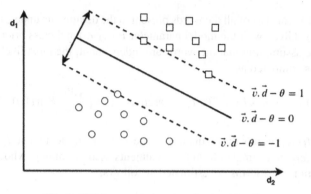

Fig. 2. SVM as maximum margin classifier [29]

alphabets Σ can be presented as $P(s)$. The chain rule of the N-gram character language model can be defined as $P(sc) = P(s).P(c|s)$ for a character c and string s. Based on N-gram Markovian assumption that considers previous $n - 1$ characters, the chain rule can be modified as

$$P(c_n|s_{c1...c_{n-1}}) = P(c_n|c1 \ldots c_{n-1})$$

Thus the maximum likelihood estimator for N-gram can be defined as,

$$P_{ML}(c|s) = \frac{C(sc)}{\sum_c C(sc)} \tag{3}$$

where $C(sc)$ represents the frequency of the sequence sc observed in the training data and $_c C(sc)$ represents the number of single character extension of sc. In this work, the used N-gram character language model is a generalized form of Witten-Bell smoothing [30]. For the experiment purpose the default value of $N = 8$ is being used.

3.4 Maximum Entropy

There is an alternative technique that was proved to be effective for sentiment classification is maximum entropy [31]. This technique sometimes performs better than Naive Bayes approach for text classification [32]. The estimate of $P(c\ d)$ takes the following exponential form:

$$P_{ME}(c|d) = \frac{1}{Z(d)} exp\left(\sum_i \lambda_{i,c} F_{i,c}(d, c)\right) \tag{4}$$

where $Z(d)$ is a normalization function. The binary function $F_{i,c}$ is a feature/class function for the feature f_i and class c. The term $\lambda_{i,c}$ represents the feature-weight parameter for the feature f_i and class c. Based on the expected values of the feature/class functions, the parameters are set to maximize the entropy. Due to the missing relationships between features, ME model performs better for the case where conditional independent assumptions are not met.

4 Experimentation and Results

This section discusses different steps being followed for finding the efficacy of the ML approaches. These steps include the corpus description, which was used for the evaluation purpose, pre-processing of the raw data, feature extraction from those data, evaluation metrics used and finally the result analysis.

4.1 Data Corpus Description

For this work, we had collected the feedback of 1344 students from our institute web portal. The feedbacks received consists of two parts, (a) unstructured textual feedback and (b) a numerical scale of 1–5 about the quality of the teaching and learning process. Table 1 presents the sample feedbacks of the students, and Table 2 reports the distribution of differently labeled feedbacks. The textual data set is manually labeled {positive, negative, neutral} by two experts with the linguistic background. The majority rule is being used to label the data, and no majority case, the neutral labels are assigned. To verify the reliability of the labels given by the experts and the students (based on numerical values), we match their labels and found high percentage of agreement (81.09%). The other measures like Krippendorff's alpha [34] was 0.631 and Fleiss kappa [33] was 0.629 are seems to be more conservative [35]. The quantitative labels of 1–5 interpreted as follows, 1–2 are considered as negative, 3 - as neutral, and 4–5 are considered as positive feedbacks.

4.2 Preprocessing

As the students' feedbacks contain unstructured text, so to extract the meaningful information from those texts need preprocessing of the data set. The well-known preprocessing steps which are applied to clean the data set may be the removal of spelling errors, stop word removal, removal of punctuations, etc. In this work, we used the following preprocessing steps to remove the noise from the data set.

Table 1. Sample of students feedbacks collected for our study

Sl. No.	Feedbacks	Sentiment labels	Feedback Score
1	This class is very boring and we are not feeling sleepy subject matter is not explained properly	Negative	1
2	faculty is very confusing while explaining the concept. He need to 1st read properly and then teach the course	Negative	1
3	The subject is very interesting and she made the class lively. She explains the subject nicely	Positive	4
4	Excellent subject, taught very nicely. Lab experiment are very well organized to understand the subject well	Positive	5

(continued)

Table 1. (*continued*)

Sl. No.	Feedbacks	Sentiment labels	Feedback Score
5	We have work out many assignments in theory and lab. That takes so much time for this subject. We get less time to study other subjects	Neutral	3
6	Subject is toooo good. Taught in a wow manner. It was really interesting in the laboratory	Positive	5
7	Subject is really boring. Thumb down for the faculty I was so happppy in skipping the classes	Negative	1

Table 2. Distribution of students feedbacks collected for our study

	Positive	Negative	Neutral
No. of instances	654	573	117

- Tokenization - It is the process of splitting the sentence into a list of words.
- Case conversion - The case conversion is used to convert the letters in to lower or upper case. The step is followed the tokenization, to match the words in the training data.
- Stop word removal - In NLP, the frequently used words in sentences like a preposition, helping verbs, articles are termed as stop-words. The removal of stop-words will reduce the number of words for further processing, and that reduces the space used for their storage and improve the response time.
- Punctuation removal - The punctuation which would not carry any useful information for the sentiment analysis is removed from the text.
- Removal of numbers - The chat like language contains numbers like 2 to represent 'to' or 'too', 4 to represent 'for', etc. So those numbers to be converted to their respective English words for better understanding and clarity.
- Normalization - Here, we are using standard normalization techniques of NLP for canonicalizing tokens so that matches occur despite superficial differences in the character sequences of the tokens i.e. converting happy to happy.

4.3 Feature Extraction

After preprocessing of the dataset, features are extracted for the analysis of the sentiments. During this phase, the preprocessed text of the training and testing dataset is converted into numerical feature vectors which are used in different machine learning models. For the N-gram model, the sequence of letters, syllables, or words is extracted for the experimentation.

Table 3. Useful information for evaluation metrics

		Predicted Class	
		Positive Class	Negative Class
Actual Class	Positive Class	True Positive (TP)	False Negative (FN)
	Negative Class	False Positive (FP)	True Negative (TN)

Table 4. Evaluation metrics for this work

Evaluation metrics
$Accuracy = \frac{TP+TN}{TP+FP+TN+FN} Precision = \frac{TP}{TP+FP}$
$Recall = \frac{TP}{TP+FN} F-measure = 2 * \frac{Precision*Recall}{Precision+Recall}$

Table 5. Performance of different approaches with considering neutral class

	Naive Bayes	ME	N-gram	SVM RB
Accuracy	0.54	0.62	0.69	0.92
Precision	0.33	0.34	0.36	0.91
Recall	0.32	0.33	0.38	0.92
F-measure	0.32	0.33	0.36	0.91

4.4 Evaluation Metrics

In this paper, we used the following evaluation metrics to evaluate the performance of different supervised machine learning approaches using the test data set. The evaluation metrics are accuracy, precision, recall and F-measure [37, 38] and those are defined with the help of Table 3 and Table 4.

From the reported results, the following observations can be inferred:

1. Support Vector Machine with radial basis kernel performed well in terms of accuracy, precision, and recall.
2. The values of precision and recall are high in SVM RB as compared to the other three models (Naive Bayes, Maximum Entropy, and N-gram).
3. Consideration of neutral classes for model building decreases the performance of the classifiers.
4. In terms of accuracy Naive Bayes model performed worst among all the four models under discussion.

Table 6. Performance of different approaches without considering neutral class

	Naive Bayes	ME	N-gram	SVM RB
Accuracy	0.55	0.64	0.71	0.94
Precision	0.48	0.35	0.38	0.93
Recall	0.49	0.34	0.41	0.93
F-measure	0.48	0.34	0.39	0.93

Table 7. Number of feedbacks used in the training of the models

Round of experiments	No. of feedbacks in each round of training		
	Positive	Negative	Total
1	25	25	50
2	50	50	100
3	75	75	150
4	100	100	200
5	150	150	300
6	200	200	400
7	250	250	500
8	300	300	600
9	350	350	700
10	426	382	808

4.5 Result Analysis

There are two parts of the experiment. In the first part to know the performance of the four models, we used 10-fold cross-validation. The results are reported in Table 5 and Table 6. Table 5 reports the performance by considering the neutral classes, and Table 6 reports the performance without considering the neutral classes.

The second part of the experiment conducted with 3-fold cross-validation [39]. In this case, we are not considering the data points of the neutral class. The 654 positive and 573 negative feedbacks are considered to make 3-fold cross validation. The total number of positive and negative data points are partitioned randomly into three folds, each with 218 positive and 191 negative feedbacks. During the experiment at each round, two-fold was used as a training data set, and the remaining one fold was used as the testing data set (shown in Table 7). This set of experiments was conducted to know the performance of the models with an increasing number of training data set. All the cases, the number of testing data set was 409 (218 positive and 191 negative).

The accuracy of the four approaches are reported in Table 8, and in Fig. 3. From the result, it is confirmed that the SVM with radial basis kernel performed best out of

Table 8. Accuracy of different models

Round of experiments	Training dataset size	Accuracy of the models				
		Naive Bayes	ME	N-gram	SVM RB	p-value
1	50	0.52	0.57	0.65	0.71	0.0000
2	100	0.54	0.58	0.71	0.76	0.0000
3	150	0.69	0.71	0.76	0.81	0.4352
4	200	0.72	0.73	0.79	0.84	0.2159
5	300	0.74	0.74	0.81	0.85	0.3178
6	400	0.76	0.77	0.82	0.86	0.2362
7	500	0.77	0.79	0.83	0.88	0.1994
8	600	0.80	0.80	0.84	0.89	0.4126
9	700	0.80	0.81	0.85	0.91	0.3024
10	808	0.80	0.81	0.85	0.93	0.4561

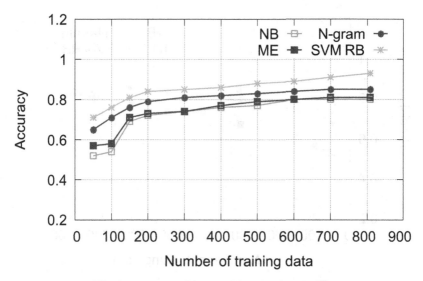

Fig. 3. Accuracy of four machine learning models

four approaches. The difference between accuracy among the four approaches was very significant ($p < 0.01$) when the number of training instances was less than equal to 100. We found from the experiment that the increased size of the training data set improved the accuracy of all the models. The accuracy of all the models reaches more than 80% when the number of training data set contains more than 700 reviews. The precision of all the models is presented in Table 9, and Fig. 4. Table 10 and Fig. 5 reports the recall of all the four models.

Table 9. Precision of different models

Round of experiments	Training data set size	Precision of the models				
		Naive Bayes	ME	N-gram	SVM RB	p-value
1	50	0.50	0.53	0.67	0.73	0.0000
2	100	0.53	0.56	0.70	0.77	0.0021
3	150	0.54	0.61	0.74	0.79	0.3525
4	200	0.66	0.63	0.76	0.81	0.3159
5	300	0.71	0.67	0.79	0.83	0.4171
6	400	0.73	0.72	0.81	0.87	0.3252
7	500	0.74	0.74	0.83	0.86	0.2594
8	600	0.78	0.78	0.85	0.89	0.3912
9	700	0.81	0.80	0.84	0.90	0.2246
10	808	0.83	0.84	0.85	0.92	0.1987

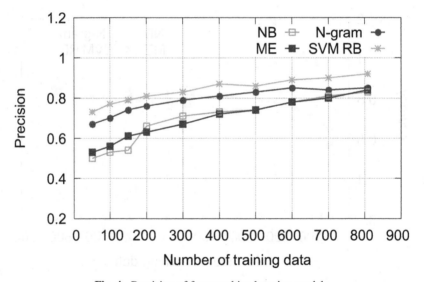

Fig. 4. Precision of four machine learning models

Table 10. Recall of different models

Round of exper- iments	Training data set size	Recall of the models				
		Naive Bayes	ME	N-gram	SVM RB	p-value
1	50	0.49	0.52	0.64	0.72	0.0000
2	100	0.52	0.55	0.67	0.76	0.0030
3	150	0.53	0.60	0.70	0.79	0.2577
4	200	0.65	0.61	0.73	0.80	0.1582
5	300	0.69	0.66	0.77	0.82	0.3271
6	400	0.72	0.70	0.79	0.86	0.4242
7	500	0.75	0.73	0.81	0.87	0.2371
8	600	0.77	0.77	0.82	0.88	0.3253
9	700	0.80	0.79	0.83	0.91	0.2361
10	808	0.82	0.82	0.83	0.92	0.1307

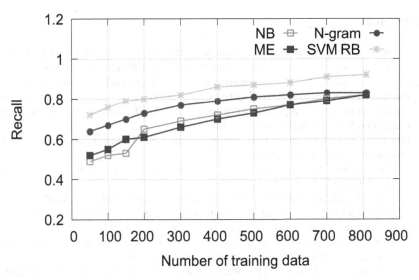

Fig. 5. Recall of four machine learning models

5 Conclusion and Future Work

The machine learning approaches have proved to be quite successful in identifying sentiments from the unstructured text documents. In the current investigation, we have used four supervised machine learning approaches of Naive Bayes, Maximum Entropy, N-gram, and SVM models to analyze the sentiments from the student's feedback. Here all the four models report more than 80% of classification accuracy. As the number of entities of the training set progressively increases, the accuracy also increases. For the fewer entities of the training dataset (50 or 100), the accuracy of the four algorithms is significant, whereas, for many entities, there is no significant change in the accuracy.

Pre-processing of the data is indispensable for the optimization of results. Such pre-processing would include named entity recognition, better tokenization, and parsing. Named entity recognition would remove the possibility of names (Alex, Bob etc.) and place names such as Delhi and Mumbai occurring in the output lexicon, which would certainly not bear any sentiment. Tokenizing could be improved to remove noisy expressions, such as numbers, dates, and words with unreadable/special characters and symbols.

In this work, there is a need to add more data in the corpus of subjective feedback from the students. The more the training data set, the more accurate is the result, which improves the performance of the model. It is noteworthy to mention that the sentiment analysis could also be done by implementing other machine learning algorithms like Decision Tree, Artificial Neural Network, etc. There may be some more extensions of this work, like combining the machine learning approach with a dictionary-based approach. With growing computer literacy and connectivity, the present investigation would gain momentum in the future.

References

1. Appel, G., Grewal, L., Hadi, R., Stephen, A.T.: The future of social media in marketing. J. Acad. Mark. Sci. **48**(1), 79–95 (2019). https://doi.org/10.1007/s11747-019-00695-1
2. Brody, S., Elhadad, N.: An unsupervised aspect-sentiment model for online reviews. In: Human Language Technologies: The 2010 Annual Conference of the North American Chapter of the Association for Computational Linguistics (HLT 2010). Association for Computational Linguistics, Stroudsburg, PA, USA (2010)
3. Das, S.R., Chen, M.Y.: Yahoo! For Amazon: sentiment extraction from small talk on the web. Manage. Sci. **53**(9), 1375–1388 (2007)
4. Routray, P., Swain, C.K., Mishra, S.P.: A survey on sentiment analysis. Int. J. Comput. Appl. **76**(10), 1–8 (2013)
5. Chinmaya Kumar Swain and Deepak B. Phatak "Evaluation model for the teacher's training program under National mission on education through ICT ", International Conference on e-Education, e-Business, e-Management and E-Learning, 7–9th Jan. 2011,
6. Drus, Z., Khalid, H.: Sentiment analysis in social media and its application: systematic literature review. Procedia Comput. Sci. **161**, 707–714 (2019)
7. Swain, C.K., Patel, A., Routray, P.: Model to evaluate the teaching enhancement of teacher's under the effect of teacher's training program through ICT. In: International Conference on e-Education, e-Business, e-Management and E- Learning, 7–9th January 2011
8. Boiy, E., Hens, P., Deschacht, K., Moens, M.-F.: Automatic sentiment analysis of on-line text. In: Proceedings of the 11th International Conference on Electronic Publishing, pp. 349–360, Vienna (2007)
9. Pang, B., Lee, L.: Opinion mining and sentiment analysis. Found. Trends Inf. Retr. **2**(1–2), 1–135 (2008)
10. Pang, B., Lee, L.: A sentimental education: sentiment analysis using subjectivity summarization based on minimum cuts. In: Proceeding of ACL 2004, pp. 271–278 (2004)

11. Jurafsky, D., Martin, J.H.: Speech and Language Processing: An Introduction to Natural Language Processing, Computational Linguistics, and Speech Recognition. Pearson Education Inc, New Jersey (2009)
12. Santi, P.K., Mohanty, S., DasAdhikary, K.P., Swain, K.C.: Design and implementation of nouns in OriNet: based on the semantic word concept. Arch. Control Sci. **15**(3), 429–436 (2005)
13. Liu, B.: Sentiment Analysis and Opinion Mining, Morgan & Claypool Publishers, May 2012
14. Swain, K.C., Santi, P.K., Mohanty, S.: Morphological analyser based on finite state transducer: a case study for Oriya language. Archives Control Sci. **15**(3), 451–460 (2005)
15. Prabowo, R., Thelwall, M.: Sentiment analysis: a combined ap- proach. J. Informet. **3**(2), 143–157 (2009)
16. Liu, B.: Sentiment Analysis: A Multi-Faceted Problem. IEEE Intell. Syst. **34**(4) (2010)
17. Panigrahi, C.R., Panda, B., Pati, B.: Exploratory data analysis and sentiment analysis of drug reviews. Computación y Sistemas, **26**(3) (2022)
18. Hu, M., Liu, B.: Mining and summarizing customer reviews. In: Proceedings of the Tenth ACM SIGKDD International Conference on Knowledge Discovery and Data Mining, pp. 168–177. ACM (2004)
19. Rajput, Q., Haider, S., Ghani, S.: Lexicon-based sentiment analysis of teachers evaluation. Appl. Comput. Intell. Soft Comput. **2016**, 1 (2016)
20. Turney, P.D.: Thumbs up or thumbs down?: semantic orientation applied to unsupervised classification of reviews. In: Proceedings of the 40th Annual Meeting on Association for Computational Linguistics. Association for Computational Linguistics, pp. 417–424 (2002)
21. Fernández-Gavilanes, M., Álvarez-López, T., Juncal-Martınez, J., Costa- Montenegro, E., González-Castaño, F.J.: Unsupervised method for sentiment analysis in online texts. Expert Syst. Appl. **58**, 57–75 (2016)
22. Altrabsheh, N., Cocea, M., Fallahkhair, S.: Learning sentiment from students feedback for real-time interventions in classrooms. In: Bouchachia, A. (ed.) Adaptive and Intelligent Systems, vol. 8779, pp. 40–49. Springer, Cham (2014). https://doi.org/10.1007/978-3-319-112 98-5_5
23. Zhang, L., Ghosh, R., Dekhil, M., Hsu, M., Liu, B.: Combining lexicon-based and learning-based methods for twitter sentiment analysis. Technical Report (2011)
24. Appel, O., Chiclana, F., Carter, J., Fujita, H.: A hybrid approach to the sentiment analysis problem at the sentence level. Knowl.-Based Syst. **108**, 110–124 (2016)
25. Domingos, P., Pazzani, M.J.: On the optimality of the simple bayesian classifier under zero-one loss. Mach. Learn. **29**(2–3), 103–130 (1997)
26. McCallum, A., and Nigam, K.: A comparison of event models for Naive Bayes text classification. In: AAAI-98 Workshop on Learning for Text Categorization, pp. 41–48. AAAI Press (1998)
27. Joachims, T.: Text categorization with Support Vector Machines: learning with many relevant features. In: Nédellec, C., Rouveirol, C. (eds.) ECML 1998. LNCS, vol. 1398, pp. 137–142. Springer, Heidelberg (1998). https://doi.org/10.1007/BFb0026683
28. RushdiSaleh, M., MartnValdivia, M.T., MontejoRez, A., UreaLpez, L.A.: Experiments with SVM to classify opinions in different domains. Expert Syst. Appl. **38**, 14799–14804 (2011)
29. Ye, Q., Zhang, Z., Law, R.: Sentiment classification of online reviews to travel destinations by supervised machine learning approaches. Expert Syst. Appl. **36**, 6527–6535 (2009)
30. Carpenter, B.: Scaling high-order character language models to gigabytes. In: Proceedings of the Workshop on Software (Software 2005), Stroudsburg, PA, USA, 86–99. Association for Computational Linguistics
31. Berger, A.L., Della Pietra, S.A., Della Pietra, V.J.: A maximum entropy approach to natural language processing. Comput. Linguist. **22**(1), 39–71 (1996)

32. Nigam, K., Lafferty, J., McCallum, A.: Using maximum entropy for text classification. In: Proceedings of the IJCAI 1999, pp. 61–67 (1999)
33. Fleiss, J.L.: Measuring nominal scale agreement among many raters. Psychol. Bull. **76**(5), 378 (1971)
34. Hayes, A.F., Krippendorff, K.: Answering the call for a standard reliability measure for coding data. Commun. Methods Meas. **1**(1), 77–89 (2007)
35. Lombard, M., Snyder-Duch, J., Bracken, C.C.: Practical resources for assessing and reporting intercoder reliability in content analysis research projects (2004). http://astro.temple.edu/lombard/reliability/
36. Chang, Y.W., Hsieh, C.J., Chang, K.W., Ringgaard, M., Lin, C.J.: Training and testing low-degree polynomial data mappings via linear svm. J. Mach. Learn. Res. **11**, 1471–1490 (2010)
37. Nasim, Z., Rajput, Q., Haider, S.: Sentiment analysis of student feedback using machine learning and lexicon based approaches. In: 2017 International Conference on Research and Innovation in Information Systems (ICRIIS), Langkawi, pp. 1–6 (2017)
38. Bouchachia, A. (ed.): ICAIS 2014. LNCS (LNAI), vol. 8779. Springer, Cham (2014). https://doi.org/10.1007/978-3-319-11298-5
39. Kohavi, R.: A study of cross-validation and bootstrap for accuracy estimation and model selection. In: Proceedings of the 14th International Joint Conference on Artificial Intelligence - Volume 2 (IJCAI 1995), vol. 2, pp. 1137–1143. Morgan Kaufmann Publishers Inc., San Francisco (1995)

Machine Learning Algorithms for Diabetes Prediction

Sudipta Priyadarshinee and Madhumita Panda[✉]

Department of Computer Science, G. M. University, Sambalpur, Odisha, India
mpanda.gmu@gmail.com

Abstract. Diabetes has emerged as one of the most deadly and prevalent illnesses in the modern society, not just in India but also everywhere else. Diabetes now impacts individuals of every age and is associated with lifestyle, genetics, stress, and ageing. Different types of machine learning approaches are now applied to forecast diabetes and also the disorders brought on by this disease. In this study we have used five machine learning classifiers such that Extra Tree (ET),Decision Tree (DT),Random Forest (RF), K-Nearest Neighbour (KNN) and Passive Aggressive Classifier (PAC) for diabetes mellitus prediction. The experimental findings demonstrate that Random Forest and Extra Tree have the lowest error rates with the highest accuracy (81.16%).

Keywords: Diabetes · Machine learning · Accuracy · Classifiers

1 Introduction

A subfield of Artificial Intelligence (AI) known as Machine Learning (ML)enables programmes to forecast outcomes more accurately even when they weren't explicitly intended to do so. In order to forecast future output values, algorithms of machine learning utilize the past data as its input. These algorithms employ mathematical approaches that are highly helpful in assessing a lot of data and making recommendations for actions based on these data. Machine learning is now being utilized in many facets of medical health. Numerous researchers [1, 2] are now using algorithms of ML to predict and manage a variety of diseases. In order to take the required steps to prevent diabetes, machine learning algorithms are being applied to investigate their potential for diabetes prediction. These algorithms may be grouped basically into 3 types: Supervised, Unsupervised and Reinforcement learning [3].Commonly referred to as Diabetes Mellitus (DM) by medical experts, diabetes disease is a collection of metabolic illnesses where an individual has excessive blood sugar due to insufficient insulin secretion, improper insulin cell response, or a combination of both. [4]. Diabetes illness is separated into 2 groups namely type 1 and type 2. The main distinction between these two is that person with type 1 diabetes can not make insulin while those with type 2 diabetes produce a small amount of insulin that is not effective enough. Urinating frequently, experiencing frequent hunger and thirst, feeling exhausted, and having impaired vision are the main symptoms of people with type 1 or type 2 diabetes [5]. The early this disease is

M. Panda et al. (Eds.): ICIICC 2022, CCIS 1737, pp. 289–298, 2022.
https://doi.org/10.1007/978-3-031-23233-6_22

detected, better chances are there to cure the patient. As forecast by International Diabetes Federation in 2017 [6] that there have been 425 million diabetics worldwide, and that population will rise to 625 million by 2045 [7].

There are three more distinct parts to this work, and they are as follows: Sect. 2 of this paper, outlines the research and studies that back up the findings on diabetes. Section 3, outlines the suggested framework and the several different machine learning classifiers utilized in the forecast of diabetes. The outcomes of the experiments are displayed in Sect. 4, while a summary and analysis of experiments are presented in Sect. 5.

2   Related Works

This section presents the many methods that has been used to foretell diabetes issues.

In this study [8], a Decision Support System that employed the Decision Stump base classifier and the Ada Boost algorithm for classification has been proposed. As foundation classifiers for the SVM, Naive Bayes,Ada Boost and Decision Tree were also used to verify accuracy. The experimental results showed that when using a Decision Stump as the base classifier, Ada Boost algorithm achieved an accuracy of 80.72%.

The following work [9] was to build a system which can more precisely judge a condition of diabetic patient. Naive Bayes, Decision Tree, ANN, and SVM methods were employed as the foundation for categorization approaches in model construction. ANN, Decision Tree, Naive Bayes, and SVM approaches offered precisions of 70%, 85%, 77%, and 77.3% respectively.

For the 2-way categorization of diabetes, the authors [10] utilized Convolutional Neural Network (CNN). With a 75/25 training/testing configuration and normalisation set at 550 for input data, the authors achieved an accuracy of 77.98% and obtained a kappa coefficient of 0.549.

Random Forest, Nave Bayes and J48 decision tree were the three ML models that were used in this study [11]. The experimental findings concluded that Nave Bayes surpassed both the J48 decision tree and random forest for accuracy in the 3-factor and 5-factor feature-selected data subsets. With an accuracy of 79.13% compared to 79.57%, the Naive Bayes on the 3-factor data subset outperformed the Random Forest on the entire dataset.

In order to identify diabetes in its early stages, the author of this study [12] utilized three algorithms of machine learning:SVM, Decision Tree, and Naive Bayes. Observed outcomes indicated that Naive Bayes provided the best results with the maximum accuracy (76.30%).

The authors [13] have used six well-known algorithms of machine learning such that SVM, KNN, LR, DT, RF, and NB for predicting diabetes disease. According to the experimental findings, SVM and KNN provided the greatest accuracy of 77%.

3   Proposed Methodology

The proposed framework is shown in Fig. 1.In our proposed methodology, data are first pre-processed for missing values, then after that the standard scalar method is used to standardize them. For prediction of diabetes illness, we have used five classification

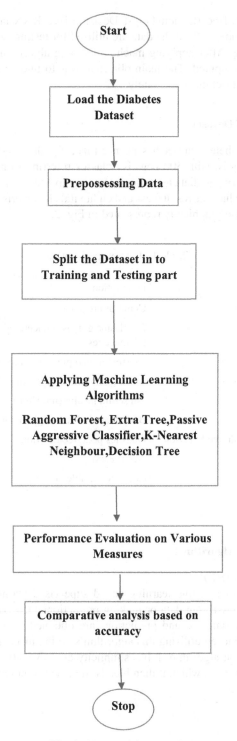

Fig. 1. Proposed framework

approaches like Extra Tree, Random Forest, Decision Tree, KNN and Passive Aggressive Classifier.For this study, 20% of the data are utilised for testing, while 80% of the data are used for training. After applying machine learning algorithms on the dataset, the accuracy rate was computed. The main objective was to find an algorithm that could classify the given dataset most accurately.

3.1 Description of Dataset

The Kaggle [14] diabetes dataset has been utilized for the experiment. This dataset consists of 768 records, with 500 negative classes referring to non-diabetes and 268 positive classes referring to diabetes patients, making up 34.9% and 65.1%, respectively, of the total dataset. It has one result class and eight vital characteristics, which are shown in the Table 1 and also graphically represented in Fig. 2.

Table 1. Dataset specification

Sr No	Attributes	Description
1	Pregnancies	Count of pregnancies
2	Glucose	2 h plasma glucose concentration in an oral glucose tolerance test
3	Blood Pressure	Diastolic blood pressure (mm Hg)
4	Skin Thickness	Thickness of the triceps skin fold (mm)
5	Insulin	2-h serum insulin (mu U/ml)
6	BMI	Body mass index (weight in kg/(height in m)^2)
7	Diabetes Pedigree Function	Diabetes pedigree function
8	Age	Age (years)
9	Outcome	category variable (1 or 0)

3.2 Classification Algorithms

A. **Random Forest (RF)**

It's a form of machine learning called supervised learning, and it's used to do things like classifying data or making predictions [15]. The decision trees are built using data samples, and predictions are obtained from each one. The best answer is then chosen utilising this algorithm's voting mechanism. Given that it is the most common algorithm, it has simplicity and diversity. This method creates several decision trees, which it then blends. It provides more reliable and accurate prediction (Fig. 3).

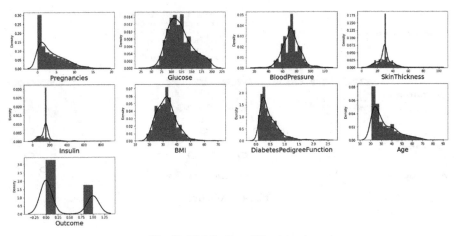

Fig. 2. Distribution of the dataset

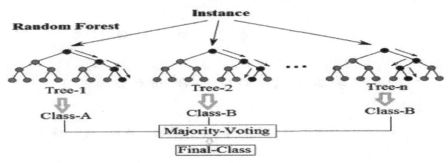

Fig. 3. Random forest

B. Extra Tree (ET)

Extra Tree is a method for enhancing accuracy and computing efficiency by combining bagging classifiers with traditional tree-based approaches [16]. The primary distinctions from other tree-based algorithms are able to separate the node by randomly selecting cut-points and building the trees utilising all of the learning samples (Fig. 4).

C. Decision Tree

It works well for both regression and classification. It functions as a classifier with a framework of tree structure having internal nodes signifying elements of dataset, branches signifying classification rules, and every leaf node signifying the classification outcomes. Two nodes,the Decision Node which are used to create decision and the Leaf Node which are the results of the decision make up a decision tree.[17] (Fig. 5).

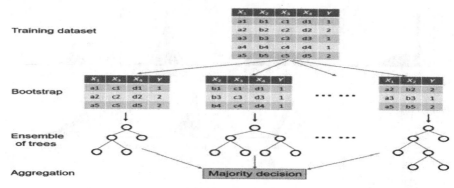

Training dataset

Bootstrap

Ensemble
of trees

Aggregation

Fig. 4. Extra tree

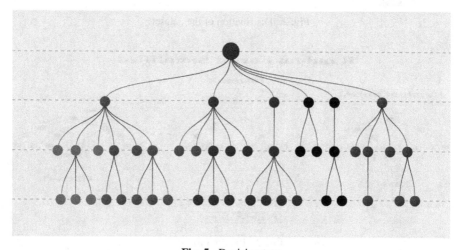

Fig. 5. Decision tree

D. Passive-Aggressive Classifier

Large-scale learning usually uses passive-aggressive algorithms. As opposed to batch learning, when the entire training dataset is applied at once, online machine learning techniques employ sequential input data and update the model of machine learning one step at a time. When there is a huge amount of data available, this is really helpful [18].

E. K-Nearest Neighbors (KNN)

A supervised machine approach called K-nearest neighbours is used to categorise label datasets. This algorithm finds neighbours for a specific data point. Additionally, predictions for the labels of unknown data points can be generated using information from these neighbours [19] (Fig. 6).

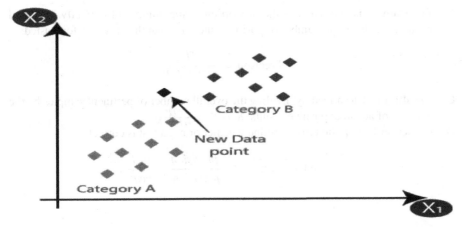

Fig. 6. k-Nearest neighbors

4 Results and Discussion

The programming language Python was employed for doing the comparative study in finding the performance matrices of the five algorithms as mentioned namely Decision Tree (DT), Random Forest (RF), Extra Tree (ET), K-Nearest Neighbour (KNN) and Passive Aggressive Classifier (PAC)on the data set of Kaggle [14]. Table 2 displays the hyper parameter values utilised in this investigation of algorithms.

Table 2. Hyper parameter values of machine learning algorithms

Algorithms	Hyperparameter Values
Random Forest	n_estimators = 500, max_depth = 5, random_state = 123
Extra Trees	n_estimators = 270,max_depth = 9, random_state = 42
Decision Tree	random_state = 123,criterion = 'entropy',max_depth = 7
Passive Aggressive Classifier	max_iter = 300,random_state = 1,fit_intercept = False
K-Nearest Neighbour	n_neighbors = 17,weights = 'distance',leaf_size = 20

4.1 Performance Measure

The performance of five algorithms were estimated on four factors as described below.These measurements rely on classification labels like TP (True Positive), TN (True Negative), FP (False Positive), and FN (False Negative) [9]. Table 3 displays the performance of various algorithms.

A. **Accuracy:** Divide the total population by the sum of TP and TN.

$$Accuracy = \frac{TP + TN}{TP + TN + FN + FP}$$

B. **Precision:** It is computed as the proportion of the number of correctly identified positive results to the number of positive outcomes that the classifier forecasted.

$$Precison = \frac{TP}{(TP + FP)}$$

C. **Recall:** It is determined by dividing the overall number of pertinent samples by the quantity of accurate positive results. $Recall = \frac{TP}{(TP+FN)}$

D. **F1-Score:** It is applied to determine whether or not a test is correct.

$$F1 - Score = 2 * \frac{precision * recall}{precision + recall}$$

Table 3. Performance of classifier for diabetes prediction

Algorithms	Accuracy	Precision	Recall	F1-Score
Random Forest	81.16	0.75	0.57	0.65
Extra Tree	81.16	0.80	0.51	0.62
Passive Aggressive Classifier	69.48	0.00	0.00	0.00
Decision Tree	70.77	0.52	0.51	0.51
K-Nearest Neighbour	78.57	0.68	0.55	0.61

As seen from Table 3, Random Forest is giving the highest accuracy of 81.16%, precision of 75%, recall of 57%, f1-score of 65% and Extra Tree is also giving the highest accuracy of 81.16%, precision of 80%, recall of 51%, f1-score of 62% for prediction in diabetes among all classifiers. The accuracies obtained from the analysis is shown graphically for better understanding in Fig. 7.

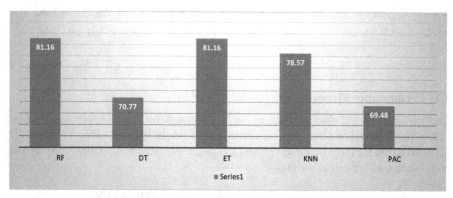

Fig. 7. Comparison of classifier's accuracy

From the above Table 3 and Fig. 7, the Random Forest and Extra Tree clearly demonstrate that they have performed the best, with an accuracy of 81.16 percent and KNN is giving the second highest accuracy of 78.57%.

5 Conclusion

One of the deadliest illnesses in the real world is diabetes mellitus, and it might be difficult to diagnose this illness in its early stages. In this study, five different machine learning algorithms were used to develop a model that successfully addresses all issues and aids in the early detection of diabetes disease. After comparing these algorithms, it was experimentally seen that Random Forest and Extra Tree have the lowest error rates and have the highest accuracy (81.16%).

References

1. Vats, V., et al.: A comparative analysis of unsupervised machine techniques for liver disease prediction. In: 2018 IEEE International Symposium on Signal Processing and Information Technology (ISSPIT), Louisville, KY, USA, 486-489 (2018)
2. Gavhane, A., Kokkula, G., Pandya, I., Devadkar, K.: Prediction of heart disease using machine learning. In: 2018 Second International Conference on Electronics, Communication and Aerospace Technology (ICECA), Coimbatore, pp. 1275–1278 (2018)
3. https://www.javatpoint.com/types-of-machine-learning
4. Joshi, R., Alehegn, M.: Analysis and prediction of diabetes diseases using machine learning algorithm: ensemble approach. Int. Res. J. Eng. Technol. 4(10), 426–435 (2017)
5. Sivaranjani, S., et al.: Diabetes prediction using machine learning algorithms with feature selection and dimensionality reduction. In: 2021 7th International Conference on Advanced Computing and Communication Systems (ICACCS). Vol. 1. IEEE (2021)
6. International Diabetes Federation, IDF Diabetes Atlas, 8th edn. (2017)
7. Li, G., Peng, S., Wang, C., Niu, J., Yuan, Y.: An energy-efficient data collection scheme using denoising autoencoder in wireless sensor networks. Tsinghua Sci. Technol. 24(1), 86–96 (2019)
8. Vijayan, V.V., Anjali, C.: Prediction and diagnosis of diabetes mellitus—a machine learning approach. In: 2015 IEEE Recent Advances in Intelligent Computational Systems (RAICS). IEEE (2015)
9. Sonar, P., JayaMalini, K.. Diabetes prediction using different machine learning approaches. In: 2019 3rd International Conference on Computing Methodologies and Communication (ICCMC). IEEE (2019)
10. Nagabushanam, P., et al.: CNN architecture for diabetes classification. In: 2021 3rd International Conference on Signal Processing and Communication (ICPSC). IEEE (2021)
11. Chang, V., et al.: Pima Indians diabetes mellitus classification based on machine learning (ML) algorithms. Neural Computing and Applications, pp. 1-17 (2022)
12. Sisodia, D., Sisodia, D.S.: Prediction of diabetes using classification algorithms. Procedia Computer Science 132, 1578–1585 (2018)
13. Sarwar, M.A., et al.: Prediction of diabetes using machine learning algorithms in healthcare. In: 2018 24th international conference on automation and computing (ICAC), pp. 16. IEEE (2018)
14. https://www.kaggle.com/datasets/kandij/diabetes-dataset

15. Breiman, L.: Random forests. Mach. Learn. **45**(1), 5–32 (2001)
16. Sharaff, A., Gupta, H.: Extra-tree classifier with metaheuristics approach for email classification. In: Proceedings Advances Computer Communication Computational Science. Springer, Singapore, pp. 189197 (2019). https://doi.org/10.1007/978-981-13-6861-5_17
17. https://towardsdatascience.com/decision-trees-in-machine-learning-641b9c4e8052
18. https://thecleverprogrammer.com/2021/02/10/passive-aggressive-classifier-in-machine-learning/
19. https://www.javatpoint.com/k-nearest-neighbor-algorithm-for-machine-learning

CRODNM: Chemical Reaction Optimization of Dendritic Neuron Models for Forecasting Net Asset Values of Mutual Funds

Sarat Chandra Nayak[1]([✉]) [iD], Satchidananda Dehuri[2], and Sung-Bae Cho[3]

[1] Yonsei University, Seoul, South Korea
saratnayak234@gmail.com
[2] Fakir Mohan University, Balasore, Odisha, India
satchi.lapa@gmail.com
[3] Yonsei University, Seoul, South Korea
sbcho@yonsei.ac.kr

Abstract. Learning algorithm and aggregation function used in the neurons have imperative influence on the approximation of an artificial neural network. Dendritic neuron model (DNM) using additive and multiplicative-based aggregation functions has been emerging as a machine learning approach and found successful in many engineering applications. This study attempts to advance the predictive accuracy of DNM through maintaining a decent steadiness between exploration and exploitation of its search space with chemical reaction optimization (CRO) algorithm, termed as CRODNM. The CRO, being a parameter free and powerful global search optimization method synergies with better approximation capability of DNM thus, able to overcome the limitations of conventional back propagation learning based DNM. In addition to this, to start the search operation with a better-quality initial population, we propose a new initial population generation method for CRODNM by incorporating several methods. The proposed CRODNM is evaluated on forecasting net asset values of four mutual funds in terms of convergence and prediction accuracy. The learning paradigm formed due to reasonable combination of CRO and DNM (i.e., CRODNM) found competitive and outperforms over DNM, multilayer perceptron (MLP), and genetic algorithm trained DNM prediction models.

Keywords: Dendritic neuron model · Chemical reaction optimization · Financial time series forecasting · Net asset value prediction · Mutual fund · MLP · GA

1 Introduction

Please Financial market data such as stock closing prices, commodity prices, energy prices, currency exchange rates, and net asset value of mutual fund companies, etc. exhibit high dynamism, chaotic in nature, following irregular movements, thus it is hard to predict their future values [1]. The inherent uncertainties and associated volatilities make the financial market data analysis a complex task [2]. Further, financial market is

© The Author(s), under exclusive license to Springer Nature Switzerland AG 2022
M. Panda et al. (Eds.): ICIICC 2022, CCIS 1737, pp. 299–312, 2022.
https://doi.org/10.1007/978-3-031-23233-6_23

highly fluctuating due to several macroeconomic factors. Regulatory bodies, political scenarios and international policies and so on. Accurate prediction of such financial data movement helps naïve investor and managers of financial institutions in decision and policy making process. During past two decades many machine learning algorithms such as artificial neural networks (ANN) have been emerging as sophisticated tools for forecasting financial data. Several applications of neuron models found effective tools in predicting financial data through modelling the underlaying nonlinearities coupled with such data [3–7]. Investing in mutual funds have been growing interest in last decades. Net asset value (NAV) is a decisive quantity to judge the financial health and stability of a mutual fund thus, it is important to predict the NAV by the fund administrators in addition to investors. The NAVs of mutual funds for a given day reflects assets and liabilities, which depend on few components that are difficult to anticipate and frequently changes. Accomplished brokers and fund managers attempt to estimate NAV in order to maximize the return from the available opportunities accessible from the dynamic international financial market with minimum risk. Therefore, an accurate and robust NAV forecasting method is essential for the smooth management of a mutual funds. A comparative analysis and review of machine learning models for NAV prediction is carried out in [8]. Few machine learning models are applied in predicting bond risk premiums [9] and asset pricing model [10, 11].

Though substantial number of ANN application exist in the literature, identification of a best model over all financial market data is difficult. Each ANN has its unique architecture, distinct characteristics and limitations as well. The multilayer perceptron (MLP) is the most frequently used model in financial forecasting. However, complex network and back propagation learning in MLP influenced its performance a lot. Also, the aggregation function used at the neurons plays a major role in the performance of a network. Single neuron models with dendritic computations are proposed in the literature [12, 13]. Lately, dendritic neuron models (DNM) using multiplicative and additive aggregations at its neurons are emerging as approximation tools [14]. Using a sigmoid function to model the synaptic nonlinearity with a single neuron, it is found capable of computing nonlinearly separable functions and approximating any multifaceted continuous function. The model uses Boolean logic to represent the nonlinear interactions in a dendrite tree instead of calculating complex functions. DNM is a model of single neuron with plastic dendritic morphology. It has a number of distinctive features which distinguish it from conventional ANNs. It eliminates the redundant synapses and dendritic branches through a neural pruning approach and thus possess a simple structure. Its simplified structure can easily transform into logic circuit classifiers through logic approximation scheme which achieves faster computation, smaller computational rate, and can resolve problems with high-speed data streams compared to other neural models. A survey on mechanism, algorithm, and real-world applications of DNM is carried out by authors in [15].

The back propagation learning of conventional DNM makes it trapping into local minima, fails to achieve the global best weights and thresholds for DNM and hence, largely limiting its performance [16]. To avoid such problems, several evolutionary algorithms are used for DNM training [16, 17]. Artificial immune system is used to train DNM and evaluated on eight classification and eight prediction datasets [17]. The study used Taguchi method to find the suitable user-defined parameters. The method found better to compared methods and able to reduce the redundant synapses and dendritic layers. In a short period of time, few evolutionary algorithms for DNM parameter tuning are found in the literature such as GA [18], biogeography-based optimization [19], social learning particle swarm optimization [20], differential evolution [21, 22], cuckoo search [23], near population size reduction [24], whale optimization [25], and particle swarm optimization [26, 27], etc. These hybrid DNMs are used for classification and forecasting problems.

In the above cited works, evolutionary algorithms are used to decide the suitable weights and thresholds of the DNM whereas, the other DNM controlling parameters such as k, k_{soma} and θ_{soma} are decided experimentally. Though such procedures have been combined with DNM and used for cracking several complex problems, their efficiency is determined by well adjustable learning parameters. In the quest of searching global optima, selection of such parameters makes the use of these technique problematic. Selection of such control parameters while solving a particular problem necessitates numbers of trial-and-error methods. Improper selection of such algorithm-specific parameters may land the search operation at local optima or erroneous solution(s). Also, these methods start their search process from a random initial population that may affect the quality of final solution. Hence, for better accuracy, techniques with higher approximation capability and fewer control parameters will be of interest. CRO is an evolutionary optimization method inspired by the process of natural chemical reactions [28, 29]. It has no algorithmic control parameter. Only the population size needs to be declared. Hence, it is easy to implement without human interventions. ANN with CRO methods is found successful applications in financial forecasting [5–7, 30].

This study is an attempt to enhance the predictability of DNM through searching its weights, thresholds and three user-defined parameters by CRO. The optimal CRODNM is obtained on fly during the evolution process rather fixing its structure at the beginning. Therefore, a self-adjustable CRODNM is formed in an automatic fashion. The CRO is parameter-free and does not necessitate any algorithmic control parameter. In addition to this, to start the search operation with a better-quality initial population, we propose a new initial population generation method for CRODNM incorporating several methods. Finally, the proposed CRODNM is evaluated on predicting NAV of four mutual funds.

The methodologies used in this study are explained by Sect. 2. Outcomes from simulation studies, comparative analysis are done in Sect. 3. Concluding remarks are mentioned in Sect. 4 followed by a list of references.

2 Methodologies

The computations of basic DNM and the mechanism of the proposed CRODNM are discussed in this section. The readers are suggested to refer the base articles as suggested in Sect. 1 for DNM.

2.1 DNM

The computations in DNM are carried out through four layers such as synaptic layer, dendritic layer, membrane layer and soma layer. For an input vector $X = \{x_1, x_2, \cdots, x_n\}$, where x_i is in $[0, 1]$, weight w_{ij}, and threshold θ_{ij} of DNM, the output Y_{ij} corresponds to i^{th} synaptic input in j^{th} synaptic layer is computed as:

$$Y_{ij} = 1/1 + e^{-k(w_{ij}*x_i - \theta_{ij})} \tag{1}$$

Here, k is a positive user-defined constant. Based on values of w_{ij}, and θ_{ij}, six different situations are arising as follows. If $0 < \theta_{ij} < w_{ij}$, then Y_{ij} is proportional to x_i and it is called excitatory state. If $w_{ij} < \theta_{ij} < 0$, then Y_{ij} is inversely proportional to x_i and it is called inhibitory state. If $0 < w_{ij} < \theta_{ij}$ or $w_{ij} < 0 < \theta_{ij}$, then Y_{ij} value is always 0 and it is called constant-0 state. Finally, for conditions $\theta_{ij} < w_{ij} < 0$ or $\theta_{ij} < 0 < w_{ij}$, the output Y_{ij} is always tends to 1, called as constant-1 state.

The nonlinear interaction of dendritic layer is computed by a multiplication unit. The output of dendritic layer is given as:

$$Z_j = \sum_{i=1}^{n} Y_{ij} \tag{2}$$

Outputs from m numbers of dendritic layers are linearly summed in the membrane layer and the result is shown in Eq. 3.

$$V = \sum_{j=1}^{m} Z_j \tag{3}$$

The final DNM output is computed at the soma layer using a positive constant k_{soma} and self-defined parameter θ_{soma} as in Eq. 4.

$$O = \frac{1}{1 + e^{-k_{soma}(V - \theta_{soma})}} \tag{4}$$

The total error signal E from N training samples at the output neuron is measured as the deviation of from target values is computed as in Eq. 5.

$$E = \frac{1}{N} \sum_{i=1}^{N} |target_i - O_i| \tag{5}$$

During the training process, the learning algorithm continuously adjust the DNM parameters, i.e., threshold θ_{ij} and weight w_{ij} values in each synapse to optimize the DNM performance.

2.2   CRODNM Based Forecasting

The goodness of initial population directly impacts the convergence rate and quality of final solution of an evolutionary algorithm. Random initialization method is the mostly used process which may not guarantee the quality of initial population. Therefore, we propose a new initial population generation method for CRODNM by fusing random initialization, opposition, quasi-opposition and generalized opposition learning based methods to avoid its premature convergence and performance enhancement. The method is described by Algorithm 1.

Algorithm 1: Initial Population Generation

---

1. Begin
2. Set *ReacNum* and design variable D.
3. Set counter $i = 1, j = 1$
4. Randomly initialize each molecule in P of size *ReacNum*.
5. for $i = 1 \rightarrow ReacNum$do
    for $j = 1 \rightarrow D$do
$$OPx_{i,j} = x_{min,j} + x_{max,j} - x_{i,j}$$
    end for
6. end for
7. Set counter $i = 1, j = 1$
8. for $i = 1 \rightarrow ReacNum$do
    for $j = 1 \rightarrow D$do
$$QOPx_{i,j} = rand((x_{min,j} + x_{max,j})/2, x_{min,j} + x_{max,j} - x_{i,j})$$
    end for
9. end for
10. Set counter $i = 1, j = 1$
11. for $i = 1 \rightarrow ReacNum$do
    for $j = 1 \rightarrow D$do
$$GOPx_{i,j} = rand * (x_{min,j} + x_{max,j}) - x_{i,j}$$
    end for
12. end for

13. Evaluate fitness of each molecule of $P, OP, QOP,$ and GOP.
14. Select best *ReacNum* molecules from $(P \cup OP \cup QOP \cup GOP)$
15. End

The CRODNM starts with the initial population as formed by Algorithm 1 and different chemical reactions are applied as search operator to explore the search space as presented in Algorithm 2. Here, the possible set of DNM parameters are considered as the search space for CRO. An individual of CRODNM in t^{th} iteration that represents a potential parameter set of DNM is depicted in Fig. 3. There are $2NM + 3$ parametersin total need to be adjusted. Prospective readers are suggested to refer literature [5–7] for detail implementation of different chemical reactions.

Algorithm 2: Chemical reactions search operation for DNM

Initialize population by **Algorithm 1**.
Set $iteration = 1, MaxIter$
While $(iteration <= MaxIter)$ do
  for $i = 1 \rightarrow ReacNum$ do
    if $rand1 \leq 0.5$
      if $rand2 \leq 0.5$
        Apply *Decomposition* reaction on molecule Mi
      else
        Apply *Redox1* reaction on Mi
      end if
    else
    Select another molecule Mj $(Mi \neq Mj)$
      if $0 \leq rand3 \leq 0.33$
        Apply *Synthesis* reaction on Mi and Mj
      else if $0.33 \leq rand3 \leq 0.66$
          Apply *Displacement* reaction on Mi and Mj
       else
          Apply *Redox2* reaction on Mi and Mj
      end if
    end if
  Apply *Reversible* Reaction for increased fitness and update reactant
  end for
  $iteration = iteration + 1$
end While
return the best molecule M_{best}

Inputs are sequentially fed to DNM along with the molecules of the population. The model computes an output as in Eq. 4. This output is compared with the target to obtain an error value. The error signal so generated is considered as the fitness of the corresponding molecule. Chemical reaction operators are applied to explore the search space. Based on the fitness values, selection process is carried out and population is updated in successive iterations. The process stops at the maximum iteration (similar to equilibrium condition in chemical reaction). The best-fit molecule is chosen from the converged population and supplied to the DNM along with the test data. The error values calculated from the test data are considered as the CRODNM prediction performance and preserved for comparative studies. Lower the error value, better is the predictability of the model. The CRODNM process is shown in Fig. 1.

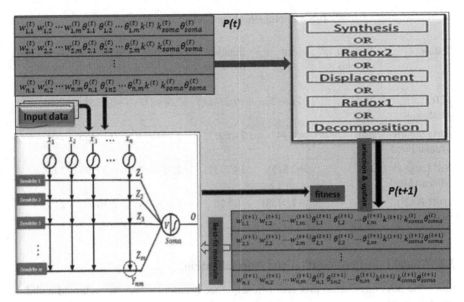

Fig. 1. CRODNM process

3 Experiments, Outcomes and Analysis

Collection of experimental data, input preparation for model and normalization, and analysis of experimental outcomes are discussed in this section.

3.1 Collection and Statistical Summary of Data

The experimental data comprising stock prices of four emerging companies such as Apple Inc., Cisco Systems, Microsoft, and Starbucks Inc. Listed in NASDAQ are downloaded from the Website: https://www.amfiindia.com/net-asset-value/nav-history.The duration of data collection is 8th September 2021 to 7th September 2022. Statistics from the datasets are summarized in Table 1. All the series showing stable and smaller kurtosis value that indicates investment opportunity. All the datasets are platykurtic. The Birla Sunlife and SBI data are deviating highly while ICICI and IDBI are stable.

Table 1. Numerical dataset and statistics.

Dataset	Total no. of samples	Mean	Standard deviation	Kurtosis	Skewness	Generated Input patterns
ICICI Prudential	243	11.48286	0.074645	2.694837	−0.23598	238
Birla Sunlife Mutual Fund	248	686.447	24.69773	2.294563	−0.14455	243
SBI Large & Midcap Fund	248	360.8158	14.77311	2.423099	−0.37398	243
IDBI B&F Service Fund	248	12.97681	0.826513	2.108236	−0.3046	243

3.2 Model Input Preparation and Normalization

Since the NAV prediction problem is a sequence prediction task, we adopted a sliding window mechanism for generating training and test patterns from the original datasets [5, 6]. For example, input patterns generated using a window size of 3 along with corresponding target values are depicted in Fig. 2.

$$
\begin{array}{ccc|c}
 & \textit{train data} & & \textit{target} \\
x(j) & x(j+1) & x(j+2) & \vdots \quad x(j+3) \\
x(j+1) & x(j+2) & x(j+3) & \vdots \quad x(j+4) \\
x(j+2) & x(j+3) & x(j+4) & \vdots \quad x(j+5) \\
 & \textit{test data} & & \textit{target} \\
x(j+3) & x(j+4) & x(j+5) & \vdots \quad x(j+6) \\
\end{array}
$$

Fig. 2. Train and test patterns generated by sliding window

The model inputs are and normalized using sigmoid method as in (6) and finally after prediction process, a de-normalization method is carried out to get the real-time data. In (6), x_{norm} is the normalized value of x_i, x_{min} and x_{max} are the minimum and maximum data value of a pattern generated by sliding window respectively.

$$
x_{norm} = \frac{1}{1 + e^{-\left(\frac{x_i - x_{min}}{x_{max} - x_{min}}\right)}} \tag{6}
$$

3.3 Experimental Design

As stated earlier, CRO has no algorithmic control parameter that need to be tuned. Only the population size needs to be defined. In this work, the population size, i.e., *ReacNum* was set to 50. The convergence criterion was set to 100 maximum number of iterations. The DNM parameters such as weight w_{ij}, threshold θ_{ij}, k, k_{soma} and θ_{soma} are decided by CRO in an evolutionary manner. Figure 3 depicts an individual representation for CRODNM. The population size, cross-over and mutation probability of GA was chosen as 80, 0.6 and 0.003 respectively. The MLP used has one hidden layer and the learning rate and momentum factor was set to 0.002 and 0.01 respectively. For a fair comparison, the same input pattern is fed to all predictors and all methods iterated for 100 times. In order to compensate the stochastic nature of predictors, for each input pattern a model was executed 30 times and average prediction errors from 30 runs are considered as the performance of a model. Only one neuron is at output layer because there is only one target variable in each input pattern to be predicted. The mean absolute percentage of error (MAPE) as in (7) is chosen as the model performance measure. For the sake of space, the error convergence graph for ICICI prudential series only presented as in Fig. 4. It can be seen that the CRODNM converged faster than others.

$$MAPE = \frac{1}{No.ofpattern} \sum_{i=1}^{No.ofpattern} \frac{|Target_i - Predicted_i|}{Target_i} * 100\% \qquad (7)$$

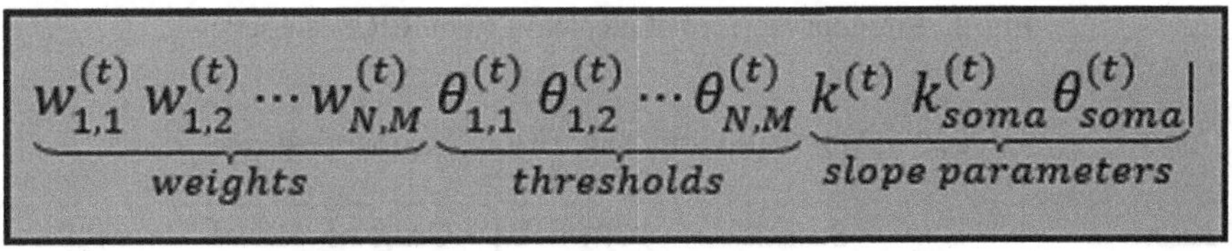

$$w_{1,1}^{(t)} \underbrace{w_{1,2}^{(t)} \cdots w_{N,M}^{(t)}}_{weights} \underbrace{\theta_{1,1}^{(t)} \theta_{1,2}^{(t)} \cdots \theta_{N,M}^{(t)}}_{thresholds} \underbrace{k^{(t)} k_{soma}^{(t)} \theta_{soma}^{(t)}}_{slope\ parameters}|$$

Fig. 3. A molecule representation of DNM

3.4 Analysis of Experimental Results

The MAPE statistics from four datasets using four predictors are recorded and listed in Table 2. The average MAPEs generated by CRODNM are 0.012816, 0.015368, 0.018815, and 0.021825 for ICICI prudential, Birla Sunlife mutual fund, SBI large and midcap, and IDBI mutual fund respectively which are lowest when compared with that from others. The GADNM model is the second good model. Both CRODNM and GADNM found efficient compared to conventional DNM. It seems that, they easily fine-tuned the DNM parameters, converged faster and thus, capable to escape the local optima. The MLP predictions are found inferior. Further, the box-whisker plots of MAPEs from ICICI dataset are depicted in Fig. 5 established the better performance of CRODNM. The predicted NAVs for ICICI data series by four predictors are plotted in Fig. 6. It shows that CRODNM predictions are much closer to actual NAVs compared to others. The error histogram in Fig. 7 shows that for most of the input patterns of ICICI, the proposed CRODNM produced error values closer to zero. These evidences from experimental work highly suggested the goodness of CRODNM predictions over others.

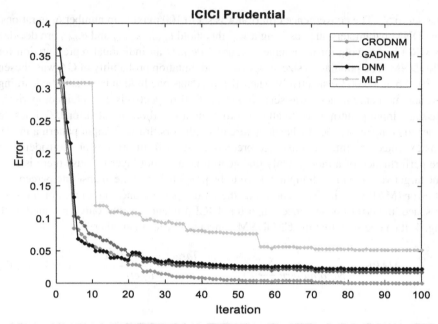

Fig. 4. Error convergence of predictors from ICICI data series

Table 2. MAPE statistics for four datasets and four predictors.

Dataset	Statistic	CRODNM	GADNM	DNM	MLP
ICICI Prudential	Minimum	2.22E-05	0.000129	4.17E-05	0.000645
	Average	0.012816	0.014045	0.013301	0.031826
	Maximum	0.126585	0.122585	0.132585	0.097585
	Median	0.00806	0.010362	0.007406	0.031674
	Standard dev	0.016763	0.015977	0.017816	0.014524
	IQR	0.012362	0.011174	0.013579	0.014113
Birla Sunlife Mutual Fund	Minimum	2.04E-05	3.29E-05	0.00349	0.009415
	Average	0.015368	0.017624	0.061509	0.134923
	Maximum	0.168562	0.195585	0.238457	0.383457
	Median	0.00806	0.014627	0.062924	0.137835
	Standard dev	0.013760	0.015223	0.015856	0.02109
	IQR	0.012325	0.01219	0.015216	0.015495
SBI Large & Midcap Fund	Minimum	2.26E-05	3.25E-05	0.00366	0.006191

(*continued*)

Table 2. (*continued*)

Dataset	Statistic	CRODNM	GADNM	DNM	MLP
	Average	0.018815	0.017624	0.061509	0.095336
	Maximum	0.106500	0.115585	0.108457	0.143457
	Median	0.007930	0.014627	0.062924	0.097835
	Standard dev	0.016337	0.015223	0.015856	0.019128
	IQR	0.011625	0.01432	0.012164	0.013458
IDBI B&F Service Fund	Minimum	1.98E-04	3.29E-05	0.004240	0.009455
	Average	0.021825	0.027465	0.060526	0.124925
	Maximum	0.100658	0.135544	0.117453	0.163457
	Median	0.007935	0.014627	0.069263	0.133572
	Standard dev	0.013703	0.017249	0.013562	0.021109
	IQR	0.011566	0.013115	0.015224	0.015485

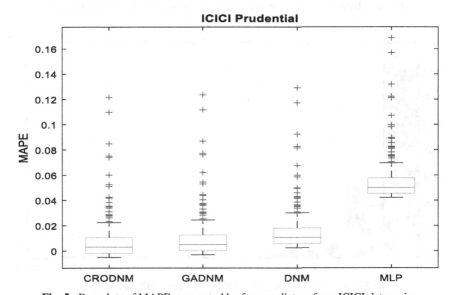

Fig. 5. Box plots of MAPEs generated by four predictors from ICICI data series

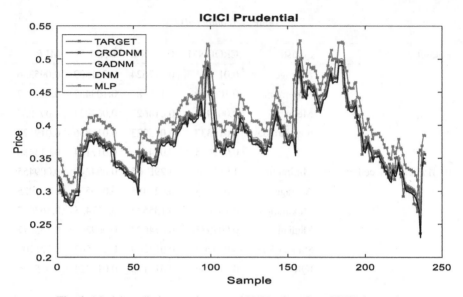

Fig. 6. Model predictions against actual NAV values from ICICI data series

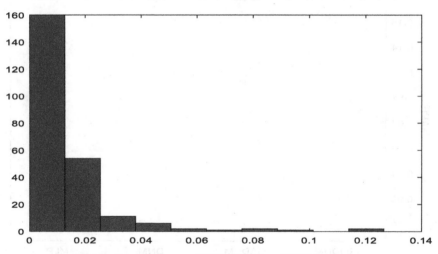

Fig. 7. Error histogram of CRODNM from ICICI data series

4   Conclusions and Further Scope

In order to improve the prediction accuracy of DNM, this study developed a hybrid forecast termed as CRODNM. The powerful global search ability of CRO hybridized with better approximation capability of DNM thus, able to overcome the limitations of conventional back propagation learning based DNM. To initiate the search operation with a better-quality initial population, a new initial population generation method for CRODNM incorporating several methods is suggested. The proposed CRODNM is applied to predict the NAVs of four real-world mutual funds exploring one-year historical data. It observed that CRODNM is quite able to model NAV historical data and capture the underlaying dynamism coupled with such data efficiently. The predictability of CRODNM is compared with three others similarly developed forecasts such as GADNM, DNM, and MLP and found superior. Experimental studies suggest that CRODNM clearly improves the NAV prediction accuracy with good convergence speed and effectively reaching the global optima. The study can be extended further by incorporating advance learning mechanisms and application to other financial time series as well.

Acknowledgement. Dr. Sarat Chandra Nayak was supported by BK21 grant funded by Korean government at Yonsei University. Dr. Satchidananda Dehuri would like to thank SERB, Govt. of India for financial support under Teachers' Associateship for Research Excellence (TARE) fellowship vide File No. TAR/2021/000065 for the period 2021–2024. Dr. Sung-Bae Cho was supported by an IITP grant funded by the Korean government (MSIT) (No. 2020-0-01361, Artificial Intelligence Graduate School Program, Yonsei University.

References

1. Fama, E.: Efficient Capital Markets: A Review of Theory and Empirical Work. R. Lowbridge (Module Leader), New York (1970)
2. Kara, Y., Boyacioglu, M.A., Baykan, O.K.: Predicting direction of stock price index movement using artificial neural networks and support vector machines: the sample of the Istanbul stock exchange. Expert Syst. Appl. **38**(5), 5311–5319 (2011)
3. Hafezi, R., Shahrabi, J., Hadavandi, E.: A bat-neural network multi-agent system (bnnmas) for stock price prediction: case study of dax stock price. Appl. Soft Comput. **29**, 196–210 (2015)
4. Wang, J., Wang, J.: forecasting stock market indexes using principal component analysis and stochastic time effective neural networks. Neurocomputing **156**, 68–78 (2015)
5. Araujo, R., Oliveira, A., Meira, S.: A hybrid model for high-frequency stock market forecasting. Expert Syst. Appl. **42**(8), 4081–4096 (2015)
6. Nayak, S.C., Misra, B.B., Behera, H.S.: ACFLN: artificial chemical functional link network for prediction of stock market index. Evol. Syst. **10**(4), 567–592 (2018)
7. Nayak, S.C., Misra, B.B., Behera, H.S.: Artificial chemical reaction optimization of neural networks for efficient prediction of stock market indices. Ain Shams Eng. J. **8**(3), 371–390 (2017)
8. Yang, Y.J., Chen, B., Zhang, L.L.: Asset price prediction via machine-learning method: a review. In: 2021 17th International Conference on Computational Intelligence and Security (CIS), pp. 168–172. IEEE (2021)
9. Bianchi, D., Büchner, M., Tamoni, A.: Bond risk premiums with machine learning. Rev. Financial Studies **34**(2), 1046–1089 (2021)
10. Fama, E.F., French, K.R.: A five-factor asset pricing model. J. Financ. Econ. **116**(1), 1–22 (2015)
11. Gu, S., Kelly, B., Xiu, D.: Empirical asset pricing via machine learning. Rev. Financial Studies **33**(5), 2223–2273 (2020)
12. Tang, Z., Tamura, H., Ishizuka, O., Tanno, K.: A neuron model with interaction among synapses, IEEJ Trans. Electron., Inform. Syst. **120**(7), 1012–1019 (2000)

13. Tang, Z., Kuratu, M., Tamura, H., Ishizuka, O., Tanno, K.: A neuron model based on dendritic mechanism. IEICE **83**, 486–498 (2000)
14. Todo, Y., Tamura, H., Yamashita, K., Tang, Z.: Unsupervised learnable neuron model with nonlinear interaction on dendrites. Neural Netw. **60**, 96–103 (2014)
15. Ji, J., Tang, C., Zhao, J., Tang, Z., Todo, Y.:. A survey on dendritic neuron model: mechanisms, algorithms and practical applications. Neurocomputing (2022)
16. Gao, S., Zhou, M., Wang, Y., Cheng, J., Yachi, H., Wang, J.: Dendritic neuron model with effective learning algorithms for classification, approximation, and prediction. IEEE Trans. Neural Networks Learning Syst. **30**(2), 601–614 (2018)
17. Tang, C., Todo, Y., Ji, J., Lin, Q., Tang, Z.: Artificial immune system training algorithm for a dendritic neuron model. Knowl.-Based Syst. **233**, 107509 (2021)
18. Ji, J., Song, Z., Tang, Y., Jiang, T., Gao, S.: Training a dendritic neural model with genetic algorithm for classification problems. In: 2016 International Conference on Progress in Informatics and Computing (PIC), pp. 47–50. IEEE (2016)
19. Wang, S., Sugiyama, D., Sun, J., Yang, L., Gao, S.: Dendritic neuron model trained by biogeography-based optimization for crude oil price forecasting. In: 2018 10th International Conference on Intelligent Human-Machine Systems and Cybernetics (IHMSC), Vol. 1, pp. 36–40. IEEE (2018)
20. Song, S., Chen, X., Tang, C., Song, S., Tang, Z., Todo, Y.: Training an approximate logic dendritic neuron model using social learning particle swarm optimization algorithm. IEEE Access **7**, 141947–141959 (2019)
21. Wang, S., et al.: A novel median dendritic neuron model for prediction. IEEE Access **8**, 192339–192351 (2020)
22. Xu, Z., Wang, Z., Li, J., Jin, T., Meng, X., Gao, S.: Dendritic neuron model trained by information feedback-enhanced differential evolution algorithm for classification. Knowl.-Based Syst. **233**, 107536 (2021)
23. Qian, X., Tang, C., Todo, Y., Lin, Q., Ji, J.:. Evolutionary dendritic neural model for classification problems. Complexity (2020)
24. Song, Z., Tang, Y., Ji, J., Todo, Y.: Evaluating a dendritic neuron model for wind speed forecasting. Knowl.-Based Syst. **201**, 106052 (2020)
25. Han, Z., Shi, J., Todo, Y., Gao, S.: Training dendritic neuron model with whale optimization algorithm for classification. In: 2020 IEEE International Conference on Progress in Informatics and Computing (PIC), pp. 11–15. IEEE (2020)
26. Yilmaz, A., Yolcu, U.: Dendritic neuron model neural network trained by modified particle swarm optimization for time-series forecasting. J. Forecast. **41**(4), 793–809 (2022)
27. Egrioglu, E., Bas, E., Karahasan, O.: Winsorized dendritic neuron model artificial neural network and a robust training algorithm with Tukey's biweight loss function based on particle swarm optimization. Granular Computing, 1–11 (2022)
28. Lam, A.Y., Li, V.O.: Chemical-reaction-inspired metaheuristic for optimization. IEEE Trans. Evol. Comput. **14**(3), 381–399 (2009)
29. Alatas, B.: A novel chemistry-based metaheuristic optimization method for mining of classification rules. Expert Syst. Appl. **39**(12), 11080–11088 (2012)
30. Nayak, S.C., Misra, B.B.: Extreme learning with chemical reaction optimization for stock volatility prediction. Financial Innovation **6**(1), 1–23 (2020)

Machine Learning Approaches and Particle Swarm Optimization Based Clustering for the Human Monkeypox Viruses: A Study

Akshaya Kumar Mandal[1], Pankaj Kumar Deva Sarma[1(✉)],
and Satchidananda Dehuri[2]

[1] Department of Computer Science, Assam University, A Central University of India, Silchar,
Assam 788011, India
pankajgr@rediffmail.com
[2] Department of Computer Science, Fakir Mohan University, Vyasa Vihar, Balasore,
Odisha 756019, India

Abstract. The world is currently battling with epidemic fear because of the prevalence of monkeypox cases in various corners of the globe, even as the threat of the COVID-19 pandemic declines. The majority of the 2022 outbreak's cases of monkeypox virus are found in Africa now found in nations throughout Europe and the Western Hemisphere. With ten instances of the monkeypox virus recorded in August 2022 in India, along with one fatality, this endemic has now spread to more than 90 nations globally. The 'Orthopoxvirus genus of the Poxviridae family' contains a large number of zoonotic viruses, including the monkeypox virus. The term "monkeypox" describes the disease because the first viral infection detected by this virus was in macaque monkeys. This article presents a summary of the most current, cutting-edge applications of "Machine Learning (ML) and Particle Swarm Optimization (PSO)" clustering to the Monkeypox instances. The literature has highlighted many large data elements where ML has promised to play a significant role. Advanced analytical techniques have proved useful in forecasting the onset of the disease as well as recognizing its symptoms and signs. Furthermore, ML-based bio-inspired big data analytics has greatly aided contact tracing, molecular analysis, and drug development. Even though it is exceedingly rare, it spreads when direct contact with the "mucocutaneous lesions" of an infected patient or respiratory droplets has been associated with the spread of the monkeypox virus.

Keywords: Monkeypox · PSO · Clustering · Zoonotic viruses · ML · Bio-inspired techniques

1 Introduction

A viral illness known as monkeypox can affect both humans and other animals [4]. 'Fever, enlarged lymph nodes, and a blistering and crusting rash' are all symptoms of monkeypox virus [11]. Between 5–21 days may pass between exposure and the development of symptoms [7, 55]. 'Symptoms of the monkeypox virus generally last between

2 to 4 weeks [7]. It can happen without any symptoms as well as with minor signs [54]. There has not been any evidence that the distinctive appearance of swelling of the glands and lesions, because of fever and muscle ache are common throughout different outbreaks [11, 54]. As shown in Table 1, Particularly in young infants, expecting women, and individuals who have weak immune systems, cases can become severe [6, 56]. The 'zoonotic virus' belonging to the 'Orthodox virus' genus is responsible for the illness. This genus includes the smallpox-causing variola virus [14, 35]. Compared to the 'Central African' (Congo Basin) strain, the 'West African' strain infects people less severely [19, 30]. Body fluids, contaminated products, handling of dumpsters, and other close contacts with an infected person are ways to spread the virus [55]. Spreading can be aided by tiny droplets and, presumably, airborne routes [53, 54]. When the same symptoms last longer than a week, people are still contagious from the moment the symptoms appear until all lesions have crusted over and fallen off [55]. The virus reportedly originated in Africa among certain rodents [30] in the first instance. A lesion of viral DNA can have retrieved to confirm the diagnosis [42].

The Democratic Republic of the Congo (DRC) (Zaire), in the city of 'Basankusu of Equateur Province', was where the first case of human monkeypox identified in 1970 [19]. Confirmed cases in total, 338 and 33 deaths (9.8% CFR) has found between 1981 and 1986 in the 'DRC/Zaire' under WHO surveillance. From 1996–1997, the 'DRC and Zaire saw the second wave of human sickness. Between 1991 and 1999, 511 occurrences in total are founds in the 'DRC/Zaire' [19, 30]. In the DRC, the Congo Basin Clade of illness is still present and has a high CFR (case fatality rate) [19]. It was once restricted to tropical jungle regions. The pattern was interrupted in 2005 when 49 instances were 'reported in Sudan' (regions that are now known as South Sudan), but there were no deaths [19]. The genomic study indicates that the virus ware imported, most likely from the DRC [30] (Fig. 1).

Table 1. Symptoms of Monkeypox Virus

Monkeypox virus category	Symptoms
Asymptotic pre-symptom	No Symptoms [11, 35]
Mild	The rash appeared, Fever, Mucocutaneous lesions, and Fatigue [35, 53]
Moderate	Mucocutaneous lesions, Muscle aches [35, 53]
Severe	High fever, Mucocutaneous lesions, Difficulty [53, 54]
Critical	Mucocutaneous lesions, Weak pulse, Respiratory failure, and Organ failure [46, 53, 54]

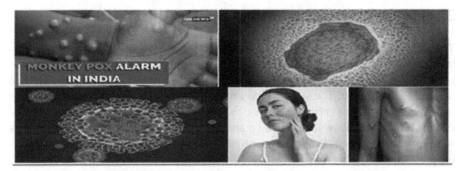

Fig. 1. Monkeypox lesion on human body and DNA of Monkeypox Virus [58]

Following that, many additional cases of monkeypox are founds in 'Central and West Africa', mostly in the DRC: 2000 cases each year between 2011 and 2014. Due to the current data's frequent fragmentation and lack of support, it is difficult to make accurate estimates of the number of cases of monkeypox over time. However, historical data showing both the quantity and geographic distribution of cases recorded in 2018 had increased [11]. By January 1, 2022, reports of monkeypox cases had come in from 42 member states across five distinct WHO regions. Table 2 displays the number of monkeypox cases and fatalities globally from January to August 2022. The geographical regions of the 'Americas are composed of Africa, Europe, the Eastern Mediterranean, and the Western Pacific. Guys who have had intercourse with other males and who have admitted to having sex lately with several or new partners are more susceptible to contracting the monkeypox outbreak. The majority of current epidemic cases were reported through "sexual health" or other health services at primary or secondary health care institutions, with a history of travel to "Europe, North America, or other countries" rather than previously unknown regions, and increasingly with recent local travel or no travel at all. Epidemiological investigations are conducted if a single case of this virus is detected then the outbreak of monkeypox in that nation is considering an epidemic. The rapid development of monkeypox in many areas raises the potential that transmission has been going on for some time without being observe given the initial absence of epidemiological linkages to previously reported monkeypox locations. This article presents a summary of the monkeypox virus based on 'machine learning and particle swarm optimization clustering'. The use of bio-inspired approaches such as machine learning may speed up diagnosis on a far wider scale than physical testing by improving screening and using the massive volumes of data generated by numerous 'laboratory tests, clinical symptoms, and radiological imaging [27]. Using current quantitative and qualitative data, machine-learning approaches can predict 'infected patients' [9, 25]. The general characteristics of monkeypox occurrences are illustrate in Fig. 2, which provides a mechanism for medical practitioners to make judgments during treatment and diagnosis. There is currently no feasible treatment available for those who have infected. In severe situations, supportive treatments such as 'tecovirimat' may be used. Because there are no clear guidelines for symptom relief as these treatments are random.

2   Machine Learning for Monkey Pox Virus

The present global monkeypox virus endemic has infected thousands of people, infrastructure stability, and global economies [53]. The ongoing COVID-19 epidemic has placed a tremendous strain on the healthcare sector due to a lack of suitable facilities to respond to the disease. The sickness has imposed a tremendous load on the healthcare system due to a lack of capacity to tackle the challenges caused by the COVID-19 pandemic [10]. Additionally, it has been demonstrate that the employment of ML enables some essential functions inside the healthcare system, saving many lives while enhancing the quality of healthcare service [25, 38]. Furthermore, like many "chronic diseases", the monkeypox virus is a global endemic that poses a threat to the health of the whole world's population. These occurrences include death, the need for hospital facilities, and the arising of these requirements. If a person has diabetes, hypertension, immunosuppressive diseases, cystic fibrosis, or cancer, they may be more susceptible to these harmful effects [31, 44]. Furthermore, children may be more vulnerable to the severity of this monkeypox virus than adults. Using the available data, machine learning algorithms may be incredibly effective in determining the risk of exposure or potential side effects in individuals infected with the monkeypox virus [59, 60]. Due to its data-driven nature, machine learning (ML) may be useful in determining the optimal method to treat individuals infected with the monkeypox virus based on recent data or features of contagious viruses [57]. It might also aid in the development of treatment regimens and even the prediction of treatment results. For individuals with persistent monkeypox virus infection, for example, an artificial intelligence model can forecast what would happen if a mechanical ventilator was delay. The medical staff may apply machine learning (ML) approaches to anticipate the probability of infection, mortality rate, and other bad event consequences with effective private-public sector cooperation using data from 'airlines, social media, traffic regions, and other monkeypox virus susceptible locations' [9, 25]. To successfully developed and enhance smallpox vaccines, find the ideal clinical trials, evaluate infected patients at different time points, and track disease transmission by the specialists in the medical profession, they are looking for innovative technology. Because of its quicker processing speed, better effectiveness, and enhanced scale-up,

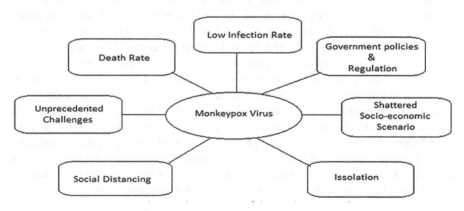

Fig. 2. Different characteristics of the monkeypox incidents

recent research has shown that using ML with bio-inspired methodologies can modernize the health industry [12, 25]. Figure 4 illustrates a variety of machine learning applications for the monkeypox virus (Fig. 3).

2.1 Screening and Treatment

The endemic monkeypox virus is control with early detection and treatment. The "nucleic acid amplification testing" (NAAT) technique, which uses real-time or conventional "polymerase chain reaction,"(PCR) is the industry standard for identifying unique viral DNA sequences. Sequencing can do independently or in conjunction with PCR [12]. However, research focuses on other ways to improve this [27]. These methods, in general, are often less costly, time-consuming, have a low true-positive rate, and require the use of sophisticated equipment. Because of this, timely identification and monitoring cannot accomplish using the traditional approach. Utilizing smart devices and bio-inspired frameworks is a quick and affordable way to identify the monkeypox virus [55, 59]. Using 'skin lesion samples, such as swabs of the lesion, and plasma antibody testing', the monkeypox virus can detect. On the other hand, monkeypox is not be detected by the use of 'plasma antibody detection. Finding LgM (Laboratory and Genomic Medicine) in recently acutely unwell individuals or lgG (Low-Grade Glioma) in matched blood samples taken at least 5 to 21 days apart, with the first sample taken during the first week of sickness, may help with the diagnosis [56], if the tested samples produce different results. Recent vaccinations may affected by blood screening. Jabeen et al. [13] provide a comprehensive overview of Monkey Pox virus replication and the requirement for antiviral treatment in humans. According to his studies, neither humans nor animals can get the monkeypox virus through the respiratory route. Human-to-human transmission is possible because of genetic alterations that may have led to the emergence of monkeypox in humans. A powerful antiviral drug that works against the monkeypox virus is urgently required since it may use as a 'bioweapon'. The efficacy of ST 246 on monkeypox [37] or Orthopox-infected people is unknown; however, it demonstrated to be effective in vivo, in vitro, and in trials on infected animals as well as non-infected humans. Suspected human transmission mechanisms for the monkeypox virus, are depicts in Fig. 5.

Table 2. The global monkeypox virus cases with death cases between January to august 2022 [57].

Region of WHO Member States	Confirmed cases	Deaths
Region of the Americas	20 438	2
African Region	404	7
Western Pacific Region	121	0
Eastern Mediterranean Region	35	0
Region of South-East Asia	14	1
Region of European	20652	2
Total	41664	12

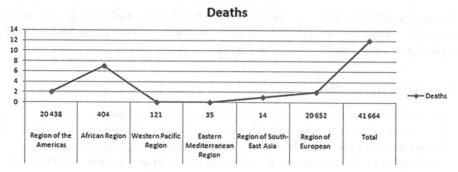

Fig. 3. The global monkeypox virus cases with death between Januarys to august 2022

2.2 Contact Tracing

To prevent the disease from spreading, it is critical to identify the person's contacts after infected with the monkeypox virus. Contact tracing is the procedure of finding and tracing people, who have recently met a monkeypox virus patient. The approach is often uses to identify the affected person for a follow-up 5 to 21 days following exposure [7, 55]. If correctly implemented, this technique has the potential to disrupt the new Monkey Pox Virus transmission cycle and lessen the epidemic by boosting the possibility of appropriate control. Several affected countries have developed various digital contact tracing methods that make use of mobile apps that use techniques such as "Bluetooth, GPS," "system physical address," and others [5]. A digital contact tracing system may operate significantly quicker than a non-digital system and is very similar to real-time. The majority of these digital tools are designs to acquire user information through machine learning algorithms evaluate to identify who is most infects with a particular virus based on recent contact chains [55]. Petersen et al. [36] meticulously prepared a list of ML-based contact tracing and diagnosis applications. The first viremia that occurs from this virus's intracellular replication spreads to neighboring lymph nodes. Infection with monkeypox can result in 'bronchopneumonia, dehydration, respiratory distress, encephalitis', and other consequences. There is no treatment for monkeypox, as cases are still report across the world. Supportive therapy, such as 'Tecovirimat', can used to treat illness. Because there are no accepted recommendations for symptom reduction, as all treatments are entirely individual.

2.3 Prediction and Forecasting

The government, public health institutions, and policymakers will be able to deal with the endemic lot more effectively if the monkeypox virus epidemic is predict and forecast. Susceptible infected and removed (SIR), "susceptible exposed infected and recovered" (SEIR), susceptible infected recovered and dead (SIRD), infected, infected, and dead (IID), infected, infected are the following terms used for prediction and forecasting the virus [25]. Several ML-based prediction models for the monkeypox virus are depicts as shown in Fig. 4. The performance of these models has to anticipate and improve, as more data is available.

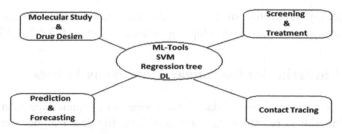

Fig. 4. ML tools for monkeypox virus

2.4 Drug Design and Molecular Research

Machine learning (ML) and molecular biology (MB) are well-known interdisciplinary research fields [13, 25]. Modern molecular biology employs advanced tools to analyze and interpret data and answer complex biological questions that traditional laboratory techniques cannot solve. Deep learning has applied to molecular design, most prominently in modeling, simulation, and drug discovery [25, 37]. With the emergence of the monkeypox virus, scientists and medical specialists from all over the world have pushed for a practical solution to build monkeypox virus treatments and vaccinations by using machine-learning approaches [25, 36, 53]. By aiding in the creation of cutting-edge medications and vaccines, recommending fresh inhibitors, looking into how structural changes affect the viral genetic variation, and other activities [16, 40], these efforts can help in the fight against the endemic spread of the monkeypox virus. The endemic may control through treatment and vaccination programs against the monkeypox virus to create potential drug designs for clinical trials, and the molecular and metabolic mechanisms of various disease pathogenesis must have understood. Drug repositioning, also known as medicinal repositioning, is a successful method for identifying new pharmacological or therapeutic uses for drug molecules that are already in use. In comparison to traditional drugs, developing new treatments frequently costs less and takes less time [8, 13, 36]. This is particularly true for the monkeypox virus, where drugs used to treat

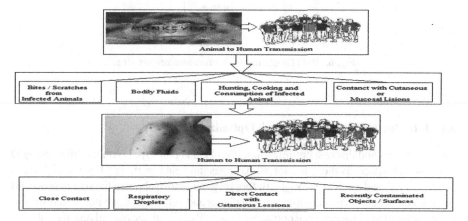

Fig. 5. Monkeypox virus Humans Transmission Suspected Models

one viral DNA group, such as smallpox, are also use to treat another. The use of ML for molecular analysis and vaccine development is discussed in Sect. 3.2.7 and Table.3.

3   PSO Clustering for the Human Monkeypox Viruses

As a result of growing biological data volume, rapid data volume expansion, and technological innovation, bioinformatics originated [50]. Big data analytics were required in the monkeypox virus case because there was a significant amount of patient data, including medical records, X-rays, images of monkeypox virus patients, lists of doctors and nurses, and their travel histories. As the number of people affected by the monkeypox virus grows, bio-inspired computing can be useful in investigating these data sets and identifying trends. Bunge et al. [6] investigated open-data tools for tracking, simulation, as well as the shifting epidemiology of human monkeypox as a potential issue. Accessible organizations, open-source communities, and geographic data resources for monkeypox viruses are represent in Tables 1, 2, 4.

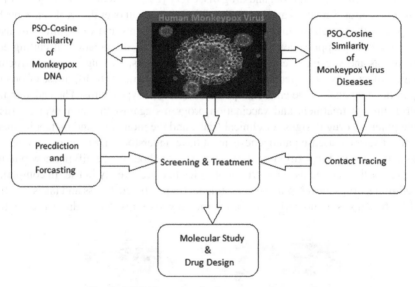

Fig. 6. PSO Clustering for human monkeypox virus

3.1   Introduction to Particle Swarm Optimization (PSO)

For continuous and discrete optimization, PSO [17] is employed with the 'dimension D of the search space' is the same for all particles, and each particle "$1 \leq i \leq N_d$" has a position"$P_{i,d}$" and a velocity "$V_{i,,d}$". Before they may move about in the search space, all particles must be assigned random starting places and velocities. Each iteration results in the identification of the personal optimal solution "P_{best}" with the overall optimal solution

"G_{best}" for each particle. According to the following equations [17], the particle's new position and velocity are:

Updated velocity: $v_i^{t+1} = w.\ v_i^t + c_1 r_1\ (p_{best}^t - p_i^t) + c_2 r_2\ (G_{best}^t - p_i^t)$.

'w' is the inertia weight in the above equation, while 'c_1' and 'c_2' are the global constants.

Updated position: $p_i^{t+1} = p_i^t + v_i^{t+1}$.

The particle updates both 'P_{best}'and 'G_{best}' in the following way:

Particle swarm optimization algorithm [17]:

- Calculate the fitness factor for each particle.
- Examine the modifications in position and speed.
- Track down 'P_{best}' and 'G_{best}' until the velocity value is zero or the specified number of iterations has reached.

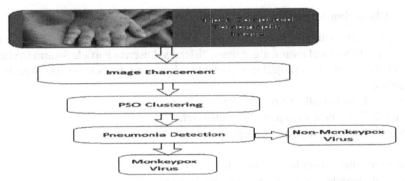

Fig. 7. PSO clustering for monkeypox virus using an image [58] of the infected patients

3.2   Clustering Based on PSO

Clustering is a technique that combines "similar data points" from a given data set into a single group [2]. Few application of clustering algorithms includes 'image compression [20], pattern analysis [22], and picture segmentation [43]'. For clustering analysis, 'particle swarm optimization, or 'clustering based on swarm intelligence, may be used [43]. Data points have treated as particles in 'particle swarm optimization approaches. Different clustering methods are use to collect the first groups of particles, until the cluster center, converges. The particle cluster is an update based on the cluster center, velocity, and position. (Represent in Fig. 6 and 7).

Using clustering method based on particle swarm optimization [43].

- Determine each particle's degree of fitness inside a cluster. $\forall x_i \in c_j$ (c_j is a 'cluster' j).
- Determine the most recent positions and 'velocities of each particle' within 'cluster' c_j.

- Replace 'P_{best}' with the ith cluster center & 'G_{best}' with the neighboring cluster centers.

Particle swarm optimization clustering iterates until it reaches the maximum number of iterations or converges. Previous sections described PSO clustering with the equations for velocity and position updates using "P_{best}" and "G_{best}" fitness matrices. The cluster centers for the PSO approach to image clustering are as follows:

$$v_i^{t+1} = w \cdot v_i^t + c_1 r_1 (p^t{}_{best} - p_i^t) + c_2 r_2 (G^t{}_{best} - p_i^t)$$
$$p_i^{t+1} = p_i^t + v_i^{t+1}$$

Where, p_i^t represents Particle position.
$\quad\quad$ v_i^t represents Particle velocity.
$\quad\quad$ c_1, c_2 represent cognitive and social parameters.
$\quad\quad$ $r_1 r_2$ are random numbers between 0 and 1.

3.2.1 Clustering Algorithm Based on PSO

The micro-aneurysms are effectively separate in this study using "blended discrete PSO clustering." In terms of swarm algorithms, "Blended Discrete Particle Swarm Optimization" (BPSO) is the best [20]. It is important to determine the "swarm size of particles" instantly as follows:

Step 1: Initialize all swarm particles.
Step 2: Determine each particle's fitness rate.
Step 3: Continue for each particle.

- Determine the cluster block's velocity.
- For each particle, use the k - nearest search method.
- Calculate the performance metric.
- 'P_{best}' and 'G_{best}' must be update.

Step 4: Go back to 'G_{best}'.

3.2.2 Image Fitness Tests

The fitness test determines the primary accuracy of the segmented computed tomography scan image. The class of the "clusters" has evaluated by applying fitness metric. The expression $x_n = (x_{n,1}, \ldots x_{n,k})$ represents each particle in a cluster. Groups of data clustering approaches are referring to swarm. The fitness function is used to rate the particle quality in the image. Figure 7 illustrates the fitness metrics used in the previously described enhanced "particle swarm optimization clustering."

3.2.3 Stages of Feature Extraction

The lesions are extracts from the segmented images during the feature extraction stage of the proposed system. Area, perimeter, circularity, and diameter are the parameters used to identify lesions. Therefore, to improve accuracy, the segmented images should be free of unnecessary and irrelevant features. This provided an automatic disease identification of lesions in patients' photos, which is extremely desirable to assist doctors in diagnosis.

3.2.4 Screening and Treatment

Monkeypox viruses have identified in 'most' or all animal fluids and excretions (including 'urine, faces, and oral, nasal, and conjunctival exudates') in addition to skin lesions [53, 54]. Consumption of infected tissues and direct injection into skin breaches are further methods of transmission. The importance of aerosol transmission varies depending on the species or habitat. Human infection can cause by 'animal bites, aerosols from proximity, or direct contact with lesions, blood, or body fluids (Fig. 5). There have a few cases when vaginal lesions increased the probability of sexual transfer, and transplacental transmission has seen. Handling, preparing, and eating wild animals have repeatedly linked to clinical cases in Africa. However, in many epidemics, the person-to-person transmission was also common [31].

Tecovirimat (chemical agent ST246), also known as 'Arestyvir', has been licensed for use in people who infected with orthopoxviruses, albeit its 'specific effectiveness' against 'monkeypox' in humans has yet to be demonstrated. Several possible treatments are also undergoing clinical trials, including a cidofovir derivative (CMX001/Brincidofovir) [45]. 'Vaccinia immune globulin', which was formerly used to treat 'smallpox', must investigate, especially in 'immunocompromised' individuals [8]. The main advantage of using this method is that it allows medical practitioners to communicate the appropriate steps to create the essential alert system. These interactions' accuracy and dependability were still major challenges for this method.

Table 3. Review of clinical research for human monkeypox virus

Monkeypox virus symptoms	Initial research	Secondary research
Respiratory symptoms	McCollm et al. [28] Quenelle et al. [37] Weinstein et al. [52] Kugelman et al. [19]	Parker et al. [33] Parker et al.(2007) [34] Jain et al. [14]
Rash	Quenelle et al. [37] Petersen et al. [36] Weinstein et al. [52] Kugelman et al. [19] McCollm et al. [28]	Breman et al. [4] Parker et al. [33] Lamet al. [21] Sale et al. [41] Parker et al.(2007) [34] MacNeil et al. [26] Petersen et al.[36]

(*continued*)

Table 3. (*continued*)

Monkeypox virus symptoms	Initial research	Secondary research
Lesions	Weinstein et al. [52] Quenelle et al. [37] Petersen et al. [36] McCollm et al. [28] Kugelman et al. [19]	Parker et al. [33] Weinstein et al. [52] Sale et al. [41] Parker et al. (2007) [34] Macneil et al. [26] McCollm et al. [28] Wawina-Bokalanga et al. [51]
Fever and exhaustion	Petersen et al. [36] Quenelle et al.[37] McCollm et al. [28] Kugelman et al. [19] Weinstein et al. [52]	Weinstein et al. [52] Macneil et al. [26] Sale et al. [41] Parker et al. [33] McCollm et al. [28] Parker et al. (2007) [34]
Lymphadenopathy	Weinstein et al. [52] Quenelle et al. [37] Petersen et al. [36] McCollm et al. [28] Kugelman et al. [19]	Weinstein et al. [52] Sale et al. [41] Parker et al. [33] Macneil et al. [26] Parker et al. (2007) [34] McCollm et al. [28] Lam et al. [21]

3.2.5 Contact Tracing

'Contact tracing' is another application of PSO clustering that is essential for 'healthcare organizations and government officials to properly manage monkeypox infections. It uses metadata from 'blog posts, social media tags, metro smartcard data, automobile records, credit card transactions, and other sources.' Extraction of important properties from geolocation to ensure that a person is in a specific area at a specific time can used to create a tracing system that can monitor people even if they are not using a tracking device, but this method is not particularly accurate [54, 60]. Bui et al. [5] proposed an approach for combining biological data with spatial analytical tools and GIS technology to make it easier to gather and integrate heterogeneous data from various healthcare information providers. The information needed to determine the data transmission on a large scale could also be accessible by improving swarm clustering. The ability to "data merge, share, and analyze" is still critical in a large data set.

3.2.6 Prediction and Forecasting

Researchers and academicians have proposed novel PSO Clustering-driven algorithms to identify monkeypox virus infections in real-time. Infection control measures, such as innovative animal isolation, aid in the prevention of epidemics in primate institutions and those that import exotic pets. Diseases have observed in Asian monkeys combined with African monkeys, so these animals should not house together. It is essential to prevent the virus from infecting other fomites. Vaccination against the vaccinia virus protects nonhuman primates (smallpox vaccine). This immunization, according to the study, may also benefit other species such as prairie dogs. If you have had monkeypox, you should avoid rats and other nonhuman primates, as well as any other animals that might be a source of infection. The design of such a robust early warning system is made possible by the combination of "Particle Swarm Optimization Clustering and ML" into a single framework. In some countries, the surveillance of infectious populations is accelerating with the use of big data analytics. For example, various governments have used Particle Swarm Optimization Clustering and ML by employing the use of numerous surveillance cameras, drones, and face recognition devices to monitor their citizens' movements and determine whether they are properly following isolation rules [17, 25]. A quick response to the spread of monkeypox viruses by Taiwan's healthcare system, which has already tested for coronavirus forecasting and prediction, was crucial in reducing the infection incidence. By carrying out an action plan for employing big data, Taiwan has led the way in the field of human healthcare [3].

Table 4. Different parameters and Symptom alleviation of monkeypox virus

Monkeypox virus different parameters	Monkeypox virus Symptom alleviation
Signs and symptoms	Fever, headache, aches in the muscles, shivering, blistering rash, enlarged lymph nodes [4, 56]
Specialty of monkeypox virus	Infectious illness [6]
Complications	Secondary infections include bronchopneumonia, sepsis, encephalopathy, scarring, and eye infections, among other conditions [6, 10]
Duration	2 to 4 weeks [7]
Usual onset	5 to 21 days after exposure [7]
Causes	Monkeypox virus [6]
Variation	West African,Central African(Congo Basin) [19]
Diagnostic Method	DNA testing [1, 12]
Differential diagnosis	Smallpox, Chickenpox [3, 12]
Protection	ST-246 vaccination, hand washing, rash cover, PPE, and staying away from sick people [15]
Diagnosis	Supportive, antiviral, and vaccinia immune globulin [27, 36]
Drug	Tecovirimat [33]
Prognosis	Most people recover [16, 35]
Frequency	Not as uncommon as previously supposed [54]
Fatality	Up to 10.6 percentage (Clade I, untreated) [53, 57] and up to 3.6% (Clade II), respectively

3.2.7 Molecular Research and Drug Development

Particle Swarm Optimization Clustering can be highly useful in getting ideas for drug discovery [22, 25, and 50]. Few attempts have previously made in this short period to develop a suitable vaccination for example CMX001/Cidofovir /Brincidofovir/Tecovirimat [45]. Hence, the development of drug and vaccination programs against the monkeypox virus is essential for controlling the endemic. The molecular and metabolic mechanisms behind disease pathogenesis are critical in finding potential treatment alternatives for clinical trials, which are required to achieve this understanding. The significance of viral-host protein-protein interactions during viral infection, as well as their potential for therapeutic applications, has previously addressed in the context of ST-246 [15, 37]. Drug reframing, also known as drug repositioning, is the process of discovering new pharmacological or therapeutic uses for old, existing, or available pharmaceuticals. It has demonstrated to be a successful strategy for discovering innovative drug compounds [33]. The Review of Clinical Research and drug design for Human Monkeypox Virus depicts above in Table 3.

4 Existing Challenges and Vaccination

There are still problems that need to overcome soon, although 'ML and Particle Swarm Optimization Clustering' have demonstrated enormous potential in the fight against the endemic monkeypox virus. As shown in Tables 3, 4, additional measures, such as 'social exclusion, mass screening, and testing, have already been implemented in response to the rapid increase in the number of confirmed cases (both infected and dying). Individuals have been encouraged to provide personal information such as medical records, GPS locations, and travel data so that "ML and Particle Swarm Optimization Clustering" can use to monitor the situation during the monkeypox virus endemic. People, on the other hand, usually refuse to disclose such information out of fear of their privacy. This challenge may overcome by employing ML-based bio-inspired techniques. Governmental agencies must also play a significant role in this field to harmonize the schemes used by multiple groups. The most common issue that big data platforms and apps have is the limited availability of standard datasets. The ML and PSO Clustering are applying for the clinical data storage and processing in a systematic approach to enable simple and safe access because further research on 'ML and bio-inspired methods' to 'predictive, diagnostic, and therapeutic 'techniques against the Monkey Pox virus and other similar pandemics will require the development of a vast cyber infrastructure to stimulate global cooperation. Smallpox vaccine recipients may be immune to monkeypox. Younger individuals, on the other hand, are unlikely to have immunized against smallpox because the disease was eliminate in most parts of the world in 1980. People who have had 'smallpox immunization' should continue to take precautions to protect themselves and others.

5 Summary and Discussion

In the past, people believed that 'Africa' was the primary source of the uncommon 'zoonotic virus known as monkeypox. Since May 2022, there have several instances of monkeypox reported in several countries that do not often experience the disease, including 'India, the United States, the United Kingdom, Spain, Portugal, and Canada'. Patients with monkeypox-related rash illnesses should investigate regardless of 'gender identity, natal sex, sex of sex partner, travel, or other special risk factors. Clinicians should strictly adhere to infection control procedures and immediately notify their local health department. This article summarizes an automated estimate of the monkeypox virus that was identifying using 'machine learning and the PSO clustering approach. Machine learning techniques, which may employ the vast quantity of data provided by various laboratory tests, clinical symptoms, and radiological scans to enhance diagnosis, will be particularly valuable in this respect for improving screening and increasing rapid diagnosis on a broad scale [55]. Machine learning techniques can predict 'infected patients' using current quantitative and qualitative data [14, 25]. The results of this strategy can help medical professionals make decisions during treatment and diagnosis, which will help battle the endemic that represents in Fig. 2, 4, and 6. Presently no effective treatments for people who are infect by this deadly virus. However, in extreme cases, supportive treatments such as tecovirimat may employ.

The following are only a few of the health recommendations for the monkeypox virus:

- Testing at Commercial and Public Health Laboratories
- 'Nucleic Acid Detection Kittest for Monkeypox virus' ('PCR-fluorescent probe method-size-48T,Cat.no-PCR0101A, PCRL0101B') [52]
- Infection Control Guidelines, Packaging, and Treatment of Monkeypox Medical Waste
- Treatment of monkeypox with a smallpox vaccine [15, 38]

It can be challenging to distinguish monkeypox from other pox-like diseases because of the "smallpox-like rash" and typical "prodromal symptoms." However, distinct monkeypox symptoms, including lymphadenopathy and lesions on the mucosa, palms, and soles, are important clinical criteria. To preserve the infection in the human population, it is believe that "recurrent animal reintroductions of the monkeypox viruses" are required [14]. Typical hypotheses include:

- Under certain temperature and light conditions, the monkeypox virus can survive longer without a host [19]
- Deforestation and flooding may result in more habitats for species that carry the monkeypox virus, increasing the likelihood that those species will come into contact more frequently and pose a greater risk of transmission.
- The monkeypox virus and its reservoirs may be able to increase their geographic range because of the rainforest's expansion brought on by warmer and more humid weather, thereby hastening the spread of the virus [29].

If the monkeypox virus spreads outside of 'Africa,' the global public health impacts will be disastrous. As a result, there would be no way to stop the virus while its geographic spread is still limited [19]. Due to inadequate resources and infrastructure, insufficient 'diagnostic resources, systemic barriers in war conditions' [19, 54], and a lack of clinical diagnosis of monkeypox [19, 28], monkeypox monitoring is challenging. Knowing the primary 'clinical characteristic' features of monkeypox will assist in 'clinical detection. Furthermore, the development of simple 'diagnostic algorithms' combined with simple, rapid testing [26] may help in the detection and hence control of a monkeypox outbreak [54].

6 Conclusion

As illustrated in Table 2, the monkeypox virus had affected around 90 countries world-wide as of August 2022, with ten cases and one fatality in India. People's social and economic security has suffered substantially because of this horrible illness. To tackle the monkeypox virus challenge, this article discusses the most recent cutting-edge applications of 'machine learning and particle swarm optimization cluster. Various researches involving big data have suggested that machine learning (ML) plays a crucial role. Advanced analytical techniques have been successful in both predicting the disease's emergence and identifying its symptoms and indications. Furthermore, the application of

Table 5. Supportive protection against of monkeypox

Component of Protection	Symptoms/Signs	Prevention/ Treatment
Protection of the skin and mucous membranes [35, 54, 55]	Rashes on the skin	➤Mupironic Acid/Fucidin ➤Clean with a basic antiseptic ➤If there is an extensive lesion, cover it with a light dressing ➤Avoid touching or scratching the lesions ➤Appropriate systemic antibiotics may be investigated in the case of a subsequent infection
	Urethral lesions	➤Sitz bathing
	Oral ulcers	➤Saline gargles with warm water and an oral topical anti-inflammatory gel
	Conjunctivitis	➤Usually self-defeating ➤If signs worsen or there is discomfort or vision loss, consult an ophthalmologist ➤Disturbances
Nutritional assistance and rehydration therapy [8, 28]	Dehydration may occur along with vomiting, nausea, diarrhea, or loss of appetite	➤Promote oral fluids or ORS ➤Intravenous fluids if necessary and a balanced ➤Nutrient-rich diet

(continued)

Table 5. (*continued*)

Component of Protection	Symptoms/Signs	Prevention/ Treatment
Symptom [35, 55]	Increase body temperature	➤Tepid sponging and, if necessary, Paracetamol
	Itching/Pruritus	➤Applying calamine lotion orally ➤Antihistamines
	Nausea and vomiting	➤Consider antiemetic
	Headache/ malaise	➤Proper hydration and paracetamol

'machine learning-based big data analytics inspired by biological systems' has considerably improved 'contact tracing, molecular analysis, and drug development. However, the lack of standard data sets and privacy issues restrict the efficiency of ML and Particle Swarm Optimization Clustering in this scenario. A single library of all the data related to the monkeypox virus is required to determine the efficacy of ML-based bio-inspired approaches in eliminating the endemic.

Acknowledgements. This work was supported by Dr.Satchidananda Dehuri, Professor of Computer Science (Erstwhile P. G. Department of Information and Communication Technology), Fakir Mohan University would like to thank SERB, Govt. of India for financial support under Teachers' Associateship for Research Excellence (TARE) fellowship vide file no. TAR/2021/000065 for the period 2021–2024.

CRediT Authorship Contribution Statement:. Akshaya Kumar Mandal (https://orcid.org/ 0000-0003-0955-4096): The general idea of literature survey, Data correction, Resources, Writing – review & editing – original draft.

Pankaj Kumar Deva Sarma (https://orcid.org/0000-0002-9748-3787): The general idea of literature survey, Research Direction, Resources, Review, and editing.

Satchidananda Dehuri (https://orcid.org/0000-0003-1435-4531): The general idea of literature survey, Research Direction, Resources, Review, and editing.

References

1. "About Monkeypox | Monkeypox | Poxvirus | CDC". 2021–11–22. Archived from the original on 2022–05–10, 2022–04–27
2. Anderberg, M.R.: The broad view of cluster analysis. Cluster Analysis for Appl. **1**(1), 1–9 (1973)
3. Bauch, C.T., Lloyd-Smith, J.O., Coffee, M.P., Galvani, A.P.: Dynamically modeling SARS and other newly emerging respiratory illnesses: past, present, and future. Epidemiology 791–801 (2005)
4. Breman, J.G.: Monkeypox: an emerging infection for humans? Emerging infections **4**, 45–67 (2000)

5. Bui, D.T., Bui, Q.T., Nguyen, Q.P., Pradhan, B., Nampak, H., Trinh, P.T.: A hybrid artificial intelligence approach using GIS-based neural-fuzzy inference system and particle swarm optimization for forest fire susceptibility modeling at a tropical area. Agric. For. Meteorol. **233**, 32–44 (2017)

6. Bunge, E.M., et al.: The changing epidemiology of human monkeypox—a potential threat? a systematic review. PLoS Negl. Trop. Dis. **16**(2), e0010141 (2022)

7. Centers for Disease Control and Prevention. Interim clinical guidance for the treatment of monkeypox (2022)

8. Centers for Disease Control and Prevention.. Monkeypox and smallpox vaccine guidance. Ultimo aggiornamento **2** (2022)

9. Davenport, T., Kalakota, R.: The potential for artificial intelligence in healthcare. Future Healthcare J. **6**(2), 94 (2019)

10. Ennab, F., Nawaz, F.A., Narain, K., Nchasi, G., Essar, M.Y.: Rise of monkeypox: Lessons from COVID-19 pandemic to mitigate global health crises. Annals of Medicine Surgery **79**, 104049 (2022)

11. https://en.wikipedia.org/wiki/Monkeypox

12. Huggett, J.F., French, D., O'Sullivan, D.M., Moran-Gilad, J., Zumla, A.; Monkeypox: another test for PCR. Eurosurveillance **27**(32), 2200497 (2022)

13. Jabeen, C., Umbreen, G.: Monkeypox transmission, need and treatment of humans with an antiviral drug. Int. J. Social Sciences Manage. **4**(2), 77–79 (2017)

14. Jain, N., Lansiaux, E., Simanis, R.: The new face of monkeypox virus: an emerging global emergency. New Microbes and New Infections (2022)

15. Jordan, R., et al.: Single-dose safety and pharmacokinetics of ST-246, a novel orthopoxvirus egress inhibitor. Antimicrob. Agents Chemother. **52**(5), 1721–1727 (2008)

16. Keasey, S., et al.: Proteomic basis of the antibody response to monkeypox virus infection examined in cynomolgus macaques and a comparison to human smallpox vaccination. PLoS ONE **5**(12), e15547 (2010)

17. Kennedy, J.: Stereotyping: Improving particle swarm performance with cluster analysis. In: Proceedings of the 2000 congress on evolutionary computation. CEC00 (Cat. No. 00TH8512), Vol. 2, pp. 1507–1512. IEEE (2000)

18. Ko, Y., Mendoza, R., Mendoza, V.M., Seo, Y.B., Lee, J., Jung, E.: Estimation of monkeypox spread in a non-endemic country considering contact tracing and self-reporting: a stochastic modeling study. medRxiv (2022)

19. Kugelman, J.R., et al.: Genomic variability of monkeypox virus among humans, democratic republic of the congo. Emerg. Infect. Dis. **20**(2), 232 (2014)

20. Kumari, R., Gupta, N., Kumar, N.: Cumulative histogram based dynamic particle swarm optimization algorithm for image segmentation. Indian J. Computer Science Eng. **11**(5), 557–567 (2020)

21. Lam, H.Y.I., Guan, J.S., Mu, Y.: In silico repurposed drugs against monkeypox virus. bioRxiv (2022)

22. Lee, R.C.: Clustering analysis and its applications. In: Advances in information systems science, pp. 169–292. Springer, Boston, MA (1981). https://doi.org/10.1007/978-1-4613-988 3-7_4

23. Li, X., Fang, Z.: Parallel clustering algorithms. Parallel Comput. **11**(3), 275–290 (1989)

24. Likos, A.M., et al.: A tale of two clades: monkeypox viruses. J. Gen. Virol. **86**(10), 2661–2672 (2005)

25. Luo, Y., Szolovits, P., Dighe, A.S., Baron, J.M.: Using machine learning to predict laboratory test results. Am. J. Clin. Pathol. **145**(6), 778–788 (2016)

26. MacNeil, A., et al.: Transmission of atypical varicella-zoster virus infections involving palm and sole manifestations in an area with monkeypox endemicity. Clin. Infect. Dis. **48**(1), e6–e8 (2009)

27. Maksyutov, R.A., Gavrilova, E.V., Shchelkunov, S.N.: Species-specific differentiation of variola, monkeypox, and varicella-zoster viruses by multiplex real-time PCR assay. J. Virol. Methods **236**, 215–220 (2016)
28. McCollum, A.M., Damon, I.K.:. Human monkeypox. Clinical Infectious Diseases **58**(2), 260–267 (2014)
29. Nakazawa, Y., et al.: A phylogeographic investigation of African monkeypox. Viruses, **7**(4), 2168-2184 (2015)
30. Nolen, L.D., et al.: Extended human-to-human transmission during a monkeypox outbreak in the Democratic Republic of the Congo. Emerg. Infect. Dis. **22**(6), 1014 (2016)
31. O'Shea, J.: Interim guidance for prevention and treatment of monkeypox in persons with HIV infection—United States, August 2022. MMWR. Morbidity and Mortality Weekly Report **71** (2022)
32. Osorio, J.E., Yuill, T.M.:. Zoonoses. Encyclopedia of Virology **485** (2008)
33. Parker, S., Handley, L., Buller, R M.: Therapeutic and prophylactic drugs to treat orthopoxvirus infections (2008)
34. Parker, S., Nuara, A., Buller, R.M.L., Schultz, D.A.: Human monkeypox: an emerging zoonotic disease (2007)
35. Petersen, B.W., Damon, I.K.: Smallpox, Monkeypox, and Other Poxvirus Infections. Goldman-Cecil Medicine. 26th ed. Elsevier, Philadelphia, PA (2020)
36. Petersen, E., et al.: Human monkeypox: epidemiologic and clinical characteristics, diagnosis, and prevention. Infect. Dis. Clin. **33**(4), 1027–1043 (2019)
37. Quenelle, D.C., et al.: Efficacy of delayed treatment with ST-246 given orally against systemic orthopoxvirus infections in mice. Antimicrob. Agents Chemother. **51**(2), 689–695 (2007)
38. Ray, S., Turi, R.H.: Determination of number of clusters in k-means clustering and application in colour image segmentation. In: Proceedings of the 4th International Conference on Advances in Pattern Recognition and Digital Techniques, Vol. 137, p. 143 (1999)
39. Reed, K.D., et al.: The detection of monkeypox in humans in the Western Hemisphere. New England Journal of Medicine **350**(4), 342-350 (2004)
40. Reynolds, M.G., Damon, I.K.: Outbreaks of human monkeypox after cessation of smallpox vaccination. Trends Microbiol. **20**(2), 80–87 (2012)
41. Sale, T.A., Melski, J.W., Stratman, E.J.: Monkeypox: an epidemiologic and clinical comparison of African and US disease. J. Am. Acad. Dermatol. **55**(3), 478–481 (2006)
42. Shchelkunov, S.N., et al.: Analysis of the monkeypox virus genome. Virology **297**(2), 172–194 (2002)
43. Shi, Y., Eberhart, R.: A modified particle swarm optimizer. In: 1998 IEEE International Conference on Evolutionary Computation Proceedings. IEEE World Congress on Computational Intelligence (Cat. No. 98TH8360), pp. 69–73. IEEE (1998)
44. Sklenovska, N., Van Ranst, M.: Emergence of monkeypox as the most important orthopoxvirus infection in humans. Front. Public Health **6**, 241 (2018)
45. Smee, D.F., Sidwell, R.W., Kefauver, D., Bray, M., Huggins, J.W.: Characterization of wild-type and cidofovir-resistant strains of camelpox, cowpox, monkeypox, and vaccinia viruses. Antimicrob. Agents Chemother. **46**(5), 1329–1335 (2002)
46. Sreenivas, S.: Monkeypox: What to Know. webmd.com. WebMD (2022)
47. Stittelaar, K.J., et al.: Antiviral treatment is more effective than smallpox vaccination upon lethal monkeypox virus infection. Nature **439**(7077), 745–748 (2006)
48. Torcate, A.S., Barbosa, J.C.F., de Oliveira Rodrigues, C.M.: Utilizando o learning analytics com o k-means para análise de dificuldades de aprendizagem na educação básica. In: Anais do XXVI Workshop de Informática na Escola, pp. 31–40. SBC (2020)
49. UK, G. Research and analysis Qualitative assessment of the risk to the UK human population of monkeypox infection in a canine, feline, mustelid, lagomorph or rodent UK pet

50. Watkins, X., Garcia, L.J., Pundir, S., Martin, M.J., UniProt Consortium: ProtVista: visualization of protein sequence annotations. Bioinformatics **33**(13), 2040-2041 (2017)
51. Wawina-Bokalanga, T., et al.: An accurate and rapid Real-time PCR approach for human Monkeypox virus diagnosis. medRxiv (2022)
52. Weinstein, R.A., Nalca, A., Rimoin, A.W., Bavari, S., Whitehouse, C.A.: Reemergence of monkeypox: prevalence, diagnostics, and countermeasures. Clin. Infect. Dis. **41**(12), 1765–1771 (2005)
53. World Health Organization. Multi-country monkeypox outbreak: situation update. 2022–06–04)[2022–06–07] (2022). https://www.who.int/emergencies/disease-outbreak-news/item/2022-DON390
54. World Health Organization. Clinical management and infection prevention and control for monkeypox: interim rapid response guidance, 10 June 2022 (No. WHO/MPX/Clinical_and_IPC/2022.1). World Health Organization (2022)
55. World Health Organization. Surveillance, case investigation and contact tracing for monkeypox: interim guidance, 22 May 2022 (No. WHO/MPX/Surveillance/2022.1). World Health Organization (2022)
56. Yuen, C.Y., Dodgson, J.E., Tarrant, M.: Perceptions of Hong Kong Chinese women toward influenza vaccination during pregnancy. Vaccine **34**(1), 33–40 (2016)
57. https://worldhealthorg.shinyapps.io/mpx_global/
58. https://www.istockphoto.com/photos/monkeypox
59. Abdelhamid, A.A., et al.: Classification of monkeypox images based on transfer learning and the Al-Biruni Earth radius optimization algorithm. Mathematics **10**(19), 3614 (2022)
60. Patel, M., Surti, M., Adnan, M.: Artificial intelligence (AI) in Monkeypox infection prevention. Journal of Biomolecular Structure and Dynamics, 1–5 (2022)

Machine Learning-Based Hybrid Feature Selection for Improvised Network Intrusion Detection

Pritimayee Satapathy$^{(\boxtimes)}$ (iD) and Prafulla Kumar Behera (iD)

Department of Computer Science and Applications, Utkal University, Vani Vihar,
Bhubaneswar 751004, Odisha, India
pritimayees@gmail.com

Abstract. With the expeditious development of network-based applications, unusual threats erupt. Therefore, distinctive security components are required so that they can boost the existing security mechanism. Network administrators depend primarily on intrusion detection programs to spot such attacks. But nowadays, Machine Learning-based approaches are overwhelmingly used towards intrusion detection, where the system is made to learn from information so that it can distinguish between anomaly and normal traffic. In this research work, we comprehensively discuss some of the established machine learning classifiers concerning network traffic invasions. Using the NSL-KDD dataset, we evaluated five ML classifiers and highlighted their adequacy by employing a rigorous experimental assessment.

Within the scope of this study, we propose a hybrid feature selection technique with the goal of enhancing the prediction performance of anomaly-based intrusion detection systems (IDS). We have used information gain (IG), gain ratio (GR) and chi-squared (CS) attribute evaluation methods for the selection of relevant features. Thereafter, we have used mathematical set theory intersection to extract the best features among the 3 evaluation methods mentioned above. Five different machine learning algorithms (MLA): REPTree, LogitBoost, J48, NB, and BayesNet were implemented to generate 32 machine learning models based on each MLA, resulting in a total of 160 models. Akaike Information Criterion (AIC) was used to select the best model out of the 160 models.

Keywords: IDS · Anomaly detection accuracy · Feature selection · Machine learning · Classification algorithms · Attribute evaluation · NSL-KDD dataset · WEKA

1 Introduction

Due to the internet's growing popularity and extensive use, security is becoming increasingly important to maintain a stable and secure network, free from unauthorized activity. The term "intrusion" refers to any malicious attempt to breach the security of a network by compromising its secrecy, integrity, or accessibility. A variety of approaches, methods, and algorithms have been developed to capture and spot the network intruder. An

© The Author(s), under exclusive license to Springer Nature Switzerland AG 2022
M. Panda et al. (Eds.): ICIICC 2022, CCIS 1737, pp. 333–347, 2022.
https://doi.org/10.1007/978-3-031-23233-6_25

example of such a mechanism is the IDS, which keeps tabs on and assesses all the activities happening on a network in real time. Thus, IDS is a crucial tool that monitors networks and alerts the network administrator to any suspicious or anomalous activity, protecting the network from both existing and emerging threats that put its resources at risk [1].

IDSs are further categorized into three types based on the nature of the attacks: signature-based, anomaly-based, and hybrid. Signature- or misuse-based IDSs look for patterns in network traffic, such as byte sequences, that are used by known threats. Consequently, it cannot identify zero-day threats. IDSs that are based on anomalies are deployed to identify attacks that were previously unidentified by generating models based on the system's behaviour. The primary challenge with anomaly-based IDS is the rise of false alarm rates. The hybrid IDS combines signature and anomaly-based IDS [2]. Typically, IDS employs machine learning (ML) methods to process enormous volumes of high-dimensional data to identify intruders, develop a trustworthy model of activity, and evaluate new behaviours in the model. Even though there are a number of IDS that employ machine learning, additional research is required to improve accuracy and reduce false positive rates [3].

The pre-processing stage is accelerated and detection accuracy is increased through feature selection, a crucial component of an ML-based solution. Because the IoT ecosystem is always changing, the detection precision of anomaly-based IDSs is regarded as the biggest issue. The goal of this study is to acquire resilient performance for ML-based IDS in the varied IoT ecosystem [4] by proposing a novel feature selection approach.

1.1   Related Work

Numerous studies have been conducted over the past decade to investigate intrusion detection based on NSL-KDD dataset, aiming to improve prediction accuracy and decrease the false positive rate. Machine learning (ML) and deep learning (DL) have been the subjects of a variety of studies aimed at enhancing IoT safety [15–17]. Utilizing the Weka tool's 10-fold cross-validation strategy [5], Alabdulwahab et al. [3] tested the effectiveness of 6 supervised classifiers [Reduced Error Pruning Tree (REPTree), Sequential Minimal Optimization (SMO), LogitBoost, BayesNet, Radial Basis Function (RBF), and Naive Bayes Tree (NBTree)] for intrusion detection on the full NSL-KDD training dataset. Compared to other classifiers, REPTree's model-building time was the shortest, and its detection accuracy was the highest (99.73%). Albulayhi K. et al. [4] used the IoT intrusion dataset 2020 (IoTID20) and the NSL-KDD datasets to test 4 ML-based algorithms: Bagging, Multilayer Perceptron, J48, and K-Nearest Neighbour (called IBk or instance-based learner in the Weka Tool) for detecting intrusion using a hybrid feature selection approach that uses both IG and GR. The J48 algorithm achieved the highest level of accuracy (99.70%) in comparison to other methods when applied to the NLS-KDD dataset. Using the NSL-KDD dataset, Mahfouz et al. [6] evaluated the efficacy of six different ML techniques (NB, LR, MLP, SMO, IBK, J48) in the context of intrusion detection. First, they used the InfoGainAttributeEval algorithm's ranker method to figure out the order of attributes. Then, they used CVParameterSelection to find the best values for the classifier's hyper-parameters. With 97.89% precision, they found that the J48 method efficiently classified the dataset.

Table 1. An overview of several methods for selecting features

Feature Selection Method	Machine Learning algorithm		Datasets	Performance Metrics		Reference
InfoGain and GainRatio	1.	Bagging	IoTID20	1.	FP Rate	[4]
	2.	Multilayer Perceptron	NSL-KDD	2.	Precision	
	3.	J48		3.	Recall	
	4.	IBk		4.	F-Measure	
				5.	ROC Area	
				6.	Accuracy	
CfsSubsetEval InfoGain	1.	REPTree	NSL-KDD	1.	TP Rate	[3]
	2.	SMO		2.	FP Rate	
	3.	LogitBoost		3.	Precision	
	4.	BayesNet		4.	F-measure	
	5.	RBF		5.	ROC Area	
	6.	NBTree		6.	Specificity	
				7.	Sensitivity	
InfoGain	1.	Naive Bayes	NSL-KDD	1.	Accuracy	[6]
	2.	Logistic Regression		2.	TPR	
	3.	Multilayer Perceptron		3.	FPR	
	4.	SMO		4.	Precision	
	5.	KNN		5.	Recall	
	6.	J48		6.	F-measure	
				7.	ROC area	
Subset evaluator feature selection method (wrapper technique)	1.	Naive Bayes	CIC IDS 2017	1.	Accuracy	[7]
	2.	Decision Tree		2.	Specificity	
				3.	Recall	
				4.	Precision	
				5.	F1-score	
				6.	Error rates	
				7.	Response time.	

The studies presented in Table 1 were limited to one or a combination of two feature selection methods. Moreover, statistical model efficiency, such as AIC comparison, was not done in any of these studies. Since an optimized method for selecting features is a key part of machine learning, more research is needed to find the best ML classifier with a high rate of correct detection and a low rate of false positives. Based on this literature review, we propose a more shrewd IDS framework that eliminates redundant features from the dataset in the pre-processing stage. Our research focuses on the application of 3 well-known individual feature reduction methods, namely information gain (IG), gain ratio (GR), and chi-square (CS) methods to get the optimal feature set. Using the concept of mathematical set theory intersection, a unique hybrid feature selection approach is proposed which will rank the best minimum relevant features. The proposed IDS will be a combination of 3 feature selection modules viz. IG, GR, and CS have been used for dimension reduction which may help the classifier to improve efficiency over alternative methods.

2 Materials and Methods

Data security and privacy are key concerns, and IDSs serves as the first line of protection. Intelligent IDS are built using a variety of rule-based methods or ML frameworks. The flow diagram describing the methods followed in our proposed work is depicted in

Fig. 1. In this section, we have described and explained the dataset, ML classifiers, feature selection and reduction approaches, performance metrics, and model evaluation methods used in our research.

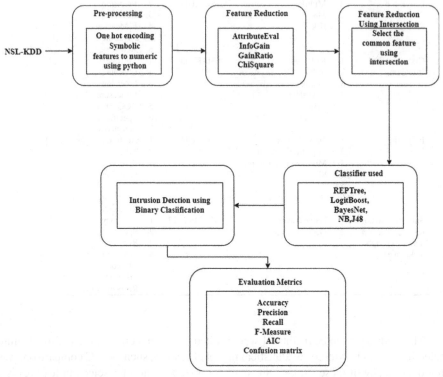

Fig. 1. Machine learning-based intrusion detection with a high-performing hybrid feature reduction approach

2.1 Dataset Description

Analysts have compiled several network traffic datasets to make it simpler to test different algorithms for discovering intrusions, allowing for a more thorough comparison of available intrusion detection approaches. These datasets may be accessible either publicly or privately or through the use of network simulation, which may be used to monitor a variety of traffic events and monitor them. The vast majority of these datasets were assembled with the assistance of a variety of tools that assisted in capturing traffic and keeping track of various traffic incidents. In our research, we have used the Network Security Laboratory Knowledge Discovery and Data (NSL-KDD) dataset, the well-known dataset for benchmarking IDSs. The well-known KDDcup99 dataset, which is exploited extensively in the field of IDS development, served as the basis for the creation of the NSL-KDD dataset, which is an upgraded version of the original. Each record in this dataset is either considered a normal operation or an attack based on the presence or absence of 41 attributes and a single class attribute [8]. The NSL-KDD datasets used for training and testing include 21 and 37 types of threats, respectively. Denial-of-service (DoS), user-to-root (U2R), root-to-local (R2L), and probe attacks are the four main types of network intrusions. Train and test data for the NSL-KDD dataset [9] are subdivided by attack type as shown in Table 2. Table 3 lists the subcategories of the four major attack types in both the training and testing datasets.

Table 2. The NSL-KDD core dataset

Dataset	Total	Normal	Denial-of-service	Probe	Remote to local	User to root
KDDTrain +	125973	67343	45927	11656	995	52
KDDTest +	22544	9711	7456	2421	2756	200

Table 3. Intrusions into the NSL-KDD dataset

Attacks in dataset	Attack type
Denial-of-service	Teardrop, Back, Worm, Land, Apache2, Neptune, Udpstorm, Pod, Processtable, Smurf, Mailbomb
Probe	Satan, Portsweep, IPsweep, Saint, Nmap, Mscan
Remote to local	Xlock,Guess_password, Named, Ftp_write, Sendmail, Imap, Httptunnel, Phf, Snmpgetattack, Warezmaster, Snmpguess, Multi hop, Xsnoop
User to root	Buffer_overflow, Ps, Loadmodule, Xterm, Perl, Rootkit, Sqlattack

2.2 Data Pre-processing

Real-world traffic data primarily contains noise, missing values, and categorical variables that prevent it from being directly employed in machine learning models. Therefore, data pre-processing is an essential prerequisite step for improving the accuracy and efficiency of a machine learning model. Out of the 41 attributes of the NLS-KDD dataset, two single-valued attributes viz. num_outbound_cmds and is_ host_login had been removed. Symbolic attributes like protocol type (3 different symbols; viz. TCP, UDP, ICMP), flag (11 different symbols; viz. OTH, RSTOS0, SF, SH, RSTO, S2, S1, REJ, S3, RSTR, S0), and service (70 different symbols) were converted to binary vector using one hot encoding method, which resulted in a total of 120 attributes (excluding the class attribute). Thus, the dataset obtained from the pre-processing stage is further used in the next stage for feature reduction, as shown in Fig. 1.

2.3 Dimension Reduction

Feature selection is crucial to the development of a better classification model because it frequently decreases the complexity of training and enhances the model's performance matrix. In our research, we implemented IG, GR, and CS attribute evaluation with the help of the ranker method to rank the one-hot encoded attributes of the NSL-KDD data set. The lowest 10, 20, 30, 40, 50, 60, 70, and 80 ranked attributes were sequentially filtered from each attribute-ranked dataset, resulting in the construction of 8 datasets for each of the three attribute evaluation methods containing 111, 101, 91, 81, 71, 61, 51, and 41 features, respectively, ultimately having a total of $8 \times 3 = 24$ datasets. The hybrid feature selection approach used by us utilizes three filter-based approaches. To design the hybrid feature selection approach, we used mathematical set theory to consider the attributes that are common (intersection) between the individual sequentially filtered datasets of the three attribute evaluation methods, resulting in a total of eight datasets. Thus, a total of 32 datasets $(24 + 8)$ were generated.

Information Gain Feature Selection: The importance of an attribute is determined by the Information Gain Attribute Analysis, which does this by calculating the information gain in relation to the class [14].

Gain Ratio Feature Selection: The gain ratio can be considered of as an extension of the information gain that was addressed earlier. It emphasizes selecting characteristics that have a high number of values in an effort to minimize the Information Gain that occurs as a result of its use. Therefore, we are able to say that the Gain Ratio feature evaluation is more accurate in certain conditions, specifically those in which the data are well-ordered and there is no redundancy [14].

Chi-Square Feature Selection: The chi-squared test is a numerical test that measures the variation from the distribution that would be predicted if the feature event were independent of the class value [18].

2.4 Model Evaluation

Several machine-learning approaches were employed to monitor traffic data for various irregularities. The majority of these approaches (classifiers) detect the abnormality by taking into account deviations from basic common network data. Typically, these models are trained using a collection of traffic data gathered over some time. There are three types of ML anomaly detection methods: supervised, unsupervised, and semi-supervised learning. In our experiments, the complete NSL-KDD dataset along with the 32 datasets generated (as described in Sect. 3.3) was evaluated based on 10 Fold Cross Validation using five well-known ML classifiers named as REPTree, LogitBoost, J48, NB, and BayesNet. We also train the classifiers without any feature reduction methods. This resulted in the generation of a total of $(32 \times 5 + 1 \times 5) = 165$ models.

REPTree: Reduced error pruning is a quick decision tree learner. A decision/regression tree is created by REPTree depending on information gained or by lowering variance [10].

LogitBoost: By reducing logistic loss, it may be applied to additive tree regression as well as binary or multi-class classification. It is suitable for managing noisy and outlier data when compared to other AdaBoost classifiers [3].

BayesNet: It is a frequently used technique that bases its operation on the fundamental Bayes theorem and builds a Bayesian network after determining the conditional probability for each node [10].

J48: The C4.5 algorithm is used to create a decision tree (DT), which is a part of supervised learning methodology and is referred to as J48 in the Weka tool [4].

NB: The Bayes Theorem serves as the foundation for the Naive Bayes (NB) classifier, one of the most traditional methods for solving classification issues. NB does not discard the features' weak predictors, in contrast to other machine learning algorithms. Each feature's information is considered, and a probabilistic model is constructed [7].

2.5 Evaluation Metrics

To assess how well the suggested IDS performs, we employed the evaluation matrices below:

Confusion Matrix: A confusion matrix is a visual aid that serves as the foundation for computing all other evaluation criteria. It has the following four values: false negative (FN), true negative (TN), false positive (FP) and true positive (TP) [3].

TP: When the IDS classifies an instance as an attack and the instance is in fact an attack, this is considered a true positive result.

FP: When the IDS classifies an instance as an attack whereas the instance is actually found to be normal, this is considered a false positive result. It is often referred to as the false alarm rate

TN: When the IDS classifies an instance as normal and the instance is actually found to be normal.

FN: Instances that should be considered attack but are misclassified as normal

Sensitivity: The percentage of true positives that are accurately determined is evaluated by sensitivity.
    Sensitivity = (TP) / (TP + FN) [6].

Specificity: The percentage of actual negatives correctly detected is regarded as a measure of specificity.
    Specificity = TN / (TN + FP) [6].

Accuracy: The result is accurate when the total amount of objects is divided by the fraction of correctly detected components, which may include either true positives or true negatives.
    Accuracy = (TP + TN)/(TP + TN + FP + FN) [3]

F-measure: The F-measure is used to evaluate the efficacy of binary classification functions, which is the harmonic mean of precision and recall. Precision is the proportion of predicted positive outcomes that actually are in the class the classifier has predicted.

Precision = (TP) / (TP + FP)

The percentage of positive cases that the classifier correctly predicted is measured by recall.

Recall = (TP)/(TP + FN)

F-measure = 2 × (Precision × Recall) / (Precision + Recall) [6]

Matthew's Correlation Coefficient (MCC): The MCC is an useful statistic for evaluating the efficiency of binary classification models developed from unbalanced data. It accepts a number between 1 and + 1, where + 1 stands for a perfect prediction, 0 for an average random prediction, and -1 for an inverse prediction.

MCC = (TP × TN-FP × FN)/$\sqrt{}$ ((TP + FN) (TP + FP) (TN + FP) (TN + FN)) [11]

Root Means Squared Error (RMSE): The percentage is determined by dividing the difference between the predicted and real values by the total number of predictions. This indicates that the RMSE is most useful when dealing with significant mistakes, the majority of which are unfavourable [12].

RMSE = $\sqrt{((p_1 - a_1)^2 + \ldots\ldots + (p_n - a_n)^2))/n}$

where a1, a2, and an are the real values and p1, p2, and pn are the predicted values for test instances.

Kappa Statistic: The agreement between expected values and values that could be expected by chance is measured using the kappa statistic. When there is no agreement beyond chance, its values tend to be zero, and it approaches 1.0 when there is a very high statistical association between the projected and actual category labels. High kappa statistics and AUC values, as well as a low RMSE value, are characteristics of a successful generalizable prediction model [11].

Akaike's Information Criterion (AIC): AIC is used to choose the best models.

AIC = n log $(\partial^{\wedge 2}) + 2(m + 1)$

The model that achieves the lowest AIC is the best option, where n is the quantity of training data, $\partial^{\wedge 2} = \Sigma \, \partial^2/n$ is a mean squared error (MSE) between what was intended to be achieved and what was actually achieved, and X = m + 1 is the number of total parameters [13].

3 Results and Discussion

Here, we present our experimental results utilising several methodologies for machine learning models and feature selection strategies that, in terms of accuracy with a minimal amount of features, are most suited for the IoT environment. The goal of this experiment is to see how well five classifiers (REPTree, LogitBoost, BayesNet, NB, and J48) can find intrusions with high accuracy while only using a few features. For this, we've used the NSL-KDD [8] training and test dataset together with the Weka ML software [5]. The examination was carried out on a computer running Microsoft Windows 11 and equipped with an AMD Ryzen 7 3700U processor, a Radeon Vega Mobile Gfx graphics card clocked at 2.30 GHz, and 8 GB of RAM. Using the Weka tool's 10-fold cross-validation, we compared three different feature reduction strategies on the entire NSL-KDD dataset for training purposes that was created following the pre-processing stage (described in Sect. 2.2) and scored each feature. This phase's goal is to not only identify many useful qualities but also to eliminate the unimportant ones. In the second step, we used 10-fold cross-validation to assess each classifier's performance on 32 datasets that are subsets of the NSL-KDD dataset and were created using various feature selection methods.

3.1 Classifier Comparison

The results of the five classifiers using 10-fold cross-validation on the NSL-KDD dataset are shown in Table 4 without the use of any feature reduction techniques. The research reveals that REPTree had a detection accuracy of 99.78% and that the J48 classifier had the highest rate of successful detection of 99.84%. Even though no feature reduction strategies were employed, the results of the investigation make it abundantly evident that the REPTree and J48 classifiers achieved the highest levels of accuracy when compared to those of the BayesNet, NB, and LogitBoost classifiers.

Table 4. Evaluation of the five different classifiers with a 10-fold cross-validation procedure

Classifier	Train Set Accuracy	Test Set Accuracy	TPR*	FPR*	Precision	Recall	F-Measure	MCC
BayesNet	96.59%	74.78%	0.966	0.038	0.967	0.966	0.966	0.933
J48	*99.84%*	*81.60%*	*0.998*	*0.002*	*0.998*	*0.998*	*0.998*	*0.997*
LogitBoost	97.10%	74.72%	0.971	0.030	0.971	0.971	0.971	0.942
REPTree	99.78%	78.72%	0.998	0.002	0.998	0.998	0.998	0.996
NB	90.09%	76.19%	0.901	0.103	0.902	0.901	0.901	0.801

TPR: True Positive Rate
FPR: False Positive Rate

3.2 Analysing the Current State of Knowledge in Comparison to the Approach that Was Suggested

Our method was compared to four other published methods that also employed the NSL-KDD dataset with binary classification. The goal of this comparison was to validate the efficacy of the strategy that we have suggested. Analysis revealed that the models generated through our approach are: (i) based on the dataset with 41 features ranked by the ChiSquaredAttributeEval method with J48 classifier, shown to have better accuracy

(99.85%) than the model generated by Albulayhi et. al. (99.70%) [4]. (ii) dataset with 41 features ranked by InfoGainAttributeEval method with BayesNet classifier, shown to have better accuracy (96.82%) than the model generated by Alabdulwahab et.al (94.89%) [3]. (iii) dataset with 41 features ranked by ChiSquaredAttributeEval method with Log-itBoost classifier, shown to have better accuracy (97.12%) than the model generated by Alabdulwahab et.al (96.66%) [3]. (iv) dataset with 41 features ranked by ChiSquaredAt-tributeEval method with REPTree classifier, shown to have better accuracy (99.77%) than the model generated by Kumar et.al (97.02%) [14]. (v) dataset with 56 features ranked by hybrid feature selection approach with NB classifier, shown to have better accuracy (91.30%) than the model generated by Mahfouz et.al (90.41%) [6]. In order to provide evidence for our assertion, we have included this comparison analysis of the NSL-KDD dataset in Table 5.

Table 5. Comparison of our analysis with published methods

Classifier	Reference dataset description		Current analysis dataset description		Reference model Accuracy	Current Analysis model Accuracy
	Reference	FRM*	FRM*	No. of Features		
J48	[4]	UMF*	CS	41	99.70%	99.85%
BayesNet	[3]	IG	IG	41	94.89%	96.82%
LogitBoost	[3]	IG	CS	41	96.66%	97.12%
REPTree	[14]	IG	CS	41	97.02%	99.77%
NB	[6]	IG	IMF	56	90.41%	91.30%

FRM*: Feature Reduction Method.
UMF*: Union Mathematical set theory.
IMF*: Intersection Mathematical set theory.
CS: ChiSquaredAttributeEval.
IG: InfoGainAttributeEval.

3.3 Evaluation of Performance Based on the Elimination of Unnecessary Features

Here, we assess the comparative effectiveness of several distinct classifiers by making use of a wide variety of feature selection strategies in order to establish whether or not the effectiveness of these strategies could be enhanced further. We used primarily the three filter-based feature reductions named as InfoGainAttributeEval + Ranker, GainRa-tioAttributeEval + Ranker, and ChiSquaredAttributeEval + Ranker, as well as a novel approach which is the intersection of these three methods, to improve the performance of five different classifiers. We have used a well-known dataset known as the NSL-KDD dataset for IDS in order to validate our suggested hybrid technique. The findings that we have acquired from the NSL-KDD dataset are displayed in Table 6, which can be found below.

Following the discussion in Sect. 3.3, we partitioned the NSL-KDD dataset into a total of 32 different datasets using the ranking of feature reduction. During the first stage, we used the ranker approach using IG, CS, and GR to determine the order in which the features should be presented. Then, from the datasets that we had gotten after one hot encoding, we eliminated the ten features with the lowest importance, and this procedure is repeated until the lowest 80 attributes have been eliminated. As a consequence of this, we now have 8 datasets, each of which has 41, 51, 61, 71, 81, 91, 101, 111 features from one of three categories—namely, IG, CS, or GR—and one from our own hybrid method. After that, each of the 32 datasets is put through training with five different classifiers, resulting in a total of 160 different models. In a similar manner, we also prepare the test datasets to contain the exact same number of characteristics as are found in the training datasets. The next thing that we did was look at the true positive (TP), false negative (FN), false positive (FP), and true negative (TN) values of 160 different models. We calculate their sensitivity, specificity, precision, recall, f-measure, accuracy, Matthew's correlation coefficient, kappa statistic, root means squared error, mean squared error, and Akaike Information Criterion based on the values of TP, FN, FP, and TN. The lower the value of the AIC, the more accurate the model will be, which will help reduce the complexity of the models, which will be very helpful for the IoT system.

Out of 160 models, the best model generated for each classifier (n = 5) chosen on the basis of AIC [13] is depicted in Table 6. It is found that J48 performed well with an accuracy of 99.855% having a model building time of 44.54 s using only 41 attributes out of 121 attributes and using chi-squared feature reduction. REPTree achieved an accuracy of 99.7746% having a model building time of 7.39 s with only 41 attributes out of 121 attributes using chi-squared feature reduction. In spite of J48's strong performance in terms of detection accuracy, the amount of time required to construct its models is significantly longer than that required by REPTree. REPTree performed well in terms of specificity %, sensitivity %, and mean squared error as shown in Table 6. Among all, J48 performed well using only 41 features with chi-squared feature reduction. Our hybrid approach which is the intersection of three feature reduction methods (IG, CS, and GR) also performed well in BayesNet and REPTree classifiers. The J48 classifier significantly performed well in terms of specificity %, sensitivity %, precision, recall, accuracy, mean square error and the kappa statistic. Also, J48 outperformed by removing the lower 80 features out of 121 features using the CS attribute evaluation method. Because of this, we strongly suggest that the J48 classifier be utilised for the purpose of intrusion detection because it has an incredibly high levels of accuracy in detection while requiring just a small number of features.

Figure 2 presents a comparison of the accuracy of the models we used in our analysis when they were trained and when they were tested. This comparison reveals that both J48 and REPTree achieved a high level of accuracy both during the training phase and the testing phase.

Table 6. Classifiers trained models accuracy metrics using feature reduction

Classifier	Features	FDT*	Se*	Sp*	Precision	Recall	FM*	AC*	MCC*	K*	RMSE*	MSE*	AIC*
J48	41	CS	99.91	99.80	0.998	0.999	0.999	99.855	0.997	0.997	0.038	0.001	−825152
BayesNet	81	Our hybrid approach	99.40	94.39	0.953	0.994	0.973	97.066	0.942	0.941	0.162	0.026	−457952
LogitBoost	41	IG	97.86	96.25	0.967	0.979	0.973	97.107	0.942	0.942	0.149	0.022	−479911
REPTree	41	CS	99.84	99.70	0.997	0.998	0.998	99.775	0.995	0.996	0.045	0.002	−77955
NB	81	Our hybrid approach	94.91	86.88	0.893	0.949	0.920	91.172	0.824	0.822	0.290	0.084	−312148

FDT: Feature Reduction Techniques: Se: Sensitivity; Sp: Specificity; FM: F-measure; AC: Accuracy; MCC: Matthew's correlation coefficient; K: Kappa statistic; RMSE: Root means squared error; MSE: Mean squared error; AIC: Akaike information criterion;

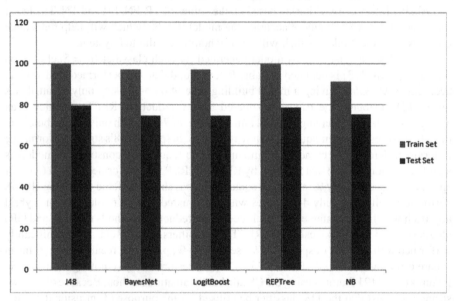

Fig. 2. Train and Test accuracy of the best model among 160 models

Figure 3 displays the accuracy of each of the five classifiers after deleting the 80 attributes with the lowest rank.

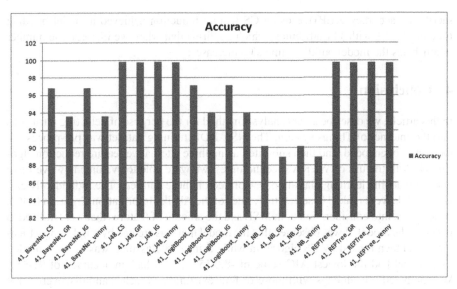

Fig. 3. Training accuracy of classifiers with 41 attributes using feature reduction

Figure 4 displays the accuracy of each of the five classifiers after removing the 10 attributes with the lowest rank. Thus, it is clear from our analysis that J48 and REPTRee achieved good accuracy with only 41 attributes out of 121 attributes using the feature reduction method. Meanwhile, REPTreee using our intersection approach of feature reduction achieves a model building time of 7.7 s with 41 attributes and uses CS feature reduction to achieve a model building time of 7.39 s. This research makes it very evident that the method that we have suggested shortens the amount of time needed to develop models while simultaneously reducing the number of attributes involved, all without

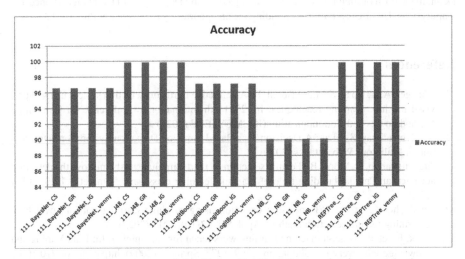

Fig. 4. Training accuracy of classifiers with 111 attributes using feature reduction

sacrificing accuracy. REPTree using CS feature reduction achieved a model building time of 18.74 s with 111 attributes, which confirms that when we increase the number of attributes the model building time also increases.

4 Conclusion

In this article, we describe a data analysis method for the purpose of detecting intrusions into the Internet of Things system. The NSL-KDD training dataset was pre-processed, then one-hot encoded, and then subsetted using three alternative feature reduction algorithms. With the use of WEKA's technologies, we were able to evaluate how well five distinct machine learning classifiers performed on these datasets. The individually created models were ranked based on the values of the Akaike Information Criterion (AIC), which takes into consideration both MSE and the amount of features that were utilised to generate the model. It was observed that the model that was created by employing 41 features, and then ranked by CS algorithm while using J48 classifier, was the best model. This model had the lowest AIC value of -825152, and it had an accuracy of 99.855. We compared our findings with those of four existing approaches and discovered that the J48 classifier performed well when compared to other classifiers while utilising the chi-squared feature reduction method with an accuracy of 99.8555%. The J48 classifier outperformed the challenge by achieving a detection accuracy of 99.7817% by utilising our hybrid feature reduction with 22 attributes. As a result, the accuracy of the model has been increased, and the rate of false positives that our proposed method generates has also been found to be minimal. In the future, we plan to extend our ML-based framework to numerous datasets with multiclass classification, and we also plan to create a deep learning-based framework for intrusion detection. Both of these things will take place in the future.

Acknowledgments. I extend my acknowledgment for the financial assistance from the UGC, New Delhi, in the form of Junior Research Fellowship (JRF) and Department of Computer Science and Applications, Utkal University for providing me an opportunity to pursue my PhD work.

References

1. Ahanger, A.S., Khan, S.M., Masoodi, F.: An effective intrusion detection system using supervised machine learning techniques. In: 2021 5th International Conference on Computing Methodologies and Communication (ICCMC). IEEE (2021)
2. Bandyopadhyay, S., et al.: A Decision Tree Based Intrusion Detection System for Identification of Malicious Web Attacks (2020)
3. Alabdulwahab, S., Moon, B.: Feature selection methods simultaneously improve the detection accuracy and model building time of machine learning classifiers. Symmetry **12**(9), 1424 (2020)
4. Albulayhi, K., et al.: IoT intrusion detection using machine learning with a novel high performing feature selection method. Appl. Sci. **12**(10), 5015 (2022)
5. Frank, E., et al.: Weka-a machine learning workbench for data mining. In: Data Mining and Knowledge Discovery Handbook, pp. 1269–1277. Springer (2009). https://doi.org/10.1007/978-0-387-09823-4_66

6. Mahfouz, A.M., Venugopal, D., Shiva, S.G.: Comparative analysis of ML classifiers for network intrusion detection. In: Yang, X.-S., Sherratt, S., Dey, N., Joshi, A. (eds.) Fourth international congress on information and communication technology. AISC, vol. 1027, pp. 193–207. Springer, Singapore (2020). https://doi.org/10.1007/978-981-32-9343-4_16

7. Shaukat, S., et al.: Intrusion detection and attack classification leveraging machine learning technique. In: 2020 14th International Conference on Innovations in Information Technology (IIT). IEEE (2020)

8. Tavallaee, M., et al. A detailed analysis of the KDD CUP 99 data set. in 2009 IEEE symposium on computational intelligence for security and defense applications. 2009. Ieee

9. Revathi, S., Malathi, A.: A detailed analysis on NSL-KDD dataset using various machine learning techniques for intrusion detection. Int. J. Eng. Res. Technol. (IJERT) 2(12), 1848–1853 (2013)

10. Choudhury, S., Bhowal, A.: Comparative analysis of machine learning algorithms along with classifiers for network intrusion detection. In: 2015 International Conference on Smart Technologies and Management for Computing, Communication, Controls, Energy and Materials (ICSTM). IEEE (2015)

11. Sarangi, A.N., Lohani, M., Aggarwal, R.: Prediction of essential proteins in prokaryotes by incorporating various physico-chemical features into the general form of Chou's pseudo amino acid composition. Protein Pept. Lett. 20(7), 781–795 (2013)

12. Joshi, M., Hadi, T.H.: A review of network traffic analysis and prediction techniques. arXiv preprint arXiv:1507.05722 (2015)

13. Karegowda, A.G., Jayaram, M., Manjunath, A.: Combining Akaike's information criterion (AIC) and the golden-section search technique to find optimal numbers of k-nearest neighbors. Int. J. Comput. Appl. 2(1), 80–87 (2010)

14. Kumar, K., Batth, J.S.: Network intrusion detection with feature selection techniques using machine-learning algorithms. Int. J. Comput. Appl. 150(12) (2016)

15. Kumar, G., Thakur, K., Ayyagari, M.R.: MLEsIDSs: machine learning-based ensembles for intrusion detection systems—a review. J. Supercomput. 76(11), 8938–8971 (2020). https://doi.org/10.1007/s11227-020-03196-z

16. Gudla, S.P., Bhoi, S.K., Nayak, S.R., Verma, A.: DI-ADS: a deep intelligent distributed denial of service attack detection scheme for fog-based IoT applications. Math. Probl. Eng. 8, 2022 (2022)

17. Gudla, S.P.K., Bhoi, S.K.: MLP deep learning-based DDoS attack detection framework for fog computing. In: Rout, R.R., Ghosh, S.K., Jana, P.K., Tripathy, A.K., Sahoo, J.P., Li, K.-C. (eds.) Advances in Distributed Computing and Machine Learning: Proceedings of ICADCML 2022, pp. 25–34. Springer Nature Singapore, Singapore (2022). https://doi.org/10.1007/978-981-19-1018-0_3

18. Thaseen, I.S., Kumar, C.A.: Intrusion detection model using fusion of chi-square feature selection and multi class SVM. J. King Saud Univ. Comput. Inf. Sci. 29(4), 462–472 (2017)

Application of Efficient Feature Selection and Machine Learning Algorithms in Mental Health Disorder Identification

Sumitra Mallick[1,2(✉)] [iD] and Mrutyunjaya Panda[1,2] [iD]

[1] Department of Computer Science, Guru Nanak Institution Technical Campus, Hyderabad, Telangana, India
sumitram.csegnitc@gniindia.org
[2] Department of Computer Science and Applications, Utkal University, Bhubaneswar, Odisha, India
mrutyunjaya.cs@utkaluniversity.ac.in

Abstract. Mental disorder is an illness that are more common in technical employees and are increasing among working professionals. It is an important and challenging issue in the world as the stress among the technical employees are high due to work culture. Mental health in the healthcare is necessary to recognize individual's situation and continue to predict diverse situations accurately. Therefore, this study proposes the mental health disorder prediction using various feature selection algorithms for a specific dataset called Tech survey Datasets. We applied multiple machine learning classification algorithms on the best features of RFE, RFECV and LASSO to obtain the performance metrics of the model and to decide the best accuracy, precision and recall of the respective models. There are 61 features in the Tech survey Dataset consisting of the data in the technical workplace worldwide that provides mental health attribute and frequency. The results are discussed and an aggregated table is developed using the performance metrics to understand the percentage of technical employees undergoes mental disorder. The proposed research evaluates various classification algorithms along with feature selection algorithm to forecast the mental disorder in a particular workplace and found to be 79% accuracy.

Keywords: Mental disorder · Feature selection · RFE · RFECV · LASSO · Associative property · Distributive property

1 Introduction

More than half of the population in different technical companies are likely suffering from mental disorder at least once during their lifetime. Depression which affects 350 million people globally suggested by World Heath Organization (WHO) (Breiman1984). Majority of people required treatment for depression may not be provided as per the report of WHO. In the United States, one of the most common mental health condition (Cuellar et al. 2005) is major depressive disorder (MDD). MDD, also referred to as clinical depression, is a significant medical condition that can affect many areas of your

M. Panda et al. (Eds.): ICIICC 2022, CCIS 1737, pp. 348–364, 2022.
https://doi.org/10.1007/978-3-031-23233-6_26

life. More than 264 people of all age globally suffering from MDD according to world health organization (WHO Mental-disorders 2019). The combination of genetic and non-genetic characteristics in AD is the diversity of MDD. A recent study which combines clinical predictors and gene study variants like rs6313 of 5-hydroxytryptamine (serotonin) receptor 2A (HTR2A), rs7430 of protein phosphatase 3 catalytic subunit gamma isozyme (PPP3CC), and rs6265 of brain-derived neurotrophic factor (BDNF) from the European Group for the Study of Resistant Depression (GSRD). A Random forest model reaching accuracy of above 79% (Kautzky et al. 2015) and in other investigation where a series of linear and logistic elastic net regularized regression (ENRR) models is used for training to achieve accuracy of 25% (Aitchison et al., 2005). The different protein level platelet has been shown among different MDD patients (Huang et al., 2014). The peripheral marker genes are considered for alzheimer's disease whereas Visinin-like 1 (VSNL1) has found co-expression with calcium for AD and long term depression (Patel et al. 2015) have worked to separate the late-life depression (LLD) patients from the normal patients for which a decision tree derived from structural imaging, age and mini-mental status examination scores and achieve an accuracy of 89%.

In feature selection process, the subset of features is selected from the larger dataset of original features. The feature selection steps include data quality, less computational time for prediction of model, predictive performance improvement and efficiency in data collection process. (Muhammad Salman et al. 2022) used filter-based feature selection technique named as ANOVA-f (Analysis of Variance test) to determine the most important features. In multi linear regression analysis, depression risk is set as target variable and for predicting the depression the context variables are set as independent variables (Zhang 2006). The two-class problem which was proposed to solve the SVM-RFE for analysis of multi class problems (Mundra et al. 2010, Xiaohui Lin et al. 2017). This multi class problem for feature selection increase the robustness of SVM-RFE, by removing the number of features with the lowest weights. Rather than removing the features one by one which is time consuming, the author has (X.G. Zhan, X.H. Lin 2015) proposed R-SVM & F-SVM to remove the noise in the data. They have followed a method AV-MI, perform to remove the noisy variable, and achieve high specificity and sensitivity. Feature selection process used in this paper (John scott 2018) are 10-fold cross validation which is used to run 10 times for validation. There are 100 features subsets that computed from the research and the feature are ranked according to their descending order. The top ranked feature is the most necessary one selected by using PCA plotted graph on the liver disease data set and selected 34 ion features.

In few cases, few samples of three liver disease are mixed due to noise and non-informative variable where MI-SVM-RFE is very constructive for obtaining the selective features. It is showing three different liver disease are clearly separated by using two intercept method- R^2 intercept and Q^2 intercept (Xiaohui Lina 2012). In the process of selecting the feature to remove the noise method used is MI-SVM-RFE, which is most popular method to select the significant features and to validate the proposed model. SVM and CRT model developed to predict the response and remission to duloxetine utilizing genome-wide genetic dataset but for selecting the features, the LASSO regression was used. LASSO model is used to predict the response or remission with the accuracy.

Finally, an optimal model was evaluated on the test subset of data with the nested cross-validation (Patel et al. 2015). The growing body of literature which addresses the role of social networks such as breakup relationship, mental illness ('depression', 'anxiety', 'bipolar' etc.) (Azorin 2013, Almeida 2010).

The paper is further organized as follows: Sect. 2 elaborates the background works given by the authors related to mental health illness, Sect. 3 generate a heat map of the dataset considered for the research, Sect. 4 proposes the mathematical modeling of the feature selection techniques, Sect. 5 discusses the experimental setup and implementation, Sect. 6 shows the results and discussions, and Sect. 7 deals with the conclusion for better analysis and classification with future models.

2 Background

In order to improve the performance of machine learning models a statistical analysis is desired as the data is huge which are collected from clinicians and pharmacists. Gaussian mixture model (Hastie 2001) is an unsupervised clustering algorithm that fits the data based on structures that determine the dimension in which the subgroup is found. The aim is to identify subgroups with inpatients rather than classify them. The depression is also detected through user's twitter by using the Bag-of-word technique i.e. the frequency of words that shows the depression level (Okser 2014, Dudek 2013). The author has used morphological stemming and categorization of Japanese tweet text, where bag-of-words is used to predict depression among participants.

The author considers a total of 571,054 SNPs genotyped samples at the Centre for Applied Genomics (TCAG) at the Hospital for Sick Children (Toronto ON, Canada). While doing data preprocessing, participants of non-European self-reported ancestry (n = 29) were excluded from the analysis (Sachan et al. 2021). The remaining sample (N = 411) follows the necessary steps to improve quality control includes the following: heterozygosity rate, relatedness (IBD), and possible population stratification due to ancestry. DNA samples were collected from clinical data and blood samples which are obtained from duloxetine and placebo arms. Gene variational characteristics are used in each step of the training set. The robust LASSO approach has been used in genomics studies to solve the 'curse of dimensionality' issue (Okser et al. 2014). Machine learning needs data to implement the algorithm (Breiman et al. 1984) of classification trees and linear support vector machines to construct a model. A predictive model is a general concept for building the model in a supervised machine learning method that classifies the observations. (Patel et al. 2016) on the MDD and CRT dataset constructed the SVM model using tenfold cross-validation, during the training stage where the best parameters are determined for the SVM model. To evaluate the model different metrics Accuracy, specificity, and sensitivity were computed. The classification performance for the training and testing of each pair of datasets implemented in R package caret. By the LASSO model, MADRS score computed on the two types of models, the first model is constructed based on the original genotype variant, and the second one is based on genotype and imputed genetic variants. Xiaohui et al. took metabolomics which is the study of small molecules composed of cells, tissues, or organisms of stimuli or genetic modifications. To determine several human diseases in the human body and to improve the diagnosis and prevention of disease. This study was also carried out in the area of toxicology and pharmacology, crop breeding plant biotechnology and drug research (Aitchison 2005). The emerging field of metabolomics can improve and explore the mechanism of cancer.

Data was collected from patients who are suffering from chronic hepatitis B (CHB), cirrhosis (CIR), and hepatocellular carcinoma (HCC) of Sixth People's Hospital (Aitchison 2005). Each patient data was collected from MRI scan, ultrasonography, CT scan and tumor markers test and the classification accuracy rate is computed firstly by comparing SVM-RFE-OA with SVM-RFE. To determine the performance of the SVM-RFE-OA, it shows that it performs outstanding for all the eight biological datasets (Xiaohui Lin 2017). The performance of the M-SVM-RFE-OA compared with SVM-RFE-OA was computed by performing the classification and determining the high-value features. Ultimately, it is observed that the M-SVM-RFE-OA performs better (John Scott).

3 Data Exploration

Data exploration is the study and correlation of huge amount of data in an easiest way for visualization. Understanding the structure and exploring data to identify how features are distributed and whether there is a link within the dataset. In the below Fig. 1, correlation within the variable is observed between the dependent variable and independent variable are depicted in this graph. it is also explained the columns in the dataset are correlated and linked between the columns of the dataset.

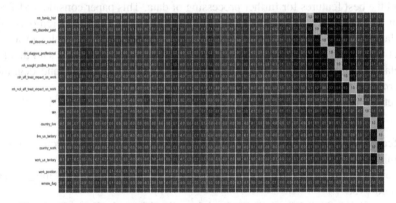

Fig. 1. The correlation values for employee in Tech survey features datasets.

The main motivation of this research is to evaluate the state-of-the-art methodologies to determine the accuracy of mental disorder prediction for technical employees. A state-of-art technique is used to assess the type of mental disorder problem a tech employee is experiencing based on the awareness of mental disorder among employees. The aim of the research is to apply machine learning model using feature selection method namely SVM, Naive Bayes, Stochastic Gradient Descent, KNN, Decision tree, Random Forest, Logistic Regression, Neural Nets, Cross Gradient Booster, Cross Gradient Booster (Random Forest) for mental disorder and the model is tested using different performance measurements. It is necessary to determine which approaches are more effective for identifying the mental disorder and which machine learning algorithm provide superior results. (Zhang et al. 2019) describe how to extract efficient features based on the weighting-and-ranking-based hybrid feature selection (WRHFS), to identify the heart stroke risk. The weighting and ranking techniques are filter based feature selection (Ruba Skaik et al. 2020).

4 Mathematical Modeling of Feature Selection

We have implemented three feature selection algorithms i.e. LASSO, RFE and RFECV to calculate the score of feature with the targeted variable. The target class feature for this research is mh_disorder_current which finds the percentage of technical people who gets mental illness compared to nontechnical people in the tech survey dataset. The best features are extracted by using all the above three feature selection algorithms. We have collected the mental health in technical survey dataset consisting of 1235 records and 61 features from various people worldwide that measure attitudes towards mental health and frequency of mental health illness in the technical workplace. In this dataset, there are a total of 61 features and mostly the NaN values are present as the data values are removed. The goal is to find a subset of size f features among N universal features to maximize the performance of the model using a machine learning classifier.

There is a requirement of computing the correlation coefficient between two variables to find the relationship. It needs to generate a correlation matrix to summarize the dataset to find the best features for further processing of data. This paper considers 51 features out of 61 features of the dataset after implementing a heatmap that removed highly correlated features. Correlation is a measure of the dependent variables in a way to reflect two variables move together and strongly relate each other. It is said that highly correlated variables become redundant for classification algorithms and degrade the performance if considers.

Let us assume N the universal set consisting of all 51 features i.e. N = { f1, f2,.........f51}.

The features set is { f1: "self_empl_flag", f2: "comp_no_empl", f3: "tech_comp_flag", f4: "mh_coverage_flag", f5: "
mh_coverage_awareness_flag", f6: " mh_employer_discussion", f7: "mh_resources_provided", f8:
"mh_anonimity_flag", f9: "mh_medical_leave", f10: "mh_discussion_neg_impact", f11: "ph_discussion_neg_impact",
f12: "mh_discussion_cowork", f13: "mh_discussion_supervis", f14: " mh_eq_ph_employer", f15:
"mh_conseq_coworkers", f16: "prev_employers_flag", f17: "prev_mh_benefits", f18: "prev_mh_benefits_awareness",
f19: "prev_mh_discussion", f20: "prev_mh_resources", f21: "prev_mh_anonimity", f22:
"prev_mh_discuss_neg_conseq", f23: "prev_ph_discuss_neg_conseq", f24: "prev_mh_discussion_cowork", f25:

"prev_mh_discussion_supervisor", f26: "prev_mh_importance_employer", f27: "prev_mh_conseq_coworkers", f28:"
future_ph_specification", f29: "why/why_not", f30: "future_mh_specification", f31: "why/why_not2", f32:"
mh_hurt_on_career", f33: "mh_neg_view_cowork", f34:" mh_sharing_friends/fam_flag", f35:
"mh_bad_response_workplace", f36: "mh_family_hist", f37: " mh_disorder_past", f38: " mh_disorder_current", f39: "mh_diagnos_proffesional", f40:"mh_sought_proffes_treatm", f41:" mh_eff_treat_impact_on_work", f42:" mh_not_eff_treat_impact_on_work", f43: "age", f44: "sex", f45: "country_live", f46: "live_us_teritory", f47: "country_work", f48: "work_us_teritory", f49: "work_position", f50: "remote_flag", f51: " tech_flag"}.

Let F_1, F_2 and F_3 be the feature subsets of universal set N.

F_1 is the feature subset that are extracted from the universal set N using LASSO technique denoted as $F_1 = \{$ f:F is a feature subset using LASSO$\}$, f is a member of feature set N, i.e. $f \in N$.

F_2 is the feature subset that are extracted from the universal set N using RFECV technique denoted as $F_2 = \{$ f:F is a feature subset using RFECV$\}$, f is a member of feature set N, i.e. $f \in N$.

F_3 is the feature subset that are extracted from the universal set N using RFE technique denoted as $F_3 = \{$f:F is a feature subset using RFE$\}$, f is a member of feature set N, i.e. $f \in N$.

4.1 Feature Selection Using LASSO

LASSO (Least Absolute Shrinkage and Selection Operator) is a regression analysis that can be used for both feature selection and regularization. LASSO Minimizes the error between data points and the actual fit points by avoiding overfitting problem i.e., it works well on the dataset where a model fit well on the training dataset but will not fit well on the testing dataset. The main objective of LASSO regularization is to find the best set of optimal features that helps to minimize the error between the actual and the target feature. The unwanted features are removed by making the coefficients to zero in the shrinking process. By using wrapper-based feature selection techniques like LASSO Regularization, F_1 features are extracted from the universal set N. The most relevant features extracted based on the rank values in the employee disorder dataset are 19 features shown below. This also helps to deal with the overfitting and underfitting problems of machine learning. Hence the feature set is derived as follows:

F_1 = {f48, f29, f46, f21, f47, f18, f17, f9, f4, f8, f22, f36, f8, f34, f39, f37, f42, f49, f43, f31}

Each feature $f \in F_1 \subseteq N$ refer to a single feature, where {f48: work_us_teritory, f28: why/why_not, f46: live_us_teritory,f21: prev_mh_anonimity, f47: country_work, f17: prev_mh_benefits_awareness, f17: prev_mh_benefits, f9: mh_medical_leave, f4: mh_coverage_flag, f22: prev_mh_discuss_neg_conseq, f36: mh_family_hist, f8: prev_mh_discuss_neg_conseq, f34: mh_sharing_friends/fam_flag, f39: mh_diagnos_proffesional, f37: mh_disorder_past, f42: mh_not_eff_treat_impact_on_work, f49: work_position, f29: age, f31: why/why_not2}.

4.2 Feature Selection Using RFECV

Recursive Feature Elimination with Cross-validation (RFECV) is a technique to evaluate the performance of all the machine learning models. This is a powerful method that helps to select the best model with its efficiency score. The paper considers the Tech survey dataset consists of 51 preprocessed features by implementing k-fold cross validation technique with the value of k equal to 5 where K data is the training dataset, and the remaining K-1 data is the test dataset. The performance of the model is computed. This process is continued multiple times with different values of k then the model performance is evaluated. All the process is done multiple times to evaluate the robustness of the model. By using RFECV feature selection technique, F2 features are extracted from the universal set N. The most relevant features extracted based on the rank values in the employee disorder dataset are 14 features shown below. Hence the feature set is derived as follows:

$$F_2 = \{f43, f2, f46, f39, f37, f41, f9, f42, f34, f40, f29, f31, f49, f48\}$$

Each feature $f \in F_2 \subseteq N$ refer to a single feature, where {f43: "age", f2: "comp_no_empl", f46: "live_us_teritory", f39:" 'mh_diagnos_proffesional',f37:" 'mh_disorder_past',f41:" 'mh_eff_treat_impact_on_work',f9:" ' 'mh_medical_leave',f42:" 'mh_not_eff_treat_impact_on_work',f34:" 'mh_sharing_friends/fam_flag',f40: 'mh_sought_proffes_treatm',f29: 'why/why_not',f31: 'why/why_not2',f49: 'work_position', f48: "work_us_teritory"}.

4.3 Feature Selection Using RFE

RFE is a wrapper method that uses random forest machine learning algorithm for its evaluation criteria. It is a backward compactable way of doing feature selection or elimination which works well in both the classification and the regression techniques. RFE builds a model using all the features and then calculates the model's accuracy. it removes one feature per iteration and then builds the model again and sees how much variation is caused in the accuracy score. It is based on the feature importance to keep the feature or remove feature. At each iteration, feature importance is measured and the less relevant one is removed to speed up the process. It is to construct a model by selecting best or worst features in each iteration and repeating the process until all features are exhausted. Features are eliminated based on their rank like Greedy optimization to find best subset of features. It is the idea of repeatedly constructing a model and choosing either the best or worst performing feature, setting the feature aside, and then repeating the process with the rest of the features. This process is applied until all features in the dataset are exhausted. Features are then ranked according to when they were eliminated. As such, it is a greedy optimization for finding the best-performing subset of features. By using wrapper-based feature selection techniques like Recursive Feature Elimination (RFE), F3 features are extracted from the universal set N. The most relevant features extracted from the employee disorder dataset are 10 features shown below. Hence the feature set is derived as follows:

$$F_3 = \{f43, f39, f37, f41, f42, f34, f29, f31, f49, f46\}$$

Each feature f ∈ F_3 ⊆ N refer to a single feature, where {f43:age, f39: mh_ diagnos_proffesional, f37: mh_disorder_past, f41: mh_eff_treat_impact_on_work, f42: mh_not_eff_treat_impact_on_work, f34: mh_sharing_friends/fam_flag, f29: why/why_ not2, f31: why/why_not, f49: work_position, f46:work_us_teritory}.

4.4 Feature Selection Using Associative Property of Union

Let F_1, F_2 and F_3 be subsets of universal set N.

The union of F_1, F_2, and F_3 written as F_1 U F_2 U F_3 = { f ∈ N | f ∈ F_1, f ∈ F_2 and f ∈ F_3}.

Union operations are associative where $(F_1$ U $F_2)$ U F_3 = F_1 U $(F_2$ U $F_3)$.

By using union operation of associative property on F_1, F_2 and F_3, the F_4 features are extracted. The most relevant features extracted from the employee disorder dataset is 15 features shown below. Hence the feature set is derived as follows:

F_4 = {f9, f43, f22, f21, f17, f41, f39, f36, f2, f49, f31, f42, f8, f38, f4, f18, f46, f47, f48, f40, f29, f34}

It is represented as F_4={f9:'mh_medical_leave',f43:'age', f22:'prev_mh_discuss_ neg_conseq', f21:'prev_mh_anonimity', f17:'prev_mh_benefits', f41:'mh_eff_treat_ impact_on_work', ',f39:'mh_diagnos_proffesional',f2: 'comp_ no_empl, f49:'work_position', f31:'why/why_not2', f42:'mh_not_eff_treat_impact_ on_work', f8:'mh_anonimity_flag', f38:'mh_disorder_past', f4:'mh_coverage_flag', f18:'prev_mh_benefits_ awareness',f46: 'live_us_teritory',f47:'country_work',f48: 'live_us_teritory', f40:'mh_ sought_proffes_treatm',f29: 'why/why_not',f34: 'mh_sharing_friends/fam_flag'}.

4.5 Feature Selection Using Associative Property of Intersection

Let F_1, F_2 and F_3 be subsets of universal set N.

The intersection of F_1, F_2 and F_3 written as $F_1 \cap F_2 \cap F_3$, is defined by the associative property as set of all element that are in F_1, F_2 and F_3.

$$F_1 \cap F_2 \cap F_3 = \{f \in N \mid f \in F_1, f \in F_2 \text{ and } f \in F_3\}$$

$(F_1 \cap F_2) \cap F_3 = F_1 \cap (F_2 \cap F_3)$ Hence, intersection operations are associative.

By using Intersection operation of associative property on F_1, F_2 and F_3, the F_5 features are extracted. The most relevant features extracted from the employee disorder dataset is 8 features shown below. Hence the feature set is derived as follows:

$$F_5 = \{f49, f43, f37, f29, f31, f41, f34, f39\}$$

F_5 = {f49:'work_position', f43:'age', f37:'mh_disorder_past',f29: 'why/why_ not', f31:'why/why_not2', f41:'mh_not_eff_treat_impact_on_work', f34:'mh_sharing_ friends/fam_flag', f39: 'mh_diagnos_proffesional'}.

4.6 Feature Selection Using Distributive Property

Let F_1, F_2 and F_3 be subsets of universal set N.

The Union of F_1, F_2 and intersection with F_3 written as $F_1 \cup (F_2 \cap F_3)$, is defined by the distributive property as set of all elements that are in F1, F2 and F3 are The Distributive law shows as:

$$F_1 \cup (F_2 \cap F_3) = (F_1 \cup F_2) \cap (F_1 \cup F_3)$$

By using union distributed over intersection of distributive property on F_1, F_2 and F_3, the F_6 features are extract ed. The most relevant features extracted from the employee disorder dataset is 10 features shown below. Hence the feature set is derived as follows:

$$F_6 = \{f49, f48, f43, f37, f29, f31, f42, f34, f41, f39\}$$

F_6 = {f49:'work_position', f48:'work_us_teritory', f43:'age', f37:'mh_disorder_past', f29:'why/why_not', f31:'why/why_not2', f42:'mh_not_eff_treat_impact_on_work', f34:'mh_sharing_friends/fam_flag', f41:'mh_eff_treat_impact_on_work', f39:'mh_diagnos_proffesional'}.

5 Implementation of Classification Algorithms

The implementation is carried out with preprocessed 51 features and 10 classification algorithms such as Naive Bayes, Stochastic Gradient Descent, KNN, Decision trees, Random Forest, Support Vector Machine, Logistic Regression, Neural Nets, Cross Gradient Booster and Cross Gradient Booster (Random Forest) to find the accuracy, recall and precision. The accuracy of Random Forest and Cross Gradient Booster (Random Forest) is around 78%, the recall of Random Forest and Cross Gradient Booster (Random Forest) is around 73% and the precision of Random Forest and Cross Gradient Booster (Random Forest) is more than 75%. Considering all the 51 features, the accuracy, precision and recall of Random Forest and Cross Gradient Booster (Random Forest) is better than all other machine learning algorithms shown in Table 1.

5.1 Classification with LASSO

We have implemented with 19 best features of LASSO and 10 classification algorithms such as Naive Bayes, Stochastic Gradient Descent, KNN, Decision trees, Random Forest, Support Vector Machine, Logistic Regression, Neural Nets, Cross Gradient Booster and Cross Gradient Booster (Random Forest) to find the accuracy, recall and precision. The accuracy of Random Forest and Cross Gradient Booster (Random Forest) is more than 78%, the recall of Random Forest and Naïve Bayes is more than 73% but equivalent to Cross Gradient Booster (Random Forest) and the precision of Random Forest and Cross Gradient Booster (Random Forest) is 77%. Considering best 19 features of Tech survey dataset, the accuracy, precision and recall of Random Forest and Cross Gradient Booster (Random Forest) is better than all other machine learning algorithms shown in Table 1.

Table 1. Considering 51 best features

Algorithms	Accuracy	Recall_score	Precision_score
Naive Bayes	0.74394	0.7074	0.70435
Stochastic Gradient Descent	0.45553	0.45735	0.45424
KNN	0.39353	0.34693	0.34917
Decision trees	0.65229	0.637	0.62987
Random Forest	0.78167	0.72876	0.75662
Support Vector Machine	0.42588	0.33333	0.14196
Logistic Regression	0.69811	0.61629	0.66023
Neural Nets	0.41779	0.327	0.14078
Cross Gradient Booster	0.74394	0.68906	0.69643
Cross Gradient Booster (Random Forest)	0.78706	0.73563	0.77349

5.2 Classification with RFECV

We have implemented with 14 best features of RFECV and 10 classification algorithms such as Naive Bayes, Stochastic Gradient Descent, KNN, Decision trees, Random Forest, Support Vector Machine, Logistic Regression, Neural Nets, Cross Gradient Booster and Cross Gradient Booster (Random Forest) to find the accuracy, recall and precision. The accuracy of Random Forest and Cross Gradient Booster (Random Forest) is more than 78%, the recall of Random Forest and Cross Gradient Booster (Random Forest) is more than 77% and the precision of Random Forest and Cross Gradient Booster (Random Forest) is 77%. Considering best 14 features of Tech survey dataset, the accuracy, precision and recall of Random Forest and Cross Gradient Booster (Random Forest) is better than all other machine learning algorithms shown in Table 1.

5.3 Classification with RFE

We have implemented with 10 best features of RFE and 10 classification algorithms such as Naive Bayes, Stochastic Gradient Descent, KNN, Decision trees, Random Forest, Support Vector Machine, Logistic Regression, Neural Nets, Cross Gradient Booster and Cross Gradient Booster (Random Forest) to find the accuracy, recall and precision. The accuracy of Random Forest and Cross Gradient Booster (Random Forest) is more than 78%, the recall of Naive Bayes and Random Forest is more than 74% and the precision of Random Forest and Cross Gradient Booster (Random Forest) is more than 77%. Considering best 10 features of tech survey dataset, the accuracy, recall and precision of Random Forest and Cross Gradient Booster (Random Forest) is better than all other machine learning algorithms shown in Table 1.

5.4   Classification with Feature Selection Using Associative Property of Union

We have implemented with 15 best features and 10 classification algorithms such as Naive Bayes, Stochastic Gradient Descent, KNN, Decision trees, Random Forest, Support Vector Machine, Logistic Regression, Neural Nets, Cross Gradient Booster and Cross Gradient Booster (Random Forest) to find the accuracy, recall and precision. The accuracy of Cross Gradient Booster (Random Forest) is more than 78%, the recall of Cross Gradient Booster (Random Forest) is more than 73% and the precision of Cross Gradient Booster (Random Forest) is 77%. Considering best 15 features of Tech survey dataset, the accuracy, precision and recall of Cross Gradient Booster (Random Forest) is better than all other machine learning algorithms shown in Table 1.

5.5   Classification with Feature Selection Using Associative Property of Intersection

We have implemented with 15 best features and 10 classification algorithms such as Naive Bayes, Stochastic Gradient Descent, KNN, Decision trees, Random Forest, Support Vector Machine, Logistic Regression, Neural Nets, Cross Gradient Booster and Cross Gradient Booster (Random Forest) to find the accuracy, recall and precision. The accuracy of Cross Gradient Booster (Random Forest) is 79%, the recall of Cross Gradient Booster (Random Forest) is 74% and the precision of Cross Gradient Booster (Random Forest) is 78%. Considering best 8 features of Tech survey dataset, the accuracy, precision and recall of Cross Gradient Booster (Random Forest) is better than all other machine learning algorithms shown in Table 1.

5.6   Classification with Feature Selection Using Distributive Property

We have implemented with 10 best features and 10 classification algorithms such as Naive Bayes, Stochastic Gradient Descent, KNN, Decision trees, Random Forest, Support Vector Machine, Logistic Regression, Neural Nets, Cross Gradient Booster and Cross Gradient Booster (Random Forest) to find the accuracy, recall and precision. The accuracy of Random Forest is 79%, the recall of Naïve Bayes is 74% and the precision of Cross Gradient Booster (Random Forest) is 77%. Considering best 10 features of Tech survey dataset, the accuracy, precision and recall of Cross Gradient Booster (Random Forest) and Random Forest is better than all other machine learning algorithms shown in Table 1.

6   Results and Discussions

The best subset of features are selected and the unimportant features are eliminated that are not contributing to the accuracy of the model from the dataset. We have implemented three algorithms for feature selection i.e. RFE, RFECV and LASSO to calculate the feature score with respect to targeted variable. The target class feature for this research is mh_disorder_current which leads to find the percentage of technical people gets mental illness compared to non technical people in the tech survey dataset. By using RFE,

RFECV and LASSO algorithms, the best features are extracted and shown in the Table 1 given above. The results are computed from the best features of RFE, RFECV and LASSO algorithms by using ten machine learning algorithms called as Naive Bayes, Stochastic Gradient Descent, KNN, Decision trees, Random Forest, Support Vector Machine, Logistic Regression, Neural Nets, Cross Gradient Booster and Cross Gradient Booster (Random Forest) to find the accuracy, recall and precision. The Table 2 is prepared as an aggregated accuracy, recall and precision to visualize the importance of the classification algorithms with respect to the feature selection methods.

Table 2. Aggregated Accuracy, Recall and Precision considering the best features

Feature selection Algorithms	Classification Algorithms	Accuracy	Recall_ score	Precision_ score
LASSO	Naive Bayes	0.77089	0.73668	0.7392
	Stochastic Gradient Descent	0.32345	0.36213	0.55758
	K-Nearest Neighbor	0.39623	0.34926	0.35247
	Decission trees	0.66846	0.64281	0.63796
	Random Forest	0.78437	0.73883	0.76686
	Support Vector Machine	0.42588	0.33333	0.14196
	Logistic Regression	0.66577	0.59539	0.64776
	Neural Nets	0.42588	0.33333	0.14196
	Cross Gradient Booster	0.75202	0.71616	0.7178
	Cross Gradient Booster (Random Forest)	0.78706	0.73563	0.77349
RFECV	Naive Bayes	0.77089	0.7392	0.7392
	Stochastic Gradient Descent	0.32345	0.55758	0.55758
	K-Nearest Neighbor	0.39623	0.35247	0.35247
	Decission trees	0.66846	0.63796	0.63534
	Random Forest	0.78706	0.76686	0.77124
	Support Vector Machine	0.42588	0.14196	0.14196
	Logistic Regression	0.66038	0.64776	0.64016
	Neural Nets	0.42588	0.14196	0.2712

(continued)

Table 2. (*continued*)

Feature selection Algorithms	Classification Algorithms	Accuracy	Recall_score	Precision_score
	Cross Gradient Booster	0.75202	0.7178	0.7178
	Cross Gradient Booster (Random Forest)	0.78437	0.77349	0.7702
RFE	Naive Bayes	0.77089	0.73668	0.7392
	Stochastic Gradient Descent	0.32345	0.36213	0.55758
	K-Nearest Neighbor	0.39623	0.34926	0.35247
	Decission trees	0.68194	0.658	0.65251
	Random Forest	0.78437	0.73883	0.76686
	Support Vector Machine	0.42588	0.33333	0.14196
	Logistic Regression	0.66577	0.59539	0.64776
	Neural Nets	0.42588	0.33333	0.14196
	Cross Gradient Booster	0.75202	0.71616	0.7178
	Cross Gradient Booster (Random Forest)	0.78706	0.73563	0.77349
LASSO ∪ RFECV ∪ RFE	Naive Bayes	0.7655	0.72738	0.7296
	Stochastic Gradient Descent	0.19677	0.3348	0.5956
	K-Nearest Neighbor	0.39084	0.34482	0.34712
	Decission trees	0.67116	0.64867	0.64162
	Random Forest	0.77628	0.72432	0.74748
	Support Vector Machine	0.42588	0.33333	0.14196
	Logistic Regression	0.69272	0.59903	0.6449
	Neural Nets	0.36927	0.30673	0.24677
	Cross Gradient Booster	0.74933	0.70566	0.71144
	Cross Gradient Booster (Random Forest)	0.78706	0.73563	0.77349

(*continued*)

Table 2. (*continued*)

Feature selection Algorithms	Classification Algorithms	Accuracy	Recall_ score	Precision_ score
LASSO ∩ RFECV ∩ RFE	Naive Bayes	0.77089	0.73933	0.74166
	Stochastic Gradient Descent	0.38005	0.38543	0.56776
	K-Nearest Neighbor	0.40431	0.35316	0.35371
	Decision trees	0.66307	0.63969	0.63403
	Random Forest	0.78706	0.7416	0.75857
	Support Vector Machine	0.42588	0.33333	0.14196
	Logistic Regression	0.68464	0.6053	0.65834
	Neural Nets	0.62534	0.51401	0.53059
	Cross Gradient Booster	0.75472	0.72314	0.7232
	Cross Gradient Booster (Random Forest)	0.78976	0.7404	0.77673
LASSO ∪ (RFECV ∩ RFE)	Naive Bayes	0.77089	0.73955	0.74172
	Stochastic Gradient Descent	0.45822	0.3969	0.40541
	K-Nearest Neighbor	0.39084	0.34482	0.34626
	Decision tree	0.69811	0.67773	0.66852
	Random Forest	0.78706	0.73873	0.75867
	Support Vector Machine	0.42588	0.33333	0.14196
	Logistic Regression	0.68733	0.59967	0.64024
	Neural Nets	0.42588	0.33333	0.14196
	Cross Gradient Booster	0.75741	0.72259	0.7251
	Cross Gradient Booster (Random Forest)	0.89706	0.73563	0.77349

The accuracy of LASSO feature selection with Cross Gradient Booster (Random Forest) is around 79% which is best among all other classification algorithms but Naive Bayes and Random Forest also performs well in this scenario. The accuracy of RFE feature selection with Cross Gradient Booster (Random Forest) is around 79% which is best among all other classification algorithms but Naive Bayes and Random Forest also performs well in this scenario. The accuracy of RFECV feature selection with Random

Forest is around 79% which is best among all other classification algorithms but Naive Bayes and Cross Gradient Booster (Random Forest) also performs well in this scenario. The classification accuracy of Cross Gradient Booster (Random Forest) is more than 78% with feature selection using associative property of union, The classification accuracy of Cross Gradient Booster (Random Forest) is 79% with feature selection using associative property of intersection, and the classification accuracy of Random Forest is 79% with feature selection using distributive property. We have concluded that Cross Gradient Booster (Random Forest) performs very well among all the classification algorithms among all the feature selection algorithms. The prediction for the mental health illness in tech survey dataset for technical people compared to non technical people is 79%.

The recall of LASSO feature selection with is around 74% which is best among all other classification algorithms but Naive Bayes and Cross Gradient Booster (Random Forest) also performs well with nearer value. Similarly the recall of RFE feature selection with Random Forest is around 74% which is best among all other classification algorithms but Naive Bayes and Cross Gradient Booster (Random Forest) also performs well with nearer value. The recall of RFECV feature selection with Cross Gradient Booster (Random Forest) is around 77% which is best among all other classification algorithms, but Random Forest also performs well. The recall of Cross Gradient Booster (Random Forest) is more than 73% with feature selection using associative property of union, the recall of Cross Gradient Booster (Random Forest) is 74% with feature selection using associative property of intersection, and the recall of Naïve Bayes is 74% with feature selection using distributive property. We have concluded that Cross Gradient Booster (Random Forest) performs very well among all the classification algorithms with RFECV feature selection algorithm is 77%. The recall for the mental health illness in tech survey dataset for technical people compared to non technical people is 77%. It means, the model correctly identifies 77% technical people have mental illness disease in the organization.

The precision of LASSO feature selection with Cross Gradient Booster (Random Forest) is around 77% which is best among all other classification algorithms but Naive Bayes also performs well with nearer value. Similarly the precision of RFE feature selection with Cross Gradient Booster (Random Forest) is around 77% which is best among all other classification algorithms but Random Forest also performs well. The precision of RFECV feature selection with Random Forest is around 77% which is best among all other classification algorithms but Cross Gradient Booster (Random Forest) also performs well in this scenario. The precision of Cross Gradient Booster (Random Forest) is 77% with feature selection using associative property of union, the precision of Cross Gradient Booster (Random Forest) is 78% with feature selection using associative property of intersection, and the precision of Cross Gradient Booster (Random Forest) is 77% with feature selection using distributive property. We have concluded that Cross Gradient Booster (Random Forest) performs very well among all the classification algorithms with feature selection using associative property of intersection is 78% but RFECV with Random Forest, Cross Gradient Booster (Random Forest) with feature selection using associative property of union and Cross Gradient Booster (Random Forest) with feature selection using distributive property also performed well with nearer value. The precision for the mental health illness in tech survey dataset for technical people compared to non technical people is 78%. It means, the classification model predicts the technical people have mental illness disease is correct 78% of the time.

7 Conclusion

We proposed a healthcare system for mental health disorders that can perform better with better feature selection algorithms. Though mental illness is a chronic illness, the results are compared by implementing various machine learning algorithms with respective feature selection algorithms for accurate predictions and justifying the suitability of the algorithms. The research was carried out with 61 features, 3 feature selection algorithms, and by implementing 10 classification algorithms. The accuracy of the classification algorithms is evaluated and the better accuracy with Cross Gradient Booster (Random Forest) with all feature selection algorithm is found to be 79%. Therefore, considering a workplace, the inference drawn is 79% of technical people are predicted that they suffer from mental health illness disease according to the tech survey dataset. We have calculated the recall with all ten classification algorithms with the best features using feature selection algorithms and the model correctly identifies 77% of technical people who have mental illness disease in the organization. We have calculated the precision with all ten classification algorithms with the best features using feature selection algorithms and the model predicts that the technical people who have mental illness disease is identified as correct 77% of the time. In the future, we will implement a model that considers various operations on feature selection algorithms by classifying the mental health disease prediction.

References

Skaik, R., Inkpen, D.: Using social media for mental health surveillance: a review Canada. ACM Comput. Surv. **53**(6), 1–31 (2021). https://doi.org/10.1145/3422824. University of Ottawa (2020)

Cuellar, A.K., Johnson, S.L., Winters, R.: Distinctions between bipolar and unipolar depression. Clinical Psychol. Rev. **25**(3), 307–339 (2005)

Kautzky, A., et al.: The combined effect of genetic polymorphisms and clinical parameters on treatment outcome in treatment-resistant depression. Eur. Neuropsychopharmacol. **25**(4), 441–453 (2015)

Aitchison, K.J., Basu, A., McGuffin, P., Craig, I.: Psychiatry and the 'new genetics': hunting for genes for behaviour and drug response. Br. J. Psychiatr. **186**, 91–92 (2005)

Huang, T.L., Sung, M.L., Chen, T.Y.: 2D-DIGE proteome analysis on the platelet proteins of patients with major depression. Proteome Sci. **12**(1), 1 (2014)

Patel, M.J., Andreescu, C., Price, J.C., Edelman, K.L., Reynolds, C.F., Aizenstein, H.J.: Machine learning approaches for integrating clinical and imaging features in late-life depression classification and response prediction. Int. J. Geriatr. Psychiatr. **30**(10), 1056–1067 (2015)

Pathan, M.S., Nag, A., Pathan, M.M., Deva, S.: Analyzing the impact of feature selection on the accuracy of heart disease prediction (2022). arXiv:2206.03239v1

Sachan, S., Almaghrabi, F., Yang, J.-B., Xu, D.-L.: Evidential reasoning for preprocessing uncertain categorical data for trustworthy decisions: an application on healthcare and finance. Expert Syst. Appl. **185**(2021), 115597 (2021)

Guyon, I., Weston, J., Barnhill, S., et al.: Gene selection for cancer classification using support vector machines. Mach. Learn. **46**(1–3), 389–422 (2022)

Almeida, J.R., Versace, A., Hassel, S., et al.: Elevated amygdala activity to sad facial expressions: a state marker of bipolar but not unipolar depression. Biol. Psychiatr. **67**(5), 414–421 (2010)

Mundra, P.A., Rajapakse, J.C.: SVM-RFE with MRMR filter for gene selection. IEEE Trans. Nanobiosci. **9**, 31–37 (2010). CrossRef PubMed

Lin, X., Li, C., Zhang, Y., Su, B., Fan, M., Wei, H.: School of Computer Science and Technology, Dalian University of Technology, Dalian. Selecting Feature Subsets Based on SVM-RFE and the Overlapping Ratio with Applications in Bioinformatics (2017). https://doi.org/10.3390/molecules23010052

https://methods.sagepub.com/book/social-network-analysis-4e/i829.xml

Polat, Ö.: A robust regression based classifier with determination of optimal feature set. J. Appl. Res. Technol. **13**(4), 443–446 (2015)

Scott, J.: https://methods.sagepub.com/book/social-network-analysis-4e/i829.xml. https://doi.org/10.4135/9781529716597.n9

Islam, M.R., Kabir, M.A., Ahmed, A., Kamal, A.R.M., Wang, H., Ulhaq, A.: Depression detection from social network data using machine learning techniques. Health Inf. Sci. Syst. **6**(1), 1–12 (2018). https://doi.org/10.1007/s13755-018-0046-0

Azorin, J.M., et al.: Characteristics and profiles of bipolar I patients according to age-at-onset: findings from an admixture analysis. J. Affect. Disord. **150**, 993–1000 (2013)

Yu, Y., et al.: How to conduct dose-response meta-analysis by using linear relation and piecewise linear regression model. J. Evid. Based Med. **16**(1), 111–114 (2016)

Hastie, T., Tibshirani, R., Friedman, J.: The Elements of Statistical Learning: Data Mining, Inference, and Prediction. SpringerVerlag, New York (2001)

Okser, S., Pahikkala, T., Airola, A., Salakoski, T., Ripatti, S., Aittokallio, T.: Regularized machine learning in the genetic prediction of complex traits. PLoS Genet. **10**(11), e1004754 (2014)

Breiman, L., Friedman, J.H., Olshen, A., Stone, C.J.: Classification and Regression Trees. Wadsworth Publishing Company, Belmont, California, USA (1984)

Lin, X., et al.: A support vector machine-recursive feature elimination feature selection method based on artificial contrast variables and mutual information. J. Chromatography B **910**, 149–155 (2012). https://doi.org/10.1016/j.jchromb.2012.05.020

Dudek, D., Siwek, M., Zielinska, D., et al.: Diagnostic conversions from major depressive disorder into bipolar disorder in an outpatient setting: results of a retrospective chart review. J. Affective Disorders **144**(1–2), 112–115 (2013)

World Health Organization (WHO). Mental Disorders (2019). WHO. https://www.who.int/news-room/fact-sheets/detail/mental-disorders

Pathan, M.S., Nag, A., Pathan, M.M., Deva, S.: Analyzing the impact of feature selection on the accuracy of heart disease prediction (2022). arXiv:2206.03239v1

Zhang, X.G., et al.: Recursive SVM feature selection and sample classification for mass-spectrometry and microarray data. BMC Bioinformatics **7**, 197 (2006). https://doi.org/10.1186/1471-2105-7-197

Zhang, Y., Zhou, Y., Zhang, D., Song, W.: A stroke risk detection: improving hybrid feature selection method. J. Med. Internet Res. **21**(4), e12437 (2019). https://doi.org/10.2196/12437

A Survey on Sentimental Analysis of Student Reviews Using Natural Language Processing (NLP) and Text Mining

J. Jayasudha[1]([✉]) [iD] and M. Thilagu[2] [iD]

[1] Research Scholar, Department of Computer Science, Avinashilingam Institute for Home Science and Higher Education for Women, Coimbatore, India
jayasudhayuvaraaj@gmail.com
[2] Department of Computer Science, Avinashilingam Institute for Home Science and Higher Education for Women, Coimbatore, India
mthilagu@gmail.com

Abstract. Sentiment Analysis (SA) is a Natural Language Processing (NLP) application. It's sometimes referred to as "opinion mining" or "emotion extraction". Sentiment Analysis is a growing area of study in text mining and a popular research subject for opinion mining in education, which analyses and comprehends students' attitudes toward their learning in order to improve the quality of decision-making. More innovative approaches have been developed in online education, which provide an efficient way to learn irrespective of Gender, geographical discrimination, age, etc. As more and more reviews or feedback are posted during online classes, these messages should be correctly classified to identify the theme behind them. Machine Learning (ML) and Deep Learning (DL) based classification models are used to solve sentiment classification problems. Machine Learning (ML) algorithms Support Vector Machine (SVM), Naïve Bayes (NB), Random Forest (RF) and Decision Tree (DT) and Deep Learning (DL) algorithms especially Convolutional Neural Networks (CNN) and Recurrent Neural Networks (RNN) are most frequently used algorithms for Natural Language processing (NLP). It allows us to have a deeper understanding of the student's emotions. It may also be used to recognize and analyse feelings in user comments or reviews on various blogs, websites, social media, online communities, and other sites in order to better understand their perspectives. Thus, the most addressed domain was the use of sentiment analysis in the context of higher education and the evaluation of teaching quality. It would be very helpful for instructors to improve learning strategies by assessing both the instructors and students' progress.

Keywords: Sentimental analysis · Opinion mining · Emotion extraction · Polarity · Natural Language Processing (NLP) · Machine learning · Deep learning · Text mining

1 Introduction

The current educational system offers a large E-Learning platform that enables students to learn new information and abilities. It also offers a means of enhancing the teaching and learning process through the analysis of feedback or Comments in order to take better decisions. Sentiment analysis has been widely used for a variety of objectives in numerous application fields. When taking into account customer ratings, social media monitoring, and other factors, the education sector should be given priority. It is very important to make a proper analysis of textual data as the data collected is unstructured. Sentimental Analysis is used for analyzing the positive, negative and neutral sentiments of user's opinion. This uses the concept of Natural Language Processing and text analysis to analyze user's sentiment using tweets, comments, reviews posted. By analyzing the context it identifies the sentiment of users and it helps them to makes some changes for better approach and make users to meet their needs. Sentiment analysis can be carried out at the word, sentence, or document level. Because handling these reviews manually is difficult due to the large amount of data, automatic processing is required.

The popularity and importance of students feedback have also increased recently especially during COVID-19 when compared to movie reviews or tweets (Santos, Cicero, & Gatti, 2014.), With a few notable exceptions, who examined the connection between a ratio based on the positive and negative phrases in the postings and dropout (Wen, 2014.). There are very few contributions in the domain of MOOCs and education evaluations. Additionally, neither a defined strategy for handling sentiment analysis in MOOCs nor a comparison of various methodologies exist nor role of teachers has surprisingly shifted over the years. Teachers must now not only get familiar with new tools, but also keep up with cutting-edge technology. The skeleton of any educational system is its teachers. A teacher's effectiveness is judged not just by his or her academic qualifications, but also by skill, and commitment. Feedback at regular intervals is considered as a most effective approach for a teacher to improve teaching methodologies. Feedback might be an open-ended or closed-ended as they are loaded with observations and insights, open ended textual feedbacks are difficult to examine manually and draw conclusions.More number of research are being carried out in identifying sentimental Analysis and Opinion mining. To be specific opinion mining helps teachers to evaluate the attitudes and behavior of students towards specific subject, platforms and teachers.

Machine Learning (Baidal, Karen, Carlota, & Vera, 2018) and Deep Learning algorithms are used to identify the meaning behind the reviews and it focuses on polarity i.e., positive, negative, or neutral. Machine Learning is classified as supervised or unsupervised, whereas the Lexicon-based approach analyses and identifies the scores for the phrases already assigned, and it is used to identify the polarity. As shown in Fig. 1. It is divided into two approaches: dictionary-based and corpus-based, (Bhalla, 2022) which use semantic approaches or statistical methods to identify sentiment polarity. If the dataset is small, algorithms such as Naive Bayes, Support Vector Machines, and Random Forest are used to find polarization. Deep Learning concepts like Convolutional Neural Networks (CNN), Recurrent Neural Networks (RNN), and Long Short-Term Memory Networks (LSTM) have also contributed a lot to Natural Language Processing (NLP).

This study aims to provide a comprehensive comparison between various approaches in ML and DL in detecting the polarity of sentiments behind students' feedback based on various datasets. Students' feedback is viewed as an effective tool in this research paper that provides valuable insights when compared to other entities such as courses,

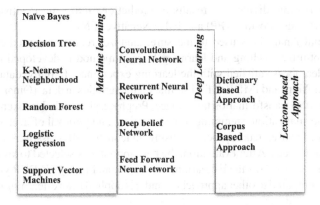

Fig. 1. Sentiment analysis classifiers

institutions, and so on. The analysis here is based on students' perspectives, taking into account all aspects of teaching and learning, including the course, teaching methodology, course structure, assessment, teachers' knowledge, behavior, and presentation, among others. During the last five years, the majority of articles published focused on gathering opinions and attitudes toward teachers, with only a few papers focusing on institution-related questions and some on general feedback. According to the literature review, a greater number of papers focus on gathering opinions and thoughts about student attitudes toward teachers.

2 Related Work: A Literature Review

Sentimental Analysis focuses mainly on polarity detection and recognition of emotions towards an entity, which could be based on any event. Sentimental Analysis uses NLP, ML and DL techniques to discover users' opinions, identify the sentiments from a vast amount of information. It can be done at the document, sentence, or aspect level (Cambria, Schuller, Liu, Wang, & Hava, 2012). SA is an interdisciplinary field that deals with data preprocessing, information retrieval, statistics, and computational linguistics. Research work related to student feedback is analyzed, which is collected from various sources, and a few research works related to other domains are also considered to analyse the various algorithms, methodologies, and models' accuracy in Machine Learning and Deep Learning.

A research mainly focuses on sentimental analysis of user preferences with Google Classroom data for Indonesian language (Situmorang, Chairunnas, & Bon, 2020). Reviews about Google Classroom are obtained through the Google Play store and data scrapping techniques for mobile applications, which are stored as .csv format for further processing. Preprocessing is performed on the collected data to remove stop words, punctuations, and stemming. A framework is being developed using impKNN and uses term weighting using the term frequency-inverse document frequency (TF-IDF) method to characterize the polarity of opinion in E-Learning. When the TF-IDF calculation is applied to training and testing data, number of matches is found using confusion matrix

(Kandhro, 2019) that divides the results of predictions into True Positive (TP), True Negative (TN), False Positive (FP) and False Negative (FN).

Sentimental Analysis is used to measure, analyze, report, and predict data about learners to optimize teaching and learning. Here, a method is developed to determine whether the learner is satisfied with the learning experience. Initially, data is collected from Amazon, Yelp, and IMDB to find similar characteristics in data. (Omar, 2020) In the second phase, data transformation takes place. Preprocessing includes tokenization, case conversion, normalization, stemming, transliteration, and removal of irrelevant content. During the third phase, data is processed using lexicon and ML classifiers such as Naive Bayes, Decision Trees. After evaluation, the best approach is selected to know the actual feedback collected towards the E-Learning environment. Finally, VADER yields the best results when compared to other approaches, and it is applied in an e-learning environment to get the best results.

A comparative analysis was carried out with 140 responses collected through Google forms (Fahmi, 2020). For the best results, Multinomial Nave Bayes, Support Vector Machine, and Random Forest with unigram and bi-gram were compared. In both cases, the Multinomial Naïve Bayes classifier produced the best results of 80% when compared with the Support Vector Machine and Random Forest. A hybrid architecture, combination of keyword-based components and learning system components, is used to detect hidden phrase patterns, used to identify syntactic and semantic details, and emotion prediction is identified based on the knowledge-rich linguistic resources and trained classifiers. Initially, text is tokenized and split into sentences.

(Dsouza, 2019) POS Tagger is used to annotate information by identifying verbs and nouns. This content is provided as input for Emotion Intelligence PR, followed by Machine Learning PR. Finally, it predicts the emotions by building a training model and applying it. So the output obtained from the keyword-based component acts as an input for the learning-based component. Here, a hybrid-based architecture is used to detect emotion that has been validated with experimental results.

An international questionnaire Turkish Tale dataset (Binali, 2010) is used to identify the sentiments where the data in tales were split into paragraphs and sentences, and typo errors were also corrected using the Zemberek Library. In supervised machine learning approaches, multinomial, logistic regression, and Gaussian NB were used. Due to insufficient data, results were not accurate, and the dataset was improved with more data to get better accuracy. A final result with 75% accuracy was also obtained using the Logistic Regression algorithm.

Students' feedback from Vietnam universities was collected through surveys and collected feedback was classified into sentiment-based tasks and topic-based tasks, and labelling was done (Osmanoğlu, 2020). The vntokenizer tool is used for tokenization, and Maximum Entropy and Naïve Bayes algorithms are compared here. Finally, MaxEnt performs well when compared to Naïve Bayes with both tasks in corpus.

The research work (Almalki, 2022) used a twitter dataset in the distance learning domain for identifying sentiments. Using the Twitter API or third-party libraries, data scraping is done. The API extracted nearly 14,000 tweets and preprocessing is done. Apache Spark is used for parallel computing, and the Flask API is used for identifying the sentiments behind Arabic tweets. Finally, Logistic Regression produced an accuracy of 91%. An approach (Nimala, 2021) collected feedback from around 4895 students and compared it with four different models like STM,ETM, SWAT, and ET were constructed, and STM has an accuracy of 86.5 and produced better results compared to other models. Another model uses the Movie Review dataset to build a model that analyses sentiments.The initial model was trained with a 50% manually annotated dataset in the Hindi language (Rani, 2019) and the experimental results are compared with other ML approaches, but the proposed CNN model overcomes the performance of other models and achieves 95% accuracy. The next model uses Deep Learning NN and Applied CNN on the Lithuanian Internet Comment dataset (Kapočiūtė-Dzikienė, 2019) to analyse the emotions behind the dataset. It is built on Word2Vec and FastText word embedding. So the best results were reported with 70.6% accuracy using CNN. So it works better and produces good results if the dataset is very small.

It was suggested to use an attention-based LSTM model that includes aspect information. A novel model was developed to predict the sentiment score of financial opinion mining and categorise it into a particular pre-defined class. The LSTM layers maintain the intermediate output to link it to the final distribution representation and take the word embedding as input. (Shijia, 2018) Additionally, 504 news headlines and 675 microblog messages are included in the dataset utilised for the experiment. In addition, there were 27 classification labels and an emotion score scale from -1 to 1. The neural network used the word2vec model as an input for word embedding. A number of deep learning models were compared, and the results showed that ALA performed the best.

To present a sentiment lexicon (Chen, 2020) established a sentiment analysis framework based on a deep neural LSTM network. The information was created using the Military Life PTT board from Taiwan's largest internet forum. The testing findings demonstrated that the suggested framework's accuracy and F1-measure were higher than the results obtained by employing solely existing sentiment dictionaries. LSTM is used to create a sentiment analysis model for the Roman Urdu language (Ghulam, 2019), When compared to other machine learning algorithms, the testing findings demonstrated significant accuracy.

A work that compared five Machine Learning techniques (Altrabsheh, 2014) using Naïve Bayes, Complement Naïve Bayes, Maximum Entropy, and Support Vector Machines that automatically analyse the student's feedback in real-time with a minimum time. Preprocessing is done to remove stop words, punctuation, and numbers, case conversions and spell checking have been done for a collected 1036 instances. Here, data is collected in two different ways: real-time collection of feedback in lectures and end-of-unit feedback. Naive Bayes will not work with uneven datasets and Complement NB addressed this problem and produced better results where the Naive Bayes algorithm was implemented in R and CNB was implemented in Weka. Maximum Entropy finds the weights of features that maximise the likelihood using search-based optimization. Its performance is very poor when dealing with real-time problems. Support Vector Machines is effective in text categorization and SVM Radial Basis Kernel works well with Natural Language Processing (NLP) and it is flexible to use in experiments, SVM performed better compared to NB. Maximum Entropy performed better for neutral class results without change in F1-Score, precision, and recall and also prevents over fitting.

In (Toçoğlu, 2020), three conventional text representation schemes and three N-grams have been used with classifiers like SVM, Naïve Bayes, Logistic Regression, and the Random Forest algorithm. Ensemble learners like AdaBoost, Bagging, Random Space, and Voting algorithms were also evaluated for producing better results. Here the dataset is divided into 10 mutual folds. When three different classifiers with text representation and stemming schemes were used, F5, raw, and snow ball stemming scheme, raw outperformed the SVM classifier and TF-IDF text representation. Again, N-gram models are compared against classifiers and text representations, which produced the results as SVM and RF with unigram performed well. Considering ensemble methods, it doesn't produce more changes in the results, so finally TF-IDF outperformed well.

The research work (Kastrati Z. A., 2020) compared Deep Learning and Machine Learning algorithms using student reviews (21,940 reviews) from an E-Learning platform. SVM, Nave Bayes, Boosting, and DT ML algorithms are combined with TF-IDF, a 1D-CNN model is built to extract sentiment, and FastText, Word2Vec, and Glove word embedding's are used for a better F1 Score of 88.2%. A work consists of 2 datasets: the rating score dataset and the textual comment dataset, and various ML classifiers (MLP, Logistic Regression, SVM,RF are compared to identify the best classifier (Lwin, 2020).For labelling the rating score dataset, K-Means clustering is used and trained with various models where SVM produced a better result, and Naïve Bayes is used for textual comment classification as it consists of both English and Myanmar language and tested using 10-fold cross validation with F-Measure-95% best results. 30,0000 textual feedback has been collected from college students. After preprocessing (Katragadda, 2020), it is evaluated using NB, SVM, and ANN classifiers. Finally, ANN produced the best accuracy of 88.2%. It clearly states that classifiers' performance is purely based on the parameters considered and the size of the dataset.

A study was conducted to improve the sentiment classifier by using TF-IDF and n-grams and ensemble techniques (Pacol, 2021). It converts text into vector values instead of count vectors in base models where it produces the minimum amount of information when compared to vector values. Teaching performance data is collected from various campuses of Pangasinan State University and consists of 9140 sentences, which are manually cleaned and labelled in an excel file. Considering the performance of n-gram and base models, n-gram with SVM performed with 0.98 accuracy, whereas n-gram shows improvement in the performance in ensemble models with Naive Bayes, Logistic Regression, and Support Vector Machine.

Large volumes of data, such as discussion statements, likes, and follows, as well as individual system interactions, including timestamps of activities, videos watched, test outcomes, and logins, are generated by MOOCs and serve as evidence of participant involvement and experience. The study's low response rate, (Lundqvist, 2020) which can skew the sample, is one of its limitations. Only 264 people commented in the free text comment section during the first week of the course, which is a reflection of how few people comment in MOOCs overall. According to the study, there is a correlation between the general tone of postings and comments made about the MOOC, and this course had a generally positive tone compared with others.

Four Machine Learning techniques such as Support Vector Machines, Naïve Bayes (NB), Maximum Entropy (ME), and Complement Naïve Bayes (CNB) were compared.

1036 responses were collected, and 641 cases were positive and 292 cases were considered negative. (Ullah, 2016) After several preprocessing steps, Maximum Entropy and Support Vector Machines perform well, and the possibility of including more preprocessing will result in a better outcome.

A model is built with different layers that use the data collected from students of Vietnam University (Sangeetha, 2021). The inputs are trained using embedding models such as Glove and Cove, and the output features are fed into the encoding layer. Next, the output of the encoding layer is fed into a dropout layer that prevents over fitting. The results of these dropout layers are combined using LSTM, which produces only minimum features. Finally, everything will be fed into the dense layer for producing output. This new architecture is less error-prone when compared to the other three models: LSTM with 86%, LSTM with Attention with 87%, Multi-head LSTM with Attention with 90%, and the proposed model with 94% accuracy.

MOOC reviews have been collected from Coursera and a framework has been proposed for aspect-based sentimental analysis. This model identified the critical factors that determine the effectiveness of online courses and also the attitude of students. With keywords and manually annotated reviews, the proposed framework (Kastrati Z. I., 2020) is being tested and validated against datasets using LSTM and CNN. LSTM with glove performed well, with an F1-Score of 86.13%.

Two algorithms have been compared to analyse the Twitter data based on hashtag keywords and compared the performance with Recurrent Neural Network and Support Vector Machine through R-Tool. SVM and RNN have been carried out with a sample of 20, 50, and 600 tweets, Recurrent Neural Network produced better results compared to Support Vector Machine (Kaur, 2021). Even though Machine Learning and lexicon-based approaches are used in feedback analysis, Deep Learning methods propose a better and more efficient system that uses Word2Vec for text processing, CNN (Asmita S, Anuja T, & Ash, 2019) for automatic feature extraction, and final classification is done using Support Vector Machine. So, Deep Learning can be used in the education domain to classify the strengths, weaknesses, and suggestions for a trainer. Various datasets from Twitter sentiment, the sentiment Tree bank, and online movie reviews (Rojas-Barahona, 2016) were considered and applied to various Deep Learning architectures such as convolutional, recurrent, and combined methods. Both fine-grained and binary classification have been carried out, and comparatively, CNN performs well in polarity detection compared to supervised models.

3   Methodology

3.1   Datasets

Most of the related research findings identified a few important aspects regarding the teaching-learning process, including students' opinions about teaching, institutions, and courses. So a study was carried out nearly using more than 25 papers based on educational feedback reviews from students. Mostly, for this kind of analysis, open datasets are limited and are not available with the required attributes that suit our needs. The data used in the research papers was taken from various sources like real-time feedback collected from students of various universities through Google forms, Survey/Questionnaire, social media, blogs or forums, MOOC educational platforms (Course era and EdX), online reviews, and some used blended datasets which may be manually annotated to obtain the result. Duplicate records should be removed after data collection and, in many cases, data collected from online forums is unstructured and should be labelled manually and trained to be used with supervised Machine Learning approaches.

3.2 Approach

The most crucial phase of every machine learning model is data preprocessing (Gottipati, 2018). The performance of the model is significantly influenced by how effectively the raw data is cleaned and preprocessed. Text preprocessing aims to clean up the data so that it can be processed in the next step. Text preprocessing makes the input documents more consistent to facilitate text representation, which is necessary for most text analytics tasks. Tokenization breaks the sentences into words, stemming obtains the root words from tokens; and lemmatization creates a single base word for various inflected forms, Part of Speech is used for identifying parts of speech in tokens, Named Entity Recognition (NER) classifies the text into various categories.

Figure 2 shows preprocessing techniques in NLP like tokenization, lemmatization, parsing, and bag of words that help us analyse the sentiments in text. Initially, after getting feedback, input is split into sentences or words, and, using tokenization, POS tagging, and lemmatization, it converts sentences into words. Then a sentiment score is calculated from these tokenized words and, based on the score, the sentiment is categorized. Sentiment can be classified using either Machine Learning or Deep Learning Models, so appropriate models should be selected to get the relevant output.

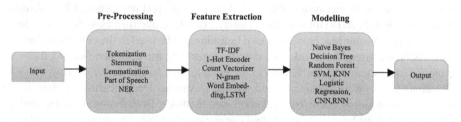

Fig. 2. Sentimental analysis using machine learning/deep learning

An automated process that analyses and discriminates sentiments as positive, negative, or neutral based on the emotions expressed by users in the form of text.NLP identifies the core data that helps us understand students' sentiments. SA classifies huge amounts of real-time data in a few seconds, which is very complicated to manually classify and it also results in erroneous results. Sentiment can be analysed through Machine Learning and lexicon-based approaches. Machine learning algorithms need data for training as it is to be collected and labelled manually and it is a time-consuming process (Singh, 2017). Supervised ML algorithms like Naïve Bayes, Decision Tree, K-Nearest Neighborhood, Random Forest, Logistic Regression (Ghulam, 2019) Support Vector Machine algorithms are mostly used to identify the sentiment of any review or sentence. Natural language processing, text analysis, computational linguistics, and other approaches are used to identify and quantify the sentiment of text in sentiment analysis. For better results, these algorithms require labelled data as a dataset and can be combined with lexicon approaches (dictionary-based or corpus-based) and classifiers such as Ada boost, N-Model, Bagging, and Random Space and Aspect based classification methods (Toçoğlu, 2020) are also used with TF-IDF statistical method (Kastrati Z. A., 2020), activation functions like Tanh, sigmoid, and ReLu (Chen, 2020) are combined with ML algorithms like SVM, Multinomial NB, and Logistic regression for better accuracy. Table 1 demonstrates various methods used in literature works, datasets used, algorithms compared, new models developed, and results.

Deep learning has emerged as a powerful machine learning technique that learns multiple layers of representations or features of the data and produces results (Zhang, 2018). Along with the success of deep learning in many other application domains, it has also been popularly used in sentiment analysis in recent years. Due to their high performance (Yadav, 2020) Deep Learning algorithms like Convolutional Neural Network (CNN), Recurrent Neural Network (RNN), and Deep Belief Networks (DBN) are the most frequently used algorithms for Sentimental Analysis. Ensemble methods and architectures can also be used to identify the polarity of words that learn features through layers that are fed directly into another layer as input (Ghorbani, 2020).

Lexicon approaches like corpus-based and dictionary-based approaches can perform sentiment analysis without training, and it needs explicit vocabulary for separate language as it is unsupervised. The tokenization process separates each word in a review or post and, based on the emotion found, it is assigned as positive, negative, or neutral flags based on words already available in the lexicon. Some tools like VADER (Kastrati Z. D., 2021; Dsouza, 2019) & (Kastrati Z. D., 2021),SentiWordNet, WordNet and SentiBank are publicly available to analyse the sentiment behind the words.

Table 1. Literature review- machine learning, lexicon based and deep learning methods for sentimental analysis

Year	Reference	Model	Dataset	Results
2022	(Almalki, 2022)	Logistic Regression with Apache spark, Flask API	Arabic Tweets from Twitter API	Logistic Regression- 91% SVM -69%
2021	(Pacol, 2021)	Naïve Bayes, SVM, Logistic regression.TF-IDF,n-grams, ensemble methods	Pangasinan State University-1827 statements	N-Gram with SVM -98%
2020	(Situmorang, Chairunnas, & Bon, 2020)	Imp KNN with TF-IDF	LMS reviews through Google Classroom and Play Store	Accuracy -84%

(*continued*)

Table 1. (*continued*)

Year	Reference	Model	Dataset	Results
2020	(Omar, 2020)	VADER Classifier, Naïve Bayes and Decision Tree	IMDB, Yelp and Amazon	VADER Accuracy– 90% NB (amazon)-81% DT (Amazon)-76%
2020	(Fahmi, 2020)	SVM & SVM-PSO, Naïve Bayes,KNN	LMS Dataset through API (2154 Reviews) (Feature Reduction)	SVM-PSO with Sastrawi – 82.27% SVM-PSO without Sastrawi – 82.09%
2020	(Osmanoğlu, 2020)	Decision tree, KNN, MLP, XGB, NB, SVM Logistic Regression,	International & Turkish Tale Dataset, Data from LMS (Study materials) 2421 Comments	Logistic Regression (CT + SC) – 77.5% DT- 76.5%
2020	(Toçoğlu, 2020)	Classifiers, Text Representations and Stemming Schemes	Student Reviews 698 Reviews	SVM Accuracy TF *idf = 73% TF – 70.6% TP – 69%
2020	(Sangeetha, 2021)	LSTM,LSTM + ATT, MULTIHEAD, FUSION	Vietnam University (16,175 statements)	Fusion Model Achieves better Accuracy
2020	(Kastrati Z. D., 2021)	LSTM,CNN	Coursera reviews (5989 reviews)	F1-score LSTM + Glove -93.3%
2020	(Katragadda, 2020)	Naïve Bayes,SVM and ANN	30000 Students Review	NB-50% SVM -60.8% ANN -88.2%
2020	(Kastrati Z. A., 2020)	SVM, Naive Bayes, Boosting, Decision Tree, 1D-CNN (Aspect based Classification)	21940 students' reviews	CNN -88.2% DT (TF)-77.9% DT(TF*idf)– 88.67%
2019	(Dsouza, 2019)	MNBC, SVM, RF for unigram and bi-gram	Google Form data (140 Responses)	MNBC -80% produced best results
2019	(Nimala, 2021)	STM,ETM,SWAT, ET Models	Feedback form (4895 Responses)	STM Accuracy = 86.5% ETM -74.5%
2019	(Kapočiūtė-Dzikienė, 2019)	ML (SVM,MNB) DL (LSTM,CNN)	Lithuanian Internet comments (10,570 comments)	LSTM,CNN– 61%,70% SVM,MNB–72%,73.5%
2019	(Chen, 2020)	LSTM,Bi-LSTM	Military life PTT	LSTM – 90.11% Bi-LSTM – 92.68%
2019	(Ghulam, 2019)	NB,RF,SVM,Deep Neural Network	Roman Urdu dataset	NB – 77.2% RF – 88.6% SVM – 92.4% DNN- 95.2%

(*continued*)

Table 1. (*continued*)

Year	Reference	Model	Dataset	Results
2018	(Rani, 2019)	CNN	Movie Review Dataset	CNN (3 Layers) - 95% CNN (2 Layers) – 93.4%
2018	(Shijia, 2018)	RNN-LSTM	504 news headlines and 675 microblog messages	ALA outperformed well (Attention based LSTM model with aspect information)
2018	(Moreno-Marcos, 2018)	Logistic Regression, NB, SVM,DT, RF, UnSup (Dictionary, SentiWordNet)	MOOC (13,300 Reviews)	AUC Performed well compared to Kappa
2018	(Van Nguyen, 2018)	Naïve Bayes and Maximum Entropy	Vietnam Students Dataset (16000 Responses)	ME(Sentiment Based)- 87.9% ME (Topic Based)-84%
2017	(Singh, 2017)	Naïve Bayes,J48, BFTree and OneR	Woodlands Wallet (100 Reviews), Camera Review (8000 Reviews), Movie Review (2900 Reviews)	J-48 & OneR performed well
2016	(Ullah, 2016)	SVM,ME,NB,CNB	University of Portsmouth (1036 reviews)	SVM- 96.2% ME – 87%
2014	(Altrabsheh, 2014)	NB,CNB,SVM Linear, Poly and SVM RB	Real-time feedback collection and end of unit feedback (1036 Instances)	CNB(With Kernal) - 84% CNB (Without Kernel) – 80% SVM(Without Kernel) – 94% SVM (with Kernel) -93%

4   Research Challenges and Future Directions

Instead of a fine-grained analysis that is related to various characteristics and the sentiments associated with them, the majority of the study concentrated on a thorough examination of sentimental analysis. Possibility of using figurative language, such as sarcasm, irony, and other complex types of discourse in which authors use language to convey the opposite meaning. Even for humans, recognizing irony can be difficult and complex, resulting in a lot of misunderstandings in everyday life. Sarcasm and irony detection in natural language processing is challenging, particularly for sentiment analysis. For a better classification, it's also important to consider identifying irony, sarcasm, and figurative speech, examining emoticons, emoji's, and emoticons, as well as assessing negative and double-negative words. Only a small number of open datasets with insufficient properties are available. Only a few sources are accessible to identify the lexical components. Therefore, there is a demand for more datasets and more emotional analysis publications. Researchers have utilized a variety of evaluation metrics to assess how well different methodologies perform, and by selecting the best measures, any mode's effectiveness is improved. The extraction of named entities, which can refer to concrete people or abstract notions, is one of the fundamental difficulties with natural texts. Expand the most sophisticated model to include sentiment analysis across several languages. Consequently, a multi-language processing paradigm must be put in place. There are over 80 dictionaries available for other languages. Very little research is done in code-mix languages, and the majority of work is done in English. So this case needs to be considered in future work. Many studies simply translate all comments into English using machine translation, although this may cause emotions to be lost in the translation.

Finding irony in Natural Language Processing (NLP), especially in sentiment analysis, is a difficult issue. Satirical statements may lead to inaccurate categorization in the findings of sentiment analysis and data mining. Huge datasets are typically needed for deep learning techniques, but real-world datasets are frequently unbalanced.

5   Conclusions

The educational sector is undergoing a tremendous transformation because of online education. Massive amounts of structured and unstructured data are collected through online platforms, which include MOOCs, EdX, Coursera, etc. Students' feelings can be gauged through posted feedback, forums, and reviews. This helps the teachers to identify the students' attitudes, feelings, and behavior to make necessary improvements in teaching methodology to maintain the students' retention rate. Sentimental Analysis research has increased in recent years, and while initially only Machine Learning algorithms were considered, Deep Learning algorithms are now being used to identify the polarity. Examining the Literature for Support Vector Machines and Naive Bayes are most frequently used in Machine Learning models, while Convolutional Neural Networks and Recurrent Neural Networks (RNN) are used in Deep Learning models (CNN). Research is required, taking into account the difficulties in analysing feedback and determining the best model in Machine Learning or Deep Learning that results in high accuracy. As a result, Sentimental Analysis based recommendation systems analyse comments and extract precise information about students' expectations, teaching methodology, their interests, and expected curriculum updates to be embedded in the education sector to vastly improve every aspect of education.

References

Almalki, J.C.: A machine learning-based approach for sentiment analysis on distance learning from Arabic Tweets (2022)

Altrabsheh, N., Cocea, M., Fallahkhair, S.: Learning sentiment from students' feedback for real-time interventions in classrooms. In: Bouchachia, A. (ed.) ICAIS 2014. LNCS (LNAI), vol. 8779, pp. 40–49. Springer, Cham (2014). https://doi.org/10.1007/978-3-319-11298-5_5

Asmita, S.S., Anuja, T.D., Ash, D.: Analysis of student feedback using deep learning. Int. J. Comput. Appl. Technol. Res. **8**, 161–164 (2019)

Mite-Baidal, K., Delgado-Vera, C., Solís-Avilés, E., Espinoza, A.H., Ortiz-Zambrano, J., Varela-Tapia, E.: Sentiment analysis in education domain: a systematic literature review. In: Valencia-García, R., Alcaraz-Mármol, G., Del Cioppo-Morstadt, J., Vera-Lucio, N., Bucaram-Leverone, M. (eds.) CITI 2018. CCIS, vol. 883, pp. 285–297. Springer, Cham (2018). https://doi.org/10.1007/978-3-030-00940-3_21

Bhalla, R.: A review paper on the role of sentiment analysis in quality education. SN Comput. Sci. **3**(6), 1–9 (2022)

Binali, H.W.: Computational approaches for emotion detection in text. In: 4th IEEE International Conference on Digital Ecosystems and Technologies, pp. 172–177. IEEE (2010)

Cambria, E., Schuller, B., Liu, B., Wang, H., Havasi, C.: Guest Editorial Special Issue on Concept-Level Opinion and Sentiment Analysis. IEEE, (IF:2.570, 5-year IF:2.632(2010)), pp. 15-21 (2012)

Chen, L.C.: Exploration of social media for sentiment analysis using deep learning. Soft. Comput. **24**(11), 8187–8197 (2020)

Dsouza, D.D.: Sentimental analysis of student feedback using machine learning techniques. Int. J. Recent Technol. Eng. **8**(14), 986–991 (2019)

Fahmi, S.P.: Sentiment analysis of student review in learning management system based on sastrawi stemmer and SVM-PSO. In: 2020 International Seminar on Application for Technology of Information and Communication (iSemantic), pp. 643–648 (2020)

Ghorbani, M., Bahaghighat, M., Xin, Q., Özen, F.: ConvLSTMConv network: a deep learning approach for sentiment analysis in cloud computing. J. Cloud Comput. **9**(1), 1–12 (2020). https://doi.org/10.1186/s13677-020-00162-1

Ghulam, H.Z.: Deep learning-based sentiment analysis for roman urdu text. Procedia Comput. Sci. **147**, 131–135 (2019)

Gottipati, S., Shankararaman, V., Lin, J.R.: Text analytics approach to extract course improvement suggestions from students' feedback. Res. Pract. Technol. Enhanc. Learn. **13**(1), 1–19 (2018). https://doi.org/10.1186/s41039-018-0073-0

Kandhro, I.A., et al.: Student feedback sentiment analysis model using various machine learning schemes: a review. Indian J. Sci. Technol. **12**(14), 1–9 (2019)

Kapočiūtė-Dzikienė, J.D.: Sentiment analysis of lithuanian texts using traditional and deep learning approaches. Computers **8**(1), 4 (2019)

Kastrati, Z.A.: Aspect-based opinion mining of students' reviews on online courses. In: Proceedings of the 2020 6th International Conference on Computing and Artificial Intelligence, pp. 510–514 (2020)

Kastrati, Z.D.: Sentiment analysis of students' feedback with NLP and deep learning: a systematic mapping study. Appl. Sci. **11**(9), 3986 (2021)

Kastrati, Z.I.: Weakly supervised framework for aspect-based sentiment analysis on students' reviews of MOOC. IEEE Access **8**, 106799–106810 (2020)

Katragadda, S.R.: Performance analysis on student feedback using machine learning algorithms. In: 2020 6th International Conference on Advanced Computing and Communication Systems (ICACCS), pp. 1161–1163. IEEE (2020)

Kaur, H.A.: A proposed sentiment analysis deep learning algorithm for analyzing COVID-19 tweets. Inf. Syst. Front. **23**(6), 1417–1429 (2021)

Lundqvist, K.L.: Evaluation of student feedback within a MOOC using sentiment analysis and target groups. Int. Rev. Res. Open Distrib. Lear. **21**(3), 140–156 (2020)

Lwin, H.H.: Feedback analysis in outcome base education using machine learning. In: 17th International Conference on Electrical Engineering/Electronics, Computer, Telecommunications and Information Technology (ECTI-CON), pp. 767–770. IEEE (2020)

Moreno-Marcos, P.M., Alario-Hoyos, C., Muñoz-Merino, P.J., Estévez-Ayres, I., Kloos, C.D.: Sentiment analysis in MOOCs: a case study. In: 2018 IEEE Global Engineering Education Conference (EDUCON), pp. 1489–1496. IEEE (2018)

Nimala, K.: Sentiment topic emotion model on students feedback for educational benefits and practices. Behav. Inf. Technol. **40**(3), 311–319 (2021)

Omar, M.A.: Sentiment analysis of user feedback in e-learning environment. Int. J. Eng. Trends Technol. (IJETT), 153–157 (2020)

Osmanoğlu, U.Ö.: Sentiment analysis for distance education course materials: a machine learning approach. J. Educ. Technol. Online Learn. **3**(1), 31–48 (2020)

Pacol, C.A.: Enhancing sentiment analysis of textual feed-back in the student-faculty evaluation using machine learning techniques. Eur. J. Eng. Sci. Technol. **4**(1), 27–34 (2021). https://doi.org/10.33422/ejest.v4i

Rani, S.: Deep learning based sentiment analysis using convolution neural network. Arab. J. Sci. Eng. **44**(4), 3305–3314 (2019)

Rojas-Barahona, L.M.: Deep learning for sentiment analysis. Lang. Linguist. Compass **10**(12), 701–719 (2016)

Sangeetha, K., Prabha, D.: Sentiment analysis of student feedback using multi-head attention fusion model of word and context embedding for LSTM. J. Ambient Intell. Humanized Comput. **12**(3), 4117–4126 (2020). https://doi.org/10.1007/s12652-020-01791-9

Dos Santos, C., Gatti, M.: Deep convolutional neural networks for sentiment analysis of short texts. In: Proceedings of COLING 2014, The 25th International Conference on Computational Linguistics: Technical Papers, pp. 69–78 (2014)

Shijia, E.Y.: Aspect-based financial sentiment analysis with deep neural networks. In: WWW (Companion Volume) (2018)

Singh, J., Singh, G., Singh, R.: Optimization of sentiment analysis using machine learning classifiers. HCIS **7**(1), 1–12 (2017). https://doi.org/10.1186/s13673-017-0116-3

Situmorang, B.H., Chairunnas, A., Bon, A.T.: Sentiment analysis of user preferences on learning management system (Lms) platform data. In: 2nd African International Conference on Industrial Engineering and Operations Management, IEOM 2020, pp. 1784–1789 (2020)

Toçoğlu, M.A., Onan, A.: Sentiment analysis on students' evaluation of higher educational institutions. In: Kahraman, C., Cevik Onar, S., Oztaysi, B., Sari, I.U., Cebi, S., Tolga, A.C. (eds.) INFUS 2020. AISC, vol. 1197, pp. 1693–1700. Springer, Cham (2021). https://doi.org/10.1007/978-3-030-51156-2_197

Ullah, M.A.: Sentiment analysis of students feedback: a study towards optimal tools. In: 2016 International Workshop on Computational Intelligence (IWCI), pp. 175–180. IEEE (2016)

Van Nguyen, K.N.: UIT-VSFC: vietnamese students' feedback corpus for sentiment analysis. In: 2018 10th International Conference on Knowledge and Systems Engineering (KSE), pp. 19–24 (2018)

Wen, M.Y.: Sentiment analysis in MOOC discussion forums: what does it tell us? In: Proceedings of the 7th International Conference on Educational Data Mining (EDM 2014), pp. 130–137 (2014)

Yadav, A.: Sentiment analysis using deep learning architectures: a review. Artif. Intell. Rev. **53**(6), 4335–4385 (2020)

Zhang, L.W.: Deep learning for sentiment analysis: a survey. Wiley Interdisc. Rev. Data Min. Knowl. Disc. **8**(4), e1253 (2018)

Rice Yield Estimation Using Deep Learning

Niyati Mishra, Sushruta Mishra$^{(\boxtimes)}$, and Hrudaya Kumar Tripathy

School of Computer Engineering, Kalinga Institute of Industrial Technology (KIIT) Deemed to be University, Bhubaneswar, Odisha, India
niyatimishra1696@gmail.com, {sushruta.mishrafcs, hktripathyfcs}@kiit.ac.in

Abstract. Global and regional food security heavily relies on effective yield estimation results. Thus precise and on-time rice yield estimate or prediction is a pivotal factor not only to ensure food security but also for sustainable development of agricultural resources. Machine learning and deep learning are proving to be exemplary support tools for decision making for rice yield estimation or prediction, such as selection of the rice varieties that need to be grown and also decisions involving the management of crops during growing season. Several researchers have put forth a variety of deep learning as well as machine learning algorithms that have helped estimate rice yield time and again. This paper proposes a LSTM based model to predict the Rice yield of the data collected for all 314 blocks of Odisha by ICAR - National Rice Research Institute (NRRI), Odisha. In this study, we get 0.07 RMSE score for training data and 0.21 RMSE score for test data. The model is also evaluated based on the various performance metrics for three rice datasets. The overall performance for the rice datasets is evaluated to be 0.989 recall, 0.979 precision, 0.989 accuracy and 0.984 F1 score.

Keywords: Machine learning · Deep learning · Rice yield estimation · Food security · Sustainable development

1 Introduction

The proper and effective estimates of rice yield helps strengthen national food security by ensuring timely export and import decisions, thereby helping the management make proper and informed decisions [1]. For instance, in order to breed superior varieties of crops, seed companies need a prediction of the relative performance measures of the newly developed hybrids in diverse environments and yield prediction would also help farmers or cultivators to make informed financial and management related decisions. Yet, estimation of rice yield is one of the most challenging field out there due to various complicated factors associated with it. One such factor being genotype data which comprises of high-dimensional marker data which in turn contains thousands to millions of markers for every individual plant which is an arduous task as there needs to an accurate estimation of the effects of these genetic markers which under control of a diversity of field management practices or environmental conditions.

Estimation of rice yield is recently heavily focused on the use of various deep learning techniques, for instance deep neural networks. Deep neural networks (DNN) are a type of

M. Panda et al. (Eds.): ICIICC 2022, CCIS 1737, pp. 379–388, 2022.
https://doi.org/10.1007/978-3-031-23233-6_28

representation learning models which help in extraction of underlying data representation without the need of custom-made input attributes. Some major instances of the use of deep learning techniques are described here. In [2], authors proposed a technique for the prompt and expeditious estimation of yield of rice at pixel level by incorporating a deep learning based model and a crop model for varied agriculture based systems available in South Korea and North Korea. Similarly in [3], authors incorporated CNN based framework using RGB images for estimating rice yield. The said model estimated a variation of 70% in rice yield along with a RMSE score of 0.22.

Although Deep Learning is one of the promising technologies used for estimation of rice yield, there are still a few challenges that are faced here in terms of accuracy of the model, inclusion of a greater diversity of features, etc. Many existing works based on different classifiers on rice dataset are implemented but majority of these models lack preciseness and are not so reliable. Also the overall error rate is found to be on higher end with all the existing models. In this study, we have developed a LSTM based model to predict the rice yield of data collected from 314 blocks of Odisha. The main objective of the study is to discuss the use of deep learning techniques in estimation of rice yield. The main contributions of the work are as follows:

- Aim is to address technical reliability issues associated with the rice crop yield prediction domain.
- Develop a novel hybrid LSTM model for predicting rice yield in farming zones with better performance.
- The proposed model is validated against performance metrics and the outcome noted were promising.

The paper is segregated into various sections which are briefly described here. In Sect. 1, a brief introduction of the previous research papers is discussed. Section 3 talks about the problem generally faced in yield prediction. Section 4 discusses the proposed model. In Sect. 5, we discuss about the result and the overall capabilities of the proposed model, and lastly, we summarize the various observations formed with the help of this model under conclusion and future scope title in Sect. 6.

2 Literature Review

In this section, we have listed quite a number of reputed works that have been done in the domain of Estimation of yield of various crops with the aid of various Machine Learning and Deep Learning algorithms. Tian et al. have proposed a model that incorporates deep learning based methods for the estimation of yield of winter wheat. The said model uses meteorological data and two remotely sensed indices [4]. The said incorporates Long Short-Term Memory (LSTM) neural network with an attention feature (ALSTM) attached to the model, where the pivotal idea is to focus the attention to the quintessential parts of the sequence of the input which has maximum impact on the target vectors, thereby ensuring the accurate extraction of the specific features or attributes. Sonal Agarwal and Sandhya Tarar have proposed a model which is enhanced by the incorporation of deep learning methodologies that not only provide accurate yield estimates but also precise information in regard to the quantities of soil ingredients needed and also the necessary monetary expenses that come with it [5]. The said model incorporates a dynamic combination of RNN, LSTM and SVM algorithms. Wang et al. have devised a model that helps estimate the yield of winter wheat in the primary harvesting areas in China with the use of various deep learning methodologies [6]. E. Banu and Dr. A. Geetha incorporated both DNN and random forest in their research work for rice yield estimation [7]. Sun et al. have proposed a model that incorporates both LSTM and CNN algorithms for the estimation of yield of soybean [8]. This paper was trained with the help of both environment parameters and crop growth parameters such as weather data, Surface Reflectance data as well as the Land Surface Temperature data. Nevavuori et al. have incorporated CNN based framework in their study that uses RGB data along with a particular index data that are collected by UAVs [9]. Chen et al. proposed a model that incorporates R-CNN (region-based convolutional neural network) for detecting the quantity of flowers, unripe strawberries, and ripe strawberries with regard to the estimation of strawberry yield [10]. A 3-dimensional CNN based framework was incorporated into the model devised by Russello for estimation of crop yield purpose which showed quite fascinating results in comparison to various dynamic machine learning methodologies [11]. Jiang et al. devised a model incorporating LSTM framework for estimating yield of corn crops by primarily focusing on soil and meteorological data which paved way to quite a good performance score [12]. Kulkarni et al. devised a model incorporating RNN framework that made use of soil data along with various rainfall sequences in a particular designated region for enhancement of yield estimates of the crops [13]. You et al. proposed a model that introduced a component involving Gaussian process into a LSTM or CNN framework into his model and this said model outperformed primitive various remote sensing methodologies by 30% with regard percentage error [14]. Alhnaity et al. incorporated LSTM framework into his model for predicting both plant growth variation and crop yield for two different layouts, i.e., Ficus benjamina stem growth and tomato yield prediction, in supervised greenhouse environments [15]. Some studies have shown that while CNN has the ability to explore more number of spatial features, LSTM can help divulge phenological characteristics [16]. Khaki et al. proposed a model that incorporates YieldNet which is one of the latest deep learning technique that makes use of a novel deep neural network (DNN) framework [17].

3 Problem Statement

Precise and timely prediction of crop yield information is crucial for making accurate agricultural resolutions and non-expendable decisions which has a direct impact on a country's economy [18]. Deep learning has emerged as a front runner among the various promising technologies in this regard. However, we can see that there are multiple challenges associated with using deep learning. These include integrating various interdependent factors into the model for better results, incorporating prior knowledge with existent and current data, increasing the accuracy and thus credibility of the model etc. So, in this paper we have tried to tackle some existing issues by proposing a deep learning based model which uses LSTM as the primary deep learning algorithm to provide more accurate and faster crop estimation results. We intend to explore further into the issues involved with the aforementioned domain of crop yield estimation so that we can build a robust deep learning model.

4 Proposed Model

In this study, we are proposing a LSTM (Long Short-Term Memory) network based model as can be seen in Fig. 1. LSTM is a better improved version of RNN that helps overcome the vanishing gradient problem [19]. LSTM has the capability of processing complete data sequences such as videos for example and not just singe data points like images. An LSTM unit normally comprises of a cell, forget gate, output gate and input gate. A cell is responsible for keeping track of values over random time periods, while the three aforementioned gates helps modulate the flow of data into and out of the cell.

Let's have a detailed explanation on how a LSTM network works. These are the steps normally followed by a LSTM network:

Step – 1: Initially we start with forget gate. Here we can make a decision as to which bits of the cell state can prove to be of use with the help of the new input data and previous hidden state. So, basically the forget gate is responsible for making a decision regarding which fragments of the long term memory can be forgotten based on the given new input data and the previous hidden state.

Step – 2: The following step includes the input gate along with the new memory network. The objective here is to decide what latest information is to be added to the network's long term memory (or) the state of the cell, with the help of the new input data and previous hidden state.

Step – 3: Once we have made changes to the long term memory of the network, we can then jump to the final step that focuses on determining the new hidden state by making use of the output gate. The output gate will make use of these three things, i.e., the new input data, the newly updated cell state and the prior hidden state.

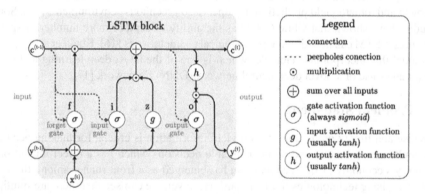

Fig. 1. Architecture of a LSTM network

In this study, we make use of a data set comprising of the various soil parameters such as soil pH, bulk density, soil organic carbon, clay fraction, soil nutrients (nitrogen, phosphorus and potassium), farm yard manure and rice yield of all 314 blocks of state Odisha collected by ICAR - National. Rice Research Institute (NRRI), Odisha. Once the data is fed to the model, it is then used to predict the yield. 70% of the data is taken as the training data while the remaining 30% is taken up as the testing data. Once the estimation of the rice yield is obtained, RMSE score is computed for both the aforementioned sets of data to give an estimate of the capabilities of the proposed model [20–22]. The overview of the proposed framework is highlighted in Fig. 2.

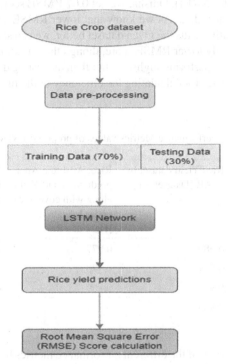

Fig. 2. Overview of proposed model

The overall pseudocode of LSTM model is highlighted below.

Algorithm: Long Short-Term Memory (LSTM)
Input: Standardized Rice dataset
Output: Rice yield prediction

Step 1: Input considered as the present value, past state and the past internal cell state
Step 2: Set values for forget gate, input gate, input modulation gate and output gate.
Step 3: Updated values for different gates computed as:
    Step 3.1: Find parameterized values of the present input and past state for each gate.
    Step 3.2: Activation function applied to each gate on parameterized vectors.
Step 4: Present internal state calculated and then find the addition of two vectors.
Step 5: Compute present hidden state and perform multiplication with output state.

5 Results and Discussion

Upon running the code in jupyter notebook using python, using the Rice crop dataset comprising of the various soil parameters such as soil pH, bulk density, soil organic carbon, clay fraction, soil nutrients (nitrogen, phosphorus and potassium), farm yard manure and rice yield of all 314 blocks of state Odisha collected by ICAR - National Rice Research Institute (NRRI), Odisha, we get 0.07 RMSE score for training data and 0.21 RMSE score for test data. As we know that lower RMSE score indicates that the said model is comparatively fits the given dataset better, we can say the model is a better fit as it has comparatively lower RMSE score, though there is still a bit of an overfitting issue as the training data performs slightly better than the testing data. We gave also used other performance metrics for calculating the efficiency of the model that is proposed in this study.

Table 1. Performance Metrics values of proposed LSTM model

Performance metrics	Rice Yield dataset by ICAR [Dataset – 1]	Rice: All-India Area, production and Yield along with coverage under Irrigation [Dataset – 2]	Rice: State wise Yield (Source: Directorate of Economics & Statistics, DAC&FW) [Dataset – 3]
recall	0.989	0.977	0.982
precision	0.979	0.970	0.969
accuracy	0.989	0.969	0.977
F1 score	0.984	0.971	0.965

Table 1 is the overview of the different performance metrics like recall, precision, F1 score and accuracy of the proposed LSTM model for different rice datasets. Precision can be measured as the ratio of number of accurately classified Positive samples to the total number of positively classified samples, thus precision indicates the reliability of the model in the classification of the Positive samples. Higher value of precision indicates that the model is capable of making more accurate Positive classifications while making fewer wrong Positive classifications. Recall can be measured as the ratio of number of accurately classified Positive samples to the total number of Positive samples, thus recall indicates the capability of the model to discover Positive samples. Higher value of recall indicates more number of positive samples identified [21]. Accuracy helps determine the overall performance of the model. It is the ratio of number of the accurately made predictions to the total number of predictions. F1 score is measured as the mean of recall and precision, so higher F1 score is achieved only when precision and recall are on the higher side. Our study shows significantly higher values and thus better performance with regard all the aforementioned datasets, for all the three different datasets that are used in this study.

The data set is fed into a LSTM network with input shape of dimension (1, 12) and run for 100 epochs. Batch size is chosen to be 10. RMSE (Root Mean Square Error) is the loss function that has been applied on the said model. The graph for the loss function is depicted in Fig. 3. This graph is based on dataset – 1. The activation function is Rectified Linear Unit (ReLU).

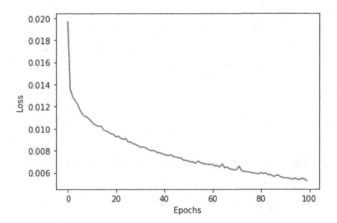

Fig. 3. A graphical depiction of the loss function, i.e., mean squared error

We also perform validation of the proposed model. Initially we split the whole dataset into a 70% training and 30% testing dataset. Further, we take 20% of the training data as the validation dataset. So, we have 30% testing data, 56% training data and 14% validation data. Then we plot a training loss versus validation loss plot to get an estimate about the performance of the model as can be seen in Fig. 4. The green curve in the plot represents the training curve which gives us an estimation of how well the model can learn based on the training dataset while, the blue curve, i.e., the validation curve gives us an estimate of how well the model is generalizing based on the validation dataset. As we can see from the plot, our model is facing some overfitting issues as the training loss happens to keep decreasing with further learning while the validation loss starts increasing again with further learning after decreasing to a certain point (Fig. 5).

Figure 4 depicts the analysis of the proposed LSTM model with other classification models in context to accuracy rate. It is observed that LSTM model generates an optimum accuracy of 0.989 as compared to other models. SVM records the least accuracy value.

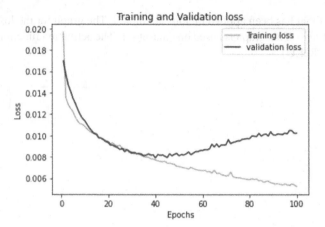

Fig. 4. Training loss vs Validation loss (Color figure online)

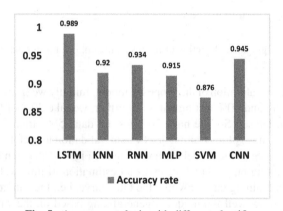

Fig. 5. Accuracy analysis with different classifiers

6   Conclusion

Estimation of rice yield plays a pivotal role in global food production. In order to strengthen national food security by ensuring timely export and import decisions, the management folks as well as farmers heavily rely on accuracy of yield predictions [23–25]. Estimation of rice yield is one of the most challenging field out there due to various complicated factors associated with. This paper focuses on integrating one of the most sought-after deep learning algorithms with the aim of estimating the yield of rice. It proposes a LSTM network based model with the intention of estimating the rice yield which makes use of a data set comprising for various soil parameters for rice research provided by ICAR - National Rice Research Institute (NRRI), Odisha. The said model still has issues like overfitting, etc. that needs to be addressed in the future works so that we can expand the research further in this domain. Another important future scope would be to avail datasets of different varieties of crops other than rice and also to integrate more features besides soil parameters that also affect crop yield.

References:

1. Chaudhury, P., Mishra, S., Tripathy, H.K., Kishore, B.: Enhancing the capabilities of student result prediction system. In: Proceedings of the Second International Conference on Information and Communication Technology for Competitive Strategies, pp. 1–6 (2016)
2. Shi, X., Chen, Z., Wang, H., Yeung, D.Y., Wong, W.K., Woo, W.C.: Convolutional LSTM network: a machine learning approach for precipitation nowcasting. arXiv 2015 arXiv:1506.04214 (2015)
3. Tripathy, H.K., Mishra, S., Thakkar, H.K., Rai, D.: CARE: a collision-aware mobile robot navigation in grid environment using improved breadth first search. Comput. Electr. Eng. **94**, 107327 (2021)
4. Tian, H., et al.: A deep learning framework under attention mechanism for wheat yield estimation using remotely sensed indices in the Guanzhong Plain, PR China (2021). https://doi.org/10.1016/j.jag.2021.102375
5. Agarwal, S., Tarar, S.: A hybrid approach for estimation of rice yield using machine learning and deep learning algorithms. J. Phys.: Conf. Ser. **1714**, 012012 (2021)
6. Wang, X., Huang, J., Feng, Q., Yin, D.: Winter Wheat yield prediction at county level and uncertainty analysis in main wheat-producing regions of china with deep learning approaches (2020). https://doi.org/10.3390/rs12111744
7. Mishra, S., Tripathy, H.K., Acharya, B.: A precise analysis of deep learning for medical image processing. In: Bhoi, A., Mallick, P., Liu, C.M., Balas, V. (eds.) Bio-inspired Neurocomputing. Studies in Computational Intelligence, vol. 903, pp. 25–41. Springer, Singapore (2021). https://doi.org/10.1007/978-981-15-5495-7_2
8. Sun, J., Di, L., Sun, Z., Shen, Y., Lai, Z.: County-level soybean yield prediction using deep CNN-LSTM model. Sensors **19**, 4363 (2019). https://doi.org/10.3390/s19204363
9. Nevavuori, P., Narra, N., Lipping, T.: Estimation of rice yield with deep convolutional neural networks. Comput. Electron. Agric. **163** (2019)
10. Chen, Y., et al.: Strawberry yield prediction based on a deep neural network using high-resolution aerial orthoimages. Remote Sens. **11**, 1584 (2019)
11. Russello, H.: Convolutional neural networks for estimation of rice yield using satellite images. Master's thesis, University of Amsterdam, Amsterdam, The Netherlands (2018)
12. Jiang, Z., Liu, C., Hendricks, N.P., Ganapathysubramanian, B., Hayes, D.J., Sarkar, S.: Predicting county level corn yields using deep long short term memory models. arXiv 2018, arXiv:1805.12044 (2018)
13. Kulkarni, S., Mandal, S.N., Sharma, G.S., Mundada, M.R., Meeradevi: Predictive analysis to improve crop yield using a neural network model. In: Proceedings of the 2018 International Conference on Advances in Computing, Communications and Informatics (ICACCI), Bangalore, India, 19–22 September 2018, pp. 74–79 (2018)
14. You, J., Li, X., Low, M., Lobell, D., Ermon, S.: Deep Gaussian process for estimation of rice yield based on remote sensing data. In: Proceedings of the thirty-First AAAI Conference on Artificial Intelligence, San Francisco, CA, USA, 4–9 February 2017, pp. 4559–4566 (2017)
15. Alhnaity, B., Pearson, S., Leontidis, G., Kollias, S.: Using deep learning to predict plant growth and yield in greenhouse environments. arXiv 2019 arXiv:1907.00624 (2019)
16. Sahoo, S., Das, M., Mishra, S., Suman, S.: A hybrid DTNB model for heart disorders prediction. In: Mallick, P.K., Bhoi, A.K., Chae, G.S., Kalita, K. (eds.) Advances in Electronics, Communication and Computing. ETAEERE 2020. Lecture Notes in Electrical Engineering, vol. 709, pp. 155–163. Springer, Singapore (2021). https://doi.org/10.1007/978-981-15-8752-8_16
17. Khaki, S., Pham, H., Wang, L.: YieldNet: a convolutional neural network for simultaneous corn and soybean yield prediction based on remote sensing data. https://doi.org/10.1101/2020.12.05.413203

18. Jeong, S., Ko, J., Yeom, J.-M.: Predicting rice yield at pixel scale through synthetic use of crop and deep learning models with satellite data in South and North Korea, Science of The Total Environment, vol. 802, pp. 149726 (2022). https://doi.org/10.1016/j.scitotenv.2021.149726, ISSN 0048-9697

19. Jena, L., Kamila, N.K., Mishra, S.: Privacy preserving distributed data mining with evolutionary computing. In: Satapathy, S., Udgata, S., Biswal, B. (eds.) Proceedings of the International Conference on Frontiers of Intelligent Computing: Theory and Applications (FICTA) 2013. Advances in Intelligent Systems and Computing, vol. 247, pp. 259–267. Springer, Cham (2013). https://doi.org/10.1007/978-3-319-02931-3_29

20. Mishra, S., Mallick, P.K., Tripathy, H.K., Jena, L., Chae, G.S.: Stacked KNN with hard voting predictive approach to assist hiring process in IT organizations. Int. J. Electr. Eng. Educ. 0020720921989015 (2021)

21. Dutta, A., Misra, C., Barik, R.K., Mishra, S.: Enhancing mist assisted cloud computing toward secure and scalable architecture for smart healthcare. In: Hura, G., Singh, A., Siong Hoe, L. (eds.) Advances in Communication and Computational Technology. Lecture Notes in Electrical Engineering, vol. 668, pp. 1515–1526. Springer, Singapore (2021). https://doi.org/10.1007/978-981-15-5341-7_116

22. Rath, M., Mishra, S.: Security approaches in machine learning for satellite communication. In: Hassanien, A., Darwish, A., El-Askary, H. (eds.) Machine Learning and Data Mining in Aerospace Technology. Studies in Computational Intelligence, vol. 836, pp. 189–204. Springer, Cham (2020). https://doi.org/10.1007/978-3-030-20212-5_10

23. Chakraborty, S., Sahoo, K.S., Mishra, S., Islam, S.M.: AI driven cough voice-based COVID detection framework using spectrographic imaging: an improved technology. In: 2022 IEEE 7th International conference for Convergence in Technology (I2CT), pp. 1–7. IEEE (2022)

24. Mishra, S., Thakkar, H.K., Singh, P., Sharma, G.:. A decisive metaheuristic attribute selector enabled combined unsupervised-supervised model for chronic disease risk assessment. Comput. Intell. Neurosci. **2022**, 1–17(2022)

25. Mohanty, A., Mishra, S.: A comprehensive study of explainable artificial intelligence in healthcare. In: Mishra, S., Tripathy, H.K., Mallick, P., Shaalan, K. (eds.) Augmented Intelligence in Healthcare: A Pragmatic and Integrated Analysis. Studies in Computational Intelligence, vol. 1024, pp. 475–502. Springer, Singapore (2022). https://doi.org/10.1007/978-981-19-1076-0_25

Sentiment Analysis on Movie Review Data Using Ensemble Machine Learning Approaches

Om Prakash Jena[1](✉) [iD], Alok Ranjan Tripathy[1] [iD], Manas Prasad Rout[2],
and Partha Sarathi Pattnayak[3]

[1] Ravenshaw University, Cuttack, Odisha, India
jena.omprakash@gmail.com,
omprakashjena.cs@ravenshawuniversity.ac.in
[2] FM University, Balasore, India
[3] KIIT Deemed to be University, Bhubaneswar, Odisha, India

Abstract. Today's machine learning application has a huge impact on the current scenario that is big changes is afoot in the marketing world and shifts are largely down to the power of machine learning. It is about finding pieces of predictive knowledge, it has capable in the field of NLP to understand, analyze, manipulate and potentially generate human language, Truly listening to a customer's voice requires deep understanding of what they have expressed in natural language. NLP is the best way to understand this and uncover the sentiment behind it. Here we have proposed a sentiment analysis for movie review, from the movie review dataset. We have implemented the data set by using of Naive Bayes, Logistic Regression, Random Forest algorithm, Support Vector Machine, Multinomial Naïve Bayes, Stochastic Gradient descent classifier along with combining all those as an ensemble with voting majority techniques with features parameters such as positive, negative, neutral, partially positive, partially negative. We get the result of the proposed ensemble technique is better than individual algorithms with 94% of accuracy.

Keywords: Sentiment analysis · Naive Bayes · Logistic Regression · Random Forest · Multinomial Naïve Bayes · Stochastic gradient descent classifier · Majority voting · Movie review · IMDB dataset

1 Introduction to Sentiment Analysis

NLP increase computational power to achieve accurate results in different area i.e. healthcare, media, finance and human. To understanding human language, speech or text for a machine is a great challenge because machine can understand any things through binary representation, the human generated data are large volume, this generated data may contain unstructured format and the difficulties is the machine could generate accurate feedback to considering the human generated data, so NLP can build a bridge in between the human and computer and solve this problem. NLP used some technique i.e. syntactic analysis and semantic analysis. Syntactic analysis refers to the arrangement of word in a

© The Author(s), under exclusive license to Springer Nature Switzerland AG 2022
M. Panda et al. (Eds.): ICIICC 2022, CCIS 1737, pp. 389–400, 2022.
https://doi.org/10.1007/978-3-031-23233-6_29

sentence that make grammatical sense. It used for, how the natural language deals with the grammatical value. There are some syntax techniques are used such that lemmatization, word segmentation, Part-of-speech tagging, parsing, sentence breaking, stemming. But semantic analysis used to know the meaning and interpretation of word and how sentence are structured. There are also some technique i.e. Named entity recognition (NER), word sense disambiguation, natural language generation.

Sentiment Analysis is also termed as emotion AI or pulling of opinion. Basically it focuses on identify subjective information. It checks the polarity of text i.e. positive or negative. By the help of these polarities, change the concept, improve productivity and advertising so it helps reduce some negativity. Sentimental analysis is also referred as opinion mining. It is component part of NLP (natural language process), that helps to distinguish and pull opinions within a given block of speech/text. Basically the aim of sentiment analysis is to determine the frame of mind, sentiments and response of writer based on the topic. Sentimental analysis have so many advantage in various field like business related area, researchers etc. It is also use for monitoring i.e. in a social media; there are huge amount of data in form of short-message, memes and emoticons. These are some challenges for the micro-blogging content that is coming from Twitter and Facebook, it is because of the kind of language used for convey the sentiments i.e. short forms, memes and emoticons. Sentimental analysis is helpful for the researchers especially in the fields like Sociology, marketing, advertising, economics and political science. Sentimental analysis is also used in companies. Companies have customer feedback, so those companies manipulate his plans/structure according to the feedback system, but it is still impossible to analyze it manually.

There are various steps to analyze sentiment data. Here we have performed several phases as data Collection, Text Preparation, Sentiment Detection, and Sentiment Classification.

The entire work is organized as follow: Sect. 1 describe the basic introduction to sentiment analysis, Sect. 2 describe the related work, Sect. 3 describe the proposed methodology with different ML methods along with ensemble method, Sect. 4 describe performance measurement for the proposed models, Sect. 5 elaborate the result analysis and Sect. 6 describe the conclusion and future work.

2   Recent Work

The author taking social media sentiment analysis using SVM and NB algorithms and using Ant Colony and particle Swarm optimization method getting 73.62%, 77.30% accuracy for NB and 76.71%, 80.54% for SVM respectively [1]. Considering the social network Uri attack tweets the author use two methods i.e. sentiment score and polarity count getting 94.3% accuracy of negative and 5.7% of positive result [2]. Taking Vietnamese student feedback corpus with LSTM using support vector machine algorithm, the author achieved the F1-score of 90.2% accuracy [3]. Using different machine learning algorithm such as NB, SVM, DT, RNN, taking movie reviews the author learn how to face ML problem and how to do data analysis to make the work easier. He noticed that applying transformation on the data can improve the performance of classification method and he found the RNN gives the better result [4]. With the help of the Urdu sentiment corpus, taking Urdu tweets to analysis and polarity detection, the dataset comprising over 17,185 token with obtain 52% of positive and 48% of as negative [5]. The author considered Particle Swarm optimization (POS) and Ant Colony optimization (ACO) with SVM and NB classifier getting 86.29% of accuracy than the SVM-PSO [6]. Taking Deep learning neural network (DNN) for customer sentimental analysis and review classification achieving high level accuracy is 0.9248% with average F1-score of 0.925% [7].

The author proposed sentimental analysis for hotel rating using NB algorithm using 60% training data and 40% of testing data and getting 45 key values for positive and 45 key for negative. He noticed that for scaling the dataset Naïve Bayes is good and implementing the linear equation on features and predicators [8]. Taking sentiment analysis using SVM with Osgood values and Turnery values obtaining accuracy 68.3% in Osgood but Turnery gives 65.8% of accuracy. But the hybrid SVM (Turnery and Lemma) gives accuracy 86.0% and hybrid SVM (Osgood and Lemmas) gives accuracy 84.6% and 86.0% with 3-fold and 10-fold experiment [9]. Taking Amazon and IMDB movie review, the author considering Naïve Bayes, J48, BF Tree and oneR classifier but Naïve Bayes is quite faster in learning whereas oneR more promising, it gives 91.3% of accuracy, 97% in F-measure [10]. The author considered 2 dataset HI-EN and BE-EN and using SVM and voting classifier with neural network obtaining 0.569% f-score of HI-EN and 0.526% F-score BN-EN [11]. The author tried to exceed domain-transfer problem with some effective measure feature, using Adapted Naïve Bayes, taking 3 Chinese domain-specific dataset and use Chinese text POS tool ICTCLAS and getting average of 600 word in education review, 460 terms in stock review and 120 word in computer review [12]. Taking movie and product reviews dataset of sentiment analysis in Turkish and English language using SVM classifier obtain 91.33% accuracy [13]. In this paper, the author takes car reviews as dataset contain pre-labeled sentence of 10,000, positive and negative of 5000, overly the author going through sentence level analysis so employing conjunct analysis with sentence level it gives better accuracy. He found that ML algorithm cannot be efficiently so using WordNet substantially enhance the accuracy is about 80% [14]. Taking dataset as movie and product reviews hat are in English and Turkish language using SVM algorithm and considering some parameter i.e. kernel type, weighting schemes (i.e. TF-IDF, tokenization,feature selection), the author getting accuracy is about 91.33% [15]. Processing micro blogs, it is very challenging task, it have noise. In this paper the author taking method as combining social and topic context to analyze micro blog sentiment. To analyze this, using Laplacian matrix of the graph model [16]. A noble approach has been discussed to improve sentiment analysis with patterns lexicons and negations with hybrid and Sentic net4 with a commendable accuracy 86.32% [17].

3 Proposed Methodology

Here we consider a dataset as IMDB movie dataset and applied different machine learning classifier as Naïve Bayes, Random Forest, Logistic Regression and applying some pre-processing steps as shown in Fig. 1.

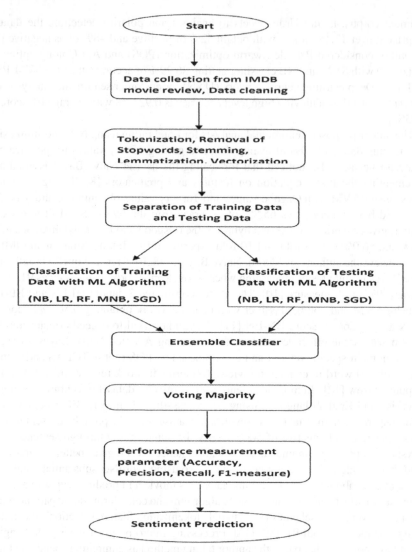

Fig. 1. Overall Diagram of Proposed Method

3.1 Naïve Bayes Algorithm

Naïve Bayes algorithm Bayes theorem for probabilistic prediction. It is used for find out assumption of independence between predictors. This is used for very large dataset because it has no complicated iterative parameter estimation.

Considering IMDB movie review as a dataset. Before applying algorithm, it should be pre-processed. Converting for word vector. We separate reviews as positive and negative. It stores like positive folder and negative folder (such as positive review in positive folder and negative reviews in negative folder. In this folder, we noted that positive reviews as "pos" tag and negative reviews as "neg" tag. After that, it finds out best word are taken by applying conditional probability. Apply Naïve Bayes classifier with testing data and best word to obtain matrix.

Steps of the Algorithm

1. Initialize the prior probability of positive or P(positive).
2. Initialize the prior probability of negative or P(negative).
3. Conversion of sentence into word.

   For each class of (Positive, negative):

   For each word in (phrase)

$$P(W|C) < num(W|C)|num(Class) + num_{total} \qquad (1)$$

$$P(C) = P(C) * P(W|C)$$

Return max $\{P (+ve), P (-ve)\}$

$$P(G|S) = \frac{P(S|G) * P(G)}{P(S)} \qquad (2)$$

$$P(G|S) = P(S_1|G) * P(S_2|G) * P(S_3|G) \ldots\ldots\cdots * P(S_N|G) * P(G) \qquad (3)$$

$P(G|S)$-- > posterior probability of class (d, target) given predictor(y, attribute).
$P(G)$ -- > class of prior probability.
$P(S|G)$ -- > likelihood.
$P(S)$ -- > predictor as prior probability.

$$P(G|S) = \frac{P(S|G) * P(G)}{P(S)} \qquad (4)$$

where S is feature and G is sentiment value.

$$P(G|S_1, S_2, S_3) = \frac{P(S_1, S_2, S_3) * P(G)}{P(S1, S2, S3)}, S_1, \ S_2, \ S_3 \text{ are feature} \qquad (5)$$

$$P(d|S_1, S_2, S_3) = \frac{P(S_1|G) * P(S_2|G) * p(S_3|G) * P(G)}{P(S_1) * P(S_2) * P(S_3)} \qquad (6)$$

$$P(G|S) = \prod_{i=0}^{n} \frac{P(S_1|G)}{P(S)}$$

Calculation of P(S) is done only once, so we calculate only

$$\prod_{i=0}^{n} P(S_1|G)$$

$$P(G_k|S_1, \ldots\ldots S_n) = \frac{1}{Z} P(G_k) \prod_{i=1}^{n} P(S_i|G_k) \qquad (7)$$

$$\hat{W} = argmax_{g \epsilon G} P(G|S) \tag{8}$$

$$P(G|S) = \frac{P(S|G) * P(G)}{P(S)} \tag{9}$$

$$\hat{W} = argmax_{d \epsilon D} P(G|S) = argmax_{d \epsilon D} \frac{P(S|G) * P(G)}{P(S)} \tag{10}$$

$$\hat{W} = argmax_{d \epsilon D} P(S|G) * P(G)$$

$$\hat{W} = P(S_1, S_2, S_3|G) * P(S)$$

$\hat{W} = G_k$ for some K as follows:

$$\hat{w} = argmaxP (G_k) \prod_{i=1}^{n} P(S_i|G_k) \tag{11}$$

To avoid underflow,

$$\hat{w} = argmax(\ln P(G_k) + \sum_{i=1}^{n} \ln P(S_i|G_k)) \tag{12}$$

If W_1 and W_2 are two independent variable,
$P(W1, W2|S) = P(W1|S) * P(W2|S)$.

3.2 Logistic Regression

It is a statistical learning technique in supervised classification algorithm. Here we used sigmoid function.

$$(A) = \frac{1}{1 + e^{-A}}$$

$m_{i,j}$--> feature vector of length 'N'.

$$j = 1, \ldots\ldots\ldots, N, i = 1, \ldots\ldots\ldots, h.$$

$$M = \begin{bmatrix} m_{11}, m_{12}, \ldots . m_{1N} \\ m_{21}, m_{22}, \ldots . m_{2N} \\ \cdot \\ m_{h1}, m_{h2}, \ldots . . m_{hN} \end{bmatrix}_{h*N} \tag{13}$$

$$R = \begin{bmatrix} r_1 \\ r_2 \\ \cdot \\ \cdot \\ r_h \end{bmatrix} \quad P(R|M) = \frac{1}{1 + e^{--f(m)}} \text{(posterior)} f(m) \text{ is the feature. } (m_j)$$

$$\log[\frac{P(R|M)}{1 - P(R|M)}] = m_0 + m_1\beta_1 + \ldots\ldots\ldots + m_N\beta_N + \epsilon = f(m)$$

Maximum likelihood estimation,

$$argmax : \log\{\prod_{i=1}^{h} P(R_i|M_i)R_i(1 - P(R_i|M_i))^{(i-R_i)}\} \tag{14}$$

3.3 Random Forest Classifier

It is based upon ensemble tree based learning algorithm. It decides the final class of the test object, considering the vote from different decision tree. Here in this classifier we have adopts boats tarp bagging aggregation.

Training set $W = w_1, w_2, \ldots\ldots, w_n$.

With responses $S = s_1, s_2, \ldots\ldots, s_n$.

Bagging repeatedly "E" times.

For $e = 1, 2, \ldots\ldots E$.

Prediction for unseen samples y', by averaging the prediction from all individual regression tree on y':

$$\hat{f} = \frac{1}{E} \sum_{e=1}^{E} f_e(y') \tag{15}$$

To find out uncertainty of the prediction,

$$6 = \frac{\sqrt{\sum_{e=1}^{E}(f_e(y') - \hat{f})^2}}{E-1} \tag{16}$$

3.4 Multinomial Naïve Bayes Classifier

It is mostly used for discrete counts. Here we have taken the feature vectors $(g_1, g_2, \ldots, g_k)$ to solve the problem of text classification task with the integer value of word frequency by using TF-IDF method.

The conditional probability distribution $\Pr ob(doc/class_m)$ can be given by

$$\text{Multinomial } \Pr ob(doc/class_m) = \Pr ob((g_1, g_2, \ldots, g_k)/class_m)$$

$$= \prod_{1 \leq n \leq k} \Pr ob(g_n/class_m) \tag{17}$$

After applying the Bayes rule we have reduced the equation to.

$$C_{MAP} = \arg\max_{c_m \in C} \overline{\Pr ob}(c_m) \prod_{1 \leq n \leq k} \overline{\Pr ob}(g_n/class_m) \tag{18}$$

With the feature available in the documents bag of word, we have calculated $\Pr ob(g_n/class_m)$. The probability of w_n in $class_m$ is calculated in training dataset as

$$\Pr ob(w_n/class_m) = \frac{count \text{ number}(w_n * class_m)}{\sum_{w \in Voc} count \text{ number}(w_n, class_m)} \tag{19}$$

3.5 Support Vector Machine

It's a supervised machine learning algorithm that aims to locate a hyperplane in a multi-dimensional space. The SVM's goal is to find the best hyperplane so that the two groups can be segregated. This ideal hyperplane divides the two groups while also increasing the margin between them. The distance between the hyperplane and the SVs is known as the margin. It is widely used because of its primary benefit, which is that it can be very efficient even in high-dimensional spaces. However, the key flaw in this method is that it does not have probabilistic estimations. High precision can be achieved by fine-tuning hyper parameters such as gamma, coat, and kernel level, but in practice, defining the exact hyper parameters can be difficult which directly enhances the computational cost and overhead.

The hyperplane optimization can be obtained by Equation.

Minimize $\frac{1}{2}||w_{(v)}||^2$, where $||w_{(v)}||^2 = w_{(v)}^T x$

Subject to $y_j(w_{(v)}^T x_j + b) \geq 1$ where $j = 0,1$

$1 - y_j(w_{(v)}^T x_j + b) \leq 0$ where $j = 1,2, \ldots$

The Lagrangian optimization problem is defined in Equation.

$$\tau = \frac{1}{2}||w_{(v)}||^2 + \sum_{j=1}^{n} \alpha_j(1 - y_j(w_{(v)}^T x_j + b)) \tag{20}$$

The first derivative of the above equation is taken with respect to $w_{(v)}$ and b, then we have the following Equation.

$w_{(v)} + \sum_{j=1}^{n} \alpha j(-y_j) x_j = 0$.

$w_{(v)} = \sum_{j=1}^{n} \alpha j y_j x_j$.

$\sum_{j=1}^{n} \alpha j y_j = 0$ where $\alpha j \geq 0$.

For the non-linearly classification problem, we introduce another dimension to create a bigger dimensional space. Here ξ_j is introduced to represent the approximated misclassified data samples. So, the classification model is represented as in Equation

$$f(x) = \frac{1}{2}w_{(v)}^T w_{(v)} + c \sum_{j=1}^{n} \xi_j \tag{21}$$

$subject to y_j(w_{(v)}^T x_j + b) \geq 1$ Where $j = 1,2,\ldots$ And $\xi_j \geq 1$

Where c represents the trade-off between the margin and training error and c is a constant. We have to minimize the $f(x)$ for a better-optimized hyperplane.

3.6 Stochastic Gradient Descent Classifier

It is mostly used for optimizing problem in machine learning which find best parameter that corresponds to best fitted predicted result.

Let input is x_i and corresponding output is y_i then

$$H = -\sum_i (y_i \log(p(x_i)) + (1 - y_i) \log(1 - p(x_i))) \tag{22}$$

Here we have used both Adam and RMSProp optimizer for our simulation based on Batch stochastic gradient descent classifier.

4 Performance Measurement Parameter

Here we have considered some measurement parameter for our model to find out the solution of our model. The parameters are Accuracy, Precision, Recall and F-measure.

$$\text{Accuracy} = \frac{Correct predictions number}{Total number of prediction}$$

$$\text{Accuracy} = \frac{T(+ve) + T(-ve)}{T(+ve) + T(-ve) + F(+ve) + F(-ve)}$$

$$\text{Precision} = \frac{T(+ve)}{T(+ve) + F(-ve)}$$

$$F_\beta = \frac{(\beta^2 + 1)RT}{\beta^2 R + T} (R and T are precision and recall)$$

where $\beta > 1$, then it is favorable for recall.

$\beta < 1$, then it is for precisions.

$\beta = 1$, here presicion and recall are equal.

When $F_{\beta=1}$ or F_1 $F_1 = \frac{2RT}{R+T}$.

5 Result Analysis

Considering on a movie review dataset we have taken 151871 amount of data out of which we segregate 101870 amount of training and 50001 amount of testing data. Simulating on python with Intel®Core™ i5-5005u cpu @ 2.00 GHz,64-bit, 8 GB RAM and we taking performance measurement parameter(precision, recall, accuracy) and implementing three classifier(such as: Naïve Bayes, Logistic Regression, Random Forest) and getting the following table with individual accuracy 84% of Naïve Bayes, 86% of Logistic Regression, 88% of Random Forest, 85%.of Multinomial Naïve Bayes, 90% of Support Vector Machine, 0.91 of Stochastic Gradient Classifier and 0.94 with our proposed ensemble technique. The output of some sample positive review words and negative review words are given in Figs. 2 and 3 respectively (Table 1).

Table 1. Result analysis of different ML algorithms.

Method Used	Confusion Matrix			Performance Parameter				Accuracy
		Prediction		Precision	Recall	F-measure	Support	
		Positive	Negative					
Naïve Bayes	Positive	4413	616	0.87	0.82	0.84	4972	0.84
	Negative	900	4072	0.83	0.88	0.85	5029	
Logistic Regression	Positive	4271	758	0.84	0.87	0.86	4972	0.86
	Negative	626	4346	0.87	0.84	0.86	5029	
Random Forest	Positive	4271	758	0.85	0.87	0.86	4972	0.88
	Negative	626	4346	0.87	0.85	0.86	5029	
Multinomial Naïve Bayes	Positive	4333	696	0.82	0.86	0.84	4972	0.85
	Negative	598	4374	0.85	0.83	0.82	5029	
Support Vector Machine	Positive	4511	518	0.88	0.86	0.85	4972	0.90
	Negative	580	4392	0.87	0.88	0.89	5029	
Stochastic Gradient Classifier	Positive	4448	581	0.80	0.82	0.84	4972	0.91
	Negative	553	4419	0.81	0.85	0.87	5029	
Proposed Ensemble Method (Majority Voting)	Positive	4671	358	0.89	0.83	0.92	4972	0.94
	Negative	442	4530	0.85	0.90	0.93	5029	

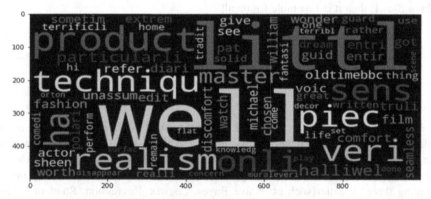

Fig. 2. Some positive review words

Fig. 3. Some negative review words

6   Conclusion and Future Work

We have performed movie review sentiment analysis by using Naïve Bayes, Logistic Regression, Random Forest, method and from which it will conclude that, due to the ensemble mechanism used in Random Forest, Multinomial Naïve Bayes, Support Vector Machine, Stochastic Gradient Classifier and ensemble technique algorithm it result 94% of accuracy which more optimistic than the other methods. Based on this result our proposed model worked efficiently for sentiment prediction of the movie reviewer to a great intent. This can be applied to collect the relevant information to model a recommender system which analyzes the marketing, advertising and promoting the movie.

In the future work, we have to focus on some ensemble method and optimization technique for other parameter, parameter reduction, so that our model will work on both robust recognition system and recommender system.

References

1. Badr, E.-S., Salam, A., Mustafa & Ali, Mahmoud & Ahmed, Hagar.: Social media sentiment analysis using machine learning and optimization techniques. Int. J. Comput. Appl. **178**, 975–8887 (2019). https://doi.org/10.5120/ijca2019919306
2. Kawade, D.: Sentiment analysis: machine learning approach. Int. J. Eng. Technol. **09**, 2183–2186 (2017). https://doi.org/10.21817/ijet/2017/v9i3/170903151
3. Vu, N., Kiet, N., Ngan, N.: Variants of long short-term memory for sentiment analysis on Vietnamese students' feedback corpus, pp. 306–311 (2018). https://doi.org/10.1109/KSE. 2018.8573351
4. Liombart, O.R.: Using machine learning techniques for sentiment analysis. University Autonoma De Barcelona (UAB) (2017)
5. Khan, M.Y., Nizami, M.S.: Urdu Sentiment Corpus (v1.0): Linguistic Exploration and Visualization of Labeled Dataset for Urdu Sentiment Analysis (2020). https://doi.org/10.1109/ICI SCT49550.2020.9080043
6. Bansal, P., Kaur, R.: Twitter sentiment analysis using machine learning and optimization techniques. Int. J. Comput. Appl. **179**(19), 5–8 (2018). https://doi.org/10.5120/ijca20189 16321
7. Shreyas, R.L.: Sentiment analysis of customer satisfaction using Deep learning. IRJCS **6**(12) (2019). https://doi.org/10.26562/IRJCS.2019.DCCS10083

8. Bhargav, P.S., Reddy, G.N., Chand, R.R., Pujitha, K., Mathur, A.: Sentiment analysis for hotel rating using machine learning algorithm. IJITEE **8**(6) (2019)

9. Mullen, T., Collier, N.: Sentiment analysis using support vector machines with diverse information sources. In: 2004 Conference on Empirical Methods in Natural Language Processing , EMNLP (2004)

10. Singh, J., Singh, G., Singh, R.: Optimization of sentiment analysis using machine learning classifiers. HCIS **7**(1), 1–12 (2017). https://doi.org/10.1186/s13673-017-0116-3

11. Mishra, P., et al.: Code-mixed sentiment analysis using machine learning and neural network approaches. arXiv abs/1808.03299 (2018)

12. Tan, S., Cheng, X., Wang, Y., Xu, H.: Adapting Naive Bayes to domain adaptation for sentiment analysis. In: Boughanem, M., Berrut, C., Mothe, J., Soule-Dupuy, C. (eds.) ECIR 2009. LNCS, vol. 5478, pp. 337–349. Springer, Heidelberg (2009). https://doi.org/10.1007/978-3-642-00958-7_31

13. Gözükara, F., Özel, S.: An experimental investigation of document vector computation methods for sentiment analysis of Turkish and English reviews **31**, 467–481 (2016). https://doi.org/10.21605/cukurovaummfd.310341

14. Meena, A., Prabhakar, T.V.: Sentence level sentiment analysis in the presence of conjuncts using linguistic analysis. In: Amati, G., Carpineto, C., Romano, G. (eds.) ECIR 2007. LNCS, vol. 4425, pp. 573–580. Springer, Heidelberg (2007). https://doi.org/10.1007/978-3-540-71496-5_53

15. Zou, X., Yang, J., Zhang, J.: Microblog sentiment analysis using social and topic context. PLoS ONE **13**(2), e0191163 (2018). https://doi.org/10.1371/journal.pone.0191163

16. El Alaoui, I., Gahi, Y., Messoussi, R., Chaabi, Y., Todoskoff, A., Kobi, A.: A novel adaptable approach for sentiment analysis on big social data. J. Big Data **5**(1), 1–18 (2018). https://doi.org/10.1186/s40537-018-0120-0

17. Pradhan, A., Senapati, M.R., Sahu, P.K.: Improving sentiment analysis with learning concepts from concept, patterns lexicons and negations. Ain Shams Eng. J. **13**(2) (2022). https://doi.org/10.1016/j.asej.2021.08.004, ISSN 2090-4479

Comparative Analysis of COVID 19 Detection from Cough Speech Using Machine Learning Classifiers

Soumya Mishra$^{(\boxtimes)}$, Tusar Kanti Dash, Ganapati Panda, Amit Kumar, and Sushant Kumar Singh

Department of Electronics and Tele Communication, C. V. Raman Global University, Bhubaneswar 752054, Odisha, India
soumya@cgu-odisha.ac.in

Abstract. Corona Virus Disease-2019, or COVID-19, has been on the rise since its emergence, so its early detection is necessary to stop it from spreading rapidly. Speech detection is one of the best ways to detect it at an early stage as it exhibits variations in the nasopharyngeal cavity and can be performed ubiquitously. In this research, three standard databases are used for detection of COVID-19 from speech signal. The feature set includes the baseline perceptual features such as spectral centroid, spectral crest, spectral decrease, spectral entropy, spectral flatness, spectral flux, spectral kurtosis, spectral roll off point, spectral skewness, spectral slope, spectral spread, harmonic to noise ratio, and pitch. 05 ML based classification techniques have been employed using these features. It has been observed that Generalized Additive Model (GAM) classifier offers an average of 95% and a maximum of 97.55% accuracy for COVID-19 detection from cough signals.

Keywords: COVID-19 · Speech feature · Machine learning classifier

1 Introduction

According to the statistics given by the World Health Organization (WHO) on October 14th, 2022, there have been a total of 620,301,709 confirmed COVID-19 cases [1]. COVID-19 symptoms include body discomfort, high body temperature, strong coughing, and significant breathing difficulties [3]. The ludicrous and rising spread of the COVID-19 virus has resulted in unprecedented coordination among several fields in order to limit the infection's spread and prevent collateral damage on a regular basis [4]. Here in this work, COVID-19 has been attempted to be diagnosed using human cough by adopting datasets from multiple databases of healthy and positive individuals. Moreover, an advanced and combative way to early speech detection is by implementing machine learning classifiers to classify COVID-19 [2, 5]. K-Nearest Neighbour (KNN) is a proven classifier [4] to detect COVID-19 because of its excellent efficiency and capacity [5] to address a variety of challenging pattern categorization tasks. Moreover, Decision Tree [6, 7], Naïve Bayes [8] and Support Vector Machine (SVM) [9] have previously shown

M. Panda et al. (Eds.): ICIICC 2022, CCIS 1737, pp. 401–408, 2022.
https://doi.org/10.1007/978-3-031-23233-6_30

enhanced classification results in speech problems. GAM classifier is compared against KNN, SVM, Binary tree and Naïve Bayes to achieve the best outcomes. In our work, we are mainly evaluating three major corpuses for extracting baseline perceptual spectral features for COVID-19 detection from the coughing sounds of different individuals. The paper proceeds with the methodology, results and discussions followed by concluding the work.

1.1 Related Works

[13] showcases exploiting temporal and spectral features with a VGGNet classifier, delivering 0.82 AUC for Cough based COVID-19 classification. A highest accuracy of 89.79% using Random Forest (RF) ML-classifier based on spectral features is delivered in [30]. [11] portrays exploiting Cepstral and spectral features through an RF Classifier, delivering 69% test data classification accuracy. Pahar.et.al. [31] have in detail experimented the cough detection using deep learning structures and achieved a maximum of 95% using ResNet50 architecture.

2 Methodology

Speech segments were obtained for baseline feature extraction, using a 25-millisecond window length [10] post normalizing the signal amplitudes as a part of pre-processing technique. Here, the audio files of the standard databases are subjected to perceptual audio feature extraction consisting of 13 feature vectors. GAM, KNN, SVM, Binary Tree and Naïve Bayes are the potential classifiers used to classify the positive and healthy cough sounds based on the extracted features in this work. The classifier hyperparameters are tuned using Bayesian Optimizer Fig. 1.

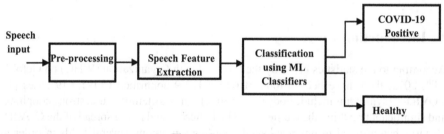

Fig. 1. System model

2.1 Databases

Three standard available labelled corpuses were adopted in the work for conducting the experiment. The databases are as follows:

2.1.1 Coswara (DB-1)

The Coswara-Cough Audio samples were originally obtained using an online tool that allows for crowdsourcing, from all over the world. The audio samples were recorded at 48000 samples per second. The dataset comprised of 6507 clean audio files, 1117 noisy files, and the remaining files are of poorer quality, all belonging to 941 test subjects [11]. Here the individual cough categories are combined together and considered for further feature extraction.

2.1.2 Coughvid (DB-2)

The Coughvid collection contains over 25,000 cough recordings from people of all ages, genders, and geographical locations. It includes over 2,800 samples used to detect medical issues in coughs, making it one of the most comprehensive cough datasets with expert annotations accessible for a variety of cough audio sample classification applications. Before downsampling, these audio samples were subjected to a lowpass filter with a cutoff frequency of 6 KHz, which was downsampled to 12 KHz [12].

2.1.3 KDD Cambridge (DB-3)

This Cambridge database, comprised of cough and breathing samples, as well as complete information about the volunteers' age, gender, demography, medical histories and symptoms collected via an app. The audio samples were captured at 44.1 kHz sampling rate. The audio samples were taken from 582 healthy individuals and 141 individuals who had COVID-19 positive tests. Cough symptoms were reported by 264 healthy people and 54 COVID-19 patients, whereas no symptoms were reported by 318 healthy people and 87 COVID-19 patients [13].

2.2 Feature Extraction

The baseline perceptual audio feature vectors in this work comprise of:

a. *Spectral Centroid:* The spectral centroid represents the centre of the spectral power distribution of a signal and also highlights the intensity of an audio signal [14].
b. *Spectral Crest:* This feature denotes the maximum power spectrum of a sound signal. Spectral crest offers easy differentiation of harmonics from noise-like sounds [15].
c. *Spectral Entropy:* Signal information and spectral distribution spikiness are measured by spectral entropy [16].
d. *Spectral Roll-off:* Speech transmissions often have less energy at high frequencies. This characteristic can be seen in spectral roll-off, which characterises an energy and frequency connection. Previous research has focused on the spectral roll-off that contains the majority of the energy or on a narrow range of spectral roll-off values [14].
e. *Spectral Kurtosis:* Spectral kurtosis highlights the transients with their indices in frequency domain. It is a statistical instrument that may detect the presence of a series of transients and their positions in the frequency domain [18].

f. *Spectral Flux:* The power spectrum's cycle-to-cycle variability is measured by spectral flux. The spectral flux was calculated as the Euclidian distance between consecutive power spectrums [14].

g. *Spectral Skewness:* A spectrum symmetricity around its arithmetic mean is computed using spectral skewness. Skewness equal to zero denotes symmetric distribution, a value less than zero denotes more energy compaction on the right hand side of the spectrum, and a value larger than zero denotes more energy compaction on the left hand side of the spectrum [15].

h. *Spectral spread:* Spectral Dispersion is another name for it. The bandwidth of the transmission has a direct impact on this aspect. The rate-average map's deviation from the centroid can be used to define it. Pure tonal sounds have a tiny spectral spread compared to the vast spectral spread of noise-like signals [15].

i. *Spectral slope:* It is determined via linear regression and represents the slope of the signal's amplitude which is vitally used in speech detection purpose [15].

j. *Spectral decrease:* The spectral decrease characterises the rate-map representation's average spectral slope, with a greater emphasis on low frequencies [15].

k. *Harmonic to noise ratio:* Harmonic to noise ratio indicates the noise amount in an audio speech signal [22].

l. *Spectral flatness:* Spectral flatness measures the similarity of the speech spectrum with a noisy spectrum. Acoustic signals include a property called spectral flatness that has proven advantageous in a variety of audio signal processing scenarios. The geometric mean of the magnitude spectrum of the signal, as determined by the discrete Fourier transform, divided by the arithmetic mean, is the standard definition of spectral flatness [17].

j. *Pitch:* Pitch represents the bandwidth or the correlation between any two sounds and measure of voice quality respectively. The delayed duration between two subsequent pitch intervals is governed by vocal fold tension and the increase of air pressure in the lungs. It may vary, resulting in pitch variations of 2–10% across two consecutive intervals [23].

2.3 Machine Learning Classifiers

2.3.1 SVM Classifier

[25] flaunts a high classification accuracy obtained by SVM in speech classification problem. It is a well-known binary classifier employing a decision boundary between two classes to create a hyperplane [21].

2.3.2 *KNN* Classifier

KNN classifier uses the Euclidian distance to determine the distance between the stored records and unidentified records to classify whether the person has COVID-19 or not [19, 20].

2.3.3 Naïve Bayes

The Naive Bayes method uses sample data information to estimate the posterior probability $p\left(\frac{y}{x}\right)$ of each class y given an item x [24].

2.3.4   Binary Tree

To construct a binary decision tree, class labels are divided into two groups at each branch of the tree until the binary tree reaches a single class label. Distance measurements between the retrieved characteristics of the class labels are utilised to create a binary decision tree. Principal component analysis is used to minimise the high dimension of the feature set in order to measure the distance between disease categories [26]. To create a speaker model with the goal of achieving a high average prediction power, as measured by the average prediction entropy of the binary tree leaf distributions Low entropy, such as anticipating unique symbols, correlates to the desirable prediction quality in this case, and vice versa.

2.3.5   GAM Classifier

The Generalised Additive Model (GAM) was created in 1990 by Hastie and Tibshirani as a statistical model. It can be used in a variety of prediction situations [29]. GAM exploits regression properties for a thorough analysis of the data using a 'Smoothing function'. This 'smoother' is competent to estimate the trend from the data plot which can subsequently establish the dependency of the mean of the response variable to the predictors.

2.4   Experimental Setup

All simulations were performed on MATLAB 2021a software, with Windows 10 operating system, 8 GB RAM. GAM, SVM, KNN, Binary tree and Naïve Bayes were utilised as potential classifiers to detect COVID-19 infection. Cross validation was performed using a k-fold with k = 10 [20]. For performance evaluation of the classifier, factors such as recall, sensitivity, F-score, precision, and accuracy were evaluated. The audio was digitised and pre-processed using suitable functions, following which the speech baseline features were extracted and reposited in MS Excel sheets. The classifiers were then applied to these extracted feature vectors to obtain the necessary outcome of the detection. The classification accuracy is evaluated as follows: [2]. The hyperparameters of all the classifiers are selected using Bayesian Optimization technique [28].

3   Result and Discussion

Cough speech classification was performed on three databases, Coswara, Coughvid, and the KDD Cambridge consisting of different categories of cough samples collected from all over the globe.

Extracted baseline perceptual audio features were fed into GAM, SVM, KNN, Naïve Bayes and Binary Tree. For performing the simulations, we have used MATLAB R2021a in windows 10 operating system with intel i5 processor, 8GB RAM ,4GB SSD and 4 GB graphics. The classification outcomes were interpreted in terms of confusion matrix and classifier parameters expressed in Accuracy, Precision, Specificity, F-Score and Area Under the Curve (AUC) Table 1.

Table 1. Classification accuracies and outcomes for DB-1, DB-2, DB-3.

Databases	Classifiers	COVID_19 & Healthy classification				
		Accuracy	Precision	Specificity	F-Score	AUC
Coswara [DB-1]	GAM	**0.9755**	**0.9677**	**0.9751**	**0.9754**	**0.97**
	KNN	0.8244	0.8462	0.7857	0.8148	0.82
	SVM	0.8062	0.8125	0.8125	0.8125	0.8
	Naïve Bayes	0.8589	0.9255	0.9060	0.8172	0.85
	Decision Tree	0.9395	0.8423	0.7875	0.8894	0.93
Coughvid [DB-2]	GAM	**0.9722**	**0.9714**	**0.9833**	**0.9645**	**0.96**
	KNN	0.898	0.9375	0.9167	0.9091	0.9118
	SVM	0.8865	0.8235	0.8865	0.8235	0.8833
	Naïve Bayes	0.8852	0.9231	0.8889	0.9057	0.9139
	Decision Tree	0.8357	0.95	0.7037	0.8085	0.8757
KDD Cambridge [DB-3]	GAM	**0.9035**	**0.7891**	**0.8055**	**0.7470**	**0.89**
	KNN	0.8357	0.95	0.7037	0.8085	0.8757
	SVM	0.7777	0.7945	0.5690	0.7893	0.72
	Naïve Bayes	0.8707	0.8296	0.7215	0.8918	0.85
	Decision Tree	0.8741	0.9882	0.9886	0.9223	0.857

From the above outcomes, it is observed that GAM classifier, delivers best results i.e. 97.55% classification accuracy, 96.77% precision, 97.51% specificity, 97% AUC, and 97.54% F-Score for DB-1; 97.22% accuracy, 97.14% precision, 98.33% specificity, 96% AUC, and 96.45% F-Score for DB-2; and 90.35% accuracy, 78.9% precision, 80.55% specificity, 89% AUC, and 74.7% F-Score for DB-3.

4   Conclusion

COVID-19 detection from speech signals can be a valuable and cost-effective method because it does not require any complex medical invasive tests or exposure to clinics. This work highlights a ubiquitous non-invasive detection strategy which can quickly diagnose a suspected patient's preliminary state of being COVID-19 positive or healthy without the need to visit a hospital or seek medical assistance. In this paper, simple baseline perceptual audio features have been used for detection of COVID-19 cough using 03 databases and 05 Machine learning classifiers. GAM outperformed the rest in obtaining best results from all the databases followed by Binary Tree based classifier delivering the second best detection performance in the first database. However, this disease detection approach is yet to be validated by hospitals and physicians. In future, attempt can be made to develop a similar ML classifier model based on perceptual baseline features for real time detection of speech related diseases such as Parkinson's disease, Alzheimer's disease, Dysarthria, dementia, oral cancer etc.

References

1. https://covid19.who.int/
2. Shaban, W.M., Rabie, A.H, Saleh, A.I., Abo-Elsoud, M.A.: A new COVID-19 patients detection strategy (CPDS) based on hybrid feature selection and enhanced KNN classifier. Knowl. Based Syst. **205**, 106270 (2020)
3. Chowdhury, M.E., et al.: QUCoughScope: an artificially intelligent mobile application to detect asymptomatic COVID-19 patients using cough and breathing sounds. arXiv preprint arXiv:2103.12063. (2021)
4. Rasjid, Z.E., Setiawan, R.: Performance comparison and optimization of text document classification using k-NN and naïve bayes classification techniques. Procedia Comp. Sci. **1**(116), 107–112 (2017)
5. Hassan, A., Shahin, I., Alsabek, M.B.: Covid-19 detection system using recurrent neural networks. In: 2020 International Conference on Communications, Computing, Cybersecurity, and Informatics (CCCI), pp. 1–5. IEEE (2020)
6. Aich, S., Younga, K., Hui, K.L., Al-Absi, A.A., Sain, M.: A nonlinear decision tree-based classification approach to predict the Parkinson's disease using different feature sets of voice data. In: 2018 20th International Conference on Advanced Communication Technology (ICACT), pp. 638–642. IEEE (2018)
7. Petti, U., Baker, S., Korhonen, A.: A systematic literature review of automatic Alzheimer's disease detection from speech and language. J. Am. Med. Inform. Assoc. **27**(11), 1784–1797 (2020)
8. Meghraoui, D., Boudraa, B., Merazi-Meksen, T., Boudraa, M.: Parkinson's disease recognition by speech acoustic parameters classification. In: Chikhi, S., Amine, A., Chaoui, A., Kholladi, M.K., Saidouni, D.E. (eds.) Modelling and Implementation of Complex Systems. LNNS, vol. 1, pp. 165–173. Springer, Cham (2016). https://doi.org/10.1007/978-3-319-33410-3_12
9. Jain, M., Narayan, S., Balaji, P., Bhowmick, A., Muthu, R.K.: Speech emotion recognition using support vector machine. arXiv preprint arXiv:2002.07590. (2020)
10. Asgari, M., Shafran, I.: Predicting severity of Parkinson's disease from speech. In: 2010 Annual International Conference of the IEEE Engineering in Medicine and Biology, pp. 5201–5204. IEEE (2010)
11. Sharma, N., Krishnan, P., Kumar, R., Ramoji, S., Chetupalli, S.R., Ghosh, P.K., Ganapathy, S.: Coswara--a database of breathing, cough, and voice sounds for COVID-19 diagnosis. arXiv preprint arXiv:2005.10548. (2020)
12. Orlandic, L., Teijeiro, T., Atienza, D.: The COUGHVID crowdsourcing dataset, a corpus for the study of large-scale cough analysis algorithms. Scientific Data. **8**(1), 1 (2021)
13. Brown, C., et al.: Exploring automatic diagnosis of COVID-19 from crowdsourced respiratory sound data. arXiv preprint arXiv:2006.05919. (2020)
14. Stolar, M.N., Lech, M., Stolar, S.J., Allen, N.B.: Detection of adolescent depression from speech using optimised spectral roll-off parameters. Biomed. J. **2**, 10 (2018)
15. Sharma, G., Umapathy, K., Krishnan, S.: Trends in audio signal feature extraction methods. Appl. Acoust. **15**(158), 107020 (2020)
16. Toh, A.M., Togneri, R., Nordholm, S.: Spectral entropy as speech features for speech recognition. Proc. PEECS. **1**, 92 (2005)
17. Madhu, N.: Note on measures for spectral flatness. Electron. Lett. **45**(23), 1195–1196 (2009)
18. Antoni, J.: The spectral kurtosis: a useful tool for characterising non-stationary signals. Mech. Syst. Signal Process. **20**(2), 282–307 (2006)
19. Hossain, E., Hossain, M.F., Rahaman, M.A.: A color and texture-based approach for the detection and classification of plant leaf disease using KNN classifier. In: 2019 International Conference on Electrical, Computer and Communication Engineering (ECCE), pp. 1–6. IEEE (2019)

20. Fushiki, T.: Estimation of prediction error by using K-fold cross-validation. Stat. Comput. **21**(2), 137–146 (2011)
21. Ismael, A.M., Şengür, A.: Deep learning approaches for COVID-19 detection based on chest X-ray images. Expert Syst. Appl. **1**(164), 114054 (2021)
22. Krom, G.D.: A cepstrum-based technique for determining a harmonics-to-noise ratio in speech signals. J. Speech Lang. Hear. Res. **36**(2), 254–266 (1993)
23. Medan, Y., Yair, E., Chazan, D.: Super resolution pitch determination of speech signals. IEEE Trans. Signal Process. **39**(1), 40–48 (1991)
24. Webb, G.I., Keogh, E., Miikkulainen, R.: Naïve Bayes. Encycl. Mach. Learn. **15**, 713–714 (2010)
25. Jain, M., Narayan, S., Balaji, P., Bhowmick, A., Muthu, R.K.: Speech emotion recognition using support vector 23
26. Yüncü, E., Hacihabiboglu, H., Bozsahin, C.: Automatic speech emotion recognition using auditory models with binary decision tree and SVM. In: 2014 22nd International Conference on Pattern Recognition, pp. 773–778. IEEE (2014)
27. Brigham, K., Kumar, B.V.: Imagined speech classification with EEG signals for silent communication: a preliminary investigation into synthetic telepathy. In: 2010 4th International Conference on Bioinformatics and Biomedical Engineering, pp. 1–4. IEEE (2010)
28. He, F., Zhou, J., Feng, Z.K., Liu, G., Yang, Y.: A hybrid short-term load forecasting model based on variational mode decomposition and long short-term memory networks considering relevant factors with Bayesian optimization algorithm. Appl. Energy **1**(237), 103–116 (2019)
29. Leathwick, J.R., Elith, J., Hastie, T.: Comparative performance of generalized additive models and multivariate adaptive regression splines for statistical modelling of species distributions. Ecol. Modell. **199**(2), 188–196 (2006)
30. Tena, A., Clarià, F., Solsona, F.: Automated detection of COVID-19 cough. Biomed. Signal Process. Control **1**(71), 103175 (2022)
31. Pahar, M., Klopper, M., Warren, R., Niesler, T.: COVID-19 cough classification using machine learning and global smartphone recordings. Comput. Biol. Med. **1**(135), 104572 (2021)

Classification of High-Resolution Satellite Image with Content Based Image Retrieval and Local Binary Pattern

Rajalaxmi Padhy, Laxmipriya Samantaray, Sanjit Kumar Dash$^{(\boxtimes)}$, and Jibitesh Mishra

Odisha University of Technology & Research, Bhubaneswar, Odisha, India
sanjitkumar303@gmail.com

Abstract. The framework of content-based image retrieval (CBIR) is based on the visual interpretation of contents that are present in the query image, which can deal with problems like image texture classification and image texture visualization. This study uses texture features to create a CBIR system for satellite image datebase exclusively for high-resolution satellite pictures. The discussed technique makes use of a block-based scheme and the local binary pattern texture feature. In order to extract LBP histograms, the query and database pictures are separated into equal-sized blocks. The Chi-square distance is then applied to compare the block histograms. According to experimental data, the local binary pattern (LBP) formulation is a potent tool for retrieving high-resolution satellite images.

Keywords: Local binary pattern · Texture feature extraction · Content-based image retrieval · High resolution satellite image

1 Introduction

Image-processing applications potentially benefit from using image retrieval techniques. A CBIR system is based on comparing the query over full images. Color, texture, and shape are common methods of retrieving images. These methods are used to retrieve an image from an image dataset. The multiple image resolutions and sizes and spatial color distribution are irrelevant to them. Therefore, none of these methods are suitable for retrieving art images. Furthermore, shape-based retrievals are only helpful in a small number of scenarios. With the development of imaging technology in recent years, satellites with extremely high-resolution spatial imaging systems, such as IKONOS, GeoEye-1, World-View-1, and Quick Bird, have been launched and are now able to make more precise observations of the world. The issue of managing image databases has arisen as high-resolution photos have become more widely available. A CBIR system returns images from an image database based on a query image. Images are provided by the content and metadata-based systems, utilizing an efficient image retrieval method. Global features including color, shape, and texture are employed by various new picture retrieval algorithms. However, the earlier outcomes indicate that using those global attributes to look for related photos produces too many false positives.

© The Author(s), under exclusive license to Springer Nature Switzerland AG 2022
M. Panda et al. (Eds.): ICIICC 2022, CCIS 1737, pp. 409–416, 2022.
https://doi.org/10.1007/978-3-031-23233-6_31

In this paper, we present a novel interpretation of image retrieval employing both content and metadata. The user-provided query image is used to extract related pictures from the picture library. Using "content-based" research implies that rather than examining the image's metadata, such as its categories and keywords, it will examine the image's actual contents. The features of query image along with the images stored in database are extracted and appropriately indexed in a typical CBIR. The system lists all those in the database. The database is searched for relevant pictures using the closest similarity distance. It calculates the distance between the features of the requested image and all those in the database. The database is searched for relevant pictures using the closest similarity distance. We use the local binary pattern (LBP) operator to evaluate texture performance for extracting high resolution satellite images.

The remainder section of the paper is structured as follow. Second segment describes the background and related work. The third segment gives the description of the system model and methodology. The fourth segment shows the results and discussions of the respective data set, and the fifth segment gives a conclusion to our paper.

2 Background and Related Work

The method of visual perception for humans heavily depends on color information. In addition, color is independent of the size and position of objects in an image. Because of these factors, the color characteristic is frequently used in image retrieval to describe a picture's contents. Creating a color space histogram is the easiest way to get color information. Color, texture, and intensity signals have been shown to be effective for identification of low-resolution satellite images [1, 2]. In order to identify the type of clouds in weather images, feature extraction has been exploited extensively [3, 4]. In collaboration with color, shape, and texture features, effective features produced by the combining of channels such as the vegetation indexes (NDVI), brightness indexes (BI), or urban indexes (ISU) are employed with multi-spectral and hyper-spectral low resolution satellite pictures (Noaa, Landsat). [5] Textural and structural features have long been known to be highly discriminative in mid-resolution images [6, 7]. High resolution satellite picture indexing and retrieval, however, is still a relatively unexplored field of study. Recent research [8, 9], in which the texture descriptor is typically paired with other features, has demonstrated the texture descriptor's capability in dividing and extracting.

Images' color information is displayed using the General Color Histogram (GCH), and the distance between two images' color histograms indicates how similar they are. This technique is susceptible to changes in intensity, color shifts, and cropping. Images are divided into blocks by local color histograms (LCH), which then provide a different histogram for each block. Thus, a mixture of these histograms serves as an image representation. Every block in one picture is compared to an equivalent block in the other image to compare the two images [1].

A content-based color picture retrieval system based on color features of the visual features and their spatial relationship was proposed by Jaehyun An et al. in [3–5]. The proposed scheme discovers numerous dominant colors for each region after extracting the salient regions using a color contrast method. Then, a binary map is used to characterize the spatial patterns of each dominant hue. Hamed Qazanfari et al. used the colour difference histogram (CDH) in the HSV colour space [20]. The perceptually different color between two adjacent pixels in terms of colors and edge orientations is included in CDH [17–19]. Utilizing entropy and correlation criteria, efficient features are chosen from the extracted features. Feature selection, feature extraction, and similarity measurement are the three steps in this methodology. It's also proposed in [24, 25] to use the primitives of colored instant as the framework for a color image retrieval system. A block-by-block division of the image comes first. All blocks' color moments are then extracted and grouped into several classes. An image's primal is assumed to be the average moments of each class. There are features for every primitive. The YIQ color model is employed in this article for images that are in color [13].

It gives details on how surfaces and objects are arranged structurally within an image. The distribution of light intensity inside an image is characterized by its texture. A picture's texture information is crucial for defining the image's contents. A new technique for content-based picture retrieval using the color difference histogram (CDH) was proposed by Guang-Hai Liu et al. [14]. The distinguishing feature of CDHs is that, for colors & edge directions in L*a*b* color space, they count the perceptually uniform color distinction between 2 points on different backgrounds [21]. Two different kinds of special histograms used in the proposed approach work together to calculate background colors and orientations simultaneously. A similar perceptual color change between adjacent pixels' edge orientations may be seen in the first histogram. The second histogram displays the consistent perceived color difference between the edge orientation data and the color indices of nearby pixels. Pictures are covered by a number of elements in an application for image categorization and retrieval. Both spatial and wavelet-changed input images are used to extract relevant features. The wavelet transformation separates smooth and sharp information into separate channels, degrading images into various resolutions.to provide further context for the image.

3 System Model and Methodology

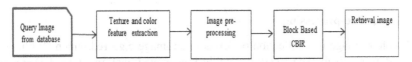

Fig. 1. System model for image retrieval

Figure 1 shows the framework of the system model for image retrieval. Here we are using several samples from the database of high-resolution satellite images. Firstly, we load the satellite picture databases in the MATLAB workspace. Resize the picture and convert it from RGB to grayscale. Then perform pre-processing exercises and register the local vector design with a reason for each pixel. Following that, extract the LBP features and retrieve the image with the help of CBIR.

3.1 Color Feature Extraction

In this case, we extracted the colour feature from each channel and merged them. Then the colour will effectively change if the location of the image changes. To locate the feature, color histograms are built in various color spaces. For color spaces like RGB, LAB, HSV, HUE, and OPP, 3-D histograms are built. Red, green, and blue make up the RGB color space. These three colors' combination coefficients function as a color component. The limitations of the color spaces are not visually constant for the acquisition. These three-color channels have a strong association. To solve issues, many color representations have been suggested. For example, the edges are determined in inspiration by biological color spaces like the opposing color space, hue saturation & brightness are indeed the color spaces connected to how people describe color, and CIE La*b* & L*uv are perceptually accurate color spaces. These two-color spaces are dependent on the device. Such histograms, which are classified as a single feature vector, were created for $8 \times 8 \times 8 = 512$ color bins.

The LBP texture generator has gained popularity as a strategy in many applications because of its discriminating capabilities & mathematical flexibility. The robustness of a LBP operator towards periodic grey-scale changes that are based on illumination changes is its most special feature in real-world applications. LBP's operator used the center pixel as a threshold when it was first operational, operating with a 3×3 rectangle neighbor. In order to determine the LBP code associated with the center pixel, threshold values were multiplied by weights whose powers of 2 then were added, as shown in (1):

$$LBP_{P,R(x)} = \begin{cases} \sum_{p=0}^{p-1)} s(g_p - g_c)2^p \end{cases}$$

$$\text{Where } s(X) = \begin{cases} 1, x \geq 0 \\ 0, x \leq 0 \end{cases} \tag{1}$$

where g_p is the value of the neighbouring pixel, g_c is the grey value of the central pixel, P is the number of neighbours, and R is the neighbourhood's radius.

3.2 Image Pre-processing

RGB colour image is a collection of pixels in an image e.g.- red, green, & blue color schemes, respectively. The 3-D RGB satellite images are transformed into 1-D grey scale image by retaining texture features in the images.

$$I_{GS} = 0.3R + 0.6V + 0.1B \tag{2}$$

The LBP operator has the problem of modifying the output if the image size changes even slightly. For complex photos, LBP might not perform as expected. The operator's thresholding strategy is too responsible for this. We suggest reducing the image's colour depth in order to increase the LBP's resistance to these small variations in pixel values. Various quantification levels were used in a set of experiments ($q = 16$, $q = 32$, $q = 64$, $q = 128$), and the quantization also applied to both the image database as well as the test image.

3.3 Block Based CBIR

For complete images, the CBIR systems compute textures. It keeps the database at a manageable size. If the feature for the image were extracted worldwide, the textures inside the image would not be represented properly. It is preferable to extract local features from the proposed feature rather than use feature descriptors. This can be accomplished by using photo segmentation or division. The segmentation procedure can be difficult to create a good segment, especially towards the edge of the textured region that might affect the retrieval outcome later. So, the CBIR approach is used to divide the image into sections without applying any segmentation at all.

Every 512 × 512-pixel database image separated into 16 unique fixed-size blocks that don't cross. Every block's LBP pattern is computed. The query image is treated identically throughout the query phase. For demonstrated consistent using their LBP attributes, a distance measure is required in the mutual information. There are a variety of heterogeneity measurements available. Due to its efficiency in terms of the both quickness and high retrieval rates, the Chi-square value is utilized in this work to assess the similarity of 2 LBPV graphs, H_1 and H_2, , referring to (3):

$$D_{1,2} = \sum_{b=1}^{B} (H_1(b) - H_2(b))^2 / H_1(b) - H_2(b) \tag{3}$$

B is the total of histogram bins, which is determined by the parameters P & R that were utilised. By computing the Chi-square distances between both i^{th} the query as well as the jth database blocks histogram, the query and dataset images can be contrasted. The total of the lowest distances shown by (4) is the final picture similarity distance D for retrieval:

$$D = \sum_{i=1}^{16} \min_j (D_{i,j}) j = 1, 2 \ldots 16 \tag{4}$$

The CBIR system's performance could be assessed using a variety of objective criteria. Return (Re), a commonly used performance indicator, is described as.

$$Re = N/Mt \tag{5}$$

Here N represents the no. of relevant objects, & Mt is the overall number of relevant objects that were retrieved.

4   Result and Discussions

In this part, we show how our High-Resolution Satellite Image retrieval technique can recognize objects. Google Earth data has been used to create the database. It has been chosen to encompass the low textural, highly textural, low structural and highly structural area using various illumination conditions and geographic resolution. It consists of 12 categories, each comprising 50 samples. To create 16 blocks of 128 × 128 pixels each, here we enlarged the pictures to 512 × 512 pixels.

We calculated the LBP$_{P,R}$ riu2 in the investigations using (P, R) parameters of (8, 1), (16, 2), and (24, 3), accordingly. The Interactive Data Language is used to create the system for retrieving images. In this paper, we acquire a set of satellite pictures exported from Google Earth2, which gives higher resolution satellite pictures up to 0.5 m to evaluate the current approach for indexing satellite pictures. In Fig. 2, some samples from the database are shown (https://captain-whu.github.io/BED4RS/). There are 50 samples of 12 types of relevant scenes, which include (a) airport, (b) forest, and (c) parking, in high-resolution satellite images. It's important to note that image samples from the same class may have different scales, directions, and illuminations because they are gathered from various regions in satellite picture resolutions.

Fig. 2. Testing samples of high-resolution satellite

All 600 pictures inside the database are deployed as query images to plot the recall curves. The number of retrieved pictures was then multiplied by the standard recall. The curves in Fig. 3 show that even more over 71% of the pictures are successfully retrieved for the first 180 comparisons. Additionally, the difficulty of the LBP algorithm for extracting features is substantially lower than that of the Gabor technique.

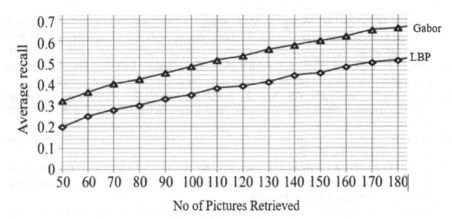

Fig. 3. Image retrieval result

5 Conclusion

In this paper, we discuss a content-based image retrieval system based on Local Binary Pattern as well as a block division technique to categories high-resolution satellite pictures. It means there are so many complicated images in satellite images that this is the medium to give clarity to the messy picture. so that we can identify the whole region using this method. The experiments demonstrate that with High Resolution Satellite Images being compressed, Local Binary Pattern texture features can still deliver effective picture retrieval. Future research and the fact that High Resolution Satellite Image has both frameworks and texturing imply that the addition of some structural features would most likely result in improved results.

References

1. Maheswary, P., Srivastava, N.: Retrieval of remote sensing images using colour and texture attribute. arXiv preprint arXiv:0908.4074 (2009)
2. Tebourbi, R., Belhadj, Z.: A texture based multispectral images indexing. In: 2005 12th IEEE International Conference on Electronics, Circuits and Systems, pp. 1–4. IEEE (2005)
3. Ma, A.L.: Indexing and retrieval of satellite images. Doctoral dissertation, Oakland University (2005)
4. Upreti, D., Saran, D.S., Hamm, D.N.:. Content-based satellite cloud image retrieval. University of Twente Faculty of Geo-Information and Earth Observation (ITC) (2011)
5. Bouteldja, S., Kourgli, A.: Retrieval of high-resolution satellite images using texture features. J. Electron. Sci. Tech **12**(2), 211–215 (2014)
6. Maître, H.: Indexing and retrieval in large satellite image databases. In: MIPPR 2007: Remote Sensing and GIS Data Processing and Applications; and Innovative Multispectral Technology and Applications, vol. 6790, pp. 24–38. SPIE (2007)
7. Bhattacharya, A., Roux, M., Maitre, H., Jermyn, I.H., Descombes, X., Zerubia, J.: Indexing of mid-resolution satellite images with structural attributes. International Society for Photogrammetry and Remote Sensing (2008)
8. Wang, S., Wang, A.: Segmentation of high-resolution satellite imagery based on feature combination. Int. Arch. Photogramm. Remote. Sens. Spat. Inf. Sci. **37**, 1223–1227 (2008)

9. Wan, Q. M., Wang, M., Zhang, X. Y., & Zhang, D. Q. (2009, October). Two-stage high resolution remote sensing image retrieval combining semantic and visual features. In MIPPR 2009: Automatic Target Recognition and Image Analysis (Vol. 7495, pp. 1291–1301). SPIE

10. Nisia, T.G., Rajesh, S.: Classification of high-resolution Images with local binary pattern and convolutional neural network: an advanced study. New Appr. Eng. Res. **3**, 1–6 (2021)

11. Kavitha, P.K., Saraswathi, P.V.: Machine learning paradigm towards content-based image retrieval on high-resolution satellite images. Int. J. Innov. Technol. Explor. Eng. **9**, 2278–3075 (2019)

12. Liu, G.H., Yang, J.Y.: Content-based image retrieval using color difference histogram. Pattern Recogn. **46**(1), 188–198 (2013)

13. Singh, H., Kumar, A., Balyan, L.K., Singh, G.K.: A novel optimally weighted framework of piecewise gamma corrected fractional order masking for satellite image enhancement. Comput. Electr. Eng. **75**, 245–261 (2019)

14. Asokan, A., Anitha, J.: Change detection techniques for remote sensing applications: a survey. Earth Sci. Inf. **12**(2), 143–160 (2019). https://doi.org/10.1007/s12145-019-00380-5

15. Afifi, A.J., Ashour, W.M.: Image retrieval based on content using color feature. International Scholarly Research Notices (2012)

16. An, J., Lee, S.H., Cho, N.I.: Content-based image retrieval using color features of salient regions. In: 2014 IEEE International Conference on Image Processing (ICIP), pp. 3042–3046. IEEE (2014)

17. Degerickx, J., Roberts, D.A., Somers, B.: Enhancing the performance of Multiple Endmember Spectral Mixture Analysis (MESMA) for urban land cover mapping using airborne Lidar data and band selection. Remote Sens. Environ. **221**, 260–273 (2019)

18. Dhivya, R., Prakash, R.: Edge detection of satellite image using fuzzy logic. Clust. Comput. **22**(5), 11891–11898 (2017). https://doi.org/10.1007/s10586-017-1508-x

19. Qazanfari, H., Hassanpour, H., Qazanfari, K.: Content-based image retrieval using HSV color space features. Int. J. Comput. Inf. Eng. **13**(10), 533–541 (2019)

20. Bu, X., Wu, Y., Gao, Z., Jia, Y.: Deep convolutional network with locality and sparsity constraints for texture classification. Pattern Recogn. **91**, 34–46 (2019)

21. Wang, Q., Wan, J., Li, X.: Robust hierarchical deep learning for vehicular management. IEEE Trans. Veh. Technol. **68**(5), 4148–4156 (2018)

22. Li, X., Yuan, Z., Wang, Q.: Unsupervised deep noise modeling for hyperspectral image change detection. Remote Sens. **11**(3), 258 (2019)

23. Pavithra, L.K., Sree Sharmila, T., Subbulakshmi, P.: Texture image classification and retrieval using multi-resolution radial gradient binary pattern. Appl. Artif. Intell. **35**(15), 2298–2326 (2021)

24. Shih, J.L., Chen, L.H.: Colour image retrieval based on primitives of colour moments. IEE Proc.-Vis. Image Sig. Process. **149**(6), 370–376 (2002)

25. Ruichek, Y.: Attractive-and-repulsive center-symmetric local binary patterns for texture classification. Eng. Appl. Artif. Intell. **78**, 158–172 (2019)

Author Index

Printed in the United States
by Baker & Taylor Publisher Services